This is a volume in

THE UNIVERSITY OF MICHIGAN HISTORY OF THE MODERN WORLD

Upon completion, the series will consist of the following volumes:

The United States to 1865 *by Michael Kraus*

The United States since 1865 *by Foster Rhea Dulles*

Canada: A Modern History *by John Bartlet Brebner*

Latin America: A Modern History *by J. Fred Rippy*

Great Britain to 1688: A Modern History *by Maurice Ashley*

Great Britain since 1688: A Modern History *by K. B. Smellie*

France: A Modern History *by Albert Guérard*

Germany: A Modern History *by Marshall Dill, Jr.*

Italy: A Modern History *by Denis Mack Smith*

Russia and the Soviet Union: A Modern History *by Warren B. Walsh*

The Near East: A Modern History *by William Yale*

The Far East: A Modern History *by Nathaniel Peffer*

India: A Modern History *by Percival Spear*

The Southwest Pacific to 1900: A Modern History *by C. Hartley Grattan*

The Southwest Pacific since 1900: A Modern History *by C. Hartley Grattan*

Africa: A Modern History *by Ronald Robinson*

GERMANY
A Modern History

The University of Michigan History of the Modern World

Edited by Allan Nevins and Howard M. Ehrmann

GERMANY

A Modern History

BY MARSHALL DILL, JR.

Ann Arbor: The University of Michigan Press

TO THE MEMORY OF
MY MOTHER,
EDNA FAY DILL,
who died on December 26, 1935

Preface

It is a challenge to write about German history. Probably no other people has been at times so much admired and at other times so much loathed as the German people. They have endured crisis, tragedy, and catastrophe but have always displayed the tenacity to recover, never more spectacularly than at the present time. When weak they have been the hapless prey of their neighbors; when strong they have often with nauseous arrogance tried to dominate and subjugate those neighbors. A talented and complex people, they have produced men with the lofty grandeur of Johann Sebastian Bach, Immanuel Kant, and Johann Wolfgang von Goethe; they have also produced men with the diabolic venom of Paul Josef Goebbels and Heinrich Himmler. When divided they have sought unity, but when united they have tended to split into their constituent parts. Although an integral part of Western culture, they have at times forsworn and challenged that culture; the challenge has been supported with such power that the West has been hard pressed to subdue it. Germany has been at different moments a threat, a friend, and even an ally. She has never been negligible.

I have tried to write a convenient, manageable, and succinct history of Germany with stress on the last century, and have attempted to make the complexities of German development as understandable as possible.

This book is directed at a varied assortment of readers. I hope that the general educated public, concerned about the state of the world, will discover in this work how one of the important components of the world developed as it did; that the undergraduate student can use it not too unpalatably as a text or as supplementary reading; that it will be helpful to the teacher as the source of lecture material or for explanations of troublesome points; and that the graduate student will find the text useful for the running thread of German history, and the Suggested Readings a competent steppingstone to research.

This is not a scholar's book, though I trust it is a scholarly one. I have cut footnotes and scholarly apparatus to the barest minimum and have limited my bibliography to works in the English language which are readily available. Many of these works will easily introduce the student to further reading in other languages, especially, of course, German.

I do not know of any other book on this subject in English that accomplishes exactly the objective I have set for myself. It is in some ways a modest objective, but one for which I have no apology since I do not disdain the use of learning for purposes of communication.

One of the most pleasant aspects of writing a book is the opportunity it affords to thank one's friends for their kindness and gracious help. Had it not been for the generosity and modesty of Mr. James Joll, Fellow of St. Antony's College, Oxford, this book would not exist. My warm friends and fellow historians, Dr. Edwin L. Dunbaugh, Hofstra College, and Dr. Carl E. Schorske, University of California, Berkeley, have each read considerable portions of the manuscript and made valuable suggestions. My stubbornness prevented me from always accepting their advice, so I must accept full responsibility for shortcomings in the following pages. I extend my thanks to Sister Mary Marguerite, O.P., librarian of the Dominican College of San Rafael, and her staff, for many kindnesses. I am grateful also to Mr. Walter W. Corriea for encouragement and help in the tedious work of proofreading.

The troubled history of Germany has much to teach us. Perhaps this volume will extend the reach of its lessons a little further.

Contents

MAPS

GERMANY

A Modern History

CHAPTER I

The Formation of Modern Germany (to 1500)

Germany is today the country of the middle. The very fact that she is currently divided into two states, one influenced by the West and one by the East, underlines this statement. Throughout modern history she has been conditioned by her proximity to the Slavic east, the Latin south, and the Gallic west. However, during the first thousand years and more of the Christian era, Germany was not the land of the middle. She was the frontier land between the classical, Christian culture of the west and south of Europe and the semibarbarous, pagan culture of the east and north. An important aspect of medieval history is the gradual integration of these areas into the Christian community. Much of this work was done through Germany and by Germans.

Unlike Great Britain, Spain, Italy, or even France, Germany has no settled natural frontiers, except perhaps in the south, where the Alps erect a massive barrier. The plain of northern Europe extending from the English Channel across Germany and Russia into Asia is not marked by any important uplands. Through the centuries armies and migrations have been able to cross and recross it almost at will. The major river systems which water it have served more often as avenues of communication than as barriers. Many scholars feel that this lack of protective geographical features has caused the heavy military emphasis in German history.

Six important rivers, the Rhine, Ems, Weser, Elbe, Oder, and Vistula, traverse German lands mostly from southeast to northwest. Each, especially the Rhine, has contributed something to German development. Dropping from the hilly south across what used to be heavily forested country to the northern plain, these rivers have enriched Germany with wild, beautiful, and romantic scenery. East and west communications are afforded by the Main, which flows into the Rhine, and the Danube, both wide and easily navigable for long distances.

Southern Germany rises from the plain through wooded rolling country to the plateau of Bavaria and then to the majestic peaks of the Bavarian Alps and the Austrian Tyrol. Germany, then, is a land of contrasts, a fact which has contributed to its typical provincialism and parochialism. A visitor even today is astonished at the dialectical differences between Vienna and Berlin, or Munich and Hamburg. Both geography and history have conspired to keep Germany apart rather than to forge it into a unity. Most of Germany, especially the north, is not warm and sunny; much of it is dour and lowering, even depressing. There are many, usually overromantic writers who insist that this has colored the German "national personality." These people forget how miserable and dreary London and Paris can be.

The earliest contact between the Romans and the Germans on German soil occurred when Julius Caesar reached the Rhine during his conquest of Gaul in the fifties, B.C. He reported briefly, but made no effort to extend his conquests any further east. During the reign of Augustus the Romans pushed east of the Rhine to the Weser, but in the year 9 A.D. Germanic forces under the first German hero, Hermann (Arminius), defeated three Roman legions in the battle of the Teutoburg Forest. This battle not only led to Augustus' alleged cry, "Give me back my legions," but also discouraged the Romans from extending the boundaries of the Empire further to the east. By the end of the first century they established a definite limit to their domain along the line of the Rhine and Danube rivers, and between the headwaters of these built the famous Roman wall or *Limes,* which they fortified against any incursion from the east.

At about the same time the Roman historian, Tacitus, wrote his *Germania,* the first literary work devoted to a description of the Germans. Tacitus, who was essentially a moralist anxious to reform the evil Romans of his day, paints a rosy picture of the barbarians. He tells of a tall, blond, virile people, decent and moral in their family life, brave as fighters, prudent as tillers of the soil and breeders of domestic animals. He even suggests a form of democracy when he describes the chieftains in consultation with the men of the tribe. The combination of the exploits of Hermann and the writing of Tacitus has helped modern German nationalists tremendously.

Rhenish and Danubian Germany remained part of the Roman Empire as long as it existed. Many of the important German cities (Trier, Cologne, Mainz, Augsburg, Regensburg, Vienna) started as Roman provincial towns. When the Empire weakened in the fourth and fifth centuries, Roman Germany entered a period of confusion marked by the "wandering of the peoples." It suffered invasion and the dilution of its Roman traditions by the influx of tribes which had not experienced Roman civilization. *AT FALL OF EMPIRE*

The Franks, who were destined to be the political organizers of both France and Germany, rose to prominence during the fifth century. At first they inhabited the east bank of the Rhine, but during the lawless days of the decline of the Empire pushed westward, occupying what is now the Low Countries and northern France. Unlike many of the wandering tribes, they did not abandon their original homeland when they started to conquer but simply expanded their territory. The greatest of the Frankish leaders was Clovis (481–511). This chieftain conquered on all sides and at death had carved out a kingdom consisting of most of modern France, Belgium, the Netherlands, and western and southern Germany. Probably the most significant act of his life was his conversion in 496 to orthodox Catholic Christianity instead of the heretical Arian Christianity which the other Germanic tribes embraced.

The family of Clovis, known as the Merovingian dynasty, continued to rule for about two hundred and fifty years. It degenerated rapidly, and the history of the Frankish kingdom is a sorry story of murder, war, and fratricide. However, during these years Christian missionaries had an opportunity to push eastward into German lands and to convert the native pagans. The most notable of these, and one of the principal German patron saints, was St. Boniface (672–754), a native of England who spent his life preaching to Germans. He converted Hesse and Thuringia, founded abbeys (in particular, the great abbey of Fulda where he is buried), and before his martyrdom had become the primate of Germany and representative of the pope.

When the Merovingian family became hopelessly incompetent in the eighth century, a new family assumed the leadership of the Franks, first as "mayors of the palace" and later, under Pepin the Short, as king with the blessing of the pope. This Carolingian family produced its greatest representative in Charles the Great, known to the Germans as Karl *der Grosse* and to the French as Charlemagne, who ruled from 768 to 814 and is a major figure in the history of both nations.

Charles was a mighty warrior and spent much of his long reign fighting in all directions—against the Lombards in Italy, the Moslems in Spain, and the pagans in Germany. One of his main contributions to Germany was the advance of the Frankish border to the Elbe River with the defeat of the warlike and stubborn Saxons. Those Saxons who were not slaughtered were forced to receive baptism. He also included Bavaria into his realm and even pushed eastward into modern Austria.

On Christmas Day, 800, when Charles was assisting at Mass in Rome in the church of St. Peter, Pope Leo III, apparently to Charles' surprise, placed an imperial crown on the king's head and saluted him as Augustus, the old title of Roman emperors. This act marked an effort to revive the old Roman Empire in the person of the Frankish chieftain. It also registered the pope's recognition of the fact that he could no longer count for help on the obvious ruler, the emperor at Constantinople, and that the church must now rely on the great Catholic barbarian kingdom which had developed to the north and west. On this day began the long fateful connection between the German political ruler and the Roman spiritual ruler, which was to have such a vast influence on German development with its concept of a universal temporal monarchy or *Reich* marching with the Roman spiritual monarchy at the head of the Christian community.

Louis, the only surviving son of Charles, was not the man his father had been, but at least he kept the huge empire together until his death in 840. Then his three sons, Lothar, Louis, and Charles, resorted to civil war to achieve the sole rule. At Strassburg in 842 Louis the German and Charles agreed on a pact of eternal friendship, a document which is interesting because it shows how the languages of the eastern Franks and the western Franks had drawn apart. The two groups could not understand each other, so the Oath of Strassburg was drawn up in two tongues—one the ancestor of modern German, the other of modern French. The following year Lothar joined his brothers in a division of the empire into three parts. By the Treaty of Verdun, Charles received the western section, which grew into France, while Louis took the eastern section, which grew into Germany. Lothar received the title of emperor and a curious chimneylike domain stretching from Rome to the North Sea. It is significant that this middle area, Lotharingia (the German word for Lorraine is Lothringen), has been a source of struggle ever since between French and Germans, both of whom claim it as their own. After the death of Lothar and his son another treaty, signed at Mersen in 870, gave Louis some territory from the old Lotharingia. Soon thereafter the imperial title passed briefly to the French branch of the family.

The period of the late ninth and early tenth centuries is a dismal one in Western history. It saw the disintegration of Charles' empire and the breakup of the west into small, parochial, feudal entities. It also saw serious incursions by alien foes—the Northmen from Scandinavia, and the Moslems from the Mediterranean. Charles the Great was a man who tried to hold back the tide, but the forces at work were too great for him. The primitive economic organization of the time was unable to hold together so great an empire. The trend was toward feudal division.

In the east Frankish kingdom there developed five great tribal or stem duchies, which tended to usurp royal prerogatives. These were Lorraine, Saxony, Swabia, Franconia, and Bavaria. During the later years of the ninth century the dukes of these areas paid little but lip service to the incapable Carolingians, and on one occasion even deposed one of them. When the German branch of the Carolingian family died out in 911, the five duchies might have pursued independent courses, but to avoid a king taken from the French branch of the family the dukes elected Conrad, duke of Franconia, thus emphasizing the electoral and not the hereditary character of the German kingship. Conrad, on his deathbed in 919, nominated as his successor the most powerful of the tribal dukes, Henry of Saxony, the king portrayed in Wagner's *Lohengrin*. As Henry I, he founded the first of the three great dynasties that reigned in medieval Germany.

Henry's son, Otto I (the Great, 936–73), was the most important of the Saxon rulers and one of the most significant figures in German medieval history. Faced with serious civil wars and with dissension within his own family, he put these down sternly. One of his solutions for the problem of civil war was to have great importance in German development. This was the system of depending on churchmen to carry out political duties. He granted large and wealthy fiefs to bishops and abbots, thus becoming a founder of the institution of the ecclesiastical principality, independent of any secular rule except the emperor's, which was to persist in Germany until the nineteenth century. Since the prelate was in many cases a political ruler, the emperor felt that he should appoint him. During Otto's time, when the church in Rome was weak and corrupt, this did not cause much trouble; but later, when the papacy reformed itself, the popes believed that since the functions of the bishops were primarily spiritual, they should be named from Rome. Here lay the roots of the investiture controversy, which filled German history for centuries to come.

Otto's most important military exploit earned him the title of "the Great." In 955 he completely defeated the Magyars or Hungarians at the battle of the Lechfeld. From then on these people, who had been a warlike nuisance, settled down to an agricultural economy as neighbors to the Germans. In the northeast Otto pushed the German culture in the direction of the Oder River, but had uneven success. During his reign the archdiocese of Magdeburg was founded as a center for conversion of the pagans.

Otto also became interested in the affairs of Italy, where the last Carolingians had divided up their territories and instituted a weak system of government. He married the widow of the king of the Lombards and declared himself king of Italy in the tradition of Charles the Great. In 962 he appeared in Rome, where the papacy had sunk to a frightful state of corruption at the mercy of the Roman nobility. The German ruler cleaned up the mess and, in return, the pope once more revived the Roman Empire in the west by crowning Otto. Thus the imperial title became anchored in the German monarchy and remained so for almost a thousand years. The emperors now insisted that they had a decisive voice in the election of successive popes.

The lasting connection between Germany and Italy and the intimate relationship between emperor and pope is often viewed as a bad influence on the steady development of Germany. It is certainly true that a number of the medieval emperors spent much of their time and effort dealing with strictly Italian and church affairs. This was particularly true during the high middle ages, when the popes made universal claims and when the north Italian cities grew and claimed their independence from the Germans. The dream of universal rule, of the *Reich,* has unquestionably been an important and disturbing preoccupation of Germans into the twentieth century.

Otto's two immediate successors, also named Otto, suffered from the imperial disease and spent most of their time in Italy. Otto III even moved his capital to Rome and spent his short life on the Palatine Hill among imperial dreams. On his death the last of the Saxons, the devout Emperor St. Henry II (1002–24), ruled from the cathedral town of Bamberg, which he greatly beautified. Devoted to Germany and to the church, he watched the further development of feudalism and carried on unsuccessful warfare with his neighbors. He insisted when he could on respect for royal authority.

Henry left no direct heirs, so the choice for the kingship fell on Conrad of Franconia, a descendant in the female line of Otto the Great. He was the first of the Salian or Franconian emperors, who reigned for almost exactly a hundred years. Conrad II was first and last a political figure, grim in personality and uninterested in church problems. He managed to acquire the title of king of Burgundy, along with its strategic possessions. He demanded obedience to the royal position and thus paved the way for the reign of his son, Henry III (1039–56), which is often regarded as the height of medieval royal power in Germany.

Henry, a pious man married to the deeply religious Agnes of Poitou, enjoyed a reign marked by relative peace and prosperity, the latter caused by the new beginnings of town life in Germany. During this reign some of the main features of the high middle ages started to assert themselves. In fact the most important development of these years, and one which Henry and Agnes encouraged warmly, was the effort of the church to reform itself from within, known as the Cluniac reform. Henry abolished the abuse of simony in his domain and supported the new reforming popes. By doing so, he sowed the seeds of the conflict which was to rage at its height during the reign of his son and successor, Henry IV (1056–1106).

Henry IV was crowned king when he was only three years old and before his father died; he succeeded to the throne at the age of six. This necessitated a regency under the control of his politically inept mother Agnes, a period of weakness during which both the feudal nobility and the papacy were able to strike powerful blows at the position of the emperor built by the two previous monarchs. By this time the reform party was in the ascendant in Rome, determined to end simony, to enforce the celibacy of the clergy, and to put a stop to lay investiture or the nomination of church officials by temporal authorities. In 1059 the Lateran council legislated anew the method of electing popes: this should be done by the college of cardinals with no reference to either the emperor or the Roman nobility. This measure was intended to end the paternalistic relationship of the emperors to the popes which had started with Otto I.

Not long after Henry reached his majority, one of the great popes of history was elected, the monk Hildebrand or Pope St. Gregory VII (1073–85). Gregory was a highly intelligent, inflexible, and determined man, who was resolved to push the reform program to success. He achieved a great deal, but at the cost of a bitter conflict with Henry. Henry at first was disposed to favor the new pope, but when he realized the lengths to which Gregory was prepared to go to end lay investiture, and also how important lay investiture was to his position in Germany, he called a meeting at Worms which declared that Gregory had been illegally elected and was not to be obeyed. A rancorous correspondence ensued between the two, and Gregory excommunicated the emperor and released his subjects from obedience to him. This move led to a general uprising among the German nobles, who invited the pope to Germany to settle affairs there. Gregory started north but had reached only the castle of Canossa in Tuscany when he heard that Henry had crossed the Alps in midwinter (1077) and was at that moment in the snow in front of the castle asking admission and absolution. After three days the pope received the emperor, absolved him, and returned his authority to him. This event is generally thought of as the supreme example of the state bowing to the church, and certainly it was a striking gesture. However, Henry was shrewd in his behavior. He knew that the pope as a priest could not refuse absolution, and so kept Gregory out of

Germany and now received papal support in his wars with his rebellious nobles.

The three decades remaining to Henry were bloody and turbulent in the extreme, but their details need not detain us. He did not maintain peace with Gregory and actually led an army to Rome where he had himself crowned by an antipope of his own choosing. He was in constant trouble with his nobles and also during his later years with his sons. This was one of the unhappiest reigns in history. The only pattern that emerges from it is the beginnings of an alliance between the emperor and the towns against the nobility. Henry died suddenly in 1106 leaving as heir his disagreeable son, Henry V (1106–25).

Henry continued the antipapal policy of his father, insisted on the right to lay investiture, and marched into Italy where he imprisoned the pope. However, in 1122 a compromise settlement, known as the Concordat of Worms, was worked out and allayed at least the worst part of the strife. By this agreement the emperor was to invest with temporal insignia, the church with spiritual. This sounds logical, but it really begged the question of appointment. In fact from this time on the emperor had more influence in German appointments, the pope in Italian. There was no way by which the problem could be definitively solved, because the claims were mutually exclusive. It was, however, temporarily shelved.

With the death of Henry V, the Salian line became extinct. The obvious candidate to succeed was Frederick of Hohenstaufen, nephew of the former emperor. However, the electors wanted to emphasize their privilege and not simply allow the imperial title to become hereditary. So they elected Lothar, Duke of Saxony (1125–37). Lothar was personally a nonentity, but his election led to a centuries-long conflict, the strife of Guelfs and Ghibellines. These names arose because Lothar's son-in-law and heir was Henry Guelf, Duke of Bavaria, while the Hohenstaufens had a possession called Waiblingen, a word which the Italians corrupted into Ghibelline. By this time the old stem duchies, which had constituted the patrimony of the high nobility during the time of the Ottos, had tended to disintegrate, and western Germany was becoming more and more divided into little feudal principalities, both lay and ecclesiastical. Thus there arose a new nobility, not so powerful as the old as individuals but very important as political functionaries. This new knighthood became the source of the feudal armies and of either support or opposition to the emperors.

When Lothar died, the electors behaved as they had in the past. They feared that the Guelf interest was becoming too powerful and elected the head of the Hohenstaufen family, Conrad III (1138–52). The new king, like his predecessor, was weak and incompetent, but his election intensified the rivalry between Guelf and Ghibelline and also opened the way for two of the most interesting figures in German history, Frederick I and Frederick II Hohenstaufen.

The most important events associated with the reign of Conrad did not involve him personally but rather the two great feudal lords, Henry the Lion (the Guelf) and Albert the Bear (of the Ascanian family). These two devoted themselves to continuing the push to the east. Henry conquered Mecklenburg for Christianity, while Albert received the new frontier area of Brandenburg and, by attracting colonists from the west to settle in the swampy regions around the little village of Berlin, laid the foundations for the later Prussian state.

At Conrad's death the electors agreed to his choice of his nephew, Frederick of Hohenstaufen, known as Barbarossa. He is the most attractive of the medieval German rulers. Reminiscent of Charles the Great, he was the perfect feudal knight and had a high opinion of the title of emperor, which he saw in direct succession from the great Romans of the past. Had Frederick been able to rule simply as a German king, his reign might have been one of the most successful in history and he might have been able to lay the bases of a national Germany. However, his position as emperor forced him into a constant relation and usually a conflict with the popes, a conflict which, in time, led to the downfall both of the Holy Roman emperors (as Frederick started to style himself) and of the temporal position of the medieval papacy. In addition, in his wars with the prosperous towns of north Italy he had to come to grips with the new force of urban life, something of which his background and training gave him no understanding.

Frederick started his reign (1152–90) with a number of pacific gestures. In particular, he wooed Henry the Lion by recognizing his position east of the Elbe, by confirming him in the duchy of Saxony, and by returning to him the duchy of Bavaria which he had lost. In return for these favors, Henry was to behave as a loyal subject of his emperor and help him with foreign problems. For some time this policy was successful. Henry did accompany Frederick on his early Italian expeditions and occupied himself with such peaceful projects as the foundation of the city of Munich.

Much of the interest of Barbarossa's reign is connected with his six expeditions to Italy and his complex relationship with the church, which will not concern us here. In Germany he insisted on the maintenance of the peace and used his German domains as a reservoir of manpower and wealth to support his activities elsewhere. He carried on an active foreign policy, usually friendly toward England and cool toward France. He married the heiress of Burgundy and thus renewed the close relationship between that kingdom and Germany. In the east he established Austria, a new duchy on the frontier, which he gave to the house of Babenberg and so prepared for important future developments.

The rupture with Henry the Lion arose out of Henry's refusal to go on Frederick's fifth, and unsuccessful, foray into Italy in 1174. On his return Frederick summoned Henry to his court on a large number of charges. Henry refused to attend, so Frederick banned him and deprived him of his holdings. Saxony was divided up and never reassumed its importance in the northwest. Bavaria was also reduced in size and given to Otto of Wittelsbach, the founder of an important German family. The shape of the future Germany was gradually unfolding itself.

Frederick's last important act, and one whose effects were to have great significance for German history, was to marry his son and heir, Henry, to Constance, heiress to the Norman kingdom of Sicily and southern Italy. Henceforward the fate of the house of Hohenstaufen was to be inextricably woven with the fortunes of Italy. Finally in 1190 Frederick set off on the Third Crusade. But he never arrived in the Holy Land for he drowned while bathing in a river in Asia Minor.

Frederick's reputation grew mightily after his death. He seemed to be a second Charles the Great. Eventually the typical German legend, at first associated with his grandson, Frederick II, was attached to Barbarossa, namely that he had not died but lived on in a cave in the Kyffhäuser mountain, from whence he would come to rescue Germany at her time of greatest need.

Henry VI (1190–97) succeeded his father. He was an imperious and ambitious prince who wanted to establish a universal Hohenstaufen empire based on both Germany and Italy. In Germany he had to face a revolt by Henry the Lion, who tried to regain his position and re-establish Guelf power, an effort in which he was almost successful. Henry VI's premature death in 1197 threw Germany into a period of chaos and civil war for almost twenty years.

For much of this confused period there were two claimants to the throne in Germany: Philip of Swabia, brother of Henry VI, and Otto of Brunswick, son of Henry the Lion. Eventually Philip was murdered and Otto completely defeated by Philip II of France at the battle of Bouvines (1214). In the French army at this battle was young Frederick of Hohenstaufen, son of Henry VI, who in the next few years, largely through the influence of the greatest of medieval popes, Innocent III, was recognized as king in Germany and crowned emperor.

It is a temptation to write at length of Frederick II. Some called him the Wonder of the World; some called him the Antichrist; some called

The Holy Roman Empire | *about 1200*

him the first modern man. Certainly he was a flashing and baffling figure. However, he is barely a figure in German history. Barbarossa made his headquarters in Germany and led forays into Italy. His grandson did the opposite. He centered his life at his brilliant court in Palermo, Sicily, and spent very little time in his German domain.

Early in his reign Frederick took an important step toward lessening the power of the king in Germany, when, in 1220, he granted almost complete independence to the German church. The clergy was declared exempt from taxation and from lay jurisdiction; henceforward the ecclesiastical princes were almost independent monarchs. In 1231 through the Privilege of Worms, by which he sought support for his activities in Italy, Frederick granted almost as much latitude to the German princes, giving them control over local justice and many other former royal prerogatives. Curiously enough, while in southern Italy Frederick was the prototype of the centralizing monarch, in Germany the effect of his rule was the opposite and gave almost full rein to the dynastic particularism which was to be such a curse to Germany in the future. He consistently favored the princes over the towns, which he disliked. On his last visit to Germany Frederick tried to reverse the process he had started, but he was unsuccessful in doing so. He died in 1250; his son, Conrad IV, in 1254—and with them the Hohenstaufen family died out and also medieval Germany. For nineteen years no German king was elected. This great interregnum is an important watershed in German history. Before 1254 the emperor had some claim to being a universal monarch; after 1273 he was the ruler of Germany only, though he kept the old title. And in fact he was hardly ruler in Germany, for dynastic particularism advanced to such a degree that the emperor increasingly could look for support only to his own feudal territories.

During the reign of Frederick II one important event occurred in Germany, which had no connection with the emperor but which was to have significance in the future. During the Crusades several military religious orders had been founded to protect the Holy Sepulchre. These orders were made up of knights, vowed to celibacy but not a religious life; they remained warriors. One of them was the Teutonic Knights, made up of Germans. By the thirteenth century there was no more Holy Sepulchre in Christian hands to guard. The Teutonic Knights wandered to Transylvania to spread Christianity. In 1229 a Polish prince, Conrad of Masovia, invited the knights to come to the shores of the Baltic Sea to continue their missionary work. They accepted and in a short time had carved out for themselves a small empire in the northeastern borderlands, which eventually became the duchy of Prussia, and, together with the lands of the Ascanians in Brandenburg, formed the nucleus of the kingdom of Prussia.

The later middle ages, the period between the interregnum and about 1500, set the pattern for modern Germany even more than the preceding centuries. A number of new and significant developments occurred. The four dynasties whose representatives were to shape Germany (Hapsburg, Hohenzollern, Wittelsbach, and Wettin) made their active appearance. It is noteworthy that the bases for each of these (Austria, Brandenburg, Bavaria, and Saxony) were in the east, and, except for Bavaria, in "colonial" Germany which had been carved out of pagan territories. The old lands in the west along the Rhine had been so divided up that they were either ecclesiastical principalities or belonged to small princelings. The large dynastic units were the decisive forces now; the political center of German gravity shifted to the east. The relation with the church differed too. No longer did German emperors meddle in the affairs of Italy; they concerned themselves with building the power of their own families and lands. In return the popes were excluded from a voice in the imperial elections. Town life reached its apogee during these centuries, and the quarrels between the towns and the knights were continuous. In the north the so-called Hanse towns banded together into a powerful league to protect their mercantile interests, with no reference to their official overlord, the emperor.

When the German electors finally got together in 1273 to elect a new emperor, they did not want to choose the most powerful prince. If they had, they would have chosen Ottokar of Bohemia, who had built a large and wealthy domain for himself but who had boycotted the election. They did not want to choose one of themselves but a prince of second-rate importance who would not be a threat to them and would confirm all their rights. They found their man in Rudolf of Hapsburg (1273–91). The Hapsburg family had lands in southwest Germany, in Switzerland, and in Alsace. Rudolf took no interest in Italian affairs and did not trouble to go to Rome to be crowned. His immediate interest was to reduce the power of Ottokar, who on the extinction of the house of Babenberg had usurped its lands in Austria. Rudolf was completely successful at the battle of the Marchfeld in 1278, in which Ottokar was killed. He permitted Ottokar's heirs to retain their lands in Bohemia and Moravia but invested his own sons with the Austrian domain and thus established Hapsburg power along the Danube, where it remained for more than six centuries. When Rudolf died, the electors, alarmed at the growing power of the house of Hapsburg, passed over his son and once more elected a middling prince, Adolf of Nassau. Adolf proved to be very ambitious and meddled abroad in the conflicts between Philip IV of France and Edward I of England. The electors, disgusted with Adolf, claimed the right to depose an emperor and in 1298 chose Rudolf's son, Albert I (1298–1308). Albert was primarily concerned with the fortunes of his own house. When the Bohemian house became extinct, he seized Bohemia and Moravia for his son. He curried favor with the arrogant pope, Boniface VIII, hoping that the pope would permit him to build a hereditary Hapsburg state. But his career ended when he was murdered by his nephew. There was not another Hapsburg emperor for more than a century.

By this time French interests were important in west Germany where the aggressive king, Philip IV, was trying to extend his power. The new election brought to the German throne a French vassal, the brother of the archbishop of Trier, Henry of Luxemburg or Henry VII (1308–13). Henry was something of an anachronism, taking seriously the old universal idea of empire. He went to Italy, was hailed with plaudits by Dante, was crowned, but accomplished little. At home, however, he was not remiss in fighting for his own family. He seized Bohemia from the Hapsburgs and granted it to his son John, thus endowing the Luxemburg family with a strong basis of power in the east, where it remained paramount for over a century.

The next election was a confused one. In fact two emperors were chosen, Frederick of Hapsburg and Louis of Wittelsbach. Civil war raged for several years, but in 1322 at Mühldorf Louis defeated Frederick and assured himself of power. Soon thereafter he did the typical thing and secured the electorate of Brandenburg for his son.

The reign of Louis IV, "the Bavarian" (1314–47), was a troubled one for Louis but a very interesting one from the point of view of constitutional history. Owing to events in Italy, Louis incurred the fury of Pope John XXII, the ablest of the popes who reigned from Avignon. It looked as if the story of Henry IV and the Hohenstaufens were to be retold. But there is a curiously anticlimactic character to this struggle. John insisted that Louis had been illegally elected and excommunicated him. Louis appealed over the pope to a council and launched an attack on the higher clergy for their wealth and luxury. Much of the interest of the conflict centers around the important figure in the history of political theory, Marsiglio of Padua, who wrote the *Defensor Pacis* as a tract in favor of imperial supremacy. This work insists that the pope has no authority over the emperor in secular matters, that in fact the emperor has the positive duty to resist such papal claims. Louis went to Rome where he was crowned by the "people" and appointed an antipope.

This last action had no practical result, but Louis won his point in refusing the pope any voice in his election. This is a far cry from the days of Gregory VII and Innocent III, and a definite step toward the anticlericalism of the coming centuries.

The electors supported Louis' claims by a document which marked a stage in constitutional history. In 1338 at Rhense they decreed that the emperor's title derived alone from his election by a majority of the electors. Thus the pope was eliminated as a factor in imperial elections. But Louis did not long enjoy his triumph. A series of unhappy events in Germany lessened his popularity; he was even deposed in 1346 and died accidentally the next year.

The deposition of Louis brought to the imperial throne the most capable man of the period, Charles IV (1346–78) of the house of Luxemburg. This was the great moment in the history of that house and also in the history of Bohemia. Charles built Bohemia and the neighboring lands he controlled (including Brandenburg, which he took from the Wittelsbachs) into a really strong state with many modern characteristics. In 1346 he established at Prague the first university in central Europe and made a show city of his beloved capital.

In German history Charles is especially notable for the most important constitutional document of the late middle ages, the Golden Bull of 1356, which regulated imperial elections until the end of the empire in 1806. For the first time a precise list of the electors was stated. They were seven in number, three spiritual (the archbishops of Mainz, Trier, and Cologne) and four temporal (the count Palatine of the Rhine, the king of Bohemia, the margrave of Brandenburg, and the duke of Saxony). The electorates were henceforth to be indivisible and hereditary. No voice in elections was given either to the pope, the princes of nonelectoral rank, or the townsfolk. Thus an electoral oligarchy was set up. The votes of any four of the electors sufficed, and as an added gift the electors received the right that no appeals could be made from the decisions of their courts.

Unfortunately for Charles' hopes his sons were lesser men than he, and the half century following his death was one of confusion and loss in prestige for the imperial power. Charles' eldest son Wenceslas, or Wenzel, succeeded his father (1378–1400) but proved himself incapable of handling a series of civil conflicts which broke out. His combination of alcoholism and incompetence led the electors to depose him in 1400, an act which he, however, did not recognize and continued to protest. A Wittelsbach of the western branch of that family, Rupert, Elector Palatine, was put on the throne (1400–1410), but his unfortunate reign proved that it was necessary for the emperor to be in immediate control of one of the large domains in the east. When Rupert died, Wenceslas' younger brother Sigismund, who had inherited the kingdom of Hungary by marriage, was elected and wielded the effective power until his death in 1437.

Sigismund's reign was troubled mainly by problems which arose in the church. The aftermath of the residence of the popes at Avignon was the scandalous great schism of the west, a period of forty years during which two and sometimes three men each claimed to be the legitimate pope. A council of the church met at Constance from 1414–18 to settle the matter. It prevailed on two of the three claimants to retire and elected Pope Martin V, who was recognized by all except the discredited third claimant.

Even more important for German developments was the treatment of John Huss at the Council of Constance. Huss was a professor at the University of Prague who was much influenced by the teachings of John Wyclif in England. Huss attacked corruption and wealth in the church and called for a return to evangelical simplicity. He also attacked theological dogma, holding the Bible superior to the church and opposing the dogma of transubstantiation. He insisted that the liturgy should be celebrated in the vernacular. His movement soon shifted from the purely religious to the political sphere because it was attractive to the Czechs in Bohemia, who were developing a strong sense of nationalism and resented the dominance of Germans in their land.

Huss was summoned before the Council of Constance and given safe-conduct by Emperor Sigismund. He refused to recant his heresies and in spite of the safe conduct was burned at the stake in 1415. This action led to the Hussite wars in Bohemia, a series of bitterly fought conflicts which lasted for twenty years. In spite of the eventual victory of Sigismund and the Catholics, the Hussite wars left tragic memories of religious and social cleavages which were to re-emerge in the following century.

Early in his reign Sigismund made a fateful appointment. In 1415 he appointed his friend, Frederick of Hohenzollern, to the electorate of Brandenburg. The Hohenzollern family, which originated in southwestern Germany, had for generations held a hereditary imperial post in Nuremberg. It now became one of the most important German families and started a career that was to lead it to Versailles in 1871 and to Doorn after 1918. It was Sigismund also who established the Wettin family in Saxony, where it too was to remain until 1918.

Sigismund died without a male heir. The beneficiary of the activities of the house of Luxemburg was the house of Hapsburg. Albert of Hapsburg, Sigismund's son-in-law, inherited temporarily the lands of Bohemia and Hungary and was also unanimously elected emperor. From this time until the end of the empire in 1806, with one short interruption, a Hapsburg always wore the imperial crown.

Albert reigned for only one year, but his cousin Frederick III (1440–93) was on the throne for over a half century. Frederick was no statesman, but he did have the usual Hapsburg sense of glorifying his own family. He achieved this through matrimonial policy, the greatest example of which was the marriage of his son and heir, Maximilian, to Mary, the heiress of the vast lands of the dukes of Burgundy.

The late fifteenth century was a relatively quiet period in German history. But great things were being gestated. The ideas and artistic achievements of the Renaissance in Italy were making their way across the Alps. Humanists and mystics in their divergent ways were attacking the fabric of the old church. The quiet of the fifteenth century was the prelude to the prodigious events of the sixteenth.

CHAPTER II

Religious Conflict and Territorial Triumph (1500-1714)

With his useful gift of hindsight, it is no problem for the historian to see that by 1500 the German world was on the threshold of momentous events. Alike in the political, economic, social, religious, and artistic spheres, developments were culminating simultaneously in such a way that an upheaval was almost bound to occur. The fifteenth century had shown the weakness of the imperial organization; the inert Frederick III had simply emphasized it. Power was certainly slipping from the head to the members, but the question was which of the groups of members would receive it: the electoral princes, the lesser princes, or perhaps the middle-class burghers of the prosperous German towns. The very prosperity of the towns based on their crafts and their extensive trade served to accentuate the misery of the peasantry, the overwhelming majority of the German population, burdened almost beyond endurance by dues and duties of various sorts levied by both state and church; in years of bad harvest their plight was tragic. To add to their sorrows, the quantity of coined money in Germany increased greatly during these years, bringing with it the evils of inflation. The German peasant was sufficiently wise to know how much better off he might be, an attitude always pregnant with trouble.

The religious situation was also charged with future problems. The influence of the Hussite heresy with its heavy anticlerical overtones was felt throughout Germany. The financial exactions imposed by the Renaissance papacy, careless of its transalpine public relations, made the established church unpopular in many places. In Germany, unlike England and France, there was no strong national government to check the most serious demands of the church. Along with the dislike of the church as a temporal institution, there was also a shift in theological emphasis. Probably some of this too was caused by the Hussite example. In this period a number of mystics flourished, men and women who achieved their religious experience through immediate intuition of God without much reference to the mediation of church and sacraments. This movement culminated in the so-called *devotio moderna,* whose adherents preached a simplified Christianity with emphasis on personal morality and a personal relationship with God. One of the schools conducted by these men trained Erasmus of Rotterdam, the greatest German scholar of the time, who, though he remained within the mother church, nevertheless bitterly attacked some of its churchmen.

By this time the new attitudes, grouped together under the label "Renaissance," had reached Germany. Humanism, scholarship, the study of Greek, and the practice of the fine arts were no longer limited to Italy. It seems no accident that the three greatest German painters of all time, Mathias Grünewald, Albrecht Dürer, and Hans Holbein the Younger, were all alive in the year 1500.

When Frederick III died in 1493, he was succeeded as emperor by his son Maximilian I (1493–1519), the "last of the knights," a flamboyant and chivalrous fellow who was, however, no fool. Familiar with the well-administered lands of his wife's Burgundian inheritance, Maximilian was anxious to institute reforms in the crumbling structure of the Empire. At a meeting (Diet) of the princes and estates of the Empire in 1495, an effort was made to modernize the old institutions. The Diet established a supreme court (*Reichskammergericht*) which was to adjudicate all quarrels endangering the public eternal peace of the Empire. The Empire was further divided into ten "circles," overlapping the boundaries of individual states to help preserve peace. These circles show the extent of the Empire according to the authorities of the time and point out that it was already a distinctly German state. As it turned out, the reforms were inadequate to handle the problems that were about to arise; they were at least a recognition of the needs of the moment.

Maximilian spent much of his reign in warfare, particularly with the kings of France. The quarrel between the French Valois kings and the Austrian Hapsburgs, arising from the settlement of the Burgundian inheritance, was to develop into a long-standing conflict lasting even after the house of Valois died out and was succeeded in 1589 by the house of Bourbon. Maximilian did not neglect the typical Hapsburg matrimonial diplomacy. By marrying his son to the heiress of Ferdinand and Isabella of Spain, he prepared for his grandson Charles one of the greatest inheritances in all history, an inheritance, however, which brought no happiness.

When Maximilian died in 1519, two powerful foreign rulers, Henry

VIII of England and Francis I of France, announced themselves as candidates for the imperial throne. The obvious candidate was Maximilian's grandson, Charles of Hapsburg, now king of Spain. The prelude to the election was full of bribery and diplomatic chicanery. It was largely the support of the great Fugger banking house of Augsburg that secured the triumph for Charles, whose dominions were now immense. From his mother, he possessed Spain with her domains in Italy and across the Atlantic Ocean; from his grandmother, he controlled part of the lands of Burgundy, including the rich and powerful Low Countries; and from his grandfather, he inherited the Austrian Hapsburg possessions. And now he was Holy Roman emperor.

Charles V's reign (1519–56) was a tragic one. Charles was not an attractive personality. He was dour and serious, but deeply devout and concerned with the high positions he held. In fact, his principal problem was that his dominions were so extensive that no sooner did he seem about to solve one conflict than he was called urgently to another. Three major preoccupations concerned him: the religious revolt in Germany, the endemic war with France, and the threat of the Ottoman Turks, who approached the gates of Vienna and convinced the Hapsburgs that the onus of the old crusading movement had devolved upon them. It is difficult not to be sympathetic with this ruler so beset by competing problems.

The religious revolt centers around the career of Martin Luther (1483–1546). Luther's father, a peasant miner, planned a career in the law for his son; but after a deep religious experience, Martin gave up his legal studies and undertook a religious life, entering an Augustinian monastery. He was ordained a priest in 1508 and sent to the new University of Wittenberg in Saxony as a professor of philosophy. Two years later he went to Rome on church business and was bitterly shocked by the luxury and extravagance he found there in high clerical circles. He was a man of violence, a man burning for God, who lived in fear of eternal damnation and was sure that no deed of his could relieve the penalties of his terrible future in hell. Eventually, from his studies of the Bible he developed the consoling doctrine of justification through faith.

In 1517 a Dominican, John Tetzel, appeared in Wittenberg preaching an indulgence proclaimed by Pope Leo X to collect money to build the new church of St. Peter in Rome. Contributors to the fund, if repentent for their sins, were promised remission of the temporal punishment due for those sins. Luther considered this an intolerable abuse, and on October 31 nailed to the door of the university chapel ninety-five theses, or propositions, concerning the doctrine of indulgences, which he declared himself ready to dispute with any opponent who might present himself. This typically medieval action is generally regarded as the opening event in the history of Protestantism.

It is beyond our scope to enter into the details of the early history of the Protestant movement or to raise the theological problems involved. During the three years after 1517 Luther took part in various public disputes, and his positions were the subject of official inquiries. Gradually, as he attacked the primacy of the pope and later the doctrine of transubstantiation, Luther moved further and further from orthodoxy until his own intellectual integrity forced him to recognize that he was closer to Huss than to Rome. By 1520 he had written his major theological tracts. In that year Pope Leo condemned a number of Luther's propositions and threatened excommunication. When this papal ruling (or bull) arrived in Wittenberg, Luther reacted by burning it publicly in the square before the university. Shortly thereafter the excommunication was decreed formally.

At about the same time the new emperor, Charles V, appeared in Germany and called a meeting of the imperial Diet at the city of Worms. The pope appealed to the emperor to place Luther under the ban of the Empire. The Diet summoned him to Worms under safe-conduct to give him one more chance to recant. In March 1521 Luther appeared twice before the Diet, on the second occasion delivering his famous speech in which he declared himself unable to change his views in any way. He then left Worms and on his way home was spirited away by his friend and patron, Frederick the Wise, Elector of Saxony, to the peaceful seclusion of the castle of the Wartburg, near Eisenach, where he spent almost a year at his translation of the Bible. Aside from its religious importance, this work set the future literary form of the German language. In the meantime the Diet placed Luther under the ban of the Empire.

After his return from the Wartburg Luther married a former nun and spent most of the rest of his life advising on the formulation of the new doctrines and on the organization of the new churches. Since he could not depend for support on the Empire, Luther based the new institutions on the local territorial princes. Each of these in Lutheran areas became a supreme bishop for his own domain and controlled his own church. This obviously gave a mighty impetus to the growing power of the individual princes and also encouraged the less scrupulous of them to embrace the new faith because they could then seize the possessions and incomes of the old church.

The decade of the 1520's was decisive for the Protestant revolution. In 1521 there was an expectation that Luther could be silenced; by 1530 the breach was complete, a statement of Lutheran beliefs had been drawn up, and Germany was divided spiritually forever. During those years Charles V was not in Germany at all. His major preoccupations were two wars against France, wars which were only peripheral to German history except that they permitted the consolidation of Protestantism without the presence of the emperor to do anything conclusive about it. In fact, in 1522 Charles abdicated further his position in Germany by making his younger brother Ferdinand regent of all the German Hapsburg lands. Ferdinand was married to the heiress of Bohemia and Hungary, lands which fell to him on the death of their king in 1526. As ruler of those eastern territories, Ferdinand's primary concern was to defend them against the Turks. From 1526 to 1532 he waged campaigns in that direction, of which the most serious moment was the first Turkish siege of Vienna in 1529. Both Hapsburg brothers thus were able to give only secondary attention to Germany during this momentous decade.

From the earliest days of his protest Luther was met with extreme popularity and enthusiasm by the masses with whom he came in contact. This was a measure of the unpopularity of the church at the time, but it was also a measure of the severe economic and social tensions of the moment. In fact, religious issues became so intertwined with social ones that it is almost impossible to separate them. As early as 1521 the towns of Wittenberg and Zwickau fell prey to leaders who not only pushed the religious revolution in an extreme radical direction far beyond anything that Luther had ever preached, but also tried to set up a semicommunist society aimed against the princes. Luther, furious at this, left his retreat at the Wartburg and in a week drove these "saints" from the new temple.

Another sign of discontent was the revolt of the imperial knights in 1522. They were not subject to any territorial prince but owed their allegiance directly to the emperor, and usually possessed a small estate from which they tried to wrest a livelihood. In the early sixteenth century they were in a very depressed condition. The prosperous elements in Germany were the princes and the towns. The knights were suffering badly from monetary inflation. Two of them, Franz von Sickingen and Ulrich von Hutten, assumed the leadership of the cause. These men espoused Lutheranism and decided to attack the ecclesiastical lands, in particular those of the archbishop of Trier. The attack on Trier failed, Sickingen was killed at a siege of his own castle, and Hutten died the next year in exile. This revolt is not intrinsically important but illustrates the turmoil of the period.

Much more important and bloody was the Peasants' War of 1524 and 1525. There was nothing new about revolts of the oppressed peasantry.

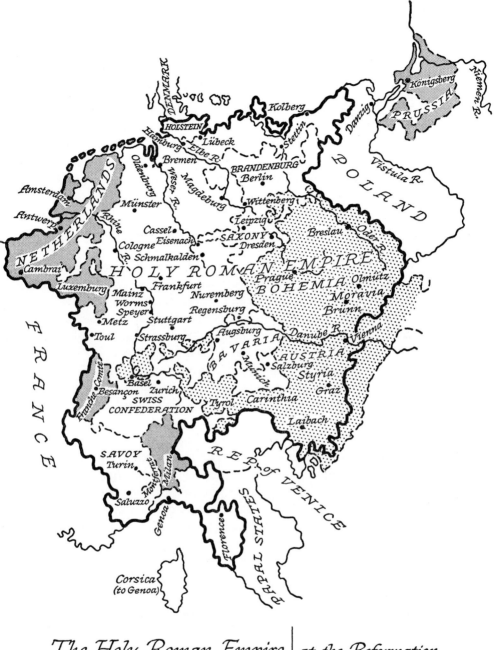

The Holy Roman Empire | at the Reformation

——— Holy Roman Empire

Austrian Hapsburg Possessions

Spanish Hapsburg Possessions

During the late fifteenth and early sixteenth centuries there was endemic unrest under the banner of the *Bundschuh,* the typical peasant footgear. There was nothing specifically religious about this peasant movement, though some of its attitudes resembled the Hussites'. However, the appearance of Lutheranism with its break from traditional authority, and the general ferment of the times, seemed to be propitious for the peasants. The peasant leaders, none of whom were men of great capability, adopted Luther's views and were impressed with the anti-Roman program of Ulrich Zwingli in Switzerland, which lay near the area in which the peasant strength was greatest.

The peasants drew up a program called the Twelve Articles, which were both religious and economic, though on the whole limited in their demands. They called for an elective priesthood and the abolition of various oppressive feudal dues. Although some German leaders saw the justice of some of the demands, there was on the whole no sympathy with them, and the peasants decided to resort to force. By the spring of 1525 several hundred thousand peasants were under arms. They conducted a campaign of reprisal against their lords, which rapidly assumed the bloodthirsty character of social wars.

This was a crucial moment for Luther, whom the peasants were hailing as a leader. He had already shown his basic political conservatism in his attitude toward the radicals at Zwickau. He now made his position very clear in a violent and passionate pamphlet entitled *Against the Murderous and Rapacious Hordes of the Peasants.* This was all the propertied classes needed. They organized troops which in the course of several months put down the peasants with appalling brutality. The peasants were crushed, this time permanently, and Luther had placed his future squarely in the hands of the territorial princes.

From this time on Lutheranism ceased to spread among the lower classes. Its attraction was now to the educated, especially the local rulers, who tended to sweep their people along when they themselves became converts. An example is Albert of Hohenzollern, Grand Master of the Teutonic Knights. Lutheran teachings had reached as far as remote Prussia and attracted Albert. He paid a visit to Luther, who advised him to renounce his vows, marry, abolish the Order, and found a dynasty. Albert did exactly that and thus helped to establish the future greatness of the Hohenzollern family. Prussia joined ranks with Saxony, Hesse, and the other Lutheran territories.

With the creation of more Lutheran states the tendency developed among both Catholics and Lutherans to form leagues based on similarity of belief. While no one wanted civil war or the disruption of the Empire at this time, there is no question that these leagues paved the way for the consolidation of the two groups and eventually for the tragic wars of religion. In 1526 Archduke Ferdinand summoned a Diet of the Empire to meet at Speyer. Ferdinand was intensely concerned with the imminent threat of the Turks and anxious to gain the support of all the German princes in his military efforts. Thus it would clearly not be possible try to enforce the decisions made at Worms in their full strength. Emperor Charles now believed that a final settlement of the religious problem was not possible until a general council of the church could be convoked. Thus at Speyer a mild resolution was taken providing that, until this council met, the estates "with their subjects, would live, govern, and act in such a way as everyone trusted to justify before God and the Imperial Majesty." Although it was not the intent, this edict seemed to consecrate the religious division in Germany and to make it easier for hesitant princes to embrace the new faith without fear of imperial reprisal.

Three years later the situation had changed a good deal. Charles V and Pope Clement VII had patched up their difficulties; the war with France was brought to a close; the Turkish peril was receding. It seemed possible to Ferdinand to take a stronger line. Accordingly he called another Diet at Speyer (1529) at which he read a message calling for no more religious innovations and announcing the imminent arrival of Charles in Germany and the immediate calling of a church council. The message was approved by the Catholic majority while the Lutherans drew up a "Protest," from which the word Protestant derives.

The following year Charles did arrive in Germany for the first time in nine years and called a Diet of the Empire to meet at Augsburg. It was a splendid affair but ended in failure. It looked like a religious council rather than a political one. There was a full representation of Catholic theologians. The Protestant cause was upheld by Philipp Melanchthon, a young follower of Luther, who hoped that a compromise might be effected between the two parties. He had drawn up a statement of belief, the Augsburg Confession, which blunted some of the sharp edges of Protestantism and which he believed might be a document of conciliation. Although Melanchthon was constantly willing to compromise, there were points beyond which he could not go. No compromise was achieved, and the Diet decreed a return to the very strict prohibition of Lutheran teachings proclaimed at Worms in 1521. The Protestant princes left the Diet, and the *status quo* was hardly changed. The Augsburg Confession has remained a creed for orthodox Lutheranism ever since.

The Diet gave the Protestants six months to return to the old faith. The Protestant reply in early 1531 was to found the League of Schmalkalden, which eventually became a firm alliance of the Protestant princes and cities to protect them against Catholic attack. The drift toward open conflict continued.

It looked as if this time the Hapsburgs meant business in their resolve to stamp out Protestantism, but again their attention was diverted by pressing problems elsewhere. Once more the Turkish danger looked ominous. The emperor was forced to agree to the Religious Peace of Nuremberg (1532), a truce which was to continue the *status quo* until a council or the next Diet. In return the Protestant princes offered Charles help against the Turks.

As it developed, this temporary arrangement of 1532 lasted for almost fifteen years. Charles was out of Germany during most of this time. He undertook a campaign against the Turks, two wars with France, and two expeditions to North Africa. It was not until 1544 that he was free to take any important action in Germany. In the meantime the Protestant area in Germany increased enormously. By the mid-forties almost all of north Germany was Protestant and even Austria itself felt the impact of the new doctrines. Among the temporal principalities only Bavaria seemed safe for Rome. A special problem arose in the case of the ecclesiastical territories. If a bishop or abbot decided to turn Protestant, should he secularize the whole territory as Albert of Hohenzollern had done, or should he simply get out of the way himself and permit a new canonical appointment? The solution differed in various places according to the relative strengths involved. In some dioceses secular administrators were appointed to run the affairs of the area while the question remained unanswered. The problem of church lands in secular territories was serious too, especially when one realizes that the church had fulfilled all social and charitable functions. The usual solution was for the prince to confiscate all church property and to assume the responsibility for the church's former duties. The temptation latent in this for avaricious princelings is obvious.

Still another serious problem arose with the introduction of the teachings of John Calvin in Germany. These teachings, far more radical in their opposition to the old faith than those of Luther, spread to southwestern Germany from Calvin's headquarters in Geneva. They made special inroads into the lands of the Elector Palatine. The Lutherans were just as opposed to Calvinism as they were to Catholicism, so the struggle became three-cornered.

When Charles V returned to Germany in 1545, he at first appeared to temporize. However, before long it was clear that he was determined to wage war and was trying to win to his side some of the Protestant princes. He was successful in obtaining the help of Duke Maurice of

Saxony (not to be confused with his cousin from the other branch of the Saxon line, the elector of Saxony, who was a leader of the League of Schmalkalden). The War of Schmalkalden broke out in 1546. For some months nothing decisive happened; the Protestants in particular were hesitant and dilatory. In April 1547 Charles won an overwhelming victory over the Saxons at the battle of Mühlberg. The Saxon elector was captured and his dignity transferred to Maurice. It looked as if Charles and Catholicism were triumphant. The following year Charles issued the so-called Augsburg Interim, an attempt at religious peace. It was in fact hardly a compromise, though it did grant a few favors to the Protestants. For instance, they could maintain a married clergy and receive communion in two kinds if they obtained a papal dispensation. There was also an effort to reform some of the abuses of the old church.

Nobody liked the Interim very much. The pope was suspicious because Charles seemed to be arrogating religious decisions to himself, particularly at a time when the Council of Trent was already meeting to deal with the problem. The Protestants were, of course, dissatisfied. Even more significant perhaps was the fact that all the princes, Catholic and Protestant, were worried about the revival of the authority of the emperor—especially an emperor who was primarily a Spaniard. They had enjoyed too long the pleasures of practical independence to be willing to give them up.

The situation simmered for several years until in 1552 the Protestant princes revolted against Charles. This time they were led by Maurice, who had changed sides and gone to the length of making an alliance with Charles' bitterest enemy, Henry II of France. This phase of the war was unsuccessful for Charles, who was almost captured at Innsbruck and fled over the Brenner Pass into Italy.

The war continued against France, but in Germany negotiations went on for some time under the direction of Archduke Ferdinand, culminating in the Peace of Augsburg of 1555, a landmark in German history. This treaty settled the religious question with the phrase, *cuius regio eius religio*. This meant that each prince might freely choose between Catholicism and Lutheranism and might require his subjects to conform to his beliefs. An "ecclesiastical reservation" provided that churchmen who henceforth wished to change their religion had to abandon the church property entrusted to them to the Catholic church, which would appoint a new incumbent. All church lands confiscated before 1552 were to remain Protestant; all others were to remain Catholic. The treaty gave no privileges of any sort to the Calvinists. This compromise agreement remained the legal basis of the religious settlement for the next century, though in practice it was often violated.

A few months later Charles V, tired and disgusted, abdicated his titles and functions, and retired to a monastery for the short remainder of his life. His Spanish and Italian possessions went to his son Philip, while his central European holdings went to his brother Ferdinand, who became Emperor Ferdinand I (1556–64). With these events a period in German history came to a close.

The focus of interest in Europe during the second half of the sixteenth century moves away from Germany. It shifts to France, which was on the eve of its long religious struggle; to England and Spain, where the long duel of the reigns of Elizabeth I and Philip II was about to be fought; and to the Netherlands, which was soon to start its war of independence under the house of Orange against Spain. Religiously speaking, the main interest in Germany lies in the loss of ground of Protestantism and the corresponding gains of Catholicism as a result of the Catholic Reformation.

The emperors of the period were not men of great strength or political competence. Ferdinand I's son, Maximilian II (1564–76), was a man of peace, who, however, was forced to protect his eastern possessions in a long struggle against the Turks. He was not fond of Spain and personally favored Protestantism, but left little imprint on history. His son, Rudolf II (1576–1612), had a curious personality. By choice he resided in Prague, where astrologers were his favorite companions. The impressive scientific names of Tycho Brahe and John Kepler are associated with his court. Content with the stars and his paintings, Rudolf displayed little political acumen.

For a time after 1555 Protestantism continued to grow and consolidate itself until within a few years it represented a considerable majority of the German population. The most extensive gains were made by the Calvinists, disliked by Lutherans and Catholics alike. The first important German prince to become a Calvinist was the Elector Palatine, who made of his capital, Heidelberg, a center of Calvinist thought. This belief spread into the lower Rhineland where it was encouraged by the neighboring Dutch. Calvinism also found adherents in Bohemia.

More impressive was the recuperative power displayed by the Roman Catholic church. The Catholic Reformation is linked with two important events. The main one was the Council of Trent, which met intermittently from 1545 to 1563. This council, from which Protestants were excluded, defined in detail the doctrine of the church, especially those parts of it which had been attacked by the Protestants. It also enacted a number of disciplinary and educational reforms which remedied many of the abuses against which Luther and the other reformers had raised their outcry. Hardly less important was the approval by Pope Paul III in 1540 of a new order, the Society of Jesus or Jesuit Order, which had been founded a few years before by St. Ignatius Loyola. The first German Jesuit was St. Peter Canisius, sometimes called by Catholics the second apostle to Germany (St. Boniface having been the first). The Jesuits were active in founding schools and sending out preachers to confute the Protestants. They were very successful, and by the end of the century Protestantism hardly existed in Bavaria, Austria, parts of Bohemia, and large sections of the Rhineland.

The settlement at Augsburg contained a number of ambiguities, most of which involved the ecclesiastical reservation. On the whole the Lutherans displayed remarkable apathy in enforcing what they felt were their rights, while the Catholic princes were more adamant. A major test case occurred in Cologne in the early 1580's when the archbishop publicly declared himself a Protestant. The pope deposed him and named a Bavarian prince as his successor. The affair burst into open warfare, but the Catholics triumphed very quickly and Cologne remained Catholic thenceforward.

The Protestants watched the resurgence of Catholicism with concern but took no important action until a series of religious disturbances broke out in the little town of Donauwörth in the early years of the seventeenth century. Here Catholic Bavaria violently repossessed for the old church a Protestant town on the grounds that it had denied rights to a Catholic monastery in the neighborhood. As a result the leading Protestant princes simply walked out of a meeting of the Diet in 1608.

The following year a military step was taken with the formation of the Protestant Union. This alliance, under the leadership of Frederick IV, Elector Palatine, included as the years went on most of the leading Protestant princes. However, the continuing conflict between Lutheran and Calvinist tended to render it less powerful than might have been the case. A few months later some of the Catholic rulers formed a competing Catholic League under the aegis of Duke Maximilian of Bavaria. Here again there was weakness because a number of the members were ecclesiastical rulers whose military strength was negligible.

A general European war threatened during these years over the extremely complicated inheritance of Cleves-Jülich in northwestern Germany. Had it not been for the murder of Henry IV of France in 1610, war might have begun. As it developed, both the Union and the League backed down and the inheritance was divided between the two principal candidates, one of whom was the Hohenzollern elector of Brandenburg who had just inherited the duchy of Prussia. An important aspect of the Cleves-Jülich dispute was that foreign powers—France, the Netherlands, Spain, and England—involved themselves actively in it, prefiguring the years to come when Germany was to become the prey and battleground for foreign antagonists.

The seedbed of the future great war lay in the Hapsburg dominions in Bohemia. Here the old Hussites were encouraged by the new German Protestants, and both Czechs and Germans of the new faith increased in spite of the efforts of the Jesuits. Emperor Rudolf, anxious to end his days peacefully with his studies, granted a charter of freedom of conscience in 1609 and even permitted a committee of Protestant leaders, called *defensores,* whose function was to defend the liberties of the Protestants. Rudolf's actions aroused the disgust of his family, particularly his brother, Archduke Matthias, who in 1612 forced him to resign all the Hapsburg hereditary lands but not the title of emperor. Rudolf tried to resist but died in 1613 before he accomplished anything, and Matthias was elected emperor (1613–19).

The major problem of Matthias' reign was the question of succession. He and his two brothers were aging and childless. The obvious heir was their cousin, young Archduke Ferdinand of Styria, whose principal quality was his devoted adherence to the Catholic church. The Austrian Hapsburgs, supported by their Spanish cousins, pressed for Ferdinand's proclamation even before the death of Matthias. He was in fact proclaimed in Hungary and Bohemia in 1618. Matthias died in early 1619, and Ferdinand II (1619–37) was elected emperor.

The Bohemian Protestant nobles were not disposed to accept the accomplished fact, insisting that their kingship was elective, not hereditary. The crisis occurred on May 18, 1618, when a number of Protestant leaders called on the royal governors in the castle in Prague to protest ill treatment. The discussion turned into a fight, and the two governors and one secretary were hurled out of a window to fall seventy feet. They were not seriously hurt, according to the Catholics because on their way down they called on the holy names of Jesus and Mary, and according to the Protestants because they landed on a soft dung heap. In any case, this so-called "defenestration of Prague" was the opening action in the Thirty Years' War.

It took a long time to get a war started in the seventeenth century. The diplomats played a slow complex game of conflicting alliances, while the generals were reluctant to expose their trained men in battle and preferred a dilatory strategy of maneuver. The Protestant princes were not anxious to unleash the full strength of the Catholic opposition —especially Saxony, the largest Protestant territory, which hated Calvinism and was determined to hold to its imperial moorings. In the summer of 1619 a Bohemian army approached Vienna while Ferdinand was being crowned at Frankfurt, but it had to withdraw.

The Bohemian nobles did not hurry to elect a king. The foremost candidate was Frederick V, Elector Palatine, young, handsome, charming, the husband of a daughter of James I of England, and a Calvinist. In August he was elected and made the mistake of accepting the election. He started his rule in Prague in great state, but there were many who predicted that he would be only a "winter king," that his kingdom would disappear with the spring thaw. He received no help from his father-in-law in London, who was at the moment dallying with an alliance with the Spanish Hapsburgs.

The most important alliance concluded was between Emperor Ferdinand and Duke Maximilian of Bavaria, head of the Catholic League. Maximilian was the most astute of the German princes. He never allowed himself to be duped by the Hapsburgs but believed at this moment that he had much to gain from Ferdinand. The agreement provided that a League army would invade Bohemia, that Maximilian would be reimbursed for his expenses, and above all that he would receive the electoral title and some of the lands of his relative Frederick, who was put under the ban of the Empire. The League army under General Tilly moved into Bohemia and at the battle of the White Mountain in November 1620 crushed Frederick and his Protestant supporters.

The White Mountain was a crucial date in Bohemian history. It consecrated the hatred of Czech for German. The Hapsburg reprisals were violent and bitter. The lands of the rebel nobles were seized and resold to a new German nobility superimposed on the Czech population. One of the main immediate gainers was Albrecht von Wallenstein, a Protestant-born noble and a staunch believer in astrology, who had become a Catholic to marry an elderly wealthy widow and ran her lands and others which he bought so competently that he eventually became one of the richest men in Europe. With this money Wallenstein was able to raise a large private army which he rented to the emperor. He was the most impressive of the soldiers of fortune during this period, who enriched themselves by warfare at the expense of the unfortunate population.

The League army under Tilly now moved west to the Palatinate and in 1622 completed the conquest of Frederick's hereditary domain. Ferdinand granted the electorship officially to Maximilian and the first phase of the war was over.

The second phase centered in northwestern Germany and was dominated by King Christian IV of Denmark. In this area there were a number of important bishoprics which had been secularized in defiance of the ecclesiastical reservation. They would be obvious targets for Catholic Hapsburg action, since they were located strategically for the Spanish Hapsburgs to get at their rebellious Dutch subjects. For the opposite reason both the Dutch and the English were anxious to keep the Catholics out of the area. France, although of course a Catholic kingdom, was primarily interested in opposing Spain; she had just come under the control of her great minister, Cardinal Richelieu, who, although a prince of the church, was more concerned with keeping down the Hapsburgs than with supporting the Catholic cause. Thus the war gradually began its shift from a war of religion to a war of dynastic interests. The king of Denmark, as duke of Holstein, was a prince of the Empire. He was elected captain of the "Lower Saxon Circle" and with his army entered Germany.

There were two armies available to the Catholics. One was the army of the League under General Tilly. The other was the large body of well-trained men which Wallenstein offered to Emperor Ferdinand with the understanding that great gains would accrue to his ambitious self and that the army would live off the land wherever it happened to be. In 1626 Wallenstein defeated a Protestant soldier of fortune, Ernst von Mansfeld, at Dessau and pursued him eastward. Later the same year Tilly defeated King Christian decisively at the battle of Lutter. Both Catholic generals followed up their victories by an invasion of Denmark in 1627. The Protestants were routed. One of their princes, the duke of Mecklenburg, was deposed by the emperor, who gave the territory to Wallenstein, an unheard of reward for an upstart member of the lower nobility. Emperor Ferdinand then decided to achieve control of the Baltic coast of Germany where imperial influence had been negligible for many years. Therefore, during 1628 Wallenstein tried to capture the islandlike city of Stralsund. He had no naval equipment and thus failed in this project, but Catholic power was at a greater height than for generations before.

The emperor seized this moment to take his most ambitious step. In 1629 he proclaimed the Edict of Restitution, which provided that all the church lands and dioceses which had become Protestant since the religious peace of 1555 were to be restored to the Catholic church. This involved fourteen bishoprics and many convents and monasteries. Immediately members of the Hapsburg and Wittelsbach families were named to the vacant sees. Shortly after, the treaty of Lübeck was signed between the emperor and King Christian by which the Danish king repossessed his lands but promised to get out of German affairs. This was the height of the Hapsburg fortunes.

By this time the Catholic princes, especially Maximilian of Bavaria, were getting very uneasy. It was admittedly desirable to restore Catholicism to as much of Germany as possible, but this now seemed to redound only to the greater glory of the Spanish and Austrian Hapsburgs. There was a real fear that Ferdinand was aiming at the establishment of a strong, centralized monarchy in Germany at the expense of the cherished independence of the territorial princes. The princes and the League could exert some check over the emperor through their control of the League army under Tilly; but they had no control over the private army of Wallenstein, who was in the emperor's personal employ and whose ambition, arrogance, and depredations seemed to have no end. They decided to force Wallenstein's dismissal. This was accomplished at a meeting in Regensburg in 1630. The soldier of astrology returned to his lands to wait until he was needed once more.

The third, or Swedish, and most dramatic period of the Thirty Years' War opened with the landing of Gustavus Adolphus, king of Sweden, on German soil in June 1630. Gustavus, the "Lion of the North," was a young man who had already displayed brilliance as an administrator in his reorganization of Sweden and as a military leader in his campaigns against the Poles. He was a devoted Lutheran, who feared a Hapsburg triumph in Europe as a direct threat to his own position. He gained the alliance of several of the lesser north German rulers shortly after he landed, but his great achievement was the treaty of Bärwalde signed with France in early 1631. By this treaty France, which was not officially in the war, promised to subsidize the Swedes generously in their "liberation" of German states from Hapsburg domination. This was Richelieu's greatest diplomatic stroke. Shortly thereafter Gustavus forced an alliance with the elector of Brandenburg and started to march south. Meanwhile Tilly's army set out to meet the Swedish king and in May 1631 captured Magdeburg, whose administrator was an ally of Gustavus. The town was put to sack and burned almost to the ground. The war was becoming more general and more ferocious; Germany was becoming a charnel house.

When Tilly's men advanced into Saxony and began to pillage, the Saxon elector, who had kept out of the war so far, joined the king of Sweden. On September 17, 1631, the battle of Breitenfeld, near Leipzig, was fought between Tilly and Gustavus with the aid of the Saxons. The Swedes annihilated Tilly's army. After this there was almost no opposition to Gustavus Adolphus' triumphant march across central Germany to Frankfurt, where he spent the winter.

The spectacular successes of the Swedes gave pause to the German rulers. What advantage was there in exchanging a Hapsburg ruler for a

Swedish one? Even Richelieu was worried. Emperor Ferdinand saw only one course open, the recall of Wallenstein. Wallenstein's price was high: he wanted supreme command, answerable to no one, and wished to make any treaty with Saxony of his choosing. Ferdinand had no alternative. Wallenstein put his forces on the move and began by pillaging Hapsburg Bohemia on his way to meet the Swedes. In early 1632 Gustavus started eastward. He defeated Tilly, who died shortly thereafter, and carried out a campaign of terror in Bavaria as bad as Wallenstein's in Bohemia. All summer the two armies lay near each other in Saxony. The battle of the titans occurred on November 16, 1632, at Lützen, also near Leipzig. It was a furious battle in which the Swedes were victorious, but, more important, Gustavus Adolphus was killed on the field.

The events of the next two years are confused. The Swedish crown passed to Gustavus' young daughter Christina under the regency of the able minister Axel Oxenstierna. The loss of Gustavus was a bitter blow; Sweden could not expect to play the large role that had been hers for two years. There was an understandable disposition on the part of the princes to end this war which had been so long and so cruel. The behavior of Wallenstein during 1633 will always remain something of a mystery. He missed various opportunities to demonstrate his force and instead busied himself negotiating with some of the Protestant princes. Some think that he saw himself as the ruler of a reorganized empire with a greater degree of religious toleration. Emperor Ferdinand turned against him and in February 1634 dismissed him. Wallenstein moved from Prague to Eger, and there on February 25 he was murdered by a group of his own officers. He remains one of the most enigmatic and fascinating characters in German history.

During 1634 and 1635 there were serious efforts in the direction of peace. The German princes, both Catholic and Protestant, realized that they had become simply the pawns of foreign interests. A feeling of common German nationality seemed to motivate them. This culminated in the Peace of Prague of 1635 between the emperor and Saxony. It modified the Edict of Restitution and set 1627 as the date of the possession of church holdings. This was a date favorable to the Catholics, but not so favorable as 1555. A number of German states acceded to the treaty, but the cause of peace was not to prevail. In the same year, 1635, Richelieu acted openly by declaring war on Spain and entering officially into the carnage in Germany.

The last thirteen years of the war are barely a part of German history. During them Germany was acted on rather than acting. The armies of France, Spain, Sweden, the Empire, and the German princes crossed and crisscrossed the German land wreaking havoc and leaving behind them burning towns, ravaged fields, and rotting corpses. The war was now really a tangle of wars whose principal protagonists were the non-German states. The issues which had originally given it birth were almost forgotten. Germany had entered the period of her history in which she was the prey of other nations. Ferdinand II, so important in the early days of the struggle, died in 1637 after assuring the succession to his son. Ferdinand III (1637–57) was a shadowy figure, dominated by his Spanish Hapsburg cousins.

By the early 1640's there was terrible war-weariness, especially in Germany, and negotiations to start real negotiations got under way as early as 1641. It took three years before the diplomats assembled and four more before the treaties of Westphalia were signed. Even then France and Spain remained at war for more than another decade. Rarely in history has diplomacy been more complex. The degree of wrangling over protocol and precedence, the squabbles on religious niceties, and the awkwardness of communication would be laughable if one did not realize that at the same time the armies were still on the march, fighting, killing, and ravaging. The representatives of the Catholic powers assembled at Münster, those of the Protestants at Osnabrück forty miles away. Somehow they agreed on a series of arrangements which became basic law for Germany for a century and a half to come.

The Peace of Westphalia of 1648 consecrated the essential independence of the German states. The Hapsburg thrust for a centralized German monarchy was never revived. Foreign nations (e.g., France and Sweden, both of which received imperial territories) became members of the German Diet. There were some territorial shifts within the Empire; Brandenburg increased considerably by receiving most of Pomerania and several secularized bishoprics, including the expectancy of Magdeburg, to the south. The Netherlands and Switzerland were recognized as independent of the Empire. Maximilian of Bavaria retained his electoral title and some of the lands of the Palatine elector, but a new electorate was set up for the "winter king's" son, the new Elector Palatine. Within the Empire two bodies were established in the Diet—one of Catholics, the other of Protestants. Henceforth each was to run the concerns of its own group, and neither could come under the control of the other. The date for the ecclesiastical reservation was set at 1624. Calvinists were given equal status with Lutherans. These religious arrangements show a sense of toleration or, more particularly, that religious issues were no longer so urgent as formerly. From this time on there were no important changes in the religious map of Germany. This was a peace of exhaustion; it did not really settle any of the basic issues, but at least it did create a pattern in which the old Holy Roman Empire could muddle along until it finally collapsed under the impact of the next general upheaval, the revolutionary period of the late eighteenth century.

The second half of the seventeenth century was a tragic period for Germany. There was almost no German history. The first great need was to recover somehow from the frightful ravages of the Thirty Years' War, ravages so severe in both men and property that Germany was seriously retarded behind the other states of western Europe. Probably the most poignant description of this pitiful period occurs in the one important literary production of the time, Grimmelshausen's picaresque novel, *Simplicissimus,* which paints a horrendous picture.

The great figure of the period was Louis XIV of France. France had now replaced Spain as the major power on the continent, and Louis waged several wars to enlarge his domains—particularly in the northeast at the expense of the Rhenish parts of the Empire and of the Spanish Netherlands (modern Belgium). The first of his wars, the War of Devolution (1667–68), hardly concerned Germany at all, although Emperor Leopold I (1658–1705) was nominally in the alliance against France. Louis claimed that the Spanish Netherlands had "devolved" upon his Spanish wife because her dowry had never been paid, and proceeded to invade that territory. A combination of English, Dutch, and Swedish forces persuaded Louis to abandon his big enterprise, but in the Treaty of Aix-la-Chapelle he received several important towns for his trouble.

The ire of the French king now turned toward the Dutch; after having by diplomacy detached from them both England and Sweden, he launched his forces against the little republic in 1672. The Dutch, who were allied with Frederick William, the "great" elector of Brandenburg (1640–88), put up a surprising and vigorous resistance, overthrew their republican leaders, placed William III of Orange in control, and opened their floodgates to protect the province of Holland from conquest. In 1674 the war became general when the Empire and Spain allied themselves with Holland and declared war on France. At about the same time England withdrew from her French alliance and made peace with the Dutch.

German participation was halfhearted. Emperor Leopold entered the war at first on behalf of his Hapsburg territories, though the Empire in general did not join in until later, and sent a force under General Montecucculi to the middle Rhine. Frederick William marched with the Austrians but became disgusted with their delays, particularly when they were soundly defeated by the great French general, Turenne, who had

The Empire at the Peace of Westphalia

The Empire ———
Spanish Hapsburg Dominions
Austrian Hapsburg Dominions
Church Lands

been ravaging the Palatinate. The elector decided to go his own way and withdrew from the war accepting instead a French subsidy. This action has been a difficult one for enthusiastic Prussian historians to explain. Frederick William maintained this policy for only a year, however, because the Swedes, allied with France, descended on his domains. He marched rapidly to oppose them and in 1675 won the battle of Fehrbellin, the source of his title "the Great." The war dragged on until 1678 when several treaties were signed at Nimwegen, by which France made a number of gains, mostly at the expense of Spain. Emperor Leopold, however, had to cede to Louis the city of Freiburg-im-Breisgau. Frederick William received nothing for his efforts because the French protected the interests of their Swedish allies.

When Louis XIV was not waging war, he was waging peace. He managed to achieve as many of his ambitions through clever diplomacy as through war. Much of this was at the expense of Germany. One device was the construction of a league of minor German princelings in the Rhineland, most of them ecclesiastical lords, to act as satellites of the great king in promoting French interests within the Empire. This was a phase of the centuries-long policy of France to keep Germany weak by luring the Rhineland into the French orbit. Napoleon I and Napoleon III undertook the same policy, as did the governments of France after both world wars in the twentieth century.

More important at the time was Louis' creation of the so-called Chambers of Reunion, which operated very successfully in the first half of the 1680's. Groups of lawyers searched the feudal records in order to discover all the territories which had at any time been dependencies of the areas which France had acquired in recent years. The French government then made legal claim to all these lands and occupied them by military force. Louis made a number of significant gains by this technique, including the important towns of Luxemburg and, most particularly, Strassburg. It is a measure of German weakness at the time that the French were nearly always unopposed in this process. In fairness, however, it should be added that during these years the Austrians were at war with the Turks, who in 1683 actually besieged Vienna.

By 1685 Louis XIV's fortunes reached their apex; from then on they declined. This was caused partly by Louis' increasing arrogance at home culminating in the revocation of the Edict of Nantes and the consequent persecution of the French Protestants, a policy which dismayed the Protestant rulers in Europe. Abroad, Louis' German policy and the "reunions" were increasingly resented, and there was always William of Orange to encourage any moves against France. Finally in 1686 the League of Augsburg was established, an anti-French alliance composed of Emperor Leopold, Sweden, Spain, Bavaria, Saxony, and the Palatinate. An immediate cause of this alliance was Louis' insistence that the Palatinate belonged to him because his sister-in-law was the sister of the childless elector, who had just died. Three years after the formation of the League, William of Orange became William III of England and was able to throw English strength and money behind the League. However, by that time the War of the League of Augsburg (1688–97) had already begun.

At its very outset the war brought fresh calamity to Germany for the French armies entered the Palatinate and completed the devastation which had been started by Turenne during the Dutch war. It was during these years that the famous castle in the lovely university town of Heidelberg was destroyed and became the picturesque ruin that it remains today. As the war continued, most of the principal fighting occurred in the Netherlands and Italy, and at sea, rather than in Germany. The fortunes of war were uneven; when the treaties of Ryswick were signed in 1697, French losses were as noticeable as French gains. In Germany Louis XIV was forced to relinquish to the Empire all of the "reunions" except the very important one of Alsace, including Strassburg, which was now lost to Germany until 1871.

The great crisis in European diplomacy in the last years of the seventeenth century revolved around the succession to the throne of Spain. Charles II, feeble and childless, was likely to die at any time without leaving an immediate legal heir to the vast Spanish possessions. The three main claimants, all of them related closely to Charles through the female line, were Louis XIV, Leopold I, and the elector of Bavaria. Neither of the two great monarchs expected to inherit this empire in his own name; Louis wished it for his young grandson Philip of Anjou, while Leopold claimed it for his second son Charles. Several treaties were made to arrange for the expected succession. Charles of Spain, annoyed that others were dividing his legacy during his lifetime, made a will granting the entire inheritance to Philip of Anjou, and died soon thereafter in 1700. Louis XIV accepted the throne of Spain for Philip and sent the young man to Madrid with the ill-judged remark, "There are no longer any Pyrenees."

Emperor Leopold was angry at the cavalier fashion in which his son had been treated; William III saw in the situation an opportunity to create further trouble for Louis XIV. The result was the Grand Alliance of all the major powers of Europe against France and Philip's Spain. Only Bavaria was allied with the French. In 1701 the War of the Spanish Succession began, which lasted for twelve years and bled further the nations which had seen so little of peace for a century.

Only one of the major figures in this war was "German"; only one of the major battles was fought on German soil. The "German" hero was Prince Eugene of Savoy, commander of the Austrian forces, who was in fact a Frenchman born in Italy. The battle was Blenheim, fought in Bavaria in 1704. In this battle Prince Eugene and his great English colleague, the Duke of Marlborough, defeated the French and Bavarians. For seven years in Germany, the Netherlands, and Italy severe battles were fought in which France was usually vanquished. During this time Emperor Leopold died and was succeeded by his son Joseph I (1705–11), an older brother of Charles, the claimant to the Spanish throne. The French nation had been bled dry, and in 1708 Louis XIV started peace negotiations. However, the terms were too high for France; the Allies insisted that France send her army to dislodge Louis' grandson from Spain. Louis refused, and the war began anew. In 1711 Emperor Joseph died; his brother Charles inherited the Hapsburg possessions and was elected Holy Roman emperor as Charles VI (1711–40). This event changed the entire situation because England, Holland, and their allies had no more desire to see the resurrection of the empire of Charles V than to see the king of France control Spain. French arms became more successful; in England an important political change occurred dislodging Marlborough from the first position in the government of Queen Anne. The result was the negotiated treaties of Utrecht (1713) followed in the next year by treaties between France and Emperor Charles.

In the treaties between Louis XIV and Charles VI, known as the treaties of Rastadt and Baden, Charles obtained control of the Spanish Netherlands, which was then called for almost a century the Austrian Netherlands. The Hapsburgs also received most of the former holdings of Spain in Italy, including Milan, Naples, and Sardinia. Although these Italian territories were shifted about in a complicated manner during the following years, the Austrian Hapsburgs now had a solid foothold in Italy, which was to have important repercussions in the future and, combined with considerable Austrian conquests from Turkey, was to move the Viennese monarchy even further from its earlier position of primary concern with German affairs.

Some of the most interesting developments of this period center about the rise of Hapsburg power in the east. The long reign of Emperor Leopold I and the short reign of Joseph I resulted in a considerable increase in Hungarian and Slavic territories. There took form the multinational Hapsburg realm familiar to students of modern history. For the first time something specifically "Austrian" began to appear. The Ottoman Empire, which had rested in a moribund fashion for a long time, took new spirit under the leadership of a dynasty of grand viziers, the Kiuprili family. During this period it waged two wars against the Hapsburgs, in the course of which Turkey sustained great losses. The first war was short and inconclusive. However, after a truce had expired, a second and lengthy war ensued. In 1683 the Turks pushed as far as Vienna and laid it under siege. It was a moment of panic for Christian Europe. The hero of the occasion was the king of Poland, John Sobieski, who led an army to the relief of the Hapsburg capital. The Turks retired and for some years lost even more ground to the Austrians. At last the war came to an end in 1699 by the Treaty of Karlowitz in which Austria received almost all of Hungary, Transylvania, Croatia, and Slavonia. The wars continued in the eighteenth century and brought millions of Magyars and Slavs under Hapsburg rule, a fact which shifted the center of the Hapsburg realm well to the east and opened a new chapter in the long, tangled question of what really constitutes German Europe.

While these events were occurring in the southeast, the Wettin dynasty of Saxony also achieved greater power in non-German territories. In 1692 Elector Augustus II of Saxony was elected king of Poland by the nobles of that land after the death of Sobieski. To assume this new dignity Augustus became a Catholic, although he did not disturb the Lutheranism of his Saxon subjects and continued to preside over the Protestant body in the Imperial Diet. Augustus' son, Augustus III, was in his turn also elected king of Poland. Thus for a considerable period Saxony was more involved in Polish, Russian, and Swedish affairs than in German.

In northwestern Germany the Guelf family in Hanover was about to reach new heights. After the English revolution of 1688 Parliament stipulated that the sovereign must be a Protestant, thus specifically ruling out any Catholic heirs of the Stuart family. Other than William III and his sister-in-law Anne, the nearest Protestant heir was Princess Sophia of Hanover, daughter of the "winter king and queen." Hanover had developed and prospered greatly during these years and had become a center of learning and intellectual achievement. In 1692 the unwilling Emperor Leopold established a ninth electorate and granted it to the ruler of Hanover.

The Wittelsbach family did not achieve any foreign honors. However, after the Palatine electorate was inherited by a Catholic rather than a Calvinist Wittelsbach, the two branches, Palatine and Bavarian, were able to work in close harmony. Furthermore, the Wittelsbachs were highly successful in promoting candidates of their family to important ecclesiastical territories. Thus this family assumed even greater importance in old Catholic Germany.

One important dynasty, the Hohenzollerns of Brandenburg, so far has been left out of account. There is no question that the rise of the electorate of Brandenburg into the kingdom of Prussia is the most important political development in Germany during the late seventeenth and early eighteenth centuries. However, this development culminates so pointedly with the achievements of Frederick the Great that it seems most logical to describe it in the next chapter.

The era of Louis XIV was a pitiable period of German weakness. Although the Holy Roman Empire still legally existed, the Peace of Westphalia had given it a death blow as far as any effective political power was concerned. Thus the interest in the years between 1648 and the French Revolution is frankly dynastic and particularist. More than ever the word Germany was simply a geographical expression. The eighteenth century was to witness the further development of the dynastic struggles and to narrow them down to a struggle between the south and the north, between Hapsburg and Hohenzollern.

CHAPTER III

The Eighteenth Century. Hapsburg versus Hohenzollern (1714-90)

The eighteenth century continued and sharpened the tendencies already observable in the seventeenth. This was the century of princely absolutism par excellence. The last significant vestiges of the old local diets or estates, which had constituted some check on the princes, disappeared. It was a century of dynastic rivalries culminating in the long struggle between the two principal German dynasties—the Hapsburgs and Hohenzollerns—which was to be a principal issue in German history for over a century. Intellectually and artistically speaking, it was a century in which Germany made enormous strides and entered fully into the mainstream of western European thought. By the end of the period no Englishman or Frenchman could disregard the German contribution.

The most spectacular development of this era was the growth of the electorate of Brandenburg in the sandy wastes of the northeast into the powerful kingdom of Prussia, which by the end of the eighteenth century ranked as one of the great powers of Europe. This feat was made possible by several lucky inheritances and by the deeds of three Hohenzollern rulers of genius, Frederick William, the Great Elector of Brandenburg, King Frederick William I of Prussia, and King Frederick II, the Great.

The geographical basis of the kingdom of Prussia was composed of three separate areas spread loosely across the whole width of northern Germany, which came to the Hohenzollerns at different times and in different ways. The electorate of Brandenburg with its capital at Berlin was granted to Frederick of Hohenzollern by his friend, Emperor Sigismund, in the early fifteenth century. A century later the Grand Master of the Teutonic Knights, who was a member of the Hohenzollern family, secularized their lands and established for himself and his descendants the duchy of Prussia, with its center in the town of Königsberg. The two branches of the family made a compact providing that if either branch died out, the other would inherit its possessions. The Prussian branch became extinct in the early seventeenth century, so the elector of Brandenburg also became duke of Prussia, for which he owed homage not to the Holy Roman emperor but to the king of Poland, the overlord of Prussia. The third component of the future Prussian kingdom was made up of the three small principalities of Cleves, Mark, and Ravensburg in northwestern Germany along the lower Rhine. They were a part of the complicated Cleves-Jülich inheritance, which was such an unsettling part of the diplomacy prior to the Thirty Years' War. The elector of Brandenburg was one of the principal claimants. When the inheritance was divided, he received the three territories mentioned above. The various Hohenzollern territories had no cohesion. Each had its own laws, customs, traditions, which it guarded jealously. Each had its own estates, or representative body, which was determined to resist any monarchical authority imposed from above.

In 1640 the young elector Frederick William came into a sorry inheritance. His lands had been the battlefield and playground of foreign armies for years. Brandenburg was one of the most ravaged areas of Germany, since the former elector had been a weak tool in the hands of the Swedes. Frederick William himself had been sent to well-organized Holland for his education. He did not forget what he learned there.

Frederick William began his reign by a policy of conciliation and a search for peace, necessitated by his weakness. He managed to get rid of many of the foreign soldiers on his lands and to reorganize his army into a small but respectable force, one of the few left in Germany. Thus his voice at the Peace of Westphalia was out of proportion to his strength. He received eastern Pomerania, Minden, Halberstadt, and the expectancy of the important archdiocese of Magdeburg when the administrator died. This was a notable increase of territory.

In 1655 the First Northern War broke out when King Charles X of Sweden attacked Poland. At first Frederick William remained neutral but took care to increase his army greatly and to demand recruits from all his territories even though they might be called upon to fight a long distance away. During the five-year conflict he was successively neutral, allied with Sweden, and allied with Poland. His army acquired a good reputation at the battle of Warsaw in 1656. When the eventual peace was signed at Oliva in 1660, Frederick William did not gain any land but instead the very important right that henceforward he was sovereign in Prussia, where he now owed no allegiance to Poland, Sweden, or the Empire.

During much of his reign Frederick William was involved in bitter conflict with the estates of his various holdings, which insisted (especially in Prussia) on privileges and local peculiarities which had been granted them from time to time, so that it was impossible to establish any centralized administration. Frederick William was determined, in the spirit of his period, to erect a firm, centralized state, controlled exclusively by himself on the pattern of the state of Louis XIV. The details of the struggles are picturesque but need not detain us. By the end of his reign the elector had achieved extraordinary success and laid the foundation for the unified army and the efficient civil service which were to remain the hallmarks of Prussia thenceforward. He began the typical Hohenzollern policy of granting almost unlimited authority to the nobles on their estates so long as they recognized the prince's authority in war, foreign affairs, and national policy. He was a patriarchal ruler with the foresight to introduce economic reform in Brandenburg-Prussia, to welcome industrious Huguenot exiles from France, and to build canals and roads. He left a far stronger state than he inherited.

In his foreign policy Frederick William pursued a devious course in the complex diplomacy and wars of the time. He realized that Brandenburg-Prussia was not wealthy enough to support the big military establishment he felt necessary to defend her unusually long and ill-protected boundaries and to support her growing pride. Thus he supported his projects by a policy of subsidy from abroad. Although usually loyal to his Hapsburg overlord, he did not hesitate at times to ally himself with France if greater advantage appeared likely. He proved a competent general, especially at the battle of Fehrbellin in 1675 when he defeated a Swedish army. Frederick William did not add any territory to his domains in the latter part of his reign, but on his death in 1688 he left a state respected and feared.

His son and heir, Frederick III (1688–1713), had none of his father's great qualities. Ostentatious and extravagant, he dissipated much of the treasure his father had accumulated. He devoted himself to the beautification of Berlin, importing the great sculptor, Andreas Schlüter, and building palaces. He founded the Berlin Academy of Sciences, the University of Halle, and also attracted a number of learned men to his court. In foreign affairs he dabbled in the wars of his time, loyal to the Hapsburg interests but gaining only a few pieces of territory here and there. Probably his greatest achievement was the title of king. The elector of Saxony was king of Poland; the elector of Hanover could look forward to being king of England. Frederick wanted the same rank. So he devoted much time and effort and, more important, the services of his soldiers to this goal. He finally achieved it and in 1701 crowned himself in the castle of Königsberg. Thus from that date he is styled King Frederick I. The royal title came from Prussia rather than Brandenburg because there he was sovereign. At first he was permitted to call himself simply king "in" Prussia, but the humiliating preposition did not stick.

King Frederick William I (1713–40) was again a great change from his father. This disagreeable, miserly, avaricious, coarse, vulgar, gouty, drill sergeant was amazingly competent and laid the foundations for Prussian power which his genius son was able to exploit. He scorned the artistic and intellectual interests of his parents and led with his big family a parsimonious existence taking pleasure only in smoking strong tobacco with his cronies or in drilling his tall soldiers on the parade ground at Potsdam.

Frederick William, like his grandfather, was determined to assert absolute authority—in his own phrase, like a "rock of bronze." To this end he was ruthless and resembles his contemporary, Peter the Great of Russia. His particular ability lay in civil and military administration, the pillars of Prussian greatness. For instance, in 1723 he established the General Directory for over-all administration, a remarkably neat and efficient institution, which however depended on the constant and minute supervision of the king. None of the ministers had any authority without the king; they were higher secretaries. This system worked with Frederick William in charge, and later with his son. These two were willing to give unlimited pains to public affairs. However, it broke down when less devoted and efficient men wore the crown.

The great joy of Frederick William's life was his army. The soldiers were his favorites, especially if they were tall. He formed units of men over six feet in height, and other sovereigns, anxious to win his friendship, would send him tall young men. He loved his army so much that he did not want to risk it in battle. During his reign the army was doubled in size to over 80,000 and became the best-trained in Europe, but it rarely fought. The king dallied with diplomacy, but it was usually over his head; he stuck to his wise policy of remaining at peace. His only campaign was a profitable one. The Great or Second Northern War raged for over twenty years involving Russia, Sweden, Poland, and some of the German states. Toward the end Frederick William entered temporarily and for his pains received an increase in his Pomeranian lands including the mouth of the Oder River and the important city of Stettin, which became the port for Berlin until it was removed from Germany in 1945.

Personal tragedy entered the Hohenzollern family with the conflict between Frederick William and his eldest son Frederick, later Frederick the Great. Their personalities were poles apart. The father was brutal, stingy, coarse; the son, artistic, literary, and dreamy. He liked to play the flute and to read and write poems and plays in French. The father felt that the son would destroy all his achievements and handled him with brusqueness and an utter lack of understanding. This situation culminated in an attempt by Frederick, accompanied by a favorite officer friend, to escape from Prussia. The fugitives were caught and imprisoned. Frederick was forced to watch the execution of his beloved friend. The king even talked of executing his son. Instead he imprisoned him for a year. Frederick spent this time learning about local administration and political affairs, and the father eventually released him and permitted him to come to Berlin. During the last years of the king's life the two managed to get along reasonably well. Frederick William presented his son with a palace, Rheinsberg, which he loved, and with a wife, whom he did not love since he never had any interest in women. At Rheinsberg Frederick spent several happy years reading, playing music, and writing a work on political philosophy, *Antimachiavel,* in which he refutes the doctrine of Machiavelli, of whom he was later to prove one of the best disciples. In May 1740 Frederick William died as a result of gout, and Frederick II ascended the throne he was to occupy until 1786.

The German situation in 1740 was dominated by the Hapsburg emperor's preoccupation with the succession to his far-flung family possessions. Charles VI's only surviving children were two daughters, the elder being the Archduchess Maria Theresa, a beautiful and deeply religious young woman. No woman had ever before inherited in the Hapsburg lands; Charles devoted his life to making sure that Maria Theresa would be an exception. Thus he promulgated a document known as the Pragmatic Sanction, which declared that the Hapsburg lands were indivisible and that in default of male heirs they should pass to Maria Theresa or to his other daughter. A good part of Charles' reign was then devoted to securing the recognition of this principle by the powers of Europe. He achieved the acceptance of the estates of the Hapsburg realms without very much difficulty, but each time that he secured an acceptance he had to make a concession. Thus his weakness forced him to cede some Balkan territory, including Belgrade, back to the Turks. Frederick William I made little trouble about accepting the Sanction. Spain agreed for a time. However, in the 1730's the short War of the Polish Succession broke out, in which the Sanction became an issue. It arose over a disputed election to the Polish throne, which was still elective. Emperor Charles supported the candidacy of Augustus III of Saxony, son of the former king. The fighting was not serious, but the Hapsburg armies made a poor showing. At the Treaty of Vienna in 1738 Augustus received the throne of Poland. The losing candidate was given the duchy of Lorraine for his lifetime, after which it was to revert to France. The former duke of Lorraine, Francis, received compensation for his loss in Tuscany, where the Medici family had just become extinct. The Hapsburgs granted back to the Spanish royal family some of their former Italian possessions which they had obtained in 1714, receiving some smaller ones in return. Charles received the acceptance by the powers, especially France, of the Pragmatic Sanction, but at a considerable cost. Francis, the dispossessed duke of Lorraine was soon thereafter married to Maria Theresa. It looked as if the succession were secure. Five months after the death of Frederick William I in 1740, Charles VI also died, and Maria Theresa claimed her inheritance of the Hapsburg realms.

It soon became clear that Charles' work had been in vain. Within six weeks the new king of Prussia invaded Silesia, and Europe started a quarter century of warfare. Very soon three claimants, the elector of Bavaria, the elector of Saxony, and the king of Spain, disputed Maria Theresa's right to the Hapsburg succession. Frederick asserted as his excuse for the invasion some old claims of the Hohenzollern family to various parts of Silesia, but there is no question that they were mere pretexts. He wanted Silesia and he wanted glory.

Frederick achieved immediate success and occupied the whole of Silesia by the spring of 1741. By this time the Silesian war had spread and had become part of the general War of the Austrian Succession, which was to last for eight years in Europe and overseas. France, Bavaria, and Spain allied against Maria Theresa, while Britain supported the lady. The beautiful young princess appealed to the chivalrous Hungarian nobility, who enthusiastically rallied to her cause. An Austrian army entered Silesia, and Frederick retired to meet it. The first of Frederick's many battles, Mollwitz, was a Prussian victory although the king, fearing defeat, rode distractedly into the night.

When the electors of the Empire met in 1742, they passed over Maria Theresa's husband, Francis, and chose as emperor the elector of Bavaria who took the name of Charles VII (1742–45). This was the only occasion since the fifteenth century that a non-Hapsburg was elected. A few days after his coronation an Austrian army captured his capital, Munich; wits parodying the old phrase *aut Caesar aut nihil* ("either Caesar or nothing") commented about Charles *et Caesar et nihil* ("both Caesar and nothing").

From the outset Frederick showed himself an undependable ally to the French and Bavarians. His interests were centered solely in Silesia and he had no intention of wasting his good army to fight the battles of the French. Twice before 1742 he negotiated with Maria Theresa and promised to get out of the war if she would cede Silesia to him. After two Prussian victories in 1742 Maria Theresa unwillingly agreed to this proposal and signed the Treaty of Berlin with Prussia. This freed the Austrians and their Anglo-Hanoverian allies to operate against their other enemies, which they did successfully, especially at the battle of Dettingen where George II of England defeated a French army. These Austrian successes frightened Frederick, who knew that Maria Theresa in her heart was not reconciled to the loss of Silesia. Therefore in 1744 he re-entered the war and invaded Bohemia.

In the beginning of 1745 the unfortunate Emperor Charles died, and his successor in Bavaria offered to get out of the war and abandon his father's pretensions. He was restored to his lands and dignities and promised to vote for Francis of Lorraine in the coming imperial election. Sufficient votes were acquired, and Francis I (1745–65) was duly elected. Militarily, it was an unhappy year for the Austrians because Frederick won the battles of Hohenfriedberg and Soor, while the French general Maurice de Saxe (an illegitimate son of Augustus II of Saxony-Poland) defeated the Austrians badly in the Austrian Netherlands at the battle of Fontenoy. Maria Theresa was again forced to deal with Frederick and in the Treaty of Dresden confirmed her loss of Silesia.

From this time on the war in Europe petered out. The British had to bring their troops home to face the invasion of Charles Stuart, the Young Pretender. The principal interest of the war was now the colonial contest between Britain and France, which did not concern Germany. A treaty was finally signed at Aachen (Aix-la-Chapelle) in 1748, which confirmed Maria Theresa in her inheritance and also her cession of Silesia to Prussia. It was an inconclusive peace to end an inconclusive war.

Both Maria Theresa and Frederick II spent the eight years of peace between 1748 and 1756 reorganizing their realms and setting the tone for an important period intimately connected with their two very different personalities. During the war Maria Theresa had proved to be a woman of determination and forcefulness, with high qualities of leadership. She far overshadowed her ineffectual husband, who is important only because he fathered her numerous children. She had observed the weakness latent in her domains, a weakness which was to lead to their collapse in the twentieth century, namely their multiplicity and variety in government, customs, and traditions. She attempted a partial cure of this weakness. Not being a child of the Enlightenment, as her eldest son was, she did not have his single-minded reforming instinct. Her reforms were tempered with gentleness and an understanding that one cannot make changes too rapidly. She attempted centralization, mostly in Austria and Bohemia, of such things as tariffs, the army, finances, and justice, where the awkwardness was most glaring.

Maria Theresa set the tone for the laughing, gay Vienna that was to become so beloved by the world in the nineteenth century. In her elaborate rococo palace of Schönbrunn on the outskirts of Vienna she welcomed to her court musicians and poets who created much of the artistic taste of Europe, as the court of Louis XIV had done at Versailles a century before. This was the Vienna of Haydn and Gluck, later of Mozart and Beethoven, which was to make the word music almost synonymous with Vienna.

Frederick II had different and, on the whole, simpler problems to deal with. He had inherited from his father an extremely efficient administration; it was necessary only to keep it operating and to integrate into it Silesia and also East Friesland, which had fallen to Frederick by inheritance during the war. The mature Frederick proved himself as competent an administrator as he was a general. He devoted the same constant and selfless attention to the minutiae of public affairs that his father had. He was if possible even more despotic than his father, rarely seeing his ministers and spending his time reading and annotating the endless written reports they were required to submit to him. Yet it was a despotism animated by extreme intelligence and by an understanding of economic and social forces rare in his time. During the years of peace Frederick built his lovely little palace of Sans Souci in Potsdam, where he was happiest. There, when work was done, this lonely, cynical, unscrupulous, and shrewd recluse would sit with a company of men distinguished in the letters and sciences and make music, listen to poetry, or read aloud his own prolific if mediocre literary output.

Maria Theresa was still not reconciled to the loss of Silesia; Frederick realized this and knew that there would no doubt be another conflict before the matter was settled. Thus the years from 1748 to 1756 were filled with diplomatic maneuvers culminating in the so-called Diplomatic Revolution. One of its principal architects was Prince Kaunitz, who after 1753 was the empress' chancellor. Kaunitz recognized that Great Britain was an undependable ally for a purely continental nation like the Hapsburg realm. Her interests were almost exclusively concerned with her struggle with France for possessions overseas. Kaunitz, who had spent some years at Versailles as Austrian ambassador, was convinced that an influential pro-Austrian party could be formed there under the aegis of Madame de Pompadour, the powerful mistress of Louis XV. Maria Theresa had drawn close to Empress Elizabeth of Russia. Thus the possibility loomed of a great continental alliance composed of Russia, Austria, and France, which would seal Frederick's fate.

Frederick was worried about the Austro-Russian relationship and thus was receptive to British advances motivated by a desire to protect Hanover, which was also ruled by the British monarch. Thus Britain and Prussia signed a neutrality agreement, the Treaty of Westminster, which much irritated France, already at war with the British overseas. Kaunitz exploited this irritation to obtain French acceptance in 1756 of a defensive treaty with Austria. The centuries-long conflict between French and Hapsburg rulers was ended, and the two prepared to fight as allies.

Frederick was not the man to wait until his enemies were ready to attack him. In August 1756 he invaded Saxony to use it as a base for an attack on Bohemia and launched the Seven Years' War (1756–63). Within a few months the opposing alliance was completed and Frederick found himself at war with Austria, France, and Russia, as well as a number of the smaller German states. Help from Britain was reluctant and spasmodic, in the form of subsidies, not of armies.

The Seven Years' War was an epic struggle between a small country and the three greatest continental powers. In it Frederick displayed himself as one of the greatest military geniuses of all time. The loving attention which Frederick William I had given his army bore fruit. Frederick was like a swordsman who confronts several enemies at the same time and has to face first one way, then another, to defend himself. The French and Austrians were to the southwest and south, while each summer a large Russian army appeared from the east to threaten the heart of Prussia. Frederick won victory after victory, but he also suffered some serious defeats; in 1759, 1760, and 1761 it looked more and more as if he had to perish under superior strength and see the breakup of the Prussian state. His greatest victories were in 1757 when, within a few weeks, he defeated the French and minor German states at Rossbach and then the Austrians at Leuthen. The following summer he triumphed over the Russians at Zorndorf, but in 1759 the Russians won a major victory at Kunersdorf and a few months later actually occupied and burned Berlin itself.

Frederick's letters and remarks during this period when he was constantly with his army tell of a neurotic and neurasthenic, often sunk in gloom, who always carried on his person a vial of poison in case worst came to worst. In spite of everything he kept hoping for a miracle.

The miracle came in the first days of 1762, when Empress Elizabeth of Russia, who hated Frederick, died and was succeeded on the throne by her nephew, Peter III, who had nurtured a cult of Frederick and Prussia.

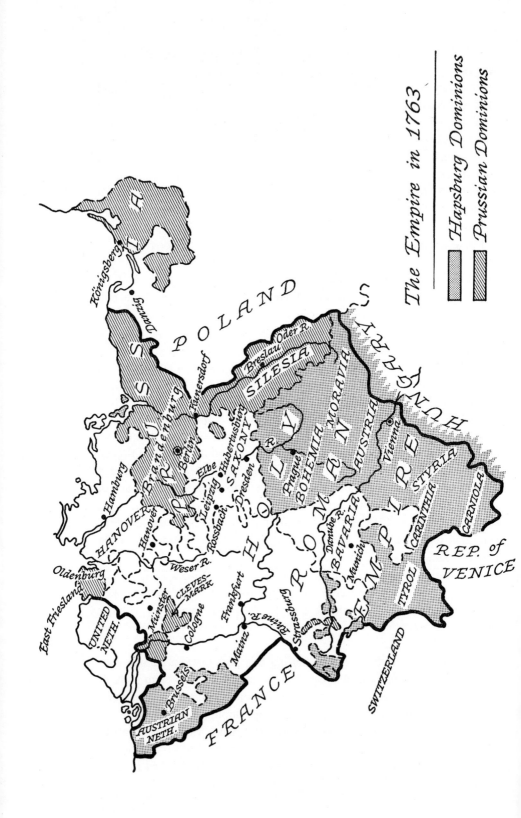

The Empire in 1763

Hapsburg Dominions
Prussian Dominions

POLAND

PRUSSIA

Königsberg
Danzig

Oder R.
Breslau
SILESIA
Rungersdorf
Brandenburg
Berlin
Hubertusburg
Leipzig
SAXONY
Dresden
Elbe
Rossbach

HOLY
Prague
BOHEMIA
MORAVIA
AUSTRIA

HUNGARY

ROMAN

Vienna
STYRIA
CARINTHIA
CARNIOLA

REP. of
VENICE

HANOVER
Hamburg
Hanover
Weser R.
Oldenburg
East Friesland
Oldenburg
UNITED
NETH.
Münster
CLEVES-
MARK
Cologne
Frankfurt
Mainz
Rhine R.
Strasburg
Danube R.
BAVARIA
Munich
TYROL
SWITZERLAND

EMPIRE

FRANCE

Brussels
AUSTRIAN
NETH.

Peter immediately made peace and, indeed, an alliance with Prussia. In the west, France, which had been defeated both in India and in Canada, was ready to make peace with Britain and was no longer interested in the war in Europe. This war too was petering out. Frederick continued to win victories over the Austrians, and finally the two combatants signed the Treaty of Hubertusburg on February 15, 1763, which confirmed the situation before the war. Maria Theresa had to recognize the final loss of Silesia. Prussia gained no territory, but there was henceforth no question that she was one of the great powers of Europe and that no general question could be settled without consulting her. This was Frederick's greatest achievement in the international field.

After 1763 Frederick II had had enough of war, and except for a short campaign in 1778 Prussia was at peace for the remainder of his reign. He did not neglect his army, however, and was happiest when reviewing his troops. He kept an intimate watch on everything that happened in his kingdom, traveling constantly through it and noting even the most insignificant details on his estates. He built the New Palace at Potsdam and continued his evenings of music and poetry. Frederick became very popular with his people during these years when they spoke of him as *der alte Fritz* and laid the groundwork for the legend which became so persistent and influential in later years.

Frederick had learned in the Seven Years' War how dangerously exposed Prussia was, and he was determined not to risk again the near disaster of those years. His role became that of a peacemaker, but he managed to maneuver it into one of great profit for Prussia. The most impressive example of this was the First Partition of Poland in 1772. The Russian empress, Catherine II, was waging a successful war against Turkey, and the expectation was that she would make large demands on the Turks when the peace was arranged. This seriously worried Maria Theresa and her son Joseph II (1765–90), who had succeeded his father as emperor in 1765 and ruled jointly with his mother in the Hapsburg lands. They feared an increase of strength for Russia in the southeast to such an extent that a war between Austria and Russia seemed very possible. This prospect worried Frederick, who was afraid that Prussia might be drawn into the struggle. He sought some alternative plan whereby Russia might make gains which would not affect Austria. Obviously he hoped for Prussian gains as well. The perfect situation seemed to exist in Poland, whose weakness made her a possible prey for aggression. Frederick's idea was simplicity itself, namely that Russia and Prussia (and if necessary Austria) should each take a slice of the old kingdom of Poland. Thus Catherine would have her glory without the danger of a European war. Frederick sent his brother Henry on a visit to St. Petersburg with instructions to sound out Catherine. She was delighted with the idea and it was implemented right away. Maria Theresa was shocked at such uncloaked robbery but was afraid not to take her share. Thus she received the province of Galicia, while Frederick received the bishopric of Ermeland and the province of West Prussia (without Danzig and Thorn), so that now East Prussia was joined geographically to the bulk of the kingdom. This was an important accretion and gave Frederick the pleasure of organizing an efficient Prussian administration for the new territories.

The one war which Frederick undertook in the later years of his reign arose, as usual, over a problem of succession, this time in Bavaria. The elector of Bavaria died in 1777, leaving no direct heirs. The legal heir was Charles Theodore, Elector Palatine, who also had no direct legitimate heirs. The presumption was that eventually the lands would go to still another branch of the Wittelsbach house, whose head was Charles, duke of Zweibrücken in the Saar area. Emperor Joseph, anxious to increase his German holdings, persuaded Charles Theodore for various favors to cede to him about one third of Bavaria. Frederick had no notion of watching Joseph succeed in so considerable a project, so he persuaded Charles of Zweibrücken to make objection, which both Prussia and Saxony supported. Negotiations came to nothing, so war was declared. It was a comic opera war dubbed by the soldiers the "Potato War," for they insisted they spent most of their time foraging for supplies during the cold winter months. There were no battles, merely a few skirmishes. In early 1779 Maria Theresa took the initiative and opened a correspondence with Frederick. This interchange resulted in the Treaty of Teschen by which the Austrians got only a very small part of what they had anticipated.

Joseph was not satisfied with the rebuff; in 1785, having been freed of the tutelage of his mother by her death five years before, he tried another plan. This time it was to be a straight trade. Charles Theodore was to cede Bavaria to Austria in return for the Austrian Netherlands, which was proving a nuisance to the Viennese government. Once again Frederick took action, but on this occasion no war developed. To help Charles of Zweibrücken, who once again resented the loss of his Bavarian expectancy, Frederick founded the League of Princes (*Fürstenbund*) composed of most of the important north German states. The pressure of this group forced Joseph to give up his ambitious plan. Some Prussian historians have seen in this action a step toward the unification of Germany under Prussian auspices. Actually it was just a pose for Frederick in his long struggle against Austria and his attempt to maintain the old ramshackle character of the Holy Roman Empire which so conveniently made possible the expansion of the Prussian state. Frederick did not live very long to enjoy his new triumph; he died in August 1786.

Only the decade of the 1780's was granted to Joseph II to carry out his contemplated reforms in the Hapsburg dominions. As long as Maria Theresa lived, she was clearly the senior partner who made the major decisions. Unlike his mother, Joseph was a full child of the Enlightenment and should be counted in the list of the enlightened despots with Frederick II, Catherine II of Russia, and Charles III of Spain. Joseph hated the untidy and cumbersome structure of the lands he had inherited, in which his position differed from place to place according to the customs and traditions in a particular area. He wanted to establish a centralized unitary monarchy in the neat eighteenth-century sense. He realized that his principal enemies were the corporate vested interests of the aristocracy and the church. In his attack on them Joseph ran the danger of encouraging those in the nonprivileged classes who believed in popular sovereignty according to natural law. These people became the so-called Austrian Jacobins, who were prosecuted during the nineties.

It is difficult to be unsympathetic to some of Joseph's goals, but he had the faults of his virtues. He was one of those reformers who try to do too much too soon at the expense of offending attitudes and beliefs that have grown up over the centuries. Thus he failed in nearly all his efforts. On his epitaph he described himself as one "who, with the best of intentions, was unsuccessful in everything that he undertook."

Joseph decreed the abolition of serfdom, he tolerated the private celebration of Protestant services, he drastically cut down the number of monasteries, and he withdrew most of the censorship so that criticism of the possessory classes could be published. In spite of his personal strong Catholicity, he paid little attention to Pope Pius VI, who traveled to Vienna to protest his actions. But constantly he was rebuffed by a population which was not willing to welcome the new order. He had even more difficulty when he tried to integrate the various nationalities into a centralized government. For instance, he removed the crown of Hungary to Vienna as a symbol of his intentions. The Hungarians reacted violently, and the crown had to be returned. He had even more trouble in the Austrian Netherlands where he revoked the constitution of Brabant. The Belgians in 1789 broke into open revolt, a movement which in the following years merged into the greater French Revolution. Joseph died in 1790, a failure whose reforms died too within a few years. At least he had addressed himself to the problems which all Austrian rulers after him had to face, especially the nationality problem which was to become so intense in the nineteenth century. Austrian imperial history down to its end in 1918 is the story of a continuing swing between centralization and some kind of federal settlement. No really workable solution was ever obtained.

During the eighteenth century Germany achieved for the first time in years a full-fledged intellectual and spiritual partnership with England and France. By the end of the century a German could no longer be scorned as a boorish bumpkin. While it is true that much of this cultural development was derivative from France, which dominated the continent culturally (Frederick the Great regularly spoke and wrote in French), this dependence became weaker as the century wore on and was diluted by the influence in Germany of English thought and letters. By the early years of the next century Mme. de Staël was able to astonish the French reading public with an account of the achievements of the Germans in her work *De l'Allemagne.*

Space precludes an adequate discussion of German intellectual developments in the eighteenth century. In fact, since the century was such a cosmopolitan one, it is almost impossible to discuss German thought without at the same time including French, English, and even Italian culture. However, some comment on the greater figures may lend clarity to the later development of German thought and the German state.

The seventeenth century was on the whole a time of cultural stagnation in Germany during which she fell behind both England and France, which were enjoying periods of brilliant creativity. Germany was trying to heal the ravages of the Thirty Years' War, while at the same time she was forced into participation in the wars of Louis XIV. By the early years of the eighteenth century things were somewhat improved, and a degree of prosperity returned. This is particularly true in the towns of north Germany where a middle-class culture was developing that was usually free from the irritating restrictions of the petty princelings. Notable examples are Leipzig and Hanover and also the newly established universities at Halle and Göttingen. Halle, in fact, became the center of the new religious movement known as Pietism. Pietism, associated with the names of Philipp Jacob Spener (1635–1705) and August Hermann Francke (1663–1727), was an effort to return emotionalism and an "inner light" to Protestantism, whose theology had become unduly rationalistic. Thus Pietism, which developed a considerable influence over eighteenth-century thought and thinkers, encouraged that sort of liberation of the human spirit which was characteristic of the greatest German writers.

One of the earliest figures in the revival and one of the giants of German thought was Gottfried Wilhelm Leibnitz (1646–1716), who was born in Leipzig but lived most of his creative life in Hanover. True to his period, Leibnitz was trained as a scientist and made some important contributions to science, notably as the discoverer of the differential calculus. However, his universal mind transcended the boundaries of mathematics and physics, and much of his importance lies in his effort to synthesize the Aristotelian-Scholastic philosophic tradition with the newer scientific approach. In his *Monadology* Leibnitz stated that everything in the universe is composed of monads—simple, indivisible, indestructible units, each of which is unique. They are not simply material, but both material and spiritual. Thus Leibnitz hoped to bridge the dichotomy between matter and spirit or form. A citizen of the world, Leibnitz usually wrote in French, but he was interested in the development of German culture. Thus he devoted much effort in persuading Elector Frederick III of Brandenburg in 1700 to establish the Berlin Academy, of which he became the first president. Correspondence among the various learned societies of the Western world was typical of the eighteenth century, and to Leibnitz goes much of the credit for including Germany in the learned sphere.

The other German philosophic giant of the eighteenth century was Immanuel Kant (1724–1804). Born in Königsberg, he attended the university there; except for a short period tutoring not far away, Kant never left Königsberg, where in later life he became a professor of philosophy. This was the complete "ivory tower" philosopher, never marrying nor venturing more than a few yards from his study or lecture room in a relatively obscure and remote town. Yet so great was the universality of his genius that philosophy has never been the same since his career, and he must surely be reckoned in any list of the few great philosophers. Kant spent his early mature years as a student and teacher of science; his philosophic position was the standard rationalism of his time. He was profoundly shocked when he read David Hume and realized the drastic limitations of unaided reason. Thus he spent the rest of his life trying to transcend reason and to find a position of certainty on which to base behavior. In his *Critique of Pure Reason* Kant establishes that man can never know the "thing in itself" (*Ding an sich*) but must content himself in the knowledge of phenomena or the reflection of the real on the human mind and consciousness. From this subjective point of view Kant goes on in his *Critique of Practical Reason* to try to discover how man should know how to act since he cannot know full truth. He finds the one inescapable value, where in a sense subjective and objective meet, in the "moral law," and sets up as the basis for human action the "categorical imperative." This imperative exhorts man "to act in such a way that the principles of his actions may at any time be applicable to all mankind; to choose such maxims as may be made the bases of a universal law and rule" (quoted from K. F. Reinhardt, *Germany 2000 Years,* Milwaukee, Bruce, 1950, pp. 372–73). Thus Kant was primarily a philosopher of the theory of knowledge and of ethics; some critics have suggested that it was because of his influence that Christianity, especially Protestant Christianity, has tended to become primarily ethical rather than dogmatic. In later years Kant turned to studies in aesthetics and also to a consideration of history culminating in his noble essay *On Eternal Peace.*

The German Enlightenment was a complicated movement. Its source stems from several strands which were interwoven intricately, especially in such a complex personality as Goethe. One of the strands was the introduction of English literature into Germany. This had the effect of liberating German writing from the tight forms imposed by older styles and by French fiat. Milton and, above all, Shakespeare received a warm welcome; it is fair to say that Shakespeare has remained almost as much a part of German literature as of the heritage of the English-speaking peoples. An early example of the fusion of English forms with the new Pietism is found in the work of Friedrich Gottlieb Klopstock (1724–1803). Klopstock, deeply religious and emotional, was very much moved by *Paradise Lost.* The result was a lengthy poem, *The Messiah,* different in style from anything that had preceded it.

The cult of individualism infected some of the younger German writers with an almost Renaissance intensity and led into the "Storm and Stress" movement of the 1760's. These young men espoused literary radicalism for its own sake. They were tired of old religious shibboleths and professed belief in the self-containment of man and his life on earth. They adopted formlessness as an end in itself and worshiped the memory of Shakespeare, neglecting the fact that only a master of form can successfully transcend the forms. Not much of the production of the Storm and Stress writers has endured with the exception of some of Goethe's early work, but the liberating influence of the revolt fertilized the minds of later and greater writers.

A more sober element entered into this ferment of ideas with the rediscovery by the Germans of classical antiquity. The urge to the south was nothing new in German history. It had been a leading motive in the Middle Ages, but the Protestant movement had lessened it by cutting the bond with Rome. Now again Greece and Rome, especially the former with its sense of limitation and formed perfection, tempered the enthusiasm of the new movements. One of the men most responsible for this new interest in the ancient past was Johann Joachim Winckelmann (1717–68), who made his way gradually south from Prussia until he reached Rome where he reveled in the remains of the past. The new excavations at Pompeii excited him enormously and his studies culminated in his *History of the Art of Antiquity,* which was to have considerable influence in his homeland.

The two great teachers of the German Enlightenment were Gotthold Ephraim Lessing (1729–81) and Johann Gottfried Herder (1744–1803). Lessing led a penurious and uncomfortable life. He was born the son of a Saxon Lutheran pastor but gave up his own theological studies at Leipzig to devote himself to literature. For short periods he was a free-lance writer, a critic at the National Theater in Hamburg, and a librarian to the duke of Brunswick, but he died in poverty and was buried at public expense. Lessing was more of a critic than a creator, a reflection of his being a good son of the Enlightenment. His Deistic beliefs also reflect the Enlightenment, although he gave much greater importance to God than did most of the French Deists. He wrote extensively on the theater insisting that the classic French dramatists had emphasized form too much, and presenting Shakespeare as a model. His theories on art are found mainly in his *Laocoön,* in which he criticizes Winckelmann's insistence on the serenity of Greek art. His fame as a creative writer rests mainly on two plays, *Minna von Barnhelm* and *Nathan der Weise.* The former is Germany's first and best classic comedy, to an extent in praise of Frederick the Great's Prussia. The latter is a long poetic drama set at the time of the Third Crusade. The three protagonists are Saladin; Nathan, a noble-minded Jew; and an equally noble-minded Christian knight. The theme of the play is tolerance and cosmopolitanism: it is not a man's dogma that counts but his charity and goodness. Once again Lessing proved himself a product of the Enlightenment.

Herder was even less of a creative artist than Lessing, but it may be argued that his influence was greater than Lessing's. He was born in East Prussia, was a student of Kant at Königsberg, and became a Lutheran minister. For some time he carried out both clerical and teaching duties at Riga in Russia; eventually, owing to Goethe's help, he settled in Weimar, where he was in charge of the church in that grand duchy. Probably his single greatest contribution was that he was one of the first literary critics to think in historical terms. He was interested in the growth of language and its development in literature. He deplored the influence of foreign literatures upon the German and initiated the study of native folk poetry (a direction of thought that was to have dire influence on the next century). In later life he developed a philosophy of history in which he saw mankind evolving toward a higher humanity, but the concept of the evolution is uppermost. Herder has been accused of being the first German nationalist. There is some weight to this accusation, but certainly it was a nationalism heavily tinctured by the cosmopolitanism of his period. All critics are agreed on his importance both as a teacher and as an influence on Goethe.

Unquestionably the greatest product of eighteenth-century Germany and one of the greatest literary figures of all time was Johann Wolfgang von Goethe (1749–1832). It is difficult to say something significant about Goethe in a few paragraphs. His long life spanned such a stirring period, his interests were so amazingly versatile, and his formulation of ideas so lofty that he comes nearer than anyone else to the Enlightenment ideal of the universal man.

Goethe was born in Frankfurt to a wealthy middle-class family. He was sent to the University of Leipzig to study law but spent much of his time consorting with the literary figures who abounded there. Bad health forced him to cut short his studies, and after a brief stay at home he continued his education at Strassburg. In 1775 he settled in Weimar at the invitation of the young grand duke, Charles Augustus, the most remarkable prince patron of the arts of the century. Except for some trips Goethe spent the rest of his years in Weimar, usually active as a political functionary in the little principality. His residence there, and that of Schiller a few years later, made the word Weimar synonymous with the Germany of poets and thinkers.

Goethe's early works breathe the spirit of Storm and Stress. In his play *Goetz von Berlichingen* he departs from the Aristotelian unities and approaches the Shakespearean form. In it he depicts a protagonist whose tragic and powerful will dooms him to disaster. Much the same theme dominates the original version of *Faust,* in which violence and passion wreck the bourgeois world of the young woman Gretchen. Finally in *The Sorrows of Young Werther* Goethe stretches the limits of lachrymose emotion almost to the breaking point in describing the passionate unfulfilled love of Werther for his Charlotte, a passion which ends in Werther's suicide. *Werther* stands high on the best-seller list of all time for it hit Europe just as the age of sentimentality was beginning and caused even such a cynical and hardheaded young man as Napoleon Bonaparte to cry himself to sleep more than once. Goethe's early works were characterized by emotion, strength, and vitality, but also by the lack of discipline of a sensuous and passionate man.

In 1786 Goethe went to Italy for a long sojourn which was to have a great influence on him. He fell a prey to the classic environment. The immediate results were several dramas that were classic and restrained in form but still clamorous for human liberty and for a cosmopolitan sense of love and humanity: *Egmont, Iphigenia,* and *Tasso.* To the period shortly after Goethe's return to Weimar belongs also the classic ex-

ample of the typically German form of the novel of educational development, *Wilhelm Meister's Apprenticeship* (*Lehrjahre*). Goethe's versatility showed itself in these years too, for he devoted much of his time to
studies in natural science: botany, morphology, mineralogy, and meteor-
ology. These studies resulted in important writings.

One of the most profound influences on Goethe's life, and one of the
most fruitful associations in literary history, was the friendship between
Goethe and Friedrich Schiller which ended only with Schiller's death in
1805. Schiller was born in 1759, the son of a medical officer in the army
of the duke of Würtemberg. As opposed to Goethe, Schiller was reared
amid hardship and privation. His superior intellect won him a scholarship in a school dominated by Duke Charles Eugene, one of the least
enlightened princes of the Enlightenment period. Here at a military
academy he was stifled by rigid discipline and censorship in an attempt
to make a lawyer out of him. He finally studied medicine but without
enthusiasm. Schiller throve on the literature which was smuggled into
his school and secretly wrote his first drama, *The Robbers,* which was
produced in Mannheim. He had to attend the production in secret; he
lost patience with this frustration and escaped from Würtemberg to
Mannheim. He was now destitute; to make matters worse, his second
play, *Fiesco,* was unsuccessful. He found temporary refuge with a friend
and completed his third drama, *Love and Intrigue,* which was more successful. These early plays cry for liberty and attack tyranny. They betray
the Storm and Stress attitudes, but in a much more restrained dramatic
form.

Schiller was rescued from his financial problems by a young admirer
with whom he lived in Saxony for two happy years, marked by the
composition of *Don Carlos* and also of the *Ode to Joy,* which Beethoven
later set to music in his *Ninth Symphony.* Finally the same enlightened
grand duke of Saxe-Weimar who was Goethe's patron came to Schiller's
rescue. He gave Schiller an appointment as professor of history at the
University of Jena, where he remained for a few years until bad health
forced him to move to Weimar where he could be nearer Goethe and
supervise the productions of his dramas at the court theater. He died in
1805 of a consumption which had ravaged him for years.

During the Jena period Schiller turned to serious historical studies
and produced a *History of the Revolt of the United Netherlands* and a
History of the Thirty Years' War. These works provided him with some
of the background for his later historical dramas.

Schiller's most important creations occurred in the last years of his
life at Weimar where he was in constant contact with Goethe. The two
men were extraordinarily complementary. Goethe provided a subjective

sensuousness and Schiller an objective idealism. They were even able to write some works together, but mostly they encouraged and inspired each other. During these years Schiller developed his remarkable lyric gift, writing some short poems which rival Goethe's unquestioned pre-eminence in this genre. However, Schiller's great achievement during these six years was the composition of five long poetic dramas (one of them a trilogy), on which much of his reputation rests. The greatest ones were *Wallenstein, Mary Stuart, The Maid of Orleans,* and *William Tell.* The first three are studies of tragedy in personality or circumstance; the last is one of the greatest songs of liberty.

Goethe lived for almost thirty years after Schiller's death. They were years of increasing serenity when Goethe assumed an almost Olympian stature. He refused to become absorbed in German nationalistic strivings. In fact, he is an embarrassment for nationalistic historians since, being the greatest figure in German literature, he was a staunch admirer of Napoleon and regarded him as the representative of the spirit of the time. If any word can be applied to Goethe, it is the word cosmopolitan; he is a pleasant relief from the nationalist fanatics in which German literature sadly abounds.

These years saw Goethe's most mature production. Shortly after Schiller's death the first part of *Faust* appeared, a recasting of the original version. Then came the novel, *Elective Affinities,* the auto-biographical *Poetry and Truth,* the collection called *Wilhelm Meister's Travels,* and finally the second part of *Faust.* These major works were interspersed with volumes of short lyrics, scientific works, and Goethe's conversations carefully transcribed by his faithful friend Eckermann.

This is no place for a comprehensive comment on *Faust.* It is one of the monumental creations of the human spirit, astounding in its archi-tectonic form and its breadth and depth of human understanding. It moves from the sensual, selfish, and passionate emphasis in the first part to the altruistic and loving strivings of the second. Faust never ceases to strive; he is never able to say that any moment is so wondrous that he would wish it prolonged indefinitely. Finally the chorus of angels sings out that he who is ever striving and aspiring can be redeemed and that if he is also conscious of love and grace from on high, he will receive there a heartfelt welcome. This characteristic of constant aspiration is always present in the *Faust.* One of the German thinkers of the twentieth cen-tury, Oswald Spengler, has diagnosed it as the touchstone of modern man, whom he calls the "Faustian" man.

Goethe is one of those authors so lofty as to defy classification. He was poet, novelist, dramatist, scientist, and political thinker. No catalog of the few outstanding creations of our literary history will omit his

Faust; yet from the grandiose conception of that work he could move to the lyric gracefulness of some of his short poems. A classicist? Sometimes. A romanticist? Sometimes. Perhaps Napoleon, who was no flatterer, summed it up when he met Goethe and said afterward, *"Voilà un homme."*

If Germany was pre-eminent in the eighteenth century in letters, she was incomparable in music. The catalog of German composers during the period is long, but six of them remain among the greatest musical geniuses of our culture.

Johann Sebastian Bach (1685–1750) was born in Eisenach of a family already known in musical circles in the vicinity. He spent his whole life in music, at first for several years handling the music, both religious and secular, for a number of the small central German courts. In 1723 he settled in Leipzig, where he passed the rest of his life as cantor of the church of St. Thomas. He was extremely busy composing *ad hoc* pieces for the services, drilling the choir, and carrying out a host of minor obligations, but still he found time to compose a prodigious number of works. Bach died as obscurely as he lived, and it was not until 1894 that his grave was identified. His works too were almost unknown until the mid-nineteenth century when the Bach revival began. The first performance, after the original, of the *St. Matthew Passion* occurred in 1829 under the direction of Felix Mendelssohn. Since that time composers and critics have uniformly acknowledged the fact that Bach is without a peer in his own fields. The *Mass in B Minor,* the *St. John* and *St. Matthew Passions,* the immense amount of cantatas, and the numerous compositions for various instruments are among the richest inheritances in music.

An almost exact contemporary of Bach was George Frederick Handel (1685–1759). His life was spent according to a far different pattern in association with some of the wealthy and great of his day. He was born in Halle and intended for the law. However, when his father died, Handel took up the serious study of his beloved music. He achieved his first success in Hamburg where an opera of his was presented. He then spent several years in Italy perfecting himself in the art of the Italian opera, which was then the vogue. He was appointed court composer in Hanover, but soon went to London where he spent the rest of his career after 1713. In fact, he is a more significant figure in the history of English music than of German. He even anglicized his name (originally Händel). For a number of years he wrote and produced Italian operas in England, writing more than forty-five himself, but in the late thirties the fashion changed and Handel found himself in serious financial straits. He eventually turned to the composition of oratorios, the form which was to bring him fame. He wrote thirty-two of them, of which *The Messiah* is the most beloved today. In addition, he composed a large number of cantatas and much incidental music, mainly for the court of George I.

Christoph Willibald Gluck (1714–87) is sometimes known as the father of opera. He was born in south Germany and during his early mature years traveled extensively with opera companies composing and producing in both the Italian and French styles. He attracted the attention of Empress Maria Theresa, who put him in charge of opera at her Court Theater. From then on his career was assured and he spent most of his time in Vienna, though there was a tumultuous period when he attempted with varying success the production of operas in Paris under the patronage of Marie Antoinette. He wrote several dozen operas, of which the most enduring have been *Orfeo ed Euridice, Alceste,* and *Iphigénie en Tauride.* Gluck's importance lies not in the intrinsic value of his operas but in the fact that he changed their form, making them more dignified and restrained, insisting on the literary quality of the librettos, and breaking the dominance of the singers. His was a work of purification which left the way open for the far greater genius of Mozart, whom Gluck knew and admired.

One of the most prolific of the great composers was Franz Joseph ("Papa") Haydn (1732–1809). Haydn, who was born and spent nearly all his life in Austria, came of peasant stock and had all the virtues associated with that class. As a child he was taken to Vienna to sing in the cathedral, but when his voice changed he was thrown penniless on the world. He started to compose and moved from patron to patron until he became the protégé of the Esterházy family with whom he remained for thirty years composing symphonies, quartets, operas, and incidental music for performance in the great Esterházy palace. By the time he was sixty, although he had never left Austria and had lived most often in the countryside, he was one of the best-known composers in Europe, a friend of Mozart and a teacher of Beethoven. He was invited to London where he had enormous success both as a composer and as a conductor. At that point in his life he moved to another genre and wrote several major oratorios inspired by the work of Handel. He composed more than a hundred symphonies, more than sixty string quartets, and a large amount of assorted vocal and instrumental music. If Gluck can be called father of the opera, Haydn should be considered father of the symphony.

Nature smiled when Wolfgang Amadeus Mozart (1756–91) was born in Salzburg. He was endowed with prodigious musical gifts which appeared in early childhood, and was trained in their development by a father who was both a competent musician and a tough taskmaster.

Mozart is perhaps the classic example of the infant prodigy. He started writing music at the age of six and was taken to most of the courts and capitals of Germany and western Europe where he appeared frequently, charming his hearers both with his music and his personality. During his teens Mozart spent much time in Italy breathing the musical air of that land. He then returned to Salzburg where he became a court musician for the prince-archbishop, who, however, was jealous and difficult to work with. In 1781 Mozart broke with the archbishop and moved to Vienna where he spent most of the remainder of his short life constantly fighting poverty. He died a pauper. Probably never in the history of music has one man possessed such versatility and mastery of a variety of musical forms. The very list of Mozart's compositions is almost unbelievable. He wrote over forty symphonies, three of which are among the greatest ever written; there are more than twenty operas, including the marvelous *Marriage of Figaro, Don Giovanni,* and *The Magic Flute.* There are also countless religious works, string quartets, and compositions for varying combinations of instruments. A lightness of touch, a sure sense of melody, and a complete mastery of form characterize Mozart. Although his work does not possess the stormy violence of some of his successors, there are moments of deep seriousness—especially in the later symphonies and *Don Giovanni*—which are a long distance from the frivolity of the earlier rococo music. Several critics have said that of all the composers Mozart would be the hardest to replace.

The last of the German musical titans of the eighteenth century was Ludwig van Beethoven (1770–1827). The word titan fits Beethoven well, for his personality, his life, and his work were all tempestuous and revolutionary. He was born at Bonn to a lower-class family of Flemish descent. He made his first musical studies in west Germany, but in 1792 went to Vienna to become a pupil of Haydn. He stayed in or near Vienna for the rest of his life. His personality was craggy, irritable, difficult; he was a revolutionary, even a democrat. He dedicated his third symphony to Napoleon Bonaparte; but when he heard that Napoleon had made himself emperor, he tore up the dedication and replaced it with the word "heroic" (*Eroica*). He despised Napoleon thenceforward and refused to be presented to him. He would not accept the servile position in which musicians had existed at the palaces of the nobility and thus rendered his own finances more difficult. Yet he would not submit. In music, too, he liberated the forms of composition and wrote passages which, though normal to our ears, were frightening to his first listeners. His first two symphonies are in the classical Mozartean style, but beginning with the third he introduced a long first movement of tightly knit, thoughtful, dramatic quality. He also replaced the traditional minuet with the scherzo, usually a tumbling rapids of ironic buffoonery interspersed with reflection on the seriousness of life. Finally in his last symphony he made a drastic innovation by introducing the human voice in the last movement; it is a massive chorale based on Schiller's *Ode to Joy*. His personal tragedy was enhanced by the fact that from the age of thirty his hearing grew faulty, and in the last years of his life he was deaf. Nevertheless, he continued to compose and left a great body of work embodying almost every musical form: his nine symphonies; his opera *Fidelio;* his religious music, including the *Missa Solemnis;* and an abundance of works, such as his later string quartets, which are considered by some critics to be among the most profound musical compositions of all time.

Germany, then, enjoyed an extraordinarily rich cultural flowering in the eighteenth century. This was aided by the very fact of her decentralization. German culture did not tend to center in one spot, as French culture in Paris and English in London. The traveler is astonished at the proliferation of palaces, churches, and dwellings that still remain from this period. Every princeling wanted his Versailles. Some of the princelings were coarse and vulgar despots, but a number of them were men of high and dedicated cultivation, like Charles Augustus of Saxe-Weimar.

This was an important century for Germany. She repaired some of the spiritual and material damage of the turbulent sixteenth and seventeenth centuries. She saw the development of two great powers, Austria and Prussia, each stronger than all the other German states put together. The Holy Roman Empire lived on as a political fiction, but the time was at hand when, as a result of the great French upheaval, it was to be buried and the German world was to take important steps toward the modern concept of the national state.

CHAPTER IV

France Triumphant (1790-1814)

During this period Europe was so dominated by the events which occurred in France that it is difficult to describe it from any point of view other than the French. However, it was a vitally important period for Germany too. The revolution and the career of Napoleon I served as a catalyst to speed up momentous changes in the German world. Germany entered the era with the old Empire still legally existing, with two major monarchies, Prussia and Austria, and with several hundred smaller principalities, duchies, counties, ecclesiastical territories, free cities, and imperial knights. She emerged from the period with the thousand-year-old Empire no longer in existence, with the two big monarchies enlarged and strengthened, and with less than forty smaller kingdoms, duchies, and principalities, and only four free cities. The ecclesiastical principalities had disappeared, and the imperial knights and many lesser princes had been "mediatized" (placed under the jurisdiction of one of the temporal rulers).

The changes were not only geographical and structural. A new spirit was abroad. The constant warfare of the revolutionary era introduced in Germany new ideas which were to be dominant in the nineteenth century. The most important were liberalism and nationalism. These are difficult words to define. The first was the legacy of the political thinking of the Enlightenment and the attempt to apply it in France, summarized roughly by the slogan "Liberty, Equality, Fraternity." The second was largely the result of the occupation of most of Europe by French troops, a situation which gave rise to a strong feeling by the occupied of their separateness, their intrinsic value as a people, their unique importance. The cosmopolitan eighteenth century made way for the nationalistic nineteenth. Another by-product of the period occurred in the military sphere. With the appeal for a *levée en masse* by the French revolutionary government to repel its enemies, the day of the professional army was over. Henceforward the conscript army took its place, and war became a national activity in which whole populations were concerned.

The reaction to the first revolutionary events in France differed from place to place in Germany. As might be expected, the most favorable reaction occurred in the west near the French frontier. Here the influence of France had been strong for centuries; in fact, some of the ecclesiastical and small temporal territories were more in the orbit of France than of the Empire. It was in these areas too that the influence of the Enlightenment had been strongest, and there were a number of authors and publicists who welcomed the happy news of the ending of the old absolutist regime in France with its feudal overtones. There were processions and festivities at which "trees of liberty" were planted to indicate solidarity with the new French dispensation. However, many of these early attitudes changed. There were legal problems, caused by the feudal overlapping of German and French territories around Alsace. Then too, the increasingly radical tone of events in France led to disenchantment among the more idealistic. The influence of the refugee noblemen and churchmen, who appeared in ever-increasing numbers in the Rhineland and made their headquarters at Koblenz, was felt. These people arrived bitterly complaining of their fate and no doubt exaggerating the atrocious treatment they had received in their homeland.

Further east there was less sympathy. The autocratic rulers in Berlin and Vienna could not watch with satisfaction attacks on the principle of royalty, no matter how pleasant might be the discomfiture of arrogant France. This was particularly true in Vienna, where both Joseph II and his successor Leopold II (1790–92) were brothers of Marie Antoinette, the suffering queen of France. However, during the early months of the revolution there was too much ill feeling between Prussia and Austria for the two to act in concert.

Frederick the Great had been succeeded on the throne of Prussia by his nephew, Frederick William II (1786–97), one of the weakest and least competent members of the Hohenzollern family. His reign shows the danger latent in the Prussian system of government. It could work well when the monarch was willing to give unstinting attention to public affairs, but when the king was either lazy or incompetent the whole edifice fell apart. Frederick William II was dissolute and licentious, and also subject to fits of odd religiosity which culminated in his adoption of Rosicrucianism. His jealousy of Austria was increased by a war which Austria was waging with Turkey and which promised territorial gains for the Hapsburgs. Leopold II, a temperate and moderate ruler, who had gained a considerable reputation from his administration in Tuscany for many years, decided to soothe Prussian sensibilities. Thus at Reichenbach in 1790 he signed an agreement with Prussia to make no major demands from the Turks, so that Frederick William would have no reason to clamor for compensation. The following year Leopold made a peace with Turkey in which he even relinquished the fortress of Belgrade, which his armies had captured. He was now free to turn his attention to domestic affairs and to try to undo some of the irritating reforms of his brother Joseph. He did this in a spirit of toleration, granting to some of the angry minority national groups the prestige and position they demanded. However, he had to restore order in Belgium by force. Leopold was also distressed with the plight of his sister and brother-in-law in Paris and engaged in a secret correspondence with them which led to their abortive attempt to escape from France in June 1791.

These events served to bring Prussia and Austria closer together. The two German monarchs met at Pillnitz in August to compose their differences. This they did in a joint declaration which mainly served to infuriate the revolutionary government in France. Leopold and Frederick William promised that they would intervene in France, if at all, only with the consent of the other powers. The mere mention of intervention was enough to set the French leaders on fire.

Leopold died suddenly early in 1792 and was succeeded as emperor by his son, the last Holy Roman emperor (Francis II, Holy Roman emperor, 1792–1806; Francis I, emperor of Austria, 1804–35). Francis was immediately faced, in spite of his inexperience, with the imminent danger of war. Some of the small German states in the Rhineland appealed to the emperor to help them get redress from France for the loss of old feudal dues in Alsace. The emperor was sympathetic to their request and, having fallen under the influence of the French *émigrés,* was not averse to a war. In France a war party, the Girondins, had come to power; they hoped that some of the domestic problems could be solved by a successful war. Thus both sides wanted war. The French Assembly forced the reluctant Louis XVI to declare war on Austria (not on the Empire) on April 20, 1792, and some days later on Prussia too. Thus a period of almost twenty-five years of terrible warfare began.

The German powers believed that the war would be merely a military parade. They felt that France was in the throes of chaos and that her army had been hopelessly crippled by the loss of many of its aristocratic officers. At first they seemed to be right, for they won a number of small victories. This impelled the Prussian commander, the duke of Brunswick, to issue in July a manifesto declaring that the allies planned to restore Louis XVI to his full power and would hold the people of Paris strictly accountable for any indignities suffered by the royal family. This manifesto had an effect opposite to that intended. On August 10, 1792, the

Paris mob stormed the palace of the Tuileries, the king fled for protection to the Assembly, the French monarchy ended, and several weeks later a republic was proclaimed. The turn of the military tide came in September when at Valmy the Prussian army was defeated by the French. It was not a great battle but became a landmark because it put heart into the despairing French and started the astonishing succession of victories which France was to enjoy for the next twenty years.

Frederick William II's heart was never really in the war with France. He was more interested in events in the east where Prussia seemed surer to gain a greater increase of territory than in the confused west. Conditions in Poland had once more reached a crisis. After the partition of 1772 the Poles, with a remarkable spurt of energy, attempted to reform their antiquated kingdom. This effort culminated in 1791 with the adoption of a new constitution establishing a hereditary monarchy for the Wettin family, strengthening the executive power, and abolishing the old feudal vestiges. Empress Catherine of Russia, quick to see the danger of a strong Poland at her border, denounced the new constitution strengthening the monarchy as "revolutionary" in almost the same breath that she denounced the weakening of the monarchy in France as "revolutionary." She sent Russian troops into Poland to restore the old anarchy; they were met by Prussian troops advancing from the west. The result, in early 1793, was a second partition of Poland in which Prussia acquired Danzig and Thorn, a considerable part of western Poland, and a total of over a million new subjects.

The last act of this sorry story occurred in the two following years. Polish patriots rose against the intolerable aggression from abroad but were no match for the combined force of Russia and Prussia. In 1795 Poland disappeared from the map of Europe. This time Austria joined in the pillage. She received the area around Cracow, while Prussia got large parts of central Poland including the important city of Warsaw. Frederick William II felt that he had reason to be proud of his achievements and that he need not lament too much his failures in the west.

Meanwhile the extraordinary and unexpected successes of French arms continued along the Rhine and in Belgium. The old dream of the French border on the Rhine seemed closer to realization than ever before. The warfare was not completely one-sided but enough so to frighten the German powers. The French captured Brussels; they occupied almost the whole left bank of the Rhine forcing the three ecclesiastical electors to flee across the river; in spots they even advanced beyond the Rhine. The enthusiasm of the republican patriots seemed to have no bounds and evoked a corresponding enthusiasm among some of the elements of the German populations. For example, some patriots proclaimed a republic in Mainz until the city was integrated into France proper. In mid-1793 the allies achieved some successes; but after the French Committee of Public Safety called a mass levy of the French population and reorganized the new army under Carnot, the French seemed invincible. By the end of 1794 all of Belgium was in French hands and the German allies had retired across the Rhine.

Faced by this situation, Frederick William II decided to cut his losses. He determined to trade the west for the east, a policy in line with Prussian tradition. He negotiated the Treaty of Basel (March 1795) with the less radical French republican government which followed the fall of Robespierre in the summer of 1794. This treaty is important because it provided a model for the breakup of the Holy Roman Empire which was to follow during the next decade. It also showed the degree to which Prussia was uninterested in the affairs of the Empire in general and concerned only with the welfare of the Prussian state. This attitude was to be repeated by the Austrians when they came to make their peace two years later.

The Treaty of Basel had both public and secret clauses. In the public clauses Prussia recognized France's occupation of the left bank of the Rhine temporarily until a final arrangement was secured with the Empire, which had officially come into the war some time before. In secret, France promised that north Germany should be neutralized and, most important, Prussia agreed to the permanent possession of the left bank by France with the understanding that she would be compensated for her own losses by land on the right bank taken from secularized ecclesiastical territories. This decision signed the death warrant of the old ecclesiastical principalities, which were to disappear almost completely in the next ten years.

The Treaty of Basel and the Third Partition of Poland were the last important acts of Frederick William II, who died in 1797. He was succeeded by his son, Frederick William III (1797–1840), a devoted, hardworking, mediocre man of distinctly limited intelligence, who was destined to a long reign full of stirring events which he hardly understood.

Those who expected the Treaty of Basel to lay the foundations of a general peace were disappointed. Austria was as antirevolutionary as ever and was carrying out an "anti-Jacobin" prosecution at home. Furthermore, the emperor's brother, Archduke Charles, was having some success in fighting the French who had advanced into south Germany.

The new French government, the Directory, had decided to launch a new series of offensives against the Austrians. This action was to comprise three separate thrusts. The two principal ones were planned for central and southern Germany, while a third was intended mainly to hold down an Austrian army in northern Italy. This third army was entrusted to a young Corsican officer, General Napoleon Bonaparte, who had achieved some reputation as an artillery officer fighting the British at Toulon. The two armies in Germany had only moderate success; against them Archduke Charles won his victories. The decision was achieved by Bonaparte's army in Italy.

The Napoleonic campaigns have been described in intense detail and must not concern us here unduly. Napoleon advanced from the Riviera coast, knocked the king of Piedmont-Sardinia out of the war, defeated the Austrians at Lodi, and in May 1796 occupied the old Austrian possession of Milan, where he set up a republic and ruled like a king. During the fall and winter he defeated the Austrians several times, most notably at Arcola and Rivoli, and in the spring of 1797 crossed the Alps and presented himself dangerously close to the Austrian homeland. The result was preliminary peace negotiations at Leoben and a final treaty signed in October 1797 at Campo Formio.

The Treaty of Campo Formio repeats the pattern of the terms of Basel. Austria ceded Belgium outright to France. She also recognized Napoleon's reorganization of northern Italy into a republic. In return she received, through an act of piracy, the possessions of the stately old republic of Venice. Austria also agreed to summon a congress at Rastadt to settle the whole tangled problem of the western part of the Empire. In secret she gave her permission to France to possess the left bank of the Rhine as far as Cologne; she stipulated that Prussia was to receive no compensation on the right bank, but that other princes would be compensated, presumably from ecclesiastical lands. Finally France offered to secure for Austria Salzburg and parts of Bavaria. The same selfish spirit animated the Hapsburg in this treaty that had animated the Hohenzollern at Basel. With this document the war of the First Coalition against France came to an end. Only Great Britain was still at war.

The Congress of Rastadt was a lamentable failure. It sat from late 1797 to the spring of 1799 and then adjourned because a new general war broke out. All the hatreds, tensions, and petty meannesses of the German princelings showed themselves nakedly. The scene was a source of scorn and derision to the publicists of the time. Bonaparte spent some days at Rastadt on his return home from Campo Formio. In his conversations he laid down the lines of his future German policy: encouragement of Austro-Prussian enmity, favoritism to the middle-sized German states (e.g., Bavaria, Saxony, Würtemberg, Baden, and Hesse-Kassel), absolute French domination of Rhenish Germany. It was the old policy of Richelieu and Louis XIV, except that now the military weight was completely on the French side. The intricacies of the organization of the tottering old Empire were too much for the Germans to handle themselves. However, another war was to intervene before the surgery was performed. Soon after his visit to Rastadt Bonaparte left on his adventuresome if fruitless expedition to Egypt.

The Second Coalition was largely the work of Emperor Paul of Russia, a near-psychotic, who resented the behavior of the French toward the Knights of Malta, of whom he was grand master. He also deplored French meddling in central Europe, so he allied himself with Britain, Austria, and various smaller nations. Russian, British, and Austrian armies attacked France from several directions during 1799. At first the allied armies swept all before them and dislodged the French from positions in Italy, Switzerland, and Germany. The only French success was the repulse of a British landing in Holland. However, in late 1799 Paul changed his mind. He became jealous of Britain and also angry at the lukewarm co-operation given his armies by the inefficient Austrians; therefore he withdrew from the war leaving Austria as the only major continental power involved. At the same time Bonaparte left his army in Egypt and returned with a few followers to France. In a *coup d'état* he overthrew the government of the Directory and made himself dictator of France with the title of First Consul.

True to his policy of rapid military movement Napoleon, in the spring of 1800, led his army over the Great St. Bernard Pass into Italy and defeated the Austrians at the battle of Marengo. Some months later the French general Moreau defeated Archduke John at the battle of Hohenlinden in Germany and advanced toward the Tyrol. Emperor Francis asked for peace, and the new treaty was signed at Lunéville in February 1801. This treaty repeated many of the provisions of the Treaty of Campo Formio, including the French possession of the left bank of the Rhine and the indemnification of the German princes who lost land there.

This time there was to be no repetition of the inconclusive Congress of Rastadt. The indemnifications and the territorial shifts in the Empire were worked out over a period of two years under the watchful eyes of the French government and also of the new Russian emperor, Alexander I. France insisted on her rights granted by the Treaty of Westphalia to guard the institutions of the Empire, as did Russia on similar rights from the Treaty of Teschen of 1779. In fact, most of the negotiations occurred in Paris where Talleyrand, Napoleon's foreign minister, interviewed the various claimants and made awards while increasing his large personal fortune from German bribes. The German princes reached new depths of ignominy as they begged for scraps of old German territory from the Corsican upstart who was ruling France and the apostate bishop who was his minister.

By late 1802 the arrangements were completed and the matter was placed in the hands of the Diet of the Empire at Regensburg. The Diet appointed an Imperial Deputation and the final act of this committee, passed in February 1803, bears the massive title of *Reichsdeputations-hauptschluss*. By this enactment the old medieval Empire came for all intents and purposes to an end. Its composition was radically altered. France bordered the Rhine for its full length from Alsace north. There were now six free cities instead of forty-eight. There were only three ecclesiastical principalities left, and they were soon to go. All the rest of the ecclesiastical lands and municipal territories were used as indemnification for the princes who lost land west of the Rhine, but in most cases the compensations were considerably greater than the losses. Two ecclesiastical electorates (Cologne and Trier) were abolished, and three lay ones (Baden, Würtemberg, and Hesse-Kassel) were added. There was no mention of the imperial knights who simply disappeared as political entities by the process of mediatization (placing them under a temporal lord).

The indemnifications benefited principally Prussia and the middle states, which received very generous grants of former church territories. Bavaria, Baden, Würtemberg, Hanover, and the Hesses became considerable states but not large enough to be a threat. Napoleon was going to find them very convenient for his purposes. In fact, he soon simply occupied Hanover because it belonged to the king of England. Germany was much simplified; this is Napoleon's principal claim to German gratitude. However, at the time it was done only for the greater power of France. The formal abolition of the Empire and the organization of much of Germany into a confederation under French auspices did not come for three more years and required another war. But the foundations were all laid in 1803.

In 1804 Napoleon affronted old Europe by two actions. In February he violated the sovereignty of Baden by sending a force across the border and arresting a Bourbon prince, the duke of Enghien, whom he brought to Paris and executed, alleging a conspiracy against the French government. Three months later he was proclaimed Napoleon I, emperor of the French. These events were viewed with extreme alarm, especially by Alexander of Russia, who was now becoming very anti-French. He was encouraged in his attitude by the British, who, after a short peace, were again at war with France. The result was an alliance between the two and efforts to include Austria and Prussia in the coalition. Austria reacted to Napoleon's proclamation with the proclamation by Emperor Francis of his new title, emperor of Austria. This action, of course, emphasized even further the impending dissolution of the old Empire. After a good deal of delay the Austrians joined the Third Coalition with Britain and Russia in 1805, but by the end of that year Prussia still refused to commit herself.

In the fall of 1805 Napoleon broke camp at Boulogne, from which he had threatened Britain with invasion, and marched rapidly across France and Germany arriving at the city of Ulm, where he found an Austrian army which he surrounded. General Mack, the Austrian commander, had no choice except to surrender all his men. Napoleon then advanced toward Moravia where the Austrians and Russians had joined forces. There on December 2 he won probably his greatest victory, the battle of Austerlitz. Austria had to ask for peace while the Russians retreated far to the east to lick their wounds.

The Treaty of Pressburg of 1805 subjected Austria to still further humiliations. She gave up all her Italian holdings to France or to Napoleon's new kingdom of Italy; she ceded the Tyrol and a great part of her German territory to Bavaria, which was allied to France; and to Würtemberg and Baden she gave the remainder of the Hapsburg possessions in the west. Austria had to recognize Bavaria and Würtemberg as kingdoms and for all these losses received only Salzburg and a small territory in its neighborhood. She hardly existed as a German state anymore.

Napoleon carried out his final organization of Germany in the early months of 1806. He made a number of changes and transfers of territory and government and in July announced the formation of the Confederation of the Rhine. This was at first an organization of sixteen states but later included almost all the German states except Prussia and Austria. These states withdrew from the Holy Roman Empire, became allied with France, and placed themselves under the protection of the French Empire. Louis XIV's dream was at length realized. Western Germany became an area tributary to France.

There was only one reaction which Emperor Francis, now deprived of force, could make to the new situation. In August he simply announced that the Holy Roman Empire no longer existed. The old institution which had lasted just over a thousand years in its various forms was crushed by the revolutionary fervor of the French and the ruthless statesmanship of Napoleon.

There still remained the humiliation of Prussia to make Napoleon's authority in Germany complete. Prussia ever since the Treaty of Basel had played a cowardly and selfish role in German politics. She had maintained her neutrality but at the cost of her reputation for bravery. In 1805 Emperor Alexander had done all he could to bring Prussia into the coalition even to the extent of going to Berlin to make a personal plea. However, the Prussians hesitated until after the defeat of Austria and the retreat of the Russians. In mid-1806, at the worst possible moment, they declared war on France because of some actions of Napoleon in north Germany and some negotiations concerning Hanover. They thought that their army was still the army of Frederick the Great. It no longer was, however, and in two battles fought on the same day (Jena and Auerstädt on October 14, 1806) the Prussians were disastrously defeated. Within a few days Napoleon was in Berlin and most of the Prussian fortresses had surrendered to the French. The king and the court fled to East Prussia where Napoleon pursued them in early 1807. The Russians joined forces with the Prussians, and Napoleon fought both in an inconclusive battle at Eylau in February. In June the decisive French victory of Friedland brought Napoleon to the frontier of the Russian Empire.

Napoleon met with Alexander and Frederick William at Tilsit immediately after the battle of Friedland. He concluded a treaty of friendship and alliance with Russia but a very humiliating treaty with Prussia. It might have been worse had it not been for the mediation of Alexander and the tearful pleas of the beautiful Prussian queen, Louise. Prussia ceded to Napoleon all her territories west of the Elbe River, most of which were erected into the kingdom of Westphalia for Jerome Bonaparte. She also ceded most of the land acquired in the partitions of Poland, from which Napoleon created the grand duchy of Warsaw under his friend the king of Saxony. Prussia was further forbidden to maintain an army of over forty-two thousand men and was required to pay France a large indemnity. Having been forced to greatness by Frederick the Great and then swollen by the booty from Poland, Prussia could now hardly rank as a second-class power. This was probably the zenith of Napoleon's fortunes and the nadir of German humiliation.

At this point interest shifts from the parade of Napoleon's victories to the efforts made by his victims to reform their states and effectively resist the conqueror. The long-term consequences of the French invasions were beginning to be felt. In the western states of the Confederation of the Rhine the new spirit of French liberalism and efficient administration were introduced, and these old-fashioned states began to join the modern world. For example, in Bavaria during the Francophile ministry of Count Montgelas serfdom was abolished, while in the kingdom of Westphalia the Napoleonic law codes were instituted.

More important was the new spirit of nationalism displayed by the occupied countries. This too was learned from France. Modern nationalism seems to have begun with the French Revolution manifesting itself in the cult of patriotism, the mass army, and the song of the revolution "Marseillaise." Sentiments like this are contagious, and when

French armies occupied their territories other Europeans began to develop a cult of patriotism directed against the French oppressors.

After her disastrous defeat in 1805 Austria tried to reform herself and become the German leader, a position she had abdicated some time before. In the long run, the dynastic selfishness of the Hapsburgs and the particularism of the non-Germanic nationality groups defeated the Austrian reform. However, in 1808 and 1809 Count Stadion, the emperor's chief minister, made impressive strides in centralizing the government and reforming the finances. At the same time Archduke Charles accomplished a good deal in the reform of the army while attempting to make it a match for the French. The Austrians were impressed by the brave stand the Spanish were making against their French oppressors; the British government encouraged Austria with subsidies; even the astute Austrian ambassador in Paris, Count Clemens von Metternich, thought the time was ripe for war. Therefore, in the spring of 1809 the Austrian government issued a call for all Germans to join it in an attempt to throw off the French yoke.

The Austrian appeal found little answer. In the north there were a few quixotic uprisings which the French put down without trouble. The only important one was that of Andreas Hofer and his brave Tyrolean peasants who stood courageously, if hopelessly, against the Bavarians and the French. Austria had to fight alone. Napoleon hurriedly left Spain and marched across southern Germany. He suffered his first defeat from Archduke Charles at Aspern in May, but in July he crushed the Austrian army at Wagram near Vienna.

The Treaty of Schönbrunn (October 1809) brought Austria almost to the depths that Prussia had reached at Tilsit. She had to cede the Salzburg area to Bavaria, Polish territories to the grand duchy of Warsaw and to Russia, and her whole Adriatic coast to Napoleon, who needed it to seal off the coast of Europe from British commerce. She also had to break off all connection with Great Britain and to pay France an indemnity. This treaty broke Austria's spirit; for several years she offered no resistance to the French. In fact in April 1810 Napoleon married Archduchess Maria Louisa, a daughter of Emperor Francis. This created a blood bond between the old Hapsburg and the upstart Bonaparte. With the birth of Napoleon's son in 1811 the Austrians had an interest in the maintenance of the new empire. From this time on their diplomacy was not intended to rid Europe of Napoleon but merely to restrict the French to predominantly French areas. This was the line followed by Metternich, who had now become Austria's principal minister, a position which he was to hold for almost forty years.

The Prussian effort at reform and the reshaping of her institutions was more successful than the Austrian and far more significant for the future of Germany. In fact German historians call the years from Tilsit to 1813 simply the "reform" period. The reforms were enacted in a number of fields: political and economic, military, and educational. Prussia rose out of the slump into which she had fallen and prepared herself for the principal role in Germany. She enjoyed the leadership of a number of remarkable men, many of whom were not Prussian by birth but drifted there to serve the independent German state which seemed to offer the most hope for the future. They found themselves opposed and blocked at almost every turn by the shortsighted and pedantic Frederick William III.

The outstanding member of this circle was Karl, Freiherr vom Stein. Stein was an immediate subject of the emperor, an imperial knight, whose little domain lay not far from the Rhine. He found the management of his estates frustratingly petty, so early in life he entered the Prussian civil service. He rose gradually through the ranks and by 1804 was in charge of the finances of Prussia.

Stein was distinctly a son of the Enlightenment. He believed in the primacy of reason and also in human liberty, being convinced that free men are more productive members of society than those in bondage. He was no lover of tradition for its own sake and invited constant trouble with the king and the conservatives by his insistence on the thorough overhauling of the habit-ridden Prussian administration. Thus in early 1807 the king dismissed him in an order describing him in abusive language. During the disastrous months that followed the king was forced to change his attitude and the day after the signature of Tilsit appointed Stein his principal minister, a position which he held for about a year. During this year he achieved several important reforms and proved to be unusual for his period since he was a German, rather than only a Prussian, patriot.

Two important enactments marked Stein's tenure of office. The first was the edict in October 1807 which liberated the serfs. Legally the serfs were now free and for the first time had the right to sell and buy property. The thought was that the edict was to be succeeded by others abolishing all manorial jurisdiction, but this complete task was not accomplished and the lords of the manors retained many of their rights until 1848. Nevertheless, Stein took an important first step.

The following year Stein issued the municipal ordinance which granted self-government to a number of the cities in Prussia and eliminated the old guild system of government. This was an important beginning of some sort of liberalism in the autocratic Prussian state. In spite of his hopes, Stein was not able to obtain the king's approval to a similar law for rural areas; thus a dichotomy was established between the semi-liberal towns and the very conservative countryside, a situation which was to have influence in Prussian politics for decades to come.

Stein was not fated to remain long in office and was unable to carry out the far-reaching plans he nourished for the future. In late 1808 an anti-Napoleonic letter of his was seized by the French censorship, and Napoleon demanded that Frederick William dismiss his minister—probably the most acceptable demand that the king of Prussia ever had to obey. After two years of return to the old conservative leadership Frederick William appointed Karl von Hardenberg as his principal adviser in 1810. Hardenberg continued Stein's work during his long tenure of office. He secularized church property, reformed the financial structure of Prussia, and introduced legislation along the lines of the new economic philosophy of *laissez faire*. This earned for him the dislike of the old vested interests, especially the noble landed proprietors, but he managed to retain the confidence of the king and to change the course of Prussian development in a modern direction.

The old army of Frederick the Great and its organization died on the field of Jena. At Tilsit Napoleon demanded that the Prussian army be shorn to a mere forty-two thousand men. The time was obviously ripe for a thoroughgoing reorganization in the military sphere. A brilliant group was at hand to effect it. As military administrators, there were Scharnhorst, Gneisenau, and Boyen; as a philosopher of war, Clausewitz; as generals in the field, Blücher and Yorck. The French had revolutionized warfare by the introduction of the mass citizen army. Now the Prussians copied their foes. They gradually formed a new Prussian army consisting of a regular professional army as the core with a militia and a general levy of the male population as reserves to be called upon when needed. This became the pattern for the Prussian army in the following century of Prussian military prowess. To circumvent the limitation on the size of the army, the new leaders devised an ingenious system in which a small number of men were trained intensively for a short time and then replaced by another group. Thus when Prussia took the field against France in 1813, the enemy was astonished by her large number of well-trained soldiers.

In the realm of education the major achievement was the foundation of the University of Berlin in 1810 under the leadership of Wilhelm von Humboldt. The older universities had been increasingly criticized for the sterility of their teaching and methods. New educational ideas were being developed; Humboldt was a disciple of the new philosophy and created at Berlin an institution which in a short time became the leader in German teaching and research and one of the principal universities in the world.

The new spirit manifested itself in other ways. Ludwig (Father) Jahn established a nationwide system of physical education for young Prussian boys, in which not only their bodies were strengthened but also their minds indoctrinated with ideas of the national grandeur of the Germans. Possibly most impressive of all was the series of lectures given in the winter of 1807–8 by Johann Gottlieb Fichte entitled *Addresses to the German Nation*. They were delivered under the immediate surveillance of French police, and were concerned first with a consideration of the sterling moral qualities of the German people and then with a call for a rehabilitation of German national greatness. Thus while Prussia seemed to be at her lowest ebb, she was in fact going through a momentous process of reform and renewal which was to bear fruit in the years to come.

The crisis with France developed after the tragic retreat of Napoleon's armies from Russia in the autumn of 1812. Both Prussia and Austria as technical allies of France had to provide contingents for the massive attack. Thousands of other Germans were in the *Grande Armée* as part of the forces contributed by the various states of the Confederation of the Rhine. The Austrians managed to avoid a good part of the fighting since they were on the right wing, well south of Napoleon himself, but the other Germans suffered along with the French in the awful retreat. By November it developed into a rout, and Napoleon left the remains of his army and hurried ahead to Paris.

At this point Tsar Alexander had to decide whether to continue the war now that the enemy was off Russian soil. His decision was undoubtedly influenced by Stein, who had some time before made his way to the Russian court and become Alexander's adviser on German affairs. Alexander, always pleased to play Sir Galahad, was receptive to Stein's counsel and led his army across the Russian frontier to undertake a general war of liberation of Europe from the French yoke.

Another important decision had to be taken, this time by General Yorck, commander of the remnant of the Prussian army near the Russian border. He could continue to fight the Russians, he could surrender to them, or he could co-operate with them. Completely on his own initiative, in an action which technically constituted treason, Yorck signed on December 30 at Tauroggen an agreement with the Russians guaranteeing neutrality. This opened the way for the Russian army into East Prussia, where Alexander appointed Stein temporary administrator of all German territories cleared by the Russian army.

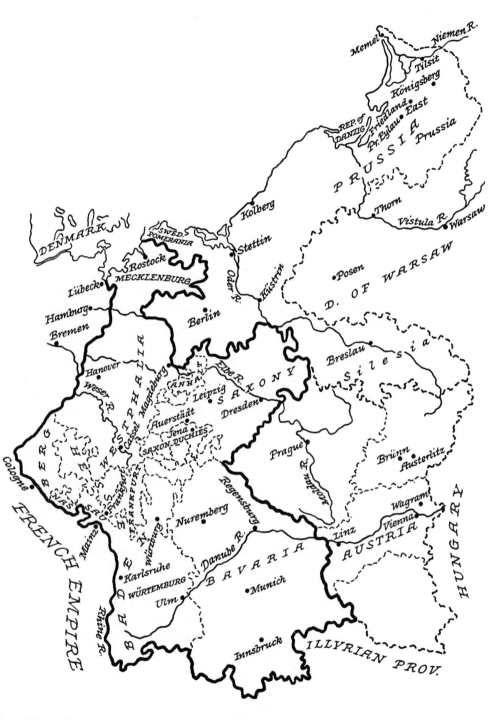

The Confederation of the Rhine and Prussia in 1812

Boundary of the Confederation of the Rhine ▬▬▬▬

These actions placed King Frederick William in a quandary and forced that vacillating monarch into some difficult decisions. He could not forgive Yorck's disobedience, something unthinkable in a Prussian officer, but nevertheless he could not avoid observing the popularity of Yorck's act. He moved to Breslau, away from French observation, and there entered into negotiations with Stein and the Russians. The result on February 28 was the Treaty of Kalisch, a full military alliance containing the promise that Prussia would be granted territories suitable to regain her position of 1806, though not necessarily the same territories she had lost because Alexander did not want Prussia to control so much of Poland.

For the next several weeks Frederick William acted as a popular monarch, which was very much out of character. He established the decoration of the Iron Cross for bravery in the field, he called for the establishment of "Free Corps" to fight the enemy, and in his proclamation "To my people" he listed eloquently the patriotic motives for war. The Prussian people responded with enthusiasm. They founded Free Corps, the most successful of which operated under Major von Lützow, and established a tradition to be exploited in the melancholy days after 1918. They advanced money while the poets and composers wrote songs. Never before had the people of Prussia felt that they were incorporated into the actions of their government.

The enthusiasm was not shared by the rest of the Germans. Austria played a devious diplomatic game for some months trying to find a compromise which would at one time preserve the Bonaparte dynasty, restore Austria as a great power, and keep the French Empire within manageable limits. Of the states of the Confederation of the Rhine only one withdrew from its alliance with Napoleon.

Napoleon, always determined to take the first steps himself, performed a miracle by raising still another French army during the winter of 1812–13. In the spring he appeared in Germany; during May he won two battles and forced the Allies out of Saxony, where the king was his stoutest adherent. In early June the two sides agreed on an armistice in the hope of arriving at some sort of compromise. The whole summer was taken up by discussions, with Metternich acting as mediator. No result was achieved. In August the Austrians realized that peace was not in sight and finally cast their lot with Britain, Russia, and Prussia. For the first time Napoleon was actively opposed by the four other major powers.

Two months later Austria concluded a treaty with Bavaria, which was certainly not decisive militarily but was important because it showed the trend of diplomatic thought concerning the future of Germany. In it the king of Bavaria, who had received more favors than any other German prince from Napoleon, abandoned his alliance with France and joined the Allies. In return he was promised that at the conclusion of peace he could retain his title of king and also the lands he then possessed, except for those received from former Austrian territories. This meant that there was no serious thought of either reviving the old Holy Roman Empire or restoring the dozens of princes and prelates who had lost their possessions in the preceding fifteen years. Obviously a whole new organization of Germany was envisaged.

The great battle was fought near Leipzig from October 16 to 19, 1813. This was Napoleon's decisive defeat. After it the French moved westward pursued slowly by the Allies. One after another the princes of the Confederation of the Rhine joined the alliance against Napoleon. The kingdom of Westphalia collapsed. Only the king of Saxony stood firm, and for his loyalty he was arrested. More and more territory fell under the administration of Stein.

The Allies were still not agreed concerning the fate of Napoleon and France. For a time they continued to think of the left bank of the Rhine as permanently French; but as the months went on and Napoleon continued to resist in his brilliantly executed campaign in France in early 1814, their opinions changed. They were not yet prepared to make the final decisions for the future of Europe, but by March, led by Tsar Alexander, they had agreed on the deposition of Napoleon and the restoration of the Bourbon family. On March 9 the Allies signed the Treaty of Chaumont, in which they mutually pledged to continue to fight until the final defeat of Napoleon and not to make any separate peace. They also agreed that there should be a great congress to remake the map which had undergone such upsetting changes in the last years. Emperor Francis invited his allies to meet in his capital city of Vienna.

The end of an era came on April 11, 1814, when Napoleon abdicated from the throne of the French Empire and from all his other titles, receiving in exchange sovereignty over the island of Elba, where he proceeded to rule his toy kingdom.

CHAPTER V

Metternich's Germany (1814-48)

In September 1814 all Europe went to Vienna—all Europe, that is to say, that counted politically—not the Europe of liberals and nationalists, the people who had overthrown their masters, the people of the future, but the dynasts and the bureaucrats, who were to reap the first fruits of the people's labors. It was a brilliant assembly including some of the ablest diplomats in modern history: Metternich from Austria, Hardenberg and Humboldt from Prussia, Talleyrand from France, Castlereagh and Wellington from Britain, and Alexander I from Russia. They had a frightening task before them, for the events since 1789 had so thoroughly disrupted the old Europe that it could not possibly be restored. They had to establish the pattern of a new Europe. They did so and created a pattern which was to endure with some changes for about a century.

As far as German affairs were concerned, the principal figure was Metternich. This astute, supple, charming, cultured diplomat came originally from the Rhineland but had early entered the service of Austria and become completely Austrian in his outlook. He was not unaware of the new forces abroad in the world; he had not wasted his time in Paris when he was ambassador there. Yet he knew that liberalism and nationalism, particularly the latter, were deadly poison to the Hapsburg realm, composed as it was of a complex mixture of nationality groups. These forces constituted for Metternich "the revolution," and he was determined to keep them in check. Thus his policy was to fight a rear guard action, to conserve, and to keep things as quiet as possible. This policy was not easy to achieve in the atmosphere of 1814 because the enthusiasm engendered by the War of Liberation did not show signs of weakening as quickly as it had been brought to life. Fervid romantic longings for a united Germany were uttered by poets, writers, and young people.

The basic dilemma of creating a united Germany is simple to understand. There were two great German powers, Austria and Prussia. How would it be possible to combine them into some kind of state without robbing one or the other of its prestige and influence? This problem has been described as the *grossdeutsch* vs. *kleindeutsch* (greater Germany including Austria *vs.* little Germany without Austria) controversy, which was to complicate central European affairs for decades until Bismarck finally solved it by harsh, direct measures. At Vienna a committee was formed (consisting of Austria, Prussia, Bavaria, Würtemberg, and Hanover) to bring in a proposal for a new German organization. In the meantime the diplomats considered territorial problems.

The angriest conflict concerned the fate of Poland and Saxony. Tsar Alexander wanted to reassemble partitioned Poland into a kingdom with himself as king. Prussia refused to give up some parts of Poland that she had acquired (West Prussia, Posen, and Danzig) and for the rest demanded the cession to her of the kingdom of Saxony, which had not deserted Napoleon. When Austria and Britain opposed this plan, it looked for a time as if a new war were in the offing. In the end a compromise was effected by which Prussia received about three-fifths of Saxony, but the shorn kingdom continued to exist. As further compensation Prussia acquired the rich provinces of the Rhineland and Westphalia, whose immense wealth under the ground of the Ruhr Valley was still unknown. She also received Swedish Pomerania. Prussia was much strengthened and, even more important, her new strength was in German lands rather than foreign. The cession of the western provinces to Prussia made it clear once again that there was no intention of restoring the prelates and princes who had ruled in that area before the revolution. The Holy Roman Empire was officially buried.

Austria did not get an increase in German lands other than regaining the areas that Napoleon had given to Bavaria. Instead she added to her non-Germanic possessions by receiving Lombardy and Venetia in Italy as compensation for relinquishing Belgium and some of the small west German possessions of the Hapsburg family.

Except for Saxony, the middle and smaller states were not much changed in their territories. Some of them actually received new lands (e.g., Bavaria gained some land in the north, and Hanover acquired East Friesland). In general, the pattern worked out by Napoleon in the first years of the century was maintained. There were no more imperial knights, and hundreds of the minor princes were mediatized. No ecclesiastical territories remained and only four free cities (Hamburg, Bremen, Lübeck, and Frankfurt). The new Germany consisted of only thirty-nine separate states.

These thirty-nine sovereign states were banded together into the

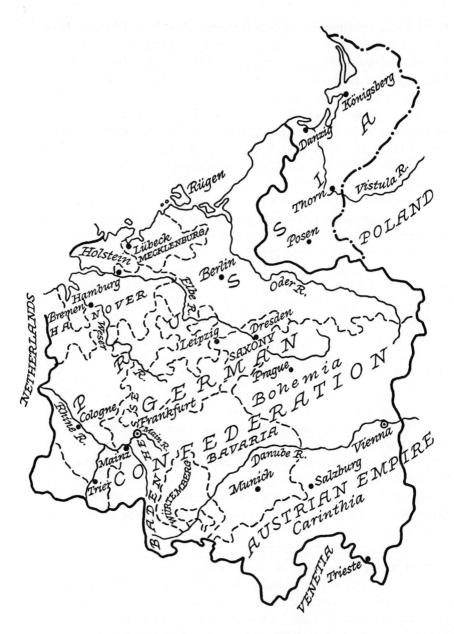

German Confederation
after the Congress of Vienna

German Confederation |————

German Confederation, a loose but allegedly eternal federal organization. Both Austria and Prussia were members of the Confederation but only for their German lands, that is, lands which had formerly been in the Holy Roman Empire. Thus Prussian Poland and East Prussia were not in the Confederation nor was the great bulk of the Austrian non-German areas. On the other hand, several non-German monarchs were members of the Confederation: the king of Great Britain because he was king of Hanover, the king of Denmark as ruler of Holstein, and the king of the Netherlands for Luxemburg.

The Confederation had a Federal Diet which met at Frankfurt under the permanent presidency of Austria. It really amounted to a conference of ambassadors because the members of it were simply named by the respective monarchs. It had the right to declare war and make peace. Each member agreed not to make alliances endangering any of the others or to go to war against another member of the Confederation. One interesting provision was the article which stated that each member of the Confederation was to be granted a constitution based on a representative body. As is the case with all constitutional states, the German Confederation could have operated in any one of a number of ways depending on the attitudes of those in charge. As things worked out, the Federal Diet became almost an annex of the Chancellery in Vienna.

With the establishment of the Confederation Germany entered what is frequently called the *Vormärz* period ("before March," in reference to the revolutions which broke out in Vienna and Berlin in March 1848). It is a dull period politically, marked by censorship, repression, and the stultification of new ideas. It is nevertheless an important period economically and socially, because during these years the industrial revolution began to make its first important impact on Germany, especially in the western provinces. This development brought with it shifts in social stratification and the whole web of German life, so that political change was bound to follow in spite of Metternich's efforts.

Much of the liberal and nationalistic agitation focused on students at the universities, particularly those outside Austria and Prussia. These youths had been intoxicated by the heady wine of patriotism during the War of Liberation. Their bodies had been trained in the physical culture schools of "Father" Jahn and their spirits urged on by the writings of Fichte and Arndt. They longed for the fine days only a few years before when Lützow had led his Free Corps of youths against the oppressor. They were in no mood now that the victory had been won to see it betrayed by a spirit of repression. This kind of attitude was especially strong at the University of Jena where the *Burschenschaft* movement was founded. The *Burschenschaften* were clubs of students who met to sing patriotic songs and indulge in beery teen-age nationalism. The movement spread throughout north Germany and culminated in the Wartburg Festival on October 18, 1817. This festival was staged at the romantic castle of the Wartburg near Eisenach where Luther translated the Bible. It was in commemoration of Luther and also the battle of Leipzig. The students sang around a great bonfire into which they threw symbols of repression and censorship, a corporal's stick and a policeman's pigtail.

One of the most extreme of the liberal leaders was a professor named Karl Follen at Jena. Among his students was a boy, Karl Sand, who became so enthusiastic about the cause of German nationalism that he resolved to strike a blow against oppression. He chose as his victim August von Kotzebue, a playwright who was in the pay of the Russian government. Sand murdered Kotzebue in Mannheim in March 1819. This act of terrorism determined Metternich to take severe action.

Metternich had become increasingly alarmed by the wave of student political activity. It led in a direction which endangered the whole conservative structure so dear to him. He was also worried about the liberal actions undertaken by some of the south German governments. In accordance with the provisions of the act setting up the Confederation, several governments, among them Bavaria, Baden, and Saxe-Weimar, had granted constitutions of a more or less liberal hue. Frederick William III in 1815 promised the Prussian people that he would grant them a constitution, but fortunately, from Metternich's point of view, he had done nothing about it. In fact he never did. Prussia had completely departed from the liberal reformist attitude of the period of Stein and Hardenberg and was now a willing seconder of Metternich's projects.

Accordingly Metternich called a meeting of several of the German states, including Prussia, at Karlsbad in July 1819 and persuaded them to pass the Karlsbad Decrees, which were later enacted as law by the Federal Diet. These decrees were reactionary in the extreme. They set up a series of commissioners at each university to see that all laws and disciplinary regulations were strictly obeyed, to check on "subversive" faculty members, and to make sure that no unauthorized societies existed. They furthermore set up a complete censorship of all written material longer than twenty pages throughout the Confederation. This was a prior censorship in which a publisher had to submit everything to the censors before publication. For years to come nothing smacking of liberalism was legally printed in Germany, and a brisk smuggling traffic developed mainly with Switzerland where many of the German liberals fled.

Although Prussia fully supported Metternich's conservative course in political matters, she showed more capacity for progress and modern ideas in other spheres, notably education and economics. The University of Berlin, now under the spiritual guidance of the major philosopher Georg Wilhelm Hegel, continued to set the pace for German learning. In economics the most important act was the foundation of the Customs Union (*Zollverein*) in 1819. This institution has been regarded by some historians as a first step toward the unification of Germany under Prussian auspices. It seems more likely that it was a practical application of common-sense administration dictated by the peculiarities of the Prussian economic scene.

As a result of her annexations in 1815, Prussia was now a varied state economically. Although the great majority of her subjects still worked on the land, there was a significant growth of industry in both Silesia and the Westphalian area. Agriculturally she was also far from homogeneous, with large estates in the east farmed by peasants just out of serfdom, while in the west the typical holding was a small plot worked by its owner. Furthermore, Prussia was so situated that she did a great deal of transit business, conveying goods to south Germany. In all her activities she was hampered by a wide variety of tariff scales and currencies. She decided to establish a uniform set of moderate duties and to invite other German states to conform to her tariffs and to merge the administration of customs on a pro rata basis. The first treaty of this sort was signed with tiny Schwarzburg-Sondershausen in 1819. Gradually the Customs Union grew, though not without difficulty because competing unions appeared in the south and west. Prussia consistently refused admission to Austria, not only on political grounds but because she feared the dumping of the large Hungarian grain crop into Germany. By 1844 most of Germany was in the Union, though certain states, notably Hamburg, stayed out even after the creation of the German Empire in 1871.

The efficient and ruthless enforcement of the Karlsbad Decrees and the general spirit of exhaustion after the Napoleonic turmoil conspired to prevent any serious outbursts of revolutionary enthusiasm in the twenties. However, by 1830 a new generation of young people had grown up for whom the old stories were ones of glory and not of suffering. A new wave of lawlessness developed, but not a very serious one.

The movement in 1830 was sparked by three revolutions abroad. In July the French deposed Charles X and replaced him with the bourgeois monarch, Louis Philippe, and a liberalized constitution. The Belgians revolted from their Dutch rulers and after some months succeeded in establishing an independent state. Even in pathetic Poland there was an effort to overthrow the Russian oppressor. In Germany the principal outbursts were in Brunswick, Hesse-Kassel, and industrial Saxony. In the first two the rulers were forced to abdicate, while in the third a modern constitution was granted. The revolutionary spirit remained active and culminated in 1832 in the Hambach Festival where 25,000 people clamored for changes, some of them even advocating a German republic.

Metternich was not slow in reprisal. He had a series of six articles passed by the Federal Diet which forbade German rulers to do anything that would reduce their sovereignty, prohibited German state parliaments to refuse appropriations as a weapon to secure concessions, and disallowed the states to prejudice any laws of the Federal Diet. There were many who felt that these laws were an infringement of local sovereignty, but Metternich succeeded in having them enforced. Repression now became an exact science. Public meetings, publications, political activity, and associations fell under the heaviest censorship and surveillance. The outbursts of 1830 had led to a worse situation than before. The immediate result was an absurd effort by some ill-trained radicals to seize the Federal Diet at Frankfurt. It failed and simply gave the authorities an excuse for even harsher measures.

Repression may have reached its high point in the kingdom of Hanover. When Queen Victoria succeeded to the throne in London in 1837, the kingdom of Hanover was separated from the British crown because of the old Salic law which forbade inheritance by a woman. So Victoria's uncle, Ernest Augustus, duke of Cumberland, became king of Hanover. He was a tough-minded old conservative who had no patience with liberal stirrings. Therefore he abrogated the fairly liberal constitution which his predecessor had granted a few years before. This became a national *cause célèbre* when the king dismissed seven of the outstanding scholars of all Germany from the University of Göttingen because they refused to take an oath to the new regime. The "seven" were immediately hired in liberal south German states, and some of the states even questioned Ernest Augustus' right to abrogate the constitution; but the Federal Diet, backed by both Austria and Prussia, supported the monarch's actions, and he was able to impose a very authoritarian constitution. The "Göttingen seven" remained a symbol of resistance to oppression.

Within five years both Austria and Prussia underwent a change of monarch. In 1835 Emperor Francis of Austria died and was succeeded on the throne by his son Ferdinand (1835–48), who was mentally incompetent. Ferdinand relied more than ever on Metternich, especially in the realm of foreign affairs, but he set up a conference of advisers in domestic affairs. In fact, the government was controlled by Metternich and Count Kolowrat, whose particular field of competence was finances.

In 1840 Frederick William III followed his colleague in Vienna, recommending on his deathbed to his heir that no constitution be granted to Prussia. The new king, Frederick William IV (1840–61), was a bizarre personality, certainly different from his Hohenzollern ancestors. He was a romantic, a dreamer, a dilettante of the arts. He enjoyed being loved and was astonished and aggrieved when he saw signs of opposition. Politically he was patriarchal, believing that a king should rule his subjects as a loving but strict father rules his children, with the implication, of course, that the child should render implicit obedience to his parent. He had no time for modern liberalism but fancied the use of the provincial estates—partly because they were a late medieval creation, and partly because with their heavily rural composition they were likely to be conservative.

Frederick William IV is in many ways a precursor of his grandnephew, Emperor William II, who shared many of his characteristics. Like William he began his reign with the relaxation of unpopular regulations, but this honeymoon period did not last very long. The people of Prussia soon discovered that Frederick William believed in divine-right rule just as much as his father had and in even a less practical way. Yet modern developments caught up with this old-fashioned monarch. During the forties the Prussian government found that its expenses exceeded its income. New types of projects, notably the building of a railroad network, were bringing the state close to bankruptcy. Frederick William was forced to take counsel with representatives of the people, but he did not envisage a constitution, which he characterized as a sheet of paper "between God in heaven and this land." He adopted instead the sham medieval idea of calling together the diets of the various provinces of Prussia into a new institution called the United Diet. The provincial diets were elected on a class basis, so that the United Diet emphasized the aristocratic classes. It met in 1847 and was presented with two government bills on financial problems. The delegates immediately developed an opposition, demanded some real control over legislation, and in particular requested a summons periodically. The king would have nothing to do with such ideas, and as a result the Diet was dismissed without accomplishing anything. However at this meeting some of the members banded into groups, incipient parties, which were to appear again the following year.

The sterile quality of political life in the *Vormärz* veils the basic importance of the period. The industrial revolution, which started in England, was now reaching the continent with increasing force. During the thirties and forties France felt its impact with the attendant incidence of strikes and the development of new social doctrines. Belgium too was quickly industrialized, thanks in part to her rich coal possessions. The movement was slower in the German Confederation where the political climate was antipathetic, but it made real progress. In the west the great coal reserves were tapped. The firm of Krupp had already laid its foundations in Essen. Towns like Düsseldorf and Cologne, which were to become industrial giants in the late years of the century, were beginning to feel the new impetus. In the east there was expansion both in Saxony and Silesia where there were important natural resources. Berlin and the eastern part of Prussia remained relatively untouched, but Vienna developed considerable industry, and new quarters of the city grew up outside the old fortifications. None of this was comparable to the phenomenal growth after 1871, but it made its influence felt.

A good part of the industrial growth revolved around the beginnings of railroad building. It had its start in Bavaria, but before long the obvious advantages of the railway became clear and the states rivaled one another in construction. In fact, the problem of financing railways forced Frederick William IV to summon the United Diet. Railways require coal and steel in large quantities; thus they started a chain reaction. The railroad system found a prophet in Friedrich List, the most important economic thinker of the period. List was banished from Würtemberg for his ideas, emigrated to the United States where he made a fortune, and then returned to Germany with diplomatic immunity as the American consul in Leipzig. He was one of the first to recognize the military possibilities of a thorough railway network. He was also a nationalist to the core and in his writings objected to the economic liberalism of the school of Adam Smith. Instead he advocated a system of economic nationalism complete with a high protective tariff.

With the increase in industrialization, even at the relatively low level of these decades, went also a change in the social organization. The new classes of the proletariat and the wealthy bourgeoisie, which were to have such importance in the future, began to appear—and with them the familiar problems of housing, labor relations, sanitation, education of the masses, etc. Until this time industrial and commercial life in Germany had been dominated by the guilds, which carefully regulated the details of the workers' lives. France abolished her guilds during the great revolution; in fact she even forbade the formation of any association of working men. However, Germany still preserved her guilds in most areas. This led to great difficulty because the new capitalistic large-scale industry which was just beginning to appear could not fit into the old guild regulations, some of which were antiquated. The introduction of new machines and techniques had the inevitable effect of causing technological unemployment, which sometimes resulted in bloodshed, as in the case of the weavers of Silesia who destroyed the new machines which were robbing them of their livelihood in the forties. Two worlds were in conflict—two worlds that were irreconcilable. The new economic forces were ready for a change, even an abrupt one, particularly since the middle forties were years of depression for both industry and agriculture.

There were plenty of people ready to suggest what form the change should take. Despite the repression, the years of Metternich's dominance produced political and social critics of all hues, ranging from a gentle liberalism through democracy to the most extreme forms of the new doctrine of socialism. And all of them, except the Marxian socialists, were wedded to the doctrine of nationalism.

At the extreme left of the spectrum there were a number of lunatic fringe theorists, usually bizarre characters, who advocated a wide variety of communal organizations. Karl Marx summed them up conveniently with the scornful phrase "utopian socialists," though some of them deserve rather better from posterity than that nickname. Marx himself was born in Trier and educated at the University of Berlin where he fell under the spell of the doctrines of Hegel, who had then only recently died. However, he reversed some of the doctrines of the master from their original idealism to a complete materialism and started to work out at length his eventual system. Returning to west Germany, he formed the association with Friedrich Engels that was to last his whole life; together, while writing for a newspaper entitled the *New Rhenish Gazette,* they developed the principles which were first enunciated in the pamphlet *Communist Manifesto* in 1847. This call to arms found very little response at the time, but later, when in exile in England, Marx and Engels composed the enormously influential *Das Kapital.*

To the right of Marx and Engels was a whole variety of political thinkers. Some of them were stirring poets like Heine and Herwegh; others were sober university professors and publicists. Some wanted a liberal constitutional monarchy on the pattern of Great Britain; others felt that only through a republican organization could the conflict between Austria and Prussia be resolved. If the country got rid of both Hapsburg and Hohenzollern, then all German people could be welded into a new pattern. A number of German thinkers studied the new United States and became devoted to the doctrine of democracy and the equality of man. Others looked back with nostalgic idealization to the Middle Ages, which, they thought, had constituted a moral, Christian, and heroic society. This attitude was given much impetus by the romantic movement in literature which was then at its apex in Germany.

It is not easy to define romanticism. It differed from country to country, and the leading romantics were themselves often such wild individualists that they defy classification. In fact, individualism is one of the main criteria of the movement. Allied with it was a strong sense of subjectivity and a desire to be free of the trammels of artistic form. The romantics condemned the men of the Enlightenment for their "cold" rationalism and their efforts to apply reforms without taking into consideration human emotions and the long period of development of so-called irrational institutions. This sense of development, of evolution, is very important to the understanding of romantic political thinking, for it merged into the school of historicism which sought to understand a phenomenon through studying its history. This kind of thinking, of which the spiritual father is probably Edmund Burke, inevitably tends toward conservatism and even the glorification of the past almost for its own sake.

Among the important early romantics were the brothers August Wilhelm (1767–1845) and Friedrich (1772–1829) Schlegel. August Wilhelm is primarily a literary figure and will be remembered for his wonderfully sympathetic translation of Shakespeare and also of a number of the masterpieces of Latin Europe. Friedrich was more concerned with history and philology and in his *Philosophy of History* invited attention to the Middle Ages. He showed consistency in his attachment to the medieval tradition by finding happiness in his later years through his conversion to the Catholic church.

One of the most characteristic of the romantic poets was Friedrich von Hardenberg (1772–1801), who wrote under the name of Novalis. His poetry was filled with the infinite longing, the bereaved love, and the burning intensity of the complete romantic. One of the themes of his prose was a glorification of the Middle Ages as the period of Christian unity when all worked in harmony under one sovereign for common goals. This naïve lack of historical understanding was typical of the period and had eventual political implications.

At a more sober level there was serious work in historiography, philology, and the study of folk literature. It is no coincidence that the great Freiherr vom Stein, following his eclipse at the Congress of Vienna, spent most of the rest of his active life in charge of a massive project to edit and publish the documents of the German Middle Ages. The resulting collection in many volumes, the *Monumenta Germaniae Historica,* remains one of the main sources for the medievalist. The brothers Jakob and Wilhelm Grimm became the founders of Germanic philology. Their taste for the past was whetted by their earlier preservation and rewriting of the immemorial fairy tales of the German people, which have remained so beloved in all lands. A similar work was done by Clemens Brentano and Achim von Arnim, who assembled and published the most famous collection of German folk songs, *Des Knaben Wunderhorn* (*"The Boy's Magic Horn"*).

Joseph Görres (1776–1848) was one of the earliest romantics to turn his thinking to politics. A devoted Rhinelander, Görres, like so many advanced Germans, at first welcomed the French Revolution; but as it advanced into the Napoleonic period, he became disillusioned and bitter. As editor of the *Rheinischer Merkur,* he was a very influential publicist and even won the respect of Napoleon. After 1815 he shifted his animosity from France to Prussia, to which his homeland now belonged. He had the Rhinelander's scorn for Prussia, which was augmented by his contempt for anything Protestant. He eventually had to escape and ended his days at the University of Munich still espousing the medieval and Catholic ideal.

Adam Müller (1779–1829) was probably the most thoroughgoing of the political romanticists. Müller was born a Prussian, but after he became an adult he turned completely against Prussianism and the Enlightenment. He joined the Catholic church and moved to Vienna where he breathed more congenial air. He knelt at the feet of Edmund Burke and thus was welcome in the circle of Metternich and his close associate Friedrich Gentz, who had translated Burke. Müller looked back with longing to the feudal society, which he felt to be most in accord with the will of God. He had the highest respect for the role and position of the state, which he believed to be above those who composed it. Thus all the liberal thinking of the seventeenth and eighteenth centuries was aberration. Such thinking occurred mostly in the west; the Germans who had adopted liberalism were slaves to Western thought; true Germans, men of the heartland of Europe, are above the pettiness of the French revolutionary ideology. Müller, then, was not only a conservative; he carried the belief in the superiority of Germans even further than Fichte or Herder.

The dramatist who accomplished most in asserting German nationalism was Heinrich von Kleist (1777–1811). Kleist was a complex character, though a Prussian, and his plays are varied and sensitive. His last two dramas, however, have Germanism as a theme. The *Hermann-schlacht* tells of the battle between the German tribal leader Arminius (Hermann) and the Romans in the time of Augustus Caesar. It is obviously a call to arms against Napoleon. Since then Arminius has been a great favorite of German nationalists. The *Prince of Homburg* is laid in the period of the Great Elector and concerns a young, rebellious nobleman who later realizes the need for complete obedience to the state because it embodies the moral law.

One of the most eccentric and influential figures in the history of German nationalism was Friedrich Ludwig Jahn (1778–1852), generally known as Father Jahn. He was born in the heart of the Prussian kingdom during the reign of Frederick the Great and early became embued with a strong sense of Prussian patriotism. Later on he expanded this Prussian-ism into a feeling for German nationalism, but always with deep admiration for the Hohenzollern tradition. His principal fame arose from his work in the training of German youth. During the years of the Napoleonic triumph he became disgusted with his own generation and concluded that the future of the German nation lay in the hands of the young men. He identified himself with the Free Corps movement during the war of 1813 and even more with the *Turnerschaft* ("gymnastic institute") and the later *Burschenschaften*. In 1811, while Jahn was an instructor in a famous school in Berlin, he started to take his students out into the open for gymnastic exercise. These exercises were intended not only to strengthen the body, but were conceived on clearly military lines to instill in the boys a strong feeling for the "German," i.e., the soldierly virtues. The movement spread throughout Germany during the century and became a characteristic expression of German nationalism. Jahn's most important writing was not unexpectedly called *Deutsche Volkstum* (perhaps best translated as *"German Racialism"*). This work glorified German race, customs, history, and language, and called on the German people to get rid of any sense of inferiority and to take unlimited pride in the fact that they were Germans. In his later years Jahn was vastly dis-satisfied with the settlement at Vienna, which had not erected a real German state. He called for further warfare to create such a state, which was to include both Switzerland and Denmark as well as the conventional German area.

A good deal more sophisticated than Father Jahn but no less devoted to the nationalist cause was Ernst Moritz Arndt (1769–1860), whose very long life almost spanned the years from the Seven Years' War to the Seven Weeks' War. Arndt, like so many others of his generation, was impelled toward nationalism by Napoleon's German conquests. He spent some time with Stein at the court of the Russian emperor in 1812 and returned with the victorious armies. He taught for a while at the Univer-sity of Bonn but was dismissed because of his connection with the *Burschenschaft* movement. One of Frederick William IV's bids for popularity at the outset of his reign was the reinstatement of Arndt, who was also elected to the Frankfurt Parliament in 1848 and hailed as a national hero. Arndt wrote many patriotic poems and songs, of which the best known is *Was Ist des Deutschen Vaterland?* (*"What Is the German's Fatherland?"*) According to the song, that fatherland exists

wherever German is spoken. In fact, much of Arndt's nationalistic thinking stemmed from the concept of language. The purity of a people's
language is the acid test of its general purity. He insisted that of the
European languages German was closest to its origins and had become
the least bastardized. For him humanitarianism and cosmopolitanism
were anathema, and he had a particular animus against the Jews because
they had become an international people.

Unquestionably the most important philosopher of the period was
Georg Wilhelm Hegel (1770–1831). Born a south German Protestant
in Stuttgart, his life was outwardly a placid one, spent almost completely
in an academic environment. He taught at Jena and Heidelberg and in
1818 was invited to the new University of Berlin, where during the
twenties he became the great figure of learning and founded a school of
younger students who were to be very influential in the future. This is not
the place to discuss the nature of Hegel's abstract and subjective thought.
It must suffice to say something about his ideas as they related to the
state, for he did a good deal to shape the thinking of later German
political figures.

Hegel thought in terms of eternal becoming, of an evolution in history
in which the so-called World-Spirit marches along taking various forms
at various times. The World-Spirit by its very nature creates its opposite,
and the result is a synthesis of the two which becomes the next World-
Spirit. (This is the dialectic of history, which Karl Marx combined with
his economic interpretation of history to develop "dialectical materialism.") Hegel insisted that "Whatever is rational is real, and whatever is
real is rational." Thus it became necessary to show that those institutions which were real were also rational, and few institutions at the time
were so "real" as the state. In fact, Hegel said that the State was the
highest and most perfect manifestation of the Universal Reason. Thus
the State came to take precedence over the individual and also over
religion, which was composed of "beliefs" only rather than "knowledge."
The State further became the representative of the World-Spirit and the
most powerful state at any given moment was that representative par
excellence. Note that the criterion is power. Hegel had recognized Napoleon as the World-Spirit during the time of his dominance. After 1815
he saw Prussia in that role and thus became the official philosopher of
the Prussian state. One almost had the feeling that the dialectic was to
come to its end with the triumph of Prussia. The point need hardly be
labored that in later decades the influence of Hegel was to prove very
useful to Bismarck.*

---

* For these comments concerning Hegel I am much indebted to Kurt F. Reinhardt, *Germany 2000 Years* (Milwaukee: Bruce, 1950), pp. 502–5.

As has been noted, the generation that grew up after 1830 differed somewhat from its forerunners. This was as true in the field of literature and intellectual speculation as it was in politics; in fact, the two were closely allied. The period between 1830 and the revolutions of 1848 was dominated by the so-called Young Germany group. This was a movement destined neither to last long nor to produce many important figures. The group had much more respect for liberalism, democracy, and general emancipation than its predecessors. It had a sense of social responsibility and a scorn for the wild individualism of the romantics. It was patriotic but not obsessed with the passionate nationalism of those who could remember the Napoleonic period better. The young people who grew up in these years were to be among the more moderate leaders of the movement of 1848.

The only major literary figure associated with the Young Germany movement and one of the greatest of all German writers was Heinrich Heine (1799–1856). Heine was a complex and interesting personality because he was drawn in several different directions. He was a Jew born in the Rhineland and, unlike many Rhinelanders, a patriotic German. His Jewishness, a racial rather than religious factor, was of constant concern to him; except in Prussia German Jews had not been granted equality of civil rights. He was also drawn by his wit and literary sensitivity toward France, where he spent most of his productive life. Soon after the French revolution of 1830 Heine moved to Paris, maintaining himself as a publicist and journalist. His last years were ones of agony for he developed a fearful spinal disease, was bedridden for years, and died a slow death.

Heine's lyrical gift was rivaled only by those of Goethe and Schiller. His short poems are among the greatest in the language; many of them, notably the *Lorelei,* were set to music by the romantic composers and have become the most beloved of German songs. His prose writing, a good part of which was political in nature, shows qualities of irony, bitterness, and wit. To an extent he was prophetic. He lamented the future he saw for his beloved Germany, where he feared the results of overnationalism and the influence of the romantic philosophers. Even if Heine had not been a Jew, his work would have been banned in Nazi Germany.

During the romantic period Germany retained her pre-eminence in music. The composers were not of the stature of Bach, Mozart, and Beethoven, but they remained the leaders in European music. Four of them were particularly outstanding. Franz Peter Schubert (1797–1828) led a short and miserable life as far as externals are concerned. He never went far from his native Vienna; he spent some of his most productive years teaching school, which he disliked; he rarely had any money and often had to live off friends; occasionally he received a taste of aristocratic patronage; his health was frequently very bad; and he died at thirty-one. Yet his output was immense. He is the father of the form of the *Lied* ("song") built around a well-known piece of poetry. Schubert wrote more than six hundred of these. He also composed eight symphonies, including the "Great" C major and the much-loved *Unfinished,* and a host of religious, piano, and chamber works. His gift for melody was supreme; for form, he was less talented and showed himself a true romantic.

Robert Schumann (1810–56) also had a difficult life. He was the son of a central German bookseller and editor. At an early age he showed great talent at the piano and was given lessons by Friedrich Wieck, father of Clara Wieck, whom Schumann later married. Until 1840 the great bulk of his composition was for the piano, the instrument with which he was always most at home. In 1840 he married Clara and started to compose songs in the tradition of Schubert and also symphonic music. The latter is not his strongest music, with the exception of the famous *Piano Concerto in A.* He was a very competent music critic and rejoiced in the discovery of large numbers of manuscripts by Schubert, which had lain neglected since that composer's death. He also was among those who discovered Brahms, with whom Clara Schumann maintained a friendship for many years. Schumann's mental powers started to fail after 1850. He tried to commit suicide, and then was put in a mental home where he died in 1856. Schumann's greatest legacy, besides the stories of the sweetness of his personality, is his wonderfully melodic piano music.

A life of refinement, money, fame, and association with the great was the fortunate fate of Felix Mendelssohn-Bartholdy (1809–47), but he never reached the musical heights of either Schubert or Schumann. He was born into a wealthy Jewish family which had converted to Protestantism. He received a very careful and thorough musical education and became as famous as a pianist and conductor as he later was as a composer. Like the other romantics, he was a child prodigy, composing the *Midsummer Night's Dream* overture at the age of seventeen. He traveled extensively in Europe, particularly in Great Britain, as pianist and conductor, and reached the height of his career in 1835 when he became conductor of the famous Gewandhaus orchestra in Leipzig. Here he had great latitude in choosing his programs and delighted in resurrecting the lost works of Johann Sebastian Bach, whose memory he admired above all others. Mendelssohn died young but left a rich legacy of symphonies (*Scotch, Italian, Reformation*), the oratorio *Elijah,* more celebrated than any work in that form since the days of Handel, and a host of minor works.

Of all the romantic composers Carl Maria von Weber (1786–1826) comes nearest to being a figure in the history of nationalism, but only accidentally. Weber came of a theatrical family and spent most of his short mature life traveling, producing operas, and composing operas of his own as well as numerous instrumental and vocal works. It was in the field of opera that he grew to fame. In 1817 he became director of German opera at Dresden; there he wrote his three important operas, *Der Freischütz, Euryanthe,* and *Oberon.* The fact that a director of German opera was appointed in addition to a director of Italian opera indicates that the German form was now recognized as separate. Weber comes between Mozart and Wagner; *Der Freischütz,* between *The Magic Flute* and *Tannhäuser,* though it does not approach either of these. In *Der Freischütz* Weber chose a German subject, in *Euryanthe* a medieval one, and in *Oberon* a fairy fantasy; opera was distinctly liberated from its preoccupation with classical and contemporary subjects. Furthermore, Weber advanced the techniques of orchestration so that he appears in the history of music as a forerunner of both Berlioz in France and Wagner in Germany. He is an important link.

Although German romantic music before Wagner was not explicitly nationalistic, in other ways it fitted in with the general romantic current, which was distinctly nationalist. Liberalism and conservatism occupied a secondary place in the minds of the leaders of thought. Either could have marched hand in hand with nationalism, but the battle that was to be fought in German history from 1848 to 1871 was to decide which it was to be. From intoxicated youth to sober age, nationalism was in the air.

Even the stodgy courts realized the universality of the feeling and suggested a wide variety of plans to create some sort of German union that would be more firm than the Confederation and still preserve something of the sovereignty (if sovereignty be divisible) of the various states. Frederick William IV suggested a sort of revival of the Holy Roman Empire as a federal state with more power given to the Federal Diet. He was willing to grant the primacy to Austria with the thought that Prussia would constitute a lord lieutenant with the particular mission of defense and the bearing of arms. This idea got lost in the turmoil of 1848.

In the middle forties the nationalists were faced with an immediate problem which was to prove a test case of nationalism and one of the most complex problems in European diplomatic history. This was the question of the duchies of Schleswig and Holstein, the Tristan and Isolde of German history. Holstein was in the German Confederation; Schleswig was not. Holstein was almost completely German; Schleswig more than half German, the rest Danish. Holstein was bound by the Salic law in which inheritance could not come through the female line; Schleswig was not bound by this law. Yet the two provinces had been ruled by the same ruler for centuries, and they were determined to remain that way. The ruler of both was also king of Denmark. In January 1848 King Christian VIII died and his heir Frederick VII was a childless divorcé. The possibility loomed that when Frederick died the throne of Denmark would pass to a cousin whose claim came through his mother; thus the problem of the Salic law in Holstein arose. Even more important at the moment was the nationalistic agitation in Denmark whose objective was to integrate Schleswig into Denmark proper. This program infuriated both the Germans in the two duchies and also nationalistically minded Germans elsewhere. It seemed clear that trouble could be expected from this quarter not only on national grounds but also because of the strategic location of the two duchies whose fate was of major interest to both Britain and Russia.

Things may have seemed relatively peaceful even by Metternich's standards in 1846 and 1847. Yet the historian today knows that there were many stirrings—political, economic, social, and intellectual—that were just beneath the boiling point. Once again it was not events in Germany that produced the actual outbreak but events in France. In late February 1848 the people of Paris arose, deposed their king, Louis Philippe, and established a republic. The year of revolution had begun.

CHAPTER VI

The Revolutionary Year (1848-49)

The revolutions of 1848 are an extraordinarily complex series of events. They almost defy description and understanding for several reasons. In the first place there is no one line of development that can be followed, because important events were occurring simultaneously in a dozen or more different places. While major occurrences were happening in Vienna, for example, events were taking place at the same moment in Berlin, Frankfurt, Baden, Dresden, Prague, north Italy, and Budapest, which had an immediate influence on the whole movement.

Even more baffling is the interdependent ideological struggle. Professor Veit Valentin, the most eminent modern scholar of the period, points out three major levels of activity during 1848: liberalism, nationalism, and socialism. These movements were the most significant ones struggling to establish themselves in nineteenth-century Europe, and all three were particularly concerned with the events of 1848 in German Europe. There was an attempt in each of the thirty-nine German states to secure liberal constitutional reforms for their obsolete governments. There was an effort to establish a united German state; Italians, Czechs, Hungarians, and Croats even tried to establish their own national states free from the Hapsburg overlord. Finally, there were attempts at social revolution, both industrial and agrarian, at several different moments in several different areas. All these efforts overlapped in time and space.

The revolutionary year began with the February revolution in France, although the first of the German outbreaks occurred before the events in Paris. The first German revolt is in many ways an exception to the rule in 1848, for it was a revolution in the conservative sense and certainly came close to being a comic-opera revolution.

In Bavaria King Louis I had been reigning since 1825. He was a highly cultured, late product of the Enlightenment who transformed Munich from a town of breweries to a city of fine buildings with a deep love of art. In his old age he took to his heart an Irish-born Spanish dancer named Lola Montez, even going so far as to give her a Bavarian title. She exerted considerable influence on the government usually in a liberal direction but managed to alienate the proud Bavarian aristocracy and, even more, the students at the University of Munich. On February 9 an outbreak of student opinion forced Lola to seek refuge; a few days later she fled from Munich. King Louis offered some reforms which would have diluted the enlightened character of his rule, but they proved insufficient; in March he abdicated in favor of his conservative son Maximilian, who established a duller rule but with more attention to the constitution. Lola made her way to the gold rush in California, where she settled for some time in the little town of Grass Valley before finally ending her career in New York.

The news of the revolt in France was influential in the southwest at first. In Baden, the most liberal of the German states, peasants, whose freedom had brought them only financial obligations, burnt mansions and threatened the aristocrats. In other western and central German states the governments were forced to change ministers and to issue liberalizing decrees. Most important, in Budapest Louis Kossuth, the great Hungarian nationalist, gave a rousing address in which he insisted on Hungary's right to autonomy and freedom under Hapsburg rule.

The first major revolt in German territory occurred in Vienna. Here there was general unrest from the time that the news arrived from France. Most of it centered around the students at the University of Vienna who were in a restive mood and started to demonstrate in favor of German unity. They looked forward to the meeting of the provincial diet of Lower Austria, scheduled for March 13, as an occasion for a public demonstration. On March 12 the students attended Mass at the university chapel, where they heard an encouraging sermon from a liberal priest, Father Anton Füster. The next morning they crowded around the meeting place of the diet where a copy of Kossuth's speech arrived from Budapest. Kossuth had called for a constitution for Austria as well as Hungary, for he insisted that even a personal union under the Hapsburg crown would be of no value if the Hungarians had a constitution while the German Austrians had none. The demonstration started to become intense and moved to the streets near the emperor's palace. It was joined by some of the new proletariat, workmen from outside the walls, until the gates were closed against them. There was some firing and several students were killed. The archdukes surrounding pitiful Emperor Ferdinand were terrified by the bloodshed and begged the emperor to make concessions. There was only one concession in which people would believe: the dismissal of Metternich. The stately old man accepted his fate with dignity and made his way to London where he remained for some years before returning to die in his beloved Vienna.

With the departure of Metternich there was little stability left in the Austrian government. The students had things their own way. A national guard was formed in Vienna of which an important and flamboyant part was the Academic Legion of the students. The government decreed freedom of the press and promised to call a constitutional assembly. One is reminded of the early days of the French Revolution when the old royal government and the people represented by the national guard tried to control affairs with some measure of decorum.

During the next weeks Emperor Ferdinand heard continual bad news from the outlying parts of his empire. In March the Italians in Milan revolted and called for a united Italy. A few weeks later a similar development occurred among the Czechs in Prague. The Hapsburg empire seemed to be falling apart as news arrived from one province after the other.

The government tried to pacify Vienna by issuing a constitution in late April. It was a fairly liberal document but did not include the workers among those who might vote. The students, now sentimentally allied with the workers, refused to have anything to do with it and demonstrated anew, calling for a constituent assembly elected by universal suffrage. At this point the imperial family became terrified and escaped to Innsbruck where it spent the next few months among the loyal peasants of the Tyrol and generals of the army, who were happy at the prospect of firing on the rebels. Elections were held for the constituent assembly which met in Vienna in July. It was a fairly radical body, eventually drew up a democratic constitution, and, as its one lasting enactment, decreed freedom for the serfs in the Empire. By midsummer it looked as if Austria were being added to the liberal democratic states of the world, and the future of the house of Hapsburg seemed very dim—especially when in June the Czechs called a Pan-Slav congress at Prague to announce to the world Slavic solidarity.

In Prussia the crucial day was March 18. There had been grumbling and demonstrations in the streets and coffee houses of Berlin for several days. The news from Paris and later from Vienna had an encouraging effect. There had even been some accidental bloodshed. Frederick William, as usual, blundered and fumbled from one suggestion to another. Finally on March 18 he announced a new ministry and also issued two proclamations. One recalled the United Diet presumably to act as a constituent assembly; the other uttered various generalizations concerning the reorganization of Germany. The people of the city were delighted and apparently satisfied by these gestures. During the afternoon thousands thronged to the large square before the palace to applaud the king and indicate their good will. Troops were lined up too, but the scene appeared peaceful until suddenly two shots rang out. No one knows who fired the shots—perhaps some trigger-happy soldier, perhaps an accidental result of the quick movement of a horse. In any case the mood of the crowd changed immediately. There was a panic to get out of the range of the rifles. Within a matter of hours barricades were built in the streets, and the peaceful Berliners turned into an angry armed mob. Throughout the night there was firing which resulted in a large number of casualties. The king was horrified; this was not the way in which he wanted to be loved. He was also the last man to desire bloodshed. Early in the morning he had a white flag raised above the palace with the word "misunderstanding" in large letters. At the same time he had the city covered with a hurriedly printed placard which had been run off during the night. It was addressed "To my beloved Berliners" and promised that if the people would withdraw from their barricades, he in turn would order the troops away. This he did; the Prussian army left its positions in Berlin, and Frederick William threw himself without defense on the mercies of the population. That afternoon he stood bareheaded in the courtyard of the palace while crowds filed past him bearing the bodies of those who had been killed during the fighting. Two days later he announced his readiness to assume leadership of a new Germany stating that "Prussia would merge into Germany," whatever that meant, and riding through the streets of Berlin wearing the black, red, and gold colors of the insurgents (a combination made up of medieval symbols which had been worn by the Free Corps of 1813). After these theatrical events the royal family moved out of Berlin to Potsdam, where they could be protected by the regular army.

Life in Berlin immediately took on the aura of Vienna. There was no more censorship; policing was done by a volunteer militia; in general, things were far freer. However, the stolid bourgeoisie of Berlin became alarmed at the increasing influence of the workers and breathed a sigh of relief as troops gradually took up their old posts in the city. The United Diet duly met and quickly approved plans for a new assembly. Elections were to be indirect, but the primary election was to be by universal male suffrage. These elections were held in mid-May and were attended with a great deal of confusion caused by the hopeless lack of experience of most of the Prussian people in such matters. The Assembly turned out to be a radical one with a good many peasants and Poles, who might be expected to vote with the radical leaders against the established order. The Camphausen ministry, which had been appointed in March, ruled from day to day without any particular philosophy guiding it, while the king displayed his characteristic ambivalence by taking one series of attitudes in public and another in private.

Throughout Germany in almost all the capitals of the smaller states revolts broke out. They followed the pattern of those in Vienna and Berlin calling for assemblies to write constitutions. The word constitution had an almost holy overtone. So throughout Germany elections were held and assemblies convened. The classic home of autocratic government endured a rash of elections. In fact, some authorities feel that one of the many causes for the failure of the movement of 1848 was the fact that there were not enough intelligent, politically conscious men in the whole land to fill the hundreds of chairs in the dozens of assemblies. In the early summer it looked as if Germany were to become a series of liberal constitutional states or, just possibly, one great liberal constitutional state.

The most colorful of the spring revolutions, and one which illustrates the radical and social aspects of the movement, occurred in liberal Baden and was the first of three outbreaks to take place in that state in little more than a year. Its leaders were Friedrich Hecker and Gustav von Struve, both republicans and idealists devoted to the concept of the brotherhood of man. They were dismayed by the wave of peasant rioting which had broken out in the area with the news from Paris. They decided to proclaim a republic for Germany and organize an army of the repressed population to achieve victory for it. They made their proclamation at Constanz near the Swiss border and advanced northward. The government of Baden employed Friedrich von Gagern, a German officer in the Dutch army, to command its troops; at a battle in April Gagern was killed, but the insurgents were completely defeated. Struve fled to Switzerland to try again; Hecker went eventually to the United States where he had a distinguished career. An absurd, pathetic, bohemian legion led by the poet Herwegh and his wife left Paris to help the German republicans; however, it arrived at the border after the battle was over.

The most important effort to establish a united national German state began even before the outbreaks in Vienna and Berlin. On March 5 over fifty liberals and republicans met at Heidelberg to discuss plans. A cleavage developed which was to become wider as time went on. Most of the liberals did not want to go so far as to establish a republic. They felt that Germany was not ready for it and that much more could be achieved by some sort of limited monarchy. The leader of this group was Heinrich von Gagern, younger brother of the general, soon to become prime minister of Hesse-Darmstadt and later president of the Frankfurt Parliament. The committee agreed to call a larger group composed of former state officials, liberals, and friends of unity to meet at the end of the month at Frankfurt. This Pre-parliament (*Vor-parlament*) met on March 31 and decided that elections should be held throughout Germany for a general parliament to represent all the people. There was some discussion about the qualifications for voting, but the group finally agreed on universal male suffrage. A rehearing of the dispute between the republicans and the limited monarchists resulted in the republican leader, Struve, leaving to establish his own republic.

The Federal Diet, also at Frankfurt, was in a quandary. In it reposed the legal power of the German Confederation, but the princes, whom it represented, were in the shadow and unable to give it any material support. Thus it became associated with the call for the elections, though privately many of the members recommended to their governments various degrees of electoral sabotage. The elections themselves were irregular. They were under the auspices of the local governments and although universal suffrage was supposed to be the rule, there was a tendency for those states which had any electoral laws to apply them. The others made up *ad hoc* regulations to suit the occasion, adding as many restrictions as they dared. Furthermore, the unsettled conditions of the time made orderly elections almost impossible. Thus the Parliament was not truly representative of the populations. In particular Austria was very much underrepresented, Prussia less so, while the states of the center and southwest (Baden, Würtemberg, etc.) were overrepresented. It is astonishing that in the chaotic state of affairs such a distinguished body of men could be brought together.

May 18, 1848, was a happy day in Frankfurt. More than eight hundred deputies marched in procession to the church of St. Paul where the Parliament was to sit. The streets and balconies were crowded; this day seemed to be a landmark in the tempestuous history of Germany. The next day the Assembly elected Gagern as president, took over the legal powers of the Federal Diet, and set up committees to work out a constitution and to see to the day-to-day administration of Germany.

The Assembly was composed of a remarkable group of men, one of the most distinguished ever elected. It represented the whole spectrum of German political thought from the right, headed by Frederick William's friend Radowitz, to the left, headed by the impoverished radical Robert Blum. This was not a body made up primarily of revolutionaries. There was a heavy emphasis on the free professions and the upper middle class. Thus, there were about a hundred university professors, about two hundred lawyers, and many businessmen, judges, clergymen, officers, and doctors. This group did not profess the overthrow of society; it was devoted to the preservation of property and of law and order, but in the direction of liberal control by the articulate people. Much of the parliamentary history of later Germany stems from this assembly because it was not many days before small groups began to disperse and to meet together in their favorite restaurants and beer halls. A system of parties rapidly developed, some of which were the predecessors of later German parties.

The Parliament took the view from the outset that since it had received the powers of the Federal Diet and represented all the German people, it was the actual government of all Germany. The question therefore arose of constituting an executive which would actually function as a government. After a good deal of discussion Gagern suggested for the post of vicar the Archduke John, an uncle of Emperor Ferdinand, who had a reputation for liberalism and had been very active in the Austrian government since the departure of Metternich. This was a shrewd choice because John was both a member of the premier German family and willing to give an appearance of democracy. John arrived in Frankfurt and was installed in a curious ceremony combining the old and the new. He named a ministry composed of Germans from a number of different states. The degree of acceptance which the new government received in Germany and abroad differed; in Austria, for instance, it was not obeyed at all, while the United States gave it diplomatic recognition. The German states went ahead with the task of making their own constitutions with little or no reference to the events at Frankfurt.

In foreign affairs the Frankfurt Parliament soon showed that in its concept of the brotherhood of man Germans were to regard each other as brothers before other peoples, for it had little disposition to be friendly to the aspirations of other nations if these conflicted with German aspirations. The oppressed Poles received no sympathy from the Parliament because a great many of them were under Prussian rule and must not be lost to Germany. Similarly the Parliament showed no favor to the Czechs and regarded the Pan-Slav congress as coldly as the Austrian government itself did.

The most urgent problem of the moment was the Schleswig-Holstein affair. King Frederick VII was clearly under the influence of Danish nationalists who wanted to integrate Schleswig into Denmark. The German nationalists in the two duchies hated this policy and also refused to recognize as their heir the Danish prince who descended in the female line. Their candidate was the duke of Augustenburg, who was the closest heir in the male line but to the Danes represented only a cadet branch of the royal family. These considerations and the occupation of Schleswig by Danish troops had led to a revolt by the two duchies and the establishment of a provisional government at Kiel in late March.

King Frederick William saw in the whole imbroglio the chance to pose as the champion of German nationalism, although he had some misgivings about supporting a people in revolt against its legitimate sovereign. He accepted the mandate of the Frankfurt Parliament to make war against the Danes. This situation revealed clearly one of the basic weaknesses of the Parliament, the fact that it had no army or navy to enforce its decrees. Prussia also had no navy; this became a major obstacle to her success in the fighting, since the heart of Denmark is located on islands. To remedy this, the Parliament bought some ships and had others built, so that the first German navy was actually the property of the Parliament and was fated after the failure of that body to be sold at auction.

A further problem was that both Great Britain and Russia took a pro-Danish position in the struggle. They had no desire to see a strong German state control the strategic lands guarding the North Sea coast of Germany and the entrance to the Baltic Sea. The fighting went badly for Prussia, and as the weeks went by Frederick William became less and less enthusiastic about his war. In August he concluded at Malmö a truce for seven months providing that both Danish and Prussian soldiers leave the duchies and that a committee of representatives of the Danish government and of the German Confederation rule them in the interim.

The news of the armistice was received with dismay in Frankfurt. This seemed to be just another example of a monarch betraying the sacred character of German national spirit. At first the Parliament voted against the armistice and planned to prosecute the war, but cooler opinions were heard. The Parliament had no army; its chances of organizing one in time to be effective were nil. Thus the moderate leaders persuaded the Parliament to accept the armistice.

This action by the Parliament was viewed by the hot nationalists as another act of betrayal, even more serious than the king's because it was done by the representatives of the people. Riots broke out at Frankfurt and the insurgents even invaded the meeting hall. The Parliament sent for help to Mainz, where there were Austrian and Prussian garrisons. The rebels fought bravely; they even murdered several of the right-wing deputies, but they were no match for the regular soldiers, who took pleasure in mowing them down and treating them brutally. This seemed like still another betrayal, this time a betrayal of the people to the forces of police repression. Struve used this moment as his occasion for a second proclamation of a republic. He gathered a large but untrained mob, and once again was defeated by regular troops and thrown into prison. These events served to discredit the Frankfurt Parliament, which now stood on the side of law and order and was opposed to extreme idealists or radicals. This explains part of the defeat of the Parliament. It suffered from what might be called sentimental attrition. As it assumed the responsibilities of government, it discovered that the extreme positions were untenable; a moderate majority developed. The coalition of ideas of the early spring dissolved and the hard disagreements remained. The same thing happened even more rapidly in the French republican experiment of the same year.

In the meantime the Parliament went ahead with its work of drawing up a German constitution. It devoted itself at first to producing a statement of the rights of the German. This is a very eloquent document embodying the dreams of liberals and democrats. It is full and far more detailed than most other statements of a similar nature. It is a lasting monument to the high quality of the philosophers and political thinkers who framed it, but it never acquired the force of law.

Naturally the principal question which the constitution makers had to deal with was the question of just who were Germans and where was Germany. In other words, should all or part of the Austrian Empire be included in the new Germany? This was the old *grossdeutsch* vs. *kleindeutsch* question, and it assumed central urgency. There were Austrian representatives at the Parliament; an Austrian archduke controlled the executive. Yet the Austrian government paid little or no attention to Frankfurt and was concerned with regathering its scattered non-Germanic territories. As things developed, the left of the Parliament demanded the *grossdeutsch* solution. It had no reverence for Hapsburg or tradition. As a practical matter the *kleindeutsch* solution seemed the only one possible. The constitution finally provided that no part of the new state might be organically connected with non-Germanic territory. This would at best give the Hapsburg emperor a chance to establish a personal union between his non-Germanic and his Germanic lands, which would have to be parts of separate states, exactly the opposite of what the Austrian government was urgently trying to achieve at that very moment. Thus the matter really became academic. By early 1849 it was clear that there was no possibility of including Austria or any part of it in the new state and that it would be necessary to name Frederick William of Prussia as the new emperor.

The constitution, finally accepted by the Parliament on March 27, 1849, created a federal state with a hereditary emperor. The emperor was to have a suspensive veto only. The legislative power was vested in a bicameral body whose upper house was to be named by the various state governments and legislatures. The lower house was to be elected by universal male suffrage. The federal government had much wider powers than the old Federal Diet, including control of economic, military, and foreign affairs. The next day the Parliament chose Frederick William IV of Prussia to be first emperor of the Germans.

Gagern and a committee of the Parliament now journeyed to Berlin to offer the crown to Frederick William. They were received coldly, even insultingly. The king temporized at first. He said that he must receive the consent of the other German states to the new organization. Many of the smaller ones expressed it right away, but some of the greater rulers, particularly the king of Bavaria, demurred, for which Frederick William expressed gratitude. Finally the Prussian king definitely refused the offer on the grounds that a ruler by divine right could not receive a crown from the people, a crown picked up from the gutter so to speak.

In late April the committee returned sadly to Frankfurt. When they arrived, they found that most of the German governments had withdrawn their representatives from the Parliament. Most of the sober, moderate deputies returned to their homes; only the radicals remained. Soon thereafter the free city of Frankfurt requested the remnants to leave the city. They made their way to Stuttgart, where they met a few more times until the troops of the king of Würtemberg drove them out. At their last meeting on June 18, 1849, in a room over a wine shop, they sang a patriotic song and formally disbanded the first general representative assembly of the German people and ended the first modern effort at the unification of Germany.

The Parliament has been criticized a good deal in the intervening years. A frequent criticism is that the schoolmasters who dominated it spent so much time arguing abstract points of natural law and political philosophy that they lost the effective moment. It is certainly true that they argued endlessly, but it would seem that there were other more important reasons for the failure. As the months of the Parliament went on, it became clear that the majority was made up of liberals both in the political and economic sense. Many of the ills of Germany were economic, and the angry masses were not to be appeased by appeals to reason and immutable economic laws. Furthermore, and in the short run decisive, was the fact that the Parliament possessed no means of enforcing its decisions. Military forces remained with the states, that is, with the monarchs. As soon as the counterrevolution got under way and the rulers again became masters in their own houses, it was clear that they would abandon their lip service to the Parliament. In the great modern successful revolutions, e.g., the French Revolution of 1789 or the Russian ones of 1917, the regular troops transferred their allegiance to the rebels. This did not happen in 1848 (or in Russia in 1905). It may be that the German armies were composed mostly of ignorant peasants who had no idea what the revolution was about and were aware only of their oath to their monarchs; this would set them apart from the French in the 1790's. It was certainly true that the German armies had not undergone the almost incredible ordeal of war, weather, and incompetence that made the Russian soldiers so receptive to the revolution in 1917. Whatever the reason, the German forces remained true to their officers and to their rulers. This was decisive and nowhere more so than in the Austrian Empire where the counterrevolution began.

Emperor Ferdinand had the unusual luck for a Hapsburg of having three competent and loyal generals, Prince Windischgrätz, Field Marshal Radetzky, and the Croat governor, Baron Jellachich. Before the year ended, he also acquired a highly intelligent and unscrupulous minister, as authoritarian as Metternich himself, Prince Felix zu Schwarzenberg. This group used the old Austrian technique of setting one part of the empire against another, which was not difficult because the mutual hatreds of the nationalities in the empire was exceeded only by their joint hatred for their German masters. The first decisive event occurred in Prague in June when Windischgrätz, whose wife had just been shot by the Czechs, ordered up reinforcements, bombarded the city, and reduced it to submission.

In Italy the kingdom of Piedmont-Sardinia had joined with the rebellious Italian subjects of the Hapsburgs in an effort to liberate north Italy and start the unification of that peninsula. On July 24 Radetzky achieved complete victory over the joint Italian armies at the battle of Custozza. Lombardy and Venetia were returned to Austrian obedience amidst the usual repressive measures. Little by little Ferdinand was being reassured that he still ruled over an empire.

The clearest use of the policy of divide and rule was seen in the treatment of Croatia and Hungary. The Croats were a part of the kingdom of Hungary and devotedly hated the Hungarians as much as the Hungarians hated the German Austrians. In early 1848, when each nationality was making its bid for independence, the Croats did so too. To appease them the emperor appointed a native Croat, Jellachich, as their governor. For some months events elsewhere prevented the Austrian government from paying much attention to what was happening in Croatia, but there was friction between the two to the extent that Jellachich was suspended from his functions during the summer. However, in September Ferdinand's government decided that it would be politic to reinstate Jellachich, and some weeks later he was put in charge of the attack against the Hungarian rebels. At first he was unsuccessful, having been driven by the Hungarians into Austria proper within a short distance of Vienna.

October was the decisive month for the Austrian revolution. The Constituent Assembly had been sitting in Vienna since July. Its tone had become increasingly radical and so had the attitude of the Viennese who declared their solidarity with the Hungarians and went so far as to murder in cold blood Count Latour, the minister of war. It was now time in the opinion of the government to settle with Vienna. This sort of outrage must not go unpunished. The first step was to order the Assembly out of Vienna to the little town of Kremsier in Moravia, where it would be away from the influence of the Vienna mob; its time would come later. The next was to order Windischgrätz to invest and besiege the city. The siege went on for several days with the regular army bombarding its own capital city. On October 31 Vienna submitted and the German part of the Austrian revolution of 1848 was over.

Schwarzenberg, who had now established himself as paramount at court, decided that it was necessary to arrange the abdication of Emperor Ferdinand. Ferdinand was clearly incompetent, and it was desirable to have a new imperial symbol for the work of reconstruction that lay ahead. Schwarzenberg was successful in persuading the emperor to give up his throne and also in convincing Ferdinand's younger brother, the heir to the crown, to relinquish his rights. In this accomplishment he was much helped by the heir's wife, Archduchess Sophia, who was ambitious for her son to be emperor rather than her husband. The son, Archduke Francis Joseph, was young, handsome, and brave. On December 2, 1848, at Olmütz, where the court was staying, he was proclaimed emperor of Austria and began one of the longest and saddest reigns in all history (1848–1916).

The Constituent Assembly was still working on the constitution at its new quarters in Kremsier. In March 1849 the task was completed and ready for presentation to the nation. The Kremsier constitution, which never went into operation, was a democratic document calling for a federal organization of the complex empire. Schwarzenberg did not approve of it and simply ordered the Assembly dissolved. In place of the new constitution Francis Joseph promulgated another, highly centralized in nature, but did not put even this one in effect because he chose to rule autocratically until things returned to normal.

The only remaining rebels were the Hungarians. Angered by the cavalier treatment given the Assembly, and even more by the centralized constitution which would put Hungary completely under the heel of Vienna, the Hungarian leaders abandoned the fiction of a personal union under the emperor and declared their independence. All out warfare ensued between the Austrians and the Hungarians, but the Austrians made little headway at first because their armies were exhausted after the tensions of the year before. At this point Austria was saved from abroad.

Emperor Nicholas I of Russia was one of the blackest reactionaries of the century. He had spent 1848 in a state of rage against the revolutions and frustration that he could do nothing about them. Now he saw a chance. He offered to Francis Joseph the loan of a Russian army to help quell the rebellious Hungarians. The Austrians accepted the offer. General Paskievitch invaded Hungary with a Russian force, while the Austrian general Haynau attacked from the west. The combination was too powerful for the Hungarians to withstand, and in August they surrendered, not to the hated Austrians but to the Russians. The Russians handed the Hungarian leaders over to the Austrians, and the reprisals were brutal. Russia now withdrew happy from a mission well performed and content in having a new friend, Austria, who could no doubt be counted on in the future. By mid-1849 Francis Joseph was in control of his whole empire, but the bitterness that had been engendered was never to be allayed as long as the empire lasted.

Frederick William IV did not have as much trouble quelling the revolution in Prussia as the Austrian rulers. He did not have the nationality problem to deal with, and furthermore the Prussians had never shown themselves very adept at revolutions. He took heart from the successes in Austria and in November decided to copy the action there and exile his Constituent Assembly from feverish Berlin. In fact the Prussian Assembly was probably the most radical of the many German assemblies of the year and was hardly representative of the sober Prussian middle class and the loyal peasantry. On November 9, 1848, the king sent General Wrangel to order the Assembly from Berlin to the village of Brandenburg. It replied that it would move only by force; Wrangel assured it that he had plenty of force. The Assembly moved. It tried a last effort by calling on the people of Prussia to refuse to pay their taxes, but this gesture accomplished nothing; even the Frankfurt Parliament disapproved of it. In early December Frederick William dissolved the Assembly and at the same time promulgated a constitution. At first blush it looked as if the king's constitution were almost the same as the one drawn up by the Assembly, but closer examination disclosed that behind all the liberal statements the king's power was remarkably intact and the royal charter was a very authoritarian one. A number of changes were made in the new constitution during the following two years; it did not assume definitive form until 1850, so it will be logical to describe it in the next chapter.

There were two last pathetic flickers of the revolutionary movement in the late spring of 1849, one in Saxony and the other in Baden. Both of them arose from the despair of liberals when Frederick William refused to accept the crown offered by the Frankfurt Parliament. Saxony was one of the most advanced areas in Germany, both intellectually (because Leipzig was the center of the book trade) and industrially. The Saxons had counted heavily on a new order in Germany and were furious that their own king had not urged Frederick William to become emperor. They rose in revolt in Dresden in early May. The revolt did not amount to much. The king of Saxony invited Prussian troops into his kingdom to put down the rebels. This they did swiftly. However, this revolt has lasting interest because involved in it were Michael Bakunin, the famous Russian anarchist, and also Richard Wagner, the composer. Wagner escaped but was forbidden to live in Germany for many years.

The revolt in restless Baden was more serious. It also was planned as a fight for the Frankfurt constitution. The rebels were numerous; it has been estimated that at one time they included half of the male inhabitants of Baden. Their leaders were impressive; Lorenz Brentano, a lawyer, became the head of the rebel government, with Struve, now released from prison, Mieroslawski, the Polish patriot, and Carl Schurz, later to become an important American political figure, as lieutenants. The Prussian army was again the agent of repression. There was a good deal of fighting but finally the rebels were driven into the fortress of Rastadt, where they were besieged during most of the month of July. Finally a shortage of food forced them to surrender. Although the rebels were promised freedom by the Prussians, they did not receive it; many of the liberal leaders of Germany languished for long periods in Prussian prisons. Schurz was one of the lucky ones who managed to escape and to enrich the United States by his presence.

With the defeat of the uprising in Baden the movement of 1848 ended. Things for some time after it were worse than they had been before, and the liberal professorial leaders were discredited for years to come. Other nations profited from the forty-eighters who left Germany to make their way abroad. At the present time, after the ordeals of the last fifty years, the new Germany may look back to 1848 with interest. Perhaps she will find that the men of that year are her best models.

CHAPTER VII

The Chastened Fifties (1849-62)

The decade of the fifties is generally thought of as a melancholy era in which the German monarchs, re-established in their authority, once more applied the old policy of repression, in some cases more stringently than before 1848. This judgment is for the most part true. The idealistic liberalism of the *Vormärz* period was almost completely discredited by the triumph of force. However, nationalism was far from dead. The first successful steps toward the unification of Italy were taken in the fifties, while similar steps occurred soon thereafter in Germany. The difference was that now the steps were taken by the diplomats, the generals, and the men in high places rather than by the poets, the professors, and the champions of the "people." Nationalism and liberalism were no longer wedded; in both of the great unifying processes of the mid-century the initiative was taken by might, not by sweet reason.

In the earlier period much of the political activity was led by professors and scholars. After the failure of 1848 most of this class retired from active political life. They concerned themselves with their studies and became devoted almost completely to nonpolitical scholarship. When they were heard on public topics, it was with the harsh nationalism of a Treitschke, far different from the attitudes of the men of the thirties and forties.

The tendency seemed to be to leave politics to the professionals, especially to the diplomats. A wave of materialism swept over Germany, perhaps as a reaction from the defeat of idealism but also as a function of the ever-increasing industrial growth. Along with the professors the proletariat had been discredited, and the middle class had learned to fear the violence of the lower classes. Thus the way was cleared for the new upper middle class to pursue its goals without much opposition. In fact there appeared to be a tacit agreement between the political leadership and the economic leadership that each would not impinge on the other's area.

In Prussia the year of storms left a good deal of debris that needed to be cleared away. Frederick William was not completely satisfied with the constitution he had promulgated in late 1848 and spent a number of months tinkering with it. In its final form of 1850 it remained the basic law for Prussia until the end of the kingdom of Prussia in 1918. The document was an authoritarian one. It provided for a lower house of parliament elected by universal male suffrage but with an electoral law so framed that the great weight of political power lay with the possessory classes. The voting population was divided into three classes determined by the amount of taxes they paid. Each of these elected an equal number of electors, who in turn elected the members of the parliament. It has been estimated that 17 per cent of the voters controlled 67 per cent of the seats. The reasoning behind this, of course, was that those with the highest stakes in society would be the most conservative. This was sound to an extent, but it neglected two major social facts of the time: the most conservative element of the population after the noble landowners was the peasantry, who were almost disenfranchised; and much of the liberal thought emanated from the prosperous middle class, which was over-represented. It took only a few years for this to be made clear to the Prussian government.

In addition to the lower house there was an upper house (*Herrenhaus*) which consisted of distinguished men, some of them appointed for life by the king. There was no ministerial responsibility, and the parliament had to vote only new laws and taxes.

Another piece of unfinished Prussian business was the war with Denmark which had been suspended by the armistice of Malmö. In the spring of 1849 Denmark denounced the armistice, and fighting began again. The Prussian army invaded the Danish peninsula of Jutland, but as in the year before the warfare was inconclusive and another armistice was arranged in July. The Prussians and Danes undertook negotiations which dragged on for a year and ended in a peace signed in July 1850 which simply begged the question because both Denmark and Prussia "reserved their rights." The dispute was finally settled at the international level. A conference of the five great European powers, plus Denmark and Sweden, was held at London. On May 8, 1852, it agreed to the London Protocol which provided that the two duchies should be ruled separately from Denmark and that the succession in them should be the same as in Denmark in spite of the Salic law. In return the claims of the duke of Augustenburg were appeased by a money payment. There the matter rested until 1863 when the conflict arose in an even more urgent way and provided a crisis which was of prime importance for the unification of Germany.

Frederick William had drunk of the heady wine of a united Germany with himself at the head of it, although in an unsatisfactory form. He was not willing to relinquish his hopes of achieving such a position in a fitting manner. The king's close friend Radowitz worked out a scheme for German unity which became known as the Prussian Union. This plan provided for a close federation of all the German states except Austria, under Prussia, with a much stronger central government than that of the old Federal Diet at Frankfurt. The federation was to be bound closely to the Austrian Empire through alliances and economic co-operation. The aim was a great central European nation operating in most matters as one unit.

The proponents of the Prussian Union drew up a draft constitution for the federation and managed to receive the tentative agreement of the important states of Saxony and Hanover. These two assumed that Bavaria and Würtemberg were also in favor of it, but the two south German kingdoms, especially Bavaria, whose king was stoutly anti-Prussian, wanted no part of it. In October 1849 an assembly met at Erfurt to promote the movement. Saxony and Hanover withdrew leaving only Prussia and most of the very small states, which were afraid of Prussian might. A parliament, also at Erfurt, in the spring of 1850 produced no better results. The Prussian Union entered a stage of suspended animation.

By this time, thanks to Russia, the Austrian government was free of its last internal revolt and ready again to assert itself on the international scene. Schwarzenberg had no notion of letting Prussia go ahead with a plan which would effectively drive Austrian influence out of the great bulk of Germany. His plan was to revive the Confederation of 1815 in which Austria enjoyed primacy. In May 1850 he called a meeting of the German states at Frankfurt. A number of the smaller ones accepted the invitation, and this assembly re-established the old Federal Diet. The two great German powers stood at loggerheads; fears arose of a war between them.

The situation reached critical proportions as the result of a conflict which broke out in Hesse-Kassel. The elector (the rulers of the territory chose to maintain this obsolete title even though there was nobody for them to elect), a tough old conservative, had reached a governmental stalemate with his more liberal local parliament, and there was danger of an armed uprising. He called on the Federal Diet at Frankfurt for help, while the Hessian parliament called on Prussia because Hesse-Kassel was a member of the Prussian Union. Both sides responded with troops and mobilized their armies. The danger of war increased greatly.

The decisive voice was raised not by a German but by the archconservative Emperor Nicholas of Russia. Nicholas was still in the mood to support Austria, whose policies coincided with his own. He was thoroughly disgusted with Frederick William, who, he thought, was conducting an absurd and sinister flirtation with liberalism. This was enough for the king of Prussia, since the idea of war always filled him with horror. Prussia backed down from her dangerous position.

The last scene in Prussia's attempt at this time to assume primacy in Germany took place in November 1850 when Frederick William sent his principal minister, Otto von Manteuffel, to Olmütz to meet with Schwarzenberg. The two agreed on the re-establishment of the German Confederation with the Federal Diet at Frankfurt. A clause was inserted into the agreement to save face for Prussia stating that open conferences could be held to organize a possible future reorganization of Germany. However, there was no question who was the victor in this diplomatic war. Prussian historians usually refer to the meeting as the "humiliation of Olmütz." Prussia entered into several years of a deep sleep of repression under the severe guidance of King Frederick William and Manteuffel.

In the Austrian Empire repression was at least as strict as in Prussia. The nationalities that had revolted in 1848 found themselves under almost martial law. Severe reprisal was constant. The Hungarians in particular suffered at the hands of their Austrian masters and embarked on a policy of passive resistance which lasted for almost twenty years until they were made equal partners with the German Austrians.

Prince Schwarzenberg died in 1852 while still young. He had been the mastermind of Austrian recovery from the revolutions. He was certainly one of the most competent statesmen of the century; it is interesting to conjecture what the history of central Europe might have been if he had lived for another twenty years. His policies continued even after his death. Now they were associated with the name of Alexander Bach, minister of the interior. At home the policy was one of strict centralization and Germanization. The government ignored the old historical national entities and simply divided up the empire into administrative units governed from Vienna. Every effort was made to oppose national instincts and to impose German ideas and ideology. The result was grumbling and dissatisfaction in all quarters. Austria had to weather the mounting crises of the fifties and the sixties with a disloyal population and a domestic situation far from stable.

In this condition Austria had to face the two international wars of the fifties. In one of them she was a diplomatic participant only, in the other an active belligerent; but both of them concerned issues close to her and had important influences on her future. In 1852 Prince Louis Napoleon Bonaparte, president of the French Republic, was proclaimed emperor of the French. This action seemed to many to overturn the settlement of the Congress of Vienna; it ushered in a period of warfare following the long period of relative peace after 1815. During the fifties and the sixties the unifications of both Italy and Germany were accomplished. In all these matters the Austrian government had an immediate interest.

The Crimean War (1854–56) took longer to get started than almost any war in modern history. The roots of the conflict arose from a dispute about who was to have control of the Holy Places in Palestine—the Orthodox or the Roman Catholics, with Russia and France as the respective protectors of these churches. In time the problem widened to include Great Britain, as Russia seemed to be demanding undue influence in the Ottoman Empire, something about which the British were sensitive. Austria became immediately affected when in July 1853 the Russians occupied the Danubian principalities as a device to force the Turkish sultan to accede to their demands. These principalities, Wallachia and Moldavia, the heart of modern Romania, were adjacent both to Russia and to the Austrian kingdom of Hungary. Eastern Hungary (Transylvania) contained thousands of Hapsburg subjects of Romanian nationality. Therefore the Austrians viewed with much alarm Russian encroachment in this area. Tsar Nicholas did not anticipate opposition from Austria; he expected gratitude in return for the good deeds he had done for the Austrians in recent years, but he was to be surprised.

Austria at first hoped to act as a mediator in the struggle and offered the so-called Vienna Note, an ambiguously worded memorandum which was supposed to regulate Russian influence in Turkey. The tsar accepted it but the sultan refused to, realizing rightly that the Russians could expand its application to almost a complete protectorate. Tsar Nicholas met with Francis Joseph at Olmütz, but as the year ended the dispute was still hanging fire.

In early 1854 the eastern dispute developed into a war. Great Britain and France joined Turkey in attacking Russia. The Russian army crossed the Danube, and Austria had to make up her mind. She decided first to take counsel with Prussia. In Prussia there was a decided difference of opinion on what attitude to take. The liberals supported the western side, while the conservatives were pro-Russian. Among their leaders was Otto von Bismarck, the Prussian representative at the Federal Diet. Frederick William as usual vacillated. In April 1854 he signed an agreement with Austria promising that neither would do anything to offend the other during this war, but agreeing with Austria to oppose Russia if she attempted to incorporate the principalities into her empire. Thus on the whole the German powers, especially Austria, leaned to an anti-Russian position. In June Austria demanded that Russia not advance further south than the Balkan Mountains and state when she intended to evacuate the principalities. She also made a treaty with Turkey by which the sultan agreed that Austria might occupy the principalities as soon as the Russians could be dislodged. Tsar Nicholas was appalled by Austrian ingratitude.

In the meantime Russia was faced with an imminent attempt by the British and French to land troops on the Crimean Peninsula and bring the war into Russian territory. She had no wish to add Austria to the number of her enemies. So in August she withdrew her troops from the principalities, and Austrian forces, already mobilized on the eastern frontiers of the empire, took up positions in Wallachia and Moldavia, to remain there until the war was over. At this point the relations between Russia and Austria were completely embittered, never to be improved until the two empires were no more.

In the same month the Austrian government presented to Russia the Vienna Four Points already agreed to by Great Britain and France as a basis for a possible peace. These are not worth exploring in detail, but in general they called for a considerable lessening of Russian influence in Turkey. The Russian government rejected them out of hand, so at the end of the year Austria went the length of forming an offensive and defensive alliance with Great Britain and France. She mobilized her armies but did not ever actually declare war against Russia.

The year 1855 was filled with one of the most inept military campaigns in all history, waged by the British and French in the Crimea. It was lucky for the western powers that the Russian army was even less efficient. In March Tsar Nicholas died and was succeeded by his son Alexander II, who was anxious to get out of the war. In September the allies managed to enter the major Russian naval base of Sebastopol. In December the Austrians further increased the ire of Russia by sending her an ultimatum threatening war if she would not accept the Four Points, neutralize the Black Sea, and cede Bessarabia back to the Ottoman Empire. Russia had no choice but to accept the ultimatum and ask for peace. The peace conference was held at Paris in March 1856.

Austria gained absolutely nothing from the Crimean War and actually lost almost as much as Russia did. She permanently lost the friendship of Russia, which would have been immensely valuable in the decade ahead; her finances were grievously affected by keeping her army in a state of readiness for months; and at the peace table she had the pleasure of hearing the astute Count Cavour, minister of Piedmont-Sardinia, who had brought his little country into the war, plead the case of Italian unity and make a violently anti-Austrian speech.

Prussia did little or nothing in the Crimean War after making her early arrangement with Austria. Frederick William pursued a policy of aimless neutrality typical of him. However, at least he did nothing overt against Russia. This paved the way in the years ahead to a Russo-Prussian *rapprochement,* which was to be extremely useful to Bismarck during the sixties. It was almost as an act of pure charity that Prussia was permitted a seat at the Paris Congress in 1856.

The next major crisis concerned Austria even more directly than the Crimean War. Napoleon III professed himself a nationalist, in particular in favor of Italian aspirations. In fact, as a young man he had served in an Italian patriot army in an attack on the possessions of the pope. In 1858 Count Cavour, premier of Piedmont-Sardinia under King Victor Emmanuel II, decided it was time to force Napoleon to take some definite action in behalf of Italy. He met secretly wtih Napoleon, and the two agreed that France would come to the aid of Piedmont in a war to drive the Austrians out of Italy if Cavour could so arrange matters that the war would look to the world like Austrian aggression.

Napoleon behaved very coldly to the Austrian ambassador in Paris at the diplomatic reception on New Year's Day, 1859. This served notice to the world that trouble was in the offing. The details of Cavour's diplomatic maneuvering are not important, but by March the Piedmontese army was on a war footing and welcoming into its ranks Italian nationalist refugees from Austrian Lombardy, who were evading conscription into the Austrian army. This was a direct provocation to Austria. The Austrian government fell into Cavour's trap by mobilizing its own army and serving an ultimatum on Piedmont demanding that Piedmont withdraw from its warlike attitude. Piedmont refused, so Austria declared war, thus appearing the aggressor as Cavour hoped.

These events occurred in April. France immediately joined the Piedmontese, and Napoleon left Paris to command his army declaring that he would free Italy "from the Alps to the Adriatic," whatever that meant. The war was a short one. The Piedmontese won some minor victories at first, but two major battles were fought between the French and the Austrians in June—the battles of Magenta and Solferino. Both were French victories, but neither was decisive. However, after Solferino the Austrians were planning to withdraw to the east, where they had a number of strongly fortified positions from which it would have been difficult to dislodge them. In fact, both sides were anxious to end the war. Napoleon had several reasons. Personally he was not a warlike man;

he was appalled by the carnage of the battles. Further, he was alarmed at the spread of nationalistic uprisings in Italy; they could easily endanger his close relationship with the pope and the Catholic church, which was so important to him at home. The government in Paris informed him with some panic that the Prussian army was mobilizing along the Rhine and the road to Paris was almost open since most of the French army was in Italy. Lastly, the prospect of forcing the Austrian strongholds was a distasteful one. On the other side, Francis Joseph was also interested in peace because the shaky Austrian financial structure, already endangered by the Crimean War, was giving signs of collapse. Furthermore, it was dangerous for the Austrians to keep their forces in Italy because of the constant threat of a Hungarian revolt at home.

Accordingly, the two emperors met after the battle of Solferino at the village of Villafranca and agreed on an armistice which eventually resulted in a peace treaty signed some months later at Zürich. The essential clause of this arrangement was that Austria was to cede Lombardy to Piedmont but retain her possession of Venetia. Napoleon had not carried out his boast; Cavour and Victor Emmanuel were disgusted with Napoleon's double dealing; Francis Joseph had at least cut his losses, the first of a number of occasions in which he was fated to do the same thing.

A large part of Austrian history during the nineteenth century can be described as a series of unsuccessful wars followed by reorganizations of the empire. This was particularly true after the unsuccessful war with France. Reform was in the air throughout Germany; the revolution of 1848 was now a decade past and some of it had been forgotten. There was a new spirit in Prussia and some of the smaller German states. If Austria wanted to maintain her premier position in Germany, it seemed clear even to Francis Joseph that something would have to be done to establish some kind of constitutional order in Austria. The bureaucratic absolutism of the Bach system had proved a complete failure. The years of 1860 and 1861 were to be years of constitutional experiment in Austria.

Francis Joseph certainly had no desire to let the nationalities prescribe their own futures; he remembered 1848. He was determined that any changes to be made were to emanate from his own council in Vienna. Counsels in Vienna in 1860 were dominated by members of the old aristocracy who felt that the solution of the empire's ills lay in a return to government through the old "historicopolitical" entities, the various component parts of the empire, with no particular reference to their coincidence with the various national groups. They envisaged a semimedieval series of local diets which would send members to a central body. This was extreme decentralization but in a direction which would favor not the new spirit of nationalism but the old feudal areas which little by little had been accumulated by the Hapsburgs. This kind of thinking was embodied in the October Diploma issued by Francis Joseph in 1860 as a new pattern for the government of the empire.

The October Diploma, which never went into effect, outlined a system of government based on the local diets. In particular, the Hungarians were rebuffed by it because they received none of the special historical privileges that they considered their right. Francis Joseph picked as the man to carry out the new order, Anton Schmerling, somewhat of a liberal, a man who saw that the new project was a relic of the outworn past. He immediately began to press for a modification of the Diploma; the result was the February Patent of 1861, which was allegedly an interpretation of the Diploma but in fact shifted its whole basis.

Schmerling's plan moved a good deal of power from the local diets to the central parliament. However, the parliament was to be elected by a curious electoral system which was to be based on social class rather than nationality, a much safer arrangement from the Hapsburg point of view. The idea was to throw the weight of power into the hands of the German Austrians who might be expected to favor the central government. Furthermore, important areas of government, such as foreign affairs and the military establishment, were to be left in the hands of the emperor.

The February Patent had no greater success than the October Diploma. Again the Hungarians led the opposition. They simply refused to take part in the elections under the Patent. The resulting parliament was called by the scornful Viennese "Schmerling's theater." The Austrian constitutional experiments of 1860 and 1861 did not lead to stability, and the empire continued to be ruled by bureaucratic administrative methods with the nationalities, led by the Hungarians, offering only sullen obedience under duress. In these unsatisfactory circumstances Austria entered the vitally important decade of the sixties, a decade that was to decide her future and Germany's for years to come.

In Prussia too the late fifties were years of significant change. The vagaries of Frederick William IV became more and more intense until by 1857 it was clear that he was a victim of real mental disorder and at times too incompetent to carry out his royal functions. During that year and the next his periods of lucidity became rarer until in October 1858 he was removed from his duties and his younger brother William became regent. Frederick William lingered on until early 1861, when William was proclaimed king of Prussia as William I (1861–88).

William was over sixty years old when he became regent. He differed in almost all respects from his older brother. Tall, erect, austere, and military, he had none of Frederick William's love of art and culture, a fact which caused regret to his wife Augusta, who had been reared at the cultivated court of her grandfather, Charles Augustus of Saxe-Weimar, the patron of Goethe and Schiller. William's virtues were those of the Prussian officer—loyalty, courage, sober piety, and devotion to duty without outstanding intelligence. His one great love was the army, with which he had spent much of his life and which he knew thoroughly. In politics William had a reputation as a thoroughgoing conservative. He left Berlin in the stormy spring of 1848 and spent some months in exile in London. On his return he led the Prussian forces in quelling the last flickers of revolution in Saxony and Baden. During the fifties William came to disapprove of his brother's repressive rule. He realized that the constitution was there to stay and that prudence dictated an effort by the king to rule according to its spirit. William separated himself from the reactionary entourage of Frederick William without committing himself to real liberalism; he tried to steer a sort of middle course. Thus when he became regent, people began to speak of his regime as the "new era."

In fact during the early months of the regency there was considerable relaxation of the repressive enactments of recent years. Civil liberties, guaranteed by the constitution, were for the first time realities. The two elections to the Prussian parliament which had taken place during Frederick William's time had returned to power a predominantly conservative body because of governmental pressure and the boycott of the elections by some of the liberal elements. This situation changed, and the house elected in 1859 contained a liberal majority. The term liberal is a misleading one. The Prussian liberals of this period were not radicals in any sense of the word but simply men who wanted to make Prussia into a constitutional monarchy and who realized that their best way of achieving this aim was to guard jealously their right to control financial appropriations. It was this parliamentary determination, added to William's equally strong determination to make changes in the organization of the army, that caused the years after 1859 to be known to Prussian historians as the "time of conflict."

William was primarily interested in the army. He had watched it in the war with Denmark and also when the Prussians mobilized on the Rhine during the Franco-Austrian War. He was deeply dissatisfied with what he saw and determined to make changes. The Prussian army was still organized on the lines laid down during the reform period before 1813. Though an admirable reform, it had had to take account of the problems of the moment; furthermore, Prussia had changed very markedly since that time.

In the first place the army was hampered by the lack of modern equipment. New types of weapons had not yet been adopted in Prussia. A more difficult problem was that of conscription. According to the law all able-bodied young men were subject to conscription for three years. In fact, the population of Prussia had increased so considerably that the army was not able to take all the recruits to which it was entitled. Thus the weight of conscription fell inequitably. Furthermore, the army had adopted the policy of releasing the conscripts on leave after two years, so that the population had accepted a two-year period as normal although the three-year law was still on the books. When the army mobilized, as in 1859, the regular army was too small; thus it had to call upon the reserve militia (*Landwehr*) right away. The *Landwehr* was controlled more democratically than the army; its officers came from different social classes; it was more popular.

In late 1859 Prince William appointed a new minister of war, General Albert von Roon, a brilliant organizer but a political intriguer and deep conservative. Roon appointed General Helmuth von Moltke as chief of staff. Together these two, with the active collaboration of the regent, outlined plans for the new army. They immediately provided for the necessary technical improvements. They also proposed to place the *Landwehr* more closely under the regular army and to make the three-year period of conscription normal. These last two proposals had political overtones as well as purely military ones. They looked to the liberals like attempts on the part of the officer class to control the popular *Landwehr* and to do a more thorough job of indoctrinating the conscripts with their own attitudes in three years instead of two.

The liberal ministry had a difficult time with the army project in the lower house of the parliament. The house made no trouble about accepting the technical changes but refused to agree to the appropriations for the *Landwehr* and length-of-service proposals. The most they would do was to grant provisional appropriations for 1860 and 1861 with the understanding that these were not to be considered permanent. The army went ahead with its reforms, but Prussia continued without a regular budget, subsisting on the old taxes which were still collectible.

In 1861 some of the more advanced liberals broke away from the old Liberal party and formed the Progressive party (*Deutsche Fortschrittspartei*), which by its title emphasized its German rather than purely Prussian quality. In its program the new party insisted on the maintenance of popular control for the *Landwehr* and a two-year period of service. In the elections of 1861 the Progressives won a decisive victory, almost ousting the conservatives completely and taking many seats from the Liberals. The new chamber proved more intractable than the last, and in early 1862 the king dissolved it and called for new elections. The results were even more distressing to the king than those of the year before.

The situation became crucial in September. By that time the ministers realized that the whole army program would never be accepted by the lower house. They further agreed that they were behaving unconstitutionally and illegally by administering the state without a budget; for a time even Roon accepted this point of view. It seemed as if the Progressives were willing to compromise; they indicated that they would accept the *Landwehr* project if the government would give up the three-year conscription. King William refused to give in one iota; he felt strongly that the control of the army was a royal prerogative and one with which the parliament had no right to meddle. To him the alternative was quite simple. He would abdicate the throne in favor of his much more liberal son, Crown Prince Frederick. He even had the document of abdication drawn up, but Frederick would have nothing to do with it.

At this point Roon offered a solution. It was to change the ministry and to call to Berlin the only man who might be able to save the day, Otto von Bismarck. The king viewed this suggestion with the utmost reluctance. He disliked and feared Bismarck. The two did not see eye to eye on foreign policy, and William feared Bismarck's violence. As late as September 19 he said he would not call Bismarck, but already the day before in Paris Bismarck received a prearranged telegram from Roon which was to shape the course of German and European history for decades to come.

CHAPTER VIII

The Decade of the "Foundation" (1862-71)

The telegram from Roon with its enigmatic message, *"Periculum in mora. Dépêchez-vous"* ("Danger in delay. Make haste"), arrived in Paris on September 18, 1862. Its recipient, Otto von Bismarck-Schönhausen, wasted no time but took a train from Paris to Berlin on the nineteenth. On the twenty-second he had an interview with King William, which resulted in his appointment as minister-president and foreign minister of the kingdom of Prussia. At this moment there entered upon the large stage of European history the man who was destined to dominate Prussian, German, and even European affairs for almost thirty years and whose statesmanlike stature was to dwarf most of his contemporaries.

Otto von Bismarck was born in 1815 on the estate of Schönhausen not far from Berlin. It seems almost symbolic that while on his father's side he descended from a typical east-Elbian aristocratic family, on his mother's side the blood was not nearly so blue, for her family was a middle-class line which had done well in the administrative service of the Prussian state. These were the two classes which Bismarck was later to weld into the German ruling elite. He received an education typical of a young man of his class and eventually spent time at the University of Göttingen, where he was an indifferent student, although he must have read voraciously and lived a full and bibulous social life. It was probably there that he set forth on his alcoholic career, which can best be described by the word prodigious.

After leaving his formal studies, Bismarck tried his hand at a position in the Prussian civil service, which he did not keep very long because of its boring routine. He then returned to his father's estates and attempted the life of his forefathers as a member of the landed gentry. This too bored him, but he found some relief in continued heavy reading. More relief was undoubtedly afforded by his marriage in 1847 to Johanna von Puttkamer, an extremely pious young woman of about his own social class. The marriage had the immediate effect of reclaiming the young Bismarck from errant agnosticism to the security of orthodox Lutheranism, a position from which thereafter he never swerved. At about the same time he became interested in politics, and 1847 found him at the United Diet in Berlin as a representative from his district. At this assembly Bismarck took a position of thoroughgoing conservatism and allied himself with those who stood for throne and altar.

When Bismarck heard the news of the uprising in Berlin in March 1848, he went immediately to the capital and informed the king that he would be glad to return home, assemble the faithful peasantry of the neighborhood, and with them disperse the disloyal rabble of the city. Frederick William, understandably alarmed by his truculent vassal, refused the offer; as a result Bismarck played little part in the events of the revolutionary year, though one can imagine him thundering over his morning newspaper.

Bismarck's first important appointment came in 1851 when Frederick William IV named him Prussian representative at the revived Diet of the German Confederation at Frankfurt, partly because Bismarck had upon occasion been sympathetic to Austria and also because, after Olmütz, the Prussian government wanted to soothe Austrian feelings. It was soon clear, however, that the king had picked the wrong man for the purpose, for Bismarck had now become anti-Austrian and, to bolster Prussian prestige, amused himself by irritating the Austrian representative in every annoying way (e.g., smoking when the Austrian forbade it, or ostentatiously going for an excursion when the Austrian had called a meeting). He adopted a strong attitude during the Crimean War, annoyed by the vacillation of the Prussian king and convinced that Prussia should not work with the western allies. He saw that Austria was losing her credit in Russia and already had a sense of the importance of Russo-Prussian friendship for the future.

After the accession of Prince William of Prussia as regent, Bismarck was withdrawn from Frankfurt and appointed to the important post of Prussian ambassador in St. Petersburg. Here he spent the three years from 1859–62. These were important years for him, for during them he made lasting friendships with leading Russians and learned at first hand to understand the sometimes mercurial and always personal character of Russian rule. At the time of the Franco-Austrian War of 1859 Bismarck once again adopted an anti-Austrian attitude and warned against Prussian aid to her Germanic sister state.

In early 1862 Bismarck's Russian period came to a close and he was named ambassador to Paris. He held this position for only a few months and spent part of the time on a visit to London. He did manage a love affair with a young Russian lady in Biarritz, and, more important perhaps, got to know Napoleon III, who was to be his principal antagonist in the diplomatic fencing of later years. It was shortly after his return from Biarritz that he received the fateful telegram from Roon.

Bismarck's personality is not an entirely easy one to understand. He was well-read, cynical, and witty. If he wished to, he could be charming; women were attracted to him in spite of his formidable appearance. Although a heavy drinker and smoker, he had inexhaustible energy when he needed it. Then he would make up for this expenditure by prolonged rests. In his later years he became irascible and grouchy; he was always imperious. The degree of his success has made his many worshipers feel that he had long-range plans which he developed with superhuman astuteness. It seems more true to say that he had a startling ability to analyze a situation as it arose, keep all its threads in his hands, and derive from it the maximum advantage for Prussia, since it was Prussia rather than Germany that he served. He was perhaps the last of the old diplomatists, happiest when dealing with foreign affairs, continental rather than global in outlook, and surely one of the most subtle political minds that the modern west has produced.

King William must not have known that in appointing Bismarck his principal minister he was chaining himself for the rest of his life to what Germans call the demonic force of the new statesman. If he had known it, he would have been well advised to think twice. In any case, he did not have to wait long to see the tack Bismarck would take. After naming a conservative group to form the ministry, Bismarck made one of his first appearances before a legislative body, the Budget Committee of the Prussian lower house. On this occasion he made the statement which contained the words "blood and iron" so often connected with the policy of the "Iron Chancellor." He declared, "The great questions of the time will be decided not by speeches and the resolutions of majorities— that was the mistake of 1848 and 1849—but by blood and iron."

After thus expressing himself, Bismarck proceeded to his solution of the constitutional conflict between the king and parliament. The solution was simplicity itself. The government simply ruled Prussia by executive decree in despite of the parliament. Bismarck sent out collectors to receive taxes and threatened that they would if necessary be accompanied by soldiers whose loyalty was to the king and not to the parliament. Needless to say, the taxes were collected. Bismarck became the target of all kinds of unpopularity and even attack. This did not bother him at all. He developed a specious theory that there were loopholes in the Prussian constitution which permitted him to act as he was doing. No one was taken in by this, but no serious effort was made to defy the government. Bismarck dissolved the parliament more than once and called new elections. Each time the liberals received greater support from the people. Bismarck's support lay solely with the king, whose plans for the army reform were now being realized. As a further challenge to constitution and parliament, Bismarck by administrative decree in 1863 established a strong and illegal censorship of the press during the electoral campaign. He went so far indeed that the heir to the throne, Crown Prince Frederick, in a public statement made in Danzig, disavowed the government's actions and absolved himself of any knowledge of them. This statement led to an angry letter from father to son and to the removal of the crown prince from any important connection with the government. It also led to an angry relationship between Bismarck and Frederick and his wife, Crown Princess Victoria, daughter of Queen Victoria, which was to last for many years until the tragic death of the semiliberal Frederick. Bismarck was the victor. In his position of sole authority he unflinchingly maintained his policy of violence, setting at naught parliament, constitution, and people. He maintained this policy for four years until military success brought him abject surrender from the parliament in the shape of a retroactive amnesty and personal gifts to the victorious statesman. This ignoble action of the deputies is one of the many tragedies of German political history.

After having established his tough position toward domestic problems, Bismarck was ready to embark upon his career as a diplomat, a role much more congenial to him. Two events occurred in 1863 which to a degree set the stage for things to come. One of these was Bismarck's attitude toward the Austrian-sponsored Congress of Princes at Frankfurt. The Austrian emperor had decided that the German Confederation needed remodeling and reform, but in a conservative spirit without taking account of popular desires. To this end he invited the monarchs of the German states to meet with him in Frankfurt. King William of Prussia was inclined to accept the invitation, flattered by the fact that it was conveyed to him by the king of Saxony in person. Bismarck, seeing in the plan only a thrust for increased Austrian prestige, set himself definitely against it. His interview on the subject with the king was a stormy one. It is said that Bismarck was reduced to tears. This was not to be the last such emotional scene between the two, and this time, as on all future occasions, the minister was the victor. King William refused the invitation; as a result, the meeting, lacking the presence of the second-largest German power, came to nothing.

More important was Bismarck's attitude and action toward the Polish insurrection which had broken out in 1863 against the Russian government. Tsar Alexander II was carrying out a policy of stern and cruel repression in Poland to such a degree that British and French sentiment was wounded. The two western powers proposed a circular letter to the tsar protesting against the severity with which he was treating the Poles. Austria and Prussia were asked to adhere to this letter. Austria regarded it favorably. Bismarck, however, to whom the Poles meant nothing, sent conservative General von Alvensleben to St. Petersburg where he drew up the so-called Alvensleben Convention which provided that Russian and Prussian troops would mutually have the right to cross each other's borders in pursuit of fugitive Poles. This arrangement, of course, was of value only to Russia. The practical result so far as the Poles were concerned was not great, but the implications were considerable. First, Napoleon lost the close relationship with Russia toward which he had been working since the Crimean War. Second, Russia was irritated as in 1854–56 by Austrian ingratitude and double dealing. Finally, Alexander realized that he had a friend in Berlin. In subsequent years this Russo-Prussian amity was to be very useful to Bismarck. In fact, the time was close at hand for its usefulness, for the next major problem facing the diplomats was one that closely concerned the Danish royal family, related to the Romanovs, and over which Russia had historically extended a hand of cousinly protection.

The troublesome problem of the duchies of Schleswig and Holstein had lain in abeyance since the Treaty of London of 1852. A new crisis loomed in 1863 when Frederick VII of Denmark proclaimed a new constitution. By this constitution the two areas of Denmark and Schleswig, although technically not merged, were brought closer together politically and the way seemed to be paved toward gradual union. This was a victory for the nationalist Eider Dane party. (The Eider is the little river separating Schleswig from Holstein.) A few days after publishing the constitution but before actually signing it, Frederick VII died; his successor, from the Glücksburg (female) line, was proclaimed as Christian IX. His first problem was whether or not to accept the new constitution. He decided to do so and signed it on November 18, 1863, three days after his accession.

This action caused a furor in Germany. It looked like an affront to the spirit of German nationalism, for it seemed to integrate the German minority in Schleswig into a foreign kingdom, to break up the old unity of the two duchies, and to violate the Treaty of London. More important, it gave Bismarck a choice pool of troubled waters to fish in, and fish in it he did with all the equipment he could bring into action. It seems clear that from the outset Bismarck was determined not to set up the duchies as a new entity within Germany but instead to annex them to the kingdom of Prussia. He claims in his memoirs that this was the case. However, he had to be very secretive about this aim since the idea would be received with horror in Vienna and also by the Diet at Frankfurt. A further complication was that Frederick, Duke of Augustenburg, now publicly revived his claim to the duchies on the ground that his father had given up his own claim but not his son's. This young duke was received with enthusiasm throughout Germany and made a trip to Berlin to secure Prussian support for his claims. Bismarck was able to avoid this, in spite of some wavering on the part of the king, by a reminder to William that Prussia had signed the Treaty of London by which Christian was to be recognized.

The next step taken by the Prussian minister was to arrive at an agreement with Austria to bring the two great German powers into harmony. This accomplishment was one of Bismarck's diplomatic triumphs, since in this way he broke free from the German Confederation. Henceforward Prussia and Austria acted together as signatories of the Treaty of London, which the Confederation as such had not signed. The agreement was rendered easier by the fact that Austria was on fairly bad terms with France and therefore more willing to have a friend in Berlin. Thus Austria and Prussia agreed that action should be taken on the basis of the Treaty of London. The next step was for the two powers to persuade the Frankfurt Diet to carry out Federal Execution against Christian IX, an action which was succeeded by the occupation by German troops of the duchy of Holstein and its small neighbor Lauenburg. This action left the basic question of Schleswig still in abeyance, for Schleswig was not a member of the German Confederation. Austria and Prussia insisted that German troops must advance further and cross the Eider into Schleswig to enforce the Treaty of London. They tried to get the Diet to take this step; the Diet, however, refused. Therefore the two powers decided to act for themselves, which Bismarck wanted in the first place, and presented an ultimatum to Denmark demanding the abrogation of the recent constitution. Denmark refused this ultimatum; as a result, on February 1, 1864, Austrian and Prussian troops crossed into Schleswig. The first of Bismarck's three wars for the unification of Germany had begun.

The war is of interest principally because it provided the newly remodeled Prussian army with its first opportunity to display itself in the field. It marks also the first appearance of the triumvirate which was to become invincible during the ensuing decade: Bismarck as head of the government, Roon as minister of war, and Moltke as chief of the General Staff. The actual commander in the field at first was the very old General Wrangel, but most of the strategy was developed by Moltke. The first objective was the allegedly impregnable Danewerk, a line of forts across the neck of the Jutland Peninsula south of the town of Schleswig. Owing to bad weather, the Danish army retired from this position without a real fight and withdrew to the peninsula of Düppel and the adjacent island of Alsen. Before the end of February German troops had crossed the northern border of Schleswig and were on territory of Denmark proper, a fact which caused some embarrassment in Berlin and Vienna where it was feared that the advance into Denmark might unleash a general European war. By April 18, 1864, Düppel was stormed and taken, but at this point military activity was suspended for a time because the other powers of Europe, notably Great Britain, had called a European conference in London to try to settle the dispute without further bloodshed. It is hardly profitable to say much about this conference since it ended in failure. All sorts of proposals were suggested which might solve the general problem. Denmark was in a weak position both militarily and diplomatically. On the other hand, the German powers, flushed with success, were no longer content to make the treaty of 1852 the basis of the solution. Denmark would go no further in conciliation. Thus the conference came to an end in late June, and hostilities were renewed.

By this time General Wrangel had been replaced by Prince Frederick Charles of Prussia, who undertook successfully on June 29, 1864, Moltke's audacious plan of landing on and occupying the island of Alsen. This action effectively broke Danish morale because the Danes realized that they were no longer safe on their islands. They therefore proposed an armistice and began peace negotiations. On October 30 a treaty was signed in Vienna, of which the most important provision was that King Christian abandoned jointly to Austria and Prussia his rights over Schleswig, Holstein, and Lauenburg.

It is clear that this arrangement was no permanent one. It dodged the question of the final status of the duchies and in particular evaded the issue concerning the duke of Augustenburg. The Schleswig-Holstein problem becomes now the pivot of the general problem of the future of Germany. All that was gained by the Danish War was the removal of Denmark from the German picture. Bismarck now let his intentions become somewhat clearer. While the war was in progress, he had indicated to Austria that Prussia was interested in annexing the duchies. He had to deal with some opposition from King William, who felt he had no right to the duchies and that Augustenburg had, but in the course of time Bismarck was able, as always, to bring the monarch around to his way of thinking. In February 1865 Prussia informed Austria of the conditions under which she would permit the duchies to be set up as a German state. They involved a permanent alliance with Prussia, naval bases, and the right to build a canal across the peninsula; in general, they were so severe that they constituted annexation to Prussia in all but name. Relations between the two German powers became more and more strained, and the possibility of war with Austria was discussed in Prussian ruling circles. However, Bismarck was not willing for a breach to occur at this moment. He presumably wanted to sound out opinion in the other capitals of Europe before acting. Accordingly an agreement with Austria was patched up at Gastein in August 1865, by which Lauenburg and the administration of Schleswig were granted to Prussia and that of Holstein to Austria. A glance at the map on page 88 will show that this again was no permanent solution. Austria had few interests that far from home. Further, Prussia could garrison Schleswig only by transporting her troops across Holstein. However, the Gastein convention did grant a breathing spell for almost a year, and Bismarck gained the title of count. (He was made a prince after 1871.)

The next months were spent by Bismarck in an extremely intricate series of diplomatic moves preparatory to war with Austria, which he now felt to be both inevitable and desirable. He studied the general European picture. Russia and Great Britain were no threat. The former was very friendly to Prussia, the latter jealous of France and not averse to a strong counterweight in north Germany. Italy would be a desirable ally against Austria, but so great was the influence of France in Italy that an alliance could hardly be achieved without the consent of Napoleon III. Accordingly Bismarck in October made a trip to France and visited the French emperor at Biarritz. We do not know exactly what they said, but it seems clear that Napoleon expressed a friendly interest in Prussian aspirations—especially if these were coupled with increase of territory to France. Probably Belgium, Luxemburg, the Saar, and the Palatinate were mentioned airily in the discussions. It seems clear that Bismarck made no definite commitments but did not oppose further negotiation after the conclusion of the war.

On his return from France Bismarck spent the winter in moves designed to increase the tension with Austria and to get the king and other leading Prussians in line with his own policy. He started to enlarge the ground of the whole problem by indicating that it transcended the simple addition of the duchies to Prussia, that in fact it involved a whole reorganization of the German Confederation. He dangled before the king the prospect of a remodeled Germany in which Prussia would play the principal role. The big decision was reached by Prussia in February 1866 when at a crown council Bismarck was given permission to seek an alliance with Italy against Austria. This of course was a violation of the constitution of the Confederation.

The alliance with Italy was not very difficult to achieve. Bismarck managed to make it favorable for Prussia. Italy obligated herself to follow Prussia into war, but there was no promise on Prussia's part that the war would have to occur. In return for her participation in a war Italy was to receive the province of Venetia, which was still under Austrian rule. One important proviso made by Italy was that for the treaty to go into effect the war would have to start within three months after its signature (April 8, 1866).

Bismarck now turned to immediate preparation for war, trying to maneuver Austria into the position of aggressor. Much of the activity occurred in the Diet at Frankfurt. For example, the Prussian delegate suggested that a general German parliament elected by universal suffrage be called. Bismarck now was posing as a liberal and a good German nationalist. His attitude, however, was really determined by the fact that he believed universal suffrage to be more conservative than a suffrage based upon taxes or land. He knew the conservative character of the peasantry, who would dominate. Bismarck's letters to the Austrian government became ever sharper. In the duchies everything was done to annoy the Austrian authorities in Holstein and to damage the position of Augustenburg, who was favored by the Austrians. Bismarck even made gestures in the direction of peace with the Prussian parliament.

The crisis occurred in June 1866. Austria, goaded beyond endurance by what she considered Prussian breaches of the Gastein arrangement, brought the whole matter before the Federal Diet. Prussia retaliated by occupying Holstein and dislodging the Austrian troops from the duchy. Austria then presented a motion to the Diet calling for the mobilization of all the member states except Prussia. Bavaria modified this to exclude Austria too from mobilization. Bismarck instructed his delegate that if either of these motions were passed, he was to announce that the vote constituted a breach of the constitution of the Confederation, which Prussia therefore considered no longer to exist. He was to propose further that a new constitution be adopted, unbelievably enough, on the lines of that of the Frankfurt Parliament of 1849, with Austria excluded. The vote was taken on June 14, the Bavarian motion was passed, the Prussian delegate carried out his instructions, and war broke out. Most of the southern and western states sided with Austria, so that Prussia was opposed by the majority of the Confederation.

The story of the war is a simple one and upset the calculations of those (notably Napoleon III) who thought that it would be a long and exhausting struggle. In fact it is sometimes called the Seven Weeks' War. There was fighting in three areas. In western Germany a Prussian army defeated Hanover at the battle of Langensalza. In Italy an Austrian archduke defeated the Italians at the second battle at Custozza, and Austria was also the victor on the Adriatic Sea. The main center of conflict, however, was Bohemia. Here Moltke directed the operations. The Austrian commander was General Benedek, who was given the command there largely because of his intimate knowledge of the terrain in north Italy. There was only one battle, the battle of Königgrätz (also known as Sadowa since the battlefield lies between the two villages), fought on July 3, 1866, a brilliant victory for Prussia and a catastrophic defeat for Austria. This battle is one of the decisive turning points of modern history. It established Prussian hegemony in Germany and shifted the European balance of power well to the east. Thus it was a crushing defeat for Napoleon, as well as for Francis Joseph. More than dimly aware of this, the French emperor debated coming to Austria's aid even after the battle and sent his ambassador in Berlin, M. Benedetti, to the front to offer mediation, but the gesture was treated with scorn by Bismarck.

Bismarck had a difficult time now with King William, who, flushed with victory, wanted territory from Bavaria and Austria and also a triumphal entry with his army into Vienna. Bismarck, however, displaying his greatest diplomatic skill, wanted a peace with Austria which would indeed get her out of Germany but also avoid humiliating her as much as possible. Stormy scenes including tears ensued between king and minister. Finally Bismarck won his point. By the preliminary Peace of Nikolsburg, which became definitive at Prague on August 23, Austria was excluded from Germany and gave her consent to any arrangement that Prussia desired in north Germany (north of the Main River). She lost no German lands. Her only territorial loss was the province of Venetia to Italy. Bismarck went even so far as to humor the Austrian emperor's request that no territorial demands be made on Saxony. Far different was Bismarck's attitude in northwest Germany. In that area four historic entities disappeared from the map and were simply annexed to Prussia. They were the kingdom of Hanover, the grand duchy of Hesse-Kassel, the duchy of Nassau, and the free city of Frankfurt, which latter was treated with surprising brutality. It looked almost like an afterthought that the old bone of contention, Schleswig-Holstein, was also annexed to Prussia, although the Prussians promised that a plebiscite would be held in north Schleswig.

This settlement was a great victory for Bismarck's policy. The force of "blood and iron" had proved decisive. At home the minister received his reward from the parliament which he had been defying for four years. He requested and received an indemnity bill, legalizing all expenditures of the past years in a gesture of forgive and forget. The parliament, in addition, voted him a grant of money for his personal use, with which he bought himself the estate of Varzin in Pomerania. The indemnity did not pass without opposition. It led to a split in the Progressive party. The group which became the National Liberal party approved the indemnity; others further to the left refused to vote for it and became the core of the later Progressive party. However, for the moment Bismarck was vindicated and now had leisure to reorganize most of Germany under Prussian auspices.

The constitution which Bismarck drew up for the new North German Confederation with slight changes served as the constitution of the German Empire after 1871 and remained in force down to the end of World War I in 1918. It was largely the personal handiwork of Bismarck, who turned his efforts to it after a period of illness and rest in the fall of 1866. It was presented to a Reichstag, elected for the purpose by universal suffrage, which passed it with a few modifications in about two months. This constitution is a masterpiece of a sort. It ensured that Prussia would be in almost complete control of the new entity known as the North German Confederation. The Confederation and the later Empire are sometimes described as Prussia writ large. The king of Prussia by hereditary right held the position of president of the Confederation. In him reposed executive authority, principally concerned with foreign affairs and the military establishment. He was to name a chancellor, the only minister of the Confederation, who was responsible to the president and to him only. The chancellor could name assistants, but Bismarck was careful to avoid anything that smacked of real cabinet government or of any type of responsibility to the parliament. The chancellor was to be chairman of the upper house of the legislature, called the Bundesrat. This house was made up of delegates representing the governments of the various states, really ambassadors. The states received votes in the Bundesrat in proportion to the votes they had had at the Diet at Frankfurt, with the exception that Prussia received in addition to her original ones the votes of the states she had annexed. Thus Prussia had seventeen votes, but only fourteen were needed to veto a constitutional amendment. The votes were cast by the unit rule. The Bundesrat met behind closed doors. It had the sole right of initiating legislation into the lower house or Reichstag, which was elected in proportion to the population by universal male suffrage. This apparently democratic device was really a façade, for the powers of the Reichstag were largely illusory. It could debate proposed legislation referred by the Bundesrat, and more important, in spite of Bismarck's wishes, it had the right to pass the annual budget. In general, however, it became the most distinguished debating society in Europe. The constitution was tailored by Bismarck for Bismarck and worked as he had planned while he was at the helm. During most of his succeeding years he was both chancellor and also minister-president of Prussia. Thus the important relationship was between the president (later emperor)-king and chancellor-minister-president. As long as Bismarck and William I worked together, Bismarck retained his ascendancy. After William's death a more aggressive emperor shifted the weight of the relationship to himself, and the result was the mercurial reign of William II.

The relationship between the new Confederation and the four south German states which were not members of it (Bavaria, Würtemberg, Baden, and the southern half of Hesse-Darmstadt) was within a few months assured by military alliances with Prussia, providing that in case of war the south German troops were to be placed under the command of the king of Prussia. These alliances were a result of negotiations for compensation between Bismarck and Napoleon III. North and south were also bound together by the old customs union, which was revived after the war.

The war of 1866 had constitutional repercussions in the Hapsburg lands as well as in north Germany. In 1867 a thoroughgoing overhaul of the Austrian Empire occurred after lengthy discussions between Vienna and the leading Hungarian political figures. The result was the so-called *Ausgleich* or compromise which set up the dual monarchy of Austria-Hungary. By this arrangement the kingdom of Hungary was separated from the rest of the empire and given complete independence in internal affairs. The relationship with Austria was solely a personal one, vested in the Austrian emperor who was also king of Hungary. Each half had its own constitution and parliamentary organization. There were three joint ministers, one each for foreign affairs, the armed forces, and finances necessary for the former two. To organize these joint affairs a system was devised whereby members of the two parliaments, known as Delegations, met together but in separate rooms alternately in Vienna and Budapest. It was a cumbersome method of government but persisted down to the extinction of the Hapsburg monarchy in 1918.

The years 1867–70 were largely filled by negotiations between Bismarck and Napoleon III, which led eventually to the outbreak of the Franco-Prussian War in the summer of 1870. It is a sorry story of French ineptitude, gaucherie, and inefficiency, and of Prussian astuteness, efficiency, and unscrupulousness. Much has been written about the relative responsibility of France and Prussia for the war. A moderate approach seems to be that if the whole four-year period is taken into account, France appears more to blame, but if only the crisis of 1870 is to be judged, Prussia is the greater villain.

Immediately after the news of the battle of Königgrätz, the French emperor tried to cash in on the promises of compensation which he professed to believe Bismarck had given him at Biarritz the year before. His first suggestion was that France should annex some of the left bank of the Rhine, including the city of Mainz, and part at least of the Palatinate, which belonged to Bavaria. It was at this time that Bismarck evolved from a purely Prussian statesman to one who concerned himself with all Germany. He stated that it was quite out of the question to cede any German territory to a non-Germanic nation. He also used this thrust of Napoleon as bait to persuade Bavaria to sign the military alliance with the Confederation.

A year later in 1867 a more serious affair arose concerning the little grand duchy of Luxemburg, which belonged to the king of the Netherlands but had been part of the old German Confederation. The Dutch king was willing to sell it to France, and Napoleon, thwarted on so many sides, thought that at least this would be something to show for his efforts. The project raised a storm of nationalistic fury within Germany. Bismarck had the question raised in the Reichstag and used the opportunity to take full advantage of national feeling in a highly theatrical speech. The result was that Napoleon had to retreat. At a meeting in London the independence and neutrality of Luxemburg were guaranteed by the powers.

A last effort of the French emperor concerned Belgium, which he hoped possibly to annex as a result of heavy investment by the French in Belgian railways. Nothing came of this either, largely owing to Bismarck's awareness of the hostility with which Great Britain would regard such a threat on the sensitive channel coast.

Napoleon seemed to be foiled on all counts. The years 1868 and 1869 were years of tension and of jockeying for position. France made a belated effort to improve the condition of her army. She also engaged in a desperate series of negotiations with Austria-Hungary and Italy to achieve an alliance that might be useful against Prussia. Some progress was made in this direction, but when the war broke out neither of these states did anything to help France. Bismarck seemed to hold all the trump cards. He simply waited for a suitable occasion to settle accounts with France and to draw the south German states into the new German unity. The occasion arose in the summer of 1870 over a problem connected with the naming of a new monarch for distant Spain, which had been without a ruler since the deposition of Queen Isabella II in 1868.

The Spanish revolutionaries, after getting rid of their corrupt and unpopular queen, had drawn up a monarchical constitution but so far had found no one to place on the throne. Among the promising candidates was the young Prince Leopold of Hohenzollern-Sigmaringen, a very distant cousin of the king of Prussia, a Catholic, and a brother of the recently established prince of Romania, Carol. Leopold's father, Karl Anton, was still alive. He and the titular head of the family, King William of Prussia, were responsible for Leopold's decisions rather than the young prince himself. A good deal of secret negotiation went on during 1869 and the early months of 1870 among the Spanish, the Hohenzollern family, and the Prussian court. The most important aspect of this is the attitude taken by Bismarck toward it. This is not absolutely clear. In his memoirs Bismarck throws a certain amount of smoke screen over his role. Modern scholars on the whole agree that Bismarck knew of and approved the plan, and in fact that he did all he could to push it in the face of the king's reluctance. Bismarck must have realized that the French reaction to the plan would be very hostile. Thus one is forced to the conclusion that Bismarck was thinking of the matter not only as it concerned Spain but more as it concerned the final unification of Germany through the adherence of the south German states, and also that he was prepared to face, if necessary, a war with France to achieve his aims.

During the early months of 1870 the affair proceeded secretly. In March Prince Leopold and his father visited Berlin, but still King William demurred. Not until well into June did he give his consent. The plan was to keep the matter secret pending a public announcement by the Spanish parliament. However, owing to a number of accidents, the news reached the French ambassador in Madrid on July 3. The excitement with which it was greeted in Paris was unprecedented. Napoleon was hurt at what seemed to him the duplicity of the king of Prussia. The French foreign minister, the Duc de Gramont, gave an inflammatory speech in parliament declaring that France would not tolerate a resurrection of the empire of Charles V. He also sent the unfortunate French ambassador, M. Benedetti, to the health resort of Ems, where the king of Prussia was vacationing, to take the matter up urgently with the king in person.

King William, alarmed by the storm which had arisen, was trying to maintain peace. In fact, during the whole crisis he behaved with moderation and courtesy. He resumed his former opinion that the prince should not accept the Spanish throne and so advised him and his father. Bismarck, on his Pomeranian estate, was becoming more and more restive as it began to appear that the affair would blow over with nothing gained. He decided to travel to Ems; but when he reached Berlin, he heard the public news that Leopold had withdrawn his candidacy.

So far the crisis had resulted in a major diplomatic triumph for France, which she desperately needed. However, the French government unwisely decided to push the matter further. Benedetti was instructed to

demand from King William a statement that no member of the Hohenzollern family would ever again be permitted to aspire to the throne of
Spain. Accordingly the next afternoon, July 13, 1870, Benedetti approached the king as they met on the promenade and delivered his foolish
message. The king received him politely, declared that he knew no more
news of the matter than Benedetti, promised that he would send him a
copy of an expected telegram from Leopold, and took his leave. Upon
returning home, the king did as he had promised; he wrote Benedetti
that he considered the matter closed and did not feel they needed to
meet again. He then asked an aide to send a telegraphic account of the
day's events to Bismarck in Berlin.

Bismarck in his memoirs gives a detailed story of the following evening. He says that he had invited Moltke and Roon to dinner to drown
their sorrows over the mishandled and unproductive crisis. During dinner the telegram from the king arrived. Bismarck read it and, jumping
from his chair, made some comment about a red flag to bait the Gallic
bull. He then went to his desk and edited the telegram, not changing the
facts, but shortening the account and coloring it to suggest both that
Benedetti had been rude to the king and also that the king had dismissed Benedetti abruptly. The telegram was made public and published
in the French newspapers the next day. The apparent insult to the
French ambassador infuriated public opinion in Paris. Crowds gathered
and an emotional orgy ensued. There was no further way to restrain
events, although Napoleon had a heavy heart. On July 19 the French
government in an almost nonchalant way declared war. Almost immediately the four south German states declared their solidarity with Prussia, and France found herself at war with all of Germany.

From the outset it was clear that Prussian efficiency was immeas-
urably greater than that of the rather shabby French. Moltke devised the
strategy, which was carried out by three German armies. During the
month of August a number of battles were fought near the Franco-German border, nearly all of them Prussian victories. The decisive battle, however, was fought on September 1, 1870, at Sédan. Here one of the two
major French armies, under Marshal MacMahon with the emperor present, found itself on the defensive in an extremely disadvantageous position. The Germans surrounded the French, who were forced to surrender
almost a hundred thousand men. The emperor gave himself up as a
prisoner to the king of Prussia and was sent to the castle of Wilhelms-
höhe near Kassel. Two days later in Paris the people arose, drove out
the Empress Eugénie, and ended the second French Empire. The following month the other major unit of the French army, under Marshal
Bazaine, was trapped in the fortress of Metz, besieged, and forced to

surrender. By this time other German forces had crossed northern France and—in spite of the heroic efforts of the French, led by Léon Gambetta and Adolphe Thiers, to raise new French levies—had encircled Paris, beginning a siege which was to cause the Parisians untold misery and to end in the surrender of the capital in January 1871. However, by that time another event had happened of decisive importance for the future, the proclamation of the German Empire on January 18, 1871.

Very shortly after Sédan, negotiations began between the south German states and Bismarck concerning the creation of a united Germany. These negotiations were difficult and several times were almost discontinued. Both Bavaria and Würtemberg demanded special concessions. In particular, the mentally doubtful Louis II of Bavaria was hesitant. Even King William of Prussia was reluctant, feeling that the title king of Prussia was far more dignified than any parvenu imperial title. Finally, however, things were arranged. Bavaria and Würtemberg received special privileges in such matters as the army (during peacetime), and postal, railway, and telegraph regulations. Bismarck wrote out a letter for the king of Bavaria to copy requesting William to accept the title of emperor. This Louis did probably in return for a handsome bribe to help him out of his serious financial straits. On January 18 in the Hall of Mirrors in the palace of Versailles a somewhat sulky William assumed the title of German emperor (he would have preferred emperor of Germany), and the united German Empire came into existence.

The war was still going on, although the Germans did not engage in much more fighting. Instead they stood aside while troops of the French republican government put down their own rebellious compatriots of the Commune of Paris. Peace negotiations between France and Germany began in February, and a final treaty was signed at Frankfurt on May 10. France had to pay an indemnity of five billion francs and to endure a German occupation until the amount was paid. Much more important was the cession by France to Germany of the province of Alsace and part of French Lorraine including Metz. Bismarck disapproved of part of this cession but for once was overruled. Thus there was introduced into the European body a cancer which was to prevent a reconciliation between the two antagonists and contribute mightily to the military competition which characterized Europe from 1871 to 1914.

CHAPTER IX

Bismarck's Germany. I, Political (1871-88)

From its foundation until his dismissal in 1890, the German Empire was dominated by Bismarck. He held the position of *Reichskanzler* ("imperial chancellor") during the whole period and was usually also minister-president of Prussia. The Bismarck of the seventies and eighties was different from the earlier man. His personality remained dominant and overbearing, becoming more irritable as he aged, but his objectives had changed. In the sixties he pursued an aggressive ruthless policy aimed at unification. After 1871 he pursued a *Friedenspolitik* ("policy of peace") in order that the new German state might digest the achievements of the earlier period. The man who had with calculation risked war now became the man who would do almost anything to avoid war. He conceived his purpose to be the consolidation of past gains and the maintenance of Germany's military and economic strength. So massive and awesome was his personality, so obvious his achievement, that the world saw in Germany a great monolith of strength and power. It was not until after 1918 that, upon closer examination, a number of cracks and crevices were seen in the structure, weaknesses which Bismarck was often able to disguise but which in the course of time became too gaping for further patchwork. This generalization is true of many aspects of the German state and is not least discoverable in the spectrum of political parties with which the chancellor had to deal.

On the far right of German politics—if we do not count the completely intransigent Poles, Danes from north Schleswig, French from Alsace-Lorraine, and Guelf supporters of the former king of Hanover—the two conservative parties, the Conservative and the *Reichspartei,* found their places. One might expect the Conservative party, whose members were mostly Prussian aristocrats from the same stratum of society as Bismarck himself, to be a main support for the chancellor. This was not the case. The Conservatives had two major interests: Prussia, and their agricultural livelihoods. As far as the first was concerned, they felt that Bismarck had neglected purely Prussian concerns in favor of general German ones; they viewed the new empire with a good deal of mistrust. On the second count, they feared that Bismarck was favoring the new commercial and industrial interests too much and that this would redound to their own disadvantage. Furthermore, they were suspicious of Bismarck's campaign against the Catholic church in the mid-seventies, fearing that the same attack could be made against their beloved Lutheranism. It was not until Bismarck's watershed year of 1879 (when the question of the protective tariff, so dear to the agrarians, arose) that the Conservatives shifted from opposition to support of the government. One of their leaders was Roon, the great minister of war. For a time he served as minister-president of Prussia, but in the end he definitely turned away from his old colleague Bismarck.

Perhaps the principal example of Bismarck's acrimony toward the Conservatives occurred in his handling of the affair of Harry von Arnim. Arnim, a young, talented, and quickly promoted member of the diplomatic service, was given the difficult post of ambassador to France after the Treaty of Frankfurt. He cut a considerable swath in French political circles and had the reputation of favoring the return of a monarchy in France. This conflicted with Bismarck's policy, for the chancellor felt that a republic was a weaker form of government than a monarchy, and above all, he wanted a weak France. Thus he supported the republicans and was at odds with his ambassador. Further he believed that conservative circles were grooming Arnim to succeed him as chancellor. This was too much. So Bismarck sent to Paris a young, brilliant misanthrope, Fritz von Holstein, to spy on Arnim, who was admittedly careless about leaving valuable documents around. Holstein amassed evidence of many misdemeanors; Bismarck recalled Arnim and tried him for treason. He was found guilty, escaped from Germany, and lived the rest of his life in exile. Many Conservatives felt that Bismarck had hounded Arnim for personal reasons, and the affair increased the tension between him and the far right.

The *Reichspartei* consisted of conservatives of a bit more liberal hue than the members of the Conservative party. It was not so exclusively Prussian in character but drew on nobility from other parts of the empire. These differences account for its orientation. It was a supporter of Bismarck, although in the eighties its membership in the Reichstag was so small as to make it unimportant.

During the decade of the seventies Bismarck looked for his principal support to the National Liberal party which at that time was the largest single party in the Reichstag. It was mainly the party of big business and industrial interests, which were rapidly becoming so very important. The

Prussian members of it were the group of liberals who, at the time of the Indemnity Bill of 1866, had voted in favor of Bismarck. In doctrine they were allied to the main tenets of Manchester liberalism, *laissez faire* or free trade. They were psychologically in sympathy with the anti-Catholic legislation because of their typical nineteenth-century liberal anticlericalism. They were also in sympathy with the general spirit of material progress and expansion, which Bismarck seemed to symbolize at the time. By the end of the decade, however, the alliance between Bismarck and the Liberals was wearing thin, and the final break came when Bismarck espoused the cause of the protective tariff. This was a complicated story, but in the end Bismarck decided to accept the support of the Conservatives and the Center. After 1879 the Liberal party went downhill in its electoral support, and liberalism became a dying philosophy in the empire.

The question of protectionism arose partly out of the peculiar financial arrangements for the support of the empire. Bismarck was fundamentally uninterested in economic problems and had no hesitation in saying so. During the first decade and more of his tenure of office he had been mainly interested in diplomacy and had relegated domestic questions to trusted subordinates. In the middle seventies, however, he began to realize the precarious nature of imperial finances. In addition to certain fixed sources of revenue, the empire had to rely on donations, called matricular contributions, made by the individual states each year to cover the imperial deficit. Bismarck disliked this system, which he felt lessened the dignity of the empire and looked like a charitable handout. Bismarck felt that if the imperial government could get the proceeds of the customs duties, it might become self-supporting. He was encouraged in his views by the agrarian interests, which were becoming more and more alarmed at the dumping on the German market of large amounts of agricultural produce underselling the local product. The introduction of a tariff bill in the Reichstag caused a parliamentary battle, which Bismarck won only at the expense of exchanging the support of the National Liberals for that of the Conservatives and the Catholic Center. This was the political watershed of his domestic policy. Even at that cost he did not achieve all he wanted, for the bill which the Center was willing to accept differed from Bismarck's original project since the Center, which had federalist rather than centralist views, wanted to preserve the principle of the matricular contributions, although granting increased revenue for the imperial government.

The other liberal group in the Reichstag, composed largely of those who had refused to vote for the Indemnity Bill in 1866, underwent various changes of name but can be conveniently described as the Progres-

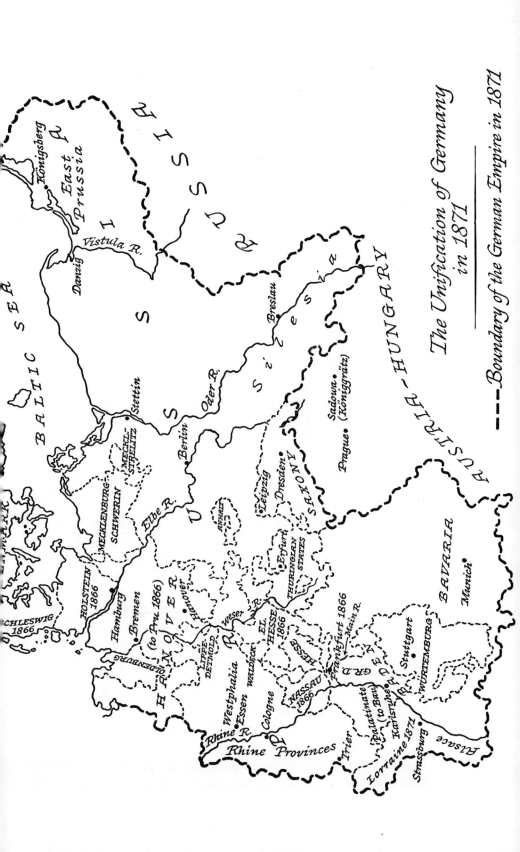

The Unification of Germany in 1871

Boundary of the German Empire in 1871

RUSSIA

BALTIC SEA

Königsberg

East Prussia

Vistula R.

Danzig

P R U S S I A

Stettin

Berlin

Oder R.

Breslau

S i l e s i a

Sadowa (Königgrätz)

Prague

AUSTRIA-HUNGARY

MECKL.-STRELITZ

MECKLENBURG-SCHWERIN

Elbe R.

ANHALT

Leipzig

Dresden

SAXONY

Erfurt

THURINGIAN STATES

BAVARIA

Munich

HOLSTEIN 1866

Hamburg

Bremen

(to Pru. 1866)

H A N O V E R

Hanover

Weser R.

LIPPE-DETMOLD

WALDECK

EL. HESSE 1866

Frankfurt 1866

Main R.

OLDENBURG

SCHLESWIG 1866

DENMARK

Westphalia

Essen

Cologne

Rhine R.

Rhine Provinces

Trier

NASSAU 1866

GRD. HESSE

Palatinate (to Bav.)

Karlsruhe

Stuttgart

WÜRTEMBERG

B A D E N

Lorraine 1871

Strassburg

Alsace

sive party. It came the nearest to representing real democracy in Germany as an American or Englishman would recognize it. Needless to say, this was a party of opposition to the government. It fluctuated very much in strength from election to election, but regularly in the person of its eloquent leader, Eugen Richter, provided liberal and democratic objection to most of the chancellor's projects.

The Catholic Center party was a unique group. While it was legally founded only in 1870, its roots go back at least to 1848. The exclusion of Catholic Austria from Germany made the remaining German Catholics, who constituted about one-third of the population of the empire, fearful that they would be submerged by Protestant Prussia; so they felt they should organize as a unit. Socially speaking, the Center was the least homogeneous of the German parties. Unlike the others it had neither a class nor an ideological basis, except for the common Catholicism of most (but by no means all) of its members. Its strength was drawn from such disparate elements as the heavy industrialists of Silesia and the west, the Catholic aristocracy and peasantry of the south, and the increasing Catholic industrial proletariat, particularly in the Ruhr area. Thus it was a microcosm of German society. The party's heterogeneity made its policy flexible. It always possessed a right wing of conservative agrarians and a left wing of advanced social thinkers, which eventually crystallized into the Christian Trade Union movement. Thus the party was susceptible of coalition either to the left or the right; generally in the imperial period it was to the right. In addition, in the person of its leader, Ludwig Windthorst, the Center had a brilliant parliamentarian, who was able and willing at times to challenge even the champion, Bismarck. During the seventies, owing to Bismarck's campaign against the Catholic church in Germany (the *Kulturkampf*), the Center was in bitter opposition to the government. However, as the decade wore on this situation changed, partly as a result of the emergence of the Social Democratic party, partly because of the defection from Bismarck of the National Liberals. In 1879 the Center made an arrangement with the Conservatives and became a government party for awhile. At that time the Catholic agrarians saw eye to eye with their Protestant colleagues and helped Bismarck in his struggle over the tariff so that he would call off his war on the Catholic church. Windthorst's policy was usually to keep the Center party in the middle, where it could ideally maintain a sort of balance of power. In spite of the *rapprochement* with Bismarck, German Catholics continued to feel treated as second-class citizens. Catholics received far fewer important posts in the government than their numbers seemed to demand. The Catholics realized and resented this; thus there was always a latent hostility to the empire and its institutions, which lessened loyalty. The result of this attitude is to be seen in the events of the late World War I and early Weimar periods.

The *Kulturkampf,* Bismarck's attack on the Roman Catholic church, is generally regarded as one of his least successful undertakings. On the surface it seems hardly credible that the astute and subtle chancellor would take a series of gratuitous actions without necessity, which would be bound to alienate a very considerable portion of the population from him and his government. Perhaps the best analysis suggests that the modern highly nationalistic state finds itself almost in the nature of things forced to oppose and attack any such great international organism as the Catholic church (or for that matter international socialism). This may be the best explanation at the philosophical level, but there are other approaches. During the sixties the papacy under the aggressive direction of Pope Pius IX had undertaken a series of forceful acts somewhat in contrast to the defensive attitude that had been characteristic of the papacy in earlier decades. The struggle with the house of Savoy over the unification of Italy, the *Syllabus of Errors,* the definition of the Immaculate Conception, and above all, the definition of Papal Infallibility at the Vatican Council in 1870—all bore witness to a Catholic renascence. These moves alarmed non-Catholic political figures. Contemporary journals witness the widespread fear that every few days the Pope might issue some infallible statement, which would bind all Catholics, on almost any subject. This was of course a complete misunderstanding of the doctrine, but it was often heard. With this sort of possibility Bismarck had no patience. He was determined to be master in Emperor William's house and would brook no division of authority with the pope or anyone else. A possible lever for Bismarck entered the scene with the formation of the "Old Catholics," a group which refused to accept the dogma of Infallibility. In addition to the foregoing considerations, there were others concerning foreign policy, always Bismarck's principal interest. In the European system of the moment Germany was most at odds with the two highly clerical states, France and Austria-Hungary. It was to be feared that the German Catholics, sympathetic to their Catholic neighbors, might be a source of disaffection and disloyalty at home. It was necessary then, reasoned Bismarck, to take preventive action against a possible Catholic plot which might undo the work of the preceding difficult decade.

Bismarck didn't wait long after the Treaty of Frankfurt to launch his offensive against the new Center party. In the summer of 1871 he abolished the Catholic section of the Prussian ministry of culture and education on the grounds that it was pro-Polish. Shortly afterwards he delivered on the floor of the Reichstag a stinging attack on the Center in general, and Windthorst in particular, and secured a law outlawing the Jesuit order. Most of the succeeding repressive legislation was passed by the Prussian parliament rather than by the Reichstag, because matters concerned with such subjects as education were the responsibility of the individual states. In the month of May in 1873, 1874, and 1875, under the direction of Adalbert Falk, Prussian minister of culture and education, a number of laws were passed which are collectively known as the May Laws. They instituted civil marriage, withdrew state support from recalcitrant clergy, placed all clerical education and appointments under the state, dissolved most religious orders, and instituted penal regulations to punish offenders. Before long many priests and bishops were in prison and the situation had become unbearable. Together with these acts went a great deal of talk and agitation. For example, the famous scientist, Rudolf Virchow, described the campaign as a *Kulturkampf*, or struggle for civilization against alleged Catholic obscurantism. Bismarck himself in a public speech stated that he would not go to Canossa, recalling the humiliation of the German emperor Henry IV before Pope St. Gregory VII in the eleventh century. He described the struggle as just one more act in the endless drama of the conflict between state and church for freedom of action.

It seems clear that Bismarck totally misunderstood the Catholic church. As the years went on, he realized that he was only solidifying opposition not only from the Center but also from many of the Conservatives and the more radical Liberals, the former because they feared for their Lutheran church, the latter because these laws were a grave infringement of a basic liberty. Therefore, in the later years of the decade he cast about for a graceful exit from the persecution. An opportunity arose in the death of Pope Pius IX in 1878 and the accession of the flexible and diplomatic but firm and highly intelligent Leo XIII. The new pope wrote to Bismarck the very day of his election. Little by little the two began to understand each other. Bismarck now began to feel the need of support rather than opposition from the Center party, the second largest party in the Reichstag. His alliance with the National Liberals was reaching its last days because of the tariff issue. Further, and this was an important consideration, Bismarck detected the growth of another group much more sinister in its implications than the Catholics and one which the Catholics could be counted on to oppose, namely the Social Democratic party, which had recently reorganized itself and was beginning to appear as a threat. All of these considerations prompted him to retreat from the untenable position into which he had maneuvered himself. The retreat was not dramatic but gradual. During the decade after 1878 most of the laws of the seventies were gradually repealed, and in the late eighties Leo XIII was able to say that the *Kulturkampf* was a thing of the past. In this whole affair Bismarck made one of his worst miscalculations. It seems to bear out the old maxim: *"Qui mange du pape en meurt."* ("He who tries to eat the pope, dies of it.")

The seventies saw also the rise of the party furthest to the left on the German political scene, a party which was to give Bismarck much cause for alarm during the remainder of his ministry. The German Social Democratic party is a complex organism since it had a dual origin and descends from two men opposed in personalities and some of their policies. The effort to compromise between the traditions of Karl Marx and Ferdinand Lassalle is the thread which binds German socialist history together and which eventually becomes decisive in the period when the Social Democrats held the future of Germany pretty much in their hands, the period from 1918 to 1923.

Ferdinand Lassalle deserves the credit for the foundation of the first party of laborers in Germany. Born of a comfortable Jewish family in Breslau, Lassalle grew up as a dilettante, a littérateur, an extravagant dandy in Berlin. He served a jail sentence for meddling in revolutionary activities and later amused himself with the study of law. His notoriety and fame in Germany arose first from the fact that he espoused the cause of the wealthy Countess Hatzfeld who was trying to obtain a divorce. Lassalle took the lady under his legal wing and after years of litigation managed to win her case. After that he had no problem of financial support. During the fifties he turned his errant mind to the "social question" and devised a philosophy aimed at the amelioration of labor. He was a strong believer in universal suffrage and in the organization of the laboring class as a political party and pressure group which would demand a better place in society for itself. He did not, like Marx, envisage the overturn of society and government; indeed he looked forward to a period when a government influenced by labor would exist and a close benevolent and paternalistic relationship would develop between the two. It was this pro-state bent that was to be Lassalle's most heretical legacy to German Social Democracy from the Marxist point of view. Lassalle and Bismarck had a number of conversations and apparently found that their ideas were not hopelessly at odds; in fact, in later years Bismarck publicly acknowledged his admiration for Lassalle. In 1863 Lassalle started seriously to organize the party he had planned. The General German Workers' Association was founded at Leipzig, and for months Lassalle toured the German industrial districts, making speeches and trying to increase the membership of the new group. It did not grow rapidly at first, but the seed was sown. Lassalle had only a short time to perfect his organization, because in the summer of 1864 he got involved in a sordid love affair and was killed at the age of thirty-nine in a duel by the Romanian noble fiancé of his sweetheart. The Association continued, however, led by some of Lassalle's friends and financed by Countess Hatzfeld. It grew gradually during the decade of the sixties.

Toward the end of that decade, as a result of the publication of the first volume of *Das Kapital* in 1867, the doctrine of Karl Marx, hitherto little known in Germany, started to spread and to compete with Lassallean thought. The two men most closely associated with the introduction of Marxism as a political force in Germany were August Bebel and Wilhelm Liebknecht, both of whom had spent some time in the Lassallean camp. Bebel, a product of the working classes, was an admirable organizer. Liebknecht, a revolutionary from the days of '48, had known and admired Marx while in exile in London. Both of them were suspicious of the statist character of Lassalle's doctrine and decided to establish a pure Marxist party, which they did in August 1869 at Eisenach. For several years there were two competing parties claiming the allegiance of the proletariat.

Finally in 1875 the two groups met together at Gotha to hammer out a unified program, and the German Socialist party, properly speaking, came into existence. The program had to be a compromise, and many overtones of Lassalle can be detected in it though it pays lip service to Marxism. Marx himself was very dissatisfied with it and wrote a severe criticism of the Gotha program.

During the seventies the votes of the socialists increased with growing industrialization and particularly as an aftermath of the depression of 1873. In the election of 1877 the socialists returned twelve members to the Reichstag. Bismarck viewed this development with grave misgiving and resolved to find an opportunity to squelch this new, potentially dangerous group. The occasion arose in 1878. In that year two attempts were made on the life of the emperor. The first left him unscathed, but the second wounded the old man badly. Neither of these attempts was directly traceable to the socialists, but Bismarck used them as a pretext for dissolving the Reichstag and calling new elections, which resulted in a gain for the right-wing parties and a loss of three seats for the socialists.

Promptly Bismarck placed before the chamber a project for an antisocialist law and secured its passage by the votes of the two conservative parties and the increasingly demoralized National Liberals. The law was very stringent. It prohibited socialist meetings and publications and provided that a state of siege could be proclaimed for enforcement. The law was renewed three times and remained in force until 1890. During that period the only place where socialist oratory could be legally heard was on the floor of the Reichstag itself, where the socialist members were protected by parliamentary immunity.

As was the case with the broadside attack on the Catholics, the antisocialist law failed miserably in its purpose. Between 1878 and 1890 the socialist vote increased from just over three hundred thousand to almost one and one half million, while the party's membership in the Reichstag jumped from nine members to thirty-five.

During the eighties Bismarck continued to rule for the most part with the alliance of Conservatives and Centrists, which had been formed at the time of the tariff controversy. Most of the major events of this period were in the field of foreign policy and will therefore be discussed later. The one major domestic contribution of the early eighties was the series of social security laws which were enacted, but they too will be described in another connection. In 1887 the chancellor enjoyed his ultimate triumph and undertook his last shift in party alignment. On this occasion the issue was the so-called Septennate, or bill by which army estimates would be considered by the Reichstag only every seven years. This proposal harked back in a sense to the period of the constitutional conflict in Prussia in the sixties. Bismarck called a new election and secured the passage of his bill by the Cartel, or coalition of Conservatives and National Liberals; the Center once more passed into opposition in spite of a suggestion from Pope Leo XIII that it support the chancellor. This achievement did not mean, however, that liberalism was rejuvenated. It meant rather that the liberals, having lost their *élan* some years before, were just submissive to the increasingly autocratic Bismarck. This was Bismarck's last victory. The next year his beloved old William I died, and gradually the supports were pulled from beneath the founder of the empire.

Taken in balance, Bismarck's achievement as a domestic political statesman cannot be praised unqualifiedly. It is true that in almost every major issue he managed to get what he wanted. However, he left behind him a heritage of discontent and bitterness veiled by his apparent outward success. The increasingly important Social Democrats were irreconcilable opponents of the regime. The Catholics, one-third of the population, were in opposition and chronically resentful of neglect. The Progressives always voted against the government. The National Liberals had lost, or been deprived of, their chance to make liberalism a vital force in German society. Only the Conservatives were dependable. As long as the old master with a vitriolic tongue and cynical shrewdness was there to dominate events, a façade of success and power could be maintained. Yet the days were drawing close when he would no longer be there.

CHAPTER X

Bismarck's Germany. II, Economic and Social (1871-88)

The great single fact about Germany in the period under consideration is her phenomenal economic development. This and its implications, both social and political, dwarf the other aspects of German life. The Germany of the early years of the twentieth century bore little resemblance to the Germany of the year of unification. From a parochial land, well behind her western neighbors, she had become an industrial giant exceeded only by the United States. Probably there is no similarly rapid development recorded in history. The only parallels are Japan at about the same period and the Soviet Union after 1927. This amazing development brought, however, a whole train of problems to Germany as the industrial revolution did to all other countries, problems by no means yet resolved either in Germany or elsewhere.

The velocity and date of Germany's economic strides made her story somewhat different from that of the other major industrial powers. Some economists suggest that one of the keys to Germany's success is to be found in the fact that she was almost a century behind Great Britain in her industrialization. She could thus profit from the mistakes and growing pains of the British economy. Furthermore, she was able to start her modernization with more highly perfected machinery and thus avoid some of the problems of obsolescence. Another peculiarity of the German development was that almost from the start she united science with technology and industry. It is commonplace today for great companies to have large laboratories where pure research is carried out and for there to be close liaison between universities and industry. That was far from usual in the late nineteenth century, and Germany must be given much of the credit for it.

A measure of the industrial growth is the growth of the population. Between 1871 and 1910 the population of Germany increased by more than half, from just over forty million to almost sixty-five million. Contrast this with France, which between 1876 and 1911 moved from about thirty-seven million to thirty-nine and a half million. Most of the growth was in the towns and cities. In 1871 about 36 per cent of Germans lived in towns; by 1910 fully 60 per cent did. During the mid-nineteenth century there was a steady drain on the German population, caused by emigration mostly to the United States and to South America. By the end of the century this stream was reduced to a trickle because German industry was able to absorb the increasing population. In fact, by the turn of the century Germany actually experienced a labor shortage and came to depend upon transient foreign labor at harvest time.

Much of the German industrial prowess is not completely the achievement of the Germans. Germany was endowed richly with natural resources, perhaps more richly than some Germans have wanted to admit. In the enormous coal deposits of the Rhineland-Westphalia district, centering in the Ruhr Basin, and in the large coal areas of Silesia she had almost the coal wealth of England. In addition, there are rich lignite deposits in central Germany. In iron ore she has not been so favored, but the iron deposits of Silesia and of the Saar area are important. After the annexation of Lorraine in 1871 her position was much improved, and conditions became even more favorable as science developed techniques for the extraction of low-grade ores. In other minerals, notably potash, Germany was relatively fortunate as well.

A major impetus for the development of heavy industry in Germany as elsewhere was the building of a railway network. This not only made the demand for steel soar, but also, by binding the country together, made easy the distribution of finished products. The first German railway resulted from the enthusiasm of King Louis I of Bavaria, who built in 1835 the earliest line between Nuremberg and neighboring Fürth. Yet the economist Friedrich List deserves the title of father of German railroads. He conceived of a great system of lines which would radiate principally from Berlin. The Prussian government, however, was at first not much interested in railway building, and it was in Saxony that the second important line was opened, between Dresden and Leipzig. However, during the decade of the forties Prussian governmental reluctance was overcome, and many concessions were granted for the laying of new track. By 1850 Germany had about half again as much trackage as France, and most of the main German cities were connected by steel. In the sixties the importance of railways as military adjuncts was realized, and Moltke in his strategic plans made full use of the well-developed system. Thus in both 1866 and 1870 the superiority of German railways was a factor in the rapid Prussian and German victories.

Almost as important for Germany as her railroad system is her canal system. The main German rivers run from southeast to northwest. The problem thus was to connect the basins by a number of east-to-west canals. This was not very difficult because of the flatness of the north German plain and the low elevation of watersheds. Canals were not new to Germany; but after the railway network was laid out, great sums were spent both on building new ones and widening and deepening existing ones. Among the best known which date from the imperial period are the Kaiser Wilhelm (or Kiel) Canal across the Jutland Peninsula and the Dortmund-Ems Canal connecting the Rhine with the Ems Basin, thus enabling Rhine shipping to get through to the North Sea without leaving German waters. This canal-building activity did not end with the imperial period but was pushed both by the Weimar Republic and by Nazi Germany. Some of the achievements of these later years were the Mittelland Canal across north Germany and the great ship elevator on the canal leading from Berlin to its port of Stettin. Along with the development of the canal system went the improvement of inland cities as deep water ports. The most impressive of them is the enormous harbor of Duisburg-Ruhrort; perhaps more unusual is the fact that Mannheim-Ludwigshafen, about three hundred miles from open water, is a deep water port with heavy traffic.

The building of great ships and the development of a large merchant marine came a little later. By the end of the century both Hamburg and Bremen had increased the capacity of their harbors, and the two greatest German steamship companies, the Hamburg-America and the North German Lloyd, were actively competing for both passenger and freight transportation with ships of other nations. In fact, in the nineties a German ship, the "Kaiser Wilhelm der Grosse," held for some years the blue ribbon for transatlantic service.

In the field of heavy industry, coal mining and steel hold pride of place in the period. Both boomed incalculably in the years between unification and war. Coal production jumped from twenty-nine million to one hundred ninety-one million metric tons. This compares with a British production of one hundred eighteen and two hundred ninety-two, and a French production of thirteen and forty respectively. In addition, by 1913 Germany was producing eighty-seven million metric tons of lignite as opposed to eight million in 1871. In Europe only Britain was ahead of Germany.

In the case of iron and steel the story is even more spectacular. Germany managed to overtake Great Britain in steel production between 1890 and 1900 and in pig iron output in the following decade, while France and Belgium were left trailing pitifully behind. The German steel industry was dominated by a few big names, or more properly dynasties, of which Krupp is the best known. The first Krupp, at the beginning of the nineteenth century, had a small forge in the village of Essen, where, as a result of experimentation, he discovered a process for making cast steel. His son Alfred developed the great industry associated with the name. As a supplier of locomotives and steel rails, he was supported by the railway boom. The munitions industry was also centered largely around Krupp, who became known as the Cannon King. By 1914 Krupp was employing almost seventy thousand workers. In 1820 Essen had a population of four thousand; by 1910 it had increased to four hundred ten thousand. The dynasty still continues under Alfried Krupp von Bohlen und Halbach. (Bertha Krupp, heiress to the fortune, married Gustav von Bohlen und Halbach, who added the word Krupp to his name. The present head of the family is their son.)

One could run the gamut of the various types of industry and see a similar frenzied activity. The textile factories increased greatly; the cutlery business was so advanced that it was possible to buy German cutlery in Sheffield, England, long the world's center for this industry. In two industries Germany approached pre-eminence. They are the chemical and electrical industries. Germany is well endowed with chemical resources. In the late nineteenth century she began to exploit them very extensively, though as yet not significantly for export. They were mainly consumed at home. Yet the foundation was laid for the creation of the famous I. G. Farben combine in the Weimar Republic period. In electricity the advances are connected mainly with two names: Werner von Siemens, inventor of the dynamo; and Emil Rathenau. These two men were the founders of the two great combines which in due course divided Germany's (and much of the world's) electrical business between them. Siemens and Halske Co. and the German General Electric Co. (Allgemeine Elektrizitäts-Gesellschaft, generally known as the A.E.G.) were the respective creations of these men and remain today a basic part of the world's electrical industry.

This industrial and commercial growth necessitated a growth in banking facilities. In finance Germany developed a modern and highly integrated system composed partly of banks that had been in existence before 1871 and partly of others founded shortly after unification. They revolved around the Reichsbank, the central bank of issue, chartered in 1875. As in the case of industry, the tendency of banking in Germany was to integrate into several very large units rather than to spread among small corporations. Thus four large institutions had the most powerful, though not the exclusive, hand in German financing. There were the Deutsche, the Darmstädter, the Dresdener banks and the Discontogesellschaft. From the start the relationship between finance and industry was very close, and a complicated system of interlocking directorates evolved. Much of the banks' energies were connected with the financing of new enterprises, and in the course of time the leading banks developed extensive relationships abroad with attendant political implications.

An important development in German economic history was the tendency to form cartels, or monopolies, which became noticeable in the seventies but gathered much more momentum in the eighties. There were many sorts of cartels, but their basic component was an agreement among the large entrepreneurs in any given industry to regulate or limit output and to fix prices. The protective tariff legislation of 1879 gave this movement a distinct push by tending to eliminate, or at least reduce, the flow of foreign goods into the German market. Thus in the eighties cartels proliferated. Before 1877 there were fourteen cartels; between 1879 and 1885 seventy-six were formed; in the following five years one hundred twenty more appeared. At the end of the century there were about two hundred seventy-five in active operation.

By the turn of the twentieth century Germany was transformed economically. Not only had she evolved an imposing economic system, but this system was largely in the hands of a relatively small number of extremely influential men. The story of the leading German industrial dynasties is an absorbing one for the social, as well as the economic, historian. It was not all clear sailing for these people. Germany endured the vagaries of the business cycle along with the rest of the world. The two or three years immediately after the Franco-Prussian War were unprecedentedly prosperous in Germany. It is said that more factories were established between 1870 and 1873 than in the preceding seventy years of the century. Part of this is traceable to the French indemnity, much of which was thrown upon the market as the government redeemed many of its obligations. The effect of the panic of 1873 in the United States was felt very quickly in Europe, and the years following were years of severe depression in Germany and central Europe in general. They led to the clamor for protection that had such important political results in Germany. However, in the long run nothing could stop the astounding German industrial boom.

The story is not quite so rosy on the agricultural side of the German economy, although there was progress in this area too. By unification, most of the settlement of the serf question was complete and the pattern of landholding pretty well crystallized. A free peasantry and a landed gentry controlled the land. The pattern varied sharply from west to east. West of the Elbe the characteristic (though not exclusive) holding was that of the small free farmer who farmed intensively a small plot of land.

The land east of the Elbe was dominated by the large landholder who employed many peasants and engaged in extensive agriculture. His farming efficiency was often called into question, and the problem of various types of subsidy for the marginal eastern farmer remained an important political question right into the days of the Nazis.

Efforts were made to improve and develop scientific agriculture throughout the century. The most important name in this connection is Justus Liebig, who was a pioneer in the application of chemistry to agriculture. His ideas were taken up and developed by new departments in the universities and by schools devoted exclusively to agricultural study, which were favored by the government and tried successfully to increase the product of the soil. This was necessary because during the period 1870–90 Germany ceased to be able to feed herself and became increasingly dependent on foreign importation. These were the years too of the migration from country to city. A result of this shift was a labor shortage on the farms, and an invitation to greater per capita productivity.

The landowners, reacting to these various changes in their position, solidified themselves into an important political lobby of the Conservative party. It has been seen how this development led in great part to the passage of the protective tariff and the change of Bismarck's party orientation in the eighties. In the reign of William II the landowners were to play an even more strategic role in government.

These economic shifts and the general transformation of German life led to basic changes in the social pattern. Perhaps the most obvious was the rapid urbanization, the changeover from a rural to an urban economy. Here again the statistics are astonishing. The most spectacular are those of Berlin, which around 1820 had been a comfortable little city of nearly two hundred thousand but which became by 1914 a megalopolis of over two million, one of the largest in the world. There was a big gap between Berlin and the second largest German city, Hamburg, which contained just under a million; but no less than four other cities, Munich, Leipzig, Cologne, and Breslau, had passed the half million mark. The Westphalian industrial area, hard to estimate because of the number of separate municipalities, must have been one of the largest concentrations in the world, containing within a radius of less than fifty miles from its center Cologne, Essen, Dortmund, Duisburg, Düsseldorf, Barmen, Elberfeld, Bochum, and many other smaller communities.

This enormously rapid growth of big cities led in Germany as elsewhere to the introduction of new and serious problems. Perhaps the most urgent was housing for the new arrivals. The industrial slum, with its human tragedy, came into being; in spite of efforts to control the problem, and great building enterprises, the lot of the worker was abject. Berlin, in particular, developed a tragic situation which any reader of Jakob Wassermann's moving novel *Christian Wahnschaffe* (translated into English as *The World's Illusion*) is familiar with. There were also problems of education, health and sanitation, recreation, parks, and transportation, which had to be faced very suddenly.

New social classes arose with the new society, blurring the old familiar trinity of nobility, bourgeoisie, and peasantry. Industry brought two new classes to Germany: a small upper middle class, and a much larger class of industrial workers. The new upper middle class was composed of the industrial magnates, bankers, and businessmen. It formed a plutocracy which overshadowed the older commercial patriciate immortalized by Thomas Mann in *Buddenbrooks*. Socially it looked upward toward the aristocracy rather than downward toward the humbler bourgeois towns-folk. Increasingly intermarriage between the two upper classes occurred, thus further blurring the class picture. A unique early example of the growing union between land and industry was the wealthy and aristo-cratic Silesian landowner, Henckel von Donnersmarck, who bought up much profitable coal-mining property in his area and also involved him-self with French financial interests, thus combining the three important strands of the new society: the land, heavy industry, and international business.

The growth of the industrial proletariat has been a typical feature of Western civilization and has caused obvious and decisive repercussions in the modern world. This was certainly the case in Germany, where the political importance of the proletariat is witnessed by the booming mem-bership of the Social Democratic party. Bismarck was probably right in 1866 when he believed that universal suffrage was a conservative in-strument; by 1890 he had realized that times had changed and that univer-sal suffrage had placed an important part of the control of the vote in the hands of the new radical class of workers.

Together with the increase in industrial workers went the development of the trade union movement for their protection. The enactment by the North German Confederation in 1869 of a law permitting the estab-lishment of workers' associations ended old prohibitions and paved the way for the development of the union movement. This development did not occur immediately, however. The union movement lagged behind industrialization and even behind the Social Democratic party. Although there were some foundations in the early years of the *Reich,* it was not until the decade of the nineties that German unionism became a major force, and even then it did not develop along unified lines. There were three main union organizations, though one far overshadowed the others both in numbers and in influence. This was the so-called Free

Trade Union movement, Marxist in coloration and closely affiliated with the Social Democratic party. By the turn of the century the membership of this group approached seven hundred thousand, but by 1912 it had passed two and a half million. Though the leadership of this movement (Carl Legien being the most prominent leader) worked closely with the Social Democrats and at times ruled in party decisions, by no means all of the union members were also members of the party. There was, however, a strong tendency for them to vote the Social Democratic ticket. It is also noteworthy, given the future importance of the party, that the trade union leadership was consistently on the conservative wing of the party. Trade unionism is not a revolutionary movement. It is a vested interest and has no desire to overthrow a social order in which it has a place of respectability and even prestige. The influence of the union leaders in the party councils was to contribute important pages to the history of the revolution of 1918 and the Weimar Republic.

The second of the union movements was known as the Christian Trade Unions. Christian social thought derived from Emanuel von Ketteler, bishop of Mainz, who back in the fifties and sixties had become conscious of the new shifts in society and of the need for the church to provide ways to keep the industrial worker close to his religion. This sort of thinking was found all over Europe but very particularly in Germany, where Catholics were conscious of their minority status. It received impetus during the pontificate of Pope Leo XIII, who was the first pope to concern himself greatly with the new social problems. The growth of the Marxist parties, specifically based on a philosophy of materialism, alarmed Christians, who saw a frightening leakage from all the churches. The early history of the Christian Union movement is a complicated one because there were some very divergent theories on its organization and ideology. By 1899, however, most of these had been ironed out, and at Mainz a united platform was adopted and a central organization formed. At that time there were about fifty thousand members of Christian unions; by 1913 there were over three hundred thousand. They remained about one-seventh the size of the Free Unions but at times had an influence disproportionate to their size. Although they were founded mainly under Catholic auspices, they welcomed Protestant membership and were technically interdenominational. Their major political allegiance was to the Center party, although this relationship was far more tenuous than that of the Free Unions and the Social Democrats. They stood on the left wing of the Center party, and the best-known Christian Union leader, Adam Stegerwald, was viewed askance by some of the conservative Center leadership.

The third group was known as the Hirsch-Duncker Unions after the two men who had been influential in their foundation. They were liberal in character, neither Marxist nor Christian. They believed in a policy of self-help in the old liberal tradition. This group was the smallest of the three, numbering by 1913 slightly over one hundred thousand members.

Bismarck was not blind to the transformation of Germany which took such rapid strides during his tenure of office. He was forced to turn from his favorite sport of the higher diplomacy and to interest himself in economic and social problems. Perhaps it is putting it too strongly to say that Bismarck did this against his will, for he had a sort of inarticulate concept of the patriarchal state which forced him to be concerned with social welfare. His heritage gave him a concept of paternalism as far as the management of an estate was concerned; from this to paternalism in the management of the state is not a very long step. There was a sense of *noblesse oblige,* not unlike that of the British Conservatives of the Disraeli type, which made it imperative for those high on the social ladder to keep a fatherly eye on those lower down. It is not too much to suggest that Bismarck's abortive friendship with Lassalle was based on this mutual acceptance of the state's responsibility to its population. Add to this Bismarck's severe distrust of the Social Democratic party and a consequent urge to take some of the wind from its sails, and you have sufficient motivation for the series of "social security" laws which he pushed through the Reichstag in the last decade of his rule.

In 1881 Bismarck introduced his new program of social legislation, perhaps the most constructive series of acts of his whole career. Both in addresses of his own and in the speech from the throne, he emphasized the right and the duty of the state to protect the welfare of the workers. He introduced a bill calling for a system of health insurance providing for both medical attention and half pay in case of illness. Insurance funds were provided, to be paid for by employer, employee, and the state. The Reichstag received these proposals very unfavorably. Particularly angry were the National Liberals who saw here the abandonment of *laissez faire.* They managed to eliminate the state as a contributor to the fund; its function became simply that of managing the fund and paying for administration. After much political juggling the bill finally became law. The following year a similar bill was introduced to cover accident insurance and was forced through the legislature. Finally in 1889 an even more grandiose project was passed, namely an old age and invalidity pension act. In this act the state did contribute one-third of the fund. During the reign of William II the system was enlarged and perfected, with the result that Germany was the first power to have an extensive social security system.

The Germany of 1871 was almost legendary to the German of 1890.

His whole life had been changed in those two decades. Germany was no longer the backward stepchild of the preceding two centuries. She was now fully competent to compete and keep up with the other great nations of the world. Indeed she was actively doing it. This fact is important to an understanding of the international tensions leading to World War I. Great Britain no longer dominated the world economically. She had grave competition from both Germany and the United States. There were some in the late eighties who wondered if the aging chancellor had not perhaps outlived his time, if his basically conservative and defensive policy were still the right one for the new Germany. There were many who were in sympathy with the new young emperor who was restive under the rule of the older generation, who looked forward to a fuller entrance of Germany into the affairs of the whole world, and who with his love for the sea typically summarized his longings with the phrase, "Full speed ahead."

CHAPTER XI

Bismarck's Germany. III, Intellectual (1871-88)

In matters of the mind and spirit, as in matters political, the Germany of the late nineteenth century was divided against itself. The similarity does not stop there, because in intellectual matters as in political the casual observer saw a monolithic structure of science, study, research, and creativity, which looked solid and presented an aspect of unity to the outside world deceiving many of the ablest critics of the time. It has taken several generations and the collapse of the German state and society for historians to realize that there were many intellectual fissures in the German fabric. The historian of today is likely to look at nineteenth-century Germany with the thought of finding reasons for the collapse in the twentieth century. This type of history can be, and frequently has been, overdone. Perhaps this is why history has to be rewritten every generation. The difference between a history of Germany written by a non-German in 1912 and such a history written today is revealing. In the earlier work the motto on the title page might have been, "Hail to the Great Chancellor"; the later one might well read, "Why the *Führer?*" And much of this revisionist approach to German history has occurred in the realm of ideas.

There is little to be gained from a mere catalog of the names and major accomplishments of the German thinkers, writers, artists, composers, and scientists of this very full period. It appears more fruitful to single out a few of the more important or more typical of them to see what they can teach by way of understanding Bismarckian Germany more fully.

The official line of the time, the one most noticeable to the contemporary observer, was one of proud, self-satisfied confidence, rather noisy, often smug, frequently vulgar, always forceful. The words grandiose and colossal (in German *grossartig* and *kolossal*) come to mind. Such artistic monstrosities as the Reichstag building, the Protestant cathedral, or the statues on the *Sieges Allée* in the *Tiergarten,* all in Berlin, seem symbolic monuments of this aspect of the period. The triumph of military might, the achievement of unity, the economic upsurge—all seemed to bear witness to the soundness of the old Prussian virtues: frugality, hard work, diligence, industry, discipline, and, it might be added, an almost complete lack of imagination or humor.

A literary work which reflects many of these typically parvenu virtues is the extremely popular novel by Gustav Freytag, *Soll und Haben* (*"Profit and Loss"*). This work is a monument of smugness and self-satisfaction. Had it been written in the United States, its author might have been Thomas Edison, Elbert Hubbard, Henry Ford, or Calvin Coolidge. A boy is left an orphan at a tender age by his father, a country clergyman, whose only heritage to his son is a letter recommending him to the care of an old friend, a successful businessman in the neighboring large town. The boy goes to the town, regretfully leaving behind the little girl to whom he is romantically attached. She is the daughter of the local squire, a feckless scion of old nobility, who, as the book progresses, tries to retrieve his waning fortune by establishing a sugar beet refinery on his estates, a project in which he fails because of a lack of business ability. He is then forced to put himself in the hands of the unscrupulous Jews. Having arrived in the town, the boy enters his father's friend's company and by dint of long hours, hard work, and obsequiousness, in due course makes good. His way is not without pitfalls however. He has to withstand the blandishments of high society when the girl's family comes to town, the temptations of Bohemianism caused by the arrival of a ne'er-do-well relative of his employer, the evil machinations of the Jews, and the ferocious foreign nationalism of some extraordinary Polish revolutionaries. All the components are there: the rising middle class, the declining aristocracy, German nationalism, and anti-Semitism (an attitude observable in almost all lines of German thinking). Freytag was a very popular author and by no means the only representative of his type.

It was not only the writers of fiction who fell under the spell of the new success. Historians too succumbed to the siren call of the Prussian trumpet. The greatest of the historians of the period, Leopold von Ranke, is to be criticized less than others. However, even he, with his naive belief in objective history, sometimes struck a blow for the German idea. It is more particularly in the work of two of his contemporaries, Heinrich von Treitschke and Heinrich von Sybel, that we find the obeisance to Bismarck and Hohenzollern. Treitschke, one of the most popular professors at the University of Berlin, left as his most enduring work his

German History in the Nineteenth Century (which does not reach beyond 1847). This work, written with a sure touch for language, is the fruit of massive learning and scholarship: all that is Prussian, Protestant, and north German is good; all that is Austrian, south German, and Catholic is decadent and effeminate. Sybel was commissioned by the Prussian government to write a history of the unification and given access to many state documents seen by a scholar for the first time. His resultant multivolume *Foundation of the German Empire,* again profoundly scholarly and rarely inaccurate in matters of fact, is also a lyric account of the wisdom, skill, and power of the Prussian kingdom. These two historians and their fellows created the historiographical background for the world's view of the German Empire which lasted at least until 1918 and to an extent until 1933.

A study of the opposing movements is more difficult. In the first place they are variant, some insisting on different lines of approach from others. The only unifying thread is general opposition to Bismarck's solution of the German question and a feeling of uneasiness caused by the triumphant materialism of the environment. There were also some who were on the whole unpolitical, influenced heavily by French literature of the period. They tended to start as naturalists in the Goncourt tradition and to end up as symbolists, affected by the general *fin-de-siècle* attitude. Examples of this group are Gerhart Hauptmann and Hermann Sudermann.

Perhaps more interesting and certainly more significant for the future of Germany is a group of thinkers who veered very far from the line set officially and proclaimed a Germany built around objectives far different from those of Bismarck. On the whole they were men who reasoned with their hearts (or guts) rather than their heads, who depended on emotion and instinct rather than on the calculated rationality of the contemporary Prussian state.

One of the earliest and most interesting of them was the turbulent revolutionary composer Richard Wagner. The very vicissitudes of his fevered life give some suggestion of his approach to artistic and political problems. Born into an impoverished musical family in Leipzig, he spent much of his young manhood fighting against the conservative musical bureaucracies of provincial German towns and trying to gain acceptance for his own characteristically styled "music of the future." When he had achieved a certain degree of acceptance in Dresden in the forties, Wagner managed to get involved in the abortive revolt there in the spring of 1849, as a result of which he was exiled from the German Confederation and spent the following decade and more mostly in Switzerland. These years were active ones of composition, writing, and amorous adventure. There followed some years of relative prosperity in Munich under the protection of the eccentric Louis II, who reveled in Wagner's re-creation of the legendary German past. However, the master's extravagance and flouting of moral convention brought this period to an end and led to a voluntary exile again in Switzerland, which was followed by the apotheosis of his last years in Bayreuth where he established the home of what he felt was the new German art, his festival theater for the performance of his music dramas.

Deeply imbedded in Wagner's spirit was the concept of the German *Volk,* a notion hard to make clear to the English speaker. *Volk* connotes more than nation or race or people; it is more than the sum of its individuals; it is a mystical commonalty whose existence is its own defense. Wagner felt that the unique quality of the German *Volk* required it to have its own specific flowering in art. The art forms of the past were inadequate. The new form which was to express the German psyche was the *Gesamtkunstwerk* ("total art work"), in which each of the arts would have its place. Germany needed a national theater where her art could be performed in its total purity; Wagner apparently felt seriously that a consecrational festival of art would purify the German soul. For the subjects of his dramas he looked to the misty past of Germanic mythology; gods and goddesses, giants, dwarfs, and heroes and heroines, rather than commonplace Mimis or Carmens, flood his stages. This was a German world in which elemental passions could have free rein, before the limiting forces of Western, Roman, or Christian rationality curbed the magnificence of the full emotional expression of the blond tribesman of the primitive forests. It did not seem to occur to Wagner that it required the sophistication of modern symphonic orchestration and stagecraft to render his visions practicable.

Wagner's ideas are most completely represented in his last two musical achievements, *Der Ring des Nibelungen* (composed of the four units, *"Das Rheingold," "Die Walküre," "Siegfried,"* and *"Die Götterdämmerung"*) and *Parsifal.* The *Ring* begins in the depths of the Rhine, where three unexplained mermaids bewail the theft by a malicious dwarf from the underworld of the hoard of gold which it was their responsibility to guard. Whoever steals or possesses the gold must renounce love. The first criticism of mammon and materialism thus appears at the outset. We are then whisked to the skies where we find that the chief of the gods, Wotan, has compromised himself and his fellows by an ungodly and unfree act. He has contracted (and the motive for contract in the orchestra is the most sinister motive in the *Ring*) a pair of outsize giants to build him a castle in the skies, in return for which he will deliver to them the goddess of love. The castle, Valhalla, is finished and the goddess is handed over, but the gods find that without love they are losing their youth. The giants are then asked what they will accept in place of the goddess. They reply that they will accept the gold hoard recently stolen from the Rhine by the dwarf. This involves Wotan in further deceit, for he must now compound his worship of mammon by stealing the gold from the dwarfs. This he does with the help of the guileful god of fire, Loge (the only intelligent person in the whole drama). The giants accept the gold, and the curse on it starts to work immediately as one giant kills the other and, transforming himself into a dragon, heads for a cave in the forest to guard his treasure.

Wotan now decides to adopt a long-term policy to salvage as much as possible from the debacle he foresees. He begets two earth children, who in turn become the parents of the greatest hero of the world, Siegfried. We first see Siegfried as a beamish boy bouncing on the stage with his playmate, a bear. In the course of that act a good deal is sung about Siegfried, but it turns out that his most outstanding characteristic is that he is fearless. Happily for his reputation no comment is made about Siegfried's intellectual qualities; it is his fearlessness that is important. This virtue qualifies him to awaken a sleeping maiden, the formerly godlike Brünnhilde, who for disobedience has been deprived of her godhood and put to sleep surrounded by fire until someone freer than the god, Wotan, awakens her. It is notable that fearlessness and physical prowess give Siegfried this power of freedom. Finally in the last drama the world is consumed by flame and a new dispensation begins because humanity has been redeemed through love, though it is never quite clear what sort of love is involved.

A similar emphasis is to be seen in Wagner's last drama, *Parsifal*, which he calls a "consecrational festival drama." In the first act we find that the guardians of the Holy Grail are in unhappy straits as the result of the sin of their leader, Amfortas. One of the older guardians predicts that this can be cured only through the ministrations of a "guileless fool." Relatively soon thereafter Parsifal makes his appearance trying to shoot a sacred swan with his bow and arrow. There can be no question that the words "guileless" and "fool" apply accurately to this young man. He is given a chance to attend the celebration of the mysteries of the Grail, but so guileless is he that he doesn't even bother to ask what he has witnessed, a condition precedent to the redemption of the knights, which is thus postponed for about twenty years. Again the emphasis is upon emotion, faith, and physical strength rather than reason. Much the same thing is to be seen in Wagner's other works, notably *Tannhäuser, Lohengrin,* and *Tristan und Isolde.*

The thrilling mastery of musical composition which Wagner possessed so richly and the revolutionary intensity of his music divided musical Germany into two camps, one worshiping him and the other despising him. In the last decade of his life, with the help of his devotees, Wagner established his festival town in the little city of Bayreuth in northern Bavaria, and there he directed the production of his dramas and in his home welcomed the growing circle of admirers who made the pilgrimage to the *Meister* until his death, which occurred in Venice in 1883. The circle continued to exist under the leadership of Wagner's widow, Cosima, daughter of the composer Franz Liszt and former wife of the Wagnerian conductor Hans von Bülow whom she left to the scandal of society to marry her lover, the *Meister*.

Given Wagner's belief in the blood and the physical aspects of life, it is no surprise that he was a leading anti-Semite, although there is just a possibility that he may have been half Jewish himself. He crusaded constantly against the alleged Jewish influence in music and politics and against banking and industrial progress which he felt to be a result of Jewish mammonism. Wagner ran across the work of an eccentric Frenchman, Count Alfred Gobineau, who in the fifties had written *Essai sur l'inégalité des races* (*"Essay on the Inequality of Races"*), and thought highly of it. He even invited Gobineau to Bayreuth. A cult devoted to the virtues of the progressive Aryans grew up around Gobineau and close to the Wagner group. In the nineties a Gobineau society was even established. However, probably the most notable contributor to German racist ideas at the time was a renegade Englishman named Houston Stewart Chamberlain. Chamberlain was distantly related to that family of hardware manufacturers which was later to furnish Great Britain with a colonial secretary, a foreign secretary, and a prime minister. He went to Germany, fell in love with it, transferred his allegiance, married one of Wagner's daughters, and eventually settled in Bayreuth. In 1899 he published his major achievement, the *Foundations of the Nineteenth Century,* a long and rambling work in which he identifies Gobineau's Aryans with the Germans and reassures the world that the German stock can be cleansed from such impurities as have crept into it in the course of the centuries. He prophesied a future German domination of the world and preached a type of expansionism which was sharply opposed to the *kleindeutsch* solution of Bismarck and the peace policy of the old chancellor. It is interesting to note that in the 1920's, when Hitler's name was first becoming known, Chamberlain was still alive and wrote to the new *Führer,* acclaiming him as the leader who was to come.

It was at a far higher level than the foregoing that the major revolutionary philosopher of the period, Friedrich Nietzsche, operated. Very few figures in modern times have been as influential as he, and yet he has not been widely understood. An unsystematic and obscure thinker whose semipoetic and semiprophetic prose increases the difficulty of comprehension, he has been vulgarized and cheapened by many of his readers to such an extent that he is at least as important for what people thought he meant as for what he actually did mean. Nietzsche was increasingly appalled by tendencies he observed in the world about him and was a devastating critic of modern culture. He hated all things in our society which lead to a leveling of men and culture. Thus democracy and socialism were anathema to him. He hated bourgeois morality and the gentle virtues of meekness and humility. Therefore, capitalist industry and especially Christianity were among his targets. The very titles of some of his works (e.g., *The Reversal of all Values, Beyond Good and Evil*) betray his thoroughgoing iconoclasm. Nietzsche received his academic training in classical philology and published his early works on ancient Greece, for which he had had a great enthusiasm. However, the Greece he loved was the archaic period of Greek history, the heroic age, an age supposedly composed of warriors and unfettered Dionysiac revels, an age not yet bound by the stultifying rationalism later imposed by Socrates, Plato, and Aristotle, and above all, not crushed by the servile morality of Christianity. This same line of thought can be traced throughout Nietzsche's later writing. He calls for aristocrats of the spirit, an elite of freedom, action, virility, and will. The power of the will is a consistent theme (one of Nietzsche's works is entitled *The Will to Power*). He developed the concept of the superman (*Übermensch*) who was to be the moral giant whose type might still regenerate the sick world, not the physical blond beast of the Nazi caricature. Anti-intellectual and amoral, Nietzsche put his trust in instinct, faith, and will. He struck sharply at the roots of the classical Western tradition of rationality and Christianity.

In view of this, it is not surprising that Nietzsche became an early disciple of Wagnerianism. As a young man he spent idyllic visits with Wagner and Cosima at their retreat at Triebschen on Lake Lucerne. There the friendship between the young enthusiast and the middle-aged master ripened into a species of hero worship. Wagner's hopes for the emancipation of the German *Volk* found immediate response from Nietzsche, who was also thrilled by Wagner's resuscitation of the heroes of German mythology. Siegfried, indeed, is perhaps the most perfect approach to the superman. In later years Nietzsche went to Bayreuth to hear the *Ring*. The relationship changed abruptly, however, when in 1882 Nietzsche made the pilgrimage to Bayreuth to hear the first performance of *Parsifal*. This work filled him with contempt. He left the festival town immediately, exclaiming that Wagner in his old age had knelt before the cross. There ensued a bitter exchange of polemic and venom in which Nietzsche had the advantage because he outlived Wagner in sanity by six or seven years. In 1889 Nietzsche was confined to a mental institution where he remained until his death in 1900.

Nietzsche was dimly aware in his last months of sanity that he was beginning to attract an audience, which had not been the case before. During the nineties he became a rage, for his writings were exciting, obscure, and somehow dangerous. The cult of Nietzsche spread throughout the world and with it the misunderstanding of what he was aiming at. The physical emphasis and the talk of violence, virility, and will are easy to vulgarize. Thus Nietzsche has become one of the most misunderstood thinkers and indeed hailed as a prophet of Nazism, from which his sensitive spirit would have revolted as the height of vulgarity and just that aspect of the modern mass world which he loathed. His reputation is an ironic one.

Wagner and Nietzsche are both figures of first rank in the history of music and philosophy respectively, so they tend to hold the center of the stage in this phase of the intellectual history of Germany in the late nineteenth century. They were by no means alone in their opposition to Bismarck's solution of German unity nor to the trends of the times. Several other lesser-known thinkers and publicists sowed some of the seeds that were to sprout in the twentieth century. One of these was Constantin Frantz (named at birth Gustav Adolf Constantin). Frantz, the son of a Protestant clergyman, was born in 1817, educated at Halle and Berlin, and after extensive travels in central and southeastern Europe became an official for a number of years in the Prussian diplomatic service. During the mid-fifties and sixties he lived in Berlin and made a livelihood from writing, but after 1871 he retired from the capital of the hated new empire and lived his last years near Dresden, where he died in 1891. He is a classic example of the *grossdeutsch* thinker in the period after 1870. Frantz insisted that Bismarck had contradicted all important tendencies of German development by settling for an empire containing far from all Germans, an empire which by its rationality, its Prussian domination, and its modernity cut squarely across the traditional, instinctive, and organic qualities of true Germanism. He objected to democracy and elections as being simply the counting of heads without regard for enduring values. For Frantz the magic word was federalism. He envisaged a central European empire including all the peoples of Austria-Hungary and even France grouped about Germany as a womb and center. There was to be a monarch, but he was not to be absolute; yet there were to be no elected officials. The solution of this dilemma was to be a council of men picked from the great institutions of the state to advise the monarch and make decisions. Frantz leaves us to guess just which institutions they were to be, except that he specifically rules out the universities, for which he had a particular dislike. There is an almost airy dismissal of the practical difficulties that would be involved in a solution of this kind, but so entrenched is Frantz in the last backwash of Hegelian idealistic romanticism that he almost gives the impression that these practical matters are beneath the attention of the higher spirits. Frantz has remained a guiding star for many later *grossdeutsch* thinkers and has experienced a revival since 1945 in the effort to discredit all German developments since 1871 as mistakes for which Bismarck must bear much of the blame.

An even more extreme example of pure German racialism was Paul de Lagarde (born Paul Bötticher), whose major work *Deutsche Schriften* (*"German Writings"*) has been a sort of Bible for racists. Lagarde was an academic personality who taught for some time at the University of Göttingen in the field of oriental studies. However, his name will be remembered for his worship of the German race. It is extraordinary to what degree his ideas were later embodied in the Nazi doctrine. Although he admired Bismarck's achievement, it was for him at best a first step. In particular, he disapproved of Bismarck's willingness to compromise, the characteristic which most historians consider one of the chancellor's most outstanding qualities. Lagarde was expansionist and pointed out the problems of a rapidly growing race hemmed in by arbitrary and unhistoric frontiers, a notion to become so familiar later under the label of *Lebensraum*. He condemned all non-German institutions that had crept into German life (i.e., Roman law, the Roman Catholic church, and even German Protestantism because it had been divisive in German development). He seems to have influenced Nietzsche in his dislike for both democracy and industrialism and preached instead the doctrine of return to the soil as a step toward the purification of the race. He even went so far as to anticipate the future S.S. (*Schutz Staffel*) plan of setting up semimonastic schools for the training of the elite of the next generation.

A somewhat different line was taken by Julius Langbehn, whose controversial work *Rembrandt als Erzieher* (*"Rembrandt as Teacher"*) appeared in 1890. Langbehn differed from both Frantz and Lagarde in that while he fell behind none in his admiration of the German race, he did not hold Bismarck responsible for the modern illnesses which all three detected. In fact, he tended to glorify Prussianism and entertained the strong possibility that Germany would become the Greece of the modern world. However, the Germany of his time was just a start for the Germany of the future. Langbehn robbed the Dutch of Rembrandt, whose artistic insight and intuitive understanding of humanity made him a model for future Germans.

The fact that considerable space has been given to several representatives of the opposition to the new empire and of the cult of the German race should not obscure the fact that these people did not represent the dominant and obvious attitudes of the new Germany. For the bulk of the population, unthinking or self-satisfied, they were prophets without honor. Yet after disaster hit the shiny new empire in 1918, more and more it was these men rather than their formerly accepted contemporaries who commanded the attention of the reading public.

On the surface all was well in the spiritual life of Bismarck's Germany, as well as in its political and economic life. The universities continued to flourish and to produce important scholars in all the intellectual disciplines. It is hardly necessary to comment on German pre-eminence in the natural sciences. Foreign students flocked to the German centers of learning. The United States viewed Germany as a model of administration, social legislation, and educational technique. Vienna became the world's medical center; she was shortly to launch Sigmund Freud on his stellar career. Such geniuses as Robert Koch and August von Wassermann loom as large in the history of medicine as Louis Pasteur. In physics, chemistry, mathematics, and the biological sciences German research was of the first order, as for example in the work of Hermann von Helmholtz. Much the same was true in the humanities and social studies. Philology, history, sociology, anthropology—all of these profited from German thought. In addition to the "political" historians already noted, mention should be made of Theodor Mommsen, whose *Roman History* has remained standard. There was noticeable, however, the tendency for the scholar in Germany to remain aloof from political affairs. He was even aloof from his students, an awesome god attired in frock coat and top hat, who upon occasion in a very formal atmosphere cast the pearls of his erudition. His library or laboratory was his world; there are many students of Germany who feel that the learned world voluntarily abdicated from the position it might have claimed, and was therefore unconsciously contributory to the perversion of learning which was to be such a scandal in the twentieth century.

In the world of fine arts Germany in the last third of the nineteenth century produced much activity, but very little of first rank except in music. The architecture of the time was heavy, eclectic, and pompous. In Berlin there appeared a heavily ornamented, massive, and overbearing style; in Bavaria some of the same, plus some copying of earlier styles, and the unique wildly romantic castles dreamed of by Louis II. Colossal statues of Germania, William I, and later Bismarck were very popular and reached their absurd climax in the statues of his forebears with which William II enriched the *Tiergarten* in Berlin. In painting, Germany did not seem to draw much inspiration from the rich new movement in France. She developed no Cézanne, no Van Gogh, not even a Whistler. However, some creditable, if uninspired, academic canvases were painted, especially in Munich, which both in the plastic arts and particularly music was rapidly earning herself the position of the artistic capital of Germany.

The musical side of the picture was, as usual, the brightest. Wagner and Brahms both lived into the imperial period, the latter, of course, in Vienna. In fact, most of the important composers of the time were affiliated with south Germany and Austria. Outstanding among them were Anton Bruckner and Gustav Mahler, who continued the great Viennese tradition although influenced by Wagner, and Richard Strauss, a follower of Wagner, whose more important work did not appear until the twentieth century. Not only was composition at a high level but also performance. Opera companies, symphony orchestras, conductors, singers, and instrumentalists reached new heights and found wide acceptance and support from a musical German public. The revolutionary theatrical techniques of Wagner and the increasingly rich and complex instrumentation of the composers of the period led to new triumphs. Munich, Vienna, Berlin, and Dresden, all supported by their governments, offered outstanding musical fare and drew audiences from the whole world, as well as performers (for example, at a later date two Americans, Geraldine Farrar in Berlin and Maude Fay in Munich). The establishment of musical festivals, of which the Bayreuth festival was the prototype, was another characteristic of the period to continue and increase as time went on.

Once again, in another aspect of life, we see apparent success and achievement on the surface; but in matters of the spirit there was also a lurking undercurrent, hardly perceived at the time, which gradually spread its infection. Today Wagner and Nietzsche are remembered, while Gustav Freytag is almost forgotten.

CHAPTER XII

Bismarck's Germany. IV, Foreign Affairs (1871-88)

There is a very real distinction between Bismarck's foreign policy in the decade of the sixties and in the years between 1871 and 1890. In the earlier years Bismarck traced a course which was often diplomatically aggressive and several times risked the possibility of war. After 1871 the reverse was true. Bismarck was satisfied with his achievement of German unity in the *kleindeutsch* form and felt strongly that Germany and Europe should enjoy a period of tranquillity so that the new state might consolidate her gains and organize herself into a modern nation.

Though the complexities of the elaborate alliance system which Bismarck constructed to keep the peace are very great, the principles underlying his moves are not difficult to discern and are logical. Since peace was the overriding consideration, it was essential to prevent any alliance of powers even potentially unfriendly to Germany. His particular horror was that an alliance might develop between France and Russia, with the result that Germany might be forced to fight a war on two fronts simultaneously. The logical consequence of this fear was that Germany had to be closely aligned with either France or Russia. After the events of 1870–71 friendship with France was out of the question; the alternative possibility had to be sought, namely to remain close to Russia. This was in fact one of the key points of Bismarck's policy. Toward each nation he directed a slightly different policy, but these policies remained remarkably constant during his whole ministry.

France was a special case. Since it was impossible for Germany to woo her directly, at least as long as Alsace and Lorraine remained in German hands, it became necessary to keep her isolated and weak so that she would not seem attractive to any nation looking for an ally. In Bismarck's eyes a republic was a weaker form of government than a monarchy; therefore, the archmonarchist became, where France was concerned, a republican. In later years Bismarck became a willing helper in France's colonial enterprises because he believed that these activities would keep her attention away from continental European problems.

Germany's relationship with Russia was perhaps the most difficult problem which Bismarck had to face. Since the time of his embassy there, he had believed that St. Petersburg and Berlin should remain in close contact. In this effort he had the enthusiastic support of Emperor William. This general attitude was reinforced by the specific fear of a Franco-Russian alliance. The difficulty, however, consisted in trying to maintain the friendship of both Austria-Hungary, whose good will interested Bismarck, and Russia. These two were constantly at odds over Balkan problems. Bismarck had no immediate interest in the Balkans but was very anxious to keep his two eastern neighbors together. This situation was the source of endless difficulty.

The relationship with Austria-Hungary was the converse of that with Russia. Bismarck valued Austria, both because of her German background and also to keep her from any *rapprochement* with France or even Great Britain. As time went on, Austria, rather than Russia, became the basis of the Bismarckian system of alliances.

Great Britain was not a serious problem. She was unlikely to inject herself into continental affairs, unless her own direct interests were concerned. The running sore of Anglo-Russian relations, however, was dangerous; Bismarck exerted himself to prevent these two from open war.

Toward Italy Bismarck maintained an almost fatherly attitude. He had little interest in her warlike potential, but regarded her as a useful friend because of her nuisance value against France.

Bismarck's first important diplomatic step after unification was the creation of the League of the Three Emperors in 1872–73. This was a stage in the chancellor's continuing desire to harness Austria and Russia together. In the fall of 1872 the three emperors, Alexander II of Russia, Francis Joseph of Austria-Hungary, and William I of Germany, met in Berlin and agreed on some vague and abstract principles for common action. Most of these sentiments can be summarized in the phrase monarchical solidarity. The monarchs agreed to stand together against the threats of the modern world and to consult on affairs in the Near East. The following year the essence of these agreements was put on paper, and the League came into existence. It was not a military alliance but rather a gentlemen's agreement, which could last only as long as no important crisis developed. This is proved by the fact that it collapsed at the time of its first serious test, the Balkan crisis of the late seventies.

The quiet surface of the European international scene was disturbed in 1875 by the so-called "war in sight" crisis. France enjoyed a spectacular recuperation from the war of 1870–71. In spite of the German indemnity, now paid in full, she had made surprising advances economically. In the political sphere it looked as if, with the election to the presidency of monarchist Marshal MacMahon, she were going to establish a strong clerical monarchy. The *Kulturkampf* was in full swing at the time, and Bismarck was becoming alarmed at possible reaction to it in clerical countries. There was evidence of such reaction in France. To make matters worse, the French government passed a law to increase the size of the French army. In view of all this, Bismarck decided to spank his former enemy. It is not clear to what degree he actually envisaged the possibility of war. He made angry remarks, and in early 1875 newspapers close to the German government published inflammatory articles, one even using as a headline the question "Is war in sight?" Moltke, who would hardly have acted on his own volition, was heard to talk about a preventive war. France stood up to the Germans and spread the alarm of a German threat. Both Great Britain and Russia were worried by Bismarck's warlike remarks. The British complained diplomatically. The Russians did more. Tsar Alexander II and his foreign minister, Gorchakov, visited Berlin in May 1875 and took the opportunity to assure themselves both from the emperor and the chancellor that no serious thought was given to war with France. In this they succeeded. Years later Bismarck claimed that he never intended a war and that Gorchakov took a great deal of unmerited credit to himself. Whatever the facts, the war scare died down, and Germany found that she could not count unqualifiedly upon Russia's support. The incident served to irritate personal relations between Bismarck and Gorchakov, a factor which was to become more serious in the next crisis.

Much more important than the war scare of 1875 was a series of events in the Balkans. In the summer of that same year the populations of Bosnia and Herzegovina arose against what they considered the intolerable government of the Ottoman Empire. In this revolt they were joined by their Slavic cousins in semi-independent Serbia and in the Bulgarian provinces of Turkey. The Turks were able to crush these revolts but they aggravated the situation by inflicting on the Bulgars a series of bloody reprisals and massacres which have become known as the Bulgarian atrocities. The Pan-Slav sensibilities of the Russians were aroused; further, the Russian government hoped in this crisis for an opportunity to drive the Turks bag and baggage out of Europe and achieve their historical aim of the control of the Bosporus. Disraeli, the British prime minister, had a difficult time, in view of the actions of the Turks, in restating Britain's basic pro-Turkish position aimed at preventing Russian control of the eastern Mediterranean. Yet he did restate it in the face of ferocious opposition from Gladstone. The Austrians, too, supported Turkey, for they feared Russian domination in the Balkans, an area that interested them a great deal since they had been driven from both Italy and Germany.

The situation worried Bismarck very much, not because he had any interest in the Balkans, which indeed he scorned, but because this matter might stir Europe into a general war, an idea that filled him with horror. He tried in a variety of ways to keep Austria and Russia together and to prevent the worst. He helped to form an international commission to insist on reforms in Turkey; he rejoiced at a meeting between the Russian and Austrian foreign ministers in July 1876. Nevertheless, by the fall of that year the situation had become so tense that the tsar asked the German emperor if he was not right in believing that in the event of a war between Russia and Austria, Germany would be as friendly to Russia as Russia had been to her in 1870. When Bismarck replied that Germany would view very seriously any threat to the independence of Austria-Hungary, the Russians felt that he was acting with shameful ingratitude and began to withdraw from the close Russo-German friendship which had existed. In the meantime Russia bought Austrian neutrality, and war broke out between Russia and Turkey in the spring of 1877. By the following Christmas Turkey was overpowered; in January 1878 she was forced to sign a treaty at San Stefano, just outside Constantinople, which was very favorable to Russia. In addition to ceding territory in Asia to Russia, Turkey had to permit the creation of a very large Bulgaria, containing Greeks and Serbs as well as Bulgars, from the Macedonian area. Russia planned this new state as a satellite through which she could control the Balkans in general and dominate the coveted Straits area.

It was at this point that Great Britain became Russia's most active antagonist. Disraeli had no notion of letting Russia get away with such prizes. For a time it looked as if war between the British and the Russians were imminent. Disraeli took the legally justified position that by virtue of earlier treaties all decisions affecting the Ottoman Empire were to be taken by agreement of all the major powers and that Russia had violated this condition ruthlessly. Bismarck gave his reaction to the situation in the Reichstag when he offered himself and Germany as the "honest broker" at an international congress to solve the Balkan problem. Russia, deserted by all of Europe, was forced grudgingly to accept this proposal and a congress was planned for the summer of 1878 to meet at Berlin.

The Congress of Berlin is one of the landmarks of nineteenth-century diplomatic history. It displayed for the first time the German capital as a

European diplomatic center. It was attended by the leading diplomats of Europe. Disraeli and Lord Salisbury represented Britain; Gorchakov came from Russia; Count Andrássy, the Austro-Hungarian foreign minister, attended; Bismarck presided; France, Italy, and Turkey were also represented. Much of the final treaty emanated from Bismarck himself, who was even vague about Balkan geography. His general idea was that the eastern half of the peninsula should be a Russian preserve, while Austria was to dominate in the west. This plan on the whole was adopted. Austria-Hungary received the administration and garrisoning, though not the legal possession, of Bosnia and Herzegovina. Russia's dream of a great Bulgaria was much curtailed. Bulgaria was divided into three areas with varying degrees of autonomy. Russia received her Asiatic spoils. Turkey was to remain, as before, in control of the Straits. Great Britain received the island of Cyprus. France was assured privately by Bismarck that Germany had no objection to French designs on Tunisia (which he knew would infuriate the Italians). The Congress ended in mid-July, and the crisis was over.

In retrospect the Congress of Berlin was not such a triumph for Germany as it appeared at the time. In the short run, war was certainly avoided, and Bismarck's Germany had glittered as the presiding genius of Europe. In the longer run, Bismarck alienated Russia, which nursed an anti-German grievance for some time to come. In the final view, the Congress, by ignoring Balkan nationalism and compromising, laid much of the groundwork for new problems which were to impede the path of Bismarck's successors and to lead in time to the war which was to lay low the German Empire. The chancellor should not have been so ignorant and scornful of the Balkans.

After the delegates had gone home and the decorations were taken down, Bismarck looked about at a rather undesirable scene. Russian friendship, on which he had counted so much, was at least temporarily a thing of the past. These years, 1878 and 1879, marked a big shift in Bismarck's domestic policies; the same is true in foreign affairs. No longer did the chancellor want to juggle with each new situation from scratch. The opportunist was changing into the conservative. Bismarck wanted agreements on paper, firm ones on which he could depend. Thus the decade of the eighties saw the construction of a network of "defensive" military alliances.

The first of this series of alliances was concluded in the fall of 1879 between Germany and Austria-Hungary. Three years later these two partners were joined by Italy in a new alliance, the Triple Alliance, which became the cornerstone of German foreign policy and endured through successive renewals down to World War I. At first blush it would seem that this new system was the negation of Bismarck's basic idea of keeping both Russia and Austria yoked together, and it has been treated in this light by some scholars who feel that Bismarck was forced to choose between his two imperial neighbors. This view is not altogether sound because, in spite of several difficult moments, Bismarck never ceased to keep some control over affairs in St. Petersburg.

After the Congress of Berlin Russia was very disgruntled at the treatment she felt herself to have received, particularly from her old friend Germany. She made various technical difficulties about implementing the provisions of the congress. She grumbled when it was revealed that Austria had agreed to abrogate the clause of the Treaty of Prague of 1866 calling for a plebiscite in north Schleswig. Tsar Alexander even went so far as to write a sharp letter to his uncle, Emperor William, deploring the bad relations between Russia and Germany and even speaking slurringly of Bismarck. The two emperors met shortly after this letter was sent and appeared to patch up their differences, but by that time Bismarck had already decided to make the connection with Austria, had had a conversation with Count Andrássy in Gastein, and was about to go to Vienna to sign the alliance.

The alliance concluded between Bismarck and Andrássy was defensive. It provided that if Russia should attack either of the contracting parties, the other would come to her ally's aid. On the other hand, Austria was specifically excused from participating in a possible future war between France and Germany. It appeared that Austria was reaping all the advantage of the arrangement and Germany was gaining nothing but responsibilities; this was the view taken on the whole by Emperor William. However, there is evidence to suggest that Bismarck was toying with the idea of integrating Great Britain into his new system, which would have been a real achievement, but that he was deflected from this plan by Russia's surprising lack of objection to the Austrian treaty.

Bismarck's principal problem during the weeks following his signature of the Austrian alliance was to get his own emperor to ratify it. William seemed at the outset irreconcilably opposed to the new course. He had a very strong sense of dynastic loyalty, and this loyalty reached in the first instance to his nephew, Tsar Alexander II, and to the Russian connection which had been bequeathed to him from the days of the struggle against Napoleon I. There followed a very interesting correspondence between William and Bismarck in which the chancellor rang every possible change of emotional and intellectual persuasion. The emperor talked of abdicating; Bismarck threatened to resign. In the end the usual thing happened. The emperor, with a heavy heart and predictions of ill occurrences, finally approved the treaty in October 1879. The new European diplomatic course of permanent peacetime alliances came into existence.

Russia's reaction was surprising. Instead of the fury which might have been predicted, it was one of complacency. Russia was enduring a period of terroristic chaos in her domestic affairs, which was climaxed by the murder of Tsar Alexander in 1881. She could not easily face foreign disturbances at the same time. In any case, she started to make overtures to Germany soon after the Austrian treaty was concluded, an attitude which appears to have made Bismarck drop his intentions concerning London. The eventual result was a revival of the old League of the Three Emperors in 1881 and the continuance of it until 1887.

The next step in the new Bismarckian security policy involved Italy. Bismarck had on the whole preserved friendly relations with the Italians. He had helped them to acquire Venetia in 1866. In the following decade the *Kulturkampf* tended to bring him closer to antipapal Italy. Italy's anger was directed toward clerical France and also toward Austria-Hungary, which still possessed areas known to Italian nationalists as *Italia irredenta* (Trentino, Trieste, Istria, etc.), which Italy claimed were ethnically properly hers. Bismarck's secret assurance to the French delegate at the Congress of Berlin that Germany had no objection to French aspirations in Tunisia was one of the motives which led France in 1881 to declare a protectorate over that area. This action, as Bismarck anticipated, angered the Italians; their reaction was to start immediate friendly overtures to Berlin. Bismarck's reply to these overtures was to point out to the Italians that his principal foreign loyalty was to Austria. He advised them to settle their outstanding differences in Vienna before trying to achieve anything important with him. Accordingly, Austro-Italian relations were improved and anti-Austrian nationalistic campaigns in Italy were soft-pedaled; the result was the formation by Germany, Austria, and Italy of the Triple Alliance, which remained in force until Italy denounced it in 1915.

It looked by then as if Bismarck had pretty completely achieved his aim of security. Germany was closely allied to Austria-Hungary and Italy; she maintained some control over Russia in the League of the Three Emperors; she had a line to Great Britain through the latter's friendship with Austria and Italy; she had even brought Romania into her orbit by acceding in 1883 to a defensive alliance between Austria and Romania, which was transparently aimed at Russia. France still languished in exterior darkness. For several years, indeed, there was relative quiet, but this quiet was broken in the mid-eighties by the periodic Balkan crisis and also by a wave of belligerent public opinion in France centering about the personality of General Boulanger.

In spite of the fact that much has been written about it, the Boulanger episode in French history remains obscure. General Boulanger was a dashing, handsome officer, whose colorful and theatrical appearance and statements served to remind the French people how colorless and tiresome was the government of the Third Republic. He represented the culmination of a release from the frustration caused by lack of glory and achievement that had inhibited France since 1815. However, he was a man of far too small stature to realize these longings. Temporarily he inflamed French patriotism and was seized upon by French nationalists of various hues to stir up opinion. He came at a moment convenient for Bismarck, who used him for the German equivalent of the "bloody shirt" in American history, namely the fatherland endangered by France. The question of the Septennate, or voting the military budget seven years in advance, was the crucial issue at home and Bismarck was waging a difficult electoral campaign. The arrest of a French border official named Schnaebele, on a trumped-up charge of espionage, served to focus German thought on an imaginary danger from France. Schnaebele was soon released and Boulanger dismissed from the war ministry, but Bismarck won his majority in the Reichstag.

The Balkan crisis of the mid-eighties concerned Alexander of Battenberg, prince of Bulgaria. This charming but restless young man had been named to the almost independent part of Bulgaria by Alexander II shortly after the Congress of Berlin. He soon made it clear that he had no intention of ruling Bulgaria as a Russian satellite and thereby incurred the furious enmity of the new Russian tsar, Alexander III. In 1885 Battenberg led a movement leading to the union of Bulgaria with its artificially constructed neighbor, Eastern Roumelia; he got involved in a victorious war with Serbia and the next year was kidnaped by a group of Bulgarian officers, possibly at the behest of the Russians. He returned triumphantly to Bulgaria only to be greeted by a severe and angry letter from the tsar, which led him to abdicate. A further complication was that he was engaged to be married to the granddaughter of the German emperor, Princess Victoria, only daughter of the German crown prince.

Pro-Battenberg feeling ran high in Germany, except in one quarter—namely Bismarck himself. He had no notion of endangering his relationship with Russia for the sake of a young Balkan adventurer. Furthermore, it was just those elements at court who supported Battenberg that Bismarck believed to be hostile to himself, the circle around the crown prince and princess. He therefore opposed the engagement with all his power.

The international implications of this crisis led Tsar Alexander to desire to break loose from the League of the Three Emperors, which was up for renewal in mid-1887. He had become very anti-Austrian and, although he had no great love for Germany either, was prepared to offer a treaty to her without any connection with Austria-Hungary. Accordingly he sent a representative to Berlin, whom Bismarck received warmly; out of the discussions between the two was formed the famous Reinsurance Treaty, Bismarck's last major accomplishment on the diplomatic level.

This treaty, kept very secret, provided that in case of war against one of the signatories by another major power, the other would remain neutral. There were, however, two exceptions to this: if Russia attacked Austria, or if Germany attacked France. Russia also received assurances from Germany on Balkan problems. The treaty was to last for three years and could be renewed in 1890.

The question arises immediately to what degree the Reinsurance Treaty was in harmony with Germany's prior and basic obligations to Austria stemming from the alliance of 1879. Technically and legally it would seem as if there were no collision between the two, although there is very serious doubt about this if the treaty with Romania is taken into account. In the event of an Austro-Russian war, it would be the German problem to decide which was the aggressor and to behave accordingly. It need not be emphasized how difficult this is when the event occurs. Morally speaking, it seems clear that the Reinsurance Treaty was far from the spirit of the arrangement arrived at with Austria. Critics of Bismarck see in this treaty a prime example of his cynicism and unscrupulousness; his admirers see in it an extraordinarily astute technique for preserving peace in any contingency.

The full complexity of Bismarck's system appears at its height in a series of agreements collectively known as the First Mediterranean Agreement and signed in the early months of 1887. Germany adhered to only one of the agreements, that between Italy and Spain, but Bismarck may be described as the godfather of the whole plan, which consisted of arrangements among Great Britain, Austria, Italy, and Spain to preserve the *status quo* in the Mediterranean area. It was intended to act as a deterrent to any French ambitions in Egypt or Morocco and to any Russian ambitions in the Straits or the Balkans. It also aligned the British, at least psychologically, with the Triple Alliance. These arrangements in 1887 were the last achievements of the old master, who, with the exception of some abortive moves in the direction of Great Britain in 1889, seemed content with his system as he had developed it.

In the peaceful years before the Battenberg crisis Bismarck engaged briefly in a new sort of policy, very much at variance with most of his background and at odds with many of his statements. He presided over the birth of a German colonial empire. Although for years he had been distinctly continental-minded and had spoken scornfully of German colonial aspirations, although indeed he had no interests even as far abroad as the Balkan Peninsula, it was during his period that Germany entered late the race for overseas colonies.

As early as the mid-seventies there had been some clamor for the acquisition of colonies. The clamor was mainly from the commercial and shipping interests in the north German ports, whose business would naturally benefit from overseas expansion. Yet it was not until the next decade that this agitation led to any tangible results. In 1882 the Deutsche Kolonial Gesellschaft ("German Colonial Society") was founded, and in the next year the merchant Adolf Lüderitz bought from the natives some territory north of the Orange River in southwest Africa. The year 1884 was the decisive one. During it a German protectorate was established over this area in the southwest, in the face of British protests. Farther north protectorates were also declared over Togoland on the Niger coast and over Cameroons on the Guinea coast. On the east coast of Africa Karl Peters, another merchant, was the leading spirit. Some trading posts had been established between British Kenya and Portuguese Mozambique as early as 1878 by the German Africa Society. By 1884 Peters had signed treaties with the natives, and in 1885 an official protectorate was declared over this area too. All these areas had indefinite boundaries, and negotiation with the European powers, especially Great Britain, followed to establish the frontiers. By the end of the decade a number of agreements were made and Germany had a respectable African empire, though one far smaller and less valuable than those of Britain and France.

In the southwest Pacific area the Germans were also at work. In the same year of 1884 Germany staked out her claim to the northeastern quarter of New Guinea and also to the Bismarck Archipelago. The next year the Marshall and Solomon Islands were declared German possessions, and by the end of the decade Germany had come to an agreement with Great Britain and the United States concerning a condominium in the Samoan Islands.

Opinions have varied as to why Bismarck reversed his decision and permitted this colonial activity. One plausible reason is that he wanted to give room for expansion to the north German merchants. Others say that he was trying to drive a wedge between the two wings of liberalism, one of which was decidedly anticolonial while the right wing favored colonies. It is even suggested that Bismarck was anxious to create a collision with Great Britain on colonial matters because he feared British influence over the crown prince, who was bound to succeed to the throne in the near future. It may be too that he became dimly aware of the degree to which his old-fashioned, continental, almost Metternichian outlook was becoming outdated by the technological modern world which had sprung up about him. If so, it was a very dim awareness indeed as far as colonies were concerned because his enthusiasm waned, and it seemed that Bismarck later almost regretted that he had permitted Lüderitz, Peters, and the others to go ahead with their plans.

The panorama of Bismarck's diplomatic achievement is an impressive one. He succeeded in preserving peace; he made himself and Berlin pretty much the pivots of European international politics during the seventies and eighties. He has been lauded on all sides for his diplomatic shrewdness. One authority likes to describe him as the successful statesman of "limited liability," as opposed to William II and Hitler whom he characterizes as the unsuccessful statesmen of "unlimited liability." It would be foolish to underestimate Bismarck's diplomatic astuteness or the massive sum of his achievement. Yet even in the field of international affairs his heritage was not without disadvantage. The tying of the destinies of Germany to those of Austria-Hungary was to prove a drag and eventually to be the direct means of leading the empire to its doom. The establishment of far-flung colonies in time called for the creation of a strong navy and Germany's consequent immersion into *Weltpolitik* ("world politics"), which was to be so dangerously tempting to Emperor William II. Even in his own chosen field of diplomacy Bismarck's achievement, though very considerable, is not to be admired without reservation.

CHAPTER XIII

Germany Jumps a Generation (1888-90)

The year 1888 was a turning point in the annals of the house of Hohenzollern and therefore in those of Germany in general and Bismarck in particular. Two German emperors died in that year. At the beginning of the year the throne was occupied by a seasoned veteran of over ninety; at its end, by an inexperienced and badly trained young man of twenty-nine. Within a few months the direction of the state jumped a generation. The main link with the past was the aging and irritable Bismarck.

The series of personal tragedies of the royal family of Prussia began several years before the death of William I. By the mid-eighties it was clear that the aged emperor could not live much longer. All eyes were therefore turned to the heir, Crown Prince Frederick, and his wife, Crown Princess Victoria, eldest child of the English Queen Victoria and her husband Albert, the prince consort. Frederick was an attractive personality. Tall and handsome, with a long auburn beard, he seemed almost a reincarnation of the medieval Holy Roman emperors. Exposed to English influences through his bride and her family, whom he often visited, Frederick developed the reputation of being a liberal. Not a great deal tangible is known of his political opinions, however, because after his one overt criticism in 1863 of the policies of his father and Bismarck, he was silenced. Thenceforth his activities were largely confined to military functions (he acquitted himself very well in the wars of unification) and decorative duties. He and his wife surrounded themselves with people of a liberal and artistic tinge, setting up a sort of rival court to the more military and less intellectual milieu of the king. The crown princess was a more positive character than her husband. She had very definite political views, most of which added up to an antipathy to Bismarck and his policies, which she shared with her mother-in-law, the Empress Augusta. The expectation was that the new reign would lead to a new orientation of policy in a liberal direction and that the ascendancy of Bismarck would end. Bismarck himself was keenly aware of this possibility and did all he could to cut the ground from under the crown prince by lessening British influence in Germany and by discrediting the various branches of liberalism.

In the mid-eighties the crown prince began to complain of a painful throat disease, which was becoming more and more noticeable. Immediately the most distinguished German doctors were called to attend him. They pretty well agreed that the proper diagnosis was cancer and recommended an immediate operation. The crown princess, horrified at this news, demanded further consultation and requested the best medical advice available in Great Britain. A Scottish doctor, Sir Morell Mackenzie, arrived in Berlin, examined the prince, and gave his opinion that an operation was unnecessary and that the disease could be cured by painful cauterization. This advice was followed and Frederick suffered a martyrdom from these very exhausting treatments. Yet the condition did not improve. It became more and more difficult for the prince to speak, and the tone of his voice became increasingly hoarse and harsh. As the winter of 1887–88 approached, Victoria and the doctors agreed that it would be beneficial to remove Frederick from the raw climate of north Germany and take him to the gentler south. Accordingly the royal couple rented a villa at San Remo on the Italian Riviera and spent the winter there hoping against hope for a convalescence.

A good deal of criticism arose at the highhanded way in which the crown princess was directing the treatment of her husband, who was also of course a political figure of the first importance. Much of this criticism emanated from her eldest son William, prince of Prussia, who had never had a close relationship with his mother. He had been kept as far as possible from his ailing father's bedside. William determined to travel to San Remo to see the situation himself. He did so, but had a difficult time gaining access to his father. By this time it was clear that the disease was gaining ground rapidly, and the fiction that it was not a cancer was no longer tenable. In fact, it was hardly possible for the invalid to speak.

Things were at this pass when on March 9, 1888, the news arrived at San Remo that the old emperor had died. The new emperor, a dying man, after some doubt about what number he should append to his name, proclaimed his accession to the thrones of Prussia and Germany as Frederick III and made his laborious way back to a wintry and snow-covered Berlin. Once there he was not physically able to attend his father's magnificent funeral, but had to content himself with saluting the coffin from a window in the Charlottenburg palace and with watching his son William act as chief mourner in his own place.

The reign of Frederick III lasted only ninety-nine days. Owing to his illness, the now-speechless emperor made no effort to effect any important changes in the government. He appealed to Bismarck to continue his control of affairs as chancellor, and there was no change in policy. Only one major stir occurred, which brought to an end the affair of Alexander of Battenberg. Since his abdication in 1886 that prince had been living in retirement with his family in Hesse-Darmstadt, but his engagement to Princess Victoria of Prussia had never been terminated although the prince had fallen in love with an actress at Darmstadt. Empress Victoria, desiring to make her daughter happy in the few months of power that appeared to be her lot, prevailed upon her husband to invite Alexander to Berlin to award him a high decoration and presumably to make the betrothal official. Upon word of this Bismarck descended upon the palace in wrath, and with the support of Crown Prince William forced the emperor to withdraw the invitation and to end all talk of the engagement. After this Bismarck permitted the facts to become public and engaged in an unhappy campaign of beating a dead horse (and a dying emperor). He raised the specter of Russian anger, although in fact the tsar had lost interest in Alexander since he gave no indication of returning to Sofia. There is some suggestion that Bismarck feared that the empress planned to replace him with Alexander as chancellor and was therefore making sure of the defeat of this possibility. In any case, the whole affair seemed unnecessarily cruel.

As spring wore on, the emperor's condition deteriorated rapidly. To give him some pleasure he was transported by boat to Frederick the Great's New Palace in Potsdam, which was renamed *Friedrichskron* in honor of the emperor. About the same time Queen Victoria arrived for a visit in Berlin to bid farewell to her son-in-law. By the beginning of June the emperor's death was only a matter of days, and he died on the fifteenth of that month with a last gesture of placing his wife's hands in those of Bismarck.

When Crown Prince William heard that his father's death was imminent, he rushed to Potsdam and surrounded the palace with troops. As soon as Frederick died, he forbade anyone to enter or leave the building. Going into an adjoining room he wrote two proclamations, both dated not from *Friedrichskron* but from the New Palace. These proclamations violated a number of sensibilities because the first was addressed not to the people, as was customary, but to the army. He then organized a funeral for his father which was markedly less magnificent than that accorded to his grandfather three months before. With these ungracious acts William II, the last German emperor, began his thirty-year reign.

William II is a tempting but difficult person to describe: he was not without virtues and intelligence; his fatuousness and his mercurial impetuosity, combined with an almost religious belief in his position and his own wisdom, make the historian recognize the tragedy of a person so constituted in so decisive a post. At his birth in 1859, owing to professional malpractice, he was delivered a cripple with a severely withered left arm. Some amateur psychologists in the historical profession use this as an explanation for many of the attitudes which William later assumed. They tell us that this physical defect led the prince to dislike his mother and thus by projection to dislike England. This may be an extreme interpretation, but it seems clear that the defect forced William psychologically to overcompensate for it in various ways, in particular physically, so that he became very strong, bluff, and strenuous in his likes. William was a bright child and interested in many types of things, but his interests remained throughout his life those of a dilettante without any real profundity. His tutor Hinzpeter was a martinet, who tried to force him into a pattern and to push his development. He was schooled at Kassel and at the University of Bonn, but suffered from the usual disadvantage of a prince at a school with less-favored colleagues. William married Augusta Victoria of Schleswig-Holstein, a member of the Augustenburg family; it was hoped that the marriage would erase the events of the sixties. The princess was a domestic and religious woman, who until the last years exercised little political influence over her husband. William was happiest in two spheres: military and naval. He loved the sea and took frequent cruises on his yacht. This love had the dubious result of leading him to the creation of a large German navy. One of his most outstanding characteristics was his genius for malapropism; he always managed to say the wrong thing at the wrong time. He viewed himself as a first-rate orator and frequently made extemporaneous remarks which cost his ministers much time and sweat to dilute. He had an implicit belief in his own charm, which was not inconsiderable, and felt that his presence could lure either foreign statesmen or opponents on the domestic scene to his way of thinking. Above all he intended to be boss and did not plan to play the secondary role which his grandfather had done so competently. Given the highly personal relationship of emperor-chancellor in the German constitution, it is easy to see that stormy days were ahead between William and Bismarck, who were both such dominant personalities.

Bismarck does not appear to have been conscious of the personality of the new emperor. He no doubt thought of him as a clever little boy. He had not given him much training in governmental affairs and seemed to believe that William would depend on him for all major decisions, so long as he enjoyed being emperor. Bismarck in fact spent very little time in Berlin during the first months of the new reign, making his decisions from the distant seclusion of his estates and assuming that the emperor would accept them without demur.

For a time the situation seemed under control. William was enjoying himself. He decided, as soon as official mourning was over, to take some trips and see the world, thus earning the nickname of the *reise Kaiser* ("traveling emperor"). He made a rather unwelcome call on his cousin, the Russian emperor; he paid a visit to his grandmother, Victoria; and he went shooting with his contemporary and friend, Crown Prince Rudolf of Austria-Hungary. He even went so far as to visit the pariah monarch, Ottoman Sultan Abdul Hamid II, known also as Abdul the Damned and the Red Assassin.

The honeymoon was not to last very long between the emperor and the chancellor. More than two personalities—one young, vital, and anxious to act; the other aging, conservative, and looking backward— were at stake. Two generations were at issue, even two worlds. Bismarck still lived in the world of the mid-century, a world limited to the European continent where the industrial revolution had not yet created problems of a social and economic nature which have concerned governments ever since; William II, though he proved to be personally incompetent to deal with what he perceived, was a man of the new period, a man who saw that the world had become much smaller and recognized at least dimly the impact of social and economic change. William was ready to forge, if blindly, ahead; Bismarck wanted to return to the more comfortable old days. It seems clear that Bismarck was very much troubled about universal suffrage. When he instituted it in the sixties, it meant the vote for the conservative peasantry; now it meant the vote for the radical proletariat. Abundant evidence shows that Bismarck was meditating some sort of *coup d'état* to reduce the franchise drastically and shear the government of its liberal trappings.

It was no accident that the final disputes between William and Bismarck arose over the social question. As early as mid-1889 William, hoping to be all things to all men, had against Bismarck's views espoused the cause of miners on strike in the west. By the end of the year the question of renewing the antisocialist law was imminent. The Reichstag, dominated by the conservative cartel of 1887, was in Bismarck's pocket, though a new election loomed. There was a strong difference of opinion between the Conservatives and the National Liberals on the antisocialist issue. The former wanted the law with a provision that socialists could be forcibly removed from their homes, but the latter refused point blank to permit this clause. The Conservatives were ready to give in if Bismarck would announce the omission of the offensive clause as government policy. At a crown council William advocated this idea strongly. Bismarck opposed it and won the day, saying that he would prefer no law, with consequent bloodshed and a final showdown, to the emasculated law. This horrified the emperor, who had no idea of provoking civil war to start his reign. The law failed, and William proposed his own solutions to the social problems. These involved concessions to the employees and, more important in the emperor's mind, an International Labor Conference in Berlin at which he would shine as the defender of the oppressed. In February 1890 decrees to this end were published but for the first time since 1871 without the chancellor's countersignature.

Soon afterwards the elections were held and resulted in a stunning defeat for Bismarck's supporters and a triumph for the parties of the left. Bismarck was now clearly in favor of provoking a constitutional crisis which would lead to changes in the organic laws. He was also trying to make a failure and nonsense out of William's plans for a labor conference. The tension was mounting rapidly.

The crisis reached its summit as a result of two new issues. One was Bismarck's revival of an order of Frederick William IV dating from 1852, which provided that Prussian ministers might report to the king only in the presence of the minister-president. William saw this as an effort of Bismarck to keep him from the center of government. The other issue involved Bismarck's hope to build some kind of majority upon a coalition of Conservatives and Catholic Centrists. He invited Windthorst, head of the Catholic party, to confer with him without informing the emperor. The conversation proved abortive, but the emperor was infuriated when he heard it had taken place.

On the morning of March 15, 1890, Emperor William appeared unannounced at the Foreign Ministry at an hour when the chancellor was still in bed. Bismarck dressed hurriedly and proceeded to face a scolding from his monarch because he had received Windthorst without permission. Bismarck lost his temper and the interview was very stormy, to such a degree indeed that William later said that he expected to have an inkpot thrown at him. However, Bismarck was not to be outdone. Accidentally on purpose, he permitted the emperor to see a recent communication from Russia in which the tsar was said to have described William as a "badly brought-up boy." This completed the interview, and William stalked out of the building in a fury.

The last straw was the emperor's fright at a routine report indicating Russian reinforcements in the Kiev area. This made William believe that Russia was planning war, and he wanted to warn the Austrians. Bismarck wouldn't stand for any meddling in foreign affairs, so he sat down to compose his carefully worded letter of resignation. The resignation was accepted on March 18, 1890, but the letter was not published by the emperor because he didn't want only Bismarck's side of the dispute to be made public. As a parting gesture William made Bismarck duke of Lauenburg, offered him a cash gift, and sent him a portrait of himself. The portrait and title were accepted scornfully and the money refused. Bismarck never made use of the new title.

Bismarck outlived his dismissal by eight years. He spent nearly all his time at his two estates of Varzin in Pomerania and Friedrichsruh near Hamburg. The first years were ones of bitter recrimination in which the old chancellor attacked the emperor and the new chancellor unmercifully, often in the Hamburg newspaper which he controlled. He also wrote his memoirs in an effort to clear his career and reputation. The government retaliated in any way possible. Perhaps the most insulting of its acts occurred when Bismarck went to Vienna to attend his son's wedding. Both the government and the emperor wrote to their Austrian opposite numbers and to the German embassy in Vienna, requesting that no official notice be taken of Bismarck's presence in the city. In spite of this sort of treatment, Bismarck's popularity continued. Groups of Germans, often young people, made the pilgrimage to his home to see and hear the great man. Finally a public reconciliation was arranged between the old statesman and the young emperor. In January 1894 Bismarck visited Berlin and was entertained at dinner in the palace. The following year, on Bismarck's eightieth birthday, William journeyed to Friedrichsruh. However, this was all on the surface; the real acrimony continued. In the chancellery a thick file was kept of all mentions of Bismarck in the foreign press so that they could be countered if necessary. The news of Bismarck's death on July 30, 1898, reached the emperor as he was cruising on the North Sea. He returned to Friedrichsruh for the funeral and no doubt sighed happily as he saw the coffin lowered into the earth.

The last years of Bismarck's life are melancholy in view of his immense contribution to German history. The dismissal of the chancellor was caricatured in perhaps the most famous political cartoon of all time, "Dropping the Pilot" in the English *Punch*. The cartoon shows a very youthful William wearing a crown and leaning over the deck watching the lumbering old man make his heavy way down the ladder to the pilot boat. There are two sides to the story. It is impossible not to feel sympathy for William's position; it is also impossible to view Bismarck's fall as other than pathetic. Less favorable are the insulting pigheadedness of the tested servant and the ignoble rudeness of the noble master.

CHAPTER XIV

Wilhelmian Germany. I, Domestic (1890-1914)

The reign of William II was Bismarck's Germany without Bismarck, as very soon became apparent. In spite of the emperor's confident remarks, the new course of the nineties was an unsteady one both in domestic and in foreign affairs. Released from the despotic control of the old master, pressure groups began to make their influence felt, and the intrinsic weakness of the emperor allowed him to be pushed first one way, then the other by the forces surrounding him. The constitution which Bismarck had tailored for himself simply did not fit lesser men. The succession of four chancellors who sat in Bismarck's chair between 1890 and 1917 illustrates this point.

Emperor William picked as Bismarck's immediate successor, to institute the so-called "new course," General Leo von Caprivi, who held the post for four years from 1890 to 1894. Caprivi stepped into one of the most difficult positions imaginable and filled it with competence, if not brilliance. He was a regular army officer and member of the General Staff, who had a good deal of experience in army administration. Also he had served for some years as Chief of the Admiralty. (The Navy was so unimportant at this time that it was controlled by the Army.) He had been highly esteemed both by William I and by Bismarck, but had a becoming modesty which made him reluctant to accept the two big tasks of German chancellor and minister-president of Prussia.

A characteristic of the Caprivi administration is a rapid relaxation of the centralization which had existed under Bismarck, who had treated his various secretaries of state as underlings and had always refused them real ministerial status. Under Caprivi the secretaries of state played a more important role, partly because of the chancellor's lack of experience. This was particularly true in the field of foreign affairs, where Bismarck's son Herbert was succeeded by Freiherr Marschall von Bieberstein, who became a major figure in German diplomacy. The same weakening of control was apparent in the relationship between Prussia and the Reich. Bismarck, it is true, had not always acted as minister-president of Prussia, but he had remained in command. After 1892 the two offices were separated for the duration of Caprivi's incumbency.

The principal immediate cause of the break between the emperor and Bismarck had been the "social question." William was now determined to appear as the protector of the underprivileged and, in spite of the failure of his labor conference, in the early nineties secured the passage of a number of progressive laws dealing with factory conditions, hours of labor, and the like. He hoped this would, by anticipation of their program, render unnecessary the continuance of any measures against the socialists. As the years went on, however, election returns belied these hopes and William became gradually antisocialist and conservative. Much the same evolution of policy occurred on the subject of the national minorities within the empire. William tried at the outset to be very generous in his treatment of the French in Alsace-Lorraine and the Polish minority in Prussia. However, little gratitude or co-operation was shown by these groups, and the emperor in time grew anti-Polish and supported a stern policy after 1900.

Three major issues dominated domestic politics during the Caprivi era and illustrate changes in the German scene. They concerned schools, the army, and tariffs, which finally forced Caprivi to resign.

In 1892 the Prussian minister of education introduced an extremely reactionary bill, which would have placed Prussian education almost completely under the control of the Protestant and Catholic churches. In fact this bill seemed in many ways to make a complete farce out of the whole *Kulturkampf* philosophy. Since the Conservatives and Center dominated the Prussian parliament, it would have been possible to push the law through, as Caprivi tried to do out of a sense of loyalty to his minister. However, the bill caused such a furor throughout the whole country that the emperor reversed his support and had the government withdraw it. The minister of education resigned; Caprivi also offered his resignation, but it was not accepted. He did learn, however, how little he could depend on the loyalty of a monarch who was going about the land talking about divine right and announcing that he was sole master.

William II's most sensitive concern was the condition of his armed forces. After 1890 he became nervous on this count, for he was alarmed at increases in the French army and also at the growing closeness of France and Russia. In 1890 Caprivi easily pushed through some moderate increases in the army, but three years later he ran into serious trouble in the Reichstag when he presented a bill to increase the army by 70,000 men and to make various other expensive changes. The bill was voted down by the Center, still angry about the school bill, and the Progressives and Social Democrats, touchy about militarization. Caprivi replied with a call for a new Reichstag. The elections did not change the situation, except that the strength of the Progressive party was cut almost in half in favor of the Conservatives. Caprivi was able now to muster enough votes to get the military bill through, but it was a hollow victory because the success of the Conservatives at the polls presaged a major defeat for him in the more important field of commercial policy.

The commercial treaties on a most-favored-nation basis signed by Germany all expired in 1892. The future seemed to hold the alternatives of tariff wars or else partial reductions in tariffs on the basis of reciprocal trade agreements. Caprivi leaned toward the latter, because, although he was not an economist, he recognized the importance of industry and the working man to Germany. He was not oblivious of agrarian problems but felt that Germany needed the improved and efficient agriculture which the rigors of less protection might achieve. Thus in 1892 he concluded a number of trade treaties with neighboring nations, which were enthusiastically ratified by the Reichstag and earned him the title of count. In the next year he expanded his program to include several other nations, in particular Russia, against which Germany had been waging a tariff war. Needless to say, the Caprivi policy raised a storm among the conservative agrarians of the east, who saw their comfortable privileged position seriously endangered. Their protest took the form in early 1893 of the foundation of the *Bund der Landwirte* ("Agrarian League"), which for years to come was to exercise strong influence in a very conservative direction. Its lobbying succeeded in achieving the passage of a number of laws to help agriculture, and it never ceased in its efforts to get rid of Caprivi. In this it was assisted by the Prussian finance minister, Dr. Miquel, and others. The emperor, too, seemed to be tiring of his chancellor. Caprivi became sick of the struggle and, together with Count Botho von Eulenburg who had been minister-president of Prussia since the education bill fiasco, resigned in October 1892. The emperor accepted the resignation without objection.

To succeed Caprivi William picked Prince Chlodwig zu Hohenlohe-Schillingsfürst, a seventy-five-year-old Bavarian liberal Catholic. Hohenlohe had had a distinguished career in the service both of Bavaria and of the empire. He had served for a time as head of the Bavarian government, succeeded von Arnim as ambassador to France, and more recently had filled with a good deal of tact the difficult post of *Statthalter* ("governor") of Alsace-Lorraine. Hohenlohe was a cultured gentleman of the old world, cool, moderate, and conservative, but too aged for heavy responsibilities, in particular to curb the impetuous master whom he had to serve and who was becoming more irresponsible in his utterances every day. He brought an element of stability to his office, but was overshadowed by the emperor and by some of his subordinates (e.g., Marschall and his successor Bernhard von Bülow in the foreign office, and Admiral Tirpitz at naval headquarters).

The domestic events of the administration of Hohenlohe, which lasted for six years (1894–1900), are not on the whole of great interest. The chancellor tried to preserve a course of moderate conservatism, moving with the emperor away from the semiliberal period under Caprivi. He attempted to get from the Reichstag an antirevolution law, which, however, failed to pass because of its arbitrary and extralegal character. In 1896 the new civil code for the empire was adopted, but in this juristic triumph Hohenlohe himself played little part. With one exception the major events of the period fell in the realm of foreign affairs.

The exception is the beginning of the construction of the new German navy, a development which was to have exceedingly important repercussions on a world-wide scale. From the moment of his accession to the throne William II had been ashamed of his German navy and anxious to do something about it. He loved the sea and was a fervent participant in yachting activities, including visits to the regattas at Cowes on the Isle of Wight. In 1895 at the opening of the Kiel Canal, and in 1897 at the celebration of the diamond jubilee of Queen Victoria, the emperor lamented publicly the poor showing which the old shabby German vessels made among those of other nations. He enjoyed himself mouthing bellicose statements about naval matters, the most famous being "Germany's future lies upon the sea." In the mid-nineties international events and colonial activities seemed to reinforce the need to increase the navy. Luckily for the emperor the right man lay at hand. In 1897 William appointed Admiral Alfred von Tirpitz head of the admiralty to create a great navy. Tirpitz was one of the outstanding men of his time. Deeply conservative but highly intelligent, he was determined to build a large fleet, including plenty of battleships, and to make the navy popular in Germany. In the succeeding year the Naval League was founded and became an influential pressure group, composed of distinguished persons who occupied themselves by creating naval propaganda which reached down to the humblest Germans. About the same time the first naval bill was presented to the Reichstag. This bill provided for a costly seven-year program of shipbuilding and expansion. Hohenlohe supported it without much interest. It passed with the support of the right-wing parties; the Center was divided; the Progressives and Social Democrats voted against it. This was a pattern which was to persist. Instead of waiting seven years for a further request for appropriations, however, Tirpitz readied a new bill which was presented and passed in 1900. The German navy was coming into existence with a tremendous initial impetus, supported to the funnels by the enthusiastic emperor. It hardly need be added that this enthusiasm was not shared abroad, especially in London. However, William was not going to let anything stand in the way of his beloved navy, which rapidly assumed size and efficiency.

Exhausted by age, the pressures of the new German international activity, and the vagaries of the emperor, Uncle Chlodwig, as the empress called him, retired in late 1900 and died shortly thereafter. He was succeeded as chancellor by a man much more interesting and much more controversial, Prince Bernhard von Bülow. Bülow, a north German who was chancellor for nine years (1900–1909), was the son of one of Bismarck's secretaries of state for foreign affairs. He had entered the diplomatic service as a young man and had served in almost all of the principal capitals of Europe, eventually becoming ambassador to Italy and later succeeding Marschall in 1897 as secretary of state for foreign affairs. He enjoyed a great reputation during his lifetime; it was the publication of his memoirs after his death that showed the essential smallness of his character. He was cultured, supple, and diplomatic; his finesse in manipulating people was considerable; but beneath the charming façade was a narrowness of vision which renders untenable the comparisons with Bismarck which were frequently heard during his chancellorship.

As in the Hohenlohe administration, the main interest of Bülow's period lies in the field of foreign affairs. However, there were some important domestic developments. At one moment in 1908 a stronger chancellor than Bülow or a more aggressive Reichstag might have achieved parliamentary responsibility, but both failed to take advantage of the situation.

By the turn of the century the emperor's early liberalism was almost dead, and the influence of the conservative pressure groups was ever increasing. This is shown by the action taken on the perennial issue of the protective tariff. A new tariff law was passed in late 1901, which not only pleased the Agrarian League by raising substantially the duties on agricultural products but also satisfied the organized industrialists by granting their similar demands for high tariffs. The diplomatic Bülow was determined to cause as little opposition as possible. He had learned the lessons taught by the fate of his predecessors. Another evidence of conservatism and favoritism to the east-Elbian agrarian class was Bülow's policy toward the Poles in West Prussia and Posen. Here, where mortgages were frequently foreclosed on land owned by Poles, German colonists were encouraged to settle on favorable terms with the aim of recolonizing these territories with Germans and reducing the Polish population to a semiservile peasantry. On the other hand, the social legislation of the time of Bismarck was not only retained but expanded, and an abortive effort was even made to change the outworn Prussian three-class franchise. The years from 1900 to 1906 were fairly peaceful parliamentary years with the control of the Reichstag in the hands of the Conservatives and the Center, who usually worked in harmony with Bülow.

The change came in 1906 over a series of colonial problems. For some years there had been uprisings of the natives in German East Africa and German Southwest Africa, culminating in the rebellion of the Hereros in the southwest, a revolt which was very serious and threatened the extermination of the German population. The blame for this unhappy situation was widely laid on the German merchant colonists, who were accused of behaving with inexcusable brutality toward the natives. The Social Democrats and, more particularly, the Center started a drive against the government's colonial policy which went even beyond the bounds of an investigation and demanded various privileges for Catholic missions in addition to a thoroughgoing reform of the colonial administration. Here was an opportunity for the second-class citizens (Socialists and Catholics) to assert themselves in a situation which had humanitarian overtones. It was also an opportunity to attack indirectly the spirit of militarism, which seemed rampant in the nation. Bülow introduced a bill to appropriate special funds to crush the native revolt, but it was refused by the alliance of Social Democrats and Centrists. Immediately he took action by dissolving the Reichstag and ending his cooperation with the Center. The election of 1907 was gratifying to the government because the Social Democrats suffered the loss of about half of their seats and Bülow was able to construct a majority, the so-called Bülow-block, of Conservatives and National Liberals. The rebellion in Africa was brought to a bloody conclusion by the slaughter of thousands of Hereros, but at least the appointment of Dernburg to the colonial office led to a far better administration of the subject areas.

The year 1908 brought a climax to the emperor's dangerous habit of irresponsible, off-the-cuff remarks, which usually managed to irritate the sensibilities of important people. On October 28 the London *Daily Telegraph* published an interview with William which has almost undisputed claim for pre-eminence in foolish and injudicious language. In this interview William made the claim that he was a sincere friend of England and the English people but that he was an untypical German, for the German people were inimical to Britain; he claimed that he had his hands full trying to keep Anglo-German relations on a warm basis. He said further that when the British were at their lowest ebb in the Boer War, he had worked out with his staff and sent to his grandmother Victoria a plan of campaign against the Boers. How remarkable it was, he mused, that this plan was startlingly like the strategy which the British later used successfully against their enemies. It should be added that this singular interview followed hard on the heels of a new and frightening navy bill.

An explosion followed in both the British and the German press, and German political leaders took the worst view of the way in which the German people had been laid open to ridicule. Bülow offered to resign and was vague about the matter. The fact emerged, however, that the text of the interview had twice passed across his desk at his country place in the Frisian Islands, where he was rather neglectful of business, and that it had also been examined by the foreign office before publication. This compounded the damage. A few days after the publication of the interview Bülow faced an angry Reichstag, in which each party tried to outdo the others in attack. He tried to pour as much oil as possible on the troubled waters and promised on behalf of the emperor a greater future reticence. Soon afterwards the emperor returned from a trip and, shocked at Bülow's cowardice but frightened by the stir he had caused, signed a statement promising to observe his constitutional responsibilities and publicly approving Bülow's action. From this time on there was little affection between emperor and chancellor, and it appears that the emperor was just waiting for a propitious opportunity to rid himself of his former favorite. The importance of the incident is that, when for once William was abashed, it might have been the psychological moment for the government and the Reichstag to make a decisive thrust for ministerial responsibility. That this did not occur can be laid to Bülow's dislike of party government and also to the Reichstag's habit of subservience to authority.

Bülow lingered on as chancellor for some months longer. He fell from power after a defeat on a fiscal measure. In order to finance the increased expenses of the army and navy, the government proposed an inheritance tax. This bill was, of course, very unpopular with the right of the house and it failed. Deserted by his own favorite parties as well as by the emperor, who had not forgiven him for the events of the previous autumn, Bülow offered his resignation in July 1909 and disappeared for some years from public life.

The last chancellor before the war was Dr. Theobald von Bethmann-Hollweg. Bethmann was a very different type of man from Bülow. His background was in the domestic civil service, and in particular the service in and around Brandenburg. He knew little of the problems of Germany in general, let alone foreign nations. He was scholarly, quiet, and businesslike, a great contrast to the quick and witty Bülow. He probably bored the emperor, but he seemed to grow with the years until during the war he emerged as a competent thinker, without, however, the force of character to make his conclusions accepted.

Bethmann's characteristic "too little and too late" attitude was illustrated in his handling of the domestic problems which arose in the years before 1914. One of these affected him in his capacity as minister-president of Prussia. The undemocratic character of the Prussian franchise had long been commonplace to all observers. The conservative groups were represented in the Prussian parliament out of all proportion to their numbers, while the Social Democrats with all their votes had hardly any representation. Early in his administration Bethmann tried to correct this abuse and in 1910 offered a bill to the Prussian parliament on the subject. However, the bill attempted to cure only a few of the cumbersome technicalities of the system and not the roots of the problem. Even so, the Prussian Conservatives would have nothing to do with it and defeated it. No change was made in the Prussian voting system until the panicky days just before the armistice in 1918.

Much of the interest of the Bethmann administration before the war lies in the province of Alsace-Lorraine. This area had been ruled as a federal district by the imperial government from Berlin. Now the government proposed to give it a constitution so that it might take its place on a basis of equality with the other German states. In 1911 a constitution was passed by the Reichstag, and it appeared as if Alsace-Lorraine might be better integrated into the Reich. However, as was so often the case in Germany, the lack of co-ordination between the military and civilian interests became apparent. In 1913 a storm arose over an incident that occurred in the little town of Zabern (Saverne), where an arrogant young officer behaved in a brutal manner toward some of the local townsfolk. Martial law was proclaimed when the citizens protested, and the affair reached the ears of the Reichstag where the left parties protested to the extent of a vote of no confidence in the government. This of course had no legal effect but showed some of the friction in Berlin. The garrison was removed from Zabern, but some months later its commanding officer was decorated. The whole problem of military vs. civilian authority was far from solved. The events of the war were to bring it into higher relief.

The last Reichstag election under the empire was held in 1912. Every important party in the country, except one, lost seats. The Social Democrats increased their delegation from forty-three to one hundred ten, almost a third of the whole, and became the largest single party. Their losses of 1907 were more than repaired, and Germany went into the greatest war thus far in history with one-third of the population voting for the antigovernmental socialists and another third, the Catholics, restive in what they felt was an inexcusably inferior position.

The evolution of the Social Democratic party during the reign of William II is a complex one. It did not simply follow the straight Marxian line. The first reason for this is that the Lassallean influence with the concept of the strong state remained influential. Secondly, Marxism in Germany suffered at least as much as elsewhere the series of heresies and schisms which plagued all social democracy during this period. Furthermore, the rapid growth of the party, its close affiliation with the trade union movement, and its presence in the Reichstag prevented the maintenance of the degree of aloof orthodoxy which Lenin insisted on in the underground Russian branch. There was a whole range of doctrines, but three positions in particular stand out. The furthest left, associated with the names of Karl Liebknecht and the brilliant Polish Jewess, Rosa Luxemburg, was frankly revolutionary and wanted to make use of violence and the weapon of the general strike. In a more moderate position, hoping to serve as a bridge between the two extremes, stood the famous theoretician, Karl Kautsky, whose doctrine probably most nearly approximated orthodox Marxism. Kautsky called for economic progress toward a socialist community but did not lose sight of the basic concept of the class struggle. Further to the right was the revisionist group, whose most articulate leader was Eduard Bernstein. Bernstein, impressed with the growth of the party and its invasion of the bourgeois parliamentary world of the Reichstag, looked for no catastrophic switch to the classless society but rather envisioned socialism as an indefinitely advancing tide, achieving victory after victory but not necessarily by force. This revisionist line coincided most conveniently with the trade union philosophy and became in the years leading up to 1914 the dominant trend in German socialism, although the disputes at party meetings were often acrimonious in the extreme. Under the guidance of Friedrich Ebert, Bebel's successor in the party leadership, the revisionist position usually won out. Within the ranks of the Social Democratic party the divisions were already discernible which were to lead, after the war started, to the secession of the Independent Social Democrats from the parent party and later to the secession of the Spartacus League from the Independents.

As the forces of the left were lining up for the conflicts that were to come, so were the forces of the right. Mention has already been made of the significant growth of pressure groups, specifically the Agrarian

League and the Naval League. There were two others, in particular, which were outstanding in representation and importance. One of these was the *Bund der Industriellen* ("League of Industrialists"), an opposite number to the Agrarian League, composed of the leading captains of industry who often co-operated with their rural counterparts. More interesting, however, was the famous *Alldeutscher Verband* ("Pan-German League"), founded in 1893, though a parent organization had already been in operation for a few years. The Pan-German League was a peak organization for the various right-wing, nationalist pressure groups. It set itself the task of reawakening the German people to an understanding of their unique importance and to measures which would implement the spread of German nationalism throughout the world. The Pan-Germans did not regard German nationality as ending at the frontiers of the Reich. They were much interested in German ethnic groups throughout Europe and the world and had in mind unifying these far-flung people under the standard of German *Kultur* ("culture"). The League was purposely kept small, but its membership was distinguished and influential and thus disproportionately significant. It issued a weekly paper and a large variety of publications on subjects concerned with German nationalism, colonialism, the armed forces, and the like. It organized lectures and meetings and in general kept up a steady barrage of propaganda to keep the mind of the population always focused on Germany's increasingly pre-eminent position in the world. Its first important leader, Dr. Ernst Hasse, was succeeded in 1908 by Dr. Heinrich Class, who in the war years was to be a leading fighter in the cause of the annexation of conquered territory.

Still further to the right was the rise of organized anti-Semitism in the reign of William II. Much of this activity is associated with the name of Adolf Stöcker, court preacher in Berlin, who founded the Christian Social party. He won the attention of the future William II before he became emperor, but Bismarck was violently opposed to Stöcker and warned the prince to keep away from him. In the years after 1887, however, there was always at least one anti-Semitic member of the Reichstag and at times the number reached as high as sixteen. Another figure associated with anti-Semitism during that period was Friedrich Naumann, who seceded from Stöcker's party in 1896 and formed the National Social Association, which, while it stressed German nationalism and expansionism, did not favor overt persecution of the Jews. Naumann eventually drifted into the Progressive party and as a publicist influenced a number of members of the younger generation including his biographer, Theodor Heuss, president of the German Federal Republic from 1949 to 1959.

The lines of cleavage which were perceptible in the Bismarck period became much more clearly defined in the reign of William II. All that was needed was the broad catalyzing action of war to bring them into combat. The struggles of the Weimar Republic were not forged out of new materials. The elements were all present in the last years of imperial Germany.

Yet on the surface things looked serene. Germany still retained her formidable appearance to the outsider and even to most Germans. Figures could be adduced to show that economic and industrial progress was still continuing on a great scale. Learning, both in and out of the universities, was impressive and drew scholars in all fields from the whole world. In the area of literature and the fine arts there was noticeable a certain refining of the vulgar exuberance of the earlier period. Under the influence of such poets as Rainer Maria Rilke and Stefan George, a new aestheticism was apparent. As for prose, Jacob Wasserman and the brothers Thomas and Heinrich Mann were beginning to publish novels with more than a touch of social criticism. In music the exciting operas of Richard Strauss (*Der Rosenkavalier, Salomé, Elektra,* and *Ariadne auf Naxos*) appeared shortly before World War I. It looked as if Germany were about to enter a new era of cultural as well as economic supremacy. However, the shots which killed Archduke Francis Ferdinand and his wife on June 28, 1914, were to bring these aspirations to an end and launch Germany on one of the most catastrophic periods which any nation in history has suffered, a period which may not yet be ended.

CHAPTER XV

Wilhelmian Germany. II, Foreign Affairs (1890-1914)

German foreign policy during the personal rule of William II is sharply contrasted with that of the period dominated by Bismarck. The steadying influence of the old master was gone and the new policy was mercurial, unpredictable, and, on the whole, unsuccessful. There are several reasons for this change. A first is the changed quality of international affairs, which were now world-wide in scope rather than continental. Secondly, of course, the personality of the emperor set the tone for his policy. Finally, after 1890, policy was never in the hands of one man; in fact, it is often hard to know who was in charge. During the Caprivi and Hohenlohe ministries the secretaries of state for foreign affairs, Marschall von Bieberstein and Bernhard von Bülow, were much more influential than their predecessors under Bismarck. Another important influence was Count Philipp von Eulenburg, the emperor's one close personal friend. Finally, and possibly most important, was the bizarre, sinister, and misanthropic figure of Baron Fritz von Holstein. After his unsavory connection with the von Arnim affair, Holstein, disliked by, and disliking, society, retired to the recesses of the foreign office and there labored under Bismarck for many years, making himself more familiar than anyone else with the business of that office. After the retirement of Bismarck and his son, Holstein became the indispensable man, and until his resignation in 1906 was the determining force in many of the most important decisions.

The first major decision of the new regime in 1890 was the question of the renewal of the Reinsurance Treaty with Russia, which was to lapse in the summer of that year. At first blush William and Caprivi were inclined to renew the treaty and so informed the Russian ambassador. However, Holstein was opposed to it and in the course of a few days convinced the emperor and chancellor that it violated the spirit of the Triple Alliance. The decision was made not to renew the treaty. Many historians, encouraged by Bismarck in retirement, have blamed this decision for the subsequent Franco-Russian alliance which followed soon after it. Probably this is pushing the point too far. Germany chose once for all between Russia and Austria. The Russian friendship would have been difficult to retain because of the forward policy which Germany later undertook in the Balkans and the Middle East. Yet it remains true that having let one relationship lapse, Germany should have sought another, probably in London. In fact, she did the opposite by a series of sniping attacks on Britain which conditioned the British to enter the opposite camp in 1904.

One episode in 1890 suggested that perhaps Germany and Great Britain were going to move closer to each other. This was the treaty by which Germany relinquished her rights in the neighborhood of Zanzibar in East Africa and in return received from Britain the little island of Heligoland off the mouth of the Elbe River. This agreement received a good deal of criticism in Germany, especially by the colonialists, who felt that Germany had surrendered far too much for what she gained. However, the importance of Heligoland in both world wars of the twentieth century suggests that Germany was not the loser.

As the decade of the nineties wore on, German policy became more and more marked by a spirit of adventurousness, described by the German word *Weltpolitik* ("world politics"). Determined that no decisions be made anywhere in the world without the voice of Germany, the emperor fished in all troubled waters and extended his undiplomatic arm as far as possible. This activity was accompanied by a good many blustering speeches indicating ambitions which alarmed the other powers. Since British interests were also far-flung, it was almost inevitable that the two powers should clash. The most spectacular example of this clash was in connection with the growing conflict between the British in South Africa and the two independent Boer republics, the Orange Free State and the Transvaal. At the end of 1895 Dr. Jameson, with the support of Cecil Rhodes, premier of Cape Colony, and perhaps with the privy knowledge of Joseph Chamberlain, colonial secretary, led an unsuccessful filibustering raid against the Boer city of Johannesburg. The news of this raised a storm in Berlin. The alleged (and unfactual) racial kinship between Germans and Boers, and the economic interests of Germany in the Transvaal, were adduced as reasons for German intervention in the area. Emperor William talked about sending German marines to South Africa and was with difficulty persuaded by his advisers to limit his activity to sending a telegram of congratulations and encouragement to President Kruger of the Transvaal. This telegram infuriated public opinion in Great Britain, and, though the two governments managed to deal with the matter with commendable coolness, Germanophobia in England and Anglophobia in Germany became significant factors in the general European picture.

Other examples can be adduced of the geographical extension of German foreign policy during these years. In 1895 the German government joined with the French and Russian in insisting that Japan abandon her demand for the Liaotung Peninsula and Port Arthur after her victory over China. This action emphasized the German emperor's constant fear of Japan, "the yellow peril," and also his dream of a continental alliance of France, Germany, and Russia. In 1897 in retaliation for the murder of two German missionaries in China, the Germans landed at Kiao-chow, on the Shantung Peninsula, and by the following year had extracted a ninety-nine-year lease of that territory from the Chinese. This action was followed by similar Russian and British leases on the north China coast. In 1898, the year of the first German naval law, a German fleet with unknown orders appeared suddenly off Manila Bay just as Admiral Dewey was attacking the Spanish fleet during the Spanish-American War. In 1899 Germany made use of British preoccupation with the Boer War to demand and gain several of the islands in the Samoan group. In 1900 the German emperor, seizing on the murder of the German minister in Peking by the Boxers, a Chinese nationalist group, demanded and obtained the appointment of Field Marshal von Waldersee as the commander in chief of the international army sent to restore peace in the Chinese capital. It was upon this occasion that William wrote a new chapter in the history of gaucherie by instructing his forces to act like the Huns of old, thus giving enemy propagandists in two great wars material for unlimited copy.

Closer to home the Germans were also undertaking an active policy in the Ottoman Empire and the Middle East. The efforts of Marschall von Bieberstein, now German ambassador in Constantinople, to woo the Turks were gradually crowned with success. In 1898 William and his consort paid a second visit to the sultan. Then, advancing on Damascus, the emperor gave a mighty speech in which he described himself as "protector of Islam," even though the great majority of members of that religion were subjects of Britain, Russia, or France. Another aspect of this diplomatic and economic advance was the scheme for a Berlin-to-Baghdad railway, a project which would have brought German influence uncomfortably close to India. In general, no stone was left unturned to make Germany both heard and unpopular in the world at large.

These years of the new century were decisive in outlining the future because it was during them that Germany repulsed several efforts by the British government to draw closer to her, even to the extent of a proposed alliance. Joseph Chamberlain appeared as the friend of Germany. Once again in agreement with the sentiments of Cecil Rhodes, Chamberlain favored an Anglo-German-American alliance and broached the subject to Emperor William and Bülow while they were visiting London in late 1899. Chamberlain went so far as to open the subject in a public speech at Leicester on November 30, which received much criticism in both England and Germany. The Germans, particularly Bülow and Holstein, were decidedly lukewarm about the matter but let negotiations continue for over a year. They felt that Britain was much more anxious for the arrangement than Germany. Thus they tried to extort more advantage from London, even to the point of insisting that Great Britain take on all three members of the Triple Alliance as her partners instead of allying with Germany alone. By the spring of 1901 the British were tired of the subject; Lord Salisbury, the prime minister, ended the negotiations and turned instead to Japan, with which Britain concluded an alliance the following year. In the years to come England moved continually closer to France and Russia, and all hope of a real Anglo-German *rapprochement* faded. It is of course impossible to speculate what would have been the result of such an alliance at this juncture, but one may criticize the rather cavalier manner with which the Germans treated overtures from so considerable a power as Great Britain.

After the turn of the century, in spite of boisterous utterances by Emperor William indicating confidence, the initiative in foreign policy slipped from Germany into the hands of her eventual enemies. Certainly the most striking development of these years was the flirtation between the two historical opponents, Great Britain and France, culminating in the Entente Cordiale of 1904. This relationship was frightening to Germany, especially in light of the Franco-Russian alliance. However, Russia was soon in trouble in the Far East, where she was being defeated by the Japanese. In reply Germany undertook a double-barreled and inconsistent policy. On the one hand, she offered her friendship to Russia with the opportunity for France to join the grouping, William's continental scheme; on the other hand, she challenged France in Morocco at a time when Russia was too concerned elsewhere to help her ally and also as a device to test the strength of the new Anglo-French relationship.

Gestures toward Russia began with aid, comfort, and coal to the Russian Baltic Sea fleet on its odyssey to the Far East to be destroyed by the Japanese at Tsushima. Emperor William, fearful of the possible rise of

Asiatic states, was willing to remain benevolent toward Russia while she was at war with Japan. The next year William encountered Tsar Nicholas II while the two were cruising in their yachts on the Baltic Sea. They met in 1905 near the island of Björkö—William in a sunny playful mood, Nicholas ending a disastrous war and fighting a serious revolution at home. William happened to have in his pocket a draft treaty calling for mutual aid between Germany and Russia in Europe and inviting France to adhere to the agreement. Nicholas signed the draft, but the two monarchs were much dismayed when, on their return home, their respective foreign offices would have nothing to do with the treaty; further, the French vetoed the idea out of hand. This abortive episode suggests the folly of placing impetuous and irresponsible monarchs at the head of great and powerful nations.

The first Moroccan crisis might have developed into a world war in 1905. As it turned out, it was a diplomatic triumph for France and a defeat for Germany, and also announced to the world that the Entente between Britain and France meant business. The position of Morocco was confused. Nominally independent, it bordered on French Algeria and caused the French a great deal of trouble from border raids of bandits and irregular detachments. Furthermore, France, Germany, Spain, and Italy all had considerable economic investment in Morocco, which they were anxious to safeguard. Finally, the strategic location of the area across from Gibraltar aroused British interest. In early 1905 France, under the direction of her active foreign minister, Théophile Delcassé, made an arrangement with the sultan of Morocco which was so binding that Morocco would have become the equivalent of a French protectorate. Germany was excluded from any participation in this arrangement. Therefore, Bülow and Holstein thought this would be a good moment to halt France's advance. They persuaded the emperor to take a trip to Morocco, where he was to land at Tangier and treat the sultan as an independent sovereign with no reference to France. The visit was a fiasco. Landing at Tangier and bounding ashore, William was first faced by a nervous and restive horse, which almost threw him. He then rushed into the town and made a speech calling for an open-door policy with an equality of opportunity in Morocco for all nations. The reaction to this was a division of opinion within the French cabinet. Rouvier, the premier, wished to back down. He did not want to run the risk of war with Germany while Russia was in serious straits and before he was sure of the new English relationship. Delcassé, on the other hand, put full faith in Britain and wanted to push the advantage. Rouvier prevailed, and Delcassé resigned. So far the crisis had been a German victory.

Lengthy negotiations ensued and resulted in an agreement to hold an international conference partly at the instance of the American president, Theodore Roosevelt. Accordingly, the Algeciras conference was held in early 1906 at a little town in Spain across the bay from Gibraltar. The conference was a disappointment to Germany. Russia backed the French position; even Italy, a partner of Germany in the Triple Alliance, supported France; and most important, Great Britain stood consistently behind her new friend, France. An agreement was finally reached, which reaffirmed the independence of Morocco and granted France more influence there than any other power but not as much as she had tried to obtain by the earlier bilateral agreement. It was at least a moral victory for France. At home in Berlin it led to the forced resignation of Holstein and the beginning of the decline of Bülow's influence over the emperor.

Once again, the initiative in international affairs passed to the anti-German cabinets in Europe. Between the Moroccan affair and the next major crisis, the leading event was the Anglo-Russian Entente which brought together France's two friends and finally divided Europe into two opposed and apparently roughly equivalent groupings—the Triple Alliance of Germany, Austria-Hungary, and Italy; and the Triple Entente of Great Britain, France, and Russia.

A year after the Triple Entente came into existence, Europe was once more brought to the brink of war by the crisis which arose over the annexation of Bosnia and Herzegovina by Austria-Hungary. In this episode Germany was not a primary agent and was content merely with supporting her Viennese partner and thus sharing in Russian anger. By virtue of the Treaty of Berlin of 1878 Austria-Hungary had garrisoned and administered the two Slavic provinces to her south. The Austrian foreign minister, Baron von Ährenthal, decided to press for the complete annexation of the provinces and the ending of the fiction of Turkish sovereignty over them. He was impelled to this partly as a result of difficulties at home and a consequent need for a victory abroad, and also because he feared that the vigorous new Young Turk government might try to regain control of Turkey's former territories. He arranged a meeting with the Russian foreign minister, Izvolski, at which Russia agreed not to object to the annexation if she could get permission from the powers to send her war vessels through the Straits from the Black Sea to the Mediterranean. Izvolski was still on his pilgrimage to the various capitals to obtain this permission when Ährenthal announced unilaterally on October 6, 1908, the annexation of Bosnia and Herzegovina to Austria-Hungary. This action caused consternation throughout Europe, particularly in Serbia, which had designs on the two provinces in order to create a great south Slavic state and which looked to her big Slavic brother, Russia, for support. The Russian emperor seems not to have known about Izvolski's share in the proceedings and to have forced him to repudiate the deal about the Straits. Germany's part in the crisis was relatively minor. She was annoyed that she had not received prior information from her ally but nevertheless resolved to back Austria. Russia, still weak from the Japanese war and the revolution of 1905, was in no position to provoke a European war, especially as she was not at all sure of the position Great Britain would take, and thus had to back down. Austria won her last diplomatic victory. However, the rancor which had been sown in the hearts of the Russian leaders did not die. From this time until the outbreak of war in 1914, Russia was bitterly opposed to Austria's aspirations in the Balkans and naturally included in her anger Germany, Austria's ally.

Before the prewar diplomatic scene centered itself in the Balkan Peninsula after 1912, one more crisis occurred over the Moroccan question in 1911. By this time the leaders of German policy had changed. Bethmann-Hollweg had succeeded Bülow as chancellor, and Alfred von Kiderlen-Wächter, long influential in German policy, had become secretary of state for foreign affairs.

During the years since Algeciras French influence in Morocco had increased and, as a result of local uprisings in the spring of 1911, the French sent troops to the Moroccan capital. The German government objected to this as a violation of treaties; to show that they were serious, they dispatched a cruiser, the "Panther," to stand off the harbor of Agadir on the Atlantic coast of Morocco. Neither the French nor the Germans wanted this crisis to develop into a war. The French were in fact prepared to offer Germany compensation elsewhere in Africa for a free hand in Morocco. The German price, however, looked too high to them. Tension was increased by a bellicose speech given by David Lloyd George at the Mansion House in London, demanding that Britain be consulted in the crisis. Negotiations followed and in November 1911 an agreement was signed by which France was permitted to do whatever she pleased in Morocco, even to the extent of establishing a protectorate, in return for the cession to Germany of a large piece of land in the Congo area adjacent to the German colony of Cameroons.

The panorama of foreign policy in the reign of William II is not an impressive one. Although Germany had meddled in areas all over the world and sought to assert herself everywhere, she was in a less secure position than in 1890. She had had to watch first France and Russia, then

Britain and France, then Britain and Russia draw closer to each other. She was beginning to talk of a policy of "encirclement" by the Triple Entente. Within her own alliance system the relationship with Italy was at best a tenuous one. Germany had only one secure friend, Austria-Hungary, a decadent empire rent with internal dissension. It was in this situation that Germany faced the series of crises in the Balkans which led directly into the war of 1914. The historian cannot help being impressed by the blindness of the German emperor and his favored advisers in establishing their priority of aims. This is not to suggest that they wanted a general war. No one did. However, an almost irresponsible attitude forced just those actions which would most irritate other powers. An example of this type of behavior occurred in 1912. Early in that year the British government sent its minister of war, Lord Haldane, to Berlin to explore the possibilities of reducing the tensions between the two nations, especially concerning naval and colonial problems. There was disagreement between German civilian and military officials. As usual, the emperor sided with his military advisers. The result was that while colonial problems appeared easy to settle, the question of the increasing German navy was insoluble. Thus the mission failed. Again, as in the case of the Chamberlain overtures a decade earlier, one cannot guess what the result might have been, but as in that case it is hard to avoid the feeling that this was another missed opportunity.

The major diplomatic interest of the years 1912 and 1913 revolved around the Balkan Peninsula, where two local wars stringently reduced the territory of Turkey in Europe and increased that of the Christian Balkan states. They also had the effect of baring, even more sharply than the Bosnian crisis had, the conflicting policies of Russia and Austria-Hungary in the area. Germany played a relatively small part in these events. Her main involvement with them was in two spheres: continued support of her ally, Austria, with consequent alienation of Russia; and her increasing penetration of the Ottoman Empire.

Although Germany on the whole backed up Austria in the various crises arising out of the Balkan wars (e.g., Austria's determination that Serbia should not receive a coastal strip), there is evidence to suggest that Germany was sometimes irritated at Austria's belligerent attitudes and on occasion did her best to curb Austrian demands. It is interesting to compare this behavior of the German leaders with that of the French who were doing much the same thing with their ally, Russia. In fact, during these years Great Britain, France, and Germany exerted a moderating influence on their allies, and there even appeared to be some sense of a concert of Europe operating at a higher level than the two systems of alliance. This at least was the effort of Sir Edward Grey, British foreign secretary, and it was not without support in Berlin and Paris.

After her poor showing in the Balkan wars Turkey was resolved to improve the condition of her army and invited a German general to come to Constantinople and undertake this task, as she had earlier invited a British admiral to do the same for her navy. General Liman von Sanders was appointed and arrived in Turkey in the closing days of 1913. His arrival caused great disquiet in St. Petersburg, and Sazonov, the Russian foreign minister, protested violently about undue German influence in Turkey and in the Straits, always a sensitive spot to the Russians. Sazonov was right in his apprehension that Germany was becoming more and more influential in Turkey. This was a continuing process that had been developing ever since the accession of William II, but particularly since the Young Turk revolutions of 1908 and 1909. The appointment of Liman was really just an incidental aspect of a much broader matter, concerning which much light is still lacking. The affair threatened to become a real crisis, but was finally settled when Liman was promoted in the Prussian army and therefore received the rank of field marshal in the Turkish army. Thus he had too much rank to be in command of the corps at Constantinople, the point about which the Russians were most exercised. He became instead inspector general of the Turkish army.

The spring of 1914 was a pleasant moment in this period of "international anarchy." It looked as if this were to be a peaceful year. The British and the Germans were agreeing on some outstanding problems. For example, the troublesome matter of the future of the Portuguese colonial empire seemed to become manageable. Britain and Germany reached an agreement on the question of the Berlin-to-Baghdad railway. Plans were made for Emperor William to take a cruise through Norwegian waters during July and for the French president, Raymond Poincaré, to pay a state visit to the tsar. Upon this peaceful scene there fell the news, on June 28, that Archduke Francis Ferdinand, heir to the thrones of Austria-Hungary, and his wife had been murdered while on a visit to Sarajevo, capital of Bosnia. This was the event whose repercussions plunged Europe, and eventually the world, into war within five weeks.

Probably more ink has been spilled on the crisis of July 1914 than on any other similar event in history. The clause of the Treaty of Versailles of 1919 which gave Germany and her allies the full responsibility for launching the war on a peace-loving world has led to the publication of thousands of pages of documents and memoirs and thousands more of analysis and interpretation. There is no reason to reassess the crisis here. An attempt will be made to describe only Germany's immediate connection with it and to make some judgment on the actions of the German government.

Emperor William was shocked and angered by the news of the murder of his friend and hunting companion, the archduke. He was thus prepared to receive encouragingly an emissary from Vienna on July 5, who was sent to ascertain the German view of the matter. The emissary, Count Hoyos, was received by both William and Chancellor Bethmann. In his message Count Berchtold, Austro-Hungarian foreign minister, described the continuing barrage of anti-Austrian activity emanating from ambitious Serbia. Although the murder had been committed by a Bosnian, an Austrian national, there was little doubt that it had been inspired from Belgrade. Berchtold felt that this outrage, commanding as it must the reprobation of the world, was an admirable opportunity for ending the Serbian nuisance once and for all, and that it was time to give little Serbia such a spanking that she would never again indulge in anti-Austrian gestures. Emperor William agreed to this and informed the Austrian government that Germany would back any action that Austria might see fit to take. He then left for his summer cruise, clearly of the opinion that this crisis would be a local one which Austria could handle with her own means.

The next Austrian step was postponed for almost three weeks. It took the form, on July 23, of an ultimatum so sternly worded that complete compliance with it would have meant abrogation of sovereignty by Serbia. Upon news of this, Russia, acting as the Slavic big brother, indicated her solidarity with Serbia and probably encouraged Serbia to make a conciliatory but evasive answer, which Austria declared unsatisfactory. At this point the crisis ceased to be a local Balkan problem and became a general European one, with Russia and Austria as the protagonists. Britain and France entered the picture as allies of Russia, Germany as the ally of Austria. Sir Edward Grey proposed an international conference to deal with the problem. Germany's attitude toward this was that a conference was not suitable for a discussion of an affair that concerned Austria's honor, e.g., the crisis with Serbia, but that one might be possible on the subject of the Austro-Russian friction. In the meantime Bethmann, convinced at last of the seriousness of the crisis, tried to dampen Austria's aggressiveness; but it was too late. On July 28, 1914, Austria declared war on Serbia.

Austria's impulsive declaration led into the third phase of the crisis, the phase in which the military leaders quickly took precedence over the civilian diplomats, especially in Germany and Russia. At that time it was military doctrine that mobilization meant war and that it was crucial to start mobilization before the prospective enemy. Furthermore, the various general staffs had worked out strategic plans of campaign for various contingencies, and these plans often had serious diplomatic implications. This was particularly true in the case of Germany. The German General Staff, under the leadership of its former chief, Count Alfred von Schlieffen, had worked out a plan for a simultaneous war against France and Russia. This plan envisaged the defeat of France before Russia, on the theory that France with her greater efficiency would be ready to fight sooner than Russia and thus was the greater menace. It therefore became essential to know what attitude France planned to take. Also the plan envisaged the attack on France through Belgium and Luxemburg, in spite of the guaranteed neutrality of those two states. In Russia the generals, knowing the inefficiency of their army and the enormous size of the country with its lack of railroads, were sure to press for the earliest possible mobilization in order to be at the least possible disadvantage. Both William II and Nicholas II were under severe and increasing pressure to order mobilization in spite of the reluctance of both to invite a situation sure to lead to war.

In Russia the problem was almost ridiculous. The tsar gave in to pressure and ordered general mobilization on July 29. However, when he heard later the same day that Germany was trying to restrain Austria, he countermanded his order and called for mobilization against Austria only. He was informed that there were no plans for such a situation. So on July 30 general mobilization was once again ordered.

On the following day Germany sent a twelve-hour ultimatum to Russia demanding that she cease mobilizing on the German frontier. At the same time she demanded to know what France was proposing to do. On August 1, 1914, the French replied evasively that they would be guided by their own interests and a few hours later mobilized. A few minutes later Germany did so too, and an hour later declared war on Russia. The next day the Schlieffen plan was placed in operation, Luxemburg invaded, and Belgium invited unsuccessfully by the Germans to remain neutral in spite of invasion. On August 3 Germany declared war on France, and on the following day Great Britain, impelled both by her commitments to France and by the violation of Belgian neutrality, declared war on Germany. The world was at war; in Sir Edward Grey's famous phrase, "the lights had gone out all over Europe."

Few scholars today would agree with the war-guilt clause of the Treaty of Versailles, that Germany and her allies were exclusively guilty of the war. On the other hand, Germany participated with the other nations in the indirect causes of the war: militarism, commercial rivalry, imperialism, and national chauvinism. On a more immediate level, the German government erred in granting so readily to Austria the so-called blank check of support on July 5. Wiser men might well have seen the implications of Austria's determination to chastise Serbia. Germany might well have participated to a greater degree in the efforts of Grey and others to prolong negotiations. She also might have restrained the enthusiasm of her military leaders. Yet in the long view it appears that if a war had not broken out at this moment, it very likely would have soon thereafter. Germany's tragedy was the world's tragedy.

CHAPTER XVI

World War I (1914-18)

Speaking to members of the Reichstag assembled at the palace in Berlin shortly after the outbreak of the war, Emperor William declared, "I know no more parties; I know only Germans." With this remark the emperor ushered in the *Burgfrieden* ("civil peace"), which continued with relatively little disturbance until 1917. The first manifestation of this unanimity occurred almost immediately when, on August 4, 1914, the Reichstag without dissent passed a request for the first appropriation bill to finance the war. The interest of this event lies in the fact that the Social Democrats, in spite of their pacifist doctrine, joined in the affirmative vote. They rationalized this action in terms of a war against the tsarist autocracy, but they also unwittingly laid the foundation for the split in the party which was to become open in 1917 and very important in the years immediately thereafter.

Meanwhile all eyes were focused on the military scene. The German mobilization proceeded with the expected clocklike accuracy, and the Schlieffen plan was placed in operation under the incompetent and ailing chief of staff, Moltke, a nephew of the great Moltke. Eight large German armies were set in motion to advance in a series of concentric arcs, the easternmost pivoting near the northeast corner of France while the westernmost, under General von Kluck, was to sweep across Belgium and down into France while keeping to the west of Paris. The idea was to make a great enveloping movement around Paris, pushing the French army continually ahead of the German in a southward and then eastward direction until the French were caught in a trap between two German elements somewhere in Champagne or Lorraine, where they could be annihilated or forced to surrender. It is impossible to judge the Schlieffen plan because it was never carried out as devised. Several factors entered into this failure. One was that Moltke was ill and remained at Koblenz, then Luxemburg, a long way from the center of activity; a hesitant and indecisive man, he was incapable of firm action.

The French attempted an invasion of German Lorraine, which was repulsed; instead of remaining on the defensive there and permitting the decisive action to be taken by the western armies, the German command ordered an offensive into France near Nancy. This came to nothing but used troops which would better have been sent to reinforce the vital army of Kluck. With the First German Army Kluck entered Brussels in triumph on August 20, 1914, and then started south into France. On August 25 Moltke made an inexcusable error. Overoptimistic about events in the west and worried at the news of a Russian invasion of East Prussia, he detached two corps from General von Bülow's Second Army, Kluck's neighbor, and sent them to the east. These troops, had they remained, might have changed the outcome of the battle of the Marne; as it was, they arrived in the east too late to be of use. By August 30 the Schlieffen plan was completely sabotaged when Kluck, worried about the gap that was developing between his army and Bülow's, ordered a shift of course to the eastward, which led him to the northeast instead of the northwest of Paris. The French and a small British army, which had arrived quickly in France, were able to take advantage of these changes and prepared a major effort to stop the German advance. By September 4 the German armies had crossed the Marne River and were at one point less than twenty miles from Paris. Here, under the command of General Joffre, the French armies stopped their retreat and from September 6 to 12 fought the first battle of the Marne or, as the French prefer to think of it, the "miracle of the Marne." The French gave their all to this battle, even ordering out the garrison of Paris under its aged general, Galliéni, who transported his men to the battlefield in taxicabs. The result of the battle was that the Germans were not only stopped but pushed back a considerable distance. Its importance is not to be measured by the territory regained but by the fact that the inertia of the German army was brought to a halt. Shortly after the Marne Moltke was replaced by a new chief of staff, General Erich von Falkenhayn, although the change was kept secret for some weeks. Moltke did not long outlive his disgrace.

The next two months on the western front are generally known as "the race for the sea." The action consisted of a gradual widening of the battle front until by November it reached the English Channel coast at a point just northeast of the Franco-Belgian border, where with a few small shifts it remained anchored for almost the duration of the war. During this period the main action in the west lay with the British who carried out a heroic, if perhaps badly planned, defense of Ypres. It was becoming clear to many observers that the defenders had the advantage in this type of warfare, but the high commands did not accept this fact willingly. By the end of the year opposing armies dug a long series of trenches extending from the channel to the Swiss border in a generally southeasterly direction; thus began the horrible warfare of position and attrition which was to last for four years, one of the most bloody holocausts in human history.

In the east, events were more decisive and quite different. The Russians astonished both their enemies and their allies by mobilizing part of their army with commendable speed. In mid-August the First Russian Army under the command of General Rennenkampf started an advance westward into East Prussia, apparently heading for the city of Königsberg; at about the same time the Second Russian Army under General Samsonov was headed northward toward the same area from the neighborhood of Warsaw. At this news Berlin became jittery; the German commander in the east, Prittwitz, lost his nerve and, immediately thereafter, his command. At this point Moltke, in spite of his usual incompetence, made an exceedingly wise choice. On the evening of August 22 an aged and retired general, whose career had been dependable if not brilliant, received the news that he had been put in command of an army in the east and that he was to be at the Hanover railway station at three in the morning where he would meet the chief of staff attached to him. Thus occurred the meeting of two men whose collaboration was to rule the army and Germany itself during the later years of the war; one of them was further reserved to be the chief executive of his nation during nine decisive years. General Paul von Hindenburg-Beneckendorff and General Erich Ludendorff entrained at Hanover and made their way eastward to take over Prittwitz' command. This combination was to be an extraordinarily fruitful one. The two men became almost a duplicate personality during the war, HL (Hindenburg-Ludendorff) the Rosencrantz and Guildenstern of the war. Hindenburg was loyal, reliable, massive, solid, not overly intelligent, but able to maintain morale and confidence; Ludendorff, probably the major military mind of the war on either side, was tough, intellectual, aggressive, active, and determined. The combination worked with remarkably few clashes almost to the armistice of 1918.

Upon their arrival in the east the new commanders were met by Colonel Hoffman, another brilliant strategist, who had worked out a plan for dealing with the Russian menace with the modest forces at his disposal. Hindenburg and Ludendorff approved the plan, and it was put into operation. The main object was to prevent the two Russian armies from joining and overwhelming the Germans by force of numbers. This was rendered easier by the general inefficiency of the Russians, by the fact that they did not use code in their messages, and because the two

Russian generals had loathed each other ever since they had engaged in a fist fight during the Russo-Japanese War. During the last week of August the Germans achieved a brilliant and complete victory over Samsonov near Tannenberg, scene of the Slavic defeat of the Teutonic Knights in the fifteenth century. A few days later an almost equally decisive victory was won over Rennenkampf at the battle of the Masurian Lakes. Lack of manpower prevented a complete pursuit of the fleeing Russians, but the threat in the east was ended and two new names entered the military pantheon.

The following months saw Hindenburg anxious to follow his earlier triumphs with a concerted drive against the Russians to force them out of the war. To accomplish this he would need more troops; here he came into conflict with Falkenhayn, whose interests centered in the west. In spite of the conflict Hindenburg, now commander of all German forces in the east, came to the aid of the Austrian ally, whose territory in Galicia had also been invaded by the Russians. During November and December the Germans pushed across western Poland along a wide front and captured the important city of Lodz. The winter lull found them not many miles from Warsaw, the Polish metropolis.

With the approach of fighting weather in 1915 the Russian commander in chief, Grand Duke Nicholas, decided to attack the Austrians in Galicia. This offensive was so successful that the Russians soon seemed to be in a position to dash down the Carpathian Mountains into the vital Hungarian plain. Austria was in dire straits, for in addition to her failures in this area she also had been unable to conquer little Serbia. Austria's plight forced Falkenhayn's unwilling hand, and he allocated large reinforcements of German troops to replace Austrians in the area near Cracow. A new army was formed under the supreme command of Hindenburg, but immediately under General von Mackensen with Seeckt as chief of staff. In April the German offensive was launched, and the great Russian retreat began. It was a melancholy year for Russia. In August Warsaw was taken, and by September the line in the east had stabilized itself where it was to remain with minor shifts until the Russian Revolution in 1917. It started in the north near Riga and pursued an almost straight north-south course to the Romanian border. Thus Russia had lost to Germany nearly all of Poland and Lithuania and part of Latvia. Germany was no longer threatened from the east. She could now turn her full attention to her British and French enemies in the west.

Little is gained by a detailed examination of the fighting in the west in 1915. Both sides were mainly occupied in learning to fight trench warfare, for which no one was trained. It became increasingly clear that matériel rather than men was the vital need; it also became apparent to some that the western front was going to remain deadlocked and that another front had to be developed to achieve victory. This consideration impelled the British to launch the ill-fated campaign against the Turks (who had entered the war on the German side in October 1914) on the Gallipoli Peninsula. On the whole, however, the belligerents stuck to the idea of drives against the line. During 1915 the Allies undertook most of the offensive fighting because Germany had committed so many of her reserves in the east. Britain launched a major attack near Ypres during which the Germans introduced the use of gas; France, a little later, undertook an offensive in Champagne. Both were unsuccessful in proportion to the men and matériel used. More and more discouragement developed at the prospects for the future.

On the diplomatic front there was intense activity during the first eighteen months of the war, resulting in an increase of the number of nations committed. The fighting was not a month old when Japan entered on the Allied side and drove the Germans out of their Far Eastern possessions. Shortly afterward in October the Turks, long under the influence of Germany, joined their friends and opened a front against Russia in the Caucasus. More important, Turkey's participation was a threat to the vital British position in the eastern Mediterranean and the Middle East. The great prize seemed to be the adherence of Italy. Both sides tenderly wooed this reluctant virgin. Germany sent Prince Bülow and his charming Italian wife with offers of juicy pieces of territory to be taken from her ally, Austria. It was easier for the western Allies, who were at war with both Austria and Turkey, each Italy's prospective prey. A treaty was signed with Italy at London in April 1915, promising Italy considerable slices of both these empires after the victory. In return, Italy declared war on Austria in May and opened a new front in the Alps, to the further discomfiture of the already weakened Hapsburg monarchy. The German bloc achieved its last diplomatic success when Bulgaria joined it in September 1915. This made it at last possible to conquer Serbia and to connect by rail the Central Powers with their Turkish ally.

At home in Germany a good deal of optimism reigned during 1915. No enemy soldier was on German soil; on the contrary, German armies were deep into Russia, Belgium, and France. It looked like merely a matter of time. This optimism was reinforced by the press, which invariably looked at the rosy side of the picture. The civil peace continued, and one of the main preoccupations of important Germans was to decide what Germany was really fighting for and what she should demand of her prostrate enemies when the time came for peace terms. Opinion rapidly crystallized into considering Great Britain the principal enemy. This is observed in the famous "Hymn of Hate" directed against England and in the slogan *"Gott strafe England"* ("May God punish England"). Much of this attitude was based on jealousy of Britain's economic and commercial dominance, which, it was argued, forced Britain to desire the destruction of Germany, her main rival. Accordingly, the idea of striking at Britain's future by continually increasing German preeminence became a popular one. The way to achieve this was to threaten Britain on her industrial front. From this to an aggressive program, aimed at annexing Belgium and the industrial areas of northern France and the harbors facing Britain, was a short step. The demands of the annexationists were completed by a plan to annex unspecified, but certainly large, territories in the east, which were to be taken from Russia to serve Germany as agricultural lands to increase her food supply. This program of annexationism dominated the minds of most of the leading German industrialists and the military and naval figures. It entered the political parties as well; the further right the party, the more annexationist. Even many of the moderate socialists were not immune, rationalizing their position by stating that if any lands were rescued from the black tsarist autocracy, it would constitute social progress. Naturally the right-wing pressure groups were most vociferous in this movement, taking their lead from the Pan-German League, which disseminated all kinds of propaganda for the cause of the *Kriegszielbewegung* ("war-aims movement").

Not all Germans were annexationists. There were a number of leaders who took a much more moderate position. The most important of these was the chancellor, Bethmann. He was a man of good sense and generally of good will, but he was a chronic straddler and not strong enough a personality to force his opinions in the way Bismarck would have done. Bethmann had long been convinced that a reform in the German government was bound to occur. In particular, he knew that the illiberal Prussian three-class system of voting had to go. He saw with dismay that the same forces which were riding the annexationist bandwagon were also those which opposed reform. He feared the extremists, so his speeches tried to temper right-wing enthusiasm, but in this effort he lost much of his former support and moved gradually to his fall in the summer of 1917 when Germany was rapidly becoming a military dictatorship dominated by Ludendorff.

The year 1916 opened with continuing German optimism. Russia and Serbia were no longer problems. The Allies had been uniformly unsuccessful in their offensives. Falkenhayn was free to move large numbers of German reinforcements back to the west and also to pick a spot for the major offensive. He concluded that he would mount so massive an offensive against the French that they would be forced out of the war. For this operation he picked a hitherto relatively quiet sector, quiet because it was heavily fortified by the French. The Germans decided to focus their attack upon the fortress of Verdun, the capture of which, they argued, would so strain French resources and so lower morale that all would be lost for France. Thus in late February the attack began, one of the great epics of military history. Descriptive language cannot depict the horror and macabre magnificence of the following several months; it requires the pen of the novelist, not of the historian. Fortunately, Jules Romains' novel *Verdun* has caught much of this grandeur and pity. The fighting went on from February to July. The Germans captured outlying outpost after outpost; they advanced yard by yard at unimaginable cost in blood and effort. However, the French held. The story can be summed up in the immortal phrase of the French general most associated with the defense, General Henri Philippe Pétain: *Ils ne passeront pas* ("They shall not pass"). And they did not pass.

Before the battle of Verdun the British and French had agreed that they would launch a major offensive in the summer of 1916. As the fighting at Verdun became more intense, the Allied offensive became more urgently needed to relieve the pressure on the French army by forcing the Germans to divide their forces. On July 1 the British opened a furious bombardment in the west near the river Somme. This again was one of the great epics of the war. It lasted until exhaustion was reached in October. Once again the story repeated itself. The British gained some ground; the line at the end of the battle was more favorable to the Allies than it had been; a new weapon, the tank, had been introduced. Yet where was this to end? No nation could continue for much longer this almost mortal attrition. All were exhausted, especially the Germans, who had strained every nerve during the year. A new factor, however, presented itself in the west. After the failure of the battle for Verdun in late August 1916 Falkenhayn was removed from command and sent to defeat the Romanians, who had just come into the war; he carried this mission out quickly and efficiently. To replace him, Hindenburg and Ludendorff were brought from the east and placed in command of all German armies, the latter with the title of Quartermaster-General. It was to be expected that a new type of strategy would develop.

However, the events of 1917, the year of decision, were not dependent upon German strategy on the western front. Other relatively unconnected events were to prove decisive in the long run. One of these was the war at sea.

The naval war can be divided into two parts: occurrences on the surface of the seas, and action underneath. The latter was much more important. Except for some romantic additions to the lore of the sea—and also the greatest naval battle in history up to that time, a battle which, however, was indecisive—the surface fleets accomplished remarkably little except escort duties. Early in the war occurred the epic of the fleet commanded by Admiral Graf Spee, who took his ships across the Pacific Ocean from the German China station and defeated a British fleet off the coast of Chile, but found defeat and death at the hands of the British at the battle of the Falkland Islands on December 8, 1914. In addition, there were the activities of the famous commerce raiders, of which the best known was the "Emden," which made the Indian Ocean perilous for the British during the first year of the war. The German High Seas Fleet itself made a number of forays out of its harbors and came in contact with units of the British Grand Fleet upon occasion. The one major battle did not occur until May 31, 1916, when the battle of Jutland was fought, with Admiral Scheer in command of the Germans and Admiral Jellicoe of the British. Naval historians still disagree about the result. The British sustained the greater losses, but the Germans retired from the scene. Thereafter the High Seas Fleet spent nearly all its time in harbor, where many of the sailors, bored with their sedentary life, became the prey of defeatist propagandists and prepared themselves for their role in starting the revolution of 1918.

Much more significant than the surface action was the activity of the submarines. The vital importance of preventing merchant vessels from bringing goods and supplies to the enemy became rapidly apparent to both Britain and Germany, and they quickly undertook such measures as they could to starve each other economically. Geography favored the British, who could pretty well control the sea routes leading to Germany. The British early declared parts of the North Sea war zones and arrogated to themselves the right to search ships and to do their best to prevent war matériel from getting through. The problem was to what degree they could do this without raising the ire of the neutrals, particularly the United States. The American government was vigilant to protect her shipping rights, and President Woodrow Wilson addressed a number of sharp complaints to London. The German problem was much more complex. Germany, in order to prevent goods from reaching Britain, had to use submarines; here international law became heavily involved because it is impossible to save the crews of ships sunk by submarines, both because it annuls the vital element of surprise and also because there is no room for extra persons on a submarine. Nevertheless, the submarine campaign was begun early in the war, although it was not a grave threat at first because Germany did not possess many vessels. By the spring of 1915 it took on a more serious aspect when, in May, an American ship was sunk; a few days later the neutral world was horrified when a German submarine attacked and sank in eighteen minutes the great British liner "Lusitania," with a loss of over a thousand lives of whom more than a hundred were American. The German government had advertised in New York newspapers warning against embarking on the ship. The vessel did carry some war matériel and was a British ship. The legal aspect of the sinking can be argued both ways; the important thing is not the event itself but the wave of anti-German revulsion which it caused, particularly in the United States. The sinkings went on, and, as they did, President Wilson's earlier profoundly neutral attitude grew stronger until by early 1916 he received a promise from Germany that no more merchantmen would be sunk without warning and without saving human life. The submarine peril receded for some months. It is not coincidence that these were the months when the Germans hoped to win the war by the Verdun offensive and were anxious not to add the United States to their list of enemies.

By the end of the year the whole picture had changed for Germany. The Verdun offensive had failed to knock France out of the war; a Russian offensive in the summer had been dangerous enough to show that Russia could not be entirely disregarded; Falkenhayn had been replaced by Ludendorff. (Although Hindenburg was the titular superior, both military and political policy was handled by Ludendorff.) Ludendorff, who was becoming more and more the dictator of Germany, became convinced that the war could not be won on land and that Germany's only hope was to starve Britain. His staff had drawn up statistics to prove that this could be done in a matter of months if the submarine offensive were pushed as hard as possible. He therefore espoused the cause of unrestricted submarine warfare. The matter became a political rather than a purely military consideration. Ludendorff was backed by most of the leading naval and military figures, as well as the leading annexationists. Their main opponent was Chancellor Bethmann, who feared the repercussions abroad. The submarine enthusiasts won the ear of the emperor, and on February 1, 1917, unrestricted submarine warfare was declared. The next day the United States broke diplomatic relations with Germany but did not yet go the full length of war. Fate at this point played very conveniently into the hands of the British, for in February they released to the United States a message (the so-called Zimmermann note) sent a few days before from Berlin to the German legation in Mexico, offering Mexico an alliance against the United States and promising the Mexicans Texas, New Mexico, and Arizona at the end of the war. During the same month five American ships were sunk. On April 2, 1917, Woodrow Wilson delivered his superb war message to Congress; on April 6 Congress declared war on Germany.

This account is, of course, a gross oversimplification of the progressive steps which led the United States into the war, but that subject has been dealt with abundantly elsewhere. One interesting aspect of it is the relative casualness with which the German leaders accepted the news. They reasoned that Britain would be forced to her knees before American help could be of importance and that no large amount of American troops could ever get across the Atlantic Ocean. They hardly realized how near the truth they were on the first count.

If ever a year can justly be called a "year of decision," it is 1917. Obviously the two most spectacular events of the year were the entry of the United States into the war and the revolution which transformed Russia from an autocratic tsardom into a Communist state. In addition, a number of events occurred in Germany which help explain things to come. There were three major developments: the passage of the Peace Resolution, the dismissal of Bethmann with the consequent consolidation of the Ludendorff dictatorship, and the split within the Social Democratic party.

Some scholars suggest that in mid-1917 the Reichstag had its first chance since the *Daily Telegraph* affair to convert Germany into a parliamentary monarchy but that it let itself be outmaneuvered by Ludendorff and the High Command. Be this as it may, for some weeks in the summer of the year the Reichstag seemed to assert itself in the cause of peace. These events hinged around the personality of Matthias Erzberger. Erzberger, a south German Catholic, had for some time been the leader of the minority liberal wing of the Center party. In spite of this, as late as the fall of 1916 he had been an annexationist and had played along with the conservative leaders of his party. However, in early 1917 he became convinced that Germany had no chance of victory in the war and decided to do what he could to get Germany out of it as cheaply as possible. His conviction arose from several bases. He traveled to Eastern Army Headquarters where he was shown figures proving that the submarine campaign was not starving Britain and never could, and that the blockade of Germany by the British was in fact worse. Secondly, he was close to events in Austria-Hungary. The aged Emperor Francis Joseph had died in November 1916 and been succeeded by his great-nephew Archduke Charles, who was at best lukewarm about the German alliance and mainly interested in preserving his ramshackle empire, which gave signs of falling apart around him. He was anxious to get out of the war and had even made gestures to Paris and London through his brother-in-law, Prince Sixtus of Bourbon-Parma, an officer in the Belgian army. Finally, Erzberger had learned through ecclesiastical sources that Pope Benedict XV was about to launch an appeal for peace. All of these factors led Erzberger to deliver a famous speech in the Reichstag on July 6, 1917, in which he outlined his fears and called for a statement by the Reichstag which would convince the world of Germany's desire for a just peace. The speech caused consternation throughout the nation. Erzberger next proceeded to enlist the support of his own party, which he received at a stormy caucus on July 12, so stormy indeed that one of the conservative Center leaders was taken from it with a heart attack. The Social Democrats and the Progressives joined with the newly oriented Center, and there was for a time a preview of the Weimar coalition. A Peace Resolution was drawn up and passed by an almost two-to-one majority. It called for a peace of conciliation and used the Socialist slogan, "no annexations and no indemnities." The resolution was passed but was little heard of again, except as a source of annoyance to the annexationist group, who about this time organized themselves into a pressure group under the name of the *Vaterlandspartei* ("Fatherland Party"). Ludendorff, in fact, was the winner; in spite of the Peace Resolution flurry, he became more completely a dictator.

The conflict between Ludendorff and Bethmann which led to the latter's resignation on July 14, 1917, was not a new one. Bethmann had been distasteful to the annexationists and extreme military party ever since the start of the war because they felt he was cowardly about the war aims. Bethmann, however, was unable to push his ideas to their logical conclusion, so an uneasy truce existed between the two groups. By early 1917, however, Bethmann had become exceedingly worried about the food shortage in Germany, the difficulties of life, and the consequent shift toward disaffection and defeatism which he sensed. In the spring he persuaded Emperor William to issue an Easter message promising the Prussian people that the three-class system of voting would be abolished, but not until the war was over. Even this partial promise infuriated Bethmann's opponents, among them Ludendorff, and they waited for the moment to get rid of the chancellor. The moment came during the Peace Resolution debates, when the Center also abandoned the chancellor. During this debate Bethmann gave in to pressure and resigned. The question of his successor was all-important, and here the degree to which the emperor had abdicated his powers and fallen under the spell of the High Command becomes obvious. After some hesitation Ludendorff proposed the name of Dr. George Michaelis, an almost unknown civil servant who had gained a reputation as food commissioner for East Prussia. The emperor had never heard of him, it is reported; nevertheless, he appointed him. One of Michaelis' first tasks was to state his position on the Peace Resolution before the Reichstag. He made the celebrated hedging statement that he believed that the aims of the Resolution were attainable "as I interpret them"; since no one ever found out how he interpreted them, the matter became a dead issue and Michaelis operated mainly as a clerk for Ludendorff. Even Ludendorff realized how incompetent his appointee was, and poor Michaelis was forced out of office in late October and succeeded by the dignified, aged, and honorable figure of Count Hertling, a Bavarian nobleman, who was no match for Ludendorff and was content to let the High Command continue to rule Germany politically as well as militarily. Until September 1918 Ludendorff was for all intents and purposes the German government.

The year 1917 was decisive also in the history of the Social Democratic party, for in that year the strains and fissures which had existed for years came into the open and the party divided in two, with a third section of irreconcilable radicals. This third group, the Spartacus League, did not grow until the end of the war and was led by Rosa Luxemburg and Karl Liebknecht, son of Wilhelm, one of the earliest German Social Democrats. Liebknecht made his break with the party in December 1914, when he refused to vote for the war credit of that month. After this he publicly spoke against the war, was put in the army, took part in demonstrations, and was court-martialed and jailed; he was the radical martyr of the German opposition to the war. In spite of a good deal of personal sympathy for him, his group was almost negligible until 1918.

More important was the group of Social Democrats who broke away from the mother party in 1917 and formed the Independent Social Democratic party. This break in the party mirrored the old cleavage between revisionists and antirevisionists, between trade unionists and theorists, which had been developing over the years; but it mirrored it in an odd way. As is so often the case in socialist history, the lines were not drawn clearly. For example, the revisionists found themselves divided, some remaining with the old party, some joining the new, and some trying to bridge the gap. Essentially the Independents grew out of the war. They refused to vote for war credits, not necessarily on doctrinaire grounds nor because they denied the right of self-defense, but because they felt that the party had surrendered its right to independent action vis-à-vis the government. In late 1915 and early 1916 a group of Social Democrats, led by Hugo Haase, voted against war credits and thus violated the unanimity of the party. They faced disciplinary action from their own leaders, formed a separate group, and in the spring of 1917 broke away completely and founded their new party. In it were some strange bedfellows. In addition to the old radicals, such as Haase and Wilhelm Dittmann, there were also Karl Kautsky and Eduard Bernstein, representatives of opposing lines of Marxist theory. The lack of homogeneity of the Independents is one of the reasons for their relative ineffectiveness in the years after 1918. The Majority Social Democratic party, as the parent party came to be called, was now almost completely the party of the trade-union organization with all its conservative social overtones.

The mighty events which were occurring in Russia during 1917 were no doubt a spur to the radicals in Germany. At first, however, they were of advantage to Ludendorff and the militarist group. The ease with which the tsar was dislodged from his throne in March gave notice of the basic weakness of the eastern enemy. The first contribution made by the German government to the situation was to permit Lenin, his wife, and several of his colleagues to pass across Germany from Switzerland on their way home to add their particular form of Bolshevist confusion to the general chaos in Petrograd. The Provisional Russian Government announced its loyalty to its allies and vowed to continue to do its share in the war, but the gradual disintegration of the Russian army by desertions was becoming an inescapable fact. Alexander Kerensky, Russian dictator after July, attempted to mount an offensive toward Galicia in the summer, but after a few days of success it was pushed back. Ludendorff decided on a partial offensive to make things worse for the Russians; in the late summer and fall he captured Riga and, in a remarkable amphibious landing, the islands at the mouth of the Gulf of Finland. By the fall the position of the Provisional Government was impossible, and in November the Bolsheviks seized control of the government with a program which called for an immediate peace with Germany.

Accordingly, the new Soviet government asked for a meeting to discuss an armistice, and the Germans (represented by the secretary of state for foreign affairs, von Kühlmann, and by General Hoffman) and Austrians met with the Russians at Brest-Litovsk on December 3, 1917. Both Germans and Russians agreed that they would be animated by the spirit of the Peace Resolution: no annexations and no indemnities; but it remained to be seen how they would interpret these aspirations. It soon became clear that the Germans thought in terms of the erection of buffer states in the area between Germany and Russia, a form of cloaked annexation. On Christmas Day the conference adjourned for ten days in a vain effort to get the western Allies to join in the discussions. When it reassembled, now with Leon Trotsky as Soviet leader, the Russians forced the Germans into the open statement that since Germany had won the war, the peace would be made on German terms. The terms included cession by Russia of claims to Finland, the Baltic states, and Poland, and the occupation of the Ukraine by German troops. Trotsky, angered beyond control by these demands, left the conference uttering the theatrical if fatuous slogan, "No war, no peace." German troops promptly started to advance and in early March had reached a point only a hundred miles from Petrograd. By this time Lenin had taken the matter in hand, had realized that as a practical statesman he had to make peace with Germany on whatever terms he could get, and had opened negotiations once again. The German terms remained the same with the addition of some territorial grants to Turkey in the Caucasus area. The Russians signed on March 3, 1918, one of the severest treaties in history. In spite of violent oratory from the two wings of the Social Democrats, the treaty received a majority in the Reichstag. When the final vote on ratification was taken, only the Independents voted against it with the Majority Socialists abstaining. The spirit of the Peace Resolution was dead. A few months later the same sort of treaty was made at Bucharest with Romania, granting to Germany among other things a ninety-year lease of the Romanian oil fields.

On the western front the German armies remained during 1917 pretty much on the defensive. They started the year by shortening their line and retiring across scorched earth to the strongly fortified "Hindenburg" line, thus making more difficult the Allied offensive. Ludendorff was banking heavily on the success of the submarine campaign and did not want to commit the army to losses. The Allies tried several offensives; none accomplished very much and one, the French offensive under General Nivelle, was a complete failure. By the end of the year things looked very discouraging to the Allies. Russia was out of the war; Italy was staggering from a terrible defeat at Caporetto; French morale was very low as evidenced by serious mutinies in the army. The only signs of hope were the improvement in the submarine situation and the gradually increasing arrivals of American troops. Ludendorff appreciated the Allied position. He also knew that German strength had been stretched almost to the breaking point and that Germany's three allies all showed serious signs of weakness. He knew further that the German people at home were undergoing terrible privations, a situation which was effectively aiding defeatist and socialist propaganda, some of it emanating from Soviet Russia. He therefore revised his earlier strategy and decided to try to end the war before the Americans should arrive in force, but to end it by land action rather than by waiting for the eventual submarine triumph. Thus he planned the greatest of all offensives, one more powerful even than the attack on Verdun.

Every kind of expert care was used in the preparation of this great and final offensive. It began on March 21, 1918, against the British and within a few days had achieved spectacular results. The width of the push increased as the weeks went by, until by the early summer it reached all the way from north of Ypres in Belgium to Rheims. The impetus of the attack brought the Germans almost as close to Paris as they had been in the first month of the war. Once again they were on the Marne. In June at Belleau Wood they encountered American troops in force for the first time. This was discouraging because it showed how time was running against Germany. There were other signs of trouble for Germany. Peace and defeatist propaganda was moving from the rear lines at home to the front. German supplies and equipment were no longer so good as they had been. This offensive seems like the last effort of a dying animal. It finally petered out in July after four months of unprecedented ferocity. On July 18, 1918, Germany lost the offensive, never to regain it.

The remainder of the story of the war in the west is quickly told, although this speed belies the heroism, the blood, and the effort. On July 18 Ferdinand Foch, Allied commander in chief since April, opened a counterattack near Chateau-Thierry at a spot where the Germans had exposed themselves unwisely. The impetus northward slowly replaced the earlier German push toward Paris. On August 8 the British started their phase of the action near Amiens. In his memoirs Ludendorff calls this day, "the black day of the German army." Slowly but relentlessly the French, British, and Americans forced the Germans back until they reached their greatly protected Hindenburg line. On September 29 the Hindenburg line was cracked. On this day also, Ludendorff, the man of steel, collapsed. After a conversation the evening before with Hindenburg, fearful that German resistance was a matter of only a few days and conscious of the threat from the south which the imminent Bulgarian surrender posed, Ludendorff asked Chancellor Hertling to start immediate negotiations for an armistice to be based on the Fourteen Points program for peace which President Wilson had outlined in January. From this time on, although the somber dying war continued to burn for six more horrible weeks, interest shifts to the diplomats who spent these days in an effort to achieve an end to the fighting.

CHAPTER XVII

Defeat in 1918

Ludendorff's urgent request to Chancellor Hertling for an armistice on September 29, 1918, was not the first intimation to those in high places that Germany's chance for victory was becoming alarmingly dim. The great offensive of the spring had accomplished too little in proportion to its enormous cost, and the numbers of new recruits for the army were not up to the High Command's expectation. Various methods of achieving a negotiated peace were discussed at high-level conferences by both the military leaders and the government, but such thought was kept extremely secret and the public was lulled into maintaining its rosy anticipation of a conqueror's peace. The first trickle of bad news came on June 24, when von Kühlmann, secretary of state for foreign affairs, gave a speech in the Reichstag about the possibility of diplomatic negotiations leading to peace. Kühlmann was justified in these disclosures in the light of what he had been hearing, but the High Command burst into fury at the report of what he had done and demanded that the emperor dismiss the offender. William did so on July 8 and named Admiral von Hintze to succeed him.

The dismissal of Kühlmann caused a storm of attack in the Reichstag led by both branches of the socialists. They felt rightly that Kühlmann had been sacrificed to the militarists and that this act showed nakedly what a farce the fiction of civilian government had become. The debates became more and more heated and focused attention on the deplorable state of the home front. By 1918 living conditions in Germany, particularly in the large cities, had become almost unbearable; the prospect of living through another winter of wartime stringency seemed beyond human endurance. During the summer the world-wide epidemic of influenza reached Germany, and before long thousands, especially children, were stricken. The supply of food and clothing was daily becoming more meager. A potato famine had cut that staple to a fraction of the usual supply. Animals were being slaughtered for lack of fodder.

The flour ration was cut, and the prospect of meatless weeks was in sight. To make things worse the Austrian ally, equally deprived, was pleading for shipments of food from Germany. The occupation of the Ukraine, which the Germans had hoped would be their granary, was an almost complete disappointment.

One result of these sorry conditions was grumbling about high prices and profiteers. The radicals made full use of these grievances to accelerate their attacks and to call for strikes. Strikes and riots broke out as a sullen people approached another winter.

It is against this background that the Allied offensive of July must be viewed. The British success of August 8 unnerved Ludendorff. The continuing Allied advance of August and September almost robbed him of his control. It was a panicky man who, on September 29 and the days immediately following, insisted that the request for peace be made not in a matter of days but in a matter of hours.

By the last days of September a number of almost unrelated issues combined to create a major crisis. In the south, Bulgaria collapsed and asked for an armistice; in Vienna the hopes of Emperor Charles and his government were limited to preserving what could be salvaged of Austria-Hungary, even at the expense of a separate peace; in Berlin a group representing several parties in the Reichstag drew up a demand for the dismissal of the conservative Hertling, whom they considered to be simply a mouthpiece for Ludendorff; at Headquarters in Spa on the evening of the twenty-eighth Hindenburg and Ludendorff had a melancholy conversation in which they agreed on the immediate necessity of negotiations leading to an armistice. With the arrival of both the emperor and Hertling at Spa on the twenty-ninth the stage was set.

On that afternoon Emperor William accepted the resignation of Hertling, who refused to support the liberalization of the government which the others insisted upon to placate the Allies, especially the United States. No successor was named immediately, but the generals insisted that October 1 should be the deadline for the commencement of armistice negotiations. The emperor also signed and published a decree stating among other things, "It is, therefore, my will that men who have the confidence of the people should have a broad share in the rights and duties of government." There was now no road back. The new government, as yet unnamed, was pledged in advance both to ask for peace and also to reform the structure of internal government. The demand for peace came unquestionably from the army, but the acceptance of it without demur by the civilians gave a basis for the later legend that the civilians were the defeatists.

It was not until October 1, the army's deadline for the armistice request, that the emperor summoned his new chancellor. He had picked Prince Max of Baden, in many ways a good choice. Max was a cousin of the emperor and was heir to the grand-ducal throne of Baden; thus he could be expected to be loyal both to William II and to the monarchical principle. He had had considerable parliamentary experience in the Badenese legislature and had achieved some reputation as a liberal. His unexpected quality was that he was able and willing to stand up to strong opposition, even from so redoubtable a figure as General Ludendorff.

Prince Max refused to be hurried into the decisive step that the generals demanded and resolved first to form his government, which for the first time in the history of the empire was to be responsible to the Reichstag and thus include members of the controlling parties, in particular the Social Democrats. Before he completed this task, however, the High Command succeeded in conveying to the leading parliamentarians its very black view of Germany's position in the war. On the morning of October 2 Vice-Chancellor von Payer called a meeting of the leaders of all parties to hear a speech by Major von dem Bussche, a representative of the High Command. The operative statement in the speech was ". . . the Army Command has had to reach the immensely difficult decision of acknowledging that, according to human calculation, there is no longer any prospect of forcing the enemy to seek peace." Bussche's speech fell like a bombshell on those who had been kept at a distance from affairs by the dictatorship. Even to those who were close to the inner circle it was a very sobering event. Men left the meeting pale and drawn. Within a few hours leaks had occurred and all sorts of dismal rumors were making their way around Berlin.

Under the shadow of Bussche's remarks the Social Democratic delegates met to decide whether they would take part in Max's cabinet. This was a major concern of Marxist doctrine. Ebert, the leader of the party, motivated by patriotism and fear of the future if the party did not try to help at this desperate moment, carried his policy of co-operating with Max against the opposition of Philipp Scheidemann, the party's second-in-command.

The new government was announced on October 4. Several members of the Hertling cabinet remained, including Payer and Dr. Solf, who received the post of foreign affairs. Appointed also were three Centrists (including Matthias Erzberger, who became a minister without portfolio), one Progressive, and two Social Democrats. Ebert preferred to remain outside the government, but Scheidemann received a seat also as minister without portfolio.

The preceding evening Prince Max sent by way of neutral Switzerland the first German peace note to President Woodrow Wilson, from whom the Germans expected the best treatment, both because the United States seemed the nation least emotionally involved in the war and also because Wilson in his "Fourteen Points" speech and in later statements seemed to offer the most reasonable and objective program for peace. The note requested Wilson "to take steps for the restoration of peace" and to organize a conference for this purpose. It declared that Germany accepted "as a basis for peace negotiations" the Fourteen Points and Wilson's speech of September 27. It further asked for an immediate armistice.

Max's next step was to implement the promises he had made in his introductory statement to the Reichstag to liberalize the German government. For this, several constitutional amendments were necessary. The most important were the requirement of the assent of both houses for war and peace and the ending of the rule whereby a Reichstag deputy had to give up his seat in the house if he entered the government. These amendments were passed toward the end of October. In the Prussian parliament a bill was introduced calling for universal male suffrage. The Prussian upper house, even after the eleventh hour, made difficulties. However, this conservative bastion fell too, and the bill became law shortly before the armistice.

This is not the place to discuss the reactions of either President Wilson or the Allied governments to the German request for peace. That is a complicated story which has been told well and often. Wilson's reply to Max was dated October 8. The president raised three issues. He asked if the German government would accept his peace program and if it were interested only in the "practical details of its application." He pointed out that further discussion was dependent on German withdrawal from all invaded territory. Finally, he asked "whether the Imperial Chancellor is speaking merely for the constituted authorities of the Empire who have so far conducted the war." The implications of this final query were considerable. There were many, a growing number, who felt that Wilson was seeking the abdication of the emperor and probably also of the crown prince as a condition precedent to further action.

The temperate quality of the American answer was well received in Berlin. Ludendorff, in conference with the government, was willing to accept the evacuation of occupied territories. But there were some who noted that the general's pressure for an immediate armistice was not so urgent as it had been a week before. Only the extreme right newspapers were angry; they began to suggest that the armistice was being forced by the civilians upon the military.

Max decided on a conciliatory answer; it was approved by the High Command and dispatched on October 12. The one new point it raised was the question of whether the other Allies also accepted the Wilsonian peace program, a wise precaution. In answer to Wilson's question about the German government, Max pointed out that his ministry had been formed "in agreement with the great majority of the Reichstag" and stated unqualifiedly that he spoke "in the name of the German Government and of the German people."

By this time the reaction to the German approach in Britain and France, and from American public opinion, was making itself heard in Washington. The consensus was clear that Wilson was behaving too leniently toward the Germans and that there should be a hard peace. A further influence was the torpedoing on October 12 of a passenger vessel in the Irish Sea, an event which strengthened anti-German sentiment. Finally, Austria-Hungary seemed closer than ever to the brink of dissolution. The result of these forces was Wilson's note of October 14, a good deal stronger than the earlier one. He pointed out that armistice and evacuation of troops were matters which had to be left to the military authorities and that any armistice terms had to guarantee the continuance of the current Allied supremacy. He made a stern indictment of the "illegal and inhumane practices" still continued by Germany, citing the sinking of passenger ships and wanton destruction during the retreat in France. He ended with a clear indication of doubt that the German government was one with which the Allies could deal, and by implication demanded further proof that Max didn't represent the "arbitrary power" hitherto exercised in Germany.

The reaction to this note was sharp. The emperor, the chancellor, all levels of public opinion, and even the Social Democrats interpreted this as an end to the chance for a negotiated peace and felt that Germany was placing herself voluntarily under the heel of a vindictive enemy. A highly dramatic and fateful conference was held on October 17, at which Ludendorff made it clear to the government that he was no longer anxious for an immediate armistice. Moreover, he declared that he had changed his mind completely and now felt that Germany should continue to fight to preserve her honor. He expressed his belief that morale at home could be repaired, and in particular based his new opinion on the promise of a much larger intake of men into the army in the next few months than he had previously thought possible. He wanted to continue the negotiations with Wilson but believed that Germany should send a strong note and risk a rupture of the interchange by Wilson. In this attitude Ludendorff was supported by Admiral Scheer, director of naval operations, who was strongly opposed to ending the submarine war.

Max, who had drafted and obtained parliamentary support for a note promising to end unrestricted submarine warfare, was astonished and angry at the position taken by the High Command. He and his ministers felt that it was an effort to place on the shoulders of the government the responsibility for Germany's future woes. They recalled that the military had forced upon Max a demand to take precipitate steps. Max called on the emperor and made his continuance as chancellor dependent on the concession regarding submarines demanded by Wilson. The emperor reluctantly agreed, and on October 21 the third German note was sent to Washington.

In this note Max agreed to military evacuation but not to anything incompatible with German honor. He took great exception to the allegation of "illegal and inhumane actions," but stated that orders had been given to end the torpedoing of passenger ships. Finally he gave Wilson a short lesson on the constitutional changes which had recently taken place in Germany and concluded with the statement, "the offer of peace and an armistice has come from a Government which, free from arbitrary and irresponsible influence, is supported by the approval of the overwhelming majority of the German people."

The debate by cable on political science between the professor-president and the prince-chancellor continued with Wilson's third note dated October 23. In it he promised to take up the question of an armistice with the Allies. He reported that he had suggested that the Allied military leaders draw up armistice conditions which would protect Allied interests. Finally Wilson said that, although important and interesting changes had apparently been made in the German constitution, there still remained a good deal to be done, particularly in the clarification of the position of the king of Prussia. He warned that if the United States would have to deal with "the military masters and the monarchical autocrats of Germany," it would have to demand "not peace negotiations, but surrender." In the meantime, in France the military leaders were losing no time in drafting armistice conditions and passing them up to Foch, the Allied commander in chief.

Faced with the necessity of taking the rostrum next in the debate, Prince Max awaited the passage of the constitutional amendments on October 26. In addition to the changes previously mentioned, the chancellor now became dependent on the support of the Reichstag, he was responsible more clearly than before for the political actions of the emperor, and he received considerable control over personnel matters in the armed forces. Yet even after accomplishing this, Max was not free to turn to the negotiations. First he had to resolve the struggle with the High Command which had been simmering for some days.

Several events precipitated the final conflict between government and army. In the first place, the cabinet felt that in getting its military advice it should consult generals other than Ludendorff, which hitherto had not been possible. At headquarters in Spa, aware that vital decisions were in the making, Ludendorff and Hindenburg decided to go immediately to Berlin. Max ordered them not to do so, for he did not want it to appear abroad that he was taking dictation from the military. Nevertheless, they left Spa on October 24 after they issued a proclamation to the troops stating that Wilson's answers were unacceptable to "us soldiers" and in effect calling for the end of the negotiations. When Max, who was ill with influenza, heard of these two actions, he wrote to the emperor and made clear that it was now a choice between himself and Ludendorff, though he hoped earnestly that Hindenburg would not resign.

When the generals arrived in Berlin, an acrimonious conference with the government took place. On October 26 Ludendorff waited on Emperor William and after an unhappy interview offered his resignation. The emperor accepted it. Hindenburg promised to remain at his post, and at his suggestion the emperor appointed General Wilhelm Groener as Ludendorff's successor. Ludendorff returned home sulkily to write his memoirs, to become a leader in the neopagan movement, and within five years to affiliate himself with the National Socialist program of Adolf Hitler. Groener was an able choice. His reputation had been made by handling the very complex transportation problems of the army; he was to live to be an important figure in Germany in the next decade.

Freed from the incubus at Spa, Max now turned to his last note to President Wilson. It was a short one, repeating comments on the changes in the government and specifying that the military power was now subject to the civilian. The final sentence read: "The German Government now awaits the proposals for an armistice, to pave the way for a peace of justice of the kind indicated by the President in his pronouncements." A few hours before the dispatch of this note the Germans learned that Austria-Hungary had asked her enemies for a separate peace.

Wilson's last note was dated November 5. It too was short and direct, stating that the Allied governments were willing to make peace on the basis of the Wilsonian program. There were, however, two reservations. At Britain's insistence, the first concerned freedom of the seas, which Britain considered impossible. Second, there was the question of restoration of invaded territories. By this the Allies understood that "compensation will be made by Germany for all damage done to the civilian population of the Allies and their property by the aggression of Germany by land, by sea and from the air." This last reservation opened the whole knotty problem of war guilt and its corollary, reparation. By this note a meeting of minds on the question of an armistice was reached, and the way was paved for the signature of the armistice itself.

Early in October the High Command had named a commission to conduct the actual negotiations with the Allies. However, after the military leaders reversed their demand for an immediate end to the fighting, Prince Max became fearful that an all-military commission would simply refuse possible Allied demands and end negotiations with the enemy. He therefore decided to name a civilian chairman of the commission and on November 6 appointed to this thankless post Matthias Erzberger, who was known to the world as the sponsor of the Peace Resolution of 1917 and as the leader of the second largest party in the Reichstag.

Erzberger arrived at Spa on the morning of November 7. There he joined the other members of the four-man commission: a general, a naval officer, and a representative of the foreign office. Contact had been made with Foch, and the commission proceeded behind the French lines first by automobile and then by train. Early on November 8 the German train drew up to a siding near the village of Rethondes in the forest of Compiègne. Nearby stood the train of the Allied command. At 9 A.M. Marshal Foch received the German delegates in a dining car which had been made into a conference room. With Foch were General Weygand and two British admirals. Foch approved the Germans' credentials, signed by Prince Max, and maneuvered Erzberger into asking for an armistice, not simply for "proposals." He then read aloud the armistice conditions. Erzberger asked for an immediate end to hostilities, but Foch replied that fighting would continue until the armistice was signed. The Germans then sent the conditions by radio to Berlin and informed the government that while they felt the Allies would be unwilling to make any substantive changes in them, the delegation would try to get concessions on the timing of the evacuation, the numbers of weapons to be handed over, and especially on the matter of victualing Germany. They reported that the German reply was required by 11 A.M. on November 11.

The task of the German delegation was rendered more difficult by the fact that the two days of grace, November 9 and 10, were the days when momentous and revolutionary events were occurring in Germany. During those days Emperor William fled to Holland, a republic was proclaimed in Berlin, and Prince Max handed over his authority to Friedrich Ebert. This news caused Foch and Premier Clemenceau to wonder if Erzberger and his colleagues still possessed legal power to treat with the Allies; Erzberger and his colleagues wondered the same thing. Almost no official news arrived from either Berlin or Spa. The fact was that the leaders of the state were so harassed by the events immediately around them that they simply did not get around to Erzberger and his plight. Finally on the evening of November 10 a message with a code number proving its authenticity arrived from Ebert accepting the armistice conditions; later another message arrived asking that the question of food for Germany be raised.

The final conference lasted from about two o'clock until after five on the morning of November 11. The main subject of discussion was the blockade of Germany and the urgent state of food supplies for the civilian population. Erzberger was successful in getting a statement from Foch that consideration would be given to furnishing food during the period of armistice. Actually, Germany endured a frightful winter and did not begin to receive food in any quantity until the spring of 1919; this rankled in German hearts for years afterward. The Germans got minor adjustments in the numbers of weapons to be forfeited, but in essence the armistice did not differ from Foch's original demands. The document was signed shortly after five o'clock on the morning of November 11 and was placed in effect at eleven o'clock.

The armistice terms were severe. They rendered Germany incapable of renewing the struggle if peace negotiations should fail. They were territorial, military, and economic in nature. Germany had to evacuate Alsace-Lorraine and all occupied territory in France and Belgium within two weeks. She had two weeks more to evacuate all German territory west of the Rhine, which was to be occupied by Allied troops. Further, a neutral strip ten kilometers deep on the right bank of the Rhine was stipulated. In the east the German forces were to retire from former Austria-Hungary, Romania, and Turkey to within the German borders as they existed on August 1, 1914. In the case of Russia, German troops were to withdraw within those same borders "as soon as the Allies shall think the moment suitable, having regard to the internal situation of these territories." German East Africa, which still held out, was to be surrendered. Very considerable supplies of cannon, machine guns, mortars, planes, locomotives, railway cars, and trucks were to be forfeited. All submarines were to be surrendered and the rest of the fleet placed under Allied control. All Allied prisoners of war were to be liberated, but not German ones in Allied hands. The treaties of Brest-Litovsk and Bucharest were declared null and void. There were various other detailed provisions concerning economic matters and shipping, the most important being maintenance of the blockade. The armistice was to remain in force for thirty days but was renewable. There was no question in anyone's mind that Germany had lost the war.

Since 1918 many people have criticized the armistice severely. Most of this criticism has revolved around two points. The first is that the Allies should not have permitted the war to end before any Allied troops were fighting on German soil. Some even say that the Allies should have pushed on to Berlin. Then the German people would have known beyond any doubt that they had been beaten. Foch's answer to this criticism was simply to give some idea of the hundreds of thousands of casualties which would have occurred in several months more of fighting.

The other criticism is that the Allies should not have refused to deal with the German High Command, that in fact they should have refused to deal with a civilian and insisted on Hindenburg's surrender of his sword to Foch. Then, they argue, there could have been no stab-in-the-back legend, no accusations that civilians, Jews, socialists, defeatists, etc., at home sabotaged the "undefeated" army. This suggestion was, of course, followed in 1945. It is certainly true that the onus for the signature of the armistice, and later the peace treaty, fell on the Majority Social Democrats and the Centrists, the two groups most likely to create a democratic Germany. However, it would have been a hardy prophet who in 1918 could have predicted coming events, in particular the Great Depression and the emergence of such a phenomenon as Adolf Hitler.

CHAPTER XVIII

Revolution in 1918

When the members of the Armistice Commission returned from their days in the forest of Compiègne, they found a new and confusing Germany. This could not have come to them as a complete surprise. Even before October ended, German sailors struck the first blows in the creation of a new regime.

The German revolution of 1918 presents a complex picture because it is so closely identified with the military defeat. The motivations of the participants are often hard to isolate. To what extent were people moved simply by war-weariness and terrible living conditions? How great was the desire for a democratic republic? How strong was the demand for a thoroughly socialist, even soviet, state? These questions are not easy to answer. Furthermore, the dissensions within the ranks of the socialists lead to further confusion.

The real revolutionists in Germany were divided into three groups: the Independent Socialists; the Spartacists; and a new grouping, the so-called Shop Stewards, technically the left wing of the Independents but often at odds with what they considered the overly theoretical attitudes of the party leadership. The Shop Stewards, whose following was mainly among the workers in heavy industry in Berlin and whose principal leaders were Richard Müller and Emil Barth, were closer in spirit to the Spartacists than to the Independent leaders. Their program called for immediate revolution with expropriation of heavy industry and landed estates and a government in the hands of workers' and soldiers' councils (in German *Räte,* a translation of the Russian "soviet"). In other words, they wanted a revolution in Germany similar to the Bolshevik Revolution in Russia. This group was in close association with the Russian embassy in Berlin, from which it obtained both arms and printed propaganda. When Karl Liebknecht, the Spartacist leader, was released from prison in late October, he found himself close to this revolutionary faction since its aims were so similar to his own. The Independent leadership, whose principal representatives were Hugo Haase and Wilhelm Dittmann, did not feel that the time was ripe for revolution and was sceptical even about the possibility of a revolution in Germany. They counseled moderation and delay, especially at a meeting of all the revolutionary groups on November 2; at that time they won a vote to postpone the outbreak of revolution until November 11, when it was hoped the war would be over.

All three of the groups just mentioned were united in their opposition to, and scorn for, the Majority Socialists, who provide an extremely interesting sociological study at this period. It is really only by courtesy that they can be called Marxists. Essentially they had won their revolution bloodlessly in October, when they were the moving force behind the constitutional reforms of the government of Prince Max. They wanted only to consolidate their gains and perhaps push them a little bit further. They had a vested interest in society and had no notion of helping to overthrow the *status quo*. In fact, within a few days some of their leaders became almost hysterical at the thought of Bolshevism. Though they were theoretically republicans, Ebert accepted the post of imperial chancellor and envisaged a regime with Prince Max as regent for a parliamentary monarch, the emperor's infant grandson. As the months went on, the Majority Socialists found it far more pleasant to collaborate with the renascent bourgeois parties than with their Marxist colleagues to the left, and indeed were willing to join forces with the old military leaders to put down the left-wing extremists.

In terms of the foregoing analysis, it would appear that the Majority Socialists came closer to reading the spirit of public opinion in Germany than their opponents on the left. Although much has been written about revolutionary infiltration into the armed forces, the fact seems to be that the army and navy were endlessly war-weary and disgusted with the imperial regime. There seems to be very little evidence that either they, or the population at home, were interested in copying the Russian pattern of social overthrow. Each time that matters came to a decision (e.g., on November 10, on December 19, and in the elections of January 1919) the majority voted for the moderates rather than for the extremists. It is fair to add that the extremists did not produce the leadership necessary for a revolution by a minority. No Lenin emerged in the Germany of 1918.

The first overt action in the revolution occurred among the sailors of the High Seas Fleet. Ever since the battle of Jutland in 1916 the capital vessels of the emperor's beloved navy had been kept wrapped in cotton in the ports of north Germany. All naval activity centered around submarines, and the crews of the large ships were constantly raided for men able to sail under the surface. The sailors had very little to do beyond the essentials of maintenance. They were bored and restless and therefore became a prey to disaffection and radicalism. Above all, they were anxious to return to their homes and to normal life.

Admiral Scheer, director of naval operations, fought hard in mid-October to keep Prince Max from ordering a cessation of submarine warfare. He backed Ludendorff in the conference of October 17 and even took the matter to the emperor, who, however, ordered him to accept Max's decision. During the following days Scheer devised a plan to help the army and to maintain the honor of the navy. This plan required a foray by the High Seas Fleet into the North Sea to harass Allied shipping in the narrow seas between Flanders and England. He hoped to inflict large losses on the British and to lure the British Grand Fleet south from Scapa Flow to engage in a final major battle in which he felt the Germans would have a good chance of victory. Some have described this plan as simply honorable suicide; others have considered it sound strategy. In any case, the order went out but no notice of it was given to the government. On the evening of October 29 Admiral Hipper, commander in chief of the fleet, briefed his officers on the proposed action. Within a very short time the word had spread among the crews, and the rumors grew out of proportion. On several of the large ships the night was one of tumult, with increasing insubordination. The officers tried to quell the trouble both by speeches and threats, but they accomplished little. By the morning of the thirtieth it was clear that the operation was impossible because of the behavior of the sailors, and it was called off. Hipper decided to send several of the mutinous ships through the canal to Kiel, a foolish decision because Kiel was a hotbed of revolutionary sentiment. He also arrested several hundred of the ringleaders and ordered immediate courts-martial.

In Kiel the situation developed rapidly. On the evening of November 2 a mass meeting was held at which inflammatory speeches were made and cheers for socialism given. The next day there were more parades and demonstrations, and the troops at the disposal of the local commandant joined sides with the mutineers. On the fourth the industrial workers called a general strike, and by the end of the day Kiel was in the hands of the rebels. Within a few days almost the entire German High Seas Fleet was flying the red flag, and the situation was out of control.

News of these events reached Berlin slowly and in fragments. Prince Max decided to send a leading socialist to Kiel to represent the government. He picked Gustav Noske, a Majority Socialist from the conservative wing of the party, a man who had long interested himself in military matters. Noske listened to the demands of the mutineers, and within a short time relative quiet was restored. However, the incident was not closed. Some of the mutinous sailors made their way to Hamburg and Hanover, where they won the support of large numbers of the garrison troops. Within a short time all of northwest Germany was in a state of revolutionary ferment. It is interesting to note, however, that most of the sailors' demands were nonpolitical. They were mainly interested in improvement of conditions within the navy (such minor matters as the use of the word "sir") and wanted the end of the war. This was no carefully prepared Marxist outbreak, but rather a spontaneous outburst of tired, bored, underfed, and angry men.

The revolutionary events in the north caused a great deal of embarrassment to the Majority Socialist leaders. They had accomplished their aims and did not desire a revolution; they simply wanted to get on with the task of building the new Germany. Yet the disturbances continued. In the following days, as news arrived from other parts of the Reich, it was clear that there was still no end in view. The leaders were alarmed about what the Independents might do. After all, the Social Democrats were the party of the people, and the worst possible strategy would be for the Majority to let the Independents take the lead in achieving the people's will. Ebert knew this. Scheidemann, who always kept a particularly sharp eye on the Independents, realized it even more vividly. Accordingly, at a party caucus on November 6 Scheidemann demanded that an ultimatum be served on Prince Max threatening immediate withdrawal from the government if William II did not abdicate without delay. Ebert managed to defeat this proposal, but that evening he had a change of heart; he began to realize how formidable was the sentiment in Germany against the sovereign and how important it was for his party to assume leadership in this matter. The next day, therefore, the ultimatum was presented to Prince Max. If both the emperor and the crown prince did not abdicate by noon of November 8, the Social Democrats would resign from the cabinet. There was still a monarchical loophole. Nothing in the demand precluded a regency for the infant Prince William, son of the crown prince.

This was the solution desired by Max. He tried without success to enlist the support of General Groener, who was on a quick visit to Berlin. In spite of this failure, he addressed strong protests to the emperor. William however, believing himself secure at headquarters under the protective wing of the army and acting on the advice of both Hindenburg and Groener, would have nothing to do with the idea of relinquishing his imperial and royal prerogatives. A few more hours and more disquieting news were needed to convince first the generals and then the emperor that the reign of William II was over.

It did not take long for disquieting news to arrive. This time it came from Munich, where on November 7 a disturbance broke out which resulted in the flight of King Louis III, the deposition of the Wittelsbach dynasty, and the proclamation of a republic in Bavaria. The leader of the Bavarian revolution and of the Independents there was Kurt Eisner, a Jew, who had moved from Berlin to Munich a decade before. Eisner was an intellectual and an idealist, who had doubts about the possibility of introducing socialism immediately and who seemed to think in the old Marxist terms of a first bourgeois revolution to pave the way toward eventual socialism. He wanted to establish councils (*Räte*) to educate the masses in democracy. He was also willing to assume for Germany the full blame for the outbreak of the war. Here again the question arises whether the Catholic peasant population which accepted the events in Munich without demur was motivated by Marxism or by war-weariness. There is no question that the Bavarians were extremely tired of war. Furthermore, the defection of Austria-Hungary now opened the possibility of an Allied invasion of Germany from the south through Bavaria. This consideration, added to the usual Bavarian dislike of Prussia, which the southerners felt had led Germany to her doom, seems to provide sufficient cause for the events of the seventh. This conclusion is reinforced by the poor showing of the Independents in the subsequent election.

The end of the monarchy in Bavaria was the signal for similar action throughout Germany. In nearly all the capitals and large cities disturbances erupted, and by the evening of the eighth all the kings, princes, grand dukes, and dukes had either abdicated or been deposed. There was one exception. The revolution had not yet reached Berlin, and the German emperor, king of Prussia, still held fast to his privileges and responsibilities. Yet time was running short.

In Berlin there was still indecision, especially on the part of the Majority Socialists. At noon on the eighth they announced a postponement of the deadline of their ultimatum calling for abdication, supposedly because of armistice negotiations. However, during the afternoon the Social Democratic leadership heard of ominous plans from the left. The Independents, led by the Shop Steward wing of the party, had decided on a major demonstration and general strike for the next day. Plans and instructions, which had been drafted for some time, were distributed to party offices and to factories. Ebert and his colleagues realized that this was the decisive moment. It was now that the Majority Socialists could lose control of the workers for lack of leadership and permit victory by default to the Independents. The shadow of Bolshevism loomed large. At a meeting that evening the Majority leaders agreed on a deadline of nine o'clock the following morning for their earlier ultimatum. This would still give them time, if the emperor remained stubborn, to go to the streets and assume the leadership of the demonstration the next day.

November 9 was the day of the Berlin revolution. Crowds roamed through the streets. Factories were closed. The parades headed for the center of the city, the government quarter. Troops refused to obey their officers, insulted them, and even pulled off their insignia of rank. It was a scene of general but peaceful pandemonium. Very little blood was shed. Berliners have never been adept at revolution or barricades. Perhaps an innate sense of status inhibits them even in moments of anger.

Meanwhile the Majority Socialists carried out their ultimatum by withdrawing their two members from Prince Max's cabinet. In Berlin Max realized the seriousness of the situation, while the emperor and his advisers in Spa did not. He kept in contact with Spa, continually urging a proclamation of abdication, but the emperor remained firm in spite of the reversal by Hindenburg and Groener of their original position. Relying on information received from the various unit commanders at the front, they came to the conclusion that the army was no longer loyal to the dynasty. William was toying with the feudal idea of leading his loyal soldiers back to Germany to crush the rebels. It was the melancholy duty of Groener to have to inform the ruler, with Hindenburg's approval, that he could not rely on the army. William countered this by the suggestion that he should resign as German emperor but not as king of Prussia, a most extraordinary notion in view of the structure of the German constitution.

Max decided that he could not wait for a decision from Spa. On his own authority, about midday on November 9, he announced that the emperor and the crown prince had decided to renounce the throne, that a regency would be set up, that Ebert would be appointed chancellor, and that elections for a constituent assembly would be held forthwith. A few minutes later Ebert and other Socialist leaders waited on Max and pointed out to him how the local situation had changed. Max extracted from Ebert a promise to call a constituent assembly and formally relinquished to him his position as chancellor. Ebert accepted the responsibility and issued proclamations calling for order and for administrative officials to remain in office. He then returned to the Reichstag building for lunch and a little peace.

On that morning Prince Max of Baden involved himself in a network of falsehood and illegality. He invented the abdication of the two Hohenzollerns and also the device by which a chancellor could relinquish his office to someone else. Constitutionally, only the emperor could appoint a chancellor. Max, however, saw no other course and preferred illegality to bloodshed.

While Ebert and Scheidemann were at lunch listening to the crowd outside shouting and singing in the large open area in front of the Reichstag building, news arrived that a similar scene was being enacted less than a mile away before the imperial palace. There the Independent leaders were surrounded by a large crowd demonstrating in the *Lustgarten*. Rumors spread that Liebknecht was about to proclaim a soviet republic. Scheidemann was urged to address the crowd outside the Reichstag. He did so from the great staircase of the building, and as he ended his harangue, he heard himself proclaiming the German republic. Flushed with his achievement, he returned inside only to be scolded by Ebert, who informed him coldly that he had no right to do such a thing. Yet Scheidemann's words could not be unsaid. The new regime was in existence. It was in this informal, casual manner that the German republic came into being.

The epilogue to this momentous day occurred at Spa, where Emperor William was still firm in his determination to remain king of Prussia. As the afternoon wore on, the advice tendered by the generals became more and more discouraging. They made it clear that there could be no question of leading the army home to rout the rebellious socialists. They even cast doubt on the possibility of continuing to be responsible for the emperor's safety at Spa. Even Hindenburg recommended that William should leave Germany. It is not clear what finally made up the emperor's mind. Late in the afternoon, without signing any document of abdication, William retired to his train where he spent the night. Before dawn the train pulled out in the direction of the Dutch border. William placed himself under the protection of Wilhelmina, queen of the Netherlands, who granted him asylum. It was not until almost three weeks later that he drew up an act of abdication. Thereafter he spent the remaining twenty-three years of his life in exile in Holland, settling in 1920 at Doorn, where he stayed until his death. He maintained a shadow court, wrote his memoirs, and exercised his dilettante mind with archeology and his body with chopping wood. During the last year of his life he was guarded once again by German soldiers, who now wore the swastika emblem. He died in June 1941, a few weeks before another German government made the same catastrophic mistake that he had made, but much more wantonly, when it invaded the Soviet Union and engaged in another two-front war.

The first major problem facing Ebert was to establish contact with the Independents. Although the Majority Socialists represented the greater portion of the German workers, nevertheless the spearhead of the revolution was the radical group of the left, who in particular commanded the allegiance of a large portion of the Berlin proletariat, which was busily creating workers' councils. Without losing any time Ebert invited the Independents to join him in a new cabinet. The reaction of the Independents showed that they were a far-from-united group. The party leadership, represented that day by Dittmann, was willing to collaborate with Ebert; the Shop Steward wing refused to have anything to do with him and his breed. Liebknecht, for the Spartacists, demanded the transfer of all power to the councils. A compromise was offered. Dittmann swallowed the idea of the councils; the others agreed to work with Ebert, but only until the war was over. Ebert replied by insisting on the principle of a constituent assembly to settle Germany's future. The Independents countered with an insistence on an all-socialist cabinet, sovereignty to repose in the councils, and no assembly until the social program was well under way. All this was reminiscent of the events in Russia a year before. Finally the urgent needs of the moment were overriding, and both sides agreed to form a Council of People's Commissioners with three members from each party. The Socialists were represented by Ebert, Scheidemann, and Otto Landsberg; the Independents by Haase, Dittmann, and Barth.

November 10 ended with a mass meeting in the Busch Circus of the workers' and soldiers' councils of Berlin, an assembly which adopted the fiction that German sovereignty reposed in it. It approved the new Council of People's Commissioners and then proceeded to the election of its own executive committee. The slate presented to the delegates was made up exclusively of Independents, including the most radical of them, Liebknecht and Luxemburg. The soldiers' councils objected to this, and thus gave notice that the rank and file of the army was not much influenced by radical Marxism. The soldiers insisted on representation on the committee in equal numbers with the workers. They won their point and even more, because when the workers' half of the committee was elected, it was composed partly of conservative Social Democrats even after a boycott by the Spartacist leaders. This was the first of several decisive moments at which it became clear that Germany was not going to follow the Russian pattern.

The similarity between events in Germany in 1918 and events in Russia in 1917 is unmistakable. There was the same drift toward dual government: People's Commissioners and councils looked like Provisional Government and soviets. There was the same radical demand to achieve "social gains" before holding elections for a constituent assembly, in addition to the same extreme left wing prepared to seize power by force. However, the spirit in Germany and the quality of leadership were different. In the weeks to come the trend was clearly in favor of Ebert and his group. To their right the bourgeois elements, which had gone underground at the time of the revolution, emerged and prepared themselves to play their parts in the new regime.

CHAPTER XIX

Birth Pangs of a Republic (1918-19)

The future of Germany for at least the next fifteen years was settled in the weeks between the revolution and mid-January of 1919. It is a confused period in which the historian cannot find dramatic and clearly defined events on which to base his analysis; more than usual, he must search beneath the appearance of things to find the leading motives. In this melancholy era it is impossible to lose sight of the disaster which had befallen Germany. The effects were multiple, both material and psychic, and a good case can be made to indicate that the psychic aspect was even more important than the material.

Up to a few weeks before the armistice, the German people—though they were sunk deep in hunger, privation, and even epidemic—were living in expectation of a victory which would raise Germany to new heights of splendor, both political and economic. War maps told them how far German soldiers had advanced on foreign soil; communiqués lulled them with tales of the constantly improving military position. Almost from one day to the next this dreamworld collapsed and the Germans had to make the difficult adjustment to defeat, a defeat shattering in its implications. Not clear at first, these implications gradually became evident. The flight of the emperor and the proclamation of a republic under socialist auspices were regarded as shameful and humiliating by all the conservative and nationalist elements in the state. All facets of German life were disrupted by the return home and rapid demobilization of a vast army. The soldiers, widely regarded as heroes and often so esteeming themselves, were cast loose upon an economy which had been overexpanded to meet wartime needs but which was now contracting rapidly as a result both of the termination of those needs and the stringency of raw materials. Many of the soldiers had been sent into the army directly from school. They knew no trade; they knew only the protective quality of military life and the comradeship of the trenches. Now they were cast adrift, alone and resentful, into an alien society. These young, neurotic front-fighters provided admirable material for activist organizations both of the left and, more particularly, of the right. In the shadow of these imponderables and of the unknown demands which might be made by the Allies in the peace treaty, the new regime had to take shape. Much of the credit or blame for the immediate results belongs to Friedrich Ebert.

Ebert was a practical man, not a doctrinaire. Ever since he had assumed the leadership of the Social Democratic party, he had devoted his efforts by skillful tactical maneuvering toward the revisionist position of socialism. This scandalized orthodox Marxists, many of whom were now among the dissident Independents and therefore no longer had voices in the party councils. Ebert and his colleagues were strenuously opposed to anything that smacked of Bolshevism; they were determined to fight the idea of government by councils of workers and soldiers; they fought for a constituent assembly to be elected promptly by universal suffrage (including women for the first time). As the weeks continued, Ebert found that he could work more fruitfully and sympathetically with the bourgeois parties to the immediate right of socialism than with his nominal colleagues on the left. Indeed most of the story of November and December 1918 is the struggle within the ranks of the Marxists. Yet it is not the whole story, for during these same weeks the army and the old bourgeois parties revived and re-established much of their former prestige and power; by the time of the elections in January the pattern was set for a new bourgeois republic with social overtones, an outcome which did not please anyone but served as a least common denominator.

Ebert demonstrated his practical qualities at the outset. Immediately upon accepting the office of chancellor from Prince Max, he issued an appeal to the imperial and state administrators to remain at their posts. It has often been said that the peculiar quality of Prussianism, dating back to the early important Hohenzollerns, was the result of the combination of the Prussian army and the Prussian bureaucracy. Efficiency, competence, humorlessness, devotion to detail: by the use of these qualities the Prussian bureaucrats designed the Prussian state. During the empire the civil servants were drawn largely from right-wing, conservative, Protestant elements; the Catholics complained that they were not represented in proportion to their population, and there were almost no socialist civil servants. Thus Ebert's appeal was directed toward just those people who would be most out of sympathy with the spirit of his own party, which was theoretically in command of the revolution. Yet it is difficult to blame him, because a breakdown in the whole vital administrative system would have been an invitation to the radicals of the left to fill the gaps. In the higher echelons socialist officials were appointed to sit side by side with the old bureaucrats, but they were at a serious disadvantage from lack of training. In general an amazing continuity was achieved, but it boded little good for democratic institutions.

No revolution can succeed or consolidate its gains without control of the instruments of force. German strength resided in the huge army scattered on the various fronts, to an extent infiltrated by socialism but on the whole intact and still subject to the orders of its officers. The purity of the officer corps had been somewhat diluted by the promotion of non-aristocratic reservists, but on the whole it was still a reservoir of conservative monarchist opinion. It was important for both the army and the new government to define their mutual relations. Ebert knew this, and realized further that the army was potentially his greatest weapon against radical insurrection which might erupt at any moment. He decided to probe the attitude of the High Command immediately and on November 10 telephoned Spa and talked to General Groener, who on this occasion, as well as generally throughout his career, displayed a sense of political reality that was not typical of a Prussian officer. Ebert discovered that he had an ally in Groener, who realized that the moderate socialists were the best weapon against the radicals and the supporters of the conciliar idea. It was not hard for Groener to convince Hindenburg of his point of view; thus an agreement was achieved by which Hindenburg consented to remain commander in chief and to recognize the new government, while Ebert on his part tacitly accepted the authority of the officer corps over the army and won the support of the army against the radicals. The importance of this deal has been stressed by historians. The old German army, with the blessing of the Social Democrats, remained intact as a future rallying point for enemies of the republic. Here is the best demonstration of the difference between the German revolution of 1918 and the great revolutions in France and Russia. In the latter cases the old aristocratic officers either emigrated, disappeared, or became overt traitors to their earlier principles. New "people's" armies were founded by Carnot and Trotsky respectively. Nothing of this sort occurred in Germany. The old spirit prevailed, even though some of the façade changed.

The events of November 10 were concluded with a statement of general policy by the new government. This document contained a number of social provisions (such as the future establishment of the eight-hour day and the restoration of social insurance), but essentially it was a liberal, democratic, non-Marxist statement of principles. It guaranteed civil and political rights (including the right of property) and promised universal suffrage with proportional representation. It was greeted with

scorn and anger by the radical socialists but with pleasure by large elements of the population, including even some of the Independents who
realized that the overwhelming tasks of the rehabilitation of defeated
Germany precluded an immediate social change.

Among the former possessory classes most alarmed by the trend of
events, the great industrial leaders held a prominent position. For some
months the more astute ones had realized that there was trouble ahead
and had looked about to see how they could best hedge and cut their
prospective losses. They recognized that the trade unions constituted
the most stable and conservative elements within the proletarian parties.
Hence it was to them that many employers turned for insurance against
the future. Conversations were begun in October, when the employers
agreed to disband company unions and to grant parity in representation
to employers and employees. After the outbreak of the revolution the
unions increased their demands and included among them the principle
of the eight-hour day. An agreement, known as the *Arbeitsgemeinschaft*
("community of work"), was signed on November 15 between leading
representatives of capital and the three main groups of unions. The
agreement granted a number of concessions for which the unions had
long clamored. The unions were recognized; freedom of association was
granted; the principle of collective bargaining was accepted; factory
councils of employees were to be established, together with mediation
boards and mixed committees to rule on problems of employment and
conditions of labor. It was a sweeping victory for the union principle,
and most notably it was an agreement arrived at not by force but by
discussion and compromise.

The *Arbeitsgemeinschaft* was greeted variously. The Christian Unions
were enthusiastic about it, for they had long espoused the principle of
co-operation between capital and labor. The employers were grouchy at
the concessions they had made but for the time being were resigned to
their necessity. The Marxists, and this was increasingly true the further
left one progressed along the Marxist spectrum, were extremely suspicious of the agreement. The extreme leftists saw it as a betrayal of the
principle of the class struggle, an example of revisionism beyond the
pale of permitted activity. It was built on the frail foundation of the
exigencies of the moment and may be viewed as a weathervane of the
political climate of the first republican months. The Marxists were the
first to disavow it, and as the threat of extreme radicalism abated, the
employers gradually drifted away from it and formed their own associations. By mid-1920 the principle of industrial solidarity was moribund.

It was not only in the economic sphere that the bourgeois groups
came back into view. Driven underground by defeat in the war and by

the threat of Bolshevism, the old parties to the right of the Social Democrats began to reappear. During November and December they emerged with new names and new programs, but no essential changes. The new programs included as many democratic principles as each group could bear to adopt. In the new names there was a tendency to include the word "people." Thus the old Conservative party became the German National People's party; the National Liberals became the People's party (*Volkspartei*); the Progressives became the Democratic party. Even the Center talked of a change of name to Christian People's party, but this move was not successful and the name Center persisted. The motive of this effort was to suggest that the party was not strictly Catholic and would welcome more Protestant membership (a position finally achieved in the reorganized party of Konrad Adenauer after World War II). The Center was particularly important in these months, as it had been during the last two years of the war and for the same reason—as a link between bourgeois and socialist. Adam Stegerwald, leader of the Christian unions, was very influential as a liaison between the Majority Socialist and the Center parties. This relationship laid the groundwork for the creation of the so-called Weimar coalition the following year.

A final significant development on the right side of the political ledger occurred in late November, when with the blessing of Ebert the High Command called for volunteer enlistments to fill the rapidly shrinking ranks of the army. Volunteer units grew apace. They were made up largely of men who were failing in civilian life, who were resentful of the loss of the war, who were violently nationalist, and who were lost in the new society. These people were given work policing and keeping order, especially in the east and in the Baltic area where they fought off the advancing Bolshevik tide from Russia. They were strongly anti-Marxist, and in the months to come were to present the republic with an almost mortal peril when they became the standard bearers of the counterrevolution under the name of the Free Corps.

The events which have just been described are very significant to the historian writing forty years later. The subsequent history of the republic and the advent of Hitler have thrown into sharp relief the forces of conservative continuity from the empire. At the time, however, with chaos almost discernible, the vital need seemed to be the resolution of the conflict among the various wings of Marxism concerning the immediate structure of the state. This conflict revolved around one or two major issues closely connected. The basic concern was whether the new German regime should take the form of a conciliar government similar to the Russian practice of control by the "working classes" (industrial workers, soldiers, and peasants), or whether the future of

Germany should be determined by an assembly to be elected on democratic principles by a vote of all classes of the nation. The corollary to
this was the conflict over when the promised elections should take place.
The Social Democrats wanted an election as soon as possible, both to
establish clear sovereignty and to fend off extremist insurrection. For
the opposite reasons, the Independents and particularly the Spartacist
group desired to postpone the voting as long as possible, until such time
as basic social "gains" should be the accomplished fact.

The fiction persisted that sovereignty resided in the Workers' and
Soldiers' Council, which on November 10 had empowered the People's
Commissioners to act as the executive and had also elected an Executive
Committee to oversee the Commissioners. The meeting, however, had
represented only the workers and soldiers in Berlin at the time, and
could by no stretch of the imagination be called a nationally representative body. Accordingly, on November 23 the Executive Committee
called a great congress representing workers and soldiers from all of
Germany to meet in Berlin on December 16. Ebert and Scheidemann
realized at once the potential danger of this congress. If it turned out to
be controlled by extremists, it could demand immediate socialization of
industry and agriculture and the establishment of an effective government by councils. They retaliated a few days later by an intelligent,
tactical move which served as bait to attract moderate and even bourgeois democratic sympathy: they set the date for the elections to the
Constituent Assembly for February 16, 1919.

The first two weeks of December were tense indeed in Berlin. The
pretense of co-operation between the two socialist parties on the Council
of People's Commissioners wore very thin, although two of the Independents on the council, Haase and Dittmann, were far from sympathetic
with the extreme wing of their party. They sought a middle path, but accomplished little. First blood was shed on December 6 in connection
with a march of unarmed Spartacists, alarmed at rumors of counterrevolution. Otto Wels, a Social Democrat and commander of Berlin,
called out troops; they fired on the Spartacists, killing some and wound-
ing more. It is difficult to be sure who benefited from this encounter. It
gave force to the extremist contention that the Social Democrats had no
love for the worker. On the other hand, moderates, even in socialist circles, were undoubtedly alarmed by this rehearsal for insurrection and
confirmed in their belief that it was essential to fight anything that suggested Bolshevism.

The congress met in Berlin from December 16–19, in the chamber
of the lower house of the old Prussian parliament. It was a turbulent
affair, constantly interrupted by incursions of various brands of demon-

strators from the streets. From the start, however, it was clear that the sentiment of the majority of the delegates was with the Ebert government. In spite of this, the four days were tumultuous. On the first day, after Liebknecht and Rosa Luxemburg had been refused seats at the meeting, a delegation of Spartacists rushed in calling for world revolution. The second day was spent hearing attacks on Ebert's policy from leaders of the Shop Stewards and the Independents, until the center of the stage was seized by a group of mutinous soldiers who burst in demanding that the army be "democratized" by the abolition of the officers and the substitution of soldiers' committees. The third day was one of harassment for Ebert because a motion was passed, but never implemented, to remove the supreme direction of the army from the High Command. There was already real fear of a military revival. December 19 was the decisive day of the congress and an important date in German history. On that day the congress defeated by a large majority a motion to make the conciliar principle the foundation of the new German government. It then went further and advanced by a month to January 19 the date for the elections. The party of Ebert and Scheidemann was victorious on all counts. For all practical purposes the German revolution was over. Germany was not going to become a soviet republic; she was going to take a middle path as a bourgeois republic, perhaps with some socialist overtones. The ensuing violence was anticlimactic; the actions of the Constituent Assembly were simply implementation of the decision of December 19.

While they may have been anticlimactic, the events of the Spartacist revolt of December and January were serious and left a wound in the body of socialism which was never healed. The Social Democrats became Cossacks in the eyes of the extremists. To moderates and conservatives the bloodshed in Berlin was an object lesson of what might be expected of Bolshevism. The extreme nationalists felt that not enough blood was shed, that this type of lawlessness must be radically wiped out.

Not long after the congress adjourned, fighting erupted. The immediate issue concerned several thousand sailors of the People's Naval Division who had installed themselves in the former imperial palace in Berlin. Already irritated by the defeat on December 19 and convinced that the Ebert government was sabotaging the revolution, these men refused to obey an order to vacate the palace and on December 23 decided on direct action. They surrounded the chancellery, thinking that Ebert was isolated there, and seized Otto Wels, who was particularly detested because of the events of December 6. Ebert, however, had a secret telephone line, which he used to call for the help of regular army units. On Christmas eve the army, under command of the old-line General von Lequis, besieged and bombarded the sailors at the palace for several hours. The sailors could not hold out and eventually agreed to a compromise. The details of the skirmish are not important. The essence of the matter lies in the fact that the Social Democratic government had relied on army units to fire on German revolutionaries in uniform. Feeling ran intensely high, and the three Independent members of the Council of People's Commissioners felt that they could no longer operate in harmony with Ebert and Scheidemann. They took their complaint to the Executive Committee of the recent congress, but that body, composed exclusively of Majority Socialists, of course supported their own colleagues and offered no redress to the Independents. Accordingly Haase, Dittmann, and Barth resigned from the government and were replaced by three Social Democrats, including as minister of war Gustav Noske, the most militaristic of the socialists. Now both the Council of People's Commissioners and the Executive Committee of the congress were one hundred per cent Social Democrat. That party was temporarily in complete control of events. The Independents had abdicated.

The Spartacists were not ready to accept defeat. They held a mass meeting on December 30 at which they broke all connection with the Independent party, which, they insisted, had been lukewarm in the revolutionary struggle. They now took the new name of German Communist party. They listened to harangues from Liebknecht and Luxemburg, and finally, against the wishes of the latter, voted to boycott the coming elections.

The next stage of the crisis started with a conflict over Emil Eichhorn, the left-wing Independent chief of police in Berlin, whom the Social Democrats resolved to force out of office. His maintenance in office became a rallying point for the Independents. The government persuaded the Prussian authorities to dismiss him on January 4, 1919, which resulted in manifestos, demonstrations, and general turbulence lasting for several days. The Communists, again against the advice of Rosa Luxemburg, resolved on a *Putsch* and called for a general strike. The Social Democrats issued a similar call in retaliation. For several days an armed truce existed in Berlin. Efforts at conciliation were made by several of the groups concerned, but Ebert became more and more adamant. He was determined to put an end to the "Bolshevik" menace once for all. On January 11, under the command of Noske, the fighting began. Both regular troops and free corps volunteers attacked the strongholds of the Communists. For four days Berlin was a shambles in which hundreds were killed. Finally by the fifteenth quiet had returned, and the army was in control of the city. Liebknecht and Luxemburg were prisoners in local army headquarters. Late that night they were driven separately into the Tiergarten, where they were murdered by officers. Their bodies were concealed, and it was several months before Rosa Luxemburg's corpse was found floating in one of the canals which wind through the German capital. The government and army won its victory, but it was an expensive one and left bitter memories. Immediately the two Communist leaders who were murdered in cold blood became martyrs of the red religion.

Four days later the elections were held and resulted in a victory for the moderate socialists and the bourgeois parties. They were held among scenes of fighting in other German cities, repercussions of the carnage in Berlin.

There remained to be enacted one bizarre series of events, which, although it occurred later than the Spartacist revolt, nevertheless breathed the same spirit. This was the abortive and bloodstrewn effort to establish a Communist republic in Bavaria.

After the abdication of the king of Bavaria, the state was controlled by the evolutionary Independent, Kurt Eisner. However, he was defeated by the Majority Socialists in the elections in Bavaria held in January 1919. He refused at first to resign, but on February 21 he decided to announce his resignation. As he was walking into the Bavarian parliament to carry out this plan, he was shot and killed by an aristocratic counterrevolutionary named Count Arco-Valley. This crime set off a wave of political tumult in Munich, including more shootings in the parliament itself. Eventually a coalition of Social Democrats and Independents, under the moderate Johannes Hoffmann, formed a new government. However, this was only a temporary lull. A small group of artistic and radical revolutionaries, led by the author Ernst Toller and the anarchist Gustav Landauer and backed by some tougher and more realistic Communists, decided that the moment had arrived for the creation by force of a proletarian state. On April 6 they proclaimed a soviet republic in Bavaria. The legitimate government fled to Bamberg and civil war began. The Communists at first interested themselves mainly in revolutionizing art and education, but soon serious bloodshed between the two parties erupted in Munich. The national government, with Noske in charge of the operation, activated units of the army and the free corps who converged on Munich and on May 1 entered the city. There were grievous atrocities committed by both sides. Bavaria lay under martial law for some weeks, and the revolt was quelled by courts-martial and military executions. A reign of terror prevailed until finally in August the Social Democratic government was restored. This violent interlude had serious repercussions affecting the psychology of Bavarian political thought and eventually that of all Germany. The excesses of the Communist dictatorship created a revulsion in the conservative and moderate groups of the population, such that Munich became the center of conservative and reactionary extremism. It was no accident that in Munich only a few months after the Communist *Putsch* the party was founded which was shortly to develop into the Nazi party of the new reactionary messias, Adolf Hitler.

CHAPTER XX

The National Constituent Assembly at Weimar (1919)

The national elections were held as scheduled on January 19, 1919, a few days after the crushing of the Spartacist revolt. They were different from any German elections up to that time. The voting age was lowered to include all Germans of twenty years, and for the first time women were given the right to vote, which had influential results. More than thirty million people voted. The seats in the assembly were allocated to the various parties according to a complicated method of proportional representation designed to equate as far as possible the division of seats with the desires of the electorate. While a strong case can be made for proportional representation as a democratic device, it had the bad effect in Germany of encouraging a large number of parties, since even a small party was almost sure of at least a few seats. As the years went on, small groups devoted to some particular ideology tended to proliferate. This trend was not noticeable in 1919; but in that election proportional representation, which was a favorite idea of the Social Democrats, prevented the Social Democratic party from capturing an absolute majority of the assembly. In fact, no party in the entire history of the republic ever received an absolute majority.

In general, the results showed that the German people were in agreement with the course that events had taken since November. The center of gravity was some distance left of center, but by no means at the extreme left. On the right the National People's party came in fourth best, while on the left the Independents were a poor fifth. Ebert was vindicated, with the reservation that it was going to be necessary for him to co-operate with some of the more progressive bourgeois groups. The Social Democrats received the greatest number of votes (11.5 million, 163 seats). Next came the Center (almost 6 million votes, 92 seats), the Democratic party (5.5 million, 75 seats), the Nationalists (almost 3 million, 42 seats), the Independents (2.3 million, 22 seats), and the People's party (1.6 million, 21 seats).

The vocational composition of the assembly sheds some light on its activities. This was not an inexperienced body. Of the 385 male members (who alone could have had legislative experience before 1918), 143 had previously been members of the Reichstag, while 244 had been members of either the Reichstag, a parliament in one of the federal states, or some municipal legislative body. The proportion of members with experience was highest on the left of the house, a fact which shows the extent to which the former ruling classes had been discredited or had voluntarily retired for the moment from the political scene. The largest single occupational group represented in the assembly was that of trade-union officials, who accounted for 77 out of a total of 421 delegates. Then followed editors and newspapermen, government officials, party secretaries, attorneys, farmers, authors, landed proprietors, and teachers.

Thus the assembly represented neither the old ruling groups nor big business. Its heavy emphasis was upon a class of middle officialdom, a fixed-income group. The bulk represented a general conservatism of opinion, conservative not in terms of the Prussian agriculturist but surely in terms of radical Marxist teaching. This judgment is particularly true for the Social Democratic party, for here the emphasis was on the trade-union group. The assembly was only technically revolutionary, not at all revolutionary in the ideological sense.

Friedrich Ebert opened the Constituent Assembly on February 6, 1919, in the lovely little city of Weimar in Thuringia. Weimar was chosen for two reasons. In the first place, the scars from the recent fighting in Berlin were too evident; there was still turbulence there and always the fear that the Berlin proletariat might seek to dominate the assembly. Secondly, the government wanted to assure the German people—and probably even more the Allies, who were already sitting in judgment on Germany at the Peace Conference in Paris—that the new Germany was going to revert to the Germany of poets and thinkers, of Goethe and Schiller, for whom the symbol was Weimar, rather than the Germany of Prussian militarism, of Frederick the Great and Bismarck, whose symbol was Berlin and Potsdam. Thus the constitution written at this assembly and the republic which it founded are known as the Weimar Constitution and the Weimar Republic. It is instructive to compare this action with that of Hitler, who in 1933 opened his first Reichstag in the Garrison Church in Potsdam above the bones of Frederick the Great.

Since no party had received an absolute majority, it was necessary to form a coalition of some sort to run governmental affairs. Such bad blood still existed between the Social Democrats and the Independents that no co-operation between these two seemed possible, even aside from the fact that the two together did not constitute a majority. The Social Democrats and the Democrats could have formed a narrow majority, but it would have been an unstable situation as was shown when the Democrats retired from the government in June rather than take responsibility for signing the Treaty of Versailles. It seems to have been Erzberger who made it clear to the Social Democrats that they could not govern alone or allied with only the Democrats, and that further the Democrats would not enter into a coalition without the Center. Erzberger also persuaded his own party to enter a government composed of Social Democrats, Democrats, and Centrists. This grouping, generally known as the Weimar Coalition, guided the new republic during its early years, sometimes without the co-operation of the Democrats.

On February 11 the assembly elected Ebert first president of the German republic. He immediately chose as chancellor his right-hand man, Philipp Scheidemann. Scheidemann formed a ministry made up of the three parties of the coalition, plus, as foreign minister, Count Brockdorff-Rantzau, an aristocrat without party affiliation but an extraordinarily astute diplomat. Gustav Noske stayed on as minister of war. The leading Democrat was Dr. Hugo Preuss, minister of the interior and principal author of the constitution. The Center was represented by Erzberger, Dr. Johannes Bell as colonial minister, and Johann Giesberts in the post office. The new government received a vote of confidence, although speeches from both the far left and the far right indicated serious latent opposition.

The Weimar Assembly had two major tasks before it in addition to the day-to-day business of government. They were the writing of a constitution for the new republic and the establishment of peace with Germany's former enemies. There was not very much that could be done about the peace terms, for no German delegation was invited to the Peace Conference and the terms drawn up by the Allies were not presented to the Germans until May. The assembly addressed itself without delay to the new constitution. On February 24 Dr. Hugo Preuss laid before the assembly the draft constitution, which he and advisers from all over Germany had prepared during the preceding weeks. From February 24 to March 4 the assembly as a whole debated the draft and passed it at a first reading. On March 4 a constitutional committee was appointed to consider the draft point by point and to report back to the assembly. This committee met for three and a half months; the draft which they delivered to the assembly was, except in detail, the Weimar Constitution as finally voted on July 31 and promulgated on August 11.

The constitution, of course, reflected the attitudes of its authors. Dr. Preuss, the most influential of them, was a distinguished jurist with a considerable liberal reputation. In the United States he might have been called a Jeffersonian Democrat. His liberalism was the liberalism of 1848, unaffected by the broad stream of socialist thinking. The constitutional committee was about proportional in its membership to the strength of the various parties in the assembly. Most of its members were chosen by their parties as experts in legal and administrative matters. The result was a committee rather to the right of the general position of the assembly as a whole. It is therefore no surprise that the eventual constitution was redolent of bourgeois liberalism and one that Marxists found difficult to stomach.

A number of general problems had to be settled early in the discussions. One was the basic problem of centralism versus federalism. There were many, including Dr. Preuss, who wanted to break down the old, but frequently artificial, boundaries of the historic German states and create a centralized nation ruled democratically from Berlin. Convenience, efficiency, and uniformity were on the side of such a solution. However, it soon became clear that German particularism was by no means dead, that in fact it was perhaps stronger than in the past. Bavaria, for example, had no notion of surrendering her peculiar attitudes to a greater whole dominated by non-Bavarian ideas. Another plan would have been to preserve the federal character of the nation, but to separate Prussia into her provincial units to avoid the Prussian dominance of the Bismarck solution. This idea too was defeated, though it might have been received warmly abroad, particularly in France. In the end, Prussia was not shorn (except by the peace treaty), and although the central government had more authority than the empire, the old historical units retained their identity, wrote their own constitutions, possessed the residual powers of government, and maintained their complete apparatus of ministries and bureaucracies. There was one exception: several of the smallest states in central Germany merged into one new state called Thuringia. The old kingdoms, duchies, etc., were now called *Länder* (singular *Land*) and were required to have republican governments. The constitution provided that in certain contingencies the Reich government could send military force into the *Länder* to preserve order.

An even more difficult problem arose concerning the councils which had sprung up all over the country in November. Sentiment for the councils was by no means dead, although their proponents did not realize that any effective implementation had been killed in the past weeks. Disturbances erupted in Berlin in March, and Scheidemann was forced to promise that the conciliar idea would be "anchored in the constitution," even though no mention of it was made in Preuss's original draft. The problem was to fit some obeisance to the conciliar idea into the bourgeois structure which the assembly was determined to erect.

The debates in the committee, and later on the floor of the assembly, betray a great confusion of ideas about the whole question of councils. Members of different parties talked of quite different things as soon as they uttered the word "council." To the Independents it meant simply the soviet system. To the members of the parties midway across the floor it represented a mixture of factory councils, participation of labor in management, and vocational representation in parliament, at least in the upper house. To the members of the Nationalist party it suggested something which resembled the old estates of the sixteenth and seventeenth centuries. In spite of all the theorizing and the immense amount of pamphlet literature which had appeared in the weeks after the revolution (or perhaps because of it), the idea remained a confused one, especially in the minds of the men on the committee, who were conservative and trained in older and more orthodox categories of politics and jurisprudence. Still another influence came from the Social Democrats. The most prominent men of that party were affiliated with the trade unions. Strong unionists were suspicious of the idea of councils because they feared that if economic government were entrusted to factory councils and councils for larger units elected by the factory councils, there would be no room left for the old, established unions.

Finally a weak compromise was effected and written into the constitution. In the first place, the legal existence and sanctity of the unions was guaranteed. Then provision was made for councils at three levels— factory, provincial, and national. It is hard to know exactly what their spheres of competence were to be. The National Economic Council (Reichswirtschaftsrat) was to have a voice in all legislation dealing with economic matters. It was to be chosen on a vocational rather than geographical basis. The factory councils were to deal directly with management and even to have access to the books and a voice in the general direction of policy within the factory, not limited solely to labor problems.

In actual practice during the following years not a great deal was done to implement these constitutional provisions. A number of factory councils were created; their activity varied from place to place according to the attitude of the employers and the aggressiveness of the employees.

A provisional *Reichswirtschaftsrat* was appointed to work out the details of a regular body, which never came into existence. Nothing at all was done about councils at the provincial level. Much the same can be said about the plans to socialize German industry. The assembly actually passed laws to socialize the coal and potash industries, but as a result of sabotage from the employers and weak enforcement by the authorities no important changes were made. Germany remained a capitalist nation. By the end of 1920 there was very little talk about the socialist program which had loomed so large in 1918.

The Weimar Constitution is a much lengthier and more detailed document than, for example, the Constitution of the United States. Not content with describing the skeleton of the future political organization, it goes into considerable detail on civil and political rights, and economic, social, cultural, and religious matters. The statement of rights betrays a warm, philosophic understanding of the ideals of 1848 and a comprehension of American, British, and other contributions to the history of freedom. All Germans are declared equal before the law; they have liberty of travel and emigration; in case of arrest, they must be informed of the circumstances within a day; communications and the home are sacred; freedom of speech is guaranteed and no censorship is to be established. In the economic realm, the right of private property is upheld as well as the right of free association (labor unions), and a system of social insurance is to be developed. The education of children, which is compulsory, is recognized as an obligation of the state. Germans were to enjoy full freedom of conscience and religious practice.

The legislative power was vested in a bicameral body, the Reichstag and the Reichsrat. Members of the Reichstag were to be elected for a maximum of four years by all Germans over the age of twenty and according to proportional representation. The electoral laws implementing this provision erected large constituencies, each electing a number of members selected from lists compiled by each party. Thus a voter really voted for a party rather than for an individual. The Reichstag had wide and full legislative powers: it could initiate and pass laws, subject to a suspensive veto, and the cabinet was completely responsible to it.

The Reichsrat represented the *Länder*. Each *Land* had to have at least one member; none could control more than two-fifths of the body. It was made up of members of the governments of the *Länder*. The Reichsrat could, with the cabinet, initiate legislation; if it disapproved of a bill passed by the Reichstag, it could return it to that body, which could override the veto by a two-thirds vote. In practice the Reichsrat never became a very powerful body.

Any German over thirty-five years of age could be a candidate for the office of president of the Reich, whose term was set at seven years with the possibility of re-election. Later legislation provided that if no candidate received a majority of all votes cast, there would have to be a second election in which only a plurality was necessary. The president was to carry out the executive power, but all his orders and decrees had to be countersigned by the chancellor. He entered into the legislative framework to the extent that if he refused to promulgate a law within three months of its passage by the Reichstag, he could call for a referendum of the people on the matter. He could also dissolve the Reichstag and call for new elections. A peculiar power of the president, one which has been criticized more than any other provision of the constitution and which led legally to the fall of the republic, was Article 48. This article provided that if any *Land* did not live up to its constitutional obligations, the president could force it to do so by use of the armed forces. It further stated: "In the event that the public order and security are seriously disturbed or endangered, the president may take measures necessary for their restoration, intervening, if necessary, with the aid of the armed forces. For this purpose he may temporarily abrogate, wholly or in part, the fundamental principles laid down in [several articles of the statement of civil rights]." (Quoted in L. L. Snyder, ed., *Documents of German History,* New Brunswick, 1958, p. 338.) A safeguard was provided in that the president had the obligation to report any such action immediately to the Reichstag, which could rescind it.

Included in the constitution were all the modern democratic devices such as initiative, referendum, and recall, as well as the provisions for economic democracy discussed above. All in all this constitution reflected the most mature and advanced democratic political thought of its period. After its passage by the Weimar Assembly it was promulgated on August 11, 1919, by President Ebert and became the supreme law of Germany.

The Weimar Constitution was not received enthusiastically by any of the political parties. To the Social Democrats it was a defeat, for not even their minimum program was realized. To the Independents it was an even greater betrayal of principle. The Nationalists disliked it because it contained neither monarchy nor corporatism. The People's party found it too progressive. For the Center it included dangerous latent secularism. Even the Democrats, though it approximated their position most closely, found too many elements of collectivism in it. Furthermore, the Democratic party began in 1920 a decline which continued as long as the republic. The Weimar Constitution was to such an extent a compromise document that it remained at best a solution based on the least common denominator. Under such discouraging auspices the first German republic had its legal start.

Political scientists often point to the Weimar Constitution as a triumph of constructive democracy. Yet the regime established by it was within fourteen years to fall before one of the most ferociously antidemocratic reactions in all history. The answer to this paradox seems to be that a constitution is only as valuable as the energy expended by the men who implement it. The twenties later demonstrated that the number of Germans who were able and willing to expend themselves for the preservation of their democracy was tragically small and ineffectual.

CHAPTER XXI

The Treaty of Versailles (1919)

On January 18, 1919, just one day before the elections for the Weimar Assembly, the victorious Allied and Associated Powers opened in Paris the first plenary session of the conference called to re-establish peace in the world. Only the victorious powers were there. There were some who had read history and had learned that at the Congress of Vienna to which France, the defeated power, was invited, the astuteness of Talleyrand, France's representative, often led to his casting the decisive vote. There was to be no repetition of this. Germany and her allies were not allowed any share in the formulation of the new peace. Their function would be simply to receive and accept the treaties presented to them. Not only were the defeated powers to have no voice in the treaty making; the smaller allied powers had little or no voice and were heard only on details which affected them immediately. The treaties were worked out by the five great powers (the United States, Great Britain, France, Italy, and Japan), and even within that group Italy and Japan often absented themselves. The basic decisions were made behind closed doors, and the leaks were relatively few; thus it was not until the first of the treaties was handed to the German delegation in May that Germany and the world at large knew what had been agreed on.

There was very little, therefore, that the German government or the Weimar Assembly could do in the first months of 1919 about the crucial matter of peace. It was of course constantly in their minds, and unquestionably influenced some of the provisions of the new constitution. Germany insisted, whenever she had the chance, that she had accepted an armistice on the basis of the Wilsonian program of 1918 and pointed to the correspondence between Wilson and Prince Max. She felt that the democratic realignment of the nation should influence the Allies, especially Wilson, heavily in her favor. However, she was to learn that the Allies acted as if they were still dealing with the old regime and thus did severe harm to the cause of democracy in Germany by providing endless ammunition to the antidemocratic elements.

In April the government worked out a program for peace which it considered to be within the Wilsonian framework and not beyond the possibility of German acceptance. Armed with this, a German delegation, headed by Count Brockdorff-Rantzau, traveled upon invitation to Versailles. When they arrived, they discovered that the Allies were not yet ready for them; they were held in a hotel and treated almost as prisoners until the final document was complete.

On May 7, 1919, the completed treaty was handed to the German delegation. Brockdorff-Rantzau was told that he would have no opportunity to discuss the terms orally and that any communication with the conference would have to be in writing. He was further informed that he had fifteen days to obtain the authorization of his government to sign the treaty. One can imagine the surprise and horror with which the Germans read page after page of the ponderous document.

The treaty is extremely long. It is far more extensive in its economic details, military provisions, and annexes than any other such document in history. In general, it falls under five headings: the Covenant of the League of Nations, and territorial, military, economic, and punitive provisions. The Covenant was of only indirect interest to the Germans in 1919 because Germany was not invited to be among the charter members of the League.

Considerable territorial excisions of German territory were made, nearly all from Prussia. Some were outright cessions; in other cases there was provision for plebiscites. The general criterion followed was Wilson's principle of the self-determination of nations, tempered in cases of doubt by decisions against Germany. The treaty called for a plebiscite to be held in Schleswig to carry out the unfulfilled promise made to Denmark in 1864, and as a result north Schleswig was ceded to the Danes. Plebiscites in Eupen, Malmédy, and Moresnet led to the cession of these territories to Belgium. Alsace and Lorraine were to be ceded to France; in fact, they had changed their colors at the time of the armistice. Furthermore, the rich Saar Basin was removed from German jurisdiction and placed under the League of Nations with ownership of the mines and economic control granted to France. After fifteen years the residents of the Saar were to vote on their future from the choice of retention of League status, cession to France, or repossession by Germany. The rearrangement of the eastern border of Germany was a much more serious matter since it raised the centuries-long conflict of Teuton and Slav. The Allies were bound to restore the ancient state of Poland, which had disappeared from the map in the eighteenth century. Germany was required to cede to the new Polish republic nearly all the Prussian provinces of Upper Silesia (containing immense industrial wealth), Posen, and West Prussia; there were to be plebiscites in large portions of East Prussia, which resulted in German victories. The cession of West Prussia to Poland, giving her access to the sea at Danzig, drove a wedge between East Prussia and the rest of Germany and constituted the so-called Polish Corridor which was to embitter European international relations for a score of years. The city of Danzig with its surrounding territory was to become a little free city republic under the authority of the League of Nations, with special privileges for port facilities reserved to Poland. The port of Memel with its hinterland in the far east of Germany was to be forfeited to the League; in due course it was granted to the newly established republic of Lithuania. Finally, since the Allies took the position that Germans were not to be trusted to promote the welfare of less developed peoples, all Germany's overseas possessions were to be given to the League to be distributed at the League's pleasure as "mandated" territories. An added restriction provided that there could be no question of a union between Germany and the new little republic of Austria without express permission of the Council of the League.

The military clauses of the treaty began with this statement: "In order to render possible the initiation of a general limitation of the armaments of all nations, Germany undertakes strictly to observe the military, naval and air clauses which follow." The German army was to be reduced to a total force of one hundred thousand men "devoted exclusively to the maintenance of order within the territory and to the control of the frontiers." Of this hundred thousand, not more than four thousand were to be officers. The General Staff was to be abolished. Enlistments were to be for a period of twelve years, while officers were to serve for twenty-five years. This provision was intended to avoid the subterfuge which Prussia had made use of in the Napoleonic period when she trained large numbers of men intensively for short periods. It had the unexpected effect of creating a small but superbly trained nucleus which Hitler was able to expand with little difficulty into the great army of 1939. Germany was refused the manufacture and possession of all poison gas, tanks, and other offensive weapons. She had to limit her munition factories to those permitted by the Allies and close down all others. No import nor export of munitions or arms was allowed. Inter-Allied Commissions of control were to be established to enforce German obedience of these provisions and similar ones relating to naval and air forces. Germany was forbidden any military air force. The navy was to be reduced to no more than fifteen thousand men, of whom only fifteen hundred could be officers. Germany was not to possess or construct any submarines. She was permitted a token force of small battleships, cruisers, and destroyers, only sufficient to patrol her coast line.

In addition to the strictly military clauses there were some which combined military and territorial restrictions. The Allies proposed to occupy the entire area of Germany west of the Rhine for an unspecified period of time not to exceed fifteen years, dependent on Germany's fulfillment of the treaty. Even after Allied evacuation of this territory, it was to remain completely demilitarized, stripped of all offensive or defensive armament or fortification. The same was to be true, starting immediately, of a zone extending fifty kilometers east of the Rhine.

The economic and punitive clauses of the treaty go hand in hand. They are based, as is the whole treaty, on the moral guilt of Germany and her allies for the war and all its losses. The Allies chose, probably as a result of Wilson's high-minded attitude, to penalize Germany not simply because she was defeated militarily, which had usually been sufficient in the past, but because she had committed a frightful crime against humanity. This reasoning is summed up in the most celebrated and disputed clause of the treaty, the so-called War Guilt Clause, number 231. It reads as follows: "The Allied and Associated Governments affirm and Germany accepts the responsibility of Germany and her allies for causing all the loss and damage to which the Allied and Associated Governments and their nationals have been subjected as a consequence of the war imposed upon them by the aggression of Germany and her allies."

Pursuant to this clause, the Allies held Germany liable for all material damage which had been caused, with the understanding that this damage was to include future expenditures arising from the war, such as veterans' pensions. The powers at Paris were unable to arrive at any sensible and acceptable total for the bill to be rendered. Hence they contented themselves by stating that an Inter-Allied Reparations Commission would be named to report a total German reparations debt by May 1, 1921. Thus Germany was asked to sign a blank check of unknown and certainly immense size.

In the meantime, pending the decision of the Reparations Commission, Germany was to transfer five billion dollars in gold to the Allies to be credited against the future demand. In addition, she was required to forfeit large amounts of goods in kind, including timber, steel, and most of her merchant marine and large passenger ships. Germany's prewar commercial treaties were abrogated, and she was forced to grant most-favored-nation treatment to the Allies.

The strictly punitive clauses announced that the Allies proposed to request the queen of the Netherlands to release to them the former German emperor to be tried for high crimes against humanity. This proposal fortunately came to nothing because of the stubbornness and good sense of the Dutch, who refused to deport their political prisoner. The Allies went further and insisted that Germany should turn over to them for trial certain individuals "accused of having committed acts in violation of the laws and customs of war." These people were to be tried and punished by the Allies, using, if they chose, evidence furnished by Germany herself. This demand was the one which affronted many Germans the most.

When the terms of the treaty were made public, every segment of the German population arose in wrath to condemn them. This "Carthaginian" peace, this "dictate," seemed a far cry from the reasonableness of Wilson's original points. From the furthest right Nationalist to the furthest left Independent, the protest rose. There was hardly a clause of the proposed treaty that was not excoriated. The war-crimes trials were impossible insults to German honor, the cessions to Poland meant the delivery of millions of Germans to government by a lower race, the economic provisions were intended by Great Britain simply to eliminate German competition, and so on. Each group outdid the last in expressions of horror. These expressions were not limited to private individuals. Members of the Weimar Assembly filled pages of the minutes with violent statements, and Scheidemann's government instructed the delegation at Versailles to declare the terms of the treaty unbearable.

While this tumult was occurring in Germany, Brockdorff-Rantzau at Versailles was preparing a reply to the conference. He produced a lengthy document which considered the treaty clause by clause, and pointed out that it was unfulfillable, not in accord with the armistice arrangements, offensive to German honor, etc. The Allies seemed startled and offended that the Germans should react in this way. They gave almost no redress to Brockdorff's alleged grievances. The only concession of any importance concerned the cession of Upper Silesia to Poland. Instead of outright cession the Allies now agreed that plebiscites might be held in that region, an action which was in fact delayed until 1921. Seeing that it could accomplish nothing further in France, the delegation returned to Weimar on June 18 with a deadline of five days given by the Allies for acceptance or rejection. Brockdorff-Rantzau counseled rejection of the treaty. The matter was now left to the Scheidemann government and to the Weimar Assembly.

At first blush the three government parties were outdone by none in their condemnation of the treaty. Ebert, Scheidemann, and all the leading

GERMANY Boundaries ------
after the Treaty of Versailles in 1919

POLAND

CZECHOSLOVAKIA

AUSTRIA

Königsberg

Danzig

Vistula R.

Breslau

Oder R.

Berlin

Hamburg

Kiel

Bremen

Elbe R.

Weser R.

Magdeburg

Leipzig

Weimar

Dresden

Essen Ruhr R.

Düsseldorf

Cologne

Rhine R.

Mainz

Frankfurt

Nuremberg

Stuttgart

Munich

FRANCE

SAAR

Social Democrats were opposed to its acceptance. They had hoped that Brockdorff-Rantzau would be able to achieve major revisions from the Allies; but when the delegation returned with minimal success, the responsible men faced a serious dilemma. They agreed with Brockdorff that the treaty should be rejected, but as responsible men they had to face the alternative. The Allies made it clear that if the Germans rejected the treaty, the war would start again—this time with Allied troops on and even across the Rhine at points, the German army in a state of rapid demobilization, and Germany on the edge of chaos and starvation. If the Allies carried out their threat to invade across the Rhine, it seemed clear that civil war would ensue and then the familiar bogey of Bolshevism hove into view. In spite of these gloomy possibilities, the Social Democrats, the Democrats, and most of the Center were in favor of rejection. In this they were joined by the other parties and also by the military leaders. Hindenburg, still commander in chief, uttered heroic sentiments along the line of "better death than dishonor."

The first person to take a realistic position and to point out that there was no alternative to acceptance of the treaty, however unpalatable, was Matthias Erzberger. With great difficulty he was able to persuade a good many of his Center colleagues of his position, but even then he insisted that war-guilt and war-criminal clauses must be deleted. As the climax of the crisis approached, it was these requirements that were the hardest to stomach. The government approached the army command to obtain a military estimate of Germany's fighting potential. Hindenburg admitted freely that although the army might hold its own in the east, the overwhelming Allied strength in the west precluded any reasonable expectation of success in that area. In spite of this, Hindenburg still counseled rejection of the treaty and even spoke of resigning.

The Catholic Center announced its willingness to accept the treaty if the guilt and war-criminal clauses were deleted and some of the economic provisions modified. At this news many of the Social Democrats indicated their willingness to go along, but the Democrats remained adamant in their refusal and both Ebert and Scheidemann still favored rejection. Scheidemann decided to resign as chancellor, and a governmental crisis took place. Finally on June 22 the decision was made to form a government without the Democrats. Gustav Bauer, a former Social Democratic member of Prince Max's cabinet, became chancellor; Hermann Müller, a conscientious if colorless Socialist who was later to be chancellor, succeeded as foreign minister; Noske remained at the war office; and Erzberger became minister of finance. Bauer announced to the assembly that in his opinion Germany had no option but to accept the terrible treaty in order to avoid bloodshed, civil war, and untold horror. However, he too held out against the "honor clauses." He managed to get a vote for acceptance of the treaty on these terms. The Allies replied immediately that they had no intention of altering a word of the treaty and that Germany had now only twenty-four hours to accept. On June 23, with only about eight hours left, Bauer turned once more to the military for advice. As the unhappy task of counseling Emperor William to abdicate had fallen to General Groener, so did the even more unpleasant task of recommending acceptance of the treaty. Groener insisted that Germany had no option in the matter; Hindenburg might persist in his attitude of heroic stubbornness, but Groener as usual took the position dictated by necessity and common sense. In view of this, the assembly met in emergency session and with terrible misgivings voted acceptance of the treaty as it stood. Still, however, the People's party, the Nationalists, and some of the Democrats and Centrists refused to accept the onus of the treaty. They preferred to shirk the responsibility and thus were able in years to come to protest their pure German honor. With only a few hours left Bauer sent a mournful telegram to Versailles announcing acceptance of the treaty. On June 28, 1919, exactly five years after the murder of Archduke Francis Ferdinand, in the Hall of Mirrors in the Palace of Versailles, the same room where forty-eight years before William I was proclaimed German emperor, the Germans signed the treaty. Germany was represented by Hermann Müller and Dr. Bell, a Centrist minister.

Even from a perspective of forty years, it is not easy to judge the Treaty of Versailles. For twenty years it remained the source of endless controversy and thousands of pages of polemic. The Germans erected the *Kriegsschuldfrage* ("war-guilt question") into almost a religion; in this they were warmly joined by scholars and publicists in nearly every nation, representing every shade of opinion. Right-wing parties in Germany used the treaty much as the Republican party in the United States "waved the bloody shirt" after the Civil War. Whenever he had nothing else to rant about, Adolf Hitler could always attack the *"Versailler Diktat,"* ("dictate of Versailles") and excoriate the parties which had voted for its acceptance. The whole of European diplomatic history between the two world wars revolved around the implementation or repudiation of the treaty.

A few things seem to emerge from this cloud of confusion. One is that, given the principle of self-determination as a criterion, the territorial rearrangements in ethnically confused central Europe were about as sensible as anyone short of an angel could have worked out. Secondly, the failure of the United States to ratify the treaty and join the League of Nations completely obliterated Wilson's fond hope that as passions cooled the League might modify portions of the treaty. Thirdly, the whole matter of reparations and the manner in which the Allies, especially France, tried to enforce them led to terrible bitterness and eventual failure, and must be counted as a grievous error. Fourthly, the refusal of the Allies to treat the new democratic Germany any differently from the way it would have dealt with the old militaristic regime led to the discrediting of just those democratic elements in Germany which the Allies should have most welcomed and aided; instead they became saddled with the hopeless responsibility of accepting, and later trying to fulfill, the treaty obligations.

The historian can amuse himself and his readers with judgments made after the fact. However, he must always bear in mind that he is dealing with a specific moment in history, and try to see what that moment demanded of the men who were acting in it. The Treaty of Versailles followed the most intense, poignant, and passionately fought war in history up to that time. It is difficult to see how the treaty could have been much different except in detail. There was bitterness, the desire for revenge, and also an honest longing to build a better world. The complexities of human motivation appear here in a strong light; they render it impossible to make final judgments.

The fact remains that the history of Germany from 1919 to 1939 is very largely the history of the Treaty of Versailles.

CHAPTER XXII

Growing Pains of a Republic (1919-23)

The history of the Weimar Republic can be neatly divided into three periods: 1919–23, 1924–29, and 1930–33, which correspond fairly closely to the ages of man: adolescence, maturity, and decay and death. They are sharply divided from one another but share one theme, the effort of the republic to defend itself from its enemies at home, both on the right and on the left, but most often on the right.

The first period was one in which the new regime strove desperately to parry attacks from all directions. It was a period of dynamism, hatred, and confusion. There was ferment of all kinds—political, economic, social, and international. While many conflicting events occurred during these years, there are several which serve to bring out the principal trends of the time. They are the Kapp *Putsch,* which tried to establish a military dictatorship; the growth of extremist nationalism, as represented in the Free Corps movement and the murders carried out under its auspices; the efforts of the Communists to seize power; the attempts to implement the Versailles Treaty and to find for Germany a place in the new international society; and finally, the invasion of the Ruhr by the French in 1923 and the uncontrolled inflation of the German currency. After these horrors the year 1924 ushered in a new period of prosperity and apparent equilibrium.

After the promulgation of the Weimar Constitution in August 1919, there was a temporary and illusory lull in domestic affairs. The government and assembly left Weimar and settled in Berlin, but, as it developed, was sitting on the edge of a volcano. The first signs of eruption had their origins in the officer corps of the old army.

Although the army had remained intact at the time of the defeat, and Hindenburg and Groener had pledged their support to the new government, and although the troops returned to Germany peacefully and with the plaudits of the people, nevertheless the officers were on the whole bitterly opposed to the new regime. Their lives had been devoted to the cause of the Hohenzollerns. Perhaps they were an anachronism now, but they were full of vitality and hatred; many of them were prepared to plunge recklessly into an attempt to restore the old Germany with its privileged position for the military. Hindenburg had retired from active service and was living in obscurity. Groener also had given up his command after his unpopular advice to ratify the treaty. Two men now emerged as the principal figures among the higher ranks, General Hans von Seeckt and General Baron Walther von Lüttwitz, men of very different personalities. Seeckt, who was to become one of the most influential Germans of the twenties, headed the strategic *Truppenamt,* the department of the war ministry which had taken over the duties of the forbidden General Staff. Although he is still a controversial character, Seeckt's approach to the problem of the army in the republic is fairly clear. His primary and almost unmixed loyalty was to the army, not to a political philosophy. Endowed with extraordinary astuteness, he believed that the principal task of the shorn army was to develop its efficiency, to keep away from direct participation in political affairs, and to constitute itself a state within the state. His amazing success in this effort and the subtlety with which he achieved it are remarkable. Lüttwitz was a much simpler character. He was simply an old-line Prussian officer, scornful of anything that did not accord with his philosophy of "king and fatherland." With the single-mindedness born of limited intelligence, he was ready for any risk. In the early months of 1920 Lüttwitz was in command of the army district around Berlin. His civilian coconspirator, whose name is remembered only for the fiasco which he led in March 1920, was Wolfgang Kapp. Kapp had had a respectable, if narrow, career in the agricultural department of the East Prussian civil service. An extreme nationalist, he had been in the group surrounding Admiral Tirpitz which had founded the Fatherland party in 1917.

Lüttwitz and Kapp tried to enlist the support of important right-wing elements for their plan to seize the government by force and install in its place a dictatorship consisting of themselves. They made contact with the Nationalist and People's party leaders, who, however, were reticent and evasive. They no doubt felt that their position was still too insecure during this revolutionary period to chance a use of force, but that, were the army leaders successful, they could rally to them without any difficulty. The responsible command in the army, Seeckt and his colleagues, were also unenthusiastic, similarly fearful for the position of the army in this time of flux and demobilization.

The insurgents found their tool ready at hand in the so-called Erhardt Brigade. Captain Hermann Erhardt was a wild, undisciplined, flamboyant fighter, reminiscent of the *condottieri* of the Renaissance. He commanded a naval brigade which had taken part in quelling the Communists in Bavaria and was now in barracks at Döberitz near Berlin. Because of the demand of the treaty for the disbanding of the German army, the government had ordered the dismissal of thousands of men and officers, including the Erhardt Brigade. The Brigade had no intention of complying with this order. During the first days of March negotiations continued, and it was an open secret that there was likely to be some sort of thrust for power.

On the night of March 12, 1920, Erhardt sent an ultimatum to Minister Noske insisting on certain stipulations that complied with the Nationalist program, and gave the government until seven in the morning to reply. The cabinet immediately sent for the army leaders to determine if it could count on their support. There were differences of opinion, but Seeckt spoke for the majority when he said that German soldiers must not fire on one another. (It was apparently all right for German soldiers to fire on other Germans who were not soldiers.) Thus in this event the regular army simply stood aside and decided to let others settle the crisis. Faced with this attitude, the government saw no course open except flight. Accordingly Ebert, Bauer, and the ministers left Berlin and fled to Dresden and then to Stuttgart. Before they left, however, they issued an important document, an appeal in the name of the Social Democratic party to the German people to stage a general strike to defeat the ambitions of the rebels.

The next morning the Erhardt Brigade arrived in Berlin, joined by Lüttwitz, Kapp, and even Ludendorff, who happened to be taking a walk thus early on a March morning. It was greeted by cheers of the police and no resistance from the regular army. Nothing prevented the rebels from taking possession of the government buildings. They proclaimed a new government with Kapp as chancellor and Lüttwitz as minister of war. However, they had seized empty buildings. Kapp proved to be utterly incompetent, the bureaucracy did not know what position to take, the banks would not co-operate, and even the right-wing parties remained aloof. On March 17 Kapp turned over his office to Lüttwitz, but it was not clear what office there was to forego.

The general strike was a great success. The workers left en masse. Life in Germany came to a sudden stop. Even the Independents supported the strike, though the Communists refused to; the government retained the support also of the Democrats and the Center. Within a few days this comic opera *Putsch* was over. Lüttwitz resigned soon after Kapp, and by March 20 the government returned to Berlin.

It was one thing to call the workers out on strike; it was another to persuade them to go back to work. Several days of negotiations were required to achieve this, and had not the Independents backed down, they might have obtained some major concessions from the government. As it was some changes were made. Noske had become very unpopular with the left for his support of the army. He resigned and was replaced by the Democrat, Otto Gessler, who was to remain minister of war for almost eight years and to work hand in hand with Seeckt in building the efficiency of the *Reichswehr,* as the republican army was called. The resignation of Noske led to a general reshaping of the cabinet. Bauer resigned as chancellor and was replaced by Hermann Müller, the former foreign minister. The three parties of the Weimar Coalition supported the new government.

The fighting was not yet over. In the Ruhr industrial district the general strike developed into a Communist-led rebellion. It assumed very serious proportions and captured control of several important cities. The *Reichswehr,* which had no qualms about firing on these Germans, put down the revolt in a bloody fashion. To do this it had to enter the demilitarized zone on the right bank of the Rhine. In retaliation French troops crossed the Rhine to Frankfurt claiming their treaty right to oppose resurgent militarism in Germany. This action led to great bitterness between France and Germany. It was also a wedge in the relationship between the French and the British, who disapproved of the action. The French withdrew in May.

Soon thereafter, on June 6, 1920, elections were held for the first regular Reichstag of the republic. The Nationalists had been pushing for elections for some time. They felt that their own strength had increased, and the radical left had grown more powerful to the discomfiture of the Social Democrats, and that the Weimar Coalition had lost much public support as a result of the Treaty of Versailles and subsequent troubles. In all of these appreciations they were correct. The election was an important one and prefigured the course of German political life for some years to come. The Nationalists gained just under a million votes (42 to 66 seats). The People's party did even better, bringing its leader, Gustav Stresemann, into the political limelight. It more than doubled its vote and increased its delegation from 22 to 62. The Center remained relatively stable, except that its Bavarian wing decided to act separately as the Bavarian People's party and was not always dependable in support of the mother party. The greatest casualty occurred in the Democratic party, which lost well over half of its votes and was reduced from 74 to 45 seats. The Social Democrats also lost over half of their votes and 51 seats, while the Independents doubled their following and jumped from 22 to 81 votes in the Reichstag. The Communists withdrew their boycott on voting but did poorly and received only two seats. The center of political gravity had moved to the right, but more important, a polarization of political opinion became evident in Germany which was typical of, and fateful for, continental Europe in general in the interwar years. The extremes were gaining at the expense of the middle. This presaged the development a decade later of the two great parties of Germany: the Communists on the far left, and the Nazis on the far right.

Faced with the fact that the Weimar Coalition no longer commanded a Reichstag majority, Hermann Müller resigned as chancellor. Efforts were made to bring the Independents into the coalition but they refused; the Social Democrats on their part would not coalesce with the People's party. In due course a government was formed, supported by the People's party, the Center, and the Democrats. Konstantin Fehrenbach, the new head of the Center party, became chancellor, and there was a tacit agreement of the Social Democrats to try to support the government at least on major issues. This also became a pattern for the future: a government of the right center with quiet backing from the socialists. Social Democracy, which had been the mainspring and spearhead of the revolution of 1918 and of the reorganization of the following months, lost much of its influence from this time on. With one exception no Social Democrat ever again became chancellor. Germany was a bourgeois republic, bitterly attacked from both extremes.

The Kapp *Putsch* was a fiasco, but the attitudes behind it were by no means eliminated. Irreconcilable German nationalism remained an important force throughout the years of the republic and finally gained ascendancy with Hitler and the Nazis. It was a direction of mind which existed at various levels, some open and honest, others subterranean, murky, and devious. The old officer corps, the Prussian aristocracy, and the monarchists in business and industry made no secret of their views. The Nationalist party and, to a somewhat lesser extent, the People's party were clear in their opposition to the Weimar spirit of 1919. They openly espoused the old Hohenzollern colors: black, white, and red; they openly voted against the government; they openly made speeches and penned pamphlets condemning the government, the constitution, and the treaty. Their support increased markedly in the election of 1920. Many of these men bore great names, were cultivated people, and had filled important posts in the old empire. They were of course a source of weakness and opposition to the government, but at least they could be depended upon to have no hesitation in airing their views.

Much more sinister were the subterranean nationalists who organized a reign of terror in the early years of the republic and became the precursors of National Socialism. These people are variously known; their several organizations, because surreptitious, are hard to disentangle. Although they became heroes in the thirties and a good deal of hagiography was committed about them, there is still some mystery connected with their activities. It is safest to lump them together under the label Free Corps.

The Free Corps had their origin in the turbulent days immediately after the armistice when the armed forces were being demobilized on a rapid scale and law-abiding Germans were paralyzed with fear of encroaching Bolshevism. Many of the demobilized soldiers remained under arms. They knew no other trade; they had been trained intensively to concepts of German victory, German glory, German honor. Now quickly the hero of yesterday became the down-and-outer of today. His Germany was gone; obviously, he thought, it had been betrayed. But by whom? Just as obviously, he concluded, by those groups who were oppositionist in the old empire and who had stayed at home while the patriots fought: the socialists, the Jews, the pacifists, the mealymouthed and obsequious. The true German virtues must win and obliterate such elements. Physical strength, virile prowess, and muscular morality: these were the qualities of the real German. In view of these ideas Free Corps psychology patterned itself. It soon became apparent, however, that a rot was setting in; these clean young heroes were becoming brutal bullies, bloodthirsty murderers, and sweaty gangsters. The teachings of Wagner and Nietzsche, in a perverted form, now began to have their triumph. Siegfried was replacing Hans Sachs.

At first the Free Corps and their spirit were welcome even to the republican government. Some of them were of great and desirable value in subduing the Spartacists. They even looked like guardians of law and order. Between the end of the war and 1921 many of the Corps made their way to the Baltic area where Communists and Poles (both equally detested) were fighting the old German colonial culture of the Teutonic Knights. Here on the misty and mournful stretches of the east they could march arm in arm, singing their lusty songs and imagining themselves in the heroic fourteenth century. The government and even the Allies winked at much of that activity, for these people were useful in preventing the spread of Russian Bolshevism. However, in time the Baltic area became pacified and settled, and there was no more fighting for the German heroes. The epilogue to 1918 was ending. They were thus forced back into shorn Germany, where they became instruments of violence in the hands of nationalism.

In Germany the Free Corps went underground to avoid the Allies, who were insisting that all irregular armed bands be eradicated in accordance with the disarmament clauses of the treaty. Here the story becomes obscure because otherwise respectable people in the army and the government saw in these men a means of evading some of the worst provisions of Versailles. There seems little doubt that the government sometimes covertly aided them, even less that the army did. There is no doubt that large landowners, especially in the east, protected and maintained them while they concealed their weapons in innocent hayricks and barns.

Not only did the east provide a haven for the Corps. An even happier hunting ground was found in Bavaria, which was undergoing a unique evolution. Always particularist and anti-Prussian, Bavaria had even less love for the socialist republic than for the Hohenzollern monarchy, which had at least preserved order. The events of the spring of 1919 in Bavaria had increased latent conservatism and separatism. Munich was a hotbed of rightist and nationalist sentiment and oratory. The Kapp *Putsch* had repercussions in Bavaria, where the socialist government was thrust out of office and the conservative Gustav von Kahr made prime minister. Many leading Free Corpsmen, including Erhardt, made their way there and received welcome. A demand by the national government at the insistence of the Allies that all Free Corps groups be disbanded by May 31, 1920, was more or less openly flouted, by the Bavarian government, as were other decrees from Berlin. The Corps had to go underground, but they did not lack supplies. It was in this culture that the germs of National Socialism received warmth and nourishment.

There is no reason here to list and describe the various Free Corps organizations which flourished in this period. Some of them were ephemeral, others unimportant. One of the more interesting was Organization C (or Consul) led by Erhardt and by Manfred von Killinger, who was in the Kapp *Putsch* and who lived to become in the thirties Nazi consul-general in San Francisco and later ambassador to Romania. The specialty of this group was murder. It arrogated to itself the right to judge and condemn in secret meetings (called Vehmic tribunals after a medieval prototype) people who it considered to be enemies of the state. Many were thus murdered, some of them very prominent men. The first man of real importance to receive this macabre distinction was Matthias Erzberger.

Erzberger was already in eclipse. In the fall of 1919, while he was minister of finance in the Bauer cabinet, he had been accused of shady financial dealings by Karl Helfferich, a leading Nationalist. Erzberger retaliated with a libel suit, which he won on a technical ground of slander, although some of Helfferich's accusations were true. Erzberger's political career was over, and he retired to his home in southwest Germany. Organization C was not satisfied with this punishment, and decided that the man who signed the armistice and advised the acceptance of the treaty must die. He was shot on August 26, 1921, while walking in the woods near his home. The murder caused a great stir. Laws were passed and resolutions made, but the Bavarian government took no definitive action. However, Kahr was forced to resign and was replaced by Count Hugo Lerchenfeld, who promised a democratic administration in harmony with the government in Berlin.

The timing of Erzberger's murder was no doubt influenced by a new crisis in the relations between Germany and her former enemies. The Inter-Allied Reparations Commission made its final report a few days before the deadline. It announced Germany's total bill to be the staggering sum of 132 billion gold marks (about 35 billion dollars at that time), payable in forty-two years. All Germany was thunderstruck at what seemed to be an exorbitant and impossible demand. Immediately the Fehrenbach cabinet fell, and while there was no government, the Allies gave Germany six days to accept the Reparation Commission's report at the peril of an occupation of the Ruhr district. Great confusion reigned in Reichstag circles. As usual, it was the Weimar Coalition which finally realized that there was no alternative and took the responsibility of further acquiescence to Allied demands. Dr. Josef Wirth, a member of the progressive wing of the Center party, received the chancellorship; with the aid of the votes of the Independents, he accepted the Allied ultimatum. The rage of the Nationalists knew no bounds, and the clamor culminated in the murder of Erzberger. Much of the right-wing rancor was directed at the man whom Wirth picked to be minister of reconstruction and later foreign minister. This was Walther Rathenau, son and heir of the electrical magnate Emil Rathenau, a Jew. Rathenau had been very efficient during the war as the official in charge of collecting and stock-piling strategic and scarce raw materials. A brilliant, cultured dilettante of the arts, enormously wealthy, Rathenau knew western Europe well and made the decision to orient German policy toward Britain and France. He and Wirth developed the policy of fulfillment, the rationale of which was simple. Rathenau believed that the treaty and in particular the reparations provisions were unfulfillable, but he felt that the only way to prove this to the British and the French was to give evidence in good faith of trying to fulfill the demands. When the inevitable failure developed, the Allies would realize that they had asked the impossible and back down. This policy earned for the government the hatred and vilification of Nationalists, who poured scorn and abuse on Rathenau because he was a Jew and therefore no "real German."

During his tenure of office one of the most perplexing problems with which Rathenau had to deal was the relationship of the new German

republic with the new Soviet state. Although his background and training made him suspicious and fearful of Communism, Rathenau realized
some of the wisdom implicit in a Russo-German *rapprochement*. Powerful voices in Berlin demanded closer relations with the Soviets. Oddly
enough at first blush, these voices came not from the left but from the
right. A closer examination shows that this line of policy was really a
continuation of Bismarck's. The leaders of the "Russian" party in Berlin
were to be found among the old-line diplomats in the foreign office and
also very notably in Seeckt, new commander in chief of the *Reichswehr*.
These men were not overly concerned with the philosophy that dominated the Russian government. They were interested in geography (convinced that Germany and Russia must never again fight each other),
economics (impressed by the virginal potentialities of the great Russian
land), and military developments (hopeful that Germany might work
out with Russia ways of evading the treaty restrictions). Rathenau was
not unimpressed by this line of argument.

The opportunity to do something about it occurred in April 1922. The
British prime minister, Lloyd George, had proposed a general European
conference to deal with the economic dislocation caused by the war.
The French premier, Raymond Poincaré, bitterly nationalist and anti-
German, had no faith in the idea but knew of no graceful way to prevent the meeting. Thus the Genoa Conference took place, the most striking feature of which was that the two pariah nations, Germany and Soviet
Russia, were invited. Wirth and Rathenau both attended, and the Soviet
delegation was headed by the people's commissar for foreign affairs,
George Chicherin. The conference itself accomplished nothing. French
intransigence caused it to fail. However, on April 16 the German and
Soviet representatives left Genoa quietly, drove to the beautiful Riviera
town of Rapallo, and signed a treaty.

There was nothing very spectacular about the terms of the treaty.
Germany and Soviet Russia mutually agreed that they would establish
diplomatic relations, that neither would ask for any reparations from
the other, and that the way was now open for closer economic relations.
The treaty, composed right under the noses of the Allies, fell like a
bombshell throughout Europe. The two hated and feared nations were
drawing close. In particular the French were affronted, and it seems
clear that the increasingly tough line taken by France toward Germany
in the next few months was a result of events at Rapallo. In Germany
most elements greeted the treaty with great pleasure. If nothing else,
it proved that for the first time since 1918 Germany was capable of an
independent foreign policy.

Soon afterwards German and Soviet military authorities joined in a number of extremely secret meetings to discuss military collaboration. So secret were these meetings that it was not until after World War II that the world knew much about them. It has even been suggested that the German government itself did not know about them, although this has been disproved. The result was an agreement to exchange information and training. Some Russians were sent to Germany for training, while the Soviet government furnished secret locations and equipment for German officers and scientists to do research and development on types of weapons forbidden to Germany by Versailles. This collaboration grew closer through the years and did not end even when Hitler, the great anti-Communist, headed Germany.

Not even the triumph of Rapallo was enough to win personal popularity for Rathenau. He still had to face constant attacks from the right because of his policy of fulfillment and his alleged subservience to the Allies. The attacks were heightened by the conflict which had erupted in Upper Silesia. The plebiscite held there in 1921 had resulted in an almost two-to-one victory for Germany. However, the Allies decided to partition the area and allotted some of the most valuable industrial districts to Poland. The result was armed conflict in which both sides committed the usual brutal atrocities. The Nationalist reaction to this was intense and was directed largely against the Jewish "friend of the Allies," Rathenau. As in the case of Erzberger, Helfferich led the charge and on June 23 delivered a virulent speech directed against the foreign minister. The next day, as Rathenau was driving through the *Tiergarten* in his open car from his home to his office, a car drew close containing several young, armed men. They fired, and Rathenau was killed.

That afternoon Dr. Wirth entered the Reichstag chamber, which was in tumult, to adjourn the session in honor of Rathenau. On this occasion he made his most memorable statement. In a world worried about Bolshevik and Communist dangers, Wirth pointed toward the conservatives and cried, "The enemy is on the right."

Some of the men involved in the murder killed themselves; others were given light prison sentences. One of them, Ernst von Salomon, lived long enough to write, after World War II, his fascinating and sinister autobiography, *Fragebogen;* after all that had happened in the interval, he still defended his political philosophy and his actions.

The murder of Rathenau caused a number of political repercussions within the nation. The first was the passage of a law for the "defense of the republic," providing for heavy punishment for terrorists. This law led to a crisis with Bavaria which was smoothed over temporarily after a good deal of negotiation. The parties changed their alignment with the People's party moving closer to the middle group and away from the Nationalists, who became more extreme than ever. The most important development, however, was the healing of the breach in the ranks of the socialists. In the early autumn of 1922 the Social Democrats and the Independents drew nearer to each other, and within a few weeks the Independent party ceased to exist. A few extremists joined the Communists, but the great majority of the Independents returned to the parent party.

A cabinet crisis developed in late 1922. Wirth wanted to reorganize his cabinet to include within it members of the People's party. The newly reorganized Social Democratic party refused to participate on the ground that the People's party represented big business and would endanger the gains which labor had made in such matters as wages and hours. The result was that Wirth was unable to form a new cabinet and had to resign. President Ebert reached far afield for his next chancellor. He invited Wilhelm Cuno, general chairman of the Hamburg-America steamship line, to form a cabinet. Cuno, a nonparty man since his withdrawal from the People's party in 1920, had succeeded Albert Ballin, William II's Jewish friend, as head of the great shipping firm after Ballin killed himself at the time of Germany's military defeat. The choice of Cuno symbolizes a typical attitude (found not only in Germany) of the twenties: that the businessman was the magician who could cure all ills. Cuno was a very competent and shrewd executive who was called into the government at a moment of terrible economic emergency.

It was certainly true that economic rather than political problems were to predominate in Germany for the next year. The main problem concerned Germany's monetary system. Ever since the war the mark, formerly so sound a currency, had been weakening at an increasing rate. Starting with the transfers required by the armistice, Germany had been depleting her gold reserves to a dangerous degree. She had financed the war not by taxes but by loans. The accumulating service charges on these loans in addition to the transfer of gold required for reparations payments endangered German financial stability more and more. If to this is added the depressed condition of German industry because of the ending of war production, and also the fact that Germany looked like a very bad credit risk for international loans, it is clear that she was heading for economic collapse. The symptom of the collapse was the ever-decreasing value of the mark with the consequent inflation of prices. In 1922 this process became more rapid and more serious. In 1923 it became catastrophic.

The German government took the line that Germany's ills were caused completely by the reparations payments, which were draining her dry.

So on several occasions, starting in 1921, the chancellors asked for mitigation of the payments or at least for a moratorium. Very little was gained by these efforts except that a further wedge was driven into the common front of Great Britain and France. The British took a serious view of the impending financial collapse in Germany and time and again proposed solutions which might be helpful to Germany. France, however, under the direction of Poincaré, assumed a tough position and maintained that the German difficulties were illusory and simply a conspiracy to evade the obligation of reparation. It is easy to oversimplify Poincaré's position and make him appear an unqualified villain. Although France appeared to be the premier power in Europe and to have made enormous gains from the Allied victory, she was by no means sure that she had achieved security from another German attack. At Versailles she had not succeeded in separating any of the Rhineland from Germany. She had been forced to rely on a mutual assistance treaty with the United States and Britain in case of German invasion, but this treaty became inoperative when the American Senate refused to consent to its ratification. The League of Nations was still a fragile bulwark. The French reasoned that they had to control more of Germany's industrial capability to make themselves secure. By late 1922 they had determined to force this by an occupation of the rich Ruhr area without the co-operation of the British, who, regardless of party, were opposed to the action. France decided to act alone.

It was necessary now to find a pretext for the occupation. Two were at hand. On December 26 the Reparations Commission declared Germany in default on the delivery of timber (telegraph poles); two weeks later it declared Germany in default on coal deliveries. France wasted no time. With the full support of Belgium and the token support of Italy on January 11, 1923, she sent French troops into the Ruhr to protect a group of technicians who were to run the German mines and plants for the benefit of France and Belgium.

The German reaction was immediate and furious. It was of course impossible to respond with force, so Germany adopted a policy of passive resistance. With the full support of their government German workers in the invaded area refused to go into the mines and factories to produce for France. Unemployment and patriotism went hand in hand. A sullen quiet fell over the most productive industrial district on the continent. France found herself in an increasingly embarrassing position. She had gone too far to retreat; opposed by Britain and by American public opinion, she had to follow force with more force. The French sent more troops into the area; they took over the operation of factories and railroads; they imported French workers into Germany to operate

them, but the French workers often did not understand German machinery and railroad devices. Accidents increased until the Ruhr became
a scene of chaos. German patriots further complicated the issue by attacks on the French soldiers and workers and by sabotage of machinery.
The French retaliated with police action and the arrest and execution
of the ringleaders. The best known was Albert Leo Schlageter, who became a posthumous Nazi martyr and for whom a monument was erected
in Düsseldorf. The French also tried to achieve their objective of de-
taching portions of the Rhineland, and supported several abortive separatist movements led by a few Germans sympathetic to the French aspirations. Nothing came of these efforts; in fact, the whole occupation
of the Ruhr was a failure and reacted seriously on the French economy,
but France felt committed to her policy.

The effect on the German economy was far worse. Not only was her
most productive area removed from productivity, but the German
government had to face the enormous expense of subsidizing the idle
population. This obligation finally smashed the precarious German
economy, and 1923 saw the inflation of the mark pass all bounds and
lead to catastrophe. By the autumn of that year it was literally true that
a paper mark was not worth the paper it was printed on. The printing
presses were busy constantly; postage stamps and bank notes were simply
surcharged with the value of the day they were issued. It cost more than
a billion marks to send a letter from Germany to the United States.
Workers needed wheelbarrows to transport their weekly pay. By the end
of the year thirteen figures were required to represent the number of
marks that equaled one American dollar.

The social effects of the inflation were most serious and left a scar on
the German population which lasted for years and provided much of the
causation of the eventual Nazi victory. As usual in an inflation it was
the people who lived on fixed incomes who suffered most. They represented a large class in Germany at that time on account of the number
who subsisted on government pensions arising from war casualties.
Widows and orphans, elderly retired couples, civil servants, teachers,
army officers: these were the groups which saw their monthly stipends
diminish in value or their lifetime savings disappear. In addition to the
distresses of the moment there was a long-term effect. The sharp stratification of German society was such that these classes clung desperately
to their white-collar status so as not to sink into the despised proletariat.
Yet they seemed to be faced with that prospect. This social group later
found in Adolf Hitler its messias, the symbol of the *petite bourgeoisie*.
At the other end of the scale, the inflation year saw many profiteers and
speculators derive great advantages. Debtors were able to clear their

slates for almost nothing. Those with capital could purchase land and other assets which were bound to become valuable again. The hatred generated against such profiteers remained close beneath the surface and was later well exploited.

The disturbances in the Ruhr and the economic collapse provided fertile ground for revolutionary activity. In fact in 1923 the chances of violent revolution were greater than in 1918. From both ends of the political spectrum the Weimar Republic was assailed. The Communists were most active in Saxony where the government was lenient toward them. Disorders occurred, and the movement spread westward into Thuringia and Brunswick. There was even talk of separatism in these three states with the thought of founding a Communist state in the center of Germany. In Bavaria, naturally, the opposite happened. Here too there was talk of separatism, but in this case it was motivated from the right. Many of the old nobility and officer class, backed by the conservative peasantry and the Free Corps, supported a restoration of the monarchy in the person of Crown Prince Rupprecht, son of the last king of Bavaria. In Bavaria too for the first time the name of Adolf Hitler became well known. Hitler was not a separatist but a strong nationalist. He envisioned, with the sympathetic approval of General Ludendorff, a national revolution of the right aimed at a dictatorship, headed by himself, which would purge Germany of the forces of liberalism, democracy, socialism, and "Jewish" capitalism. Hitler's agitation culminated in a thrust for power in Munich in November 1923. It looked as if Germany were falling apart.

Negotiations with France to end the occupation resulted in a deadlock. The Germans insisted on evacuation of the area before the reparations problem could be discussed; the French insisted on the end of passive resistance before evacuation could be considered. As the months passed by, no solution appeared in sight and Germany sank more and more into an economic morass. Finally in August 1923 the Social Democrats decided on action and announced that they were about to withdraw their support from the government, and that they were determined that Germany should have strong leadership to protect the very existence of the republic. Faced with insufficient support in the Reichstag, Chancellor Cuno resigned on August 12. Ebert named as his successor Gustav Stresemann, leader of the People's party and without question the most important statesman of the Weimar Republic.

Stresemann came from the ranks of small business in Berlin. However, his essential shrewdness and ability made him successful in the business world in the decade before the war. He entered the Reichstag as a member of the National Liberal party and during the war was an outspoken annexationist and monarchist. After the revolution he was the main organizer of the new People's party and was generally regarded as a spokesman for big business. Stresemann's chancellorship lasted only a hundred days, but during it a number of important steps were taken.

The first was the decision to abandon the policy of passive resistance, which was costing the government millions of marks a day and increasing the economic chaos. Furthermore, the French were not prepared to negotiate as long as resistance continued. Courageous common sense dictated abandonment. Accordingly, Stresemann proposed it to the Reichstag and despite bitter opposition from the Nationalists and the Communists, who were posing as patriots, received a vote of confidence on September 26, 1923. The Ruhr workers were ordered back to work and reparations deliveries were resumed to France and Belgium.

The next step was to do something about the revolutionary disturbances which were threatening the existence of the republic. To this end and to the end of righting the financial chaos, Stresemann obtained from the Reichstag an enabling act giving the government the right to rule in most spheres by decree and even to abrogate temporarily the civil rights guaranteed by the constitution. The first and most violent action was taken against the Communists, who had made great headway in Saxony and Hamburg and threatened serious civil war. The federal government, acting extralegally, removed the Communists from the Saxon government and appointed a commissioner to rule that *Land*. In protest against this highhanded action, the Social Democrats withdrew their support of Stresemann.

The situation in Bavaria came to a head in early November with the forceful effort of Hitler and Ludendorff to capture the Bavarian government as an initial step toward all of Germany. The *Putsch* was a miserable failure, and Hitler was put in prison. Nevertheless, separatism and monarchism persisted in Bavaria, where the federal government, always lenient to the right, was not willing to take drastic action as it had in Saxony.

The last important action of Stresemann's chancellorship was the solution of the inflation. It was a surgical solution engineered by two men, Dr. Hans Luther, a conservative, nonparty figure who was later to be chancellor and also ambassador to the United States, and Dr. Hjalmar Schacht, financial "wizard" of both the Weimar and Nazi periods. Schacht, as Reichsbank president, was to control German finances for most of the next fifteen years and to give them at least an appearance of stability. The device he used in 1923 was to set up the so-called Rentenbank, based supposedly on a mortgage of all German land and industry. This bank issued the new temporary currency, the

Rentenmark, theoretically equal to the old gold mark and to about three trillion of the inflated paper marks. The government undertook a strict policy of retrenchment, discharging many civil servants and taking all possible deflationary economies. These actions restored stability but at a great price, the price of practically wiping out the public and private debt and with it the accumulated savings of a whole people.

The Social Democrats now treated Stresemann as they had Cuno a few months before. They were opposed to the intervention in Saxony, felt that Bavaria was being treated too leniently, and feared the wave of conservative economic policy which was apparent in the deflationary attitude of the government. Thus they joined, but for opposite reasons, their opponents, the Nationalists; together they forced the chancellor out of office, though he remained foreign minister for the rest of his life. The new government was headed by a member of the Center party, Wilhelm Marx, a former judge.

Germany weathered the year 1923, but just barely. During that year all sorts of wounds—political, economic, and social—were inflicted on her which were glossed over by a veneer of prosperity in the next few years, but were never healed and always ready to burst open. By the end of 1923, however, the immediate problems seemed to be on the road to solution. Even the struggle with France appeared to be ending. An international commission under the chairmanship of the Chicago banker, Charles G. Dawes, was named to re-examine the problem of reparations. Furthermore, in the French election of 1924 Poincaré was defeated and succeeded by the moderate and conciliatory Edouard Herriot. The next few years were to be ones of apparent success for the German republic. Prosperity and international amity were their keynotes. Nevertheless, the wounds remained and were to rupture even more violently under the impact of the next great international crisis, the world depression of 1929.

CHAPTER XXIII

The Origins of National Socialism

Among the many misfortunes which befell Germany in 1923, probably the most serious was the first appearance on the national scene of Adolf Hitler. The absurd Munich *Putsch* of November was the prologue to a world drama of frightful and frightening dimensions. Few noticed the portent at the time, but among those few was the aged Houston Stewart Chamberlain, who, speaking from the grave of Richard Wagner, recognized in Hitler the messias for whom he had been longing.

Adolf Hitler was born on April 20, 1889, in the village of Braunau-on-the-Inn on the Bavarian frontier of Austria, where his father, Alois Hitler, was a customs official. All members of the Hitler family, as far back as it can be traced, were peasants working the land of Upper Austria near the border of Bohemia. Alois was the first to improve his social status. As a civil servant of the Austrian Empire, he was entitled to wear a uniform and exert his minor authority. Thus his son was born into that lower middle class of which he was to become the prophet.

Adolf and his father were a bad combination. The father wanted to make a civil servant of his son, but as early as his eleventh year Adolf was determined to become an artist. To his father this meant a loss of his hard-earned social status, a descent into uncharted bohemianism. The problem was solved by the death of Alois in 1903, after which the indulgent Clara Hitler supported her son by her own drudgery and permitted him to continue at school in Linz and even to take art lessons. His aim was to enter the Vienna Academy of Fine Arts, to which he applied in 1907. He was refused admission on the grounds that the samples he had supplied were unsatisfactory. Hitler would not believe this; he preferred to think that he was the victim of a conspiracy, that some undefined "they" were against him. Soon afterwards he was also refused at the Technical Building School where he hoped to be trained as an architect.

In 1908 Hitler's mother died, and Adolf found himself without family or financial security. He made his way back to Vienna where he stayed until 1913 earning a precarious living by painting postcard views of the monuments of the city and also shaping his political opinions. These were the decisive formative years.

Vienna was a cosmopolitan city, inhabited by the numberless ethnic groups that composed the old Austro-Hungarian Empire. It was also a cauldron of raging political controversy. Socialists, racialists, and nationalists of all hues held constant meetings and published endless pamphlets. It was a tailor-made atmosphere for the young wastrel who liked to wander from meeting to meeting.

People who knew Hitler during his Vienna period tell of his way of life. He was usually desperately poor. When he managed to sell a few pictures, he lived in a furnished room; more often he slept in flophouses maintained by the city or charitable institutions for the down-and-out. His clothes were shabby; he did not always have enough to eat. At times when his income was especially poor he took whatever job offered itself in the construction industry. On at least one occasion he was discharged from a building job because he got in many arguments with the other workmen, who were mostly socialists. He read voraciously but apparently at random in order to confirm his own opinions.

In his autobiography *Mein Kampf,* Hitler maintains that his basic political attitudes were formed in Vienna. He writes lyrically of his pride in being a German; his rabid nationalism was fully developed thus early and correspondingly his loathing for "inferior" races, especially if they were in any position of authority over real Germans. This nationalistic bias led Hitler to scorn Marxism with its international creed. For him all men were not brothers; and of all the peoples to whom Hitler refused to be a brother, he felt most virulently about the Jews. To him Jews were an alien malignant growth sapping the roots of Germanism. One looks in vain for any rational ingredient when Hitler writes of the Jews. It is pure emotion and hatred. The Jews were responsible for everything Hitler disliked in art, politics, social life, etc. A psychologist might say that Hitler made the Jews a scapegoat for his own inadequacies.

Hitler grew to hate the city of Vienna and the Austrian state in general. He was infuriated by what he felt was the undue power given to non-German elements in the society. More and more he longed for a purely German state. Accordingly in 1913 he moved across the border to Munich, with which he fell immediately in love. He led more or less the same sort of life in Munich that he had in Vienna; yet this time he was happier, for he was in a completely German atmosphere.

The account in Hitler's *Mein Kampf* (New York, 1940, p. 210) of his reaction to the outbreak of the war in 1914 is instructive. He writes: "I am not ashamed today to say that overwhelmed by passionate enthusiasm, I had fallen on my knees and thanked Heaven out of my overflowing heart that it had granted me the good fortune of being allowed to live in these times." After this prayer Hitler immediately volunteered for the Bavarian army and started his four years of front-line life.

There is no reason to suppose that Hitler was not a good soldier. He was promoted to corporal and was twice awarded the Iron Cross, though it is not clear what acts of heroism led to such decorations. Usually he served as a messenger at the front line, where he was often exposed to fire. He was wounded twice, once in 1916 in the leg, and later in 1918 when he was caught in a gas attack and temporarily lost his sight. He was sent for treatment to Pasewalk near Stettin, and it was there, blind like Samson, that he heard the dread and shameful news of the armistice. He was ashamed for his nation; he was afraid for himself. The war years had provided Hitler with happiness. For the first time he had enjoyed human companionship; the camaraderie of the trenches was his life. Now that was gone, and he would have to face once again the coldness and brutality of the outside world. In his background Hitler was the symbol of the lower middle class; in his war experience he became the symbol of the Free Corpsman.

Hitler soon recovered his sight and made his way, still in uniform, across Germany to his beloved Munich. However, it was a different Munich now, having been racked by revolution and insecurity. Hitler was in Munich for the Communist revolt of the spring and for the brutal repression which followed it. He saw and heard Communists, socialists, nationalists, Bavarian separatists, all making full use of the newly granted freedoms of speech and press. It would have been impossible for him to find any laboratory richer in political viruses.

In mid-1919 Hitler got a job with the army as a sort of political training official to keep the men away from left-wing infection and to investigate new political groups that were spawning. Here he came in contact with the general in command in Bavaria, Major General Ritter von Epp, later to become Hitler's regent (*Statthalter*) in Bavaria; and with Captain Ernst Röhm, one of the most important figures in the early days of the Nazis. Röhm was a swashbuckling freebooter, happy only when fighting or in the company of fighting men, but nevertheless a person of real administrative and organizational ability. As one of his routine duties, Hitler was told in September 1919 to attend and report on a meeting of a new, small party called the German Workers' party.

This little group descended from a circle organized about a year earlier by Anton Drexler, a toolmaker, who had conceived the idea of founding a rigidly nationalist party but on a principle different from existing nationalist groups, which tended to appeal to the upper and middle classes. He had the insight to realize that nationalism needed mass support, and thus he proposed that his party would appeal to the working classes. This was undoubtedly one of the aspects that appealed to Hitler, who had admired the great mass parties in Austria before the war. Drexler's party had affiliations across the Austrian border, where there was a similar group, to which belongs the credit of adopting the swastika as a symbol. Drexler had very little success at first, even when he merged with another circle led by a journalist named Karl Harrer. In 1919 a few interesting persons joined the group. One was Major Roehm; another was Dietrich Eckart, a journalist and poet of extreme nationalist views; still another was Gottfried Feder, an odd economist, who was in thrall to his hatred of big business and the "slavery of interest" and who wanted a world safe for the proprietor of the corner grocery store.

Hitler, angered at a speech favoring Bavarian separatism, arose at the first meeting he attended and delivered himself on the theme of German unity. The party leaders were impressed and invited Hitler to a meeting of their committee soon afterward. In a short time he became member number seven of the committee of the German Workers' party. This was the germ of the future Nazi party.

Within a few months Hitler discovered two gratifying things about himself. One was that he had competent, if unorthodox, organizational ability; the other, that he was an extraordinarily persuasive public speaker. At first he was nervous about facing an audience, but as his audiences grew, he developed the techniques which made him one of the greatest demagogues in history. Endless repetition, short powerful slogans, no concepts inaccessible to the meanest mentality: these were the keys to his oratorical success. His voice was harsh; his German had a strong Austrian accent; but he managed to exercise an almost hypnotic power over his hearers. Soon Hitler quit his job with the army and devoted himself full time to the party.

In early 1920 the party, soon to be renamed the National Socialist German Workers' party (the German initials N.S.D.A.P. or the slang term Nazi were used in abbreviations), issued its twenty-five point program, which remained official until the end. It was drawn up by the early leaders of the party, and though Hitler occasionally paid lip service to it, he certainly never felt bound to it. The first point reads: "We demand the union of all Germans to form a Great Germany on the basis of the right of self-determination enjoyed by nations." The treaties of 1919 were to be abolished; Germany was to regain her colonies; no Jew was to be a member of the nation. In economic matters the program bore a strong lower middle class tinge: no unearned incomes, limitation of profits from wholesale operations, land reform, nationalization of all trusts, communalization of big department stores, and no land speculation. The program ends by calling for general progressive reforms in such fields as health and education.

Although the Twenty-Five Points were never officially abandoned, a characteristic of Nazism is its lack of positive program. It is easy to say what Hitler opposed; it is almost impossible to give a neat list of the issues he supported. During the twenties in particular, the movement was destructive rather than constructive. The Nazis were against communism, socialism, democracy, liberalism, the Jews, "plutocracy," the Western powers, the treaties of 1919, etc. Those things were clear, but as far as a positive program was concerned, there was nothing but vague mouthings about racial purity, national regeneration, the leadership principle, etc. Both Nazism and its Italian cousin, Fascism, were essentially opportunistic. The genius of Hitler and Mussolini was their ability to take advantage of a given situation using shopworn slogans of easy application. Their failure lay in their increasing belief that they were invincible and their consequent wild overreaching.

Between 1920 and 1923 Hitler hammered out the main bases that were to characterize the party for its entire existence. Less and less is heard of Drexler, Eckart, and Feder. Hitler quickly assumed complete command. He describes in *Mein Kampf* at great length the effort he devoted to what might seem minutiae in party organization. He was an expert psychologist of the classes he was dealing with, and knew the importance of such details as the party uniform, its flags, and its songs. He was giving to an uprooted people a sense of "belongingness" that had been lost with the old traditional society. The arresting character of the swastika emblem; the memories of the old imperial red, black, and white colors; the simplicity of the brown shirt and arm band: these were appreciated by Hitler who labored over them personally. As early as 1920 Hitler decided that the party must have a uniformed group of strong, devoted young men to protect the meetings from violence. They had another use, which was not kept secret: preventing and breaking up meetings of any opposition groups. This was the kernel from which grew the *Sturm Abteilung* (otherwise known as S.A., the fighting wing or "storm troop"), which was composed of ex-Free Corpsmen, veterans, and hoodlums. It took part in all sorts of demonstrations and made the nights hideous with street fighting and bloodshed.

Another important step forward was taken in late 1920 when Roehm persuaded General Ritter von Epp to raise a collection to enable the new party to buy a moribund Munich newspaper, the *Völkischer Beobachter* (*"Racial Observer"*). Now the party had an organ, at first weekly but soon afterwards daily, which could spread the word beyond the beer halls in which meetings were held. Eckart became the first editor, but not for long. He was succeeded by Alfred Rosenberg.

Some of the men who later became paladins of Nazi Germany joined Hitler in these early years. The most interesting of them was Hermann Goering, born on January 12, 1893, the son of a German consular official. He became a professional soldier, attended the Lichtefelde military academy, and fought for four years in the war. He entered the new flying corps, and by the end of the war was the leading German war ace in command of the famous Richthofen squadron after Richthofen's death. The armistice took him from the heights to the depths. He left Germany for Sweden, became a commercial pilot, contracted the morphine habit, and married a wealthy Swedish noblewoman. The Goerings returned to Germany and settled near Munich, where Hermann heard of the National Socialist party. He joined it and soon found himself at the head of the S.A. A fat, bluff, flamboyant character with an almost pathological love for uniforms and ostentation, Goering possessed considerable personal charm which disguised a brutal and amoral ruthlessness.

The relationship between Hitler and Rudolf Hess was more personal. Like a number of the important Nazis, Hess was not a native German. He was born in Alexandria, Egypt, son of a German merchant there. He was only twenty when the war broke out; he fought throughout it, first as an infantry man and then as a flyer. After the war he spent a little time in a Free Corps and then attended the University of Munich, where he fell under the spell of the geopolitician, Dr. Karl Haushofer, whose thinking he introduced to Hitler. He was even more captivated by Hitler, joined the party as early as 1920, and was never far from Hitler's side. Hess became Hitler's secretary and in the mid-twenties recorded *Mein Kampf* as the leader dictated it. A colorless personality, Hess was content to remain in Hitler's shadow. As deputy leader of the party, he did much of the dirty work. He was like a puppy dog following his master. It must, therefore, have been a personal, as well as a political, shock to Hitler when Hess made his spectacular flight to Scotland in 1941.

Alfred Rosenberg was an even more pitiable case. Born of German stock in the Baltic provinces of Russia, Rosenberg was trained for architecture at Russian schools. He fled from the Russian Revolution with a passionate hatred for Bolshevism and also for the Jewish people, whom he equated with the Bolsheviks. He was a natural candidate for the new party and soon rose to a high position, succeeding Eckart as editor of the *Völkischer Beobachter*. He took his ideology seriously, even to the point of recommending a return to the worship of the old Nordic Germanic gods. As party ideologist he penned a long, turgid, racialist book called *The Myth of the Twentieth Century,* which became after *Mein Kampf* the second Nazi bible, although toward the end of his life Hitler himself admitted that he had never read it through.

With these companions and with this preparation, Hitler marched into the turbulent year 1923, a year which was to have great importance for his thinking and for the future of National Socialism. The impact of the French invasion on the nationalistic circles in which Hitler moved was profound. Hatred mounted daily; this hatred was directed in the first place against France, which was once again demonstrating its anti-German virulence. The action of the Berlin government in sponsoring the campaign of passive resistance made even that government look patriotic to the fire-eaters in Bavaria. There was talk of rallying the nationalistic bands—regular army, irregulars, Free Corps, whoever could be depended on—to form a massive and spontaneous movement to drive out the hated invader. Roehm, who always thought as a soldier, was attracted by this sort of talk and wanted to commit the S.A. Hitler, however, was determinedly against it for reasons which must be understood if his actions during the year are to be comprehensible.

To Hitler the enemy was not France; it was the liberal, democratic, Jewish-controlled, socialist-tinged government in Berlin. His aim was to seize control of the central government. To this end the French invasion was a useful tool, for it had aroused the Germans to an orgy of national emotion. The important thing was to control this emotion and prevent it from rallying behind the current government.

The Bavarian nationalists posed another serious problem for Hitler. Many of them nursed as their hearts' desire the restoration of the Wittelsbach family on its throne in Munich; some of them even wanted Bavaria to separate itself from the rest of Germany and to constitute an independent monarchy, or perhaps one united with little Austria as a strong Catholic south German state. This kind of thinking was anathema to Hitler, who was committed to German nationalism and to no particularism and whose platform called for a strong all-German state including his native Austria. Yet the Bavarians were very important to him. His following and prestige all stemmed from Bavaria; only there would he find support in his efforts to overthrow the regime in Berlin. Thus Hitler had to steer a course not simply between two obstacles but among several.

In January 1923 Hitler planned a mass meeting of five thousand S.A. men in Munich. He immediately ran up against the opposition of General von Lossow, in command of the *Reichswehr* in Bavaria. Lossow was suspicious of the wild-eyed young man whose violent views might lead to serious trouble. At first he banned the meeting but finally relented after he had made sure that the regular army would not hesitate to fire on the Nazis if real difficulties developed. He felt this kind of assurance necessary after the army's performance during the Kapp *Putsch*. At the meeting Hitler reviled not the French but the "November criminals" who had sold Germany into the hands of evil.

Hitler's next major effort occurred in the spring when he decided on an armed mass meeting of storm troopers from all over Bavaria to break up the socialist celebrations of May Day. He gave Lossow very little time to consider the matter, and without receiving the army's permission ordered his men to gather. This time he overextended himself. The S.A. men gathered with arms, some of which had been simply commandeered from an army barracks; Hitler, Goering, and others were waiting on the field. Finally Roehm arrived from headquarters with the news that the meeting had to disband; accompanying him were units of the army to enforce the order. The demonstration was a complete fiasco. Hitler, furious at the behavior of the army, capitulated, and for the next several months retired to obscurity.

By the autumn affairs had changed. In Berlin the Stresemann government succeeded Cuno and passive resistance was ended. Now Hitler could shift his ground and attack the government for being unpatriotic and giving in to France. In Bavaria the relationship with the central government became continually worse. Bavaria was in a state of almost open revolt against Berlin. The local government resigned and placed a high commissioner with dictatorial powers in charge of the *Land*. General von Kahr, the commissioner, was a right-wing, monarchist, particularist Bavarian. In these circumstances Hitler reasoned that he might be able to use Bavarian hatred of Prussia as a lever to get control of the Bavarian government and army and then to march on Berlin to assume control of the whole nation. He was encouraged in this belief by his friend Ludendorff, the national hero, who had stood beside him at a demonstration on the anniversary of the battle of Sédan. As October wore on, things became more tense. The relationship between Berlin and Munich reached the point of open hostility. Furthermore, it looked as if Germany's major problems, the occupation of the Ruhr and the great inflation, were on the way to solution. Time therefore became important to Hitler if he were going to strike while passions were still high. An announcement was made of a major political meeting to be held on the evening of November 8 at one of Munich's large beer halls, the *Bürgerbräu Keller*. Both Kahr and Lossow were to be there. An attack on this meeting seemed feasible; this was the psychological moment.

After the meeting started and Kahr was speaking, Hitler surrounded the building with several hundred armed storm troopers. He himself rushed into the hall, brandishing a pistol. He jumped onto a table, fired the pistol into the air, and shouted that the "national revolution" had begun. No one was to leave the hall. Hitler declared that the government was in his hands. He shunted Kahr, Lossow, and the head of the police into a side room. Here he informed them that they had no alternative but to join him. They seemed to have made no dependable reply, but Hitler ran back into the meeting room and announced a new government for Germany with himself as dictator, Ludendorff (who had no advance knowledge of the plot) as commander of the armed forces, and Kahr and Lossow in important posts. The unfounded implication, of course, was that Kahr and Lossow agreed to all this. About this time Ludendorff appeared, and the conference in the side room recommenced. Kahr and Lossow appear to have succumbed to Hitler's charm and Ludendorff's majesty. How sincere they were remains still a question. In any case the quartet returned to the meeting apparently in a state of warm amity. It was then that Hitler made his principal tactical error. He was called out of the hall and in his absence most of the audience, including Kahr and Lossow, made its escape. Hitler lost control of his key prisoners.

When Lossow returned from the beer hall, he was greeted by a telegram from his commander, Seeckt, in Berlin, ordering him to put down the revolt immediately and threatening that if Lossow failed, he himself would come to Munich and do the necessary work. Lossow spent the rest of the night assuring himself of the support of his troops and preparing them against any attack that might be made either by Hitler and his storm troopers or by a group under Roehm, which had occupied the local army headquarters.

Hitler realized that he had failed. He was undecided about what to do next and spent the night in the beer hall with Ludendorff discussing possibilities of retreat. Ludendorff, conscious of his own position, insisted that no one would fire on him and advised a march across the river into the center of Munich to capture Lossow's headquarters. Hitler agreed to adopt this plan.

The next morning the Nazis and their allies, now numbering well over a thousand, forced the bridge over the Isar and advanced into Munich flying the swastika banner and singing nationalistic songs. They turned into the narrow Residenzstrasse which, at the Feldherrnhalle, a military memorial, opens into the wide Odeonsplatz. At this easily defensible spot, the police were waiting. Shots rang out. No one fired at Ludendorff, who simply kept walking straight ahead and presumably went home to breakfast. Sixteen Nazis were killed. Goering was badly wounded in the leg but managed to escape across the border into Austria. Hitler fell or was pushed to the ground, was spirited away in an automobile, hid for two days at the home of friends, but was found and put into prison. The *Putsch* was a miserable failure.

It would be reasonable to imagine that after such a disastrous fiasco the career of Adolf Hitler would have been at an end. The most astonishing aspect of the story is the manner in which Hitler turned failure into success. In fact, the beer hall *Putsch* taught him lessons which he never forgot and which he put to use. One is reminded of the lessons learned by Peter the Great from his defeat at Narva.

Ludendorff, Hitler, and eight others were accused of high treason at a trial that lasted almost a month in February and March 1924. The trial was attended by reporters, both German and foreign. For the first time Hitler had a national audience and a rent-free rostrum from which he could use his remarkable persuasive gifts at such length as he chose. He made full use of the opportunity and became for the first time a national figure. He openly attacked the revolution of 1918 and declared that anyone who fought that aberration was not a traitor but a hero. It was a very shrewd performance. In the end Ludendorff was acquitted, but several of the rest were convicted, Hitler to a term of five years in prison. However, he served a total of only thirteen months including the period of detention before the trial. Weimar Germany was not severe toward its enemies on the right.

Hitler spent his months in prison to good purpose. He devoted much of the time to dictating *Mein Kampf* (*"My Struggle"*). He also spent time digesting the lessons of the past few years. He realized several important facts. In the first place, there was no chance to control Germany with only Bavaria as a stronghold; it was imperative to build the shattered party throughout the nation. Secondly, the possibility of assuming power by means of force simply did not exist, particularly in view of the attitude of reserve taken by Seeckt, who refused to permit the army to get involved in domestic politics. The conclusion to these meditations was that when the party started to reorganize itself, it should do so by legal means. The revolution of which Hitler dreamed would take place only after full control of the government had been obtained peacefully. The Nazis should continue to preach their doctrine in season and out of season. They should try to enlarge their following to the highest possible number. They should take part in all elections, trying to achieve control at municipal, local, provincial, and national levels. The lawless freebooter of the period of struggle now earned the nickname Adolphe Légalité. He had not changed his principles but only his tactics. He was going to have trouble converting his lieutenants to his new policy, but in the end he was going to be able to boast of the accuracy of his analysis.

CHAPTER XXIV

Fools' Paradise of a Republic (1924-29)

The five years from 1924 to 1929 witnessed a sharp turn of affairs in Germany. Much of the gloom, turbulence, and uncertainty of the period after 1918 seemed to be dispelled. A new spirit was abroad in Europe, a spirit of prosperity, optimism, and conciliation. In international affairs there was a real desire to heal the wounds of the war and to admit Germany again to partnership. In literature and the fine arts Germany once more displayed her genius. Above all, in the economic sphere she appeared to regain the prodigious pace she had set in the days of Bismarck. The continuing political feuds and bickerings, the murky conspiracies beneath the surface, were veiled by a façade of success and progress. As in the late nineteenth century Germany appeared strong and powerful; as in the early twentieth century an international catastrophe was required to lay bare the inner decay.

The key to Germany's economic upsurge lay in the "solution" of the problem of inflation and the gradual easing of the connected problems of the occupation of the Ruhr and of reparations. Schacht and Luther had "solved" the monetary problem in late 1923 by the introduction of the *Rentenmark*. It was a drastic solution which left unhealed wounds throughout the social fabric, but at least the German currency remained reasonably stable during the years to come. The reparation problem was eased gradually during 1924 and 1925 by a more conciliatory policy on the part of France, but particularly by the acceptance of the Dawes plan. In April 1924 the Dawes committee made its report which became known as the Dawes plan. The committee recommended that the Ruhr be evacuated, that a sliding scale of payments starting at one billion gold marks and in five years reaching two and one half billion gold marks per year be instituted, that an international bank be founded to handle the problem of the transfer of payments, and that a large loan be granted to Germany to finance the first year's payments. The whole structure was to be based on bonds issued against Germany's highly profitable and sound railway system, an arrangement to be supervised by a foreign agent general. Reparations seemed to be put at last on a businesslike and realistic basis. The German cabinet approved the scheme rapidly. So did the Allies, although France required a new election. The real problem was to get the plan approved by the German Reichstag.

The Reichstag, elected in 1920, was nearing the end of its constitutional tenure. A date in May was set for new elections. Chancellor Marx went to the people, warmly supported by Stresemann, confident in the gains of the past months and the advance toward normality which was apparent. The Nationalists, however, entered the campaign with fire in their eyes and seized upon the Dawes plan as their major issue. They insisted that the government had sold the German economy into the hands of foreigners and was completing the havoc wrought originally by the Treaty of Versailles. They were joined in the cry by both the Communists and the Nazis (who were allied with several other racialist groups). It was a bitter campaign. When the votes were counted, the main winners were the Nationalists, whose representation rose from 66 seats to 96. The Nazi group won 32 seats, and the Communists 62. The government parties all lost, especially the Social Democrats, whose delegation fell from 171 places to 100. The People's party and the Democrats suffered similarly, while the Center as usual maintained about its earlier strength. The formation of a new government held the political stage for several weeks after the election. The question was whether the Nationalists should enter the cabinet, and if so, which other parties would be willing to work with them. It emerged that there was dissension within the Nationalist ranks between the intransigent right-wing monarchists and the more realistic conservatives. Finally Marx returned to office with the same cabinet which he had led before the election and, as so often during the republic, with the tacit support of the Social Democrats. The new Reichstag approved the Dawes plan.

The next problem to arise involved the fact that in order to put the Dawes plan into operation, some basic legislation was required. Some of it concerning the railways would in fact amend the Weimar Constitution and thus require a two-thirds vote in the Reichstag. However, the votes of a considerable number of the Nationalist members were needed for a two-thirds majority. Once again a conflict ensued. The Nationalists uttered the same outcry that they had made in the election campaign. The other parties used every persuasive device they could think of. President Ebert threatened to dissolve the Reichstag. Finally the People's party conceived the idea of offering the Nationalists a proportionate share in the government if they would give in. Marx agreed and furthermore promised that acceptance of the Dawes plan in no way altered Germany's fundamental attitude toward the treaty. The Nationalists relented to the extent of permitting their delegates to vote as individuals rather than by the unit rule. On August 29, 1924, a sufficient number of them voted for the amendment.

With this action the period of economic prosperity began. Banks and investment firms in the United States eagerly undertook the Dawes plan loan. This was only the first of a large number of loans, some of them involving tremendous sums, which were granted in the next few years by Wall Street and to a lesser extent by London. The loans went to the German federal government, to the *Länder,* to municipalities, and to private industry. A boom started in Germany which paralleled similar ones in Great Britain and the United States. A large part of the proceeds of the loans went right out again to the Allies as reparations payments, but a great deal remained in Germany. The remainder was used principally in two ways.

The first was a program of public works undertaken by every level of government. For the first time since 1914 the civilian construction industry started to work at full capacity. Town halls, stadiums, roads, schools, and all kinds of public buildings sprang up throughout Germany. This activity both helped employment and showed the world that Germany was regaining her stature. The second use of the money was even more important. This was the so-called rationalization of industry. The mid-twenties saw Germany rebuild, remodel, and retool her whole industrial plant. Obsolete and obsolescent machinery, buildings, and equipment were destroyed and replaced by shiny, new, efficient models. By 1929 German industry was an example to the world. Other nations, notably Great Britain, were later to wish that they had done the same, for this fine new plant was a welcome legacy from the Weimar Republic to Nazi Germany.

Along with the general prosperity of the period went corresponding social gains. Unemployment almost disappeared by 1928. In Prussia particularly, where the government was very stable and nearly always under the control of the Social Democrats with the able Otto Braun as minister-president, social legislation resumed where the old empire had left off. Budgets soared, but that seemed no problem since the deficit could always be absorbed by foreign loans, many of them short-term loans from the United States. An occasional Cassandra warned of the folly of thus tying the Germany economy to the vagaries of the New York Stock Exchange, but as usual such voices were little heeded.

Not only public agencies expanded their operations during this period. The same was true of private enterprise. One of the outstanding features of the time was the advance in the process of cartelization, which had been typical of the reign of William II. The Germans have always felt that huge monopolies make for efficiency and economy; in the twenties several more were established. The two major ones are sufficient illustration. In 1925 eight of the principal chemical and dye firms merged into the famous Interessengemeinschaft Farbenindustrie, A.G. (usually known as I. G. Farben). This giant corporation monopolized the chemical business not only of Germany but of central Europe and a good part of the world as the years progressed. Much the same can be said of the great steel combine, the Vereinigte Stahlwerke ("United Steel Works"), which was composed of a number of very large iron, coal, and steel operations. The heady atmosphere of the mid-twenties gave Germans the impression that although they had serious problems still in the political and international field, they had once again achieved dominance in the economic sphere.

The Nationalist party had released its members from the obligation to vote against the Dawes legislation on the understanding that it would receive a greater voice in the government. Accordingly, during October 1924 Chancellor Marx tried to reshuffle his cabinet. He wanted a wide coalition reaching from the Nationalists on the right through the Social Democrats on the left. This proved to be impossible, mainly because of the refusal of the Social Democrats. These people were anxious for new elections in the belief that the "inflation Reichstag" (as they called it) of May 1924 represented only the remaining discontents arising from the sorrows of the year before and that an election at this time would provide very different results. They won their point. President Ebert dissolved the Reichstag, and new elections were held in December. The Social Democrats were partially correct in their analysis and gained more than thirty seats. The Nazis lost appreciably, and the Communists suffered severe losses. The middle parties made small gains, but the Nationalists not only held their ground but increased their representation to 103, a formidably large number. The result was a new cabinet with a new chancellor, Hans Luther, the conservative, former finance minister. This was a right-wing bourgeois cabinet with the members ranging from Centrist to Nationalist. The Social Democrats took a firm stand of opposition, except for their support of Stresemann's foreign policy.

On February 28, 1925, just a few weeks after the Luther government took office, President Friedrich Ebert died after a short illness and an operation. A steady, untheatrical figure, Ebert had done his best to govern constitutionally and to maintain a balance among the conflicting groups. Now there had to be a presidential election, an event which opened the way for all sorts of political combinations. At first the bourgeois parties tried but failed to agree on a common candidate. Therefore each party named its own, except for the Nationalists and the People's party which united on Karl Jarres, mayor of Duisburg, who had earned an outstanding reputation during the Ruhr struggle. The other principal candidates were Otto Braun, the efficient Social Democratic minister-president of Prussia, and Wilhelm Marx, the Centrist former chancellor. Others were named by smaller groups. The election was held on March 29. Jarres received the most votes, about ten and one half million; Braun was second with almost eight million, and Marx third with close to four million. Since no one received a majority, there had to be a second election in which a plurality would suffice.

The parties between the People's party and the Communists decided to support Marx. It was easier for the Social Democrats with their high degree of party obedience to get their people to vote for a Centrist than for the Center to ask its members to vote for a Social Democrat. The Communists refused to join the bloc and put up their own leader, Ernst Thälmann. The right-wing parties had a hard time making a decision. Some of the leaders reasoned that Jarres had already received as many votes as he was likely to, and that if all the former supporters of Braun and Marx now voted for Marx, he would be elected. They felt that they needed someone of overwhelming national stature. Much against Strese-mann's advice, because he feared the foreign repercussions, the National-ists and People's party picked as their candidate Paul von Hindenburg, the heroic field marshal who was now almost eighty years old. The Hindenburg myth, so potent ten years before, still carried its magic but only by a bare margin. At the election on April 26 Hindenburg beat Marx by only about a million votes, fewer than Thälmann received. If the Communists had supported Marx, he would have won. A campaign based on German "honor" was victorious over a campaign based on German "democracy."

Monarchists were jubilant, for it seemed as if Hindenburg would serve only to keep the throne warm for a Hohenzollern restoration. Certainly the old soldier was a monarchist at heart. However, he surprised the world. Once he had taken his oath to the Weimar Constitution, he remained loyal to it. For the first five years of his presidency he always acted constitutionally, except perhaps in relation to the army where he felt himself to be still in command. His myth and popularity continued to increase.

The main interest in German history during the middle twenties centers around foreign affairs, which were directed for six years by Gustav Stresemann. The last word has not been written about Stresemann. He was without doubt the foremost statesman of the Weimar Republic, but his reputation has suffered from his adorers, who are more interested in him as a great internationalist or a "good European" than as a first-rate German foreign minister. None, however, questions his dexterity and astuteness. Like all Germans, Stresemann wanted to release Germany from what he felt were the unwarranted and inexcusable shackles of the Treaty of Versailles. His career can be viewed as a very considerable achievement of part of this aim. Stresemann differed in his tactics from many other leading Germans and was extremely unpopular in a number of influential quarters, especially among the Nationalists. The extreme Nationalists, especially that wing of the party led by the newspaper, radio, and motion picture tycoon, Alfred Hugenberg, were completely intransigent regarding the treaty. For them even the appearance of compromise or acceptance was treason. Their technique was that of the verbal bludgeon. Another approach, represented most ably by General von Seeckt, who disliked Stresemann, was simply to build Germany's might with the eventual aim of winning the nation its proper place by force. Stresemann, however, realized that Germany was hopelessly inferior to the Allies in military power and could not think of fighting for a long time to come. He reasoned that the only way to improve her position was to undermine the treaty in detail rather than to attempt to topple it as a whole. He worked patiently but relentlessly to improve the attitude of other nations toward Germany, to make friends wherever possible, and to bring up for discussion with a view toward compromise such matters as disarmament, reparations, and in particular the eastern frontier.

During the negotiations on the evacuation of the Ruhr the question arose of the admission of Germany to the League of Nations. The idea had merit from the French point of view. By becoming a member of the League, Germany would place herself under the authority of that institution, which was so heavily influenced by France. It would also be a recognition of the treaty, of which the Covenant of the League was an integral part. The idea appealed also to Stresemann, who saw in the League a forum where Germany, accepted as an equal, could bring her grievances to the eyes of the world. There remained the difficulties of the war-guilt clause of the treaty and also the fact that under Article 16 disarmed Germany might be called upon to attack an offender (especially the Soviet Union in defense of hated Poland). In spite of this, in September 1924 the German government consented to the idea that Germany should join the League, but with reservations on Article 16. The League agreed to study the matter, but the French attitude toward German reservations was very cold.

The possibility of a regional pact guaranteeing the western border of

Germany against all future hostilities was also not a new one. As far back as 1922 it had been suggested by the Cuno government. Since French foreign policy was haunted by the dream of security, the Germans reasoned that if they recognized the loss of Alsace-Lorraine and guaranteed the Rhine frontier, the French would become less adamant. Such an agreement might also lead to important economic co-operation between France and Germany in a territory which demands it.

In the early months of 1925 Stresemann sent notes to both London and Paris suggesting a regional guarantee of the western frontier. The French were attracted by the idea but felt strongly that it should be matched by a similar project in the east, namely a guarantee of Germany's frontiers with France's allies, Poland and Czechoslovakia. Germany was unmistakably firm in her refusal to consider such a suggestion. The French official reply insisted that German membership in the League with all its responsibilities should be a condition of the regional pact and that Belgium should be included in it. Negotiations continued for several months with Stresemann patiently trying to win a few concessions from the west. During this time he was beset by violent criticism from the Nationalists. The idea of consecrating the loss of Alsace-Lorraine was untenable to them; it was treason to the soldiers of 1870. They much preferred the old Prussian idea of friendship with Russia; Stresemann hastened to assure them that he did not plan to break with the Soviets, but he earned no good will.

Finally a conference met at Locarno on the Swiss shore of Lake Maggiore. It was attended by Great Britain, Germany, France, Italy, Belgium, Poland, and Czechoslovakia. The major figures were the foreign ministers of Britain, France, and Germany: lanky, bemonocled Sir Austen Chamberlain; swarthy, shaggy Aristide Briand; and fat, bald, volatile Stresemann. The treaties were signed on October 16. In them the five Western powers guaranteed the borders between France and Germany and between Belgium and Germany as drawn by the Treaty of Versailles. In addition, Germany signed with Poland and Czechoslovakia agreements calling for arbitration of any future dispute.

In retrospect the "spirit of Locarno" seems more important than the actual terms of the treaties. Chamberlain, Briand, and Stresemann formed a personal relationship at Locarno which was to be fruitful in leading toward further conciliation. For the first time since the war a spirit of warmth rather than acrimony pervaded international affairs. In spite of this, on his return to Berlin Stresemann was greeted with fury by many elements of the German people. The Nationalists unleashed their anger and withdrew their members from the government. Stresemann pointed out that now Britain was guaranteeing the German border, that a formula had been agreed on to circumvent Article 16 of the Covenant, and that Germany had been treated as an equal. The Allies continued to help him in his effort to get the Locarno agreements through the Reichstag. The Treaty of Versailles provided that the first zone of the occupied Rhineland (around Cologne) might be evacuated by 1925; the Allies had so far not withdrawn because they insisted that the Germans had not observed faithfully the disarmament clauses of the treaty. Now, however, they consented to evacuate the zone by the first weeks of 1926. The government parties with the decisive addition of the Social Democrats agreed to Locarno, and Stresemann won an important battle.

To cap the edifice of Locarno, in January 1926 Germany applied officially for membership in the League of Nations, with the understanding that she would be awarded a permanent seat on the Council. Unexpected complications arose; several of the second-rate powers—of whom the most annoying were Poland, Spain, and Brazil—announced that if Germany were to receive a permanent seat, they should too. Since both Spain and Brazil at that moment held nonpermanent seats, and since the election had to be unanimous, a real problem arose. This was particularly irritating to Stresemann since he realized that the delay played into the hands of his opponents, who in fact left nothing undone to increase his difficulties. The confusion endured for almost a year. At last in September a compromise was arranged by which Germany received her permanent seat while three more nonpermanent seats were established for the malcontents. All accepted the solution except Brazil, which resigned from the League. On September 10 Stresemann gave his maiden address before the League, the first of a series of inspiring speeches which were to make him internationally famous and to win him his reputation as a "good European."

The Soviet Union was very much alarmed by the Western orientation of German policy symbolized by Locarno. The Russians feared that Germany was entering the camp of their potential enemies in the West, and that she was turning her back on the policy of Rapallo. In fact, Stresemann was more interested in the West than in the East, but he had no desire to lose friends anywhere and he sympathized with the army's insistence on maintaining the valuable tie with the Soviets. Accordingly he did all he could to soothe them and was successful. On April 24, 1926, a Russo-German treaty was signed at Berlin which continued and broadened the Rapallo agreement of 1922. Each state was to remain neutral if the other were attacked by a third power, and both were to refuse to take part in any economic boycott against the other. They also promised a continuing, warm political and economic relationship. This treaty remained in effect until 1934, even after Hitler had been in control for more than a year. Unlike the Locarno agreements, the Russian treaty was welcomed by all parties in the Reichstag and ratified almost unanimously. It was less warmly accepted abroad, but Stresemann was resigned to that. The states between Germany and Russia became very alarmed and drew closer together; France and Romania signed an alliance. However, in time the clamor died down.

During the years after Stresemann's first appearance at the League he went there often and conducted much of his business in informal conversations with leaders of the other countries. In particular, he formed a warm personal and useful friendship with Aristide Briand. He achieved complete success in only one matter. In January 1927 the Military Control Commission, which inspected and supervised Germany's disarmament, was withdrawn; the task was turned over to the more pliable League Council. Constantly, in an atmosphere of informal cordiality and at a moment of warmth toward Germany, Stresemann brought up in season and out Germany's grievances: evacuation of the Rhineland, reparations, the eastern frontier, disarmament (wherein he stressed the idea that Germany's disarmament was only a prelude to world disarmament), and the union with Austria. It was like water wearing down a stone. If Stresemann's health had not become so precarious and if the world depression had not been so imminent, his policy might in time have solved Germany's problems with a minimum of friction. This is, of course, only speculation.

On August 27, 1928, Stresemann crowned his triumphs when he appeared in Paris to register Germany's adherence to the Pact of Paris, often described as the Kellogg-Briand Peace Pact. This pact grew out of conversations between France and the United States in which the two were to agree never to wage war against each other. Secretary of State Frank B. Kellogg suggested that the plan be broadened to become a statement by the whole world "outlawing war as an instrument of national policy." Briand approved and suggested an international meeting in Paris to sign the declaration. Germany was to be invited; Stresemann in fact seemed to be the honored guest. A German foreign minister was welcomed with enthusiasm in the French capital. The Paris pact is today often mentioned with scorn and cynicism. However, it marked a serious landmark in idealism and optimism for the future of the world. Certainly Stresemann was one of the principal architects of this attitude.

Internal affairs in Germany during the years 1926 through 1929 have none of the world interest of Stresemann's intricate diplomatic game. They revolved about issues which were intrinsically unimportant but which continued to betray the class cleavages which made any unified organization so difficult. One of these, which actually caused the fall of a government, was the dispute over the flag. On May 5, 1926, Chancellor Luther issued an ordinance providing that German offices abroad might fly the red, white, and black colors of the old Germany alongside the black, red, and gold of the republic. This decree aroused such fury on the left side of the Reichstag that a vote of no confidence passed and Luther had to resign. Hindenburg appointed Wilhelm Marx as chancellor again, with exactly the same cabinet as Luther's.

At the same time another seemingly trivial affair rocked German politics. This time it was the question of whether the deposed ruling families should be compensated for their confiscated properties. The Communists insisted on no compensation; the Social Democrats were ready to compromise but were maneuvered into demanding a referendum on the question. Although more than fourteen million people voted for no compensation, that figure was less than the required percentage in a referendum and the old families were secured in their incomes.

Still another crisis developed about the Hohenzollerns and provided the left with an opportunity of settling its score with General von Seeckt, who was widely considered to have run the army highhandedly and without proper consideration for the Reichstag in such matters as appropriations. Seeckt invited the eldest son of the former crown prince to take part in maneuvers as a temporary officer. When this became known, the outcry left the highly competent but arrogant Seeckt friendless. Gessler, the minister of defense, would not defend him. Hindenburg, who wanted more direct control of the army than Seeckt would grant him, was glad of the mischance. In October 1926 Seeckt was dismissed and replaced by General Heye, who was content to remain a mouthpiece for the field marshal. A few months later Gessler, who had been minister of defense since 1920, also fell into disgrace over some shady dealings with army money. He was forced out of office and replaced by Hindenburg's old colleague from the days of defeat, General Groener.

During 1927 two events occurred which were to lead to important results in the years of depression just ahead. One of these was the passage of a major piece of legislation, strangely enough by a cabinet containing more conservatives than at any time since the war. This new law set up machinery for a complete system of unemployment insurance which would protect a man for six months after losing his job out of funds amassed both by him and his employer. At the same time an elaborate system of labor boards provided for state mediation in labor disputes.

The other event concerned Hindenburg personally. A group of eastern landowners and industrialists conceived the idea of buying by popular subscription the estate of Neudeck, ancestral home of the Hindenburgs, and presenting it to the old soldier as a public testimonial on his eightieth birthday. This was done amid great ceremony. The result was to equate Hindenburg's personal interests with those of the agrarian class, which was constantly in need of subsidies to maintain its uneconomic holdings in the east. In 1932 this act was to have serious repercussions and to vindicate the foresight of the donors.

By the beginning of 1928 Stresemann was ready to launch a new diplomatic offensive against the Allies, this time to improve the German position on reparations and, if possible, to secure the evacuation of the Rhineland earlier than was stipulated in the Treaty of Versailles. Hoping to avoid some of the opposition at home which had greeted Locarno, he wanted to broaden his support in the Reichstag and called new elections. These were held on May 20 at the moment of the greatest prosperity of the Weimar Republic when the German people were grateful to the regime for the well-being it had provided. Accordingly the Social Democrats, the party most closely identified with the Weimar system, received a very large vote, increasing their seats in the house from 131 to 152. The triumph of the left was completed by a jump in Communist seats from 45 to 54. Most of these gains were at the expense of the Nationalists, who decreased from 103 to 78 seats. The other nonsocialist parties each lost some votes, except for the new Economic party (*Wirtschaftspartei*), a lower middle class, free-enterprise group, which won 17 seats. The Nazis were almost eliminated.

The elections led to a change of government. For the first time since 1920 a Social Democrat became chancellor. Once again it was the colorless old party wheel horse, Hermann Müller, who promised a program of stable and gradual social advances. The only crisis of the year occurred when the Social Democrats, traditionally pacifist, tried unsuccessfully to defer the construction of the first of several ten-thousand-ton "pocket" battleships, a type permitted by the treaty. They did not, however, lose control of the government on this issue.

During the years of prosperity Hitler and the Nazis had not been idle, although their lack of success in the elections suggests that they had still not accomplished very much. Immediately after his release from prison in December 1924 Hitler decided to reform the party and in particular to assure for himself the absolute leadership. Several tendencies had developed during 1924 which Hitler considered deviationist. One of these was identified with Ernst Roehm and the S.A. Roehm, the fighter, had not given up the idea of conquest of power by force. Furthermore, he was willing to ally himself with other groups, which were superficially in agreement with the Nazis but which in Hitler's opinion were a source of weakness. To Hitler the S.A. was to be used for purposes of propaganda and protection, not as a substitute for the army. He took prompt action against Roehm, who in early 1925 resigned as head of the S.A.; this remained a source of friction for some years. Eventually Hitler found the solution in the creation of the S.S. (Schutz Staffel), an elite corps founded at first for the personal protection of the leader and composed of men chosen with the greatest care for their racial background and qualities of obedience and vowed by oath to Hitler and to him alone. The S.S. did not come into full power until 1929, when Heinrich Himmler became its national leader (*Reichsführer*). Himmler, the most bestial of the Nazis, is an almost impossible man to understand. He was born in Bavaria in 1900 the son of a schoolteacher, was reared in modest respectability, and served as a youth in the army. After the war he took a course in agriculture and settled near Munich as a poultry farmer. With his little rimless pince-nez glasses and his neat clothes Himmler looked like a rather spinsterish schoolmaster. Yet this is the man who, with a few strokes of his pen, was later to order tortures and murders on a scale unprecedented in human history. He seemed the acme of mediocrity, but he had unquestionable talents for organization and administration and, at least until his last months, an unqualified devotion to his master.

The other deviation with which Hitler had to deal was of a more doctrinal nature. This was the "radical" line of thinking brought into the party by Gregor Strasser and Josef Goebbels. Strasser was a Bavarian druggist who joined the party in 1920; while Hitler was in prison, he used his abilities in public speaking to keep the party alive. He was not noted for his willing subordination to Hitler. In 1925 Hitler sent Strasser to north Germany to build the party there, a task which he undertook with gusto. He founded several periodicals and appointed as editor of one of them a young, unsuccessful author from the Rhineland named Paul Josef Goebbels. Goebbels, born in 1897, had received a good education under Jesuit auspices. In fact he was the only highly educated Nazi leader, a man who could really write the German language. He wrote a number of unsuccessful works, wandered about Germany after the war, heard Hitler, and joined the party. During 1925 his close affiliation with Strasser led him into the group of those who took seriously the word socialism in national socialism. An anticapitalist, left-wing movement grew within the party. Hitler decided to crush it and did so at a party meeting in early 1926. At this meeting Goebbels became a convert to Hitler's way of thinking and remained a devoted follower of the leader to the day of his suicide. A dwarfish little man with a club foot, he had a striking large head with piercing eyes. His almost uncanny ability to manipulate human weaknesses made him invaluable to Hitler as an expert on propaganda. Strasser remained in the party but was regarded by Hitler with continuing suspicion.

One of the problems with which Hitler had to deal was that he was forbidden to speak publicly in most of the German states. By 1927, however, this ban was removed in Bavaria, and in August of that year the first of the annual Party Congresses was held in Nuremberg. This occasion was a landmark in Nazi history because it demonstrated to anyone interested that the party was again a going concern. The election results seemed to show that not many people were much interested, but Hitler was willing to bide his time until some catastrophe should occur which would boost him into prominence. He did not have to wait very long.

Much of the year 1928 was used by Stresemann in an effort to have the reparations problem once more re-examined. While the Dawes plan had accomplished much for Germany, and while she had paid her debts punctually thanks to foreign loans, the Germans felt that a new total of payments should be established and foreign supervision removed. In August Stresemann raised that question with Briand and Poincaré, and also the question of evacuation of the Rhineland. Briand was not unwilling to discuss the matter, but Poincaré, the premier, as usual was less friendly. He insisted that German reparations were tied up with Allied war debts to the United States, a position which the American government had never been willing to accept. At the League of Nations a short time later Müller, representing Germany instead of the ill Stresemann, was not very diplomatic and received a stinging rebuff from Briand. However, negotiations began on the appointment of a committee of experts with unofficial American participation. In December agreement was reached, and on February 9, 1929, the committee met under the chairmanship of the well-known American businessman, Owen D. Young. Hjalmar Schacht represented Germany.

The meetings were long and difficult. For a time it looked as if the Allies and the Germans could never be brought together, but on June 7, 1929, the report was signed. By it Germany was obligated to make payments for fifty-nine years. The payments were to start at 1700 million marks the first year, reach a peak of 2428 million in 1966, and then diminish to 1700 million. The plan provided for a Bank of International Settlements to handle the problem of transfer; the bank was to be controlled by all the nations involved, including Germany. All foreign controls in Germany were to be abolished.

The government of Hermann Müller promptly accepted the Young plan as the basis for a general discussion of reparations, which was to be held at the political level following the purely economic discussions of the committee of experts. Immediately the Nationalists launched a campaign of opposition even more bitter than those they had launched against the Dawes plan and Locarno. Led by Alfred Hugenberg, now the official leader of the Nationalists, they neglected nothing in their excoriation of Stresemann and the parties supporting him. However, mainly thanks to the Social Democrats, Stresemann was able to control a majority in the Reichstag.

The conference on reparations met at The Hague during most of August 1929. After much conflict, with the new British Labor government proving its main foe, the Young plan was accepted. Furthermore, in spite of some French opposition Stresemann won his plea for the evacuation of the Rhineland. The Allies agreed to start the evacuation in September and to complete it by June 30, 1930.

Stresemann had won his last victory. He was not destined to lead the fight to get the agreements ratified in the Reichstag. Although he had been ill for a long time, he refused to relent in his strenuous work. He died on October 3, 1929, almost literally of overwork. One can be glad that he did not live a few weeks longer to see the beginning of the catastrophe that was to lead to the wreckage of his work, the Great Depression of 1929.

The campaign against the Hague agreements was almost unprecedented in its ferocity. The principal device used by the opposition was a draft law called "A Law against the Enslavement of the German People." It was drawn up by a committee including Hugenberg and Hitler. The draft attacked the war-guilt clause, provided that no more reparation agreements should be negotiated, and declared that members of the government could be tried for treason if they undertook any further financial commitments. This preposterous project shows the distance the opposition was prepared to go. The so-called "freedom law" caused dissension even within the Nationalist party and led to a secession from it headed by Captain Treviranus. Nevertheless, it was introduced into the Reichstag by initiative action and after its defeat was placed before the people in a referendum where it received less than six million votes. The Nationalists were losing ground but were still ready to take advantage of any calamity which might occur.

In March 1930 the Reichstag passed the legislation necessary to implement the Young plan. By midsummer the Rhineland was evacuated by the Allies. However, an era was over. Already in the preceding autumn the crash of the New York stock market ushered in a new period marked by economic catastrophe and then political collapse.

CHAPTER XXV

The Cultural Afterglow of the Twenties

Although the Weimar Republic lasted so short a time, there are certain qualities in its culture which separate it from the pomposity of the style of William II and from the sterility of the Nazi era. In the first few years release from the tensions of the war and from the inhibitions of the old regime led to rapid, even frenzied, productivity. In the last few years there was an urge to speak before it was too late. It was a rich and full period but one marked in all forms of art by a certain despondency, as if it recognized that it was an epilogue to the story of German art. More specifically, literature and the arts reflected the diversity and conflict that were evident at the political and social levels.

If the period had a prophet, it was Oswald Spengler. In 1917 and 1922 respectively, appeared the two volumes of his ponderous philosophy of history, *The Decline of the West,* a title that sounds much more melancholy in its German form, *Die Untergang des Abendlandes.* In this work Spengler, using many biological analogies and an impressive amount of scholarly jargon, examines his three great periods of Western man which he called the Apollonian, the Magian, and the Faustian. He compares each of these to the four seasons of the year and concludes that the latest, the Faustian, is in its late autumn phase and that its inevitable death and decay is not far in the future. Spengler adduces all sorts of arguments to prove his thesis. Every great period has its time of "culture," when it is vibrant and alive with great ideas and great artistic output. It then moves into the time of "civilization," when it has crystallized in its forms and produces only technical and mechanistic achievements. Spengler had no trouble in finding proofs of the latter in the twentieth century. He was almost devoid of spirituality and thus of any sense of salvation. *The Decline of the West* seemed to fit into its moment of publication all too well. It was immensely popular both in Germany and abroad. It caused people to think that perhaps they were dancing on their graves and that they should eat, drink, and be merry.

Spengler continued his line of thought in later works, especially his *Years of Decision,* in which he comments obliquely on the Nazi triumph and warns the world of the dangerous rise of the nonwhite races.

The protest against mechanization, which had played such a considerable role in the literary production of the empire, continued to dominate much of the writing of the republic. There were some who felt that Germany had earned her downfall in the war by neglecting the specific German virtues of inwardness and spirituality and substituting for them the worship of mammon. Others felt that now was the time for the Germans to rebuild their lost world by getting rid of the modern mechanized democracy so alien to real "Germanity."

Walther Rathenau, the martyred foreign minister, was not only a political figure but also a social, political, and economic thinker who published several volumes of essays on a wide variety of subjects. Although his large fortune arose from the unchecked capitalism of the late nineteenth century, Rathenau was very suspicious of that system. When he wrote approvingly of socialism, it was not of the Marxian brand that he was thinking. He was interested in an organic society as opposed to the "horizontal," vote-counting organization of modern democracy. His own background made him conscious of the importance of the technician in the twentieth century. He seemed, although he is a difficult author to condense, to conceive of a controlling elite of education and ability, which would contribute the necessary technical knowledge and inventiveness. It is interesting to find in Rathenau this concept of a ruling elite, a concept so typical of contemporary social thought.

Another leader in the protest against mechanization was Count Hermann Keyserling whose best-known work is *The Travel Diary of a Philosopher.* Keyserling traveled a great deal and delivered many lectures in a variety of countries including the United States, lectures which were well attended, especially by women. His study of Asia impressed him with the differences between the West and the East. He contrasted the concreteness of the West with the spirituality of the East and developed the idea that Germany might become the agent to spiritualize the West. Keyserling was one of a number of thinkers during this period who established schools or circles to propagate their ideas. His, called the School of Wisdom, was at Darmstadt, where he attracted a number of disciples.

Thomas Mann was unquestionably the outstanding German writer of the period; a good case can be made for the judgment that his *Magic Mountain* (1924) was the major work of the period. It is impossible to deny Mann's importance; it is possible not to admire much of his writing. He was a many-faceted man who lived to a considerable age in a time of great change. Thus the evolution of his thought is complex, but there seems to be one pervasive quality running throughout his work: decay, disease, putrescence. Part of this is derived no doubt from Mann's family background; he was born in Lübeck of one of those commercial patrician families whose decline he describes in his first important work, the realistic social novel *Buddenbrooks. Death in Venice,* perhaps his most artistic achievement, is laid in an epidemic-ridden city. *The Magic Mountain* takes place in a tubercular sanatorium. His last major work, *Doctor Faustus,* concerns a syphilitic composer of genius who sells his soul to acquire some years of productivity. The coincidence of Thomas Mann with Oswald Spengler is instructive.

Mann was a considerable artist and was constantly concerned with the position of the artist, who for him was central. He stresses the dichotomy between the artist and the bourgeois society in which he exists. Mann was an artistic snob; bourgeois vulgarity was anathema to him. In *Death in Venice* the protagonist is content to lose his life to gain a few glimpses of the absolute beauty represented by the little boy Tadzio. In *The Magic Mountain* Hans Castorp achieves salvation and release from the sanatorium through the dazzling beauty of a fruitless dash to the battlefields of World War I. Much of this artist-*vs.*-bourgeois attitude can be considered an allegory of Germany or the Western world in general, a world in thrall to vulgarity.

Mann's political opinions underwent changes during the years, although he did not like to think of himself in a political context. Toward the end of World War I he published a strange book called *Reflections of an Unpolitical Man,* which he described as his contribution to the war effort. In it he takes a radically German view and attacks Germany's enemies along the old line followed by so many Germans: rationalism, lack of emotional depth, lack of inwardness, etc. During the twenties his attitude evolved into one of conservative democracy. Mann was early convinced of the danger of Hitler, and soon after the Nazis came to power, left Germany and lived in exile until after World War II. He conducted much anti-Nazi propaganda and became a citizen of the United States, where he wrote a good deal that was overtly democratic.

Among those who believed that Germany now had a chance to rebuild herself in terms of her own deepest qualities, perhaps the best known was Arthur Möller van den Bruck; his work, *The Third Empire (Das Dritte Reich),* gave the Nazis a phrase which they used to describe their regime. The First Reich was the medieval empire; the Second Reich, Bismarck's Germany. Möller van den Bruck was the prophet of the "conservative revolution," which, led from the right, would emphasize the purely German emotional and instinctive qualities and avoid the arid rational forms developed by the West. He was opposed to Spengler's pessimism and believed that Germany had a future which depended on the integration of the national spirit. He detested democracy and socialism as they are usually interpreted, but believed in an organic German socialism in which there would not be an attempt to level men but to place each according to his talents, an idea not far from the Nazi principle of leadership. Möller disliked any form of internationalism; his socialism was distinctly national socialism, a concept which he made popular when the phrase was still little known. Once again we have the old German protest against reason and the support of instinct.

Möller van den Bruck was not the only thinker to be attracted by the concept of the conservative revolution. A great many people, especially young men, felt that the Weimar Republic represented decadence and that Germany should restore herself through a return to her traditional values. Some of these people were active on a journal called *Die Tat ("Action")* and are generally referred to as the *Tatkreis*. While it is not fair to call them Nazis or even proto-Nazis, it is true that they were influential in undermining the faith of intellectuals in the Weimar state.

Rainer Maria Rilke, who died in 1926, and Stefan George, who lived a few months into the Nazi period, remain the leading names in poetry, although both of them made their reputations before the war. Rilke's last volume of verse, the *Duinese Elegies,* was tinged with the melancholy and despair which came of the war and revolution. He seemed to long for death. George was the pure artist; anything that smacked of vulgarity was hateful to him. A high priest in his ivory tower, George constantly purified his language and sought for the embodiment of divine beauty in the heroes of the past. He formed around himself a circle (the *Georgekreis*) of younger writers, who did translations of great foreign works and also biographies of great leaders of the past. Although George would have been repulsed by the blatant vulgarity of the Nazis, he and his circle have been criticized both for remaining so aloof from the currents of the time and also for glorifying the concept of the leader.

It is not accurate, of course, to suggest that all literary production in Germany during the Weimar period was conservative, traditional, or decadent. The extreme intellectual freedom of the period led to all sorts of political tendencies and wide experimentation. Among the socialist writers was the tragic Ernst Toller, one of the leaders of the Communist revolt in Bavaria in 1919 who finally committed suicide in New York in 1939. Another was Bertold Brecht, who is probably best known to American readers for the sardonic and satirical, even mordant, libretto he wrote for Kurt Weill's *Threepenny Opera.* Less violent and more democratic was Thomas Mann's older brother Heinrich, who moved with the times so that his works have in recent years been prominently displayed on book stalls in the eastern sector of Berlin.

Pacifism contributed at least three major figures to the period. One of these was Fritz von Unruh, an aristocratic Prussian who served as an officer during the war. He was so horrified by his experiences that he devoted his considerable talent to writing against war and calling for the brotherhood of man. Perhaps less of an artist but a more popular writer was Erich Maria Remarque, whose famous novel *All Quiet on the Western Front (Im Westen nichts Neues)*, stressing the squalor and brutality of war, became a handbook for pacifists. During the last years of the republic it was usual for Nazis to attend showings of the motion picture made from this book in order to boo, hiss, and shout it down. Of course, it was banned in Germany after 1933, along with many other works mentioned in this chapter. A popular satire on the army and militarism was Arnold Zweig's *The Case of Sergeant Grischa*. Another author who lamented the social fate of mankind was Hans Fallada, whose *Little Man, What Now?* is perhaps the best description of the sufferings of the proletariat during the Great Depression.

Among the Catholic authors one of the most outstanding was a woman. This was Gertrud von Le Fort, whose spirituality pervades her writing. Her novels are usually set at a poignant moment in church history, medieval or modern, and show the constant conflict between the lovers of God and His haters. An example is *The Song at the Scaffold,* which tells of the martyrdom of a group of Carmelite nuns during the French Revolution. She relates it without affected pathos and straightforwardly analyzes the personalities of the nuns and their approach toward death. Another major female writer of the time was Ricarda Huch, who was also fascinated by history. She wrote both historical novels and scholarly historical works dealing with an extraordinary variety of subjects. She seemed to be happiest when looking back with reverence at the period when an imperial German and Christian crown bound Christendom together in the empire of the Middle Ages.

Ernst Jünger is a special case and a man whose changes in attitude make an instructive study. His main writing, *The Worker,* published as late as 1932 but representative of other things he had written, is a complete statement of the veneration of the young, vigorous male who was to create the new world and who is so beautifully portrayed in the war memorial in Munich. The war ended the cult of the idea of progress; it also ended slavery to the bourgeois ideology. It is now the time for the young man, front fighter or worker, who will accept the elementary forces of life with all their dangers and their challenges. This young man is not an individual and does not want to be one; he wishes to embody an anti-Christian group will in the new nationalism.

The Weimar Republic offered literary fare of almost any sort. In the fine arts there was also great stirring and experimentation with new forms. In architecture Germany provided the world with new styles and new types of building, some of them extremely interesting. Much of this experimentation centered around the Bauhaus in Düsseldorf, led by Walter Gropius and Marcel Breuer. New structural concepts stressing simplicity and functionalism introduced there remain the basis for much of the work of today.

The unique contribution of Weimar Germany to painting was the school of expressionism (e.g., the work of Franz Marc), much of which involved piercing social criticism of bourgeois society. Perhaps the work that will endure longest is the extraordinarily compassionate drawing of Käthe Kollwitz, whose delineation of the poor and downtrodden in their misery is unique.

In music it may be that greater achievements were made in the twenties in performance than in new composition. A few of the old giants were still alive, notably Richard Strauss and Arnold Schönberg. Strauss had passed his great period; he is one of those artistic geniuses whose important work is accomplished in youth. His last thirty years saw little significant production. Schönberg, however, maintained his activity and continued to be a central figure of musical controversy because of his atonal ideas and his use of the twelve-tone scale.

Of the younger generation of composers Alban Berg and Paul Hindemith are the most noteworthy. Berg, who died at fifty, composed in *Wozzeck* the most important opera since Puccini. Its atonality and difficulty have kept it a subject of dispute, but it has been performed in most of the major opera houses of the world. Paul Hindemith, a somewhat more orthodox composer, became famous in later years.

The performance of music remained at the same high level that was set in the nineteenth century. The great orchestras and opera houses of Berlin, Munich, and many other cities maintained a standard which can be inferred simply from the mention of the names of three conductors who were directing simultaneously: Wilhelm Furtwängler, Bruno Walter, and Hans Knappertsbusch. At Bayreuth the annual Wagner festivals continued under the direction of the master's son, Siegfried Wagner, while just across the border in Salzburg a new festival began in honor of Mozart.

It was not only in the field of serious music that the Weimar Republic made important achievements. The old German tradition of comic opera and musical comedy was not neglected. Perhaps the best example of this was the enormously popular *Jonny Spielt Auf* (*"Johnny Strikes Up"*) by Ernst Krenek, which was first produced in 1927 at Leipzig and swept Germany and Europe. The legitimate stage was dominated by the rich talent of Max Reinhardt, whose famous production of *The Miracle* toured the Western world. The German motion picture industry produced important artistic successes with such stars as Elizabeth Bergner, Marlene Dietrich, Emil Jannings, and Erich von Stroheim. Probably in America the best-known German film of the period is *The Blue Angel* with Jannings and Dietrich, which is still revived as a classic.

It goes without saying that Germany maintained her high level of scholarship in both the social and natural sciences. It will suffice merely to mention the names of Max Weber in sociology, Friedrich Meinecke in history, Albert Einstein in physics, Max Planck in mathematics, and in psychology Sigmund Freud, who lived most of his life in nearby Austria.

Germany participated to the full in the jazz-age madness characteristic of the whole world in the twenties. During these years Berlin has been described as one of the most libertine and dissolute cities in modern history. There was an almost unrestricted outlet for any kind of sexual drive or bohemian activity. The puritanical strain in the lower-middle-class Nazis was grossly affronted by this; the party launched tirades against what they termed *Kulturbolschewismus* ("the bolshevization of culture"), although the connection between the artistic world of Weimar Germany and the Bolshevik party was not always discernible.

In retrospect the frenzied and agitated decade of the twenties looks like a *danse macabre*. The observer today knows where all this was to lead, but at the time prosperity looked endless and the chance for gaiety and abandon without limit. Some of the creative minds of the period, with the sixth sense of the artist, saw where Germany was heading and put their fears on paper or canvas or in musical notation, where they are easily perceivable. However, they were the minority. The great mass danced on heedlessly, recklessly, until in 1929 and 1930 the cock crew and the dancers had to return to their graves.

CHAPTER XXVI

Death Agony of a Republic (1929-33)

The last years of the Weimar Republic were tragic in the extreme. They were of course dominated by the world-wide depression which, spreading quickly from the United States, devastated the other advanced nations. It was the most industrially sophisticated countries which suffered worst. Of these Germany was the first to feel the severe impact because her false prosperity of the years before had been based almost completely on short-term loans, which were called in as soon as credit became tight. Within a matter of months, even weeks, after the first New York crash in October 1929, German industrialists were forced to curtail their operations and discharge workers. The process spiraled, moving with ever-increasing velocity, so that by the spring of 1930 Germany was in a worse position than in 1923 because this time the crisis was world-wide and the Germans could not look for succor abroad.

The economic tensions had the result of reopening the political and social wounds which had lain dormant for some years, plastered over by prosperity. The years from 1930 to 1933 are years of naked class warfare with extremism constantly gaining over moderate attitudes. A characteristic of the four Reichstag elections held in these years is that the parties of the extreme right and extreme left gained at the expense of the old ruling parties near the center. As a result, constitutional, parliamentary government became almost impossible and the way was open to invoke Article 48 and to rule by presidential decree. When that was done, the important factors in German developments became the relationships between a number of individuals and the aged and increasingly senile Hindenburg. Thus in this period it is individuals (Brüning, Papen, Schleicher, Hugenberg, and, of course, Hitler), with their deals and their chicanery, who must be analyzed rather than the principles which allegedly guided them. The years remind one of the less savory moments of the Byzantine Empire rather than of a great modern state in the twentieth century.

Germany started to feel the economic pinch even before the Wall Street crash. In early 1929 credit started to become tight and unemployment statistics began to mount. The political reaction was immediate. It took the form of an attack on the unemployment insurance scheme which had been worked out two years before. The problem with this type of insurance is that the moments when it is urgently needed are exactly the moments when credit is most difficult to obtain. The parties of the right, representing the interests of the employers, started to clamor for the lowering of insurance premiums, while the Social Democrats, in control of the government, refused to see the law diluted when it was most needed. The result was a long parliamentary battle lasting through most of 1929 and into 1930 at the same time that the even more bitter conflict over the acceptance of the Young plan was being fought. Stresemann was seriously worried about the insurance struggle because he feared it would raise tension among the parties and endanger his beloved foreign policy, so he spent the last day of his life in a temporarily successful plea to his own party to follow the path of moderation. The result was a stroke the next morning which felled him. Without his influence the problem grew worse and a few months after his death, in March 1930, as soon as the Young plan legislation had finally been passed, Chancellor Müller gave up the battle and resigned.

The next day, March 28, President Hindenburg appointed a new chancellor, Heinrich Brüning, leader of the Center party. Brüning was a new figure in German politics and came from a younger generation. He was the first of the chancellors to have been a front fighter in the war. Deeply Catholic, Brüning was undecided after the war whether to go into politics as a career or to enter the religious life. He elected the former and soon became the Center party expert on financial matters. He climbed the party ladder rapidly and in due course became the chairman. Brüning is a cold, dour man, almost completely devoid of personal charm or magnetism. His appeal was through logic and statistics, never through the emotions. It is difficult to think of anyone less adapted personally to fight against the passionate intensity of Hitler or the deep-seated rancor of Hugenberg. Brüning has been much criticized as the slayer of German democracy because he was willing to rule by presidential decree and to undermine the Reichstag. However, in the circumstances which prevailed after the election of 1930, it seems impossible to imagine how else any kind of government could have been maintained.

Brüning's appointment was not popular on the left because he had been associated with the project to curtail unemployment insurance. Thus on his first appearance before the house as chancellor he was greeted with the phrase "hunger chancellor," which remained with him during his two years in office. His cabinet included a number of carryovers from Müller's ministry but no Social Democrats, with the result that it was weighted much more heavily on the right. Brüning's program was one of conservative liberalism. He was an orthodox economist who believed that in times of stress the government should retrench and make every possible economy. However, he realized that there were some areas in which this was not possible. In particular, to please the Nationalists he supported the *Osthilfe,* or subsidy of the marginal large landholders in the east, a subject close to Hindenburg's heart. Brüning held over the Reichstag the threat of dissolution and left little doubt that he and the president were thinking actively of the possibility of ruling by presidential decree if the Reichstag were unco-operative. He won a first vote of confidence. The Social Democrats and the Nazis voted against him, but the Center party and the Nationalists (to the fury of Hitler) supported him.

In the months from April to July 1930 there was a good deal of soul-searching among the parties; Brüning made a number of financial proposals but was never sure of his precarious majority. He had to depend on either the Social Democrats or the Nationalists. The Social Democrats were opposed to him because they felt that his program would harm the working class and that the cuts in the budget should be made elsewhere, especially in the military appropriations. The Nationalists were angry at Brüning for the opposite reasons; they believed that the proposed taxes to balance the budget would fall inequitably on the upper classes of society, and reiterated that Germany's problems stemmed from reparations and from the Young plan. The Communists would have nothing to do with the government, while the Nazis, though small in number in the Reichstag, were becoming more insolent because of gains they had made in local elections. For example, in Thuringia in late 1929 a Nazi leader, Wilhelm Frick, became minister of the interior and started to conduct a violent racist campaign, while in mid-1930 the Nazis became the second largest party in the Saxon parliament. Gangsterism and violence were growing apace in Berlin and the other large cities. The nights were made hideous and dangerous by armed street fighting, fomented by the Nazi strong-arm boys but joined in too by Communists and other dissidents. This became so serious that in June 1930 the Prussian minister of the interior forbade the Nazis to wear uniforms or emblems. In spite of this, the violence continued.

The showdown came in July. On July 15 Brüning went to the Reichstag and demanded that the house show its sense of responsibility by approving his fiscal policy and passing a balanced budget. His threat to rule by presidential decree was thinly veiled. Hindenburg backed up his chancellor by promising him the use of Article 48 if he didn't get his way and also by promising a dissolution of the Reichstag. Even in the face of this, however, the opposition parties held their ground. On July 16 a bloc of Communists, Social Democrats, Nationalists, and Nazis defeated several of the government projects. The executive carried out its threat that very evening. The government did not resign but decreed its program as an emergency measure. The Reichstag now, according to the constitution, had an opportunity to approve the decrees or to demand their withdrawal. This was a last chance for agreement. The Social Democrats were very much aggrieved and insisted that the moment had not warranted the drastic action. They declared that not all constitutional possibilities had been explored, particularly the possibility of inviting themselves into counsel since they were still the largest party. The Nationalists weakened a bit, only Hugenberg's extreme supporters remaining adamantly anti-Brüning. When the votes were counted, enough Nationalists opposed the government that by a majority of only fifteen votes the Reichstag demanded the withdrawal of the presidential edicts. Hindenburg simply signed a decree of dissolution of the Reichstag and set September 14 as the date for new elections. In the interim he decreed a number of other projects developed by Brüning, which called for a deflationary program with increased taxes, a balanced budget, and government economies even in the field of social welfare, especially in unemployment insurance.

From this moment on it can hardly be said that Germany was governed by a parliamentary system. The focus of interest shifts to the strong executive where everything depended on Hindenburg, who alone could ensure the passage of the government's program. The field marshal was now eighty-three years old and much reduced in vigor, both physical and mental. In particular, his eyesight was affected and he had to depend on his son Oscar, who acted as his secretary, to write out for him in very large letters the matters which Oscar believed the president should see. This, of course, gave Oscar Hindenburg a key position at a moment of emergency. Like many old and senile men, Hindenburg was highly susceptible to the influence of those frequently around him. During this period the man of greatest influence in the president's inner circle was General Kurt von Schleicher.

Schleicher was an extraordinary person, almost comparable to Father Joseph, Cardinal Richelieu's "gray eminence." He rose rapidly through the ranks of the officer corps and had very little contact with the fighting troops. From his school days he had been close to the Hindenburg family. During the war he served almost always at headquarters, where he attracted the admiring attention of General Groener. During the

Weimar period he stayed on at the war office, becoming an immediate assistant to Seeckt and, of course, profiting from the appointment of Groener to succeed Gessler as minister. He was shrewd, highly intelligent, a manipulator of men, the perfect political general, a person who wanted to wield power, but always from the background without the responsibility resulting from action in the public limelight. By 1930 he was the key man in the army and had richly improved his friendship with the Hindenburgs, father and son. His political ideas, so far as we know them, were conservative, but not reactionary like Hugenberg's. From 1930 until 1932, when he overreached himself, he was the most important figure in the presidential group; Brüning had to rely upon him for his entrée to the field marshal because the old man did not much like his cold and austere chancellor.

It is difficult to convey an idea of the bitterness and ferocity with which the election campaign of 1930 was fought. The proliferation of parties reached the point of absurdity; in 1930 fifteen offered themselves to the electorate. As might be expected, the Nazis made the most noise. They devoted their efforts, financed by some of the leading west German industrialists, to the middle-class unemployed and to the despairing peasantry. They were rewarded by remarkable success. The Nazis polled almost six and one half million votes, and their representation jumped from a paltry 12 to 107, making them the second largest party in the Reichstag. The Social Democrats maintained their position as the largest party but lost a number of seats; they now had 143. The third party in the nation was now the Communist party, which, like the Nazis battening on distress, raised its delegation from 54 to 77. Obviously the losers were the bourgeois parties, including the Nationalists who suffered seriously and the Democrats who had changed their name to State party and almost disappeared from view.

The most important event in the weeks between the election and the assembling of the Reichstag was the decision of the Social Democrats to support Brüning and thus assure him of a majority. Brüning had announced that he was determined to push his program even at the cost of establishing a dictatorship. In view of this the socialists, though there were many parts of the program that were hateful to them, decided to make a sacrifice to preserve some semblance of democratic government.

The new Reichstag met on October 13, 1930, amid tumult. The Nazi deputies marched to their seats in full party uniform and proceeded to make nuisances of themselves by singing, shouting, and unseemly behavior. Not to be outdone, the Communists replied in kind, and these two set the pace for the parody of parliamentary government which was to be enacted in Germany for the next several years. Brüning was greeted by shouts and boos, but presented his program with extraordinary imperturbability. His address was followed by Hermann Müller speaking for the Social Democrats and stating their grudging willingness to support the chancellor. When a vote of confidence was taken, the government won its majority and the Reichstag adjourned for six weeks during which Hindenburg issued more decrees, including the deflationary and conservative budget for the following year.

Little is gained by retelling the shameful story of the antics of the Reichstag during the early months of 1931. The extremists on both sides continued their policy of obstruction with increasing vigor. Poor Brüning had to put up with every kind of abuse and attack; he comported himself with a calm serenity that showed his conviction that these were just temporary days of chaos and that better times would restore Germany to the democratic pattern in which she belonged. Finally in March the Reichstag admitted its own incompetence and adjourned for the unusually long period of seven months.

Brüning's hope that conditions would soon improve was not to be fulfilled. The year 1931 started as inauspiciously as possible. Unemployment continued to soar, and all of Europe fell further into the morass of depression. One of the most afflicted countries was the little Austrian republic, which had never been a workable economic unit and was now in a bad way because of the withdrawal of short-term loans. The desire in Austria for a union (*Anschluss*) with Germany was strong and reciprocated. This was, however, specifically prohibited by the treaties of 1919. Brüning and the Austrian government worked out a plan for a customs union between the two which would not infringe the treaties and which might help to alleviate the serious condition of each. The plan was announced to the world in March 1931 but met with unalterable opposition from France and some of her allies. Germany was required to put the plan before the World Court at The Hague for a decision as to whether it was a breach of the treaties. A few months later the court ruled that it was a breach, so nothing came of the idea.

In May catastrophe loomed. The Kreditanstalt, the largest Austrian bank and one which had close and vital ties throughout Germany and central Europe, declared bankruptcy. The impact on Germany was very serious and for some weeks it looked as if important German banks would follow suit and create a desperate situation.

The American president, Herbert Hoover, came to the rescue with the suggestion that there should be a moratorium for a year of payments both for reparations and for war debts owed to the United States. The French were doubtful about agreeing to this plan but finally did so after they had insisted on several political concessions from Germany.

However, this was not enough. The flight of capital from Germany continued at an alarming rate. At last in the autumn of 1931 Germany's creditors agreed not to recall any more loans for a period of six months. This so-called "standstill" agreement was later extended for several years and helped Germany to weather the crisis.

Probably the most significant event of late 1931 for Germany's future was the formation of the Harzburg front. On October 11 in the little town of Harzburg a powerful group convened, including among others Hitler, Hugenberg, Schacht, Fritz Thyssen (head of the giant United Steel Works), and Franz Seldte (head of the Stahlhelm, the Nationalists' paramilitary organization). Here an alliance was formed which was to have great significance. Even more important was the fact that Hitler was beginning to make himself respectable. He was anxious to push a wedge into the world of business and industry, and therefore he toned down any possible radical implications in the Nazi program. He continued this campaign successfully in January 1932, when on the birthday of William II he was invited to address the Industry Club in Düsseldorf. His speech was largely an invective against Communism, the bugbear which alarmed the industrialists so fearfully. He managed to convince a good part of his powerful audience that not only was Nazism no threat to big business but that on the contrary it would serve the purpose of preventing any radicalism from the left. The leaders of industry grievously misjudged their man because they were so anxious to win to their side the huge following which Hitler had amassed.

In early 1932 Hindenburg's presidential term was drawing to a close. Many German leaders were appalled at the idea of an election during the severe crisis of the moment and loath to incur the expense. Brüning in particular was of this opinion and felt that the Reichstag should pass special legislation continuing Hindenburg's term for a year or two. This would necessitate an amendment to the constitution and a two-thirds vote, but a two-thirds vote would require the Nazi vote. Brüning had a meeting with Hitler, but Hitler refused to permit the Nazis to vote for the project, saying that it was simply a way for Brüning to continue his political career.

Hindenburg was at first reluctant to stand for re-election for a term of office which he almost surely would not survive. However, he allowed himself to be persuaded, no doubt by Schleicher, and announced his candidacy in February. All the parties between Nationalist and Communist declared their support of him. These included the parties which had opposed him in 1925. Hindenburg was now the paladin of democracy in this topsy-turvy period. The right-wing parties were angry at Hindenburg for placing himself in the hands of the republicans. A few days later the Nazis announced that Hitler would be a candidate. He was now eligible because he had at last become a German citizen by being appointed to a government job in Nazi-controlled Brunswick. The nationalists nominated a candidate of their own, Theodor Duesterberg, and the Communists once more ran Ernst Thälmann.

The campaign was a short, sharp one. Hindenburg was obviously too old to do much campaigning for himself. Brüning became his manager and wore himself out for the old man. People who were in Germany at the time recall how Brüning transcended himself during those weeks. His drab and colorless personality took on color and emotion. His efforts were successful. The election took place on March 13. Hindenburg received eighteen and one half million votes; Hitler, eleven million; Duesterberg, two and one half million; and Thälmann, almost five million. Hindenburg missed a majority by less than one per cent. Duesterberg withdrew from the second election, and in it Hindenburg amassed over nineteen million votes while Hitler polled almost thirteen and one half million.

It looked for a few days as if democracy had received a new lease on life. The government immediately issued an order disbanding both the S.A. and the S.S. However, bad news lay ahead. At the end of April *Land* elections were held throughout Germany, the most important of which was in Prussia. The Nazis became much the largest party in the Prussian parliament, although they did not control a majority. For the time being the old Center-Social Democrat coalition under Otto Braun continued in office.

In spite of his achievements, Brüning's days were numbered. For some months Schleicher had been poisoning the old president's mind against him. Schleicher had decided that the chancellor was a man of too much independence and stubbornness to move Germany into the conservative path that the army wanted. Some of the industrialists, who were now not averse to flirting with Hitler, alleged that Brüning's program of low prices and deflation was bad for business. Schleicher warned Hindenburg that Brüning was becoming socialistic. Hindenburg's democratic veil fell off, and it became apparent that he was still the Prussian militarist allied with the agrarian class.

Brüning was not unaware of the cabal against him. He tried desperately to achieve a victory in foreign affairs, either on reparations or on equality of armaments for Germany at the World Disarmament Conference which had just opened in Geneva. He failed in both attempts. The powers were unwilling to grant to Brüning, the democrat, what they later granted to Papen, the aristocrat, or to Schleicher, the militarist.

The final crisis arose over a project of Brüning's to split up some of the bankrupt estates in the east to make more jobs. This plan struck Hindenburg where he was most sensitive, since he was a landowner in that part of the country. On May 29, 1932, he simply asked Brüning for his resignation. This was much more the action of a William II than of a constitutional president in a parliamentary state, but the president was now in control. Brüning left the stage of German history and Germany itself after Hitler became chancellor, accepted a post on the faculty of government at Harvard, and did not return to Germany until after 1945.

On the day after Brüning's resignation, Hindenburg, on the advice of Schleicher, named as chancellor a relative newcomer in politics, Franz von Papen. Papen was a Catholic aristocrat from west Germany, who was trained as an army officer. During the war he served for some months as military attaché in Washington, but his removal was requested by President Wilson because of alleged sabotage of American munitions plants. Later he was placed on active duty on the Turkish front. After the war Papen and his very rich wife, who was connected with powerful industrial interests in the Saar, lived the life of wealthy country gentry at which Papen shone. He was handsome, charming, glib, a first-rate horseman. He played with politics but never let it take up too much of his time. For several years he was a member of the Prussian parliament where he was affiliated with the extreme right wing of the Center party, although he was never very keen on party solidarity. He won his way to the heart of Hindenburg through his ability as a raconteur and entertainer; the old gentleman spoke of him as *"Fränzchen"* ("little Franz").

Schleicher's reason for choosing Papen was to have him serve as the head of a cabinet of experts, nonpolitical in character, which would push Germany in the direction of conservative, aristocratic rule. In fact, he had the slate of names ready when Papen arrived in Berlin. He had even taken the trouble of securing Hitler's "toleration" of the new regime in return for legalizing the S.A. and the S.S., which Hindenburg wanted too, for it did not seem fair to him to outlaw the Nazi formations and not those of the other parties. There was not even a pretense at forming a government which could command a majority in the Reichstag. It remained to be seen even how much Hitler's "toleration" would mean.

When the names of the new ministers were published, it was clear that the cabinet of experts was really a cabinet of barons, so large was the proportion of aristocratic names. Schleicher himself became minister of defense, and three men who were to last into the Nazi period were introduced to the world. They were Baron Constantin von Neurath at the foreign office, Count Schwerin-Krosigk at the ministry of finance, and Franz Gürtner at the ministry of justice. Within a few days the new government dissolved the Reichstag and called for new elections. As it turned out, this too was a Nazi demand, for the Nazis were sure that their following had grown immensely since 1930. Once again the hungry and impoverished German people were faced with the expense and nuisance of a political campaign.

Two important events occurred in the interim between the dissolution of the Reichstag and the new elections, which were held on July 31, 1932. The first was an international conference held at Lausanne during June and early July. On its agenda was a final settlement of the reparations problem. This would have been a fitting climax to Stresemann's and Brüning's careful preparation, but it was delayed so that the glory became Papen's. The Germans asked for the termination of all reparation payments, but the French were not willing to go so far so soon. After several weeks of wrangling a solution was reached by which the Young plan was abolished, Germany was to make one token contribution to a fund for general European recovery, and then reparation payments were to cease. At last this problem, which had so bedeviled the international scene for thirteen years, was out of the way. It need not be emphasized to what degree Papen considered this arrangement his own personal triumph.

The other development, which concerned the government of Prussia, was much more sinister. After the April elections in Prussia no government had been formed. The parties were still jockeying for position and the Nazis, as usual, were behaving in a completely recalcitrant manner. The old Social Democratic cabinet headed by Otto Braun and Carl Severing, which had served during most of the history of the republic and had governed Prussia so wisely, was still in office as a caretaker ministry. Papen kept ordering the Prussians to form a new government, which he knew was impossible at the moment. He hoped to find a pretext to intervene by presidential decree, appoint a federal commissioner to take power, and thus gain control of the largest state in Germany and in particular of the large and efficient Prussian police force.

It was not hard to find the pretext. Ever since the Nazi armed formations had been legalized, Germany was in a state approaching civil war. There was constant fighting in the streets between the Nazi gangsters and the formations of the other parties. Bloodshed became usual, not exceptional. Matters reached an apex on July 17 when the Nazis planned a provocative procession through the streets of Altona, a very left-wing, impoverished dockyard community across the river from Hamburg but in Prussian territory. The procession turned into a street brawl, open firing occurred, and a number of people were killed.

On July 20 Papen summoned Braun and Severing, the Prussian minister of the interior, informed them that the Prussian government was not maintaining peace, and showed them a decree from Hindenburg removing them from office and placing Prussia under the control of the federal chancellor. The Social Democrats denied the accusations and declared that this was an unconstitutional action. Severing returned to his office. Papen declared a state of emergency and sent the local army commander to dislodge the Social Democrats. Finally after a threat of force Severing left his desk. The question was what action the Social Democrats would now take. Would the events of the Kapp *Putsch* be repeated? In fact the Social Democrats did almost nothing except to protest and take the matter to the German Supreme Court. The trade unions were afraid of a general strike. Papen was left with the spoils and proceeded to replace a large number of Prussian officials with people of his own choosing.

The election campaign was even more tumultuous than usual. The Nazis staged a magnificent show. Hitler and his subordinates took to the air and flew to every village, hamlet, and town to carry the Nazi message. They hoped desperately to achieve an absolute majority so that there could be no question of their control of the government. The keynote was Hitler's promise to abolish unemployment, which was still increasing frighteningly every day.

The Nazis did not achieve their majority, but they came alarmingly close to it. They more than doubled their representation, receiving now 230 seats, but in fact their popular vote was not much more than the votes Hitler had received in the presidential election in April. This suggested that perhaps the Nazis had reached the apex of their fortunes. The Communists also made gains, increasing their membership to 89, at the expense of the Social Democrats who lost a number of seats. The only two parties that Papen could count on to vote for him were the Nationalists and the People's party. Together these two mustered only 44 votes.

It had now become mournfully clear that there could be no kind of government in Germany without some participation by the Nazis. Even Papen declared as much in a public statement. Hitler was determined to achieve full power and engaged on a policy of "all or nothing," which was daring but was considered unsound even by some of the leading Nazis who felt that force could now win the day. Hitler, however, still remembered November 1923. The first two weeks of August were consumed by dickerings and conferences among Hitler, Papen, Schleicher, and later Hindenburg. Papen was willing to offer Hitler the vice-chancellorship but he held out for the chancellorship. Papen assured Hitler

that Hindenburg insisted on maintaining a nonparty, presidential government and would not accept the Nazi leader as chancellor. If Hitler refused to believe Papen, he could have the information from the president himself. On August 13, 1932, Hitler had a meeting with the field
marshal, who detested him and spoke of him as the "Bohemian corporal." Hindenburg offered Hitler a position in a cabinet headed by
Papen. Hitler refused. Hindenburg then read Hitler a lesson in good
manners, chivalry, and patriotism. The interview lasted only a few minutes and was a severe humiliation for Hitler, but it did not change his
mind. Hitler continued to play his waiting game. He was having troubles
within the party where Gregor Strasser was urging a more elastic attitude
and hoping to get support from the more radical Nazi groups. Supported
by Goering and Goebbels, Hitler maintained his firm position.

The Reichstag elected in July performed its functions for a few hours
only. On September 12 it met with Goering, chairman of the largest
party, as presiding officer. Papen arrived armed with a decree of dissolution already signed by Hindenburg. He had decided on a policy of attrition and planned to force election after election in the belief that the
Nazis had reached their climax, would now lose votes, and furthermore
would not be able to finance the expensive campaigns.

Goering pointedly ignored Papen and called for a vote on a motion
of no confidence prepared by the Communists. Papen protested to no
avail, so he simply placed the decree of dissolution on Goering's desk
and left the hall with his ministers. The voting continued, and the motion
was carried by 512 to 42. Goering called upon the government to resign,
but Papen announced that the vote was illegal since the Reichstag had
already been dissolved. New elections were set for November 6. The
episode would have made a hilarious scene in a comic opera had not
the stakes been so high.

The usual violent campaign ensued, this time accompanied by a serious strike of transport workers in Berlin. The election results justified
to an extent Papen's reasoning, but showed what a long way he had
to go. He almost doubled the support for his own government, it is
true, but he still commanded a hopeless minority. More important was
the fact that the Nazis lost about two million votes and thirty-five seats.
It was the first time since the depression started that they had lost ground
in an election. On the left the Communists did very well and raised their
representation to one hundred, mainly at the expense of the Social Democrats who had lost much prestige after Papen seized the Prussian government from them. The Nazi leaders were seriously discouraged by the
returns. They realized that their movement was of the sort that thrives
on inertia; once that was lost, they could easily slide downhill. They

realized too that their financial support would diminish with their votes. These were very tense weeks for them.

Papen felt that the election had been a personal triumph, but he now encountered a new obstacle. Schleicher regretted that he had sponsored Papen. Papen was behaving too independently and had won his way too securely into the affections of Hindenburg. Furthermore, Schleicher decided that Papen would never be able to lead some sort of broadly national government and that in fact he seemed to be heading for a personal dictatorship based on army support. Schleicher was prepared to make a deal with the Nazis, especially with their left wing, for he had recently become very friendly with Gregor Strasser. Schleicher had adherents in Papen's cabinet, and they persuaded Papen to interview the various party leaders in an effort to gain greater support in the Reichstag. Nothing came of these efforts, so on November 17 Papen offered his resignation with the thought that Hindenburg would continue the conversations with the various parties. There seems little doubt that Papen expected the old gentleman to fail and then recall him to the chancellorship.

Hindenburg spent several days in these conversations. On November 21 he summoned Hitler to his office and offered him the chancellorship with several conditions attached. Hitler demanded full powers, which Hindenburg refused, saying quite rightly that this would amount to a party dictatorship. The president now wanted to reappoint Papen, but Schleicher was firmly opposed to this; he persuaded several of the cabinet ministers to announce that they would not serve under Papen, and produced a memorandum from the army stating that Germany did not possess sufficient force to face a possible civil war with Polish intervention if Papen attempted any unconstitutional projects.

Hindenburg and Papen were outmaneuvered by Schleicher, but at a considerable cost; the president was now disgusted with him, and the former favorite was faced with a cold, rancorous old man. Hindenburg demanded that Schleicher assume the chancellorship and try to save the situation. This was the last thing Schleicher wanted, for his talent was to work behind the scenes. However, on December 2 he became chancellor.

During the months of December 1932 and January 1933 the state of naked gangsterism into which the German government had fallen became even more evident. In Berlin Schleicher made desperate efforts to achieve some sort of broad support. He offered the vice-chancellorship to Strasser in an effort to woo the Nazis and perhaps break up their united front under Hitler. Strasser played with the idea, but after a series of conferences with his party leaders decided not to compete with Hitler. He resigned his party offices and soon thereafter left for a vacation in

Italy. He was little heard of again until his murder in 1934. Schleicher had no better success with the other parties. The Social Democrats were suspicious of him, and the Center still remembered how he had treated Brüning. He received an important gift from abroad when the World Disarmament Conference announced it was prepared to accept the principle of equality in armament for Germany, but even this did little good. On December 15 Schleicher announced his new program over the radio. It was devised to placate as many segments of the population as possible, and held out a good deal of bait to the middle parties and even to the left on such matters as taxes, wage cuts, and censorship. Nevertheless, Schleicher won few friends. He was too left for the right, too right for the left.

Decisive events were occurring elsewhere. Papen was furious at his betrayal by Schleicher and ready to make advances to the Nazis. Hitler was desperately worried about lack of money and the dissension in the party symbolized by Strasser. He too was in a more tractable frame of mind. The two were brought together secretly in Cologne on January 4, 1933, at the home of the powerful banker Kurt von Schroeder. Hitler and Papen settled their old feud. In essence, the Harzburg front was reestablished and wealthy steel interests started to pour money into the Nazi coffers again. No details were settled at the meeting. Weeks of tangled negotiation were required, but the foundations were laid.

Schleicher concluded that his only hope of dealing with the Reichstag, which was about to reconvene, was to hold over the head of the Nazis the threat of dissolution. So he asked the president to sign a decree. Hindenburg, however, decided not to be helpful and sternly refused the request. Schleicher, seeing that he had lost, resigned on January 28, 1933.

The next hours were sleepless ones filled with urgent bargaining. Papen seems to have been at the center of the web. He managed on the one hand to persuade Hitler to become chancellor in a coalition cabinet, and on the other to persuade Hindenburg that with himself as vice-chancellor Hitler would be restrained from a one-party dictatorship. The decision was made on January 30. Shortly after noon a new government was announced. Hitler was chancellor and Papen vice-chancellor. Only two other Nazis, Goering and Frick, were included. Neurath remained foreign minister, and Alfred Hugenberg became minister of economics and agriculture. General Werner von Blomberg, supposedly sympathetic to the Nazis, was minister of defense. The political deal was effected which later was glorified by the word *Machtergreifung* ("seizure of power").

That evening a torchlight procession made its way along the Wilhelmstrasse past the aged Prussian field marshal and the more youthful Austrian corporal. A new era of history had opened, the era of the Third Reich. German democracy was now dead.

CHAPTER XXVII

The Nazi Revolution (1933-34)

The years of Hitler's control of Germany up to the outbreak of the war in 1939 can be divided into three sections. The first of these is the Nazi revolution proper, which occupied about eighteen months until August 1934. Although Hitler was appointed chancellor as the result of a shady political deal, he nevertheless was appointed legally and peacefully. The revolution took place after the Nazis achieved the highest positions in the German state. They effected a complete overthrow of the traditional relationships between the national government and the great fulcrums of social responsibility and power: the federal states, the political parties, the trade unions, the army, big business and industry, and the organized Christian churches. By August 1934 only the army, business, and the churches preserved any considerable measure of independence. As the years went on, even these, except for some heroic individuals, underwent synchronization (*Gleichschaltung*) into the total state.

One of the astonishing aspects of this overturn of society is the relative ease with which it was achieved and the lack of opposition which it encountered. Aside from the fact that the Nazis controlled most of the available force and were ruthless in their use of it, this success would seem to stem in great measure from the weaknesses and divisions in German society dating back for many years and brought into sharp relief during the turbulent period of the Weimar Republic. Furthermore, the weakening effects of the depression and the terrible figure of over six million unemployed in early 1933 had so cooled the Germans' lukewarm devotion to democracy that they were hardly likely to strike many blows for its preservation. The historian must also not discount the fact that the appeal of the Nazis in 1933 contained a very considerable measure of idealism. Such slogans as national regeneration and German awakening were attractive to the downtrodden, the defeated, and the resentful. Young people in particular were possessed by the idea that it was now possible for them to live in a Germany which was again strong, virile, dynamic, and clean. By the time they realized the extent of their deception, it was too late to do anything about it.

Rarely in history has a man been so underrated as Adolf Hitler. Papen and Hugenberg felt sure that their superior experience and culture plus their majority in the cabinet would make it possible to tame the demagogue while retaining the support of his enormous following. Much the same attitude was taken all along the political line. The Communists, in fact, were under orders from Moscow not to oppose the Nazis too much. Instead they were to let them have a few months of power to expose their incompetence and fatuity so that they would lose their followers to the far left and thus actually facilitate an assumption of power by the reds. The Communists continued even at this late date to treat the Social Democrats as their principal foes.

Hitler's first act as chancellor was to carry out his promise to Hindenburg to try to achieve a working majority in the Reichstag. This required support by the Catholic Center. The chancellor had a conference with the Center leader, Monsignor Kaas, which Kaas thought was just to be a preliminary discussion. Hitler, however, clearly insincere in his effort, declared after a few minutes that there was no basis for agreement. Therefore he obtained a decree from Hindenburg dissolving the Reichstag and set March 5, 1933, as the date for new elections.

This time the Nazis were not reluctant to hold an election campaign; now they could control much of the state apparatus. They made it clear that this was going to be the last election for years to come. Hitler raced to and fro throughout the land, ably seconded by Goebbels with his intensified propaganda machinery, now heavily subsidized by big business. Hitler did not announce any definite program or make election promises. He devoted his time to violent attacks on Marxism and to denouncing the Weimar system for its decadence and corruption.

Although Papen held the title of commissioner for Prussia, Goering had been appointed Prussian minister of the interior. This was perhaps the most strategic spot in the whole government, for it placed the large Prussian police force under Goering's control. The burly aviator was tireless in his dismissals of opponents in the Prussian government. He established an auxiliary police made up largely of S.A. and S.S. men. He delivered tirades against the Communists and the red terror. He made it clear that in the street brawls which abounded during the campaign the police were on the side of the Nazis. The brown terror had begun. Its first big overt act was a raid on February 24 on Communist headquarters in Berlin. Not very much of interest was found, but the newspapers the next morning reported that plans for a Communist revolution had been uncovered.

On the evening of February 27 Hitler, Goering, and Goebbels were all in Berlin, an extraordinary fact considering that the election was only a few days off. While they were at dinner, word was received by telephone that the Reichstag building was on fire. They raced to the scene to find flames high in the air over the great dome. Through the large french windows on the main floor could be seen a half-naked man with shaggy hair rushing about with burning rags in his hands. Hitler hardly paused to catch his breath, but shouted words to the effect that this was a beacon light which would show the world the depths of Communist infamy.

The mysterious stranger turned out to be a young, imbecilic, Dutch Communist pyromaniac named Marinus van der Lubbe. The fact that he was a Communist gave credence to the Nazi story. The next day Hitler issued a decree "for the protection of the People and the State," giving the government almost complete power to suspend the most basic personal and civil rights and to take authority in any of the states. It went far beyond the provisions of Article 48 of the constitution. However, the Communist party was not yet outlawed. It still had one more useful service to perform for Hitler. During the next days the campaign was intensified with all the emotional overtones of the fire adding fuel to the national conflagration.

The full story of the Reichstag fire will probably never be known, but certain facts seem to emerge pretty clearly. First, it is physically impossible for one moron with only an hour or two and some gasoline at his disposal to start a fire of such proportions in a massive stone and mahogany building. Second, there was a basement corridor from the house which Goering occupied as president of the Reichstag leading to the main building. There is hardly any doubt that a number of S.A. men went through this corridor armed with all sorts of inflammable materials and that they did a thorough job. Then they planted the innocuous van der Lubbe, who had been picked up drunk by some storm troopers a few days before in a Berlin bar.

Months later van der Lubbe and several leading Communists, including Ernst Torgler and Georgi Dimitrov, were publicly tried before the supreme court at Leipzig with Goering as witness. The Nazis had not yet suborned the German legal system. The Communists made a fool of Goering and all were acquitted except van der Lubbe, who was beheaded. However, that was not important; by then there were other things to worry about. The Reichstag fire more than served its purpose.

The last relatively free election in Germany until after World War II produced rather disappointing results for the Nazis. Although they increased their votes by five and one half million, they did not achieve the majority for which they longed; they polled seventeen out of thirty-nine million, just under 44 per cent of the total vote. However, if the Nationalist votes were added to the Nazis', the two together had a small majority; but the Nazis were not concerned about that. As soon as the eighty-one seats won by the Communists were disqualified, the Nazis alone would have their majority. This was to be the last service to Germany of the Communist party.

March 21, 1933, was set for the meeting of the Reichstag to be held at the Garrison Church at Potsdam, tomb of Frederick the Great and the central shrine of the old cult of Prussian militarism. It would be difficult to imagine a greater contrast from the inception of the republic at Weimar. To the flag-bedecked royal town hobbled in full regalia the remains of the senior officers of imperial Germany, led by bushy old General von Mackensen wearing his shako bearing the skull and crossbones of the death's-head hussars. Hindenburg in his field marshal's attire tottered from his car and was met by the new chancellor, dressed not in his corporal's uniform but in cutaway and striped trousers. Inside the church the relics of the past sat across from the masters of the present, the Nazi delegates in their brown uniforms and swastika decorations. The ceremony was brief. Hindenburg read a dedication of a new Germany, and Hitler emphasized the continuity between Hohenzollern and National Socialist. When the field marshal visited the crypt, guns fired in salute for miles around. The rest of the day was spent in parades, demonstrations, and concerts. The bridge was connected from 1918 to 1933 with the interval forgotten. The Nazis spoke of this occasion as the Day of National Regeneration.

On March 23 the Reichstag met again, this time for business, in the Kroll Opera House in Berlin. However, there was only one piece of business, the Enabling Act. This act provided that for four years the government would have the right to decree any law or treaty independently of the Reichstag. It was an invitation to the Reichstag to vote itself out of effective existence. Since it was a constitutional amendment, it needed a two-thirds vote. Therefore Hitler had wooed the Center, even giving Monsignor Kaas a written promise that he would always act legally. At the meeting Hitler called for the passage of the bill, even threatening that the National Socialists would go ahead regardless of the result of the vote. Otto Wels spoke for the Social Democrats and announced that his party would vote against the measure. It was a brave gesture, but it infuriated Hitler, who jumped back on to the rostrum and lashed out against the socialists. The other party leaders spoke, and the vote was taken amid tumult from the galleries and the streets. The only opposition came from ninety-four Social Democratic members.

Everyone else voted for the act. The Reichstag ceased to exist except as a ceremonial body which Hitler addressed from time to time on important policy developments.

The passage of the Enabling Act was the signal to go full speed ahead. It provided the legal basis for all subsequent acts. Hitler had outwitted his non-Nazi colleagues in the cabinet, for now he could act on his own authority without even the approval of Hindenburg. From this time on there was to be no halt.

In the spring of 1933 the Nazis initiated a thoroughgoing purge from German government and society of anti-Nazi groups. The purge was carried out through the whole nation but was particularly noticeable in Prussia, where Goering conducted it with ruthless brutality. By the national Civil Service law of April 7 Jewish officials of all levels could be retired. The phrase "concentration camp" was added to the world's language of despair, as Jews, Communists, Social Democrats, and other anti-Nazis were cast out of the government, the teaching profession, and other liberal professions, and sent to endure an existence of sadistic ferocity such as the world has rarely witnessed. As early as April 1 a boycott was ordered against all Jewish businesses and professions; the Jews were gradually deprived of all civil and political rights, and often forced to pay large indemnities to maintain their bare existence from day to day. The brown terror of arrests, beatings, imprisonment, and shootings was on full rampage and shocked civilization; it was efficient and thorough.

More important than the outrages committed against individuals was the Nazi determination to eradicate institutions. Individuals are ephemeral, but institutions endure. During 1933 the Nazis launched attacks against three major institutions—the federal states, the political parties, and the trade unions—all of which were potential focuses of opposition. By the end of the year all three were crushed.

The first big step to eliminate the autonomy of the federal states was taken six months before Hitler became chancellor when Papen seized control of Prussia in July 1932. He rendered the Nazis an important service in advance.

On March 31 Hitler ordered that all the parliaments of the states be dissolved and reconstituted without elections, giving the parties in each state (except the Communists) the same proportion that they had in the Reichstag. A few days later he appointed governors (*Reichsstatthälter*) for each state, in whom reposed all effective executive authority. The *Statthalter* was usually also the *Gauleiter* or local party chief; thus the unification of state and party was advanced. Hitler named himself *Statthalter* in Prussia, but appointed Goering minister-president to do the actual work. In Bavaria, where some opposition might have been expected, Hitler was wise enough to select the old free corpsman, General Ritter von Epp, who was popular there. By January 1934 the liquidation of the states was completed by the abolition of the Reichsrat or national upper house, which had been intended to represent the states. Although the Nazis paid much lip service to the unique qualities of the various Germanic areas and encouraged folk dancing and local costumes, Germany was ruled from Berlin.

The abolition of all political parties except the National Socialists occurred rapidly. The parties of the left were the first to disappear. The Communists were not allowed to seat their members in the Reichstag. In fact, most of them were in concentration camps within a few weeks. At the end of May the government simply confiscated the property of the party. The Social Democrats seem to have imagined that they could continue as a legal opposition. They did not yet know Hitler. On May 10 their property and funds were confiscated, and some weeks later the party was officially banned. It might have been expected that the center and right-wing parties, some of which actually had representatives in the cabinet, would have been able to endure. But in late June the Nationalist party simply dissolved itself, and Hugenberg retired from the government. In early July the Center and Bavarian People's party ended their careers voluntarily. By July 14 Hitler was able to decree that the Nazi party was the only legal party in Germany and to prescribe a penal sentence for anyone who tried to start another. It seems hard to believe that institutions with the traditions and prestige of the German parties would simply surrender without a fight. The fact is that they did.

Much the same was true of the trade unions. The socialist unions had been one of the most powerful units in German society; in 1918 and 1919 they almost controlled Germany. During the depression they lost members, but their position still seemed secure. Hitler cleverly decreed May Day, the traditional socialist holiday, as a national holiday and addressed a large rally of workers. The next day Nazi forces confiscated and occupied the union offices and sent many of the leaders to prison. The union assets were transferred to a new institution called the German Labor Front under the leadership of an ardent Nazi, Robert Ley. All German workers became members of the Labor Front. The old techniques of collective bargaining were abolished, and the state assumed direct control of labor-management relations.

Politically speaking, Hitler was in almost complete control of Germany by mid-1933. He had eliminated his opponents outside the party with a brutal speed and a lack of opposition, both of which were amazing. During the year from the summer of 1933 to that of 1934 he had to conduct a more difficult struggle, this time against elements within the party interested in pushing the revolution further and in directions of which Hitler disapproved. The struggle was directed against the "socialist" groups in the Nazi party who found their principal spokesmen in the S.A. leadership and in particular in its chief of staff, Hitler's longtime associate, Ernst Roehm. Their aim was an attack on two remaining important constellations of power: business and industry, and the army. They wanted to wipe out the strongholds of what they called the "reaction." Much of the detailed story of the yearlong crisis is obscure and probably will remain so, but sufficient facts have emerged for a fairly coherent account.

By the spring of 1933 the S.A. numbered between two and three million men. Some of them were the "old fighters" who had come into the movement at its start and remained loyal to it over the years. Many were later acquisitions—unemployed, unsuccessful, or ambitious—who saw in the brown shirt formation the path to riches. During the early months of the regime they were the heroes; they carried out the actual work of the terror, the raids, and the confiscations. By July their work was almost done. They looked around and saw that they were without personal possessions and authority, while many non-Nazis were in important places. In particular, they noticed that the old aristocracy of German industry had not been budged from its high estate and was in fact operating closely with the new government.

The latent socialist tendency within Nazism began to make itself articulate. Goebbels, who in March had become minister for propaganda and public enlightenment and who, though personally loyal to Hitler, had always been associated with the left wing of the party, filled his editorials and speeches with invective against capitalistic evils and with pleas for the downtrodden. Some of the early party leaders, men like Gottfried Feder, tried to secure the adoption of their lower-middle-class principles, which had made up the party credo in the early twenties. Even Gregor Strasser emerged somewhat from obscurity.

Hitler was opposed to this tendency in 1933 as he had been in 1926. He was no economist; he was little interested in economic theory. He was a manipulator of men and so far had had remarkable success with the lords of industry. He was wise enough to recognize the immense power of the German economy as then constituted. His plan was to harness and control the existing leadership rather than to venture on a new untried revolutionary experiment which might not be successful. In this thinking he was supported by Goering and Hjalmar Schacht.

Even more of a worry to Hitler than the economic attitude of the S.A. was its designs on the army. The S.A. was now twenty times as large as the army; it had carried the whole brunt of the Nazi revolution, from which the regular army had held deliberately aloof. Roehm, first and always a fighter and military man, would have loved a position of importance in the regular army. He would have enjoyed social recognition from the stiff-necked Prussian officer corps, which his social background, his wild and perverse life, and his rough personality had always denied him. He felt that the army and S.A. should be merged into the new large German military establishment, with the S.A. free corps attitude in control and a wild, free, all-German spirit succeeding the old narrow-minded bemonocled ethos.

Once again Hitler was in sharp opposition. He respected the army from his front-line days; more important, he remembered his defeat in 1923 when he had tried to pit the S.A. against the army. He also had a sound political understanding of the prestige attached to the army and in particular its importance to Hindenburg, who was not yet completely negligible. Time and again he asserted that the army was the legitimate bearer of arms and that the S.A. had as its function internal political matters only. He had to tread a narrow path.

The winter of 1933–34 was filled with maneuvering among the several groups. Hitler tried various techniques, including a kind of bribery. For example, he gave Roehm a seat in the cabinet at the same time that Hess received one. Even then Roehm would not be quiet. There seems little doubt that Hitler was constantly fed anti-Roehm sentiments by Goering and also by Heinrich Himmler, who chafed at the fact that the S.S. was technically subordinate to the S.A. and saw in the struggle an opportunity to increase the prestige of the S.S. and thus his own.

The situation was complicated by the evident fact that Hindenburg had very little time to live. The doctors made this clear to Hitler, for whom it was an extremely important matter. Hitler had determined to succeed the old man in the functions of the presidency, but knew that this would require the support of the army because of the need for a new oath of allegiance. The crucial day seems to have been April 11, 1934.

On that day Hitler went aboard a naval vessel to watch maneuvers. In the party were General Werner von Blomberg, minister of defense, General Werner von Fritsch, commander in chief of the army, and Admiral Erich Raeder, commander in chief of the navy. There is reason to believe that on that occasion Hitler made a deal with the military that they would support his succession to Hindenburg if Hitler would quiet the S.A. and not touch the army's sacrosanct position.

The events of the following weeks are obscure and confusing, especially the workings of Hitler's mind. It eventually became clear to him that Roehm was the key to the whole triple problem: the position of the army, the socialist "second" revolution, and the imminent death of Hindenburg. The days of June were filled with inventing a plausible story of a *coup d'état* supposedly plotted by Roehm, Strasser, Schleicher, and others to take control of the new Nazi state and lead it in their sinister direction. In the meantime the S.A. was ordered to go on leave during July without uniform, and Roehm himself left for a convalescent vacation at a hotel in the Bavarian Alps. Tension mounted high in the capital.

June 30, 1934, was the blood-soaked day. The events of the blood purge, or the night of the long knives as it is sometimes called, are familiar. On June 29 Hitler and Goebbels flew from the Rhineland to Munich. During the night they arrested a number of S.A. leaders. In the early morning they drove to Roehm's hotel, where they found him still in bed. Some of his companions were shot on the spot. Roehm and others were returned to Munich, where they were shot as the day went on.

In Berlin Goering and Himmler were in charge. There, too, numbers of S.A. leaders were rounded up in barracks, where S.S. firing squads shot them at intervals during the day and night. No accurate figures are available, but the number killed was certainly upwards of one hundred, many of them well-known people. The carnage was not limited to the S.A. Among the list of the dead were Gregor Strasser, General von Schleicher and his wife, Papen's secretaries, and several of the Catholic Action leaders. By some mysterious fate Papen himself, who had given an anti-Nazi speech some days before, was spared. A figure from the past was General von Kahr, who in 1923 had put down the beer hall *Putsch;* his aged and battered corpse was found in a swamp outside Munich. The ferocity of the attack is shown by the fact that a newspaper man named Willi Schmidt was killed by mistake by S.S. men looking for another Willi Schmidt, who was listed as a victim. Panic and uncertainty reigned throughout Germany.

Two weeks later on July 13, 1934, Hitler called together the Reichstag to hear his version of the purge. He gave a long speech in which he alleged that Roehm had been planning a coup to depose him and thus had forced him into violence. He attacked the behavior of the S.A. leaders, stressing Roehm's homosexuality, of which he must have known for years. Hitler promised that the revolution was now over.

If it is true that Hitler was hurried into the purge by the approaching death of Hindenburg, he was just in time. On August 2, 1934, the old soldier died at his estate at Neudeck. The army lived up to its promise. Hindenburg was dead only a matter of minutes when it was announced in Berlin that the offices of president and chancellor would be merged. Shortly afterwards the armed forces took a new oath. This oath was personally to Adolf Hitler, the leader (*Führer*) of the German land and people. Hindenburg was buried with great state in a crypt at the foot of the monument to his victory at Tannenberg.

On August 19, 1934, the German people were invited to register in a plebiscite their approval of the new situation. About 88% of the population indicated approval. The Nazi revolution was over. The *Führer* was in complete control.

CHAPTER XXVIII

The Nazi State to 1938. I, Political and Military

The years from mid-1934 to early 1938 are the years of the consolidation of the Nazi dictatorship. Narrative history almost ceases except in foreign affairs, and the historian must analyze the pattern as it develops in the various spheres of human activity. Gradually and sometimes unobtrusively the net tightened around the German people until by 1938 the total state had for all practical purposes been achieved.

An important key to understanding the political relationships is the position held by Adolf Hitler. He occupied three separate functions, that of chancellor, party leader, and president. After he inherited the presidential office, he never used the title; it smacked too much of republicanism. At first he was referred to as leader and national chancellor; after the war started, simply as leader (*Führer*). In fact, he was of greater significance than the combination of his three functions would suggest. He assumed a sort of magico-religious position. He embodied the collectivity of the racial Germanic urge for existence and power. He was the court of last resort. He was the law. Otherwise intelligent people, including foreigners, were held in thrall by his eyes, his personality. They would answer questions on some outrageous Nazi aberration with paragraphs beginning with the words, "Adolf Hitler has said. . . ." That was the end of it. Humble Germans identified themselves with their leader, who incarnated what Plato might have called the archetype, or Rousseau, the general will.

Hitler's extraordinary position in the eyes of the faithful was partly rationalized by the "principle of leadership" (*Führerprinzip*). This principle established a hierarchy of command such that each person gave unconditional obedience to those above him and was entitled to the same from those below. No more elections were held in Germany. All officials in every area of government and party life were appointed. At the apex of the pyramid was Hitler.

In fact Hitler was at the apex of several pyramids. The party and the state were not one, though they impinged and overlapped heavily upon each other. It is difficult for an Englishman or an American to grasp the concept of the totalitarian party because it is in no sense equivalent to the British or American political parties. In fact a sharper meaning is rendered by the word movement. Admission to the party was an invitation to exercise the vocation of leadership. The party members constituted a leaven in the dough of the society, an elite, a pattern for the led. At least until the war the party was kept relatively small so that the members could be highly qualified in Nazi terms. The party can be thought of as the dynamic or male force; the state, as the static or female constraint.

Immediately below Hitler on the party ladder came the *Reichsleitung* ("national leadership"). By the end of the war there were about forty *Reichsleiter*. Some of them held important state positions; others held none. A few did not even have a specific party position. Some of them were well known throughout the world: Goering, Himmler, Goebbels, etc.; others were little known even in Germany but commanded important spheres of influence, such as the party courts, its finances, or its studies of foreign affairs. In fact some of the *Reichsleiter* headed divisions which paralleled the work of state ministries. Neither the party nor the state was symmetrical or rationally organized; both were the result of a series of *ad hoc* creations, of which some were tailored simply for one man.

The next level below the national leadership was the provincial (*Gau*) leadership made up before the war of just over thirty *Gauleiter*. These men were often but not always identical with the *Statthälter*, who were of course in the state hierarchy. Some of them were well known, e.g., Goebbels, who was *Gauleiter* of Berlin; others were known only locally. It was their duty to receive orders from party headquarters in Munich or from the *Führer* in Berlin and see to it that they were enforced in their respective *Gaue*. Beneath them were whole armies of district, municipal, local, and block leaders, who brought the gospel and commandments of Nazism to every individual in the nation.

The state hierarchy was of course not entirely the creation of the Nazis. Much of it carried over from the republic and indeed from the empire, and many of the bureaucrats had been civil servants for a long time. In fact, it is extraordinary how much continuity existed. If a man were not a Jew, a socialist, or an overt opponent of National Socialism, he had a good chance of keeping his job. An outstanding example of this is the influential Erich Meissner, head of the presidential chancellery and thus immediately under Hitler, who had held the same position under both Ebert and Hindenburg.

At the top of the state ladder were the ministers. Naturally, many of them were Nazis, but the remarkable thing is that a considerable number (e.g., Papen, Neurath, Schwerin-Krosigk) were not. Hitler tended to think of them as technical experts in their departments and not as political advisers. Full cabinet meetings became rarer and rarer, until during the war they were hardly ever held. Hitler liked to make his decisions alone or with a small group of his intimates. He would usually hear advice or conflicting opinions, then retire by himself and announce the decision later; and that decision was binding.

There emerged from this system what is often called the dual state, a duality of state and party paralleling each other from the *Führer* at the summit down to the meanest functionary of either. However, no one should assume that it was a neat or even premeditated parallelism. The overlapping of nominal authority was hardly credible and became even more confusing during the war when economic controls constantly had to be tightened and when an empire all over Europe had to be governed. By 1945 it was almost impossible to locate authority, certainly not on a neat chart of organization. The answer was that authority lay with Hitler and with the men in whom he chose to repose it at any given moment. In spite of all the proliferation of organizations and officialdom, and all the lip service paid to the leadership principle and the united action of the people, Nazi Germany was one of the most intensely personal governments that the world has ever seen.

During this middle period of Hitler's rule the army was one institution in Nazi Germany which seemed to be sacrosanct. Hitler lived up to his statement after the purge of 1934 that the regular army would continue to control Germany's military force. He needed the army officers during these years more than they needed him. They were essential to create the great armed force which Hitler planned. Step by step, and rather more rapidly than some of the more conservative generals wanted, they were given ever-increasing latitude until by 1938 the German military establishment was well on its way to becoming the formidable instrument of the war years.

From the earliest days of his political career Hitler had inveighed against the Treaty of Versailles. Now that he was in control, it was to be expected that he would try to implement his invective. Reparations were already a thing of the past; there was no possibility at the moment of risking war to restore the old frontiers; the military clauses seemed to be the one area in which repudiation was feasible.

The long-planned World Disarmament Conference had been sitting in Geneva since early 1932 without much achievement to its credit. The German delegation took the position that according to the treaty German disarmament was to be only a prelude to world disarmament. They insisted that since the rest of the nations had done nothing important about disarming, Germany was entitled to build up her forces to a level of equality with her peers. The other nations recognized that this argument had some force, and in December the conference admitted "in principle" Germany's right to equality.

This was not enough for Hitler; he was in a hurry. During the 1933 session the Germans insisted that the S.A. must not be counted as effectives in granting increased numbers to Germany; they also demanded that they should start right away to build up to equality. In June the conference adjourned for several months. In October Hitler took his first major step in foreign policy. On the fourteenth he withdrew his delegation from the conference and announced Germany's resignation from the League of Nations. It would be hard to think of a sharper reversal of the Stresemann policy. The following month, in the first of Hitler's plebiscites, the German people were asked whether they approved of these two steps; 93 per cent voted yes.

The year 1934 was devoted mainly to the quarrel between the army and the S.A. which culminated on June 30, but there can be no doubt that plans were being rushed for the expansion of the army and navy and the creation of an air force. The culmination of Hitler's attack on the military clauses of Versailles came on March 16, 1935, when he simply abrogated them unilaterally. On that date he returned to the old prewar policy of the conscription of all young men, who now had to spend a year in the armed forces. To show the change in spirit he even altered the name of the army from the Weimar word *Reichswehr* to the new *Wehrmacht*.

World opinion, not yet accustomed to Hitler's tactics, was appalled at this unquestionably illegal action. There is no doubt that Britain and France could have forced Hitler to withdraw from his new position if they had chosen. However, they did nothing except to protest and to start to negotiate with Germany on nonaggression pacts, limitations of armaments, etc. Nothing came of these discussions except a naval treaty with Great Britain.

The following months were hectic for the army high command. It is not an easy matter to transform an army from one hundred thousand to six hundred thousand men almost overnight. The logistic problem alone is a tremendous one, to say nothing of the problem of training so many raw recruits simultaneously. Although the *Reichswehr* had been developed by Seeckt as a nucleus for eventual enlargement, it was a number of months before the army was actually admitting all the new personnel to which it was entitled. The munitions industry had started to increase its productivity even before 1935, but there were many problems here too in the acquisition of raw materials, retooling, and rapid expansion. However, the work went on without cease.

Almost exactly a year after the return of conscription Hitler took his next big military step. He took advantage of the fact that Europe was in the midst of a crisis in international affairs, the Italian invasion of Ethiopia. On March 7, 1936, he repudiated another part of the Treaty of Versailles and the entire Locarno system by announcing the remilitarization of the Rhineland area to the Belgian and French frontiers. The Allies had ended their occupation of this territory in 1930. This was a very daring step; it touched France at her most sensitive spot. The Germans were aware of their daring, but received no French opposition. Once again Hitler had gambled and won.

Activity in the air paralleled activity on land. From the moment the Nazis took control, interest in aviation advanced by leaps and bounds. Boys were encouraged to study aeronautics, flying clubs were founded, glider races were frequent, and commercial aviation was expanded. Hermann Goering, the old war ace, was able to find time from his conquest of Prussia to look about for a future staff for the air arm and to cheer on air-minded youngsters. It was an open secret that Germany was going to establish a military air force. Britain and France seemed to accept the idea in advance. The official creation of the air force (*Luftwaffe*) occurred a few days before the announcement of conscription in 1935. Goering became commander in chief in addition to his other responsibilities. Within a year the air force was on a war footing and ready to make its first live experiments in Spain.

The navy was to an extent a stepchild in Nazi Germany; Hitler does not seem to have understood the principles and importance of naval warfare. However, it shared in the expansion. In fact, after the announcement of the abolition of the armament restrictions, incredible though it may seem, Great Britain made a naval treaty with Germany whereby Germany was entitled to a surface navy one-third as large as the British and to a submarine fleet equal to the British. Plans were immediately put into operation for two big battle cruisers (the eventual "Scharnhorst" and "Gneisenau") and two super battleships (the eventual "Bismarck" and "Tirpitz"), as well as a respectable number of smaller surface vessels and submarines.

The regular armed forces were not the only reservoir of trained manpower. The S.A., tamed and shorn of its imperialistic ambitions, remained a force of about two million men under its new leader, Viktor Lutze. The S.S., now independent of the S.A., already had several armed battalions which were to grow into the redoubtable armed S.S. (*Waffen S.S.*) of the war. By 1936 Himmler, in addition to being leader of the S.S., became chief of the German police, another formidable armed group. In addition, there were the Labor Service (*Arbeitsdienst*) and other paramilitary organizations which, at need, could swell the *Wehrmacht*.

Hitler's birthday, April 20, 1936, was a happy day for the high-ranking officers. On that day the *Führer* promoted the minister of defense, General Blomberg, to the rank of field marshal, the first time that rank had been granted since the war. The three commanders in chief also received promotions, Fritsch and Goering to colonel general and Raeder to general admiral.

Germany was fast becoming an armed camp.

CHAPTER XXIX

The Nazi State to 1938. II, Economic and Social

There can be no question that the promise which won Hitler the most votes in the black depression days was to end unemployment. The figure of six million unemployed was ferocious. This was a challenge which had to be met immediately, and the Nazi government lost no time. The astonishing fact is that in a very short period the promise was redeemed and Germany approached full employment. However, this statement must be hedged about with qualifications in view of the methods used to achieve the goal. Certain classes of society (e.g., Jews, Communists, etc.) were declared incapable of filling certain sorts of jobs, and in many cases positions were created for jailers to control them in concentration camps. Every effort was made to remove women from employment; there was no element of feminism in Nazism, which instead preached a traditional social order dominated by males. In any time of unemployment one of the groups to suffer most is that composed of young men who have just completed their education and cannot find jobs. The Nazis took care of these people by creating the Labor Service (*Arbeitsdienst*). All young men were required to spend six months in camps in the countryside working on such projects as reclamation of land, prevention of erosion, etc., which were allegedly noncompetitive with private industry. After 1935 they then spent their period of conscription in the armed forces, an effective method of keeping them out of the labor market. Finally, the new impetus given to normal industrial production by rearmament, road building, and public works further lessened the number of unemployed.

In fact, during the mid-thirties Germany enjoyed a boom period. The industrial plant that had been built during the Weimar years was now producing for Hitler and the Nazis. Credit was extended freely and the production figures mounted steadily. Germans had lost their freedom;

they had exchanged it for a sort of economic security that had been lost during the depression.

The government and numberless speakers announced as their economic goal the achievement of autarky or self-sufficiency. They deplored the earlier dependence of Germany on other nations and promised that she would stand on her own feet. It was made clear that this aim would require much sacrifice and deprivation from the population, but this was glorified as a heroic effort by such slogans as "guns before butter" or *"Gemeinnutz über Eigennutz"* ("the general good before the individual good"). In fact, the goal of autarky for Germany was impossible because she was not overly endowed with natural resources except for coal. Since the heavy emphasis on production was on capital goods rather than consumer goods, it was obvious that Germany was going to have to import huge amounts of raw materials. Furthermore, because the government was always conscious of the likelihood of war, there would have to be large-scale stockpiling of strategic materials. These needs raised difficult problems of financing and payment.

One of the most astounding aspects of the whole Nazi story is the way in which the Germans managed to finance their operations. Shortly after he assumed power Hitler reappointed Hjalmar Schacht to his old position as president of the Reichsbank, and some months later, after Hugenberg's resignation, Schacht also became minister of economics. He had several basic problems to surmount. In the first place, Germany's gold reserves were dwindling rapidly and frighteningly, until it was hardly possible to speak of her being on the gold standard. On the other hand, the government insisted on importing great quantities of raw materials, a program that was bound to give Germany an unfavorable balance of trade, no matter how much effort was devoted to building up exports. Schacht maintained his reputation for wizardry by devising a number of novel expedients.

He established a strict control of all German currency and international trade. No one could take out of Germany more than ten marks without special permission. No one could import anything without approval. Every possible effort was made to increase German holdings of foreign exchange: exports were increased as much as possible, tourists were encouraged to visit Germany by granting them extremely favorable rates for money bought outside, and foreign firms were required not to remove their assets from Germany but to spend them there.

The German government made barter agreements with other countries to which they sent German finished goods in return for raw materials. In particular, eastern Europe, the Near East, and Latin America were chosen for these treaties. The foreign countries soon found them-

selves in a state of bondage to Germany or glutted with unsaleable mer-
chandise, e.g., thousands of Leica cameras. The treaties had obvious
political implications and paved the way for Hitler's conquest of the
Balkans, which until then had been dominated by French influence. A
combination of unorthodox devices and economic daring made possible
German recuperation and rearmament under the Nazis.

By 1936 Hitler came to the conclusion that the period of recovery
was over and that new goals had to be instituted. He further seems to
have felt that it was time for the government and party to tighten their
control over industry. Up to that time business and industry had not
been much disturbed by the new government, except of course for Jewish businessmen, many of whose firms had been "Aryanized." Now it
was time to take off the gloves, at least partially. Accordingly in October
Hitler decreed the Four Year Plan for the German economy and appointed Hermann Goering head of the Four Year Plan organization as
a sort of economic dictator. Schacht took this appointment as an affront
to him and his ministry.

The year 1937 was the decisive year in which Nazi Germany moved
from the defensive to the offensive in the international sphere. The economic reflection of this change of course is seen in the replacement of
Schacht by Walther Funk in the ministry of economics. Although Schacht
was willing to attempt daring expedients and to tread the doubtful
side of the line of orthodoxy, he was basically an old-fashioned economist, conservative as compared to some of the Nazis who were prepared to flout all the laws of classical economics. He was also apparently willing to tell the *Führer* that some of his wildly ambitious plans
were impossible to achieve. As a result, in November 1937 the more
pliant party man, Funk, replaced Schacht, although Schacht remained
president of the Reichsbank until 1939. At about the same time the
word autarky was heard less frequently and replaced by *Wehrwirtschaft*
("defense economy"). The decision for aggression was made.

It is very difficult to decide what the Nazi economic philosophy really
was. Probably there was none, certainly not a fully developed, coherent
philosophy. In this realm, as in so many others, Hitler was an opportunist, an improvisor. The old "unchangeable" twenty-five-point program of the early days is no guide for the analysis. It had called for
extensive nationalization and freedom from the "slavery of interest."
After 1933 very little nationalization occurred except in the case of
Jewish-owned enterprises, in which the usual procedure was to sell the
businesses or to surrender them to some dependable non-Jew as trustee.
The general tendency was in the direction of monopoly.

Some have insisted that Nazi economics was a sort of state socialism.

This is undoubtedly true in some aspects, but it is far from being the whole story. Most of German industry remained legally private. Men like Krupp, Thyssen, and Röchling remained at the head of their respective enterprises, unless, like Thyssen, they committed political offenses. In fact, they were heaped with honors and new holdings. However, at the next level it is instructive to note the infiltration of boards of directors by deserving Nazis: government officials, *Gauleiter,* etc. The network of interlocking directorates was impressive. On the other hand, the government by no means always refused to establish direct ownership and control of industry. This was particularly the case if the industry in question were one which might not be immediately profitable, but would be useful for the wartime economy (e.g., the utilization of low-grade ores or the synthetic fuel industry). The principal example of direct government participation in industry was the huge Hermann Goering combine, which by the end of its career managed operations ranging from steel mills to the control of canal-boat shipping. Yet even in this case ownership was really vested in the party rather than in the state.

As the war drew near, and especially during the war years, it becomes more difficult to apply the phrase private enterprise to the German economy. It is of course normal in any country in the conditions of modern warfare for the government to dominate industry. In Germany the situation was more far-reaching than elsewhere. The proliferation of control offices, chambers of commerce, and officialdom of one sort or another resulted in a bureaucracy which was very difficult to penetrate. The businessman was plagued by a series of import quotas, raw material allocations, price controls, limits on output, labor regulations, and the like, which must have made him feel bound and fettered in every direction. He was for all practical purposes a servant of the state. Perhaps the best phrase to describe the economy as fully developed under the Nazis is "command economy," a term used by Franz Neumann in his remarkable book *Behemoth* (New York: Oxford University Press, 1944).

As management gradually lost control of its operations, so even more rapidly did labor. The German Labor Front, which replaced the old unions in 1933, became a patent fraud as far as the protection of labor was concerned. It was a party "formation" rather than a governmental agency and became an instrument for the control of individuals and for Nazi indoctrination. Before long it included all German salaried workers except for the civil service. Its true character became clear in 1936 when all the basic functions of a union (wages, hours, etc.) were transferred to other agencies, mainly the ministry of economics. Much was made of groups concerned with the uplift of labor, such as *Schönheit der Arbeit* ("beauty of labor") which persuaded employers to such good deeds as decorating factories with gardens and window boxes or installing modern bathing facilities. Even more lauded was the *Kraft durch Freude* ("strength through joy") organization, a part of the Labor Front, which provided leisure-time entertainment and vacations for the chosen few, including trips on special cruise ships to countries friendly to Germany.

One of the most telling methods of controlling labor was the workbook. Every worker had to have one. It contained the basic facts of his life, the jobs he had held, why he no longer held them, and a statement of any acts of insubordination or political deviation. A German worker could get a job, but he had to be careful to keep it or to get another.

Other classes of society were watched and guided at every step just as much as labor. A list of all the National Socialist associations for various groups of the population would fill many pages. There were Nazi associations for civil servants, teachers, students, women, farmers, lawyers, doctors, etc. Each devoted itself to the same task: control and indoctrination at the intellectual level deemed suitable by the propaganda ministry.

In addition to the various professional leagues, there were the general associations for the whole population which kept a careful eye on all Germans. Needless to say, tremendous emphasis was placed on the indoctrination of youth, the reservoir of the future party. Most of this was under the supervision of the *Reichsjugendführer* ("national youth leader"), Baldur von Schirach, later *Gauleiter* of Vienna. From the moment of dawning consciousness a child was subject to indoctrination. His fairy tales and schoolbooks were all slanted to develop a love for *Führer* and Germany. When he was ten, he was eligible to join the uniformed Hitler *Jungvolk* ("young people"), or, if a girl, the *Bund deutscher Mädel* ("league of little German girls"). Four years later he almost had to join the Hitler *Jugend* ("youth"), which had constant meetings, went on camping trips, and took part in Nazi festivals, often at times when the members would otherwise be at church. Next came his months in the labor service followed by the armed forces. Then he might join the party, and perhaps the S.A. If he were a fine Nazi physical specimen, he might be admitted to the ranks of the S.S. If he were among the most perfect, he might be selected to attend for four years the course at the *Ordensburgen* ("castles of the order"—the reference is to the medieval Teutonic Knights), where in romantic spots, famous for their connection with some heroic moment in German history, he would be trained to be one of the leaders of the future. If he were not eligible for any of these honors, he would enter vocational work, still under the watchful eye of the party.

A similar gamut of organizations was available to girls, although the antifeminism of the Nazis prevented the development of these organizations as completely as their male counterparts. Women were under the direction of Frau Gertrud Scholtz-Klink, the *Frauenführer* ("leader of women").

Obviously one of the most important influences on youth is the educational system. The Nazis lost no time in synchronizing it. This action had important implications because it brought the party squarely into conflict with the churches, which had always been an important influence on education. However, it was too basic a matter for the Nazis to neglect. They had to achieve an education in Germany which would be technically competent but also nationalistically German and ideologically Nazi. Therefore a purge of teachers and curricula was high on the party agenda. Jews, Communists, and socialists were dismissed out of hand and replaced by "clean" German racial types. The textbooks and curricula were revised to present the Nazi outlook in its completeness. The crucifix on the wall of a Catholic classroom was replaced by a photograph of the *Führer*.

Even the austere and aloof German universities felt the impact of National Socialism. They had always been corporate bodies, supported by the state but sacrosanct in their autonomous self-government. The faculties actually ran their institutions and elected their own *Rektoren* ("presidents"). This happy arrangement had to end; the *Führerprinzip* was to prevail. Despite some resistance from the professors, the ministry of education appointed new officials. Jews and opponents of the regime were either dismissed or resigned voluntarily and in many cases left Germany to the immense advantage of their adopted homes. Their roll call is a roll of honor of German learning.

Probably the most appalling single act in the muzzling of learning in Nazi Germany was the famous burning of books in the courtyard of the once-great University of Berlin in late 1933. While students danced around the pyre waving swastika flags and singing Nazi songs, hundreds of banned books from the university library were consumed by flames. The list of books is a partial roster of German greatness. Not only works by Jews and Marxists were burned but, to give only one example, the works of the distinguished non-Jew and non-Marxist, Thomas Mann. It is hard to imagine a longer step in the return to barbarity. The Nazis were thorough in pursuit of their aim.

All these formations, organizations, and leagues were inspired by a sound psychological principle perverted to evil ends. The principle was the establishment of a community of thought, word, and deed. The common flags, songs, uniforms, meetings, and indoctrination gave to the individual a sense of identity, mutuality, and belongingness that he had missed in the impersonal and businesslike atmosphere of the Weimar Republic. Human warmth was cultivated to produce inhuman brutality. This is unquestionably an important factor in accounting for the success of the Nazis in winning popular support. Hitler was able to respond to the old longing of the free corpsmen for a community of destiny, but the quality of that destiny became fully clear only in the courthouse in Nuremberg in 1946.

CHAPTER XXX

The Nazi State to 1938. III, Religious and Cultural

It seems no exaggeration to insist that the greatest challenge the Nazis had to face was their effort to eradicate Christianity in Germany or at least to subjugate it to their general world outlook. Here they were not dealing with economic freedom for which acceptable substitutes could be offered, nor even with political liberties for which a degree of security could be bartered. They were attacking the deeply spiritual, traditional values, ingrained for over a thousand years, of a people which had shown itself profoundly religious and willing to fight for its faith. The French and Russian revolutionists could claim with some justification that the churches which they fought were corruptly allied with an evil old regime. This was not the case in Germany, where the churches had not been intimately affiliated with the Weimar system. Hitler was wise enough to realize that in this area he could not use the overt direct attacks which had been so successful against the Jews, the Communists, the unions, and even the political parties.

Yet there was no way to avoid the conflict. Christianity is itself a total way of life, based on supernatural authority and dedicated to a charitable brotherhood of man which transcends all political and racial frontiers. Nazism also was a total ideology, based on faith in the *Führer* and geared to a brotherhood of only Germans and "Aryans," with contempt and violence for all others. There could be no question of coexistence without such dilution that one or the other would lose its whole purpose and function.

During the years before 1933 Hitler did not say much on the subject of religion. It was known that he had been born a Catholic, but there was no record of his ever having taken part in religious observances. One of the twenty-five points of the party program called for "positive Christianity," but it was anyone's guess what that meant. Hitler had associated over the years with a variety of people dedicated to the establishment in one form or another of neopaganism. Alfred Rosenberg, General Ludendorff, Count Ernst von Reventlow, and Wilhelm Hauer all wanted to revive the worship of the ancient gods and were prepared to offer sacrifice at dawn on mountain tops on strategic dates of the year. They and others wrote a great deal of fuzzy mystification in which it was not clear whether God was embodied in the memory of Wotan or in the actual Hitler. There were some who thought that when the Nazis achieved power they would try to push a program of this sort.

To Hitler, however, the neopagans were extremists, just as Roehm and his companions were extremists of another sort. He understood that the fight against religion would have to be fought obliquely and gradually. He also realized that different tactics had to be used with the Protestants and the Catholics. The Catholic church was part of a vast international society owing spiritual allegiance to an authority outside of Germany. It possessed a coherent body of changeless doctrine to which it was firmly wedded. Protestantism, however, had been traditionally affiliated with the state since the days of Luther; also, it was divided among many organized groups, both doctrinally, as between Lutheran and Calvinist, and territorially, according to the old separate state entities. Clearly the two big groups would demand different treatment.

In 1932 a group called the German Christians was founded under the leadership of a former Free Corpsman, Pastor Joachim Hossenfelder. This group aimed at a sort of Nazified Protestantism, an accommodation of Christianity and racism. It wanted to establish the *Führerprinzip* in the church by uniting the twenty-nine Protestant groups into a single national church headed by a national bishop (*Reichsbischof*). It professed belief in Christ, but belief in the German manner, and insisted that God had granted a specific mission to the pure German race. Accordingly, it professed its abhorrence of Judaism, Freemasonry, pacifism, and other anti-Nazi doctrines.

When Hitler became chancellor, he soon decided to take in hand the "problem" of the Protestant church. He planned to use the German Christian movement as his agent, and as commander of the attack he picked Pastor Ludwig Müller. Müller was a former army chaplain who had been the leader of the German Christians in East Prussia. One wondered whether he was more soldier or clergyman. It is reported that he managed to integrate the Nazi anthem, the Horst Wessel song, into the Lutheran liturgy. Hitler appointed him first bishop of Prussia and then *Reichsbischof,* with Hossenfelder as his assistant. When the various territorial churches were asked to confirm their union into one national church under Müller, they replied by electing not Müller but Pastor Bodelschwingh, a devout minister famous for his charitable social work. This gave some warning to the government of what it might expect from the Protestant clergy. By the end of the year, however, the new constitution of the church was imposed, and after an offensive drive of Nazi propaganda Bodelschwingh disappeared from the scene and Müller was in control.

From 1933 until 1935 Müller instituted a reign of terror to force German Protestantism into the Nazi mold of blood, race, soil, and *Führer*. Clergymen were arrested and churches closed; gradually most of the territorial churches, with the exception of those in Bavaria and Würtemberg, toed the line. Yet as they did so, the opposition became strong and vocal. On the doctrinal level it was led by the theologian Karl Barth of the University of Bonn. On the organizational level it was led by the Confessional church (*Bekenntniskirche*), a group made up of anti-Nazi clergymen and lay people, eventually numbering thousands and including most of the bishops and well-known ministers. It was clear that Müller had failed to make the German Christians the leading force in Protestantism.

In September 1935 Hitler appointed Hans Kerrl as minister for church affairs. Kerrl got rid of Müller and tried to administer the church as a part of the state. He used all the weapons at his disposal. Seminaries were closed, clergymen were forbidden the right to preach, and religious newspapers and schools were shut down. Yet the resistance continued.

By 1937 the resistance of the Protestants crystallized in the person of Pastor Martin Niemöller, whose church was in Dahlem, a wealthy district of Berlin. Niemöller had had a curious career. During World War I he was a naval officer in command of a submarine. After the war he fought the Communists in the Ruhr as a Free Corpsman and then tried farming. In a short time he decided that the ministry was his true vocation and took orders. Politically he was conservative, even monarchist. At first he rather favored the Nazis, who, he thought, would restore Germany to a state of law and order and put down the wicked Communists. Slowly he realized that Hitler was enforcing not the law of God but the law of Hitler. His strong, narrow sense of duty forced him to speak out. His sermons became famous, and the congregations overflowed the church, while government agents took verbatim notes. Niemöller was a serious problem for the government. The last thing Hitler wanted to do was to create a popular anti-Nazi hero, a situation which he had on the whole successfully avoided. However, Niemöller was too outspoken. During 1937 he was arrested several times, released, subjected to an inconclusive trial, and finally simply thrown into a concentration camp where he remained until his release by the American army in 1945.

After 1939 the persecution of the Protestants, as of the Catholics, relaxed a great deal. The churches became essential to bolster morale during the war. However, there seems no question that, had Germany been victorious, the attack would have started again on an even larger scale. The important thing is that the Confessional church still existed with large numbers of supporters, that Niemöller was still popular, and that Protestantism was not broken. The *Führer*'s only major domestic failure was his war against religion, both Protestant and Catholic.

Hitler faced a different sort of problem in his effort to subdue the German Catholics. They are part of a far-flung international organization which the *Führer* respected. The Nazis were already tempting world opinion by their persecution of the Jews and had no desire to solidify Catholic opinion against them. However, there could be no accommodation between Christian brotherhood and Nazi racism. The church had already made this clear when it put Rosenberg's *Myth of the Twentieth Century* on the *Index of Prohibited Books*.

At first Hitler tried the path of conciliation, and the church advanced a distance to meet him. With the disappearance of the Center party as a political force, the Catholics in Germany were left without any defenders and Pope Pius XI was concerned about his responsibility for the souls of his German flock. Thus the church was receptive to Hitler's overtures, and in the summer of 1933 Papen, a Catholic and not a party member, went to the Vatican; there on July 20 he and Cardinal Pacelli, the later Pius XII and at that time secretary of state, signed a concordat between Germany and the Holy See.

The concordat covered the whole extent of the legal relationship between church and state. It protected the church in her rights to her property, the appointment of ecclesiastical officials, Christian education for the young, Christian marriage, etc. On paper it looked as if the Catholics in Germany were going to be secure. The concordat was greeted with glee in Berlin as a sign that the Roman Catholic church, the most conservative and traditional institution in the world, had recognized and blessed the new Nazi state.

It became clear very rapidly that the Nazis had no intention of living up to either the spirit or the letter of the concordat. As might be expected, the first clashes came in the field of education and the youth organizations. Catholic teachers were dismissed; all teachers had to join the National Socialist League of Teachers; crucifixes were removed from classrooms; every kind of pressure was used to force children into the Nazi youth organizations rather than the Catholic ones. Baldur von

Schirach became more and more overt in his attacks on Christianity in his addresses to the youth. Increasing efforts were made to muzzle and eliminate the Catholic press. As early as Christmas 1933 Michael Cardinal Faulhaber, archbishop of Munich, the most articulate anti-Nazi in the Catholic hierarchy, made clear in a sermon the sharp cleavage between Christian teaching and Nazi ideology.

It would take many pages to catalog the studied insults and attacks which the Nazis launched against the Catholic church. Some of them were petty and some grievous. Churches were not closed; millions attended them, but the faithful were made to feel that they were not good Germans and that their spiritual leaders were both treasonable and despicable. All sorts of indirect methods were used, no less dangerous for being indirect. Two in particular should be singled out.

The first was an attack on the clergy as traitors because they broke the regulations against exporting currency from Germany. German Catholics had of course for many years helped to support missionary and other religious endeavors outside Germany. The German church authorities were conscious of the problem involved and ordered that such support cease and that no money be sent abroad. In spite of this, some clergymen, nuns, and lay people, out of misguided zeal, did smuggle funds out of the country. This resulted in trials and imprisonment, and more important, a barrage of publicity implying that all Catholics were breaking the law, that the church was treasonable, and that the main characteristic of priests was an unholy lust for gold.

Even more sinister were the morals trials. Some clergymen and employees of Catholic schools were accused and convicted of illicit and perverse sexual activities. Needless to say, the stories were exaggerated out of all perspective and context. The German people were given to believe that the Catholic clergy was made up only of sexual criminals. Accounts and cartoons of unbelievable obscenity were published wholesale. Among the most active journals in this disgusting campaign were the *Schwarze Korps,* an organ of the S.S., and the pornographic *Stürmer,* edited by the notorious Jew-baiter, Julius Streicher, *Gauleiter* of Franconia.

The Catholic leaders were quick to try to refute these calumnies, but their work was difficult because the media of communications were closed to them. Cardinal Faulhaber, Clemens von Galen, bishop of Münster, and Konrad von Preysing, bishop of Berlin (the latter two eventually named cardinals by Pius XII), were the best known and most courageous leaders of the hierarchy. They were helped by many anonymous parish priests, a great number of whom were sent to suffer in concentration camps.

The anti-Catholic campaign reached its heights in 1935 and 1936. By 1937 Pius XI felt called upon to make his position clear and public. On March 14 his encyclical letter, *Mit brennender Sorge* ("With Burning Anxiety"), was smuggled into Germany and read aloud in most of the parish churches at great risk to their respective priests. The letter was impassioned and moving; it made Catholic doctrine clear and also the evil devices of the Nazis in trying to eradicate Christianity. This was a direct and unmistakable challenge. The following year when Hitler visited Mussolini in Rome, the pope made his attitude once more obvious. He ostentatiously left Rome for Castel Gandolfo while Hitler was in the city, closed the Vatican museums, and commented that the cross which was decorating the streets, the swastika, was not the cross of Christ.

The whole situation became more intense in March 1938 when Germany occupied Catholic Austria. At first, Theodor Cardinal Innitzer, archbishop of Vienna, welcomed the Germans and even flew the swastika flag from the spire of St. Stephan's Cathedral. He was soon called to Rome and cautioned by the pope. Later he suffered the fate of his brothers in Munich and Würzburg; mobs in the street attacked his home and threatened personal violence.

As in the case of the Protestants, the attack on the Catholics died down with the coming of the war; in 1941 there was even an effort to enlist the sympathy of the Catholic church in a crusade against Bolshevism. Again, as in the case of the Protestants, there is not the slightest doubt that if Germany had won the war, the onslaught would have resumed in an even more violent manner.

It is almost too heart-rending to tell again the tragic story of the Jews in Nazi Germany, surely one of the sorriest pages in the annals of humanity. In 1933 the Jews were less than 1 per cent of the population, but they had high places in society out of proportion to their numbers. It was possible to focus unreleased hatreds upon them, to make them a scapegoat for all ills in a way that would have been impossible against the millions of Catholics and Protestants. Everyone knew from Hitler's frank and virulent statements that when the Nazis came to power, the Jews would suffer; few could have guessed the almost endless extent of their suffering.

From the moment of the Nazi accession to power, the persecution of the Jews began. Jews were dismissed from all governmental or teaching posts and gradually from the learned professions and important business positions. Jewish-owned firms were seized and "Aryanized." On April 1, 1933, there was a one-day boycott of all Jewish firms. The concentration camps, hurriedly constructed, started to fill; synagogues were burned and plate-glass windows broken. Elderly Jews were exposed to all sorts of indignities, such as being forced to clean the streets with their tongues while gangs of "Aryan" hoodlums jeered at them. Placards and signs made it clear that there would be little or no punishment for attacks on Jews. The visitor to Germany became woefully used to signs on park benches stating that Jews might not sit there, to anti-Semitic exhibitions of pornographic hideousness, and to slogans painted on fences saying "The Jew is the enemy of the world" or "Who kills a Jew does a good deed."

The legal plight of the Jews was established by the Nuremberg Laws of September 15, 1935. A Jew was defined as anyone with even one Jewish grandparent. He was no longer a German citizen, could not vote, had no civil rights, might not marry an Aryan, could not fly the German flag nor teach nor take part in the arts, and did not even have the rights of a serf, but was the plaything and victim of his venomous masters. The police knocked at Jewish doors in the dead of night and removed the inhabitants. The entire period from 1933 to 1945 was a long passion for the Jewish people, a pogrom without relaxation. The only fortunate Jews were those who managed to escape from the country with help from abroad and only the clothes on their backs.

The orgy of violence reached its prewar height in November 1938 when a young official in the German embassy in Paris was murdered by a Jew. In retaliation, the worst of the pogroms was unleashed. A fine of one billion marks was levied on the Jewish community, and the beatings and the sadism knew no bounds.

Germany was a police state. The degree of control by terror achieved by the Nazis probably exceeded anything ever before known in history. The infamous Gestapo (*Geheime Staats-Polizei,* "secret state police") was only a small part of the huge police organization led by Himmler. Since he was in charge of the police and the S.S., Himmler integrated the two into a fearsome complex, some men detailed to ordinary criminal police, some to political police, and some to the management of concentration camps. The pitiful accounts of inmates of the camps have made the words Dachau, Buchenwald, Belsen, and the rest synonymous with torture, murder, sadism, and sordid cruelty. The world still had to learn the uttermost reaches of horror in the extermination camps of the war period where the "final settlement of the Jewish question" was to be carried out.

As Himmler and his police represented the negative or deterrent aspect of Nazi culture, Goebbels in his capacity as minister of propaganda and public enlightenment represented the positive. All media of communications, as well as the fine arts, fell under the authority of this ministry. Goebbels immediately set up a strict censorship and forbade the printing of any material not completely in accord with the Nazis. All Jewish-controlled agencies of news or entertainment were seized, and very quickly the newspapers, radio, and motion pictures gave the public only what Goebbels prescribed. Even such a famous liberal newspaper as the *Frankfurter Zeitung* published only the handouts of the press section of the propaganda ministry; to read one paper was to read them all. It became a serious punishable offense to listen to broadcasts from a foreign country over short-wave radio. Germans lived in a sealed cocoon to the extent that a powerful government was able to enforce its will.

Hitler considered himself an authority in the fine arts, and Goebbels was quick to implement his master's wishes. The *Führer's* taste ran to the conventional and banal. He disapproved of almost everything that had happened in the world of art since Manet, labeling modern art degenerate. In fact, he organized an exhibit of "degenerate" art in Munich as a warning to the people, but had to close it prematurely when it drew far larger crowds than the nearby showing of orthodox German art.

The Nazis undertook great projects of public works, building government offices, stadiums, art galleries, housing developments, etc. Hitler concerned himself personally in the architectural designs for these, picking Albert Speer as his favorite assistant. Typical were the enormous stadiums and meeting halls built on the outskirts of Nuremberg for the annual party congresses. They are massive, plain, and dull. Munich, the "capital city of the movement," received unadorned buildings to house the party offices and archives and two simple but awkward temples for the coffins of the men who were killed in the beer hall *Putsch* in 1923. Berlin was fated to become a suitable capital for the new Germany with monumental buildings and wide, straight thoroughfares driven through its center. Fortunately for the Berliners most of these plans either were not carried out or were destroyed in the war.

One looks in vain for important creation in literature, art, or music during the Nazi period. Most of the creative minds of the Weimar years fled abroad or lived in quiet obscurity. Artistic and spiritual Germany went under cover and waited for release. It was a dull, drab, and sterile time.

CHAPTER XXXI

The Nazi State to 1938. IV, Foreign Affairs

Adolf Hitler was as unorthodox and personal in his management of foreign affairs as in other aspects of his behavior. He had only scorn for the old-fashioned diplomacy of calculated politeness and for its frock-coated and striped-trousered priesthood. Consequently, he tended to trust the foreign office and the foreign service officers abroad with only minor and routine matters. Neurath remained minister of foreign affairs until 1938, but he seems to have been only a bureaucrat and administrator with little access to matters of high policy. Ambassadors and officials in the ministry complained of the degree to which they were kept in ignorance. They served as a respectable cloak covering the inner workings of the government.

The real source of decisions in foreign policy was Hitler himself. He liked to brood over a matter in solitude, often at his home near Berchtesgaden, and then without warning announce his conclusions to the world over the radio or in a speech to the Reichstag. His combination of intuition, bluff, shrewdness, and aggressiveness led to remarkably successful results for some years. At least he was never on the defensive; he had a highly developed sense of timing for surprise and shock tactics. He was unpredictable; he could be charming and gentle or violent and ruthless, as the situation seemed to demand. In all of his efforts he was ably seconded by Goebbels, whose propaganda barrages served to soften the enemy before the final thrust.

The one adviser to whom Hitler often gladly listened was Joachim von Ribbentrop. Ribbentrop was good-looking, well-dressed, smooth, and versed in both the English and French languages. He had traveled extensively, mainly as a salesman of champagne. He had been adopted by a noblewoman from whom he inherited the aristocratic "von." His combination of lack of intelligence, wishful thinking, arrogance, and bluster, added to complete obsequiousness before the *Führer,* won Hitler's high regard. He was in charge of the Foreign Policy Office in the party, generally known as the Ribbentrop Bureau, a group which meddled in foreign affairs, irritated Neurath, and provided Hitler with information independently of the foreign office. Appointed ambassador to Great Britain in 1936, he made a fool of himself and a failure of his work by his preposterous antics. The result was a hatred of Britain combined with a serious underestimation of her potentialities, which shaped Hitler's gross misjudgment of the British. However, not until shortly before his death did Hitler realize the hollowness of his favorite adviser.

Another favorite device of Hitler's was the use of Germans living abroad (*Auslanddeutsche*). German law did not recognize the nationalization of Germans as citizens of another state; thus the Nazis claimed that these people were still Germans. They were organized into a *Gau* of the party with Ernst Bohle in command. Propaganda was released and conventions of Germans from abroad were held in Stuttgart, which was declared to be their home city. They were trained to use divisive tactics in their respective countries so that they could be a weakening influence there when it became necessary. In some cases German ships even stood off the three-mile limit to permit the Germans resident in the area to vote in Nazi plebiscites. The success of these measures overseas was doubtful, but in central and eastern Europe the *Auslanddeutsche* served a useful purpose.

The first important step in foreign affairs taken by the Nazis has already been mentioned, namely the withdrawal of Germany from both the League of Nations and the World Disarmament Conference in October 1933. This action was popular in Germany because it was an assault on the hated Versailles system.

The year 1934 was concerned mostly with affairs in the east and the south. Most important was the German relationship to Austria. A permanent plank in the Nazi foreign platform was that all ethnic Germans should be integrated into a Greater Germany. Naturally, since Austria was almost completely German and was immediately adjacent to Germany, she was of great interest to the Nazis. The idea of *Anschluss* (the merging of the two states) was of course not new. Ever since 1918 there had been clamor for it on both sides of the frontier for both sentimental and economic reasons, but it was expressly forbidden by the treaties of Versailles and St. Germain.

In 1934 Austria had been governed for two years by the Catholic authoritarian, Engelbert Dollfuss. Dollfuss abrogated parliamentary government in 1933 and took action against the Nazi party, which was growing rapidly. Relations between Germany and Austria became very strained. The following spring Dollfuss took another step toward establishing his own sort of totalitarian rule by abolishing all parties except his own, the Fatherland Front. The result was an armed uprising in Vienna by the Social Democrats, which was quelled by blood and violence. In international affairs Dollfuss placed his reliance on Mussolini, who had taken both Austria and Hungary under his wing. The Italians had no enthusiasm for a common border with aggressive Nazi Germany because they recalled that they ruled a sizable minority of Germans in the South Tyrol. Shortly after the defeat of the Social Democrats, Dollfuss promulgated a new constitution which turned Austria into a type of Fascist dictatorship.

The clash with the Nazis came on July 25, 1934, a few weeks after the Roehm purge in Germany. A band of Austrian Nazis seized the Vienna radio station and the chancellery, where they shot Dollfuss and let him bleed to death without doctor or priest. However, the whole affair was badly managed and failed. The German Nazis, who undoubtedly had supported the attempt, had to disavow it when Mussolini announced mobilization of the Italian army on the Brenner Pass. Germany was in no position to force a decision of arms with Italy. Shortly afterward Hitler sent Papen as a conciliatory ambassador to Vienna; in 1936 an agreement was signed with Kurt Schuschnigg, Dollfuss' successor, which smoothed over German-Austrian relations for the time being. This coup, a premature forceful effort, is reminiscent of the beer hall *Putsch* of 1923. It taught Hitler a similar lesson—that he must wait until he was prepared to back up his threats.

The other important action taken abroad by the Nazis in 1934 was even more sensational than the events in Vienna. Very unexpectedly the first state with which Nazi Germany signed a nonaggression pact was Poland. The Poles were all too aware of the danger from an aggressive, nationalistic Germany on account of Danzig and the Polish Corridor. On January 26 the two states announced a nonaggression pact valid for ten years, during which there was to be no change in the relations between them. The world did not yet realize that this was part of Hitler's standard practice of lulling future victims before he was ready to pounce. He was very successful in keeping his enemies divided during his early years. The pact was also important because it indicated that Poland, traditionally friendly with and allied to France, had now reconsidered her position and decided not to antagonize the new Germany. Thus it was a prelude to the decline of the formerly powerful French position in eastern Europe.

These events caused some stirring in the capitals of Europe, where statesmen were beginning to realize dimly the danger that lay ahead.

France had at the moment an able and adventurous foreign minister, Louis Barthou, who traveled all over Europe in an effort to reinforce France's alliance system with the smaller states and to develop a warm relationship with the Russians. The Soviet government went so far as to accept membership in the League of Nations, which it had never considered seriously before. However, France lost much of her initiative in the latter part of 1934 when Barthou was murdered together with King Alexander of Yugoslavia at Marseille. A pact was eventually signed between France and the Soviet Union, but the French were never enthusiastic about it. The general picture of the years up to 1939 reveals a gradual shift of the focus of power on the continent from Paris to Berlin, in some ways reminiscent of the events from 1866 to 1870.

The year 1935 opened auspiciously for the Germans. In January the plebiscite called for by the Treaty of Versailles to decide the final disposition of the Saar area was due to be held. The Saarlanders were to choose among being granted permanently to France, being returned to Germany, or maintaining their neutral status under the League of Nations. It was a foregone conclusion that the Saar would opt for Germany since the population is almost completely German. Nevertheless, Hitler wanted the decision to be an overwhelming one and sent batteries of speakers and propaganda experts to the area. The vote was taken on January 13 and resulted in a 90 per cent victory for Germany. This was Hitler's first territorial achievement.

The next month Great Britain and France made overtures to Germany in the direction of strengthening the Locarno pact and of extending its philosophy to central and eastern Europe. Hitler played along with these suggestions for some weeks while he was planning the announcement of the formation of the air force and the return of conscription. It was apparent to even casual observers that Germany was no longer thinking seriously about disarmament, and both the British and the French announced increases in their own armed forces.

The reaction to Hitler's repudiation of the arms clauses of Versailles was immediate, but hardly alarming to Germany. The Western powers and the League issued formal protests. More important, representatives of Britain, France, and Italy met at Stresa in northern Italy. There they established the so-called "Stresa Front," which issued a joint protest against the German move. However, the Stresa Front had no future because within a few months each of its member states had taken action of varying sorts dooming it to ineffectiveness. France took direct action by signing a defensive treaty with the Soviet Union and acting as the intermediary for a similar treaty between the Soviets and France's ally, Czechoslovakia.

The British action was less explicable. Even before the Stresa conference met, Sir John Simon, the foreign secretary, accompanied by Anthony Eden, visited Berlin, where they found a gentle and cooing Hitler. Nothing immediate came of the meeting, but Hitler dropped the remark that he would be prepared to sign a treaty with Britain to limit naval armaments. It probably came as a delightful surprise to the *Führer* that the British were interested in this idea and continued to negotiate about it. Finally in June Hitler sent Ribbentrop to London as his special envoy, and on the eighteenth the two governments signed the Anglo-German naval agreement, surely one of the most unaccountable treaties in all history. By this arrangement the Germans agreed to limit their surface navy to 35 per cent of the British navy, but if they deemed it necessary, the Germans were authorized to construct submarines up to 100 per cent of the British submarine fleet. This occurred less than twenty years after Germany had almost won a world war because of her submarine prowess. The treaty also seemed to imply a British belief that the Treaty of Versailles was no longer a binding document.

Italy had even bigger plans in view. Within a few months the Ethiopian crisis began and diverted the world from its immediate preoccupation with German affairs. There followed the dismal story of the imposition of economic sanctions against Italy by the League, the Hoare-Laval "deal," and the proclamation of King Victor Emmanuel of Italy as emperor of Ethiopia. Italy emerged from these months of crisis swollen in her conceit and charged with hatred against Great Britain. British policy was disastrous. It did not achieve the protection of the Ethiopians but pushed Italy into the arms of Hitler, who was the principal gainer.

Hitler behaved during this crisis with unusual and intelligent forbearance. He was no doubt delighted that the spotlight of the world was temporarily removed from Germany. He took absolutely no part in any action against Italy. Of all the powers Germany was the only one which did not berate the Italians for their African adventure. This policy won the gratitude of Mussolini, who was already disposed to sympathy with the Nazis because of the similarity between the two political philosophies.

As far back as 1924 when he was dictating *Mein Kampf,* Hitler had admired Mussolini and had recommended an alliance between Germany and Italy. In June 1934 Hitler made his first trip across the German border to visit Mussolini in Venice. The visit was not very successful, and relations between the two countries became very strained that summer when Dollfuss was murdered and the designs of Germany upon Austria became clear. However, the events of the Ethiopian crisis went a distance toward reconciling the two fascist nations.

In March 1936 Hitler was ready for his next big step, the remilitarization of the Rhineland and the denunciation of Locarno. He gave as legal justification the treaty recently ratified between France and the Soviet Union, which, he insisted, was an implicit breach of Locarno. At the same time he offered an elaborate peace plan composed of nonaggression pacts and guarantees. This was typical of Hitler; when he wanted to, he could talk with the voice of Stresemann, but the aims were quite different. Nothing came of Hitler's peace plans. No foreign action was taken about the Rhineland problem except for votes of censure, but the German people in another plebiscite registered their wholehearted approval.

A major crisis arose in the summer of 1936 when a number of high-ranking officers in the Spanish army led a revolt against their republican government. This revolt broadened into the brutal and bloody Spanish civil war, which raged for almost three years and ended with the victory of the leader of the rebels (or nationalists), General Francisco Franco. Internationally speaking, this war had a catalytic effect on the European scene and divided the powers into two camps (or possibly three, depending on how the Soviet Union is to be classified). From the outset Italy and Germany supported Franco's cause. Mussolini permitted thousands of Italian soldiers, flushed with their African victory, to sail to Spain to support the rebels. Hitler offered help also, but was not prepared to damage many of his new soldiers. The Germans sent technical assistance, cartographers and mechanics capable of keeping motorized equipment in good condition. More important, they also sent units of the new air force, the so-called Condor Legion, which introduced the world to the horrors of mass bombings of civilian populations. The Soviet Union sent aid to the government forces, and while Britain and France officially declared a policy of nonintervention, their sympathies were with the government and thousands of British and French volunteers went to fight in Spain. Thus once again Germany and Italy were on the same team.

The time was ripe in Hitler's opinion to register more formally the friendship between Italy and Germany. The Germans were able to point to their recent treaty with Austria which regularized relations between the two countries; they were able to dangle the bait of recognition of the Italian empire in Africa; they were anxious to secure tangible benefit from the mutual fight against Bolshevism in Spain. Discussions began in both Rome and Berlin. In late October 1936 Mussolini's son-in-law, Count Galeazzo Ciano, the Italian foreign minister, visited both Berlin and Berchtesgaden, where Hitler received him with warm cordiality. The result was the signature of agreements covering all the possible points of conflict between the two states. A few days later Mussolini mentioned the agreement in a speech and referred to it as an "axis." Thus a new word entered the history of international affairs.

During these central years of his career Hitler harped a great deal on the theme of anti-Communism, although he did not cease profitable Russo-German economic relations. This policy was useful at home in focusing attention on a common foe. It was judged to be useful abroad as well. Hitler hoped that he might use it as a wedge to pry his way into closer relations with Great Britain. In *Mein Kampf* Hitler had called for an alliance with Britain as well as with Italy. In his attitude toward the British Hitler displayed some of the same ambivalence that had characterized William II; he loved and hated, feared and envied. He sent his beloved Ribbentrop to London as his ambassador in the hope that he could gain the favor of those well-known anti-Communists, Stanley Baldwin, the prime minister, and Neville Chamberlain, his right-hand man. If ever a diplomatic mission was a complete failure, it was this one. Neither Hitler nor Ribbentrop understood the British. While British foreign policy in the thirties was weak and misguided, it did not go so far in its incompetence as to envisage intimate co-operation with Nazi Germany. Ribbentrop returned from his mission full of hatred for the British but nursing the misconception that Britain was now a negligible power.

If the anti-Communist line did not succeed in London, it did in Tokyo. Japan had been a pariah nation since 1931 when she seized Manchuria from China, renamed it Manchukuo, installed a puppet government, and later withdrew from the League of Nations. During these years she was waging an undeclared war of major proportions against the Russians on the remote border of Manchukuo and Soviet Asia. Thus the German suggestion of an "anti-Comintern" pact was attractive to her. This was a pact to which other nations could be invited to adhere, for it was primarily an ideological statement rather than a military alliance (though there were some secret anti-Soviet clauses). Japan and Germany signed this pact in November 1936. The Germans had some difficulty in presenting Japan as their close associate in view of the patent fact that the Japanese people were non-Aryan, but this problem was rather easily resolved.

The year 1937 was a relatively quiet one on the international scene. Hitler did not contrive any major surprises. It was a year of growing strength and the development of past gains. The most spectacular event was the ostentatious visit of Mussolini to Germany in September. He was given a tremendous reception and treated as he thought befitted him. From this time the relationship with Italy was secure. Its first fruit was harvested in November when Italy adhered to the anti-Comintern pact.

The new British prime minister, Neville Chamberlain, made a gesture toward Germany in November 1937 when he sent his foreign secretary, Lord Halifax, to confer with Hitler. The conversations came to little or nothing; Hitler was in an unyielding mood. He had ended his courtship of Britain.

By 1938 the European picture was far different from that of five years earlier. Italy was a secure friend of Germany, while Britain and France had shown themselves weak and irresolute. Events had colored the attitudes of the smaller states as well. The government of Prince Paul, regent of Yugoslavia, was not unfriendly to Germany. King Carol II of Romania had instituted a royal dictatorship, patterned to an extent after Nazi Germany. Hungary was almost a satellite of Italy. The Poles were trying hard not to irritate their newly powerful German neighbors. Perhaps the most striking shift of attitude was taken by Belgium, which in 1937 ended her alliance with France and announced once again her earlier policy of neutrality in the hope that this step might save her from another German invasion.

A combination of economic penetration, diplomatic ruthlessness, ideological propaganda, and shrewd timing had done its work. Hitler had cause to be pleased with his achievements. He was now ready to start the campaign of unveiled aggression which was to lead into World War II.

CHAPTER XXXII

Prelude to War (1938-39)

On November 5, 1937, Hitler summoned five of his principal subordinates and subjected them to a four-hour monologue on the subject of Germany's immediate possibilities in foreign policy. Present were Field Marshal von Blomberg, Generals von Fritsch and Goering, Admiral Raeder, and Foreign Minister von Neurath. Hitler's general theory was that the achievement of autarky was basically impossible and that therefore Germany must occupy more land adjacent to her. The direction of advance was marked out as south and east; Austria and Czechoslovakia had to be overrun. Beyond this he did not go into specific detail. There was no evasion of the threat that the Germans might find themselves at war. Hitler declared himself in certain circumstances ready for war the following year and certainly within six or seven years, by which time Germany would be starting to lose her lead in war equipment. The period of preparation was over; the time of achievement was at hand.

The program was greeted with mixed attitudes by Hitler's listeners. The minutes record that the two army officers put up some protest on the ground that German armed might was not yet great enough and the potential opposition abroad too great. It is no accident that these men lost their posts in the next few months.

In fact, the most important development of the next weeks was the replacement of leading independent and critical officials by people who could be counted on to do only what Hitler told them. Already the axe had fallen on Schacht, who was no longer minister of economics; he was soon replaced by Funk, who recognized that he was subordinate to the head of the Four Year Plan, Hermann Goering.

Ever since the Roehm purge of 1934 Hitler had treated the officers of the growing army with honor and favor. There had been no great effort to synchronize the officers with the party. This did not arise from any warmth which Hitler felt toward the generals; in fact, he felt socially inferior to them, but he needed their technical services badly. Now, however, he felt stronger and was determined that the army should be an unquestioning instrument to enforce his foreign policy. He received unexpectedly just the material he needed to carry out his plans to control the high command.

In January 1938 Blomberg quietly married a woman with an admittedly obscure past. Both Hitler and Goering were at the wedding. Immediately thereafter Himmler unearthed from the police records information that the field marshal's bride had a record as a former prostitute and as a model for indecent photographs. The generals were infuriated at this affront to the officers' code and insisted that Blomberg be dismissed. Hitler agreed to this.

It looked as if Fritsch were the obvious successor to Blomberg, but an even less attractive story was developed to get rid of him. Himmler delved into the records and came up with an accusation of homosexuality against Fritsch. He even produced a professional blackmailer to confront the general. The accusation was quite groundless; it developed that the blackmailer had had relations with a retired officer with a similar name. However, Fritsch chose not to defend himself and was sent into retirement, although he was later officially exonerated. By these methods Hitler tamed the army, but he also created a core of resentful officers who were later to constitute the nucleus of the principal anti-Nazi resistance movement, which culminated with the attempt on the *Führer*'s life on July 20, 1944.

To succeed Fritsch, Hitler reached down the list of generals and picked General Walther von Brauchitsch. The succession to Blomberg was arranged differently. Hitler abolished the ministry of defense and replaced it with a staff called the High Command of the Armed Forces (*Oberkommando der Wehrmacht,* or OKW). At the head of this Hitler placed himself immediately in command. To control the administration of the OKW, he appointed General Wilhelm Keitel, an obsequious timeserver.

The final purge was made in the foreign ministry. Neurath dated as minister from pre-Nazi days. He was a respectable, if unimpressive, figure. Now, however, Hitler asked for his resignation and gave him a decorative but meaningless title. As his successor Hitler named Joachim von Ribbentrop. Some changes were also made in important posts abroad.

The first crisis came immediately. Hitler did not plan events in advance; no one can do that with exactness. Yet during 1938 he proved himself a brilliant, brutal, and bullying improviser in the field of foreign policy, as he had already done in domestic affairs.

For some months Austria's international position had deteriorated rapidly. The treaty of 1936 between Germany and Austria provided that each would respect the independence of the other. At that time Austria felt that she could rely on the protection of Mussolini. During 1937 the situation changed with the increasing intimacy between Germany and Italy. At home Schuschnigg, Dollfuss' successor, maintained his dictatorial one-party government, refused to take any Nazis into his cabinet, imprisoned a number of them, and talked publicly about the possibility of a restoration of the Hapsburg pretender to the Austrian throne. All these attitudes grated seriously on the Nazis.

On February 12, 1938, Schuschnigg traveled to Berchtesgaden for a conference with Hitler. It turned out to be not a conference but one of the *Führer*'s most venomous monologues. He turned on the unfortunate Austrian and for several hours upbraided him with wild fury, informing him that he would have to agree immediately to an ultimatum. The ultimatum provided that Austria would release all imprisoned Nazis, that Nazis might join the one party in Austria, the Fatherland Front, and that two Nazis would be admitted to the cabinet. The more significant one was Arthur Seyss-Inquart, who was slated for the important post of minister of the interior. Schuschnigg had no alternative but to accept Hitler's demands.

During the next few weeks there was a lull. Seyss-Inquart went to Berlin for orders. Schuschnigg gave a major speech calling for continued Austrian independence. However, all over Austria outbreaks of violence fomented by the Nazis occurred to such an extent that the police were no longer in control. On March 8, 1938, Schuschnigg decided to hold a plebiscite on the following Sunday, the thirteenth, in which the Austrian people would vote on whether they wanted Austria to remain independent.

When Hitler heard of Schuschnigg's move, his rage was intense. This was undercutting his whole policy. On the tenth he ordered the mobilization of the army on the southern frontier ready to invade Austria if necessary to protect the German character of Austria. He also sent a personal letter by air to Mussolini explaining his position and asking for a friendly attitude. The next day Hitler halted rail traffic on the Austrian border and sent an ultimatum to Vienna demanding that the plebiscite be postponed. Later the same day he demanded that Schuschnigg resign and be succeeded by Seyss-Inquart. President Miklas of Austria demurred at this last demand and refused to agree to it for several hours until the moment had passed at which the German army was to start to cross the frontier. However, Seyss-Inquart had time to send a telegram inviting the German army into Austria.

Meanwhile in Berlin Hitler heard by telephone the happy news that

Mussolini would not oppose the entrance of German troops into Austria. His hysterical gratitude knew no bounds, and he promised undying affection for the Italian dictator and that he would never endanger the new frontier on the Brenner Pass. The German troops started to move. Hitler flew to the south and crossed the border to the town of Linz, where he had spent much of his childhood. With public emotion he decorated his parents' graves. The next day he received Seyss-Inquart, whose one action as Austrian chancellor had been to sign a decree integrating Austria into Germany. On the fourteenth the *Führer* made a triumphal journey from Linz to Vienna, greeted by flags, music, and enthusiasm. Standing by the palace of the Hapsburgs in the city where his life had been so squalid, he received the homage of the Viennese. The *Anschluss* was accomplished.

Nazi methods immediately went into operation: arrests by the thousands, suicides, beatings, the whole panoply of Nazi horror. Yet there is no doubt that the change was popular. For the first time in twenty years Austria was assured of economic security and a position as an integral part of a great power once again. In April a plebiscite was held under Nazi auspices, and almost 100 per cent of the Austrians voted for the *Anschluss*. Abroad there was not a great deal of stir. Britain and France protested but in a halfhearted way, for it was undeniable that the Austrians were ethnically German and many felt that they should have been permitted to join Germany earlier. During 1938 Hitler's actions had just enough plausibility that it was difficult to condemn them out of hand.

Hitler did not rest long after his success in Austria. Within a few weeks he started making plans against his next victim, Czechoslovakia. Ever since his early Vienna days Hitler had hated the Czechs, who at that time, being Austrian subjects, were waging a nationalistic war of nerves against the German Austrians. Czechoslovakia had almost alone in central Europe maintained a democratic government; geographically it was a sort of wedge pointed toward Germany; also it was allied with France and the Soviet Union. All these things provoked Hitler's hatred. On the other hand, ever since the *Anschluss* the German position was much improved, because now Germany surrounded the most populous part of Czechoslovakia on three sides.

Hitler had a ready-made pretext in his anti-Czech moves. Around the western border of Czechoslovakia lived between three and four million ethnic Germans, the so-called Sudeten Germans. These people had been Austrian subjects before 1918. At the peace conference there was even talk of permitting them to join Germany, but not very much talk. They were granted as a large minority group to the new Czecho-slovak state. They lived in a reasonably cohesive area immediately adjacent to Germany. Strategically their location was important because it was on the eastern slopes of the mountains. If Germany included the Sudeten area, Czechoslovakia would have no natural barrier against attack from the west. Furthermore, this was the area in which the Czechs had built their strong defense positions against Germany.

Hitler, of course, regarded the Sudetens as Germans forcibly ruled by inferior foreigners. He encouraged the formation and growth of a Sudeten Nazi party, whose leader was Konrad Henlein. This party and other Sudeten parties caused constant disturbances in the parliament at Prague, until in November 1937 they left it and became even more vocal about their alleged disabilities. This hue and cry was eagerly taken up in Germany.

Immediately after the *Anschluss* Hitler began to see more and more of Henlein and to give him instructions. The general tenor of the instructions was to demand more and more. Every time the Czech government offered a concession, the Sudetens were to demand others and thus maintain a constant state of unrest. This was to be coupled with demonstrations, propaganda, and purposeful confusion of all sorts. In April 1938, Henlein announced an eight-point program and went so far as to demand a shift in Czech foreign policy. The Czech government felt that this was too much and refused the demands, in spite of continuing advice from London and Paris to make as many concessions as humanly possible.

Hitler spent early May on a state visit to Italy, where he received a tremendous ovation from all but the pope, although Mussolini still refused to sign an actual military alliance with Germany. When the *Führer* returned home, he found that a crisis was in the immediate offing. President Beneš of Czechoslovakia, outraged by the constant disturbances at home and by information of German troop concentrations near the border, ordered a partial mobilization of the Czech army. France and Britain warned Germany of the possibility of general war; both France and the Soviet Union announced their intention to carry out their treaty promises to Czechoslovakia. The Germans, who were in no position to face Britain, France, and Russia, plus the efficient Czech army, had to back down, and Henlein was ordered to continue to negotiate in Prague. However, Hitler's fury was unlimited; his hatred of Beneš and the Czechs increased. He decided to bide his time and started the construction of the West Wall or Siegfried line along the French frontier.

The crisis simmered during the summer. Henlein negotiated half-heartedly with the Prague government and got a statute published which did not go as far as the eight points. German diplomats did what they could to weaken the Czech position in eastern Europe. In August Prime

Minister Chamberlain sent Lord Runciman to Czechoslovakia as an official mediator. Runciman continued the British policy of urging concessions on Beneš, but in the meantime all the powers tightened up their military preparedness.

In September the crisis reached its apex. Serious fighting between Czechs and Sudetens erupted in the town of Moravska Ostrava, and the Sudetens broke off negotiations. On the twelfth Hitler addressed the Nazi party congress at Nuremberg with an unheard-of degree of venom directed at the Czechs and at Beneš personally. Within Czechoslovakia the fighting was almost out of hand.

At this point with French agreement Chamberlain decided to act personally. On the thirteenth he informed Hitler that he was willing to leave immediately for Germany to try to solve the problem by a personal interview. On the fifteenth, after his first trip by plane, he arrived at the *Führer's* home in Berchtesgaden. Hitler delivered a diatribe against the Czechs and insisted that the question of the Sudetens had to be solved immediately by their integration into Germany. Chamberlain got Hitler to promise no action by force until he had discussed the matter with the British cabinet and with the French.

On his return to London and upon consultation with France, Chamberlain managed to persuade the Czech government to cede the Sudeten area to Germany in return for a guarantee of the remainder to Czechoslovakia. Now Chamberlain was doing Hitler's work for him.

On the twenty-second Chamberlain again flew to Germany. This time the two met at Bad Godesberg on the Rhine, but now Chamberlain found that Hitler had stiffened and raised his price. The fact was that Hitler did not want merely to annex the Sudeten area; he wanted all of Bohemia and Moravia. Chamberlain was playing the part of a meddling peacemaker, who, however, was too important to be rebuffed publicly. Hitler insisted on a very short time limit for the cession and on further plebiscites; he also brought up what he said were the legitimate claims of Poland and Hungary against Czechoslovakia. Chamberlain was simply not equipped emotionally to deal with a personality like Hitler. He was despondent and promised only that he would convey the new German demands to London and Prague.

No one who lived through the next few days will forget them. Italy announced its solidarity with Germany. Hitler gave another speech packed with hatred. The French premier, Daladier, went to London to confer. President Roosevelt proposed a conference; so did Chamberlain. Finally Chamberlain appealed to Mussolini to make a move for peace. Mussolini agreed; he was not happy at the thought of a war, and so proposed a general conference. Hitler accepted the proposal and set the date for the next day. Chamberlain, Daladier, and Mussolini were invited to meet with Hitler in Munich on September 29. It is instructive to note that neither Czechoslovakia nor the Soviet Union was invited. Stalin never forgot this insult and held it against the Western powers.

At the Munich conference Hitler received all that he had asked at Godesberg, except that the time schedule for the German occupation was somewhat modified. Britain and France agreed to guarantee the new Czech state. Germany and Italy agreed to do the same, once Poland and Hungary had been satisfied in their claims. Czechoslovakia had no choice but to accept.

Before the conference ended, Chamberlain wrote out a statement promising Anglo-German accord in the future and asked Hitler to sign it. He did so, and it was this sheet of paper which Chamberlain waved in his hand as the crowds enthusiastically greeted him at the London airport. This document was to bring, in Chamberlain's words, "peace in our time." After the British awoke from their intoxication with peace, their outstanding leaders, notably Winston Churchill, realized that Great Britain had suffered perhaps the most humiliating defeat in her history.

Still Hitler was not very happy; he did not consider Munich an overwhelming victory. Quite the contrary, for there was still a Czech state in existence. During the winter of 1938–39 the Germans laid the foundations for further action in the east. Hitler had convinced himself, quite rightly as it turned out, that France was seriously weakened through internal dissension. He hoped, therefore, to detach her from her alliance with Britain. He did not achieve this, but in December 1938 Ribbentrop visited Paris and signed a treaty guaranteeing the Franco-German frontier and promising consultation on any disputes. Hitler kept insisting that he had given up all claims on Alsace-Lorraine. In the southeast the Germans worked hard to solidify their relations with the Balkan nations: Romania, Bulgaria, Yugoslavia, and also Hungary.

After the Munich conference the Czechoslovak state was much changed. Poland was appeased with the cession of the Teschen area, and Hungary received a slice of territory along the southern border of Slovakia and Ruthenia. President Beneš resigned and was succeeded by Emil Hacha. The Czechs granted full autonomy within the new Czecho-Slovakia (the hyphen was added to indicate the new federal state) to both Slovakia and Ruthenia, now called Carpatho-Ukraine and possibly useful to Hitler in the future for Ukrainian propaganda against either Poland or the Soviet Union. Germany, oddly enough, became the godfather of an autonomous Slovakia.

In the early months of 1939 the Czech government became alarmed that the Slovaks and Ruthenians were plotting independence rather than simply autonomy. In March President Hacha deposed their two governments on these grounds. The Slovak premier, Monsignor Tiso, appealed to Hitler, who saw the opportunity offered him. German agents went to the Slovak capital, Bratislava, to spur on the Slovak leaders to insist on independence. Hitler invited Tiso to come to Berlin on March 13. The *Führer* persuaded him to call a meeting of the Slovak parliament for the next morning, fly to it, and proclaim Slovak independence. This he did somewhat to the astonishment of the Slovak parliamentarians.

On the same day President Hacha was ordered to Berlin. When he arrived, he was treated to the same kind of tirade as Schuschnigg the year before. After Hitler delivered himself of a lengthy polemic against the Czechs, he told Hacha that there was only one thing he could now do for his country. German troops were on the march and Hacha could telephone Prague and order that there be no resistance to them. The unfortunate Hacha fainted. After he revived, he made the call and then officially placed "the fate of the Czech people . . . trustingly in the hands of the *Führer.*"

Hitler now took another victorious trip—this time to Prague, where he arrived on March 15. There he proclaimed that the Czechoslovak state had ceased to exist and set up the Protectorate of Bohemia and Moravia under the supervision of Germany, with Neurath as protector. Slovakia was recognized as independent. Hungary eventually annexed Carpatho-Ukraine. The whole operation had taken a week. Hitler slept that night in the Hradschin palace built by Emperor Charles IV in the fourteenth century.

The world reeled again; the protests came in, but no forceful action was taken. However, the seizure of Prague did have the important effect of turning Chamberlain once and for all against Hitler. Up to this time he had been impressed by the plausibility of the German argument based on national self-determination. This argument had no weight so far as the Czechs were concerned. The British attitude stiffened, and Chamberlain decided to offer British guarantees to nations which seemed to be threatened by Germany.

The events of March 1939 were not completely over. Within a week of his entrance into Prague Hitler enjoyed one more small triumph. Ribbentrop sent an ultimatum to Lithuania demanding the return to Germany of the port of Memel and its hinterland, which had been separated from Germany by Versailles. There was certainly nothing the Lithuanians could do to stop the Germans, so they agreed. Hitler went aboard a German naval vessel, presumably to avoid crossing the Polish Corridor, and on March 21 had the pleasure of welcoming the people of Memel into Greater Germany. It was a happy month for the *Führer.*

Hitler had no idea of resting on his laurels. His successes of the past year had been so spectacular that he saw no reason why their momentum should not increase rather than diminish. A few weeks after the Munich conference and several months before the Czech state was destroyed, the Germans started negotiations directed toward their next objective, a settlement of matters with Poland. Ever since 1919 all German governments had been bitterly resentful of the treaty arrangements on the east: the loss of Danzig; the wedge between East Prussia and the rest of Germany constituted by the Polish Corridor; and the inclusion into Poland of considerable German minorities in Silesia, Posen, and the Corridor. Even Stresemann in his most conciliatory moments refused to sign an "eastern Locarno" to guarantee the border with Poland.

Poland was in an unenviable position surrounded by her two historical enemies, Germany and Russia, both of which were growing stronger every day. During the twenties she had cast her lot with France and the "Versailles" powers, but in 1934 the Polish government welcomed the advances of Nazi Germany and signed a nonaggression pact with Hitler to last for ten years and to complement the nonaggression pact already in existence with the Soviet Union. Both the Polish dictator Marshal Pilsudski and his successor Marshal Smigly-Rydz, as well as the foreign minister, Josef Beck, seemed to be more anti-Soviet than anti-German.

Hitler, too, pursued an ambivalent policy toward Poland. While there is no doubt that he was determined to regain Danzig and other German-populated areas, he seems to have considered Poland a possible ally in an eventual war with the Soviet Union. In any case, he maintained friendly relations with Warsaw, and frequently his speeches boasted about the warm spirit which had prevailed since the treaty of 1934. By late 1938 his attitude had solidified, however, and he decided to settle the Danzig problem. In Danzig itself events had moved favorably to Germany. As early as 1933 the local Nazis elected a majority in the Danzig Senate and over the years increased their numbers until by 1938 they held 70 of the 72 seats. The *Gauleiter* of Danzig, Albert Forster, effectively ruled the city and treated his nominal master, the high commissioner appointed by the League of Nations, with scorn and neglect. The weakened League was unable to do anything about it.

The negotiations began in a friendly way on October 24, 1938, when Ribbentrop invited the Polish ambassador, Lipski, to lunch and outlined Germany's wishes. They included the return of Danzig to Germany and the construction of an extraterritorial railway and highway across the Polish Corridor. As for the rest, Ribbentrop promised a German guarantee of the Polish-German border and even hinted at a future Polish-German collaboration aimed at the Soviets. This talk was followed by others and by visits of Beck to Germany and of Ribbentrop to Poland. The Poles were very suspicious and ostentatiously renewed their non-aggression pact with the Soviet Union. They continued to be friendly toward the Germans but nevertheless maintained a firm policy of refusal of the German proposals.

Immediately after the seizure of Memel the German attitude toward Poland stiffened. Ribbentrop once more called in Lipski and reiterated his proposals, this time insisting on an immediate answer. Beck's reply was that although the Polish government was willing to discuss any matters with Germany, the specific German requirements were impossible. The last few days of March were filled with angry exchanges both in Berlin and Warsaw, with the Germans now beginning to talk about outrages committed by the Poles against German minority groups in Poland.

At this point the gradual attrition of the Poles, which Hitler counted on, was interrupted by action taken in London. On March 31 Neville Chamberlain, at last definite in his opposition to Hitler, extended in a speech in the Commons a guarantee of support to Poland by force of arms if necessary to preserve Polish independence. Immediately the French government associated itself with the British action. Hitler had an ugly surprise; for the first time he had to face clear defiance from the west. However, he was wise enough not to push the Polish matter right away. He imitated the tactics of Bismarck, who in 1865 waged a diplomatic campaign to assure himself of the attitude of the other powers before he pounced on Austria. The *Führer* had to assure himself of the general European situation now that he was threatened with the opposition of Great Britain and France.

In mid-April another country made itself heard. President Roosevelt, angered by the German aggressions and the recent seizure of Albania by the Italians, sent a note to Hitler and Mussolini asking their future intentions and specifically if they had aggressive designs on a list of over thirty countries. Hitler replied to the president in a full-dress speech delivered to a delighted Reichstag on April 28. It was a brilliantly derisive piece of irony and invective, but it did not answer Roosevelt's question. Hitler simply reiterated his old demands, attacked warmongers, and defended his actions in foreign policy. The only new element added to the situation was the *Führer*'s denunciation of both the Anglo-German Naval Treaty of 1935 and the Polish-German nonaggression pact of 1934. After this outburst Hitler retired from the public scene, while the German newspapers intensified their campaign of hate against Poland describing Polish atrocities in vivid and imaginative detail.

During the late spring and the summer of 1939 the German government devoted itself to mending international fences. It signed nonaggression pacts with Denmark, Latvia, and Estonia. Hitler welcomed high officials of Hungary, Yugoslavia, and Bulgaria to Berlin. In particular, the Nazis worked to tighten their already close relationship with Italy. Mussolini was in a happy frame of mind because of his recent cheap conquest of Albania, but he and Ciano were worried by the possibility of a European war arising out of the Polish problem. The Italian leaders knew that their armed forces were not ready for major combat and were anxious to restrain their German partners. Ciano therefore invited Ribbentrop to meet him in Milan in early May. The German minister managed to quiet the Italian's fears and even to obtain Mussolini's agreement to a real military alliance, hitherto unobtainable. The alliance was drawn up by the Germans and agreed to in Rome. It was a clear military alliance by which each power promised full support to the other in case of war. Ciano went to Berlin for the ceremonious signing of the treaty on May 22. Mussolini christened it the Pact of Steel, but in spite of all this ostentation he sent Hitler a secret message a few days later in which he warned that Italy would not be ready for war for more than three years.

Much more important than the treaty with Italy was the possibility which had loomed in Hitler's mind of an arrangement with the Soviet Union which would open the way to a direct attack on Poland. In view of the consistent anti-Communism of the Nazi philosophy and particularly of the anti-Comintern pact, such a possibility seemed to exist only in a dream world. However, Hitler was not a man to be deterred simply by ideology; he knew that there were powerful voices both among his generals and in the foreign ministry which would applaud a warmer relation with the Russians. The advantages to Germany were obvious. Without Russian support the British and French guarantees to Poland would be weak and Hitler would be spared the prospect of a long, grueling two-front war. In fact, British and French representatives were even then in Moscow trying to enlist Russian sympathy for their cause, although halfheartedly because of Chamberlain's extreme anti-Russian attitude. Hitler reasoned that Russia had a good deal to gain by an agreement with Germany. Although he no doubt anticipated an eventual war with Russia, he felt that Stalin would be happy for a breathing space and also a share of possible Polish spoils to be acquired without any Russian effort. An important straw in the wind was the replacement in May of the Western-oriented Soviet foreign minister, Maxim Litvinov, by V. M. Molotov. During the first months of 1939 Hitler's and Stalin's pronouncements seemed to be oddly free of the usual mutual invective.

The first steps were taken in May when the two governments agreed to undertake trade negotiations which had been overdue for some time but postponed. The negotiations occupied most of the month of June but were discontinued because of a lack of definite results. They were reopened in late July in Berlin, and it was then that the German representative suggested that they be supplemented by political agreements. At the same time von der Schulenburg, the German ambassador in Moscow, made the same suggestion to Molotov and engaged in several friendly conversations with him.

On August 11 a British and French military mission arrived in Moscow for detailed conversations with the Soviets. On the same day Ciano and Ribbentrop met at Salzburg. The Italians were becoming very jittery at the prospect of a general war. Ribbentrop, and Hitler too, quieted Ciano with a promise that the war would be short and easy, and dangled the prospect of an agreement with the Russians as if it were an accomplished fact.

In Moscow the Soviets played a game of delay with the Germans. Throughout the negotiations it was the Germans who were eager and the Russians who were reluctant. Stalin knew well his value to Hitler and was determined to keep his price high. Molotov turned the conversations away from simply Poland and discussed Asiatic problems and the affairs of southeastern Europe. Ribbentrop ordered acquiescence to anything the Russians would propose and suggested that he himself would like to visit Moscow to sign a final agreement. However, Molotov kept postponing the date, thus raising havoc with the German timetable. On August 20 Hitler sent a personal telegram to Stalin asking him to receive Ribbentrop on the twenty-second or the twenty-third, not later. Hitler spent an anxious thirty-six hours waiting for a reply. It came on the twenty-second. Stalin wired that he would be willing to receive Ribbentrop the next day. Hitler immediately gave full powers to his minister, who left Berlin the same day and arrived in Moscow the following afternoon.

Ribbentrop spent less than twenty-four hours in Moscow. Most of them were passed in cordial conversations with Stalin and Molotov, during which the world situation was explored and the agreements drawn up. The public agreement looked relatively innocent. It was a simple nonaggression treaty to last for ten years, calling for consultation and arbitration in the event of differences. Much more important was the secret protocol which divided eastern Europe into two spheres of influence. Lithuania was in the German sphere; Finland, Estonia, and Latvia in the Soviet. In case of changes in the political organization of Poland, a line was drawn to indicate the two spheres. Germany declared that she had no interest in the Romanian province of Bessarabia, which Russia had lost after World War I. The agreements were signed on the twenty-fourth, and the world rocked with the news that the two great ideological enemies had come together.

While Ribbentrop was in Moscow, Hitler received Sir Nevile Henderson, the British ambassador. Henderson handed the *Führer* a communication from Prime Minister Chamberlain which stated in absolutely explicit terms Britain's determination to honor her pledge to Poland with all the forces at her command. Even then Hitler hoped that the news of the Russian accord would detach Britain and France from Poland; he had set the early hours of the twenty-sixth as the moment for the attack across the eastern frontier. On the twenty-fifth he made a last effort to placate the British. It took two forms—one unofficially through a Swedish intermediary named Dahlerus, the other officially through the ambassador. Shortly after Henderson left for London, Hitler heard that that very day a pact of mutual assistance had been signed by Britain and Poland. This gave Hitler pause. His hesitation was increased by a letter from Mussolini in which the Italian dictator stated that in case of war, while he would give every political and economic assistance to Germany, he would not fight unless Germany could guarantee to Italy huge quantities of raw materials and munitions, which was manifestly impossible. In the light of these two developments Hitler postponed the attack on Poland.

The events of the remaining six days of peace were confused and kaleidoscopic. Hitler did not for a moment give up his plan to attack Poland. He accepted Mussolini's refusal to come into the war with such grace as he could muster, though he was obviously disappointed. He exchanged letters with the French premier, Daladier, asking what France had to gain from a war for Danzig. He engaged in more serious negotiations with Great Britain, sending both Dahlerus and Henderson once again to London with proposals, which, however, did not include a retreat on the questions of Danzig or the Corridor. It is interesting that until the last moment there was no serious thought of negotiating with the Poles. Hitler treated them as he had treated the Czechs a year earlier. In Berlin Ribbentrop was the leader of the war party and Goering the leader of those who sought to keep Britain out of the struggle. On the twenty-eighth a British note recommending negotiations between Germany and Poland arrived in Berlin. The British had won Polish agreement to this course. On the twenty-ninth Hitler agreed to the British proposal on condition that a Pole with full powers should arrive in Berlin the next day. On the thirtieth the Germans drew up a sixteen-point demand to be presented to the Poles. It was rather moderate in tone, but was obviously window-dressing. This was made clear when

Ribbentrop read the demand to Henderson on the night of the thirtieth but declared that it was already out of date since no plenipotentiary had arrived from Poland during the day.

By the thirty-first the negotiations ceased. Hitler wanted his war. In the evening some S.S. men faked a border incident which was used as one of the pretexts for armed action. At dawn on September 1, 1939, the German army and air force crossed the Polish frontier. World War II had begun. Later that day Hitler drove through an unenthusiastic Berlin to address the Reichstag and declare that the war had started and that he was "the first soldier of the German Reich." He nominated Goering and then Hess to succeed him in case of his death.

Even at this juncture Hitler hoped that Britain would back down, an opinion which was supported by Ribbentrop. Instead, on the morning of September 3 Sir Nevile Henderson handed an ultimatum to Hitler, stating that if German troops did not withdraw from Poland in a matter of hours, Great Britain would declare war. Shortly afterward the French ambassador arrived with a similar note. There was no question of a withdrawal from Poland, so on that day for the second time in twenty-five years the lights went out all over Europe.

CHAPTER XXXIII

World War II. The Victorious Phase (1939-42)

In 1870 and in 1914 the German armies marching off to fight were accompanied with enthusiasm, bands, speeches, and parades. Those wars were popular and welded the population into a unit prepared to do its share willingly and with gusto. This situation did not obtain in 1939. Tears, quiet, a deep seriousness—such was the atmosphere of Berlin and the other German cities. There were still too many alive who remembered the privations and horrors twenty years before and who could not help but believe that Britain and France were the same formidable foes of yore. The Nazi leadership was dismayed at this attitude, and Goebbels had to account for it by talking of the spiritual maturity of the Nazi-trained people.

Good news came, however, from the front in Poland. The lightning war (blitzkrieg) tactics worked out by the Germans were put into effect almost like an operation in a textbook. The German air force wiped out the Polish aviation in a few days and caused terror and destruction in its attacks on military objectives and large cities alike. Speedy mechanized units of tanks and armored cars raced ahead of the infantry and neutralized much Polish territory, simply bypassing the centers of heavy defense. This was a war of movement, not of position. There was no time or desire to dig in. Within little more than a week the Polish army was disorganized and demoralized. Centers of resistance stood heroically, notably Warsaw and the Hela Peninsula on the bay of Danzig, but the later weeks of the campaign constituted simply a mopping-up operation. The Polish leaders escaped to the south through Romania, and before a month had elapsed the Polish state ceased to exist.

In accordance with the secret provisions of the treaty signed in Moscow, the Red army entered Poland on September 17, 1939. It advanced from the east without opposition and joined its German friends at approximately the line established in the treaty. Ribbentrop flew a second time to Moscow to settle the details. He found that Stalin had stiffened in his attitude a good bit and now demanded that Lithuania be placed within the Soviet sphere of influence. The Germans were willing to agree to any Russian demands, and the two powers drew up a new line of demarcation. The Germans reintegrated into Germany proper all the territories (Upper Silesia, Posen, West Prussia, and Danzig) which had formed part of Germany before 1918. The remainder of Poland, an area roughly the same as the old "Congress Poland" of the nineteenth century, was organized under the name of the Government General, a state dependent on Germany and without any native government. Its capital was moved from Warsaw to Cracow, and it was placed under the brutal control of Hans Frank and the S.S. Immediately the familiar story of terror, torture, and fear began; thousands of Poles, Christian and Jewish, were arrested and placed in camps. The Germans had not the slightest sympathy for the Poles, whom they considered a barbarous race. The plight of Poland was tragic in the extreme and has probably been best told in John Hersey's poignant and brilliant novel, *The Wall* (New York: Knopf, 1950).

There was little or nothing that Britain and France could do to help Poland directly, given the attitude of the Soviet Union. The British sent an expeditionary force to France and placed it under the unified command of the French general, Maurice Gamelin. The two armies settled into the heavily fortified Maginot line facing Germany. The French tried a minor offensive into the Saar region, but soon withdrew. On October 6, after the conquest of Poland, Hitler in a speech in the Reichstag invited Britain and France to withdraw from a futile war, since the Polish question was settled once and for all. However, both Chamberlain and Daladier announced their intention to persist.

The period from October 1939 to April 1940 was one of almost complete quiet on land. Some called it the Phony War, others the *Sitzkrieg.* The British and French armies were entrenched behind the Maginot line, the Germans behind the West Wall or Siegfried line. They fired a few shots at each other every day, but undertook nothing of importance. The general feeling seemed to be that this would be a war of economic attrition in which the vastly superior industrial resources of the western allies would prove decisive. This attitude neglected the impressive preparations which the Germans had made and also the fact that Germany was not nearly so isolated in 1939 as she had been in 1914. Now she had access to Russia and through Russia to the Far East.

The interest of the early months of the war lies mainly in the war at sea. Hitler lost no time in getting his submarines into action. In fact, on the first day of the war the Germans sank the British passenger liner "Athenia" and revived memories of the "Lusitania." During September and October the Germans sank two major British naval vessels—one of them, the "Royal Oak," in Scapa Flow itself, the British base in the Orkney Islands. Most impressive was the career of the German pocket battleship, "Admiral Graf Spee," which broke out to the open sea and, after destroying a good deal of British tonnage, was finally caught and pursued by several British vessels off the east coast of South America. She put in to the harbor of Montevideo, where her crew scuttled her in order to avoid capture.

Hitler was more active than his armies during the winter of 1939–40. He had made up his mind to open a heavy offensive in the west as soon as possible. His eventual aim was to achieve "living space" for Germany in the east, and he did not lose sight of the attack on Russia which had to come sooner or later. Yet at the moment, spurred on by his success in Poland, he found himself in the happy position of being temporarily secure in the east. Thus he had to behave properly toward the Soviets and to sit back while they reduced the three little Baltic republics to dependent status and opened war on the Nordic Finns. This was not palatable to Germany; neither was the Italian attitude, which was very suspicious of the Russian friendship. Mussolini dared to be sharply critical of the *Führer* in these months. The need for action in the west appeared urgent. So from November dates were set for the attack planned against the Netherlands, Belgium, Luxemburg, and France, dates which were always postponed. Hitler seemed to be very fearful of assassination; since he considered himself indispensable, this was a serious matter— especially after a bomb, probably placed by the Nazis themselves to increase Hitler's popularity, exploded a few minutes after he left the old beer hall in Munich on November 8. The generals did not share Hitler's enthusiasm for an attack on the west. They were fearful of French superiority and very much worried about the outcome. It was from this time that Hitler's scorn of the military mentality seems to have dated. In any case, the attack was postponed because of the bad weather that winter.

In early 1940 a new idea captured Hitler's imagination. It seems to have originated with Admiral Raeder. Raeder was dismayed that the war had broken out before the German navy had completed its building program. He was also unhappy that Germany's geographical position made it relatively easy for the British to bottle up the German fleet. His desire was to acquire naval bases on the northern coast of Norway, less accessible to British power. Control of Norway, he reasoned, would also ensure the vital shipments of Swedish iron ore via the Norwegian port of Narvik. Vidkun Quisling, leader of the small Norwegian Nazi party, might be counted on for assistance. Hitler approved the idea right away and appointed General Falkenhorst to work out the details.

On the morning of April 9, 1940, German troops occupied Denmark without any opposition. King Christian X bowed before superior force and ordered no resistance. Denmark maintained her own organs of government but operated under a German military occupation.

The same morning German naval and air units appeared at the main Norwegian ports, where they met British units which were mining Norwegian territorial waters to stop the ore shipments. The Germans suffered severe losses but not enough to endanger the operation. In Oslo Quisling's attempted coup was a failure, but German troops seized control of the city. King Haakon VII and his son, Crown Prince Olav, retreated with their army into the north where they tried to hold off the Germans. On April 14 British troops started to land at various points in central and northern Norway, but the Germans maintained control of the air and in early May the British had to withdraw from everywhere except Narvik. Here they remained for another month under relentless attack, but in early June had to retire. The Germans tried to set up a native Norwegian government under Quisling; when this failed, they appointed a *Gauleiter,* Josef Terboven, who ran the country with the help of the German military and police. The king and his son escaped to London, where they set up a government in exile. The British sense of humiliation from the Norwegian campaign led to the fall of the Chamberlain cabinet and the appointment, on May 10, of Winston Churchill as prime minister.

Hitler, of course, was delighted at this campaign which, inexpensive in men and materials, had so profitably extended his base of operations. There could be no further talk of delay. The attack on the west was scheduled for early May.

On the morning of May 10 German forces swept into Holland, Belgium, and Luxemburg under the pretext that they were simply forestalling the Allies. The events of the next six weeks have been told and retold, and yet the imagination is staggered by the nightmarish quality surrounding the fall of France. The German plan was not markedly different from the Schlieffen Plan of 1914, except that this time there were light, highly mobile, mechanized units which could dash ahead of the infantry, and also quantities of bomber and fighter planes which could bombard, strafe, and demoralize the civilian population. In spite of efforts to flood their canals, the Dutch were able to hold out for only five days. Queen Wilhelmina, the Dutch gold reserve, and most of the Dutch navy sought refuge in England. Belgium resisted a bit longer, although her great fort of Eben Emael fell in a day. Four French armies raced north to help the Belgians, but French equipment was no match for the new equipment and tactics of the Germans. Probably the most important moment in the campaign was the breakthrough of the principal German mechanized army under General Kleist at the Ardennes Forest, which the French had thought would be a formidable obstacle. On May 28 King Leopold surrendered himself and the Belgian army.

The German army entered France at several points, including historic Sédan, spreading out over the terrain like a gigantic hand. One finger swept along the Channel coast cutting off from the bulk of the French nearly all the British army and a number of French units, which retreated to the only available port, Dunkirk. Here occurred the extraordinary and heroic evacuation of almost three hundred fifty thousand British, French, and miscellaneous refugees, stripped of their equipment but rescued to fight again.

Paul Reynaud, who had succeeded Daladier as premier earlier in the spring, dismissed Gamelin and appointed General Weygand. He also reformed his cabinet and appointed Marshal Pétain, the aged hero of Verdun, as vice-premier. The government moved from Paris to Tours and then to Bordeaux. Paris was declared an open city and surrendered on June 14, 1940. The Maginot line was turned. The battle of France was over.

It was at this moment that Mussolini, sure of an easy victory, in a particularly squalid gesture abandoned his policy of neutrality and came into the war against France and Britain on June 10. This action made no difference to the immediate outcome. Reynaud resigned on the sixteenth and was succeeded by Pétain, who immediately asked for an armistice.

It was typical of Hitler's vindictive personality that he chose as the spot for the armistice to be signed the same place where the armistice of 1918 was signed and indeed the same railway dining car in which Foch had dictated to Erzberger. There on June 22 Hitler experienced possibly his most exhilarating moment. The armistice terms were strict but not overwhelming. More than half of France, including both the Channel and Atlantic coasts, was to be occupied by the Germans. The only concession Hitler made was that he promised not to use the French navy in the war. Pétain and his government retired to the little resort city of Vichy, where they reorganized the French state in a conservative sense and maintained a policy of collaboration with the victors. Hitler visited Paris, went to the top of the Eiffel Tower, and stood in awe before the tomb of Napoleon. Some days later he created a new rank of *Reichsmarschall* for

Goering and promoted a number of his generals to field marshal. His speech on that occasion included a "final" invitation to Great Britain to get out of the war.

Hitler seems to have been aggrieved that the British did not follow the French example of surrender. He permitted almost a month to elapse after the French armistice before he signed the order for operation Sea Lion, the code name for the invasion of Britain. As always, his preoccupation was with the east. He had thought of the campaign in the west simply as a means to free his rear to carry out the major warfare against the Soviet Union. France was now defeated; by all the rules Britain should surrender. However, the British did not oblige, and, in fact, Churchill's speeches became more determined and more bellicose than ever. The only alternative was to cross the Channel and defeat the British on their own home island.

The Germans envisaged this invasion with very little enthusiasm. In particular, the navy was worried. It had suffered serious damage in the invasion of Norway and was far from optimum strength. It was not equipped with much in the way of self-propelled landing craft. It would have to depend on towed barges across a very rough stretch of water toward an enemy which would not be surprised and which was full of high morale for resistance. The only possibility for success lay in the achievement of absolute superiority in the air. Thus everything depended on the *Luftwaffe*. The invasion date was at first set for August 15; the air attack was to begin a week earlier.

On August 8 Goering launched his *Luftwaffe* into the battle of Britain, concentrating at first on the south coast of England, the eventual invasion point, and some days later shifting the main impact to R.A.F. bases, aircraft factories, and defense installations. The resistance of the R.A.F. to the German attack has been sung time and again and has become legendary in military history. Although there was exaggeration on both sides, the fact is that the R.A.F. prevented the *Luftwaffe* from controlling the air over England. The Germans shifted their target again to London and began the intensive grueling raids over the British capital which lasted all through the following autumn and winter. However, the danger of invasion was over. The date for the operation was postponed until October, when it was put off until 1941. In fact, it was shelved and never seriously thought of again. The raids continued on the off-chance that they might force a decision in Britain. In any case the planes, otherwise unemployed, could certainly cause serious damage to the British and lower their morale.

By the fall of 1940 the friendship with Russia was wearing thin, and the Russians were achieving entirely too much to please the Germans.

During the French campaign the Russians quietly annexed Estonia, Latvia, and Lithuania. They also demanded and obtained from Romania the cession of Bessarabia and northern Bukovina. Once again affairs in the Balkans were leading to serious rivalry between Germany and Russia. Hitler had no notion of letting the Soviets entrench themselves in areas which he considered part of the German living space. A straw in the wind was the ceremonious signature on September 27, 1940, of the Tripartite Pact among Germany, Italy, and Japan, calling for mutual aid if a presently nonbelligerent power should attack one of them. The Soviet Union was explicitly excepted from this provision; the pact seemed to be directed against the United States, but it did not please the Russians.

It is puzzling to decide exactly when Hitler resolved on his attack on the Soviet Union. He was the sort of man who likes to play with alternative possibilities until the last minute. In any case, there was no possibility of attacking Russia until the following spring. In November Molotov visited Berlin at German invitation. The *Führer* grandly described to him a future in which the world would be divided among Germany, Italy, Japan, and Russia, and tried to get Molotov interested in rosy pictures of a future Soviet expansion south to the Persian Gulf and maybe India. The hardheaded Molotov replied with factual questions about such nearby places as Finland, Sweden, and Bulgaria, and indicated Russian discontent at German activities in the Balkans. Ribbentrop handed Molotov a draft treaty dividing up the Eastern Hemisphere. Molotov took it to Moscow but gave little expectation that it would find favor there. Stalin, to everyone's surprise, was interested and sent a letter to Berlin asking for fuller details. Perhaps he, too, was stalling for time. It does not really matter, for the Germans never answered this letter. Hitler had made up his mind. By December 18, 1940, the plan for the invasion of Russia, whose code name was Barbarossa, was ready and approved.

This plan called for a gigantic push along a front reaching from Finland to the Black Sea. It became important, therefore, to ensure the loyalty of the Balkan states. Romania was the first sufferer. She had already lost territory to Russia, and King Carol announced his solidarity with Germany. Yet worse was to come. Romania had to part with land to Bulgaria; moreover, in August 1940 at Vienna Ribbentrop in a lordly way handed down the Vienna Award, by which Romania was forced to relinquish to Hungary a large part of the gains she had made in the Treaty of Trianon in 1919. The result was that King Carol abdicated, and Romania fell under a military dictatorship subservient to Germany. In November 1940 Hungary, Slovakia, and Romania adhered to the Tripartite Pact, and early in 1941 Bulgaria followed suit. Only Yugoslavia remained out of the system, but this appeared to be only a matter of time because the government of Prince Paul, regent for his young nephew, Peter II, was very pro-German. The Yugoslavs adhered to the Tripartite Pact on March 25, 1941. The only obstacle that seemed to be in Germany's way arose from the visit of the Japanese foreign minister, Matsuoka, to Berlin in the spring of 1941. He received rather casual treatment from the Germans, but Hitler promised that if Japan became involved in a war with the United States, Germany would stand by her. The bombshell was thrown, however, when Matsuoka, on his way back to Japan, stopped at Moscow and signed a nonaggression treaty with the old enemy of the Japanese, the Soviet Union. This served notice to Hitler that he could not expect Japanese help in his invasion of Russia. The Japanese did not want to have their hands tied in Siberia when their ambitions were directed against the United States, Britain, France, and the Netherlands.

Hitler's timetable for the spring of 1941 was upset mainly as a result of Mussolini's precipitate action. In October 1940, against the advice of his generals, he invaded Greece through Albania. The result was pitiful. The Greeks not only held off the Italians but actually pushed them back into Albanian territory. At the same time the British repulsed an Italian invasion of Egypt and drove them well back into their colony of Libya. Hitler was disgusted at the ineptitude of the Italians and did not plan to pull their chestnuts out of the fire. However, he did permit a force under the command of Erwin Rommel to cross to North Africa to train for African fighting. This was the origin of the famous *Afrika Korps,* which eventually took over the command in North Africa from the Italians.

In early 1941 Hitler began to consider the necessity of invading Greece to free Europe of any foothold for British troops, even though this might postpone the invasion of Russia. The British made the difficult decision of reinforcing Greece at the expense of their own undermanned army in Libya. This decided Hitler to invade Greece through Bulgaria. However, the unforeseen occurred. A few days after Yugoslavia adhered to the Tripartite Pact, a military coup in Belgrade overthrew the pro-German government of Prince Paul and installed young King Peter on the throne with an anti-German ministry. The Soviet reaction to this was most instructive. The Russians signed a treaty of nonaggression and friendship with the new government. The Nazi-Soviet pact was clearly a thing of the past.

Hitler was, of course, furious at these developments; his reply was immediate. On April 6 the Germans bombed Belgrade and invaded Yugoslavia and Greece both from the north and through Bulgaria, where German troops were assembled. Yugoslavia capitulated after little more than a week. The Greeks, aided by British reinforcements, held out longer, but by the end of April the British and Greek armies had to evacuate the mainland and try to defend Crete. In late May the Germans launched an amphibious attack on Crete and conquered the island in about ten days. At the same time Rommel pushed the British back into Egypt. Except for the loss of the largest German battleship, the "Bismarck," in the North Atlantic, it seemed a triumphant spring for Germany. However, it did not become clear until much later that the Balkan campaign, which forced the Germans to postpone their invasion of Russia for five or six weeks, might have been decisive in this much greater effort—for if anything is determinant in an invasion of Russia, it is the weather.

Military preparations for the invasion of Russia had been going on since late 1940. By the spring of 1941 the German armies were lined up along the eastern boundaries ready to spring. Plans were co-ordinated with Finland to provide for a simultaneous "reopening" of the Russo-Finnish war in the north and with the Romanians, who were prepared to march in the south to regain Bessarabia. Political preparations were made too. In March Himmler, in his function as *Reichsführer* S.S., was given almost unlimited political authority in the territories to be conquered to effect the change from Communism. This was the legal basis for the frightful crimes of the future. A month later Hitler appointed the party ideologist, Alfred Rosenberg, commissioner for the eastern occupied areas. To these contradictory arrangements must be added the responsibilities of the army in the operational areas. The groundwork was thus laid for the foolish ineptitude and frightful brutality of German behavior in occupied Russia.

The most bizarre prelude to the attack on Russia occurred on May 10 when Rudolf Hess, Hitler's beloved old party comrade, piloted himself from an air base in Germany to a field in Scotland, where he claimed to be looking for the duke of Hamilton. The world will probably never know just what was in Hess's mind, which has lacked lucidity ever since. He seems to have convinced himself that when Germany attacked Russia, Britain would reverse herself and join the Germans in the anti-Communist crusade, and that he could warn the right-wing forces in Britain to be ready. Hitler was shocked at the defection of his old friend. In the party councils Martin Bormann took over Hess's former functions and became one of the most powerful Nazis in the years to come.

Hitler launched his great attack on the morning of June 22, 1941, without official warning. On that day along a front of over a thousand miles Finnish, Romanian, and German planes, tanks, and infantry were set in action. Along with the military action came confident predictions by Goebbels and his assistants that the Soviet Union would be crushed in a matter of weeks. These promises were constantly repeated, and by October the world was told that the Soviet Union was in fact defeated. Yet there was no Russian request for peace.

It is difficult to describe the epic magnitude of the German campaigns in Russia where no less than nine million men were deployed at a single time. This was no old-fashioned warfare in which the movements of an army can be followed by a pencil line on a map, nor was it the warfare of 1914–18 in which the shifting front can be indicated by lines moved back and forth. There really was no front. Sometimes the "front" was many miles in depth where rapidly moving units bypassed strong points, where air attacks were miles removed from infantry fighting, where pockets of resistance held out sometimes for months. It was the French campaign enlarged many times; it was an elemental struggle of vastly powerful and complex forces locked in combat unto death. The author had the official responsibility for many months of following this front from day to day and never felt that he could visualize it; how then to describe it in retrospect?

For a number of weeks it looked as if Hitler's optimistic prediction about the duration of the fighting were accurate. Within about a month the Germans swept through the defenses the Russians had constructed in the areas they had gained since 1939 and went into Russia proper. From week to week the names of cities captured were spread across the communiqués: Smolensk, Novgorod, Kiev, Kharkov, Orel, and Rostov, to name only a few of the larger ones. By late fall the Germans had advanced about six hundred miles. Together with the Finns, they had encircled Leningrad. They were within a few miles of Moscow itself, and the Russian government offices were moved to Kuibyshev on the Volga. Goebbels seemed to be right.

The world now knows that these months were not so easy for the Germans as they looked at the time. Hitler was so fascinated by the progress of his forces that he began to conceive of himself as one of the master military minds of all times. He spent most of his time for the rest of his life at his headquarters in the east and constantly interfered in the decisions of his generals, whom he often treated with scorn. There was a real difference of opinion in the autumn of 1941 when Hitler ordered concentration on the industrial areas in the Ukraine, while the generals wanted to center their attention on the capture of Moscow. More important was the weather. As the autumn wore on toward winter, the soldiers started to suffer frightfully. They were not outfitted with cold-weather equipment. The high command expected the campaign to be over before it would be necessary. By November the snows had started, daylight was brief, and one of the severest winters in years set in. In the early days of December the Germans, within sight of the towers of Moscow, made a desperate effort to capture the capital before they had to cease fighting, but failed in their attempt.

Worse was in store. Immediately after the Germans had ended their offensive, the Russians with about a hundred fresh divisions opened a counteroffensive which lasted throughout the winter and not only relieved Moscow but pushed the Nazis back a considerable distance on the central front. The importance of this lay not only in the actual achievement but also in the fact that it was the first time in the war that the Germans had suffered a setback, which showed that the Russians were far from defeat.

Hitler's reaction was rapid. He ordered his soldiers to stand firm and dispute every step with the enemy. Now the Germans had to retreat over barren wasteland, which the Russians had burned in their original withdrawal. Many thought of Napoleon's retreat in 1812. Yet in spite of the most lamentable suffering the Germans did not break, and in the spring of 1942, reinforced by new levies from home and from satellite lands, were ready for a new offensive. Sometime later every soldier who had been in Russia in the winter of 1941–42 was declared eligible for a new medal, which German slang called the "frozen meat" medal. The propaganda ministry whined in complaint to God Who had decreed such a severe winter; it also complained that the Soviets had not informed the world of their immense reserve manpower.

One of the most important results of the Soviet counteroffensive was a shift in the high command of the army. Hitler blamed most of the misfortunes of the army on the generals and in early 1942 dismissed the commander in chief, Brauchitsch, as well as other important generals, including Rundstedt, Leeb, and Guderian. In addition to his title of commander in chief of the armed forces, he made himself commander in chief of the army. From this point on Hitler was in daily immediate command of the forces. Since the war the German generals in their memoirs have lamented this development. Most of them agree that Hitler had a sort of intuitive genius which was often of great importance, but they blame him for a lack of detailed training and also for a careless refusal to enter into the details of administration.

In December 1941 another event occurred which was in the long run to prove decisive in the defeat of Germany. This was, of course, the entry of the United States into the war. This is not the place to describe the gradual American drift toward war between 1939 and 1941. That subject has been combed thoroughly, and some parts of it are still unsettled. By 1941 the United States was helping Great Britain and the other anti-Nazi powers through the technique of lend-lease. In 1941 the

Allies lost over four million tons of merchant shipping, mostly in the Atlantic and mainly to German submarines. This brought the war home to Americans. However, affairs in the Far East seemed to concern the United States most, and it was the Japanese attack on Pearl Harbor on December 7, 1941, which pushed the United States into the war.

One of the extraordinary aspects of German behavior at this moment is the cavalier, and indeed casual, attitude which Hitler, Goebbels, and others took at the prospect of American intervention. One is reminded of 1917. The Germans seemed to think that the United States would be so occupied in her struggle with Japan that she would have little or no energy left to help Britain and Russia in the war against Germany. They also thought that the United States was simply a flabby, luxurious, materialistic democracy, which in time of trial would prove as rotten as France or Britain from the German view. On December 11 Hitler went to the Reichstag and gave a violent speech devoted mainly to personal attacks on President Roosevelt and the American Jews. He stood by his promise to Japan and declared war on the United States.

By the end of 1941 things looked bad for the Allies. The victories of the Axis since 1939 had been stupendous and unimagined. They were to be further immensely increased by the conquests of the Japanese in the next few months. However, in the broader picture the whole situation had changed. The Axis wantonly called down upon itself forces against which it would be ultimately powerless. However, it was going to take more than three years of bitter warfare before this truth was brought home to the *Führer*.

CHAPTER XXXIV

World War II. The Defeat Looms (1942-45)

The home front did not constitute a serious problem for the shapers of public opinion in Germany until after the first campaign against Russia. The brevity of the Polish and Norwegian campaigns, and even more, the colossal and relatively easy victory over France, seemed to bear out Hitler's contention of the superior qualities of the Germans and specifically of Germans led by the Nazi movement. In Germany there was not much distress. Food supplies remained sufficient for a normal diet, and the government's prudence in stockpiling strategic raw materials assured a constant flow of munitions. In fact, after the defeat of France Germany received a supply of luxury items such as she had not seen for years. Soldiers on leave in Paris and other French towns sent home silk stockings, perfumes, wines, and women's clothing of a far superior quality to anything that German austerity had produced. All this gave to the war a sort of Alice in Wonderland quality which blinded the German people to possible dangers in the future. Even the beginning of British air raids over German cities, relatively ineffective at first, did not hurt German morale particularly, though it did serve to reduce Goering's prestige.

The situation changed rapidly after the attack on Russia. In the first place, the invasion itself was a shock. After the Nazi-Soviet treaty of 1939 radio and newspapers told of the new friendship for the Soviet government and the Russian people. This line continued right into the spring of 1941, so that the Germans were psychologically unprepared for the new war. After June 22 the German propagandists discounted Soviet power and promised a victory as cheap and complete as the earlier ones. Even the German leadership seems to have succumbed to this over-optimism. As the months wore on and Moscow was still not captured, the truth gradually began to dawn. Casualty lists became longer and more tragic. At first Goebbels blamed the setback on the abnormally early and severe winter, but soon he had to pay tribute to Russian might. At about the same time Germany's supplies of accumulated materials began to run short. The usual wartime nuisances—delays in transportation, failures of consumer goods, and reliance on substitutes—began to make their appearance. By early 1942 the honeymoon period of the war was over, and Germany entered a period of sacrifice and austerity. The bright, shiny façade of the Nazi state became tarnished and eventually grimy and squalid.

In the first weeks of 1942 the German government decreed a national emergency program to repair at least some of the shortages and failures which had made their appearance simultaneously. In February the minister of armaments, Fritz Todt, whose reputation was largely connected with the construction of the great German highway system, the *Autobahnen,* was killed in an airplane accident. Hitler replaced him with one of his wisest appointments, Albert Speer, until that time the *Führer's* architect, with whom he had planned vast remodeling of Berlin and other German cities. Speer proved himself an extremely efficient administrator and became almost a dictator in the economic sphere.

Obviously one of the most pressing problems was the supply of labor. As the fighting continued, the demand for more and more recruits for the *Wehrmacht* developed. It was necessary to conserve skilled workers in strategic industry and keep them from becoming cannon fodder. In March 1942 a new office was established, the commissioner general for labor supply. Its head was Fritz Sauckel, *Gauleiter* of Thuringia, who in the course of time became an absolute dictator for labor problems. Together, he and Speer ran the German economy. It is interesting to note which leading Nazis retained their power and importance during the trying years of war. Of the old names, Himmler and Goebbels increased in power and importance until by the end of the war Himmler was second only to Hitler. Others, notably Goering, declined in stature. The significant new men were Bormann, Speer, and Sauckel.

Sauckel immediately undertook an elaborate campaign to use the available labor force as efficiently as possible. Women were encouraged to go into industry and agriculture for the first time. A hierarchy of essential services was established. All sorts of programs to increase the output of the individual worker were undertaken. Perhaps most important, the importation of foreign laborers was started. They came from all over German Europe. By late 1942 there were several million foreign workers in Germany; by the end of the war, over five million. At first there was an effort to treat these people in terms of their racial provenance, from the favored Nordics to the despised *Ostarbeiter* ("workers from the east"). Nevertheless, their working conditions and lives were in general deplorable. They were the slave laborers who later bcame the tragic displaced persons of the years after the war. Germany became a welter of industry, propaganda, and personal tragedy.

The military events of 1942 can be grouped under three general headings: submarine warfare, desert warfare in North Africa, and the Russian campaign. During that year the Allies lost close to eight million tons of shipping to the Axis, three-quarters of it in the Atlantic and six-sevenths as a result of submarine attack. This was the most urgent problem for the United States and Britain. Admiral Karl Doenitz, commander of submarines, established for himself a reputation as one of the greatest naval commanders of all time. Later he was to replace Grand Admiral Raeder as commander in chief of the navy.

In North Africa General Rommel led his *Afrika Korps* and its Italian allies in a powerful offensive against the British. It reached El Alamein, dangerously close to Alexandria and Cairo, where the Germans stopped and allowed British General Montgomery a period to reform and re-equip his army, mostly with American supplies which began to arrive in large amounts.

The German command decided that the campaign of 1942 in Russia would be fought in the southern sector, perhaps with the initial objective of the Russian Caucasus oil fields and the eventual aim of encircling central Russia from the southeast. In May and June Generals Manstein, Bock, and Kleist undertook a ferocious campaign which started as auspiciously as the first attack the year before. The Crimea, the industrially important eastern Ukraine, and the Kuban steppes were captured. The right wing of the German army pushed rapidly to the southeast and reached as far as the Maikop oil fields, almost to the Caspian Sea. By August the left wing had reached the Volga in the neighborhood of the city of Stalingrad. There one of the most important battles of the war and of history was to be fought, but first the Germans paused to regroup and take a breathing spell.

By the autumn of 1942 German conquest reached its fullest extent. It was reasonable at that time to speak of German Europe. On the continent only Switzerland, Sweden, Turkey, and the Iberian Peninsula were maintaining a precarious neutrality; the coast of North Africa eastward well into Egypt was under Axis control. Hitler controlled more of Europe at this moment than anyone since the days of the Roman Empire.

This vast territory became the laboratory for what Hitler liked to describe as the "new order in Europe." It is not easy to describe the new order briefly because here as everywhere in Nazism there was no uniform philosophy. The Nazis were opportunistic and variant in their treatment of the conquered areas. There was some effort given to observing a racial hierarchy: conquered Nordics were treated better than conquered Latins or Slavs. Strategic, geographical considerations also determined in part the treatment of these areas.

Some territories were annexed into Greater Germany proper. These were lands occupied mainly by Germans or which had belonged to Germany before 1919. Among them were Austria, the Sudetenland, Posen (called the Wartheland), Danzig, West Prussia, Memel, Alsace-Lorraine, Luxemburg, Eupen-Malmédy, and parts of Slovenia. Cleansed of their foreign populations, these areas were to be part of the German core of the new Europe. The typical administrative process was to erect *Reichsgaue,* districts in which the government and the party leadership were merged, which had never been accomplished completely in Germany.

The protectorate of Bohemia-Moravia and the Government General were in a unique category. Their populations were technically part of Greater Germany but without the privileges of German citizenship. These areas were dependent territories. Here the Germans unleashed a particularly ferocious reign of terror designed to eliminate all educated people, who were potential forces of resistance. The future assigned for them was colonial, useful only to provide unskilled workers for the glory of Germany. They were left to the mercies of such tyrants as Hans Frank and Reinhard Heydrich with the support of the S.S. police organization.

Some areas were placed under military occupation. In this group were Belgium, Occupied France, Serbia, Macedonia, Crete, and parts of the conquered Soviet territory. Here the German police co-operated with the army in maintaining the peace of the grave, and recruited thousands for work in Germany.

In some places there was a mixed military and civilian occupation, sometimes with the aid of natives who were willing to collaborate with the Germans. Denmark, which the Germans tried to make into the ideal occupied state, was an example of this sort of control. So were Norway, the Netherlands (where Seyss-Inquart supervised a collaborationist government), and Unoccupied France. The lands conquered from Russia were a variant of this form, except that no natives took part in the control. Rosenberg, as minister for eastern occupied territories, established two commissariats, Ostland and the Ukraine, which were headed by two *Gauleiter.*

Italy was permitted to occupy some territories in France, Yugoslavia, and Greece. The satellite states—Hungary, Romania, Bulgaria, and Finland—each received increases of territory.

Territory Annexed and Occupied by Germany, 1942

Annexed Territory   Occupied Territory

Economically, every effort was made to despoil the conquered areas. In each case after conquest there was immediate seizure of assets. Jewish possessions were confiscated. An enormous amount of booty was transported to Germany. The nations were forced to pay the expenses of their own occupation. It is difficult to know just how the Germans intended eventually to organize Europe. They themselves probably did not know, except for some vague concept that the periphery of Europe would have the function of supplying raw materials to be manufactured in Germany for the benefit of the Germans. There was a good deal of talk in books and periodicals of *Grossraumwirtschaft* ("the economics of great space"), but much of it seems to have been the merest theorizing.

In the short run, except for the labor force which Germany recruited from the occupied countries, she did not receive the economic aid from them which she had counted on. This is particularly true of the Ukraine, which she hoped would solve her food problems. Removal of labor, resistance, sabotage, and the brutal treatment by the victors were all factors which militated against the usefulness of these areas. Except for industry close to Germany proper or for certain individual plants like the Phillips electrical works at Eindhoven, Holland, the Germans did not put the industrial machine of Europe to work at anything like its full capacity while the war was going on. Apparently it proved too hard a task to achieve. In other words, the new order never really came into existence.

The latter years of the war witnessed the culmination of German barbarism. This aspect of the struggle is intimately associated with the name of Heinrich Himmler, who in addition to his other functions became commissioner for the strengthening of Germanism and, late in the war, minister of the interior. He was in charge of the policy of Germanization. This was simply a euphemism for the destruction of all those whom the Germans considered inferior and the transplanting of good racial Germans into the cleared areas. The most tragic and virulent part of Himmler's work was the almost incredible drive to exterminate the entire Jewish people, a program lightly described as the "final settlement of the Jewish question." The German Jews had been almost wiped out or imprisoned before the war. Now it was the turn of the much larger Jewish populations of Poland, western Russia, and the Balkans. This was the worst period of tortures, hangings, mass shootings, gassings, and extermination camps. The accounts of these diabolic activities must not be considered as simply wartime atrocity stories. Their documentation is beyond question. In fact, they must be considered understatements, because words and statistics are unable to convey a full account of such unprecedented human misery. Probably not since the time of Tamerlane has a conqueror been so brutal and inhuman as the Nazi conqueror.

The autumn of 1942 is generally considered to be the turning point of the war. At several widely distant spots events occurred that were to have important consequences. The first took place on October 23, when General Montgomery opened a major offensive against Rommel's forces at El Alamein in Egypt. It was a triumphant success. The British pushed on across North Africa until by early 1943 the Germans and Italians were forced out of Libya and into Tunisia.

On November 7, 1942, a large force of American and British troops landed at a number of points along the coasts of Algeria and Morocco without serious opposition. The plan was to consolidate possession of these territories and then advance eastward to take Rommel's German and Italian troops from the west while Montgomery was pushing them from the east. After a good deal of initial hesitation, resulting probably from inexperience, the plan was successful; by May 1943 the last Axis soldiers departed from African territory.

Far more impressive to the Germans at the moment was the tremendous and sanguinary battle of Stalingrad. The German army reached that neighborhood in the late summer of 1942 and started an attack on the city which lasted until November, when the Red army passed from the defensive to the offensive and launched the greatest battle of the war. The streets of Stalingrad and the waters of the Volga ran red with blood. The Russians succeeded in surrounding a large part of the German forces under the command of General F. Paulus. General Manstein, the senior group commander, tried to pierce his way through to the isolated units but without success. Hitler ordered Paulus to stand firm, and the bitter fighting dragged on through the frozen months of December and January. On January 31 Paulus could hold out no longer and surrendered himself and the remains of his forces, which numbered close to one hundred fifty thousand men.

It was not only in the neighborhood of Stalingrad that the Russians attacked. All along the southern half of the front they went on the offensive; by the spring of the new year the Germans, who had retreated steadily but stubbornly, found themselves approximately where they had been a year before. The Germans never managed to launch a general offensive again. For the rest of the war they were on the defensive, both in Russia and the west.

Stalingrad came as an appalling shock to the German population. When Paulus' surrender was announced, the government ordered a period of national mourning; for days German radio stations played only elegiac Wagnerian music. Goebbels and Sauckel tried to make a victory out of the defeat, as the British had done after Dunkirk, by calling on the German people for even greater sacrifices than they were already making. They decreed a total mobilization of labor, presumably even more complete than that of a year before. New comb-outs of manpower were ordered, and each German was expected to give unstintedly of his time, energy, and possessions. The bitter period of the war for Germany had begun, for in addition to the tragedies on the Russian front, the British and Americans were constantly increasing their air attacks on German cities, which wrought havoc in production, and even more, in transportation and morale.

The Germans made one last attempt at an offensive in Russia in July 1943. They launched a heavy attack on the central front near Kursk. However, the Soviets also had planned a thrust in the same general area and had built up their forces. The two great armies locked; after about a week of stubborn fighting the German impetus lessened and the Soviets assumed the offensive, which they maintained for the rest of the year. The German army retreated stubbornly according to plan, without panic, and selling dearly every inch of land; it was in this retreat that General Manstein proved himself one of the ablest German leaders. However, gradually the roll call of towns recaptured from the Germans became familiar through the daily Soviet communiqués. By the end of the year the Russians had liberated almost all of the Soviet Union as it had existed in 1938. The fighting was now in the newly acquired territories which had previously belonged to the three Baltic republics, Poland, and Romania.

In Italy serious developments from the German point of view filled the year 1943. After the British and Americans drove the Germans and Italians out of North Africa, they followed their success by landing a large force on Sicily in July. Within about a month the island was in Allied hands. However, the main development occurred in Rome, where on July 25 King Victor Emmanuel announced the dismissal of Mussolini and the appointment of a new government under Marshal Pietro Badoglio. The new authorities had to face almost immediately an invasion of the Italian mainland, for the Allies started to cross the Straits of Messina in mid-August. In less than a month the king decided that Italy had suffered enough. Accordingly his government offered to surrender to the Allies, and an armistice was announced on September 8.

The Germans reacted immediately. The Allies had hoped that they would be able to occupy most or all of Italy without serious fighting, but they were mistaken. The Germans solidified their control of northern Italy and rescued Mussolini from his prison. He promptly proclaimed a republican government with its headquarters in the north, another puppet state under German control. Field Marshal Kesselring, the German commander in the area, rushed all possible troops southward; after a period of confusion a line was formed across Italy about halfway between Naples and Rome. Here the Allied advance halted throughout the autumn and winter. Bitter fighting ensued, particularly in the neighborhood of the great old Benedictine monastery, Montecassino. It was not until June 1944 that the Allies entered Rome, and August that they entered Florence. A new line was established in the last winter of the war in the mountainous country north of Florence.

The Allies had good reason to be proud of their progress in 1943. Both on the Russian front and in the west great gains were made, and at sea the statistics of German sinkings started to decrease. However, there was still a large reserve of German manpower in France and the Low Countries, which were poised to repulse any Allied landings in that area, the "second front" for which Stalin was so constantly clamoring. During the first months of 1944 the plans were completed for the great invasion under the supreme command of the American general, Dwight D. Eisenhower, while the British and American air forces continued to hammer relentlessly with their air raids on Germany.

The story of the Normandy landings has been told many times, but one cannot but marvel still at the sheer size of the operation and the multiplicity of detail involved. In the early hours of June 6, 1944, the first British and American units landed on French soil. Within a month almost a million equipped men were in northern France. The Germans had guessed that the landings would occur farther east where the Channel is narrower, but they had tried to entrench themselves along the whole coast and gave great publicity to their rapidly constructed fortifications, collectively known as the Atlantic Wall. The commander in the west was Field Marshal Gerd von Rundstedt, under whom was serving the hero of North Africa, Erwin Rommel. However, the German commitments in Russia were too great for them to maintain a sufficient force in the west. This was no longer the German army of several years before.

According to the Allied plan the British held the main weight of the German armor around Caen, while the Americans carried out a successful breakout to the west and south. By the end of August Paris was liberated. In southern France the Allies landed on the Riviera coast on August 15 and pushed northward through the Rhone Valley to meet the main force in the north. The Allied success was staggering in its rapidity, and optimists began to talk of an end to the war in Europe by Christmas. However, the Germans closed their ranks as they approached their own country, and the Allies, whose logistic lines were getting overextended, had to pause. By the end of the year there was still heavy fighting in Belgium and the Netherlands.

The Russians continued their triumphant march across central Europe, synchronizing their thrust with the landings in France. The events were similar to those of 1943. Mile by mile the Soviets advanced and the Germans retreated. In January 1945 Finland, Romania, Bulgaria, and Hungary had all submitted to the Soviet Union, and Russian troops were on German soil in East Prussia. Still Hitler was determined not to give in. He planned instead to make Germany a desert of destruction to serve as his sepulcher.

While these astonishing events were taking place at the front lines, a highly dramatic event occurred within Germany itself. On July 20, 1944, an attempt was made to kill Hitler which narrowly missed success. A young officer, Colonel Claus von Stauffenberg, placed a briefcase containing a bomb against the leg of a table at which Hitler was sitting during a conference at his eastern headquarters in East Prussia. The bomb exploded, but, although four people in the room were killed, the *Führer* suffered only cuts and burns. There were two principal reasons for his escape. It was a hot day, and the conference was held in a flimsy wooden building with open windows instead of the usual underground concrete shelter. Secondly, a moment before the explosion Hitler got up from his chair and walked across the room to look at a map. These two accidents saved his life. Stauffenberg heard the explosion, assumed that Hitler was dead, jumped into a plane, and flew to Berlin to help in the transfer of power to the anti-Nazi group which had planned the attempt.

In Berlin confusion reigned. The military heads of the conspiracy, General Ludwig Beck (chief of staff of the army until 1938) and Field Marshal von Witzleben, appeared at the war ministry, assumed control, and established contact with German army groups throughout Europe to announce the end of Hitler's rule. They had trouble in convincing General Fromm, commander of the home army, that Hitler was dead. Fromm put in a call to Hitler's headquarters and managed to get through, although the conspirators had tried to disrupt communications. He talked to General Keitel, who assured him that the *Führer* was alive and only slightly wounded, but the rebels refused to believe Keitel. Stauffenberg was back in Berlin, where he insisted that the bomb had done its work. The rebels actually surrounded the government quarter of the city with their troops.

The situation was clarified only when a propaganda officer persuaded Major Remer, commander of a guards battalion, to get in touch with Goebbels, who was in Berlin. Goebbels promised Remer that Hitler was alive, and indeed got Hitler on the telephone on his direct line. Hitler orally give Remer and Goebbels plenary power to wipe out the rebels, in spite of Remer's relatively low rank. By the end of the day the conspiracy had failed. That evening a shaky Hitler spoke over the radio to the German people. A wave of suicides, arrests, trials, tortures, and executions took place over the next few months accompanied by a new extreme of ferocity, the more extreme no doubt because it was a death agony. Very few of the conspirators escaped.

As the investigations progressed, the world was amazed at the widespread ramifications of the plot and the length of time it had been simmering. The two principal leaders were Beck and Dr. Karl Goerdeler, ex-mayor of Leipzig. These two were slated to become respectively the military and civilian heads of the new Germany. A surprising number of high-ranking military men were involved. Besides Witzleben and Beck, they included Rommel, Stuelpnagel, and even Admiral Canaris, head of the intelligence service. A special center of disaffection was the command in Paris, where the attempt came closest to success. Among the civilians there were Catholic intellectuals and others, of whom the best known was Ulrich von Hassell, a former ambassador to Italy. Some of the few remaining left-wing leaders were involved. Of the very few who were not executed the best known are Fabian von Schlabrendorff and Hans Gisevius. Some of these men had been in contact as early as 1937 and 1938. They had hoped for victory at the time of the Munich conference, but were dismayed when the west yielded so completely and gave the Nazis another cheap triumph. During the war there were several assassination plots, but only the one of 1944 came within any measurable distance of success.

The mood of Germany in the winter of 1944–45 was desperate. For many months the propaganda ministry had been trying to revive failing spirits with predictions of new secret weapons, so lethal that the enemy would not be able to endure them. Observers were mystified at Allied air attacks on remote spots in Norway or at Peenemünde in the Baltic Sea. Later they were revealed to be experimental stations. A few days after the Normandy landings the Germans launched the first V-1 pilotless plane or "buzzbomb" toward London. This new mysterious weapon caused terrible damage. The Londoners had been free from attack for many months, and the prospect of its renewal brought many close to panic. The summer of 1944 was fraught with terror in the English capital; in fact, some wits talked of going to Normandy for a rest. However, as the Allies conquered more and more of the launching sites for these weapons along the coast of France and Belgium, the attacks lessened, since now the V-1's had to be launched from distant Holland or from the air. In the fall the Germans shifted their attack on London to attacks on the liberated coast, particularly Antwerp, where casualties were severe.

That same fall the V-2 rocket appeared. This weapon traveled faster than sound, so there was no defense against it. If the Germans had been able to produce these rockets in real quantity and to launch them rapidly, they might have created a desperately serious situation for the Allies. However, they did not succeed in this, and by the early months of 1945 the secret weapon scare was allayed.

By this time intelligent Germans realized that the end was in sight and could not be delayed much longer.

CHAPTER XXXV

Defeat in 1945

The German armed forces, under the immediate control of Hitler, made one final effort at an offensive to repulse the British and American troops, some of which were already on German soil. In mid-December 1944 they launched the Battle of the Bulge in the Ardennes Forest in eastern Belgium. This desperate drive had intelligent reasoning behind it. It was an effort to drive a wedge at the point of juncture of the British and the Americans. It was aimed at the possession of Antwerp, the one major port which the Allies had captured in a reasonably usable condition. General Eisenhower sent every possible reinforcement to the threatened area and placed the American troops in the north under the command of Montgomery. Air attacks were intensified in spite of the bad weather. The fighting was severe, but by the end of January the Germans were pushed back to their original lines. Thenceforward there were no German successes.

The last three months of the war witnessed uninterrupted advance of the Allied armies into Germany from the west, south, and east. On March 7 an American unit crossed the Rhine at Remagen, not far south of Cologne. Some days later the British crossed in their sector. In Italy the Allies continued their offensive northward and by late April had cleared the Germans from almost the whole peninsula. Mussolini was killed by Italian partisans on April 28, and on May 2 hostilities in that area ceased. The Russians captured Warsaw in January, Budapest in February, Danzig in March, and Königsberg and Vienna in April. By that time the suburbs of Berlin were invested by Soviet forces. On April 25 American and Soviet units met on the Elbe River. Germany was cut into two parts. This was the end.

Hitler had spent most of the later years of the war at his eastern headquarters near Rastenburg in East Prussia. He devoted himself almost exclusively to intimate supervision of military operations, and for relaxation held lunch parties at which he delivered himself of pontifical statements on all subjects. After the attempt of July 20, 1944, his physical and mental health deteriorated noticeably, not as a result of his injuries but of general nervous strain, physical inactivity, and the increasing numbers of phony and even dangerous pills and injections with which he stuffed himself. At times he burst into hysterical tantrums, railing against the German people for not measuring up to his greatness.

In the early winter Hitler made a brief visit to Berlin and then went to his western headquarters near Bad Nauheim, where he directed the offensive in the Ardennes. Then on January 16, 1945, he returned to Berlin, never again to leave the chancellery building and its air-raid shelter. He refused to face the inevitable and accused as traitors those who talked of defeat or surrender. He was determined to bring down all Germany around him in a final immolation. The comparison with the last scene of Wagner's *Götterdämmerung* is hackneyed and threadbare but almost irresistible. Hitler ordered the most complete sort of scorched-earth policy. If his commands had been carried out to the letter, Germany would have consisted only of charred wood, twisted steel, and broken stone. It is to his credit that Albert Speer determined to avoid this tragedy. He sabotaged Hitler's policy at great personal risk by countermanding the *Führer*'s orders and substituting for them directions to retire without destruction.

Hitler celebrated his fifty-sixth and last birthday on April 20, 1945. For some weeks he had existed in the cramped conditions of the underground shelter (*Führerbunker*). On that day occurred the last gathering of the faithful. Eva Braun, Hitler's mistress, had arrived from the south. Goering was there; so were Himmler, Goebbels, Doenitz, Keitel, General Jodl, Ribbentrop, Bormann, and Speer. After they tendered congratulations, they sat once more in council. The paladins pleaded with Hitler to leave Berlin and go to the south. Berlin was not defensible, but the so-called Alpine Redoubt in Bavaria and Austria, where most of the remaining German troops were located, could, it was thought, be held almost indefinitely because of the difficult mountainous terrain. Hitler had not made up his mind. That evening he took a cool last farewell of Goering, whom he now despised on account of the failure of the *Luftwaffe*. The paladins separated, some never to meet again and others only as prisoners.

Two days later Hitler had made his decision. He determined to remain in Berlin to the last and to kill himself when the final moment came. All who wished could go, but he would stay in his capital. Bormann remained; so did Goebbels with his wife and children; and so did a shifting group of military figures, secretaries, aides, and servants. By April 25 the Russians had surrounded Berlin and the only possible means of egress for the group around Hitler were improvised airstrips in the *Tiergarten*. The only communication was by radio.

The last few days of Hitler's life are not important to German history. He had done his worst and the rest was out of his hands. However, these days are fascinating and macabre as a study in abnormal psychology. A good deal of the time was spent in attacking "traitorous" high Nazis. Speer paid a last visit to the *Bunker* and admitted the degree to which he had undermined Hitler's demand for a scorched-earth policy. Hitler let him go unscathed. He was exhausted, and his affection for Speer had been remarkable. Goering, acting on verbal information from the *Bunker,* sent a message to Hitler suggesting that since Hitler was no longer a free agent, he, as successor to Hitler, should assume control. Goering set a deadline after which he would start to act as *Führer*. Hitler replied violently, stripping Goering of all his titles and positions and threatening him with death. A final blow came with the news, intercepted from a British report, that Himmler had been negotiating with the Swedish Count Folke Bernadotte to act as an intermediary to obtain peace from the Western Allies. Himmler was prepared to assume personal responsibility. This defection was almost unbearable to Hitler; even the faithful Himmler had deserted. After a frightful scene Hitler ordered the arrest of the S.S. leader.

On the night of April 28–29 Hitler made his final plans. Shortly after midnight a municipal official of Berlin was brought into the *Bunker* to perform a brief marriage ceremony uniting Hitler and Eva Braun, with Bormann and Goebbels as witnesses. There followed hours of conversation and reminiscing over champagne. In the intervals of the conversation Hitler retired and dictated his two testaments, a political one and a personal one. The political testament begins with sweeping generalities in the old familiar manner. It then expels from the party both Goering and Himmler and names Grand Admiral Doenitz as president and commander of the armed forces. It names other officials to carry on the work: Goebbels as chancellor, Bormann as party chancellor, and Seyss-Inquart as foreign minister. The personal testament explains to the world Hitler's marriage, announces his impending death, and bequeaths his personal possessions. These testaments were drawn up in several copies and sent out of the *Bunker* by messengers. They never reached their destinations and were discovered accidentally months later.

Hitler carried out his decision on April 30. After a formal lunch he and Eva Braun took leave of their companions in the *Bunker* and retired to their rooms. A few moments later a shot was heard. Frau Hitler had taken a rapid poison, but her husband had shot himself through the head.

The faithful carried the bodies outside, poured gallons of gasoline on them, and set them alight. They burned for hours until they were charred bones. Outside the walls a greater fire, the fire of Berlin, was burning too. The two conflagrations were not unconnected.

There was a curious confusion about getting the news of his appointment and of Hitler's death to Doenitz, who was at his headquarters at Ploen in Schleswig-Holstein. It was obviously up to Bormann and Goebbels to carry out the *Führer*'s wishes. Bormann sent a radio message to Doenitz informing him that he was the successor to Hitler but not telling him that Hitler was dead. It would appear that Bormann still nursed political ambitions and wanted to reach Doenitz as soon as possible after the news of Hitler's death. Goebbels, however, had decided to disobey Hitler's appointment of him as the new chancellor and instead to commit suicide. The two made an unsuccessful attempt to negotiate with the local Russian command. The next morning, May 1, Bormann sent a cryptic message to Doenitz. It read: "The Testament is in force. I will join you as soon as possible. Till then, I recommend that publication be held up." (Quoted in H. R. Trevor-Roper, *The Last Days of Hitler,* New York: Macmillan, 1947, p. 210.) He was still anxious to reach the new seat of power. Some hours later Goebbels sent a more informative message announcing the time of Hitler's death and listing the officials whom Hitler had named for the new government. Goebbels then returned to his private rooms and poisoned his six children. He and his wife walked out of the *Bunker* and stood still while they were shot by an S.S. man. Their bodies were only partially burned and were discovered by the Russians the next day.

Late that night the remaining occupants of the *Bunker,* including Bormann, attempted a mass escape. Some were successful, but Bormann was never heard of again. There is a reasonably reputable story that he was seen dead on a Berlin street.

Doenitz was astonished at the news, which he heard for the first time in Bormann's message, that he was Hitler's successor. He apparently assumed that Himmler would get the appointment and was prepared to work with him, though he disliked him. However, as a military man, he was ready to obey. On the evening of May 1 over the Hamburg radio, to the strains of music by Wagner and Bruckner, Doenitz announced the death of Hitler to those Germans who had the time or energy to listen.

Doenitz was not, and never claimed to be, a political figure. He was a highly competent naval officer and a man endowed with solid common sense, a quality which he used during the next few days. He immediately moved his headquarters from Ploen to Flensburg on the Danish border and started to form a government. He realized that the Nazi leaders would be a liability in his efforts to negotiate with the Allies. He thus disobeyed Hitler and, instead of appointing Seyss-Inquart as foreign minister, appointed the innocuous former finance minister, Count Schwerin Krosigk. Doenitz' greatest annoyance during the first few days was the presence of Himmler and a large entourage of the S.S. The admiral, anxious to be rid of this specter, simply sent him a note relieving him of all his functions and thanking him for his services to Germany. Himmler, irresolute and confused, stayed around for some days; after the surrender he tried to escape, wandered into a British control post, gave himself up, and swallowed poison as British soldiers were searching his body.

The men at Flensburg realized that their only hope for favorable treatment from the victors lay with surrender to the British and Americans rather than to the Russians. They tried to approach General Montgomery. However, Montgomery, supported by his chief, Eisenhower, had to remain true to the Allied policy of no separate peace and of unconditional surrender. On May 4 Admiral von Friedeburg, who had succeeded Doenitz as commander in chief of the navy, surrendered the troops in northwest Europe to the Allies. On May 7 he and General Jodl of the OKW traveled to Rheims where they offered the unconditional surrender of Germany to the Allies in the presence of a Russian observer. On May 9 he and General Keitel performed the same duty in Berlin to the Russians before British and American observers. World War II in Europe was over, and Nazi Germany was at an end.

Life at Flensburg was unreal for the next ten days. As small groups of Allied control officials arrived there, they were greeted aboard the headquarters ship, "Patria," as guests rather than victors, and guarded by armed German soldiers and sailors. Doenitz arranged meals and conferences. This fiction became unbearable, and on May 21 Doenitz and his shadow government were arrested and sent to join the other Nazi leaders who had been found.

The epilogue to the career of the Nazi hierarchy occurred a year and a half later in a courtroom on the outskirts of Nuremberg. The four major victorious powers—the United States, Great Britain, the Soviet Union, and France—organized an international military tribunal to try the Nazi leaders for war crimes, crimes against peace, and crimes against humanity. A good deal of criticism has been levied against the right of victors to try the vanquished for crimes which had not been defined previously. At least it can be said that the trial was not a kangaroo court, but was held soberly with every possibility given to the accused for their defense. It lasted for almost a year from November 1945 to October 1946. The testimony was mostly documentary from German sources.

Twenty-two men were tried, including Bormann *in absentia*. Three were acquitted: Papen, Schacht, and Fritsche (an underling from the propaganda ministry standing in for his master Goebbels). Seven were given prison terms ranging from ten years to life at an international prison at Spandau in Berlin: Doenitz, Neurath, Speer, Schirach, Raeder, Funk, and Hess. Twelve were condemned to be hanged: Goering, Ribbentrop, Keitel, Jodl, Rosenberg, Frick, Seyss-Inquart, Sauckel, Bormann, Kaltenbrunner (one of Himmler's principal subordinates), Frank, and Streicher. At the last moment Goering managed to cheat the hangman by somehow procuring poison and committing suicide. The rest were executed. The drama which began when Adolf Hitler made his first speech at a beer hall in Munich in 1919 had reached its terrifying catharsis.

CHAPTER XXXVI

Occupied Germany (1945-49)

No one who did not visit Germany in the period immediately after the defeat can really grasp the magnitude of the chaos and devastation. Having spent some days in Frankfurt, Berlin, Bremen, and the Rhineland as late as October 1945, the author found it impossible upon returning to England and then to the United States to give a convincing picture of what he saw. Some memories remain. The sight from the air of miles of gaunt chimneys in residential Berlin; the sight of old women dragging heavy wooden carts piled high with firewood from the Grünewald, and sometimes with little children sitting on top of the faggots; the sight of a young man in tattered *Luftwaffe* uniform staring dazedly at a wrecked plane in the woods near Frankfurt; the hysterical and corrupt gaiety of the only nightclub open in Berlin; the statue of William I hanging by one stirrup from an enormous bronze horse in Koblenz; trains so crowded that people were hanging on outside; the hundreds of notices pasted on bulletin boards asking for news of the whereabouts of a child, a parent, or a beloved; the sweet smell of putrefaction in Berlin: these tell the story better than statistics, though the statistics are sufficiently frightening. A ride along Unter den Linden or the Wilhelmstrasse was like a visit to the temple of Karnak or to the Mayan ruins in Yucatan. Here was a powerful society in dissolution.

So it seemed at the time. The world knows now that the destruction was not so complete as it appeared in 1945. Germany actually increased her productive capacity during the war. The air raids, though destructive of morale, communications, and military installations, were not nearly so destructive of basic industrial apparatus as had been thought. Under the debris many of the machines were still there. The problems of 1945 were immediate ones: food, shelter, clothing, purging, disarmament, refugees, and displaced persons. The occupation authorities have been criticized and often justly for their mismanagement of various issues.

The fact that any order came out of the chaos, given the varying aims of the four occupying powers, seems to border on the miraculous.

This is happily not the place to trace the complex history of postwar planning in the Allied capitals. Most of it was done in Washington and London, but it seems fair to say that except for some broad directives, the victory found the victors without any definitely agreed-upon philosophy. There were advocates of a "hard" peace and a "soft" peace. On the whole the Americans favored a hard peace, the British a softer one. The Russians were mainly interested in securing reparations. The French were completely absorbed in their own problems and interested only in their own security. In the summer of 1945 thousands of men—many of them barely trained for their positions, many ignorant of Germany or the German language, some brilliant, and some venal—were sent to Germany to carry out badly defined policies. The history of the occupation is one of improvisation, but through it runs the increasing realization that any intimate co-operation between the Western powers and the Soviet Union was impossible. The result of this realization was the policy of strengthening, rather than weakening, the new Germany.

At their meeting in Teheran in 1943 the Big Three (Roosevelt, Churchill, and Stalin) set up the European Advisory Commission (EAC) to sit in London and draw up postwar plans for Europe. This commission had no easy time in dealing with its respective governments, but by 1944 succeeded in drafting a division of Germany into zones of occupation. It was accepted by the three governments, although the British and Americans quarreled over which Western zone was to go to whom. At Yalta in February 1945 the zones were formally agreed upon, and Stalin grudgingly permitted the French to have a zone if it were taken out of the British and American zones. The Big Three also agreed upon several proclamations describing the structure of the military government to be made public by the powers after victory. It was further decided that in addition to the four zones the area of Greater Berlin, an island in the middle of the Soviet zone, would be divided into four sectors and governed by the four powers co-operatively.

As the various Allied armies pushed into Germany, they set up *ad hoc* military government units in each town as it was conquered without any particular reference to an over-all plan. The urgencies of the moment were so great that nothing else could have been done. The authorities tried to locate reputable anti-Nazis to put in official positions, but the main job was to distribute food, to get utilities into working condition, and to see that the security of the Allied armies was not endangered. The urgency of work was immense. By the time of surrender the positions of the Allied armies did not coincide with the proposed zones.

The Americans had advanced to the Elbe and occupied parts of Thuringia and Saxony, which were allocated to the Soviets. During May and June there was no change in these positions; the armies were busy setting up their own administrations in their zones, moving their headquarters, and preparing for the Big Three conference which was planned for July at Potsdam.

On June 5, 1945, General Eisenhower, Field Marshal Montgomery, and General de Lattre de Tassigny journeyed to Berlin; there, with Marshal Zhukov, the Soviet commander, they issued the proclamations drawn up at Yalta. By these the four Allied governments assumed supreme authority in Germany. They announced the formation of the four zones in Germany and that "Greater Berlin" would be occupied by forces of each of the four powers. An interallied governing authority (*Kommadatura*), consisting of four commanders appointed by their respective commanders in chief, was to direct the administration of Berlin. For Germany in general the four commanders in chief were to constitute the Control Council, which was to be in charge of working out the unconditional surrender and controlling Germany until the four powers set up a substitute. The Control Council was entitled to have various subordinate bodies attached to it and to maintain liaison with other members of the United Nations. Its decisions had to be unanimous. This last provision was to prove very important. Nowhere in these documents was there any detailed assurance of access to Berlin for the Americans, British, and French, although Berlin was to be the seat of the Control Council.

Part of June and July was spent in setting up headquarters in Berlin. This was not an easy job because the Soviets raised all kinds of small, detailed difficulties, which began to give the Western officials some idea of the literal-mindedness of their ally. By early July the headquarters were established, and American troops withdrew from the areas of the Soviet zone they had conquered. On July 30 the first meeting of the Control Council was convened.

In the meantime the Big Three also arrived in Berlin. The personnel had changed because in April President Truman had succeeded President Roosevelt. Furthermore, during the Potsdam Conference the victory of the Labor party in the British parliamentary elections was announced, and during the second part of the conference the new prime minister, Clement Attlee, replaced Winston Churchill. No election had unseated Joseph Stalin. The conference lasted from July 17 to August 2 and established the only fundamental agreed-upon directives which the Control Council ever received. It is important to note that France was not represented at the Potsdam Conference, though she was a member of the Control Council. Thus France was not bound by the decisions at Potsdam and actually had a veto power over them in the council.

In addition to the general statements about the disarmament, denazification, demilitarization, and re-education of Germany that might have been expected, the protocol of the Potsdam Conference laid down certain specific new directives. Some of these were territorial. The Big Three awarded without qualification the northern part of East Prussia, including the port city of Königsberg, to the Soviet Union. In respect of the Polish claims they were not so generous. The main statement was that an adjudication of these claims would have to await a final peace treaty. In the meantime, however, Poland was permitted to administer all of Germany east of the Oder and western Neisse rivers. Thus Poland "administers" Silesia as well as large parts of East Prussia, Pomerania, and Brandenburg. Later the Soviets gave the Poles a valuable slice of land on the west bank of the Oder, including the important port of Stettin. Immediately the Polish government started to displace all German inhabitants of the area, and has acted ever since, with the support of the Soviet Union, as if this were a full cession. Thus Germany lost a large percentage of her best agricultural land.

Another important pronouncement concerned the forced removal of the remaining Germans from Poland, Czechoslovakia, and Hungary into Germany. The Big Three felt that the only way to solve the minority problem was to get rid of the minorities. The protocol called for an "equitable distribution" of the refugees among the four zones. In fact, this involved the movement of about ten million people with all the tragic dislocations that always accompany such an undertaking. The refugee problem remained an urgently serious one for a number of years. The refugees did not want to go where they were sent, and the population in the receiving areas did not want them. To say that the move was to be made equitably was of course a dream. Actually the British and American zones had to receive the bulk of the refugees. Thus within a few years Germany, with her much reduced agricultural and industrial capacity, had a larger population to support than before the war.

The statement of economic principles is of great interest, particularly in view of what was to occur in the future and also the change it marked from the earlier American policy of hands off the German economy short of danger to the American forces. The key statement read: "During the period of occupation Germany shall be treated as a single economic unit." The protocol went on to specify areas of economic activity in which common policies were to be established by the four powers acting through the Control Council. There was certainly no intent

Division of Germany

According to the Potsdam Agreement

U.S.S.R.

POLISH Administration

POLAND

POLISH Administration

CZECHOSLOVAKIA

AUSTRIA

Berlin (Joint Admin.)

RUSSIAN ZONE

BALTIC SEA

NORTH SEA

DEN.

FIN.

U.S. ZONE

BRITISH ZONE

U.S. ZONE

Frankfurt

Bonn

U.S. ZONE

FRENCH ZONE

SWITZERLAND

NETH.

BELG.

LUX.

SAAR

FRANCE

to divide Germany into four airtight zones, each ruled by one of the powers independently of the others. Yet that was what developed.

In the matter of reparations, so vital to the Soviets, the Potsdam protocol did not mention any definite sum, although the Russians kept talking about ten billion dollars. The protocol provided that Russian and Polish reparations should come from the Soviet zone, with the addition that 15 per cent of the productive capacity of the Western zones unnecessary for the future German economy would be available to be sent to Russia in exchange for food and raw materials and another 10 per cent could be made available outright. There were two obvious omissions in this plan. The first was that there was no statement of how much the German economy was to produce; the second was that no reference was made to the possibility of taking reparations from current production. Details of this sort were to be decided by the Control Council. In fact the Russians had started to dismantle German factories as soon as they established themselves, and even before the Potsdam Conference large quantities of equipment had been sent eastward, reportedly in so haphazard a way that it was almost impossible to reassemble upon arrival.

The Control Council met regularly and apparently amicably during 1945 and into 1946. In bulk the number of laws it issued is impressive. However, as one analyzes the topics they dealt with, it is remarkable that they are almost all negative, carrying out in detail the abolition of Nazi institutions, decartelization, etc. The positive enactments were mostly unimportant, e.g., a law ordering the reopening of certain museums. The council busied itself with a policy on the level of industry to be permitted to the future Germany, essential before reparations deliveries could begin. The four powers differed greatly on this issue, with Britain willing to grant the highest level of steel production to the Germans. On the American side there was confusion owing to lack of co-ordination in the state department. By the spring of 1946 a figure was agreed upon, but the issue had become almost academic because the Russians were simply requisitioning current production from their zone to such an extent that they sent little or nothing to provision the West. The result was that the United States and Britain, which were sending needed supplies to their zones, were simply subsidizing Russian confiscations. This constituted a clear refusal on the part of the Russians to treat Germany as an economic unit. Accordingly on May 3, 1946, General Clay, deputy for military government to General McNarney, the American military governor, suspended all reparations deliveries from the American zone to the Russians. This of course opened a breach between the United States and Russia, which became wider as time progressed.

The Russians were not the only ones who impeded any real progress in the Control Council. The French proved themselves difficult colleagues. They refused to be bound by the decisions at Potsdam and in particular were adamant against any move to treat Germany as a unit. Their main interests were to remove the Ruhr from German control and to integrate the Saar into France. Thus they made life easier for the Russians, who could always count on a French veto in the Control Council if the question were one of carrying out the order from Potsdam to treat Germany as an economic unit.

Events outside Germany during 1946 and 1947—in the Balkans, in Greece, in the Far East, and at the stalemated meetings of the Council of Foreign Ministers—widened the gap between the two sides of the iron curtain and forced the United States in particular to do some serious rethinking about its German policy. The results of this thought appeared gradually over the months. Within Germany the four zones went their separate ways, and the inhabitants were far more affected by the philosophy dominating the zone they lived in than by anything the Control Council might do. The new Germany was forming itself on a zonal, not a national basis.

The American occupation reflected some of the typical characteristics of Americans: a blend of puritanism, naïveté, generosity, and warmheartedness. The authorities were limited by the terms of their directive, J.C.S. 1067, which prescribed the general philosophy of American military government. This document stemmed from the hard peace doctrine associated with the name of Henry Morgenthau, Jr., though it was somewhat watered down. It forbade any fraternization between Americans and Germans, the distribution of food other than to prevent epidemic or unrest, and any general control of the German economy. It was somewhat diluted by the Potsdam agreements, but remained technically in effect until well into 1947. The Americans took most seriously their responsibility for denazification. They tried more than four times as many suspect Germans as the other three occupying powers together. They distributed twelve million *Fragebogen* ("questionnaires"), in which Germans were required to answer one hundred thirty-one questions about their early lives. They carried over the historical American antitrust attitude into the decartelization program and forced some of the large firms to divide. They were stern in general about all forms of disarmament.

If the Americans were stern about the negative aspects of the occupation, they were almost overenthusiastic about the process of rebuilding German democracy. They rapidly started to set up a new political life for the Germans. An immediate problem was the division of the various zones into sensible units, for the zone boundaries often did not follow the old historical frontiers and there was a determination not to resurrect Prussia as an entity. The U.S. zone was divided into three *Länder:* Bavaria, with almost its historical area; Würtemberg-Baden, made up of the northern halves of these old states; and Hesse, a conglomeration composed mainly of old Hesse-Darmstadt and some of the areas annexed by Prussia in 1866. A special case was the Bremen enclave, which was first ruled under general British direction with American officials but later included into the U.S. zone proper.

As early as August 1945 the Americans authorized the rebirth of political parties, and within a few months permitted them to operate at the *Land* level. They assumed a similar pattern in all four zones. The two largest were the Social Democratic party (SPD), the heir of the Weimar party of the same name, and the Christian Democratic Union (CDU), a sort of descendant of the old Center party but with a much higher proportion of Protestant membership. These two were respectively a bit left and a bit right of center. On the left the Communist party (KPD) was authorized, and by 1946 a number of smaller groups combined into the Free Democratic party (FDP), favoring free enterprise and cautious political liberalism.

The Americans wanted to hold elections as soon as possible, but to start the process at the "grass roots" level. Accordingly the first village elections were held as early as January 1946. To the delight of the authorities, a very large percentage of the electorate voted and registered a return to democracy with enthusiasm. During the year elections were held in larger units. In the summer the appointed minister-presidents of the three *Länder* designated committees to draft constitutions. These were ratified by large majorities, and by the beginning of 1947 the three states had parliamentary governments run by coalitions of the major parties except for the Communists, who won very few votes.

The stern policy of the American occupation persisted until 1947, although it was always tempered by the soft hearts of individual GI's. It took the increasing intransigence of the Russians, the realization that Europe in general could not recover if Germany did not, and the frightful suffering of the winter of 1946–47 to persuade Washington that the United States would have to take an active lead in the policy of recovery.

The British attitude was consistently far less doctrinaire than the American. Although Great Britain had suffered from the Germans much more than the United States, President Roosevelt always had trouble to get the British to agree to his policy of a hard peace. During the early days of the occupation Britain followed a line of getting essential services into operation without paying very much concern to the personnel employed. Thus by the autumn of 1945 observers commented that Hamburg was functioning better than any other German city. In the summer of 1945 the Labor party assumed control in Britain. It was elected on a program of nationalization at home; it was to be expected that it would favor a similar policy in Germany and thus run counter to some American ideas of decreasing the size of German firms and encouraging free enterprise. The victory of free enterprise in Germany is probably the result of American economic dominance there after 1947 and also of German tradition. An overriding consideration for the British had to be the terribly serious economic condition in which Britain found herself after the war. She could not afford to pour vast sums into Germany and consequently had to take some decisions that she did not like. She had to encourage German recovery even at the expense of future competition in order to lessen the current burden on the British taxpayer.

The British zone consisted of large former Prussian areas, several smaller *Länder,* and the free city of Hamburg. By 1947 the British organized their zone into four *Länder.* One is Hamburg, another the Prussian province of Schleswig-Holstein. The former Prussian provinces, Rhineland and Westphalia, were united into a new *Land,* Rhineland-Westphalia, including the whole Ruhr industrial empire. A fourth *Land,* Lower Saxony, was constituted out of old Hanover and some of the small units nearby. The British moved more slowly than the Americans in granting self-government to the *Länder,* which at first adopted only provisional constitutions. Some of them did not adopt their final constitutions until after the formation of the German Federal Republic. The British instituted some of the forms of English local government and tried to avoid proportional representation but had varying success in different areas.

The French zone, carved out of the British and U.S. zones, consisted of two triangles composed of miscellaneous parts of western Germany. The southern one, which consisted of the southern halves of Baden and Würtemberg, was organized into two separate *Länder,* although now they are integrated with the larger *Land,* Baden-Würtemberg. The northern one included the Saar and an area composed of various prewar territories which the French called Rhine-Palatinate. During the years of the occupation France was so involved with her own domestic problems that she was able to give only scant attention to her responsibilities in Germany. The important part of her zone from her point of view was the Saar, which she integrated unilaterally into the French economy in 1946, a situation which persisted for over ten years. As for the rest, she viewed her position as an occupying power as a recognition of her great power status and a lever to prevent German reunification. Perhaps her most interesting contribution was in the cultural sphere. She established a university at Mainz and arranged exchanges of exhibitions, music, lectures, etc., in an effort to make good Europeans out of these Germans on the fringe of French culture.

As usual, it is more difficult to analyze what the Russians had in mind as an occupation policy. Certainly they expected to strip Germany of huge amounts of reparations and anticipated carrying out a land reform, but the degree to which they thought they could communize their zone remains in question. When they established themselves in Germany, they plastered Berlin and other cities with large placards quoting anything nice about Germany which they could find in the Communist canon, e.g., Stalin's remark, "Hitlers come and go, but the German people and the German state remain." The other powers criticized the Russians for being lax about denazification and for hiring former Nazis after a perfunctory recantation. Any German good will that the Russians hoped to earn this way was more than counteracted by the brutal behavior of the Red army, which looted, raped, and pillaged to its heart's content.

The Soviet Military Administration, at first under Marshal Zhukov, established itself at Karlshorst in eastern Berlin with five subsidiary headquarters, each under a general, for Mecklenburg-Pomerania, Brandenburg, Saxony-Anhalt, Saxony, and Thuringia. The Russian occupation continued to have a more military character than that of the Americans, British, and French, who gradually replaced their military officials with civilians.

The Soviets permitted the re-establishment of political parties as rapidly as the Americans. Here again there appeared the four usual parties, with the Communists as the smallest group. In their early appointments the Soviets were not able to find enough Communists to fill posts, so that they were in a minority. In early 1946 the Russians devised a plan to increase Communist strength. They proposed a fusion between the Communists and the Social Democrats to form a new party, the Socialist Unity party (SED). Otto Grotewohl, a former SPD leader, headed the fusion group from his party. Most of the SPD members in the Soviet zone joined the new group; in fact they had little choice, but the SED made little or no headway in Berlin or the Western zones. In the elections of October 1946 the SED polled a little less than half of the total votes cast in the Soviet zone. On the same day in Berlin, however, the SED received less than half the vote of the old SPD and also ran behind the CDU. Where there was real freedom of choice, the SED was a failure; however, in the Soviet zone it has remained the favored and dominant party.

One of the most interesting aspects of the Soviet occupation has been the land reform, which the Russians seem to have planned in some detail before the end of the war. The Soviet zone and the territory handed to Poland comprised the traditional area of the landholding aristocracy of Prussia. More than 20 per cent of the land of the Soviet zone belonged to holdings of more than twenty-five hundred acres. The general rule applied by the Russians was to redistribute holdings of over two hundred fifty acres to landless peasants and refugees. It is significant that the Soviets did not collectivize the land; it was given to individuals who had the responsibility of making it produce at the peril of losing it. Eastern Germany is no longer a land of great holdings, but neither did it become one of collective farms; it became a land of smallholders.

Signs of disenchantment with the control machinery can be noted in 1946, signs that were precursors of events to occur during the next two years. One of the first was the offer of James Byrnes, American secretary of state, on July 11, 1946, to merge the American zone in economic matters with the zone of any other power interested. This was a pretty clear admission that the U.S. despaired of fulfilling the order of the Potsdam Conference to treat Germany as an economic unit. A few days later the British government accepted the American offer, and the two powers spent the rest of the summer implementing the plan. On September 5 the agreement was announced. The idea was to set up a number of boards manned by Germans to supervise economic policy for the new Bizonia. Much stress was laid on the fact that this was not a political arrangement but only an economic one. The boards were made responsible to a committee of the minister-presidents of the eight *Länder* involved. The breakdown of the zonal wall was intended to develop an exchange of food and industrial goods where they were most needed. It was hoped that the new plan would also lead to an increase of German export trade, essential if Germany were ever to support herself.

The following day Secretary Byrnes gave a momentous address at Stuttgart to an audience composed mostly of Americans but with some Germans present. It was a measured and cautious speech, but its significance lies in the fact that for the first time since the war an Allied official was speaking to the Germans as if they were human beings with a democratic political future before them. Byrnes accepted the French future of the Saar, but very carefully did not speak of the Polish border as permanent. He pointed out that America looked forward to a democratic central government for Germany to be devised by Germans and run by them. "The American people want to return the government of

Germany to the German people. The American people want to help the German people to win their way back to an honorable place among the free and peace-loving nations of the world." This speech is often considered the turning point of the occupation.

The winter of 1946–47 was one of the coldest in the history of Europe. From December to March there was no relief. The suffering of the Germans from cold and malnutrition was intense. People slept in railway stations or in old air-raid shelters, where there was a little warmth. Mines and factories had to shut down because the workers were not strong enough to work.

President Truman had asked Herbert Hoover the year before to study the food situation in Europe in general. Now he asked him to go to Europe again and report on Germany in particular. Hoover's report makes dismal reading; he found the situation in Germany far worse than anywhere else in Europe. He recommended emergency shipments of foodstuffs. Army stocks of food were now allocated for the population.

By early 1947 the administration in Washington was fully aware of the Communist menace and ready to believe that the German menace was a thing of the past, that in fact Germany should be encouraged and helped to recover. In March President Truman formulated the Truman Doctrine when he asked Congress for a large loan to help Greece and Turkey fend off Communism. In June General George Marshall, Byrnes's successor at the state department, announced the Marshall Plan, a promise to extend vast grants and credits to promote European recovery. The original Marshall Plan included all of Europe except Germany, but by December Germany was included after the Soviet Union and its satellites had refused any American aid. In the summer of 1947 a new directive from the joint chiefs of staffs replaced the old severe J.C.S. 1067 and repeated American plans to help German recovery. The old attitudes were completely reversed.

An essential condition precedent to economic recovery in Germany was a reform of the currency. During the Nazi period and the war years Germany underwent a considerable inflation, although the controls imposed by the Nazis veiled the fact. With the collapse in 1945 the currency system collapsed also. The Allies printed occupation marks at a ratio of ten to a dollar, but unfortunately a set of plates to print this money was given to the Russians, who kept their presses constantly busy. Thus the United States was underwriting the Russian financial system in Germany. In fact currency became so valueless that it virtually passed out of circulation and was replaced by the cigarette as the standard of value. The author can recall blackboards on which the current prices of different brands of American cigarettes for that day were chalked up.

The situation was chaotic in the extreme and realized as such by all concerned, including the Russians.

Negotiations went on between East and West to reform the currency, but as usual the Russians were recalcitrant. Finally fearing that the Russians would unilaterally issue a revalued currency, the Western powers decided to get ahead of them. The French agreed to this, and for all practical purposes after the summer of 1948 Bizonia became Trizonia. The details of the currency reform are complex and need not detain us here; they are reminiscent of the year 1923. The reichsmark was withdrawn and replaced by the new Deutsche mark at a ratio of 6.5 to 100. This, of course, again hurt the saver and the fixed income groups, but it gave an enormous impulse to production. The Germans went on a shopping spree. They discovered that there were things to buy which had been withheld from the market while the currency was so unstable. Production increased by leaps and bounds as the currency remained dependable and as Marshall Plan money started to pour in. These events were the watershed between collapse and recovery in Germany. The Soviets retaliated by issuing a new ostmark for their zone and their sector in Berlin, thus further complicating the topsy-turvy state of Berlin, where at this same time the most dramatic events of the occupation were occurring.

By late 1947 there was no further attempt by either Russia or the Western powers to conceal their mutual antipathy. The earlier efforts to wash dirty linen in private was a thing of the past. The Russians were openly critical, even vituperative, about such actions as the Marshall Plan, the establishment of Bizonia, which they called an effort to keep Germany permanently divided, and the forthcoming currency reform. When the U.S. and Britain met at London with France to concert plans to establish a west German government, the Russians struck. The Control Council met for the last time on March 20, 1948. At this meeting Marshal Sokolovsky, who had succeeded Marshal Zhukov, demanded to know the results of the conference in London. The American military governor, General Lucius Clay, replied that he could not provide the information without reference to the three Western governments. Sokolovsky then read a long prepared statement of grievances against the West, declared the meeting adjourned, and walked out of the room. This was the end of quadripartite government in Germany.

Within a few days the blockade of Berlin began. It developed gradually, as the Soviets little by little cut off all surface access to the city. Their position was that Berlin was really in the Soviet zone; that the Western powers had been allowed there only to take part in the Control Council; and that since joint government of Germany had ended, the

Westerners must leave. General Clay and his British and French colleagues insisted that they were there by right of conquest and of the Yalta and Potsdam conferences. Unfortunately, they could not produce any document guaranteeing access to Berlin. That had been taken for granted in the optimistic days of 1945. By the summer of 1948 all approaches to Berlin by rail, road, and water were closed. Only the air remained open, and even here the Russians made difficulties. While it would not be very difficult to supply Allied personnel by air, the prospect of providing the German population of over two million in the three Western sectors with food and fuel by air looked impossible. More than anyone else, General Clay deserves the credit for attempting it. He received constant support from the Truman administration, the Air Force, and his British and French allies. Little by little the airlift (or airbridge as the Germans called it) became effective with a goal of supplying eight thousand tons of supplies a day in spite of the severe north German winter which lay just ahead.

The blockade of Berlin became involved with the currency reform. In fact, the Soviets acted as if the blockade were caused by the reform, a patently untrue position, since the blockade was well under way before the reform was announced. Numerous conferences ensued, mostly at the diplomatic level and usually in Moscow, with Stalin himself taking part in one of them. The details were very complicated, hinging around the introduction of a new currency in Berlin and around the new organization of Western Germany. On several occasions it looked as if the questions were settled, but then the Russians would raise new difficulties. They were playing for time in the hope that the airlift would fail. They tried to woo the inhabitants of West Berlin with all kinds of blandishments, including food and fuel, hoping that they could lure the Germans away from the West; but they failed. The Berliners exhibited a stoical stubborn loyalty to the West which was amazing; they preferred to suffer privations rather than to accept handouts from the East.

In early 1949 the Soviets realized that the airlift had been successful and the winter was over. In March the Western powers introduced the Deutsche mark into their sectors of Berlin, and thus made Berlin a city divided economically as it already was politically. At about the same time the North Atlantic Treaty Organization came into existence. The Soviet government now decided to retreat as gracefully as possible. As a result of negotiations held at a United Nations meeting, surface traffic started to move between Berlin and the West on May 12, 1949. Three days later General Clay left Germany because now the state department was to exercise control rather than military government. The Berliners have erected a monument to the airlift in front of Tempelhof airport.

They have named a principal street Clayallee. One wonders how many vanquished cities have perpetuated the memory of the head of a military occupation.

The end of the blockade ushered in a new period in German history. In May 1949 the German Federal Republic was proclaimed at Bonn. A few months later the Soviets proclaimed the German Democratic Republic in the east. Now there were two Germanies.

CHAPTER XXXVII

The Two Germanies (1949-   )

The obvious failure of the Control Council convinced the American and British authorities in 1947 that the time was ripe for the formation of a German government for Western Germany. There was no hope of associating the Russians with this plan. They talked only of a strongly centralized government, something the three Western powers, especially France, would not consider. Furthermore, the refusal of the countries influenced by the Soviet Union to have anything to do with the Marshall Plan ruled out the possibility of a uniform economic program for all Germany. An important step toward unity was taken by the formation of Bizonia, but that had been kept purposely unpolitical; now joint political institutions would have to be worked out. It became highly desirable to integrate the French zone with the other two. This was not easy because the French seemed adamant on a far looser federal structure for Germany than the U.S. and Britain wanted. The French also wanted to prevent the Germans from controlling the Ruhr. However, as time went on the French realized how difficult it would be to remain aloof from their partners, particularly when the U.S. pointed out that it would be impossible to have two Marshall Plan programs for Germany. Therefore, they accepted an invitation to meet with the Americans and British in London. This conference was opened on February 23, 1948, over the vehement protest of the Russians.

It looked at first as if the French were hopelessly far from the Anglo-American attitude, but they relented and compromised at various points. The Russian ending of the Control Council in March helped to convince the French, but discussions continued on into the summer. The French government finally approved a plan to invite the minister-presidents of the eleven *Länder* to call an assembly to draw up a constitution for a democratic federal republic with little guidance from the occupation authorities, who simply listed areas in which they wished to maintain jurisdiction and who would have the right to approve the final document. France was promised that the Ruhr question could be reopened.

The next step was to get German agreement to this plan. This proved surprisingly difficult. The German officials were very reluctant to take steps which might consecrate the division of Germany. Thus they objected to the words "constitution" and "constitutional assembly" and felt that the assembly should not be elected by the people but rather by the *Land* parliaments, a less formal gesture. In July the Germans were not at all sure how the Berlin blockade was going to result, and were anxious not to antagonize the Soviets any further. General Clay made it clear that the decisions of the Western allies would have to be carried out, but compromised on language. Thus the word *Grundgesetz* ("basic law") was used, and the assembly was called the "parliamentary council." The minister-presidents then appointed one expert on constitutional law from each *Land;* they met at Chiemsee near Munich and drew up a preliminary draft, which became the basis for the eventual Bonn Constitution.

The minister-presidents then called on each *Land* parliament to elect members to the new council on the basis of population and also in proportion to party affiliations at the last election. The council was made up of sixty-five members, with twenty-seven from each of the two major parties (CDU and SPD). It met at Bonn on September 1, 1948, and elected as its president the CDU leader, Konrad Adenauer, who was to be the leading German political figure for the next years. Adenauer, then a man of 73, had a long political career behind him; in his native Cologne he had been lord mayor from 1917 to 1933 and again briefly after the war. A devout Catholic, he became leader and spokesman of the CDU in the British zone. The council struggled over the basic law during the winter and spring of 1949, finally agreeing on it in May. The three military governors approved it on May 12, when it became law.

The basic law was complemented by an occupation statute, which defined the areas in which the occupying powers would maintain jurisdiction. This document proved very difficult to write, and in fact the German basic law was drawn up with very little co-operation from the allies. In general the allies eventually reserved control only over matters immediately concerned with the occupation: the maintenance of troops in Germany, foreign policy, reparations, disarmament, etc. They protected themselves with the right to protest any law passed by the new government within a fixed period of days and with a statute for an international authority for the Ruhr. The occupation statute was proclaimed on September 15, 1949; the military governors were replaced by high commissioners; and the occupation of West Germany was technically ended. Elections to the new Bundestag had been held on August 14; the body convened shortly afterward; and with the election of Theodor Heuss as president and Konrad Adenauer as chancellor, the new government began to operate.

The Bonn basic law, originally intended to be a short interim law until Germany became again united, emerged as a lengthy complete constitution. Its authors tried to avoid the pitfalls of the Weimar Constitution, but in many respects the two are similar. As did the Weimar, the Bonn document starts with a long detached enumeration of basic rights. It then analyzes the relation between the central government and the *Länder*. Although the republic is called a federal republic, the central government has very considerable powers, and the tendency since 1949 has been to develop them rather than the local powers. The legislative body consists of two houses. The lower, the Bundestag, is elected by universal direct suffrage. It is the basic lawmaking body. The upper, the Bundesrat, represents the states as in earlier German constitutions. The members are appointed and withdrawn by the governments of the *Länder* in rough proportion to population; it has a suspensive veto and certain emergency powers greater than its opposite number at Weimar. The president of the republic is not elected directly by the people but by a convention called for that purpose and composed of the members of the Bundestag and an equal number of delegates picked by the parliaments of the *Länder*. His term of office is five years, and he may be re-elected only once. His office is largely decorative; there is no provision analogous to the notorious Article 48 of Weimar. The chancellor is more powerful than under Weimar, as the president is less powerful. He is elected by the Bundestag on the nomination of the president. His position is more secure than in most parliamentary governments because the Bundestag can vote no confidence only if it simultaneously nominates a successor. This device was planned to eliminate the lengthy government crises that plagued Weimar. The ministers are directly responsible to the chancellor, who controls them almost as absolutely as Bismarck did. The basic law goes into much detail on such matters as finance, administration, and religion, and has at least one unique provision. Article 24 reads: "The Federation may, by legislation, transfer sovereign powers to international institutions." It is certainly true that the Bonn Republic has so far operated in a more stable fashion than the Weimar Republic. Whether this is a tribute to the constitution, the new party system, or the firm hand of Adenauer is, of course, a question; but at least no serious loopholes in the basic law have so far developed.

A few weeks after the election of Heuss and Adenauer the People's

Congress of the Soviet zone proclaimed in force the constitution that had been drawn up some time before for the German Democratic Republic. As it became clear that the Western powers were going to organize the Western zones, the Soviet occupiers picked a People's Congress, dominated by the SED, to draw up a constitution allegedly for all Germany. The constitution was held in abeyance for two years until the Federal Republic was proclaimed. Then the Eastern constitution was placed before the people of the Soviet zone for confirmation. However, so high a proportion of the population refrained from voting that the congress simply picked a number of its own members to become the People's Chamber, as the new parliament was to be called, and announced on October 7, 1949, that the new government was in force. In 1950 another election was held for the chamber, but this was a completely unfree one. The voters could elect only a list of candidates in which the SED had a considerable majority, while there was a token representation of CDU and liberals. This was like a Nazi plebiscite and achieved similar results.

The constitution has the appearance of liberalism and democracy. It is supposedly based on the *Länder* and is therefore federal in character, but this is only window dressing. Not only does much more power go to the central government than in the Bonn document, but the *Länder* themselves have virtually ceased to exist. Their local parliaments and governments have been abolished, and the Soviet zone has been divided into fourteen districts for administrative purposes. In many cases the borders of these districts are not the same as those of the former *Länder,* and it is clear that they are just local units formed to receive directives from the center.

The opposition parties are represented in the cabinet of the central government, but their function is really to support the measures of the SED rather than to provide a real opposition. The constitution can be amended by the People's Chamber itself, and since for obvious reasons the Chamber usually votes unanimously and is controlled by the dominant party, it is easy to see that the democratic quality of this constitution is delusive.

In fact, the German Democratic Republic is simply one more satellite state in the orbit of the Soviet Union. Its president, Wilhelm Pieck, an old-line Communist who died in 1960, and its premier, Otto Grotewohl, leader of the secession from the SPD, have been figureheads. The real authority lies in the Politbureau of the SED and its secretary-general, Walter Ulbricht, a dependable Communist who spent the Nazi years in Moscow and who presumably still receives his orders from there. East Germany was granted the right to conduct her own international affairs as early as 1949, and the Soviet control commission disappeared from the scene in 1954; but the huge, newly built, and ugly Soviet embassy on Unter den Linden is an ever-present reminder of the source of power.

It is hard to find reliable information on East Germany, but there is no question that the standard of living has improved very markedly since the end of the war. It is, however, an illuminating experience to walk through the Brandenburg Gate from bustling West Berlin to the shadows of the East. The visitor is usually shown the Stalin Allée, a street of massive new apartment buildings with attractive restaurants and shops along the sidewalk. However, if the visitor were to walk a few feet along one of the intersections, he would find terrible ruins and rubble of much worse appearance than in the West.

It was in connection with the building of Stalin Allée that the most spectacular event in the history of East Germany occurred—the strikes and riots of June 17, 1953. A few days earlier the workers on the new apartments were informed that their daily production quotas were to be raised without any increase in wages as an example of socialist competition. The new situation rankled in the workers' minds, and on the sixteenth and seventeenth they broke into violence. They struck and marched in parades along Unter den Linden toward the Western sector. The workers were joined by other strikers and even by youth groups in Communist uniform. They sang songs, insulted the government, and pulled down Red flags. The local police and the armed force of the republic (*Volkspolizei*) were slow to retaliate, but eventually they did and the Russians lent support by sending tanks into the streets of Berlin. The revolt was put down, of course, although it simmered for days both in Berlin and other cities. However, it was at least an indication of true feelings. There have been no other such uprisings, but the event is not forgotten. One of the poignant sights in West Berlin is the wooden cross erected to the East Berliners who fell on June 17; perhaps even more poignant is the stone near the cross, erected in memory of the Russian officers and men who were shot because they refused to fire on the East Berliners on June 17.

In Western Germany the spirit is far different. There the visitor is immediately impressed by what has been called the "miracle" of Germany, her economic recovery and amazing prosperity. A combination of the currency reform, Marshall Plan aid, the ability of the German economy to help fill the world's needs, and the general industrial efficiency of the Germans has wrought marvels. Moreover, it has not been done either by socialization or by the historic German emphasis on cartels. Bonn Germany is devoted to the economic philosophy of free enterprise. Constant pronouncements on this subject by Ludwig Erhart, minister of economics, make this abundantly clear. In fact, the great prosperity has made it impossible for the SPD to achieve control of the government since there seems no reason to change over to socialism.

Politically, Adenauer has maintained a firm control over the government. Many insist that he has exerted too much control and ruled Germany too paternalistically. German wits call the government a *Demokratur* (a pun implying "democratic dictatorship"). Certainly he has been reluctant to step down, even after having promised to do so in the spring of 1959. There is fear that when age forces him to move from the scene, there will be no one trained to replace him. His vigor and ability have been extraordinary and have undoubtedly contributed to the stability of the Bonn Republic for nearly as long as the Weimar Republic existed.

During his first four years in office Adenauer headed a coalition government of CDU and FDP, which was sometimes precarious since the FDP was not always easy to keep in line, especially in the matter of rearmament. Until his death in 1952 Kurt Schumacher was leader of the SPD opposition and one of the ablest political figures of Europe. The election of 1953 gave Adenauer's party, the CDU, a clear, if small, majority, and he has been able since then to control the Bundestag in all major matters. The Communist party has remained negligible, and in spite of occasional fears none of the so-called neo-Nazi groups has been able to win any important percentage of votes.

In the field of foreign affairs Adenauer has made himself best known. At first this meant relations with the former occupying powers, because by the occupation statute Germany was forbidden to conduct an independent foreign policy. From the first Adenauer has shown himself to be completely oriented to the West. He has done everything possible to maintain warm relations with the United States, and, more surprising, has constantly indicated a desire to draw closer to France. He has realized the seriousness to Germany of the cleavage with Russia, has chosen to align himself with the democratic powers, and has recognized that the old disputes in western Europe have to be forgotten if Europe is to play any important role in the future. In this attitude Adenauer was often opposed by Schumacher, whose overriding interest was in the reunification of Germany and who felt that this might be best accomplished by offers of friendship toward the Soviet Union.

Among the gestures made by Germany toward the West was its membership in the Council of Europe, the European Payments Union, and the Organization for European Economic Co-operation. In April 1951 Germany joined France, Italy, and the three Benelux countries in signing the project for the European Coal and Steel Community to create an international body to control these basic industries. This had the importance for Germany of ending the old statute on the Ruhr and of paving the way for future negotiations concerning the Saar.

With the outbreak of the war in Korea in the summer of 1950 the Western allies became even more conscious of building up defense forces against Communist aggression. They began to think of the large reservoir of manpower available in Germany and to change their ideas about the permanent disarmament of the Germans. As early as September 1950 the foreign ministers talked not of a German army but of German units integrated into a European army. In fact it was the French premier, René Pleven, who first made a definite proposal along these lines. During 1951 a number of conferences were held about the possibility of re-arming Germany. Steadily the Germans were losing more and more of their disabilities. In March Adenauer took the additional title of minister of foreign affairs. In July Great Britain, the Commonwealth, and France ended the state of war between themselves and Germany; in October the United States followed suit.

At home Adenauer was not having an easy time on the matter of re-armament. Since 1945 the Germans had been taught that they would never have to fight again; their constitution provided for no armed forces; they were sick of war and its terrible results. In particular, the SPD was opposed to rearmament. However, the chancellor persisted in his policy since he felt it was the only way to achieve the complete sovereignty that Germany desired.

A further step toward sovereignty was taken on May 26, 1952, when the allies watered down their occupation rights still more and entered into a contractual status with Germany by which, short of an emergency to be decided by them, they would limit their rights to maintaining troops and to dealing for Germany with the Soviet Union. The next day the foreign ministers met Adenauer in Paris to sign the agreements for the European Defense Community. This would have constituted an automatically functioning defensive alliance by which an attack on one member would constitute an attack on all, with Germany as an equal partner in defense. All the signatory nations except France ratified the EDC. The French postponed action for a long time and put up a number of objections. Finally in the summer of 1954 the French national assembly definitely refused to ratify the agreements, and the EDC did not come into existence. There was still to be delay before Germans once again wore uniforms. When they did, it was under the auspices of NATO, to which Germany was admitted in May 1955.

The climax of an era in German history came on May 5, 1955, exactly ten years after the capitulation, when Germany received notice of full sovereignty from the ambassadors of France and Great Britain. The United States had acted a few days before. Except for the right to maintain troops on German soil and the denial to Germany of the right to include Berlin in its territory, since that would endanger allied rights there, the German Federal Republic now became sovereign. Thanks to the threat from the East and the firm policy of Adenauer, Germany was free much sooner than anyone ten years before would have predicted.

Political life in West Germany since 1955 has been relatively placid. The Germans seem to have achieved for the first time an orderly two-party government far removed from the multiparty folly of the Weimar period. In 1956, in anticipation of the general elections of the following year, the Communist party was outlawed. A mark of the progress of democracy in Germany is the fact that in the 1957 election almost 90 per cent of the population voted. It gave an absolute majority once again to the CDU and thus to the pro-Western policy of Adenauer. Fears of a neo-Nazi revival were allayed by the fact that the strongest of the right-wing parties, the German Reich party, received only 1 per cent of the votes and some months later was declared unconstitutional by the highest court.

Probably the most serious rift in the smooth surface of the CDU arose during the presidential election of 1959. On July 1 the term of Dr. Theodor Heuss was to expire. Heuss had endeared himself to the population. Scholar, disciple, and biographer of Friedrich Naumann, a representative of liberal southwestern Germany, he had presided over the state with dignity and serenity. In 1954 he was re-elected without question, but the constitution forbids more than two terms for the president. In April 1959 the CDU offered the candidacy to succeed Heuss to Konrad Adenauer. This looked like a seemly end to the career of an old man who might not be able to stand up against the buffets of active political life much longer. Adenauer accepted the nomination, and his election appeared to be a foregone conclusion. There was speculation about the next chancellor, but it seemed clear that this position would go to Ludwig Erhard, minister of economics. However, in early June, while Erhard was on a visit to Washington, Adenauer addressed a letter to his party withdrawing his candidacy for president. He declared that since the renewed Soviet threat to Berlin had grown into crucial proportions at the Geneva Conference, which was going on at the time, he would be shirking his duty not to see it through. He concluded, "I cannot, therefore, assume the responsibility of leaving my post during so critical a time." The CDU delegation after some debate accepted Adenauer's decision and gave him a vote of confidence. Erhard swallowed his disappointment and pride and remained in his cabinet position.

To replace Adenauer, the CDU nominated Heinrich Luebke, who had been minister of food and agriculture since 1953. Luebke is a Westphalian, a veteran of World War I, and has devoted much of his life to farm problems. He was a member of the Prussian parliament for the Catholic Center party in the last years of the Weimar Republic, and has a respectable anti-Nazi record. The SPD nominated Carlo Schmid, who had been first vice-president of the Bundestag since its inception.

The special electoral assembly met in Berlin. This was a symbolic gesture to reassure the threatened Berliners and to show the world that West Germany claims Berlin as its own. It was greeted with some criticism abroad on the grounds that Berlin is not technically a part of the Federal Republic (though it has nonvoting representatives in the Bundestag and accepts Bonn legislation as binding) and cannot be, for the position of the West in Berlin depends on the fiction that the city is still under four-power control. At the election Luebke received a clear majority of all votes cast.

The SPD has found itself in an awkward position since 1949. The extraordinary and increasing prosperity of the country has robbed the socialists of their principal platform, the nationalization of industry. Things seem to be going so well that the German voter sees no need for a change. In fact, the SPD no longer favors a drastic change in economic organization. Its points of issue with the CDU have concerned mainly matters of foreign policy. During the life of Kurt Schumacher the SPD maintained a nationalist position. It insisted that the big issue was the reunification of Germany. It opposed Adenauer's policy of close adherence to the West, calling instead for a policy of neutralism in the hope that by not antagonizing the Soviet Union, there would be more chance to bring the two Germanies together. Since Schumacher's death in 1952 his rather colorless successor, Erich Ollenhauer, has modified this line considerably, especially as he has seen the election returns go against the SPD at the federal level. (In a number of the *Länder* there have been SPD majorities.) At the present time the most interesting SPD leader is Willy Brandt, the forceful and magnetic mayor of Berlin, who has achieved national stature and may be the SPD's hopeful when Adenauer resigns or dies.

On the economic side, the second half of the fifties has seen a continuation of the enormous strides made in the first half. The recession of the period was little noticed in Germany, and unemployment has remained at a low figure. In the basic heavy industries German production continues to soar over the 1938 figures. This is not completely true in the case of coal because other fuels have to a considerable extent replaced it in certain industries and in late 1959 several noneconomic collieries were shut down in Bochum. However, the government envisages the relocation of other sorts of industry in the Ruhr to take up the slack of possible unemployment.

The German export trade is a particular pride of the Federal Republic. It has been maintaining a consistently favorable balance of trade, which is vital to Germany because owing to her large population and to the loss of agricultural territory in the east, she must import large quantities of foodstuffs. The label, "made in Germany," once more is seen throughout the world, and German industry is actively competing for the business of developing underdeveloped lands. For example, the firm of Krupp, almost completely restored to its former power, is able and willing to provide almost anything in the way of engineering that a foreign state may want, from the earliest blueprints to the finished vast project. It is astonishing that the country which only fifteen years ago seemed damaged beyond repair is now offering to finance and construct for the rest of the world.

Germany has achieved her economic triumph with a free-enterprise system; but it is free enterprise tempered with a number of the aspects of the welfare state, to which the Germans have taken kindly since the time of Bismarck. Most of the workers are members of the one large union organization, the *Deutscher Gewerkschaftsbund* ("German Federation of Trade Unions"), which has replaced the three separate organizations of the Weimar period. Early in the occupation the principle of codetermination (*Mitbestimmungsrecht*) was adopted, by virtue of which the workers have a voice in policy decisions. In many large corporations one of the directors is chosen to represent the workers' interests. Whatever the cause, the fact is that there have been extremely few labor conflicts during the past decade.

In cultural and artistic matters Germany has made a respectable recovery from the abyss of 1945. She lost a large number of her artistic and intellectual leaders by emigration during the Nazi years. Undoubtedly also she lost in the war many of the young men who would be the leaders of today. It is remarkable, however, how quickly the Germans restored themselves to the forefront in the performing arts. The author can remember as early as October 1945 an announcement of the forthcoming performance of one of the German classic dramas in the courtyard of Heidelberg castle; performances of operas and symphony orchestras often in makeshift surroundings were among the few joys of the occupying officials in the early period after the war. Now many of the opera houses and concert halls have been restored or built anew, and the tourist has more to choose from than he has time for. For example, two grandsons of Richard Wagner have taken control of the

Bayreuth festivals and are giving performances of their grandfather's music dramas with revolutionary and controversial settings. Among the younger German composers probably the best known in the United States is Carl Orff, whose works, especially his *Carmina Burana,* have been given numerous performances.

Germany has much to offer the visitor today. Munich is being steadily and tastefully rebuilt; Düsseldorf has become the show city of the West; and in Berlin the Kurfürstendamm gives the appearance of being one of the gayest and liveliest streets in the world (unless by daylight one notes that some of the neon signs are built on scaffoldings against old ruins).

Religious life has developed very actively and apparently with real depth of intensity. This is true of both Catholics and Protestants. As a result of the changed boundaries, the two groups are almost equal in number in the Federal Republic, with just a small Protestant majority. No doubt the religious fervor of the Germans has been whetted by the persecution which continues in the Soviet zone. Every persecution creates its heroes. In East Germany the best known hero is Dr. Otto Dibelius, who is both bishop of Berlin-Brandenburg and also chairman of the council of the synod of the whole German Protestant church. His sermons in his cathedral in Berlin (which is located in the Eastern sector) have been constant exhortations to the people of East Germany to stand firmly by their Christian belief.

In view of the unspeakable ordeal which the Jewish people endured during the Nazi regime, it is encouraging to observe the efforts made by the Federal Republic to make reparation, in cases where reparation is still possible. The federal basic law specifically outlaws any attack based on religion or race, and all responsible German leaders can be quoted in the same vein. Any German Jew who suffered during the Nazi years or his heirs can apply for restitution for the goods taken from him. Thousands have done so, and restitution of about two billion dollars has been made out of funds collected by the German government as reparation taxes. Jews have been invited to return to Germany to settle and some thousands have done so, giving contemporary Germany a Jewish population of about thirty thousand. The government has built synagogues and centers for the Jews and tried to integrate them into the new society. On September 10, 1952, the Federal Republic signed at Luxemburg an agreement with the government of Israel. Germany will pay to Israel $822,000,000 by 1964, of which over $500,000,000 has already been paid. Much of this has taken the form of machinery, agricultural equipment, rolling stock, and shipping, without which the early years of Israel would have been much more difficult.

There is latent anti-Semitism in Germany as in most countries. However, in Germany it is a more frightening matter on account of the past. From time to time offenders have been tried and imprisoned. In the last days of 1959 and the beginning of 1960 a wave of anti-Semitism, taking the form of swastikas and abusive remarks painted on synagogues, swept Germany and other countries as well. The reply of the government was immediate. The president, chancellor, Bundestag, and various key groups all disavowed the actions in strong terms. Almost a hundred persons were arrested and many of them given prison terms. A good proportion of them were juvenile delinquents looking for publicity. The government remains watchful, but there seems no reason to expect significant anti-Semitism or neo-Nazism in the near future.

The most important and controversial aspect of German development in recent years has been in the realm of foreign affairs. Four major issues are involved: rearmament, the Saar question, reunification, and since 1958 the new Berlin crisis. The entrance of the Federal Republic into NATO in 1955 required the Germans to pool their armed forces into the general NATO military organization. It took a year for the government to push approval of military service through the Bundestag. The SPD led the opposition, insisting that Germany's tragedies had arisen from militarism and that it was unwise to invite them again. It also insisted that military co-operation with the West would serve only to antagonize the Soviet Union and make reunification more difficult. Finally in July 1956 the bill was passed, originally calling for a force of one half million men by the end of 1957. In early 1957 General Hans Speidel was appointed commander in chief of army forces. Great care was taken to make sure that the new army would have democratic foundations and not be in danger of becoming the autocratic state within a state which it had been during the empire, the Weimar period, and the Nazi state. It was put clearly under civilian control, with Franz Joseph Strauss as minister of defense. Even with all these qualifications it was hard to get the organization in existence, and the estimates of manpower had to be lowered. Now it is expected that German ground forces will reach three hundred fifty thousand by the end of 1961. The Germans had been permitted at the end of the war to maintain a few small naval units for coastal defense and police purposes. The permitted number has been increased and more units have been added, none larger than a destroyer. In 1958 a new German air force came into existence, but it will not be an important force for some years.

The successful settlement of the Saar question has probably been Adenauer's greatest diplomatic triumph. After the war the Saar became a part of the French occupation zone. The French separated it from the rest of their zone, and it was clear that they intended to annex it to France

politically as well as economically. The economic union was established forthwith. As the years went on and Germany became stronger,
while France was immersed in the weakness and confusion of the Fourth
Republic, the Saar issue became an even greater source of discontent.
The two governments agreed in 1955 that subject to the approval of the
Saarlanders the area should remain under international control, technically under the Western European Union (successor to the ill-fated
European Defense Community). However, at an election in late 1955
the population turned down this idea decisively. The following year the
two governments undertook bilateral negotiations and reached a conclusion late in the year. The Saar became an integral part of the German
Federal Republic at the beginning of 1957 with the status of a *Land*. It
was to maintain its economic relationship with France for three years;
however, in July 1959 these ties were broken, and the Saar is now part
of Germany. One of the remarkable features of international affairs in
the last few years has been the increasing warmth between France and
Germany. This *rapprochement* has been carefully cultivated by Adenauer and has been strengthened since Charles De Gaulle has become
the dominant political figure in France. The two leaders have met on a
number of occasions in both countries and seem to be making a strong
bid to forget the unhappiness of the past.

It goes without saying that the most urgent problem in the minds of
most Germans is reunification. The separation of Germany into two
hostile states, each operating under the aegis of one of two hostile world
powers, strikes them as unnatural and tragic. No German political figure
could hope for any success in his career if he did not pay frequent lip
service to the goal of reunifying East and West. Yet realistic Germans
realize that it is a problem outside their control and simply a function of
the far greater problem of the split between the Communist and non-
Communist worlds. The Soviet Union has no intention of relinquishing
its hold on Germany with its industrial wealth and potential for continuing the general unrest upon which Communism thrives. Similarly,
the Western powers have no idea of letting powerful and rich West
Germany drift into the Soviet orbit. As long as these attitudes continue,
and there is no reason to expect their abatement, the division will persist. It would be fruitless here to rehearse the conferences, personal
visits, and negotiations concerning the subject of the division of Germany. The Soviet Union and the Federal Republic have extended diplomatic recognition to each other, Adenauer has made the pilgrimage to
Moscow, and every conceivable combination of statesmen and diplomats
has discussed the matter from every angle; but as the years have progressed, the division of Germany has become more and more an enduring

fact. If this is true for the German Democratic Republic, it is even more true for the areas "under Polish administration" east of the Oder-Neisse line. This territory has been almost cleared of German nationals, the names have been changed, and the Poles have done everything possible to Polonize the land and create a *fait accompli*.

A certain amount of "reunification" goes on every day at a voluntary and extremely informal level. A week has never passed since the war without the surreptitious crossing of several hundreds of Germans from the East to the West. This is almost impossible along the zonal frontier, where there are barbed wire fences, many sentries of the East German uniformed police, and cleared strips along the border. It is much easier in Berlin, where it is possible to pass from East to West in the subways because the inspections are sporadic and not always efficient. Thousands have made successful efforts to reach the West. There is no way of knowing how many have failed. It is true that some have returned to the East, but their number is very small compared to those who have stayed. Those who return are the ones who find that the West is not the paradise they had expected; the very fact that that is what they expected speaks volumes concerning the opinion held in the East about the West.

The emigration from East to West has varied in its quantity in proportion to the pressure toward communization of the East German government. In 1959 and 1960 this pressure has become more intense. The original "land reform" in the Soviet zone resulted in turning the area from one of great estates into one of small holdings. No effort was made in the early years to collectivize agriculture. This has been changed, and heavy pressure is now exerted to force the individual farmers to enter collectives. Sometimes brutal measures have been used by the Communists, with the result that the stream westwards has increased though the Eastern government has also toughened its measures to prevent the leakage. There is no question but that living conditions in the East have gradually improved, but also no question that they have not improved to a degree equal to the West. The East Germans are not slow to notice this fact, which is most obvious in Berlin; it is to the interest of the East German authorities to hide it.

Berlin has undergone an experience since the blockade almost unique in history. This enormous city, itself divided in two, stands as an island of freedom about a hundred miles within the Communist border, with precarious and easily severable communication with its friends to the West. The economic prosperity of Berlin has not paralleled that of the Federal Republic, mainly because of its remoteness. In fact, the Federal Republic has had to subsidize the former capital by various devices, including a tax on all postal revenues. The Berliners have striven with great energy to develop types of industry suitable to their location, especially light industry. The result has been very satisfying. Berlin has also sought to increase tourist revenues by developing its entertainment possibilities on both the serious and lighthearted levels. Foreigners have been interested in visiting this outpost of freedom with its gaiety and fun. However, beneath the surface Berliners have continued to be apprehensive about their situation. For instance, it is noticeable that the population of Berlin is relatively older than that of the rest of Germany. Many young people, afraid of the future and conscious of the greater opportunity in the West, have left Berlin to make their careers. However, for years after the failure of the blockade it appeared that the Soviets had decided not to tamper with the Berlin settlement.

This period of relaxation ended on November 10, 1958, when Nikita Khrushchev demanded that an end be made to the four-power control of Berlin and indicated that the Soviet Union would yield its part of the occupation to the East German government. The implication was clear that the Russians consider West Berlin to be simply a part of Berlin and thus part of East Germany. It was further clear that once the Soviets had handed over their authority to the East Germans, they believed that the East Germans would have clear sovereignty in Berlin, could thus control access to the capital, and could then order Western forces and citizens out of the city.

The United States promptly replied that the status of Berlin had been drawn up by the four powers working together and that therefore no one of the four had any right to change that status without the consent of the other three.

On November 27, 1958, Khrushchev proposed that Berlin be made a demilitarized free city and announced that the Soviet government would transfer the control of access to Berlin to the East Germans by June 1, 1959, no matter what the Western powers might care to do about it. This seemed to give a six-month period of grace for the West to make up its mind to accept the inevitable.

Within the next few weeks the United States was joined by Great Britain, France, and the German Federal Republic, as well as by the NATO Council, in statements that the West refused to accept Russia's proposal and would defend its position in Berlin. President Eisenhower, Prime Minister Macmillan, and other leaders in speeches, radio broadcasts, and by all other available means confirmed their determination to maintain their position and rights in Berlin.

The early months of 1959 were filled with negotiations. The Russians offered a proposed peace treaty on Germany which would perpetuate the division, recognize the Eastern state, and consecrate the Oder-

Neisse boundary. In reply, the West proposed a general conference on the German problem at the foreign minister level, with participation by the Germans. Khrushchev countered with the suggestion for a summit conference, an idea which won no support in Washington, for the American government felt that there should be some assurance of success before it would be worth while to risk failure at the summit. Prime Minister Macmillan made the journey to Moscow in March and even accepted a rebuff from his host, who left the capital while Macmillan was there. However, Khrushchev did promise the British leader that the six-month deadline did not apply and that the Russians would not take any precipitate action in late May. Before the end of March the four powers had agreed to hold a conference at the foreign minister level in Geneva, with the understanding that if there were a possibility of a successful issue, a summit conference would be held to make it final. Accordingly, the Geneva Conference met on May 11, 1959.

The conference remained in session sporadically until early August. At the outset both the Soviet delegation and the Western powers presented drafts of their proposed plans to solve the whole German problem. Needless to say, these plans were mutually unacceptable. At times the conference bogged down over trivia and reminded onlookers of the negotiations at Westphalia in the 1640's (e.g., the first meeting was delayed for hours by a dispute over where the representatives from the two parts of Germany should sit). Finally the American secretary of state, Christian Herter, decided that the conference had no future and by his departure brought it to a close. There were no tangible results. However, it is noteworthy that the deadline announced by the Soviets came and went without any action, and the situation in Berlin remained as it had for ten years. This fact itself was possibly an achievement.

In the autumn of 1959 Premier Khrushchev visited the United States and held several private conversations with President Eisenhower. The atmosphere seemed to be friendly, even jovial, and announcement was made of a summit conference to be held in May, 1960, and of a visit by Eisenhower to the Soviet Union shortly thereafter. Khrushchev denied that there had been any ultimatum about Berlin intended or that there was any deadline after which the Russians would take unilateral action. There seemed to be a relaxation in the cold war.

Events proved that the relaxation was only temporary, if indeed it existed at all. When the heads of state assembled in Paris for the summit conference, Khrushchev ended the meeting before it began on the issue of the capture of an American plane performing espionage duties over Russian territory. A few hours later he announced at a press conference that the Soviet Union was planning to make a separate peace treaty with the German Democratic Republic which would give the East German authorities control of the access to Berlin. However, shortly afterward in a speech in East Berlin he announced that the treaty would not be signed immediately but at some indefinite date in the future.

Thus the Berlin crisis persists. It may persist for years. No one can possibly predict the next actions of the Soviet government, but the informed concensus seems to be that Berlin and its anomalous situation is a convenient weapon for the Soviets to use whenever they wish to increase the tensions in a world already tense.

History never stands still. There is never a moment at which one can stand back and make a thorough appraisal of the development of a nation, certainly not a nation with so troubled a history as Germany's. However, perhaps a few tentative remarks are possible. Germany is a full partner in the world's plight. She is heavily involved in the cold war, the division of the world of which her own division is a symbol. She cannot afford the luxury of neutralism and gives little indication of wishing it. West Germany seems to be firmly allied with the Western world and for the last ten years has given evidence of a devotion to the democratic process that is noteworthy and unprecedented in her history. She has come an astonishingly long way, much farther than anyone in 1945 would have dared to predict. In a world so torn with strife as the world of 1961, it is extremely encouraging to be optimistic about any segment of it. And one can afford at least moderate optimism about the new Germany. Surely all men of good will must hope that this optimism may continue to be warranted.

SUGGESTED READINGS

I have framed the following bibliography with strictly limited ends in view. It is intended for the general educated reader who has become interested in some phase of German history and wants to know more in detail. It will be useful both for the undergraduate student and for the instructor of an undergraduate course who may not be a specialist in the field. A graduate student building a field in German history for his doctoral examination will find this list of use, partly because many of the works mentioned in it contain more extensive and detailed bibliographies.

With the foregoing in mind I have ruthlessly eliminated all works not available in the English language. I have also ruled out monographs on highly technical subjects. I have contented myself with giving only the date of publication because the books can be found easily in standard reference works or in libraries of any size. I have entirely neglected the immense field of periodical material. I have tried to place each book in the general area which it most concerns, but many books refuse to be categorized. Thus, a student should look in paragraphs adjacent to the one of his main interest. This is particularly true in biographical and memoir material if the subject has lived through several periods. I have made the list fuller as it becomes more modern, both because that is the general plan of this series and also since there is much more available in English on Germany in the last century than for the earlier periods. I should like to remind the reader that he can often derive a more satisfactory picture of a moment in history from a good contemporary or historical novel than from scholarly works. I have not included any fiction in this bibliography, but have mentioned a number of novels at appropriate spots in the text.

Within these limitations I hope that I have brought together a substantial number of the best titles in English on German history.

GENERAL TEXTS

Probably the best general history of Germany is Veit Valentin, *The German People* (1946), although my students have sometimes complained that it is too allusive. An older work reaching only to 1871 but still useful, though over-Prussian, is Ernest F. Henderson, *A Short History of Germany* (1902). Kurt F. Reinhardt, *Germany 2000 Years* (1950) is an invaluable compilation of dates and facts with heavy emphasis on cultural history. Several modern works, each sound and brief, are S. H. Steinberg, *A Short History of Germany* (1944); G. Shuster and A. Bergstraesser, *Germany: A Short History* (1944); H. Pinnow, *History of Germany* (trans., 1933); J. S. Davies, *From Charlemagne to Hitler* (1948); and Johannes Haller, *The Epochs of German History* (1930). Prince Hubertus zu Loewenstein,

The Germans in History (1945) is subjective, Catholic, and Ghibelline, but stimulating. G. P. Gooch, one of the greatest British scholars, treats of scattered topics in *Studies in German History* (1948). One of the most exciting and highly interpretive treatments of German culture is Edmond Vermeil, *Germany's Three Reichs* (1944). A new and very comprehensive collection is Louis L. Snyder, ed., *Documents of German History* (1958).

THE MIDDLE AGES

There is not a great deal devoted specifically to medieval Germany. An old classic is James Bryce, *The Holy Roman Empire* (1904). Two works which give frequently opposing interpretations are James W. Thompson, *Feudal Germany* (1928) and G. Barraclough, *Medieval Germany: The Origins of Modern Germany* (1946). A biography which has become a classic and has been recently reissued is Ernst H. Kantorowitz, *Frederick the Second* (trans., 1957). A. L. Poole, *Henry the Lion* (1912) is an older biography of a significant person.

THE REFORMATION AND THE WARS OF RELIGION

An enormous amount has of course been written about the religious revolt of the sixteenth century, most of it theological, apologetic, and tendentious, thus not suitable for this list. Undoubtedly the most important recent book is Hajo Holborn, *A History of Modern Germany: The Reformation* (1959), in which one of the outstanding contemporary scholars carries the story to 1648. Two multivolume old classics, the first pro-Protestant and the second pro-Catholic, are L. von Ranke, *History of the Reformation in Germany* (trans., 1845) and J. Janssen, *History of the German People at the Close of the Middle Ages* (trans., 1896). Convenient one-volume summaries, both rather pro-Protestant, are T. M. Lindsay, *History of the Reformation* (1906) and Preserved Smith, *Age of the Reformation* (1920). Interesting source material consisting of letters to a great banking house is found in V. Klarwill, ed., *The Fugger News Letters* (1924–26). Emperor Charles V has had several biographers; two of the best are E. Armstrong (1902) and Karl Brandi (1939). The best work on the Thirty Years War, and a very interesting book indeed, is C. V. Wedgwood, *The Thirty Years War* (1938). The mysterious Wallenstein has found a competent and stimulating biographer in Francis Watson, *Wallenstein—Soldier Under Saturn* (1938).

FROM WESTPHALIA TO THE END OF THE EIGHTEENTH CENTURY

Two standard works are C. T. Atkinson, *History of Germany, 1715–1815* (1908) and W. H. Bruford, *Germany in the Eighteenth Century* (1935). The best short account of early Prussia is Sidney B. Fay, *The Rise of Brandenburg-Prussia to 1786* (1937). Biographies of early Hohenzollerns include Ferdinand Schevill, *The Great Elector* (1947) and the delightful R. R. Ergang, *The Potsdam Führer* (1941), which concerns Frederick William I. There are a number of biographies of Frederick the Great, including Thomas Carlyle's lengthy and rhapsodic effort. The two most recent are by Pierre Gaxotte (trans., 1941), and G. P. Gooch (1947). Sir Richard Lodge, *Great Britain and Prussia in the Eighteenth Century* (1923) deals with a specialized phase of diplomacy. A really good biography of Maria Theresa is lacking. J. F. Bright, *Maria Theresa* (1897) and his *Joseph II* (1897) are almost exclusively diplomatic. More recent and inclusive biographies are Saul K. Padover, *The Revolutionary Emperor: Joseph the Second* (1934) and Walter C. Langsam, *Francis the Good: The Education of an Emperor, 1768–1792* (1951). A specialized work which fills some of the gaps in Austrian history is Ernst Wangermann, *From Joseph II to the Jacobin Trials* (1959).

TEXTS ON MODERN GERMAN HISTORY

A number of scholars have chosen to write general works on Germany beginning at various points between 1500 and 1815. We are promised shortly a second volume of Hajo Holborn, *A History of Modern Germany*, which will deal with the period from 1648 to the present. Without question it will be excellent. At present the best work is Koppel Pinson, *Modern Germany* (1954), a highly intelligent and thoughtful book containing many excellent quotations. Sir Adolphus William Ward, *Germany, 1815–1890* (1916–18) can still be recommended. Ralph Flenley, *Modern German History* (1953) is a very competent work starting with the Reformation and devoting much space to cultural history. A. J. P. Taylor, *The Course of German History* (1945) begins in 1815 and is extremely well-written and interesting, but frequently tendentious and irritating. The most recent of these books is E. J. Passant, *A Short History of Germany, 1815–1945* (1959). G. P. Gooch, *Germany* (1925) stresses the early twentieth century. It is important to refer the reader to pertinent chapters in two major co-operative works, one American and one British: William L. Langer, ed., *The Rise of Modern Europe*, volumes of which have appeared intermittently since 1934, and *The New Cambridge Modern History*, which started to appear in 1957. A very valuable recent work which constitutes almost an intellectual history of Germany since the eighteenth century is Hans Kohn, *The Mind of Germany* (1960).

GERMANY DURING THE FRENCH REVOLUTION
AND THE NAPOLEONIC ERA

The two basic works for this period remain G. P. Gooch, *Germany and the French Revolution* (1920) and H. A. L. Fisher, *Studies in Napoleonic Statesmanship: Germany* (1903). One of the most important works written at the time was Mme. de Staël, *Germany* (trans., 1883). Another major contemporary source is J. G. Fichte, *Addresses to the German Nation* (trans., 1922). R. Aris, *History of Political Thought in Germany from 1789 to 1815* (1936) is standard. The reform period in Prussia has been treated by Guy S. Ford, *Stein and the Era of Reform in Prussia* (1922), and by Eugene N. Anderson, *Nationalism and the Cultural Crisis in Prussia, 1806–1815* (1939).

A commanding old classic in three volumes is J. R. Seeley, *Life and Times of Stein* (1878).

THE METTERNICH ERA

The bibliography for this important period is not as full as one would wish. A classic by one of the greatest German historians is Heinrich Treitschke, *History of Germany in the Nineteenth Century* (trans., 1915), which ends in 1847 and, though accurate, is very biased in favor of Prussia. Metternich's incomplete *Memoirs* (trans., 1881–82) cast some light on that statesman. His English biographies leave a good deal to be desired; probably the two best are by Algernon Cecil (1933) and Helene Du Coudray (1935). E. L. Woodward has a stimulating essay on Metternich in *Three Studies in European Conservatism* (1930). Golo Mann, *Secretary of Europe* (1946) is a biography of Metternich's right-hand man, Gentz. Peter Viereck, *Conservatism Revisited* (1949) is an attempt at a favorable reappraisal of the period. Two works on the rise of nationalism continuing on into later periods are A. G. Pundt, *Arndt and the Nationalist Awakening in Germany* (1935) and Louis Snyder, *German Nationalism: The Tragedy of a People* (1952). W. O. Henderson, *The Zollverein* (1939) is a useful monograph on an important subject.

THE REVOLUTIONS OF 1848

As in the case of the preceding period, one hopes that more and better material will appear in English. Probably the best available work at the moment is Veit Valentin, *1848: Chapters of German History* (trans., 1940), which is by the greatest recent historian of the movement but is only a partial translation of a much longer and fuller account. Three other recent works which deserve attention are L. B. Namier, *1848: The Revolution of the Intellectuals* (1944); Arnold Whitridge, *Men in Crisis: The Revolutions of 1848* (1949); and Priscilla Robertson, *Revolutions of 1848* (1952). T. S. Hamerow, *Restoration, Revolution, Reaction* (1958) is an important work which breaks new ground in its consideration of the economic and social aspects of the years before 1848 and of the revolutions themselves. Josephine Goldmark, *Pilgrims of '48* (1930) is mainly concerned with the refugees who came to the United States. A. Schwarzenberg, *Prince Felix zu Schwarzenberg* (1946) is a readable and favorable biography.

THE PERIOD OF UNIFICATION

The classic German work is H. Sybel, *The Founding of the German Empire* (trans., 1890 ff.), based on Prussian sources and pro-Prussian. The Austrian historian, Heinrich Friedjung, wrote an Austrian reply of which *The Struggle for Supremacy in Germany, 1859–1866* (trans., 1935) is a partial translation. Two important American monographs on the earlier diplomacy of the unification are Lawrence D. Steefel, *The Schleswig-Holstein Question* (1932) and Chester W. Clark,

Franz Joseph and Bismarck: The Diplomacy of Austria before the War of 1866 (1934). W. E. Mosse, *The European Powers and the German Question* (1958) deals with the attitudes of the non-German great powers. On the origins of the war of 1870 the two most useful works, respectively pro-French and pro-Prussian, are R. H. Lord, *Origins of the War of 1870* (1924) and H. Oncken, *Napoleon III and the Rhine* (abridged trans., 1928). Biographies of Bismarck carry over into the next period. The best is Erich Eyck, *Bismarck and the German Empire* (trans., 1950), a sadly abridged rendering of a very important work. Others are J. W. Headlam, *Bismarck and the Foundation of the German Empire* (1899); C. G. Robertson, *Bismarck* (1919); and Frederick Darmstaedter, *Bismarck and the Creation of the Second Reich* (1949). Bismarck's memoirs, of which the first two volumes were translated as *Bismarck, the Man and the Statesman* (1899) and the third as *The Kaiser vs. Bismarck* (1921), make fascinating if not always dependable reading. P. Weigler, *William the First* (trans., 1929) is the only available biography.

THE GERMAN EMPIRE—POLITICAL

For the internal history of the empire to 1914, William H. Dawson, *The German Empire, 1867–1914* (1919 ff.) is still not surpassed. Robert H. Fife, *The German Empire Between Two Wars* (1916) may also be consulted. The best description of the constitutional structure of the empire is in A. Lawrence Lowell, *Governments and Politics in Continental Europe* (1896). A stimulating work on political theory in the period is Rupert Emerson, *State and Sovereignty in Modern Germany* (1918). For a highly perceptive analysis of the weaknesses of the empire from a socialist point of view, see Arthur Rosenberg, *The Birth of the German Republic* (trans., 1931). A good deal has been written about William II, much of it overemotional. Probably the best biography is J. von Kürenberg, *The Kaiser, a Life of William II* (trans., 1955). Emil Ludwig, *Wilhelm Hohenzollern, the Last of the Kaisers* (1927) depends heavily on debatable psychiatry. Christian Gauss, *The German Emperor as Shown in His Public Utterances* (1915) is a very illuminating collection of the emperor's speeches. Johannes Haller, *Philipp Eulenburg, the Kaiser's Friend* (trans., 1930) is useful for the early part of William II's reign. J. Alden Nichols, *Germany After Bismarck* (1958) is a competent account of the chancellorship of Caprivi. The development of the Social Democratic party is charmingly described from the international point of view in James Joll, *The Second International* (1955). A detailed and perceptive work which accomplishes more than its title suggests is Carl E. Schorske, *German Social Democracy, 1905–1917* (1955). A. Joseph Berlau, *The German Social Democratic Party, 1914–1921* (1949) is useful for the later period. Of the several biographies of Ferdinand Lassalle, a good one is by David Footman (1947). A number of studies have been made of the German army. They cover different periods, most of them extending into the Weimar and Nazi periods. The two best are J. W. Wheeler-Bennett, *Nemesis of Power* (1953) and Gordon Craig, *The Politics of the Prussian Army* (1956).

Other useful titles are H. Rosinski, *The German Army* (1940) and Walter Görlitz, *History of the German General Staff* (1953). The naval problem is dealt with well in E. L. Woodward, *Great Britain and the German Navy* (1935). The following important monographs are described by their titles: Mary E. Townsend, *The Rise and Fall of Germany's Colonial Empire, 1884–1918* (1930); Mildred Werthei-mer, *The Pan-German League, 1890–1914* (1924); Ross J. H. Hoff-man, *Great Britain and the German Trade Rivalry* (1933); Pauline R. Anderson, *The Background of Anti-English Feeling in Germany* (1939); and Bernadotte Schmitt, *England and Germany, 1741–1914* (1918). Ludwig Dehio, *Germany and World Politics in the 20th Century* (1959) is a series of interesting if overphilosophical essays on Germany's relation to the rest of the world.

THE GERMAN EMPIRE—ECONOMIC

Three basic works on economic developments during the empire, and in two cases also covering the succeeding period, are J. H. Clap-ham, *Economic Development of France and Germany, 1815–1914* (1923); W. F. Bruck, *Social and Economic History of Germany, 1888–1938* (1938); and Gustav Stolper, *German Economy, 1870–1940* (1940). A stimulating work by one of the most distinguished American economists is Thorstein Veblen, *Imperial Germany and the Industrial Revolution* (1915).

THE GERMAN EMPIRE—INTELLECTUAL

The following is a very incomplete list; it has particular reference to the lines of thinking that eventually led into National Socialism. A good introductory work is Rohan D'O. Butler, *The Roots of National Socialism, 1783–1933* (1942). Peter Viereck's *Metapolitics, from the Romantics to Hitler* (1941) is a very readable if occasionally too glib account of some of the proto-Nazis. William M. McGovern, *From Luther to Hitler: The History of Fascist-Nazi Political Philoso-phy* (1941) is dogmatic but scholarly. Paul W. Massing, *Rehearsal for Destruction* (1949) is devoted to anti-Semitism before the Nazi period. G. P. Gooch, *History and Historians in the Nineteenth Cen-tury* (1920) is a classic, while the small book which Gooch and others compiled under the title of *The German Mind and Outlook* (1945) has some very perceptive essays on this period and the Weimar Republic. Ralph H. Bowen, *German Theories of the Corporative State* (1947) explores untouched ground. The best biography of Richard Wagner is the multivolume *Life of Richard Wagner* by Ernest Newman (1933 ff.), and one of the best works on his music is the same au-thor's *The Wagner Operas* (1949). There is an extensive literature on Nietzsche. His sister, Elisabeth Foerster-Nietzsche, wrote a stand-ard life of her brother, *The Life of Nietzsche* (trans., 1912–15), which is usually considered an effort to whitewash the philosopher's reputa-tion. C. Crane Brinton, *Nietzsche* (1941) and Frederick Copleston, S.J., *Friedrich Nietzsche* (1942) are useful introductory works. Three basic contemporary works are Houston Stewart Chamberlain, *Founda-*

tions of the Nineteenth Century (trans., 1912); Friedrich Naumann, *Central Europe* (trans., 1917); and General Friedrich von Bernhardi, *Germany and the Next War* (trans., 1914).

THE GERMAN EMPIRE—DIPLOMATIC

An enormous amount has been written on the diplomatic causes of World War I. The question of war guilt and the opening of large parts of the archives of the various nations gave scholars an almost unprecedented opportunity. The standard work is Sidney B. Fay, *The Origins of the World War* (1928). Other general treatments with varying interpretations are Bernadotte E. Schmitt, *The Coming of the War, 1914* (1930); Harry E. Barnes, *The Genesis of the World War* (1929); and the recently translated work of the Italian scholar, L. Albertini, *Origins of the War of 1914* (1952 ff.). For the period from 1871 to 1902 the basic works are the extraordinarily complete volumes by William L. Langer, *European Alliances and Alignments, 1871–1890* (1931) and *The Diplomacy of Imperialism, 1890–1902* (1935). Other standard works are Raymond J. Sontag, *European Diplomatic History, 1871–1932* (1933); Erich Brandenburg, *From Bismarck to the World War: A History of German Foreign Policy, 1870–1914* (1927); J. W. Fuller, *Bismarckian Diplomacy at Its Zenith* (1922); Karl F. Nowak, *Germany's Road to Ruin* (1932); Otto Hammann, *The World Policy of Germany* (1927); and G. P. Gooch, *Recent Revelations of European Diplomacy* (1940). Two important specialized works are Raymond J. Sontag, *Germany and England, Background of Conflict, 1848–1918* (1938) and E. Malcolm Carroll, *Germany and the Great Powers, 1866–1914: A Study in Public Opinion and Foreign Policy* (1938).

THE GERMAN EMPIRE—MEMOIRS

A large number of important figures of this period have left their memoirs. Some of them are of course undependable, but all cast interesting light. Among the more significant are the recollections of Bismarck, William II, Hohenlohe-Schillingsfürst, Bülow, Bebel, Waldersee, Bethmann-Hollweg, and Holstein. Sir Frederick Ponsonby, ed., *Letters of the Empress Frederick* (1928) gives a good deal of basic background information and much insight into the life of that unhappy lady.

WORLD WAR I

There are three extremely good books on domestic Germany during World War I, each of them broader in scope than their titles suggest. They are Hans W. Gatzke, *Germany's Drive to the West* (1950); Arthur Rosenberg, *The Birth of the German Republic* (trans., 1931); and Albrecht Mendelssohn-Bartholdy, *The War and German Society* (1938). A convenient military history is C. R. M. Cruttwell, *History of the Great War* (1934). Harry Rudin, *Armistice, 1918* (1944) is an exhaustive monograph. Friedrich Wilhelm Foerster, *Europe and the German Question* (1940) is an indictment of Germany as the cause of its own doom. J. W. Wheeler-Bennett has written the best biography of Hindenburg, with the charming title of *The Wooden Titan* (1936). His *Brest-Litovsk, The Forgotten Peace* (1938) is also useful. A number of the leading German participants in the war wrote their memoirs. Among them are Crown Prince Wilhelm, Generals Hindenburg, Ludendorff, and Falkenhayn, Admiral Tirpitz, and Prince Max of Baden.

THE WEIMAR REPUBLIC—POLITICAL

An excellent and detailed general account is S. William Halperin, *Germany Tried Democracy* (1946). Ralph H. Lutz, *The German Revolution of 1918–1919* (1922) and *The Fall of the German Empire, 1914–1918* (1932) are largely collections of documents amassed by the German committee appointed to study the causes of the defeat. The following list includes general standard works, some of them written too early for completeness or perspective: H. Quigley and R. T. Clark, *Republican Germany* (1935); Elmer Luehr, *The New German Republic* (1929); Frederick L. Schuman, *Germany Since 1918* (1937); and G. Scheele, *The Weimar Republic* (1946). Arthur Rosenberg, *A History of the German Republic* (trans., 1936) is a continuation of his earlier work but does not include the whole period. Paul Kosok, *Modern Germany* (1933) is particularly concerned with social problems. R. T. Clark, *The Fall of the German Republic* (1935) and Arnold Brecht, *Prelude to Silence* (1944) deal with the depression years. J. H. Morgan, *Assize of Arms* (1946) is the story of the effort to disarm Germany, while Jacques Bénoist-Méchin, *History of the German Army, 1919–1936* (1938) tells of the German effort to maintain her military establishment. Ruth Fischer, *Stalin and German Communism* (1948) is an inside account of Communist history in the decisive years around 1923. The best book on the Free Corps movement is Robert G. L. Waite, *Vanguard of Nazism* (1952). P. Frölich, *Rosa Luxemburg* (trans., 1940) is a competent biography. René Brunet, *The German Constitution* (1922) contains the text and an analysis of the Weimar Constitution.

THE WEIMAR REPUBLIC—INTELLECTUAL

There is a grievous need for more work on this important subject; no good general work exists. Something of the flavor of the period can be obtained from Franz Schoenberner, *Confessions of a European Intellectual* (1946), and from Moritz Bonn, *Wandering Scholar* (1948). S. D. Stirk, *The Prussian Spirit: A Survey of German Literature and Politics, 1914–1940* (1941) has some interesting insights. C. H. von Kessler, *Walter Rathenau* (trans., 1934) is devoted more to politics than to thought and is written by a close friend of Rathenau. An excellent study of some little-known figures, centering about the *Tatkreis,* is Klemens von Klemperer, *Germany's New Conservatism: Its History and Dilemma in the Twentieth Century* (1957). Several basic available. nonliterary sources are Oswald Spengler, *The Decline of the West* (trans., 1934); his *The Hour of Decision* (trans., 1934); and Moeller van den Bruck, *Germany's Third Empire* (trans., 1934).

THE WEIMAR REPUBLIC—DIPLOMATIC

A major source for this and the Nazi period, made up from captured German documents, is U.S. Department of State, *Documents on German Foreign Policy, 1918–1945* (1948 ff.). Two good general accounts are Edward H. Carr, *The Twenty Years' Crisis, 1919–1939* (1939) and Paul Birdsall, *Versailles Twenty Years After* (1941). Controversy has surrounded the figure of Gustav Stresemann. Two examples of the earlier adulatory approach are Rudolf Olden, *Stresemann* (1929) and A. Vallentin, *Stresemann* (trans., 1931). The newer attitude is best represented by Hans W. Gatzke, *Stresemann and the Rearmament of Germany* (1954), and Henry L. Bretton, *Stresemann and the Revision of Versailles* (1953). On the relations between Germany and the Soviet Union two good accounts are E. H. Carr, *German-Soviet Relations between the Two World Wars, 1919– 1939* (1951) and Gustav Hilger and Alfred G. Meyer, *The Incompatible Allies—A Memoir-History of German Soviet Relations 1918– 1941* (1953).

THE WEIMAR REPUBLIC—MEMOIRS

This period is not so rich in memoirs as its predecessor or its successor. Available are those of Philipp Scheidemann and Lord D'Abernon, British ambassador to Germany. Eric Sutton, ed., *Gustav Stresemann, His Diaries, Letters, and Papers* (1935–40) is a selection from Stresemann's papers. Albert Grzescinski, *Inside Germany* (1939) is interesting from the socialist point of view.

NAZI GERMANY—GENERAL

There is a tremendous literature on Hitler and the Nazis, much of it occasioned by the passions of wartime. Examples of the bulk of the available documentation are the forty-two volumes of *The Trial of the Major War Criminals before the International Military Tribunal* (1947–49) and U.S. Government Printing Office, *Nazi Conspiracy and Aggression* (1944–48), also a multivolume compilation. A recent, lengthy, and substantial work is William L. Shirer, *The Rise and Fall of the Third Reich* (1960). The best biography of Hitler and an excellent achievement is Alan Bullock, *Hitler, A Study in Tyranny* (1952). Konrad Heiden, *Der Führer* (1944) is good but ends in 1934; his *History of National Socialism* (1935), though still important, suffers from its date of publication. Probably the best general work on the whole Nazi creation is Franz Neumann, *Behemoth: The Structure and Practice of National Socialism* (1942 and 1944). S. H. Roberts, *The House That Hitler Built* (1937) is a good readable early account. Several standard works, most of them prewar, are Calvin Hoover, *Germany Enters the Third Reich* (1933); Robert A. Brady, *The Spirit and Structure of Ger-*

man Fascism (1937); Oswald Dutch, *Hitler's Twelve Apostles* (1940); and Henri Lichtenberger, *The Third Reich* (trans., 1937). On economic matters, see C. S. Guillebaud, *The Economic Recovery of Germany from 1933 to March, 1938* (1939), and Douglas Miller, *You Can't Do Business With Hitler* (1941). On governmental organization, see F. Morstein Marx, *Government in the Third Reich* (1937), and J. K. Pollock, *The Government of Greater Germany* (1938). A good geographical study is Arnold Brecht, *Federalism and Regionalism in Germany* (1945). A brilliant analysis of the intellectual implications of Nazism is Aurel Kolnai, *The War against the West* (1938). The United States was well-served by her foreign correspondents at this time, many of whom wrote about what they had witnessed. Some of the best of these books are Wallace R. Deuel, *People Under Hitler* (1942); L. P. Lochner, *What About Germany?* (1942); William L. Shirer, *Berlin Diary* (1941); Edgar A. Mowrer, *Germany Puts the Clock Back* (1933); Ferdinand Oechsner, *This Is the Enemy* (1942); and Otto Tolischus, *They Wanted War* (1940). A unique witness is Hermann Rauschning, who at one time saw a good deal of Hitler. After his break with Nazism he wrote *The Revolution of Nihilism* (1939), *The Voice of Destruction* (1940), and *The Conservative Revolution* (1941). H. E. Fried, *The Guilt of the German Army* (1942) and Telford Taylor, *Sword and Swastika* (1952) deal with the army in the Nazi period. The struggle with the Catholics is described in Robert D'Harcourt, *The German Catholics* (trans., 1939); Nathaniel Micklem, *National Socialism and the Roman Catholic Church* (1939); and a volume of translated documents entitled, *The Persecution of the Catholic Church in the Third Reich* (1942). On the treatment of education, see Edward K. Hartshorne, *The German Universities and National Socialism* (1937), and Frederic Lilge, *The Abuse of Learning* (1948). On the S.S. concentration camps, etc., see the tragic volume, *The Theory and Practice of Hell*, by E. Kogon (1950), and Gerald Reitlinger, *The S.S., Alibi of a Nation, 1922–1945* (1957). A few of the many works on diplomatic history are J. W. Wheeler-Bennett, *Munich, Prologue to Tragedy* (1948); Elizabeth Wiskemann, *The Rome-Berlin Axis* (1949); and three books by Sir Lewis Namier: *Diplomatic Prelude* (1948), *Europe in Defeat* (1950), and *In the Nazi Era* (1952). For life in Germany during the war, see G. Pihl, *Germany, the Last Phase* (trans., 1944), and Max Seydewitz, *Civil Life in Wartime Germany* (1945). The story of the conspiracy against Hitler has been told in a number of works, four of the best of which are Allen Dulles, *Germany's Underground* (1947); Fabian von Schlabrendorff, *They Almost Killed Hitler* (1947); Gerhard Ritter, *German Resistance* (trans., 1959); and Hans Rothfels, *The German Opposition to Hitler* (1948). Felix Gilbert, *Hitler Directs His War* (1950), shows us Hitler, the war lord. One of the most absorbing books to come out of the war is H. R. Trevor-Roper, *The Last Days of Hitler* (1947), which tells the dour story of the shelter in Berlin. An elaborate symposium of uneven merit, dealing with very varied aspects of the Nazi phenomenon, is Maurice Baumont, *et al.*, eds., *The Third Reich* (1955).

Friedrich Meinecke, *The German Catastrophe* (trans., 1950) is one of the most mature estimates of the whole tragedy by a great historian.

NAZI GERMANY—MEMOIRS

The Nazi period has produced a spate of memoirs; no doubt more are to come. Naturally, the most significant are the writings and utterances of Hitler himself: *Mein Kampf;* a collection of his speeches entitled *My New Order;* and *Hitler's Secret Conversations,* a collection of table talk during the war in Russia. Other leading Germans who have left their recollections in one form or another include Goering, Goebbels, Papen, Schacht, Rosenberg, Meissner, Raeder, Doenitz, Kesselring, Manstein, Guderian, Halder, Hossbach, Schwerin von Krosigk, Schellenberg, Gisevius, von Hassell, Weiszäcker, Dirksen, Niemöller, Otto Strasser, and Thyssen. Among non-Germans the memoirs of Ambassador Dodd, Sir Nevile Henderson, and Kurt Schuschnigg are interesting. Attention is directed to the memoirs of leaders of the United Nations such as Winston Churchill, Dwight Eisenhower, Charles De Gaulle, and many others.

THE OCCUPATION PERIOD

A straightforward account, packed with facts but not very readable, is General Lucius D. Clay, *Decision in Germany* (1950). Eugene Davidson, *The Death and Life of Germany* (1959) is an outstandingly complete recent work. Early and tendentious are James P. Warburg, *Germany—Bridge or Battleground* (1946) and Victor Gollancz, *In Darkest Germany* (1947). Three standard accounts which appeared during the occupation are Hoyt Price and Carl E. Schorske, *The Problem of Germany* (1947); J. K. Pollock and J. H. Meisel, *Germany under Occupation* (1947); and G. A. Almond, ed., *The Struggle for Democracy in Germany* (1949). Drew Middleton, *The Struggle for Germany* (1949) is a good account by a leading journalist. A somewhat less successful but more recent similar effort is Charles W. Thayer, *The Unquiet Germans* (1957). G. Schaeffer, *The Russian Zone of Germany* (1948) and J. P. Nettl, *The Eastern Zone and Soviet Policy in Germany, 1945–50* (1957) furnish information otherwise difficult to find.

SINCE 1949

This period is so recent that most of the information about it is still contained in periodical literature only. However, a few works may be cited. Probably the best is John Golay, *The Founding of the Federal Republic of Germany* (1958). Paul Waymar, *Adenauer: His Authorized Biography* (1957) and Edgar Alexander, *Adenauer and the New Germany* (1957) are the most considerable works about that statesman. Boas International Publishing Co., *Germany, 1945–1954* (1955?) tells a good deal with good illustrations and statistics about the "economic miracle." Press and Information Office of the German Federal Government, *Germany Reports* (1953) has a great deal of useful material, including chronologies and statistics.

INDEX

(Roman numerals indicate chapters; Arabic numerals indicate pages. Roman numerals are used in cases when the subject is so frequently mentioned in a chapter that it would be useless to give individual page references.)